SPEAK·TRUTH·TO·POWER

COMMANDER
STEVEN HAINES
ROYAL NAVY

THE INTERCEPTION OF VESSELS ON THE HIGH SEAS

The principal aim of this book is to address the international legal questions arising from the 'right of visit on the high seas' in the twenty-first century. This right is considered the most significant exception to the fundamental principle of the freedom of the high seas (the freedom, in peacetime, to remain free of interference by ships of another flag). It is this freedom that has been challenged by a recent significant increase in interceptions to counter the threats of international terrorism and WMD proliferation, or to suppress transnational organised crime at sea, particularly the trafficking of narcotics and smuggling of migrants. The author questions whether the principle of non-interference has been so significantly curtailed as to have lost its relevance in the contemporary legal order of the oceans. The book begins with an historical and theoretical examination of the framework underlying interception. This survey informs the remainder of the work, which then looks at the legal framework of the right of visit, contemporary challenges to the traditional right, interference on the high seas for the maintenance of international peace and security, interferences to maintain the *bon usage* of the oceans (navigation and fishing), piracy *jure gentium* and current counter-piracy operations off the coast of Somalia, the problems posed by illegal, unregulated and unreported fishing, interdiction operations to counter drug and people trafficking, and recent interception operations in the Mediterranean Sea organised by FRONTEX.

Volume 43 in the series Studies in International Law

Studies in International Law

Recent titles in this series

For the complete list of titles in this series, see 'Studies in International
Law' link at www.hartpub.co.uk/books/series.asp

The Interception of Vessels on the High Seas

Contemporary Challenges to the Legal Order of the Oceans

Efthymios Papastavridis

·HART·
PUBLISHING
OXFORD AND PORTLAND, OREGON
2013

Published in the United Kingdom by Hart Publishing Ltd
16C Worcester Place, Oxford, OX1 2JW
Telephone: +44 (0)1865 517530
Fax: +44 (0)1865 510710
E-mail: mail@hartpub.co.uk
Website: http://www.hartpub.co.uk

Published in North America (US and Canada) by
Hart Publishing
c/o International Specialized Book Services
920 NE 58th Avenue, Suite 300
Portland, OR 97213-3786
USA
Tel: +1 503 287 3093 or toll-free: (1) 800 944 6190
Fax: +1 503 280 8832
E-mail: orders@isbs.com
Website: http://www.isbs.com

British Library Cataloguing in Publication Data
Data Available

ISBN: 978-1-84946-183-2

Typeset by Hope Services, Abingdon
Printed and bound in Great Britain by
TJ International Ltd, Padstow, Cornwall

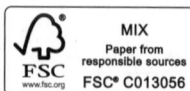

Foreword

Debates regarding the permissible scope of restrictions on the freedom of the high seas may be traced back to Grotius and Selden. While the Grotian view of the importance of the freedom of the high seas for navigation and communication persists, today there are many challenges of potentially equal common concern, such as the prevention and suppression of acts of terrorism, piracy and the smuggling of drugs. The increasing use of maritime interception on the high seas, whether exercised unilaterally or pursuant to multilateral treaty or UN Security Council authorisation, has led to the need to re-examine the conditions for the lawful exercise of maritime interception and the human rights safeguards and other conditions which should apply. In this thorough and penetrating modern study, Dr Papastavridis conducts such a re-examination in historical and contemporary context, and critiques the extension of the 'threat to maritime security' framing to new issues including illicit migration and illegal unreported and unregulated fishing. The depth and breadth of his analysis provides a valuable guide to the current law and practice of maritime interception on the high seas.

Catherine Redgwell
Oxford, 14 February 2013

Preface

This book is based on a PhD thesis awarded by University of London (University College London) in October 2009. It reflects the law as it stood, to the best of the author's knowledge, on 25 November 2012. An earlier draft of chapter two was published as 'The Right of Visit on the High Seas in a Theoretical Perspective: *Mare Liberum v Mare Clausum* Revisited' (2011) 24 *Leiden Journal of International Law* 45–69, and of chapter eight as 'Interception of Human Beings on the High Seas: A Contemporary Analysis under International Law' (2009) 36 *Syracuse Journal of International Law and Commerce* 145–228. An earlier version of the author's arguments relating to piracy off the coast of Somalia in chapter six has appeared in 'Piracy off Somalia: The Emperors and the Thieves of the Oceans in the 21st Century', in A Abass (ed), *Protecting Human Security in Africa* (Oxford, Oxford University Press, 2010) 122–54.

Acknowledgements

This book began as a doctoral thesis undertaken at University College London and was concluded almost three years after submission of the thesis in August 2009. They say that every book has its own history; this one has been written in many different libraries, such as the IALS library in London or the Peace Palace Library in the Hague; in many different parts of the world, from an apartment in New York to the beaches of several islands in the Aegean Sea including Amorgos or Karpathos and even in a hospital in Athens, where I had to stay for a week in July 2012.

It is a very pleasing – albeit daunting – task to endeavour to thank everyone who has been of support, not only during the four years of doctoral study but also during the years following my return to Greece. The reason is simply that I was extremely fortunate in having received the support, the assistance and the love of many remarkable persons. First and particular thanks are due to my PhD supervisor, Professor Catherine Redgwell, whose commitment and help has been invaluable. I am certain that this work would have been very much the poorer without her influence and her detailed comments upon numerous drafts. Her dedication and her patience with regard my infamous 'punctuality' and my propensity to use Latin maxims have been extraordinary. I was fortunate also in having Professor Vaughan Lowe and Professor Malgosia Fitzmaurice as my doctoral examiners, who, with their valuable comments, greatly improved the present work.

I am also grateful to those academics and those practitioners in the United Kingdom, in Greece and in other parts of the world who were kind enough to speak to me about and support my research, or to offer comments on earlier drafts of certain chapters. I am especially thankful to Dr Douglas Guilfoyle, Richard Gardiner, Lt Commander Brad Kieserman, Captain J Ashley Roach (Ret), Professor Myron Nordquist, Professor Maria Gavouneli, Dr Anastasia Strati, Professor Ilias Bantekas, Dr Erieta Skalieri, Judge Linos-Alexandros Sicilianos, Professor Emmanuel Roucounas, Professor Achilles Skordas, Professor Antonios Bredimas, Professor Tulio Scovazzi, Professor Tulio Treves, Dr Seline Trevisanut, Dr Irene Papanikolopulu, all of whom, by providing valuable assistance during different stages of writing, have each made their unique contribution to this work. I must particularly thank my 'anonymous source' for providing me with priceless information and for enlightening me in many respects about contemporary policing on the high seas. Furthermore, special thanks are due to all my teachers in International Law in all academic institutions in which I have studied, both in Greece and in the UK, for being the source of my inspiration and love for the discipline of public international law. Similar thanks must go to people with whom I have worked in Greece since 2009, for their encouragement and support, namely Professor Emmanuel Roucounas, Professor Costas Antonopoulos, Dr Ioannis Ktistakis, Professor Maria Gavouneli, Professor Stavros Tsakyrakis and Dr Anastasia Strati. Nothing in this book should be taken, however, as representing the views of others or the organisations for which they work.

I gratefully acknowledge the generous financial support of the Greek Institute of State Scholarships (IKY) and of the Academy of Athens throughout my doctoral studies, as well as funding provided by the UCL Old Students Association and by the UCL Graduate School (UCL Alumni Scholarship). In addition, I am especially thankful to the Directors of Research Studies at the UCL Faculty of Laws, Professor Eric Barendt and Dr Diamond Ashiagbor, for having funded my research trips to New York, Heidelberg and The Hague, which have proven particularly helpful for the completion of my doctoral thesis. Furthermore, I would like to thank all the librarians working at the IALS Library, the Peace Palace Library, the Max Planck Institute and the NYU Law Library for their kind assistance during my research in those places. Grateful mention should be made of the Hellenic Society of International Law and International Relations for its Honorary Mention for Doctoral Thesis on International Law (2009-2010) awarded to me in December 2011.

Particular thanks must go also to my friends and colleagues in London and in Greece who have been extremely helpful and supportive and have made this solitary activity a joyful and unforgettable experience. Without wanting to exclude any of my dearest friends, special thanks are due to my bright law colleagues Panos Merkouris and Anastasios Gourgourinis, who have read parts of this work in draft and have offered their valuable comments, as well as to my lovely flatmates Ilias Papapoulios and Kyriaki Bouri for their enormous patience and compassion at the difficult final stage of my studies. I am also thankful to my other young colleagues, all members of the 'Greek Mafia', with whom I spend hours discussing international law – including but not only – Dr Ilias Plakokefalos, Dr Antonios Tzanakopoulos and Dr Markos Karavias.

My final word of gratitude is due to my mother Vasileia, to whom this is dedicated.

Contents

List of Abbreviations

ACHR	American Convention on Human Rights
AJIL	American Journal of International Law
AIDI	Annuaire de l'Institut de Droit International
AFDI	Annuaire Français de Droit International
American University ILR	American University International Law Review
ARIEL	Austrian Review of International and European Law
ASIL PROC	American Society of International Law Proceedings
AYIL	Australian Yearbook of International Law
Brooklyn JIL	Brooklyn Journal of International Law
BYIL	British Yearbook of International Law
California Western ILJ	California Western International Law Journal
CYIL	Canadian Yearbook of International Law
Chicago JIL	Chicago Journal of International Law
Chinese JIL	Chinese Journal of International Law
Columbia JTL	Columbia Journal of Transnational Law
Cornell JIL	Cornell Journal of International Law
CYIL	Canadian Yearbook of International Law
Denver JILP	Denver Journal of International Law and Policy
ECOMOG	Economic Community of West African States Monitoring Group
ECOWAS	The Economic Community of West African States
ECtHR	European Court of Human Rights
EHRLR	European Human Rights Law Review
EJIL	European Journal of International Law
Emory ILR	Emory International Law Review
EPIL	Encyclopedia of Public International Law
Florida JIL	Florida Journal of International Law
Fordham ILJ	Fordham International Law Journal
FRONTEX	European Agency for the Management of Operational Co-operation at the External Borders of the Member States of the European Union
FYIL	Finnish Yearbook of International Law
GA	General Assembly
Georgetown ILJ	Georgetown Immigration Law Journal
Georgia JICL	Georgia Journal of International and Comparative Law

GYIL	German Yearbook of International Law
Harvard ILJ	Harvard International Law Journal
Hastings ICLR	Hastings International and Comparative Law Review
Houston JIL	Houston Journal of International Law
HRQ	Human Rights Quarterly
HRLR	Human Rights Law Review
ICJ	International Court of Justice
ICLQ	International and Comparative Law Quarterly
IJMCL	International Journal of Marine and Coastal Law
IJRL	International Journal of Refugee Law
ILA	International Law Association
ILC	International Law Commission
ILM	International Legal Materials
ILS	International Law Studies
ILSA JICL	ILSA Journal of International and Comparative Law
IJMCL	International Journal of Marine and Coastal Law
Int CLRev.	International Community Law Review
ISPS	International Code for the Security of Ships and of Port Facilities
IYHR.	Israel Yearbook on Human Rights
IYIL	Italian Yearbook of International Law
JCSL	Journal of Conflict and Security Law
JEA	Journal of European Affairs
JHIL	Journal of the History of International Law
JICJ	Journal of International Criminal Justice
JIML	Journal of International Maritime Law
JSAS	Journal of Southeast Asian Studies
JTLP	Journal of Transnational Law and Policy
Keesings	Keesings' Record of World Events
LJIL	Leiden Journal of International Law
LNTS	League of Nations Treaty Series
LRIT	Long-Range Identification Tracking
Max Planck YBUNL	Max Planck Yearbook of United Nations Law
Mediterranean JHR	Mediterranean Journal of Human Rights
Melbourne JIL	Melbourne Journal of International Law
Melbourne ULR	Melbourne University Law Review
Michigan JIL	Michigan Journal of International Law
MP	Marine Policy
Naval LR	Naval Law Review
Naval WCR	Naval War College Review
NILR	Netherlands International Law Review

Nordic JIL	Nordic Journal of International Law (previously: Nordisk Tidsskrift for International Ret)
North Carolina JILC	North Carolina Journal of International Law and Commerce
Northwestern ULR	Northwestern University Law Review
NYIL	Netherlands Yearbook of International Law
NYUJ Int'l Law & Pol	New York University Journal of International Law and Politics
ODIL	Ocean Development and International Law
ÖzöRV	Österreichische Zeitschrift für öffentliches Recht und Völkerrecht
Pacific Rim LPJ	Pacific Rim Law and Policy Journal
PCA	Permanent Court of Arbitration
PCIJ	Permanent Court of International Justice
PSI	Proliferation Security Initiative
QUTLJJ	Queensland University of Technology Law and Justice Journal
RBDI	Revue Belge de Droit International
RCADI	Recueil de Cours de l'Académie de la Haye de Droit International
RDI	Rivista de Diritto Internazionale
REDI	Revista Española de Derecho Internacional
RGDIP	Revue Générale de Droit International Public
RHDI	Revue Hellénique de Droit International
RIAA	Reports of International Arbitral Awards
SC	United Nations Security Council
Sri Lanka JIL	Sri Lanka Journal of International Law
Syracuse JILC	Syracuse Journal of International Law and Commerce
Temple ICLJ	Temple International and Comparative Law Journal
Grotius Society	Transactions of the Grotius Society
TS	Treaty Series
Tulane MLJ	Tulane Maritime Law Journal
LOSC	United Nations Convention for the Law of the Sea (1982) 21 ILM 1261
UN	United Nations
UNHCR	United Nations High Commissioner for Refugees
UNHCR EXCOM	United Nations High Commissioner for Refugees Executive Committee
UNSC	United Nations Security Council
UNTS	United Nations Treaty Series
UChicago LR	University of Chicago Law Review
UCLA LR	UCLA Law Review

UMiami I-ALR	University of Miami Inter-American Law Review
UQueensland LR	University Queensland Law Review
Vanderbilt JTL	Vanderbilt Journal of Transnational Law
Virginia JIL	Virginia Journal of International Law
VCLT	Vienna Convention on the Law of Treaties
VN	Vereinte Nationen
Wisconsin ILJ	Wisconsin International Law Journal
Working Group	UN, Working Group on Contemporary Forms of Slavery
WMD	Weapons of Mass Destruction
Yale JIL	Yale Journal of International Law
YbILC	Yearbook of the International Law Commission
ZaöRV	Zeitschrift für ausländisches öffentliches Recht und Völkerrecht

Table of Cases

International Judgments, Advisory Opinions and Arbitral Awards

National Decisions

Table of Treaties and other International Agreements

Multilateral Agreements

Bilateral Agreements and Treaties

1

Introduction

I. INTRODUCTORY REMARKS: ENQUIRING MARITIME INTERCEPTION ON THE HIGH SEAS

MARITIME INTERCEPTION, OR the right of visit, as it is called under the UN Convention on the Law of the Sea (article 110),[1] is the most significant exception to the fundamental principle of the freedom of the high seas, which is predominantly of a negative nature. According to the UN Memorandum on the Regime of the High Seas (1950):

> The freedom of the high seas, essentially negative, may nevertheless contain positive consequences . . . All maritime flag-States have equal right to put the high seas to legitimate use. But the idea of the equality of usage comes only in second place. The essential idea underlying the principle of freedom of the high seas is the concept of the prohibition of interference in peacetime by ships flying one national flag with ships flying the flag of other nationalities.[2]

From this prohibition of interference with non-national vessels flows the principle of exclusivity of flag-state jurisdiction, namely that ships on the high seas are, as a general rule, subject to the exclusive jurisdiction and authority of the state whose flag they lawfully fly.[3] This principle is firmly rooted in the axioms of state equality and of the freedom of the high seas.[4] However, it is not an absolute rule from which no derogation is

---

[1] See United Nations Convention on the Law of the Sea, 1833 *United Nations Treaty Series* 397; entered into force 16 November 1994 (hereinafter: LOSC); as at 7 November 2012, LOSC has 164 parties, including the EC; see at www.un.org/Depts/los/reference_files/chronological_lists_of_ratifications.htm#The United Nations Convention on the Law of the Sea.

[2] Memorandum on the Regime of the High Seas, by the Secretariat, (14 July 1950), UN Doc. A/CN 4/32, reprinted in (1950-II) *Yearbook of the International Law Commission*, 67, 69 (translation) (hereinafter: *UN Memorandum*). The Memorandum is believed to be the work of Gilbert Gidel.

[3] See generally I Brownlie, *Principles of Public International Law*, 7th edn (Oxford: Clarendon Press, 2008) 225 (hereinafter: Brownlie, *Principles*); DP O'Connell, *The International Law of the Sea* Vol II (ed IA Shearer) (Oxford: Clarendon Press, 1984) 796 (hereinafter, O'Connell); R Jennings and A Watts, *Oppenheim's International Law*, 9th edn (London: Longman, 1992) 737 (hereinafter: Oppenheim's *International Law*).

[4] It was famously given judicial imprimatur in the dictum of Lord Stowell in the *Le Louis* case: 'All nations being equal all have an equal right to the uninterrupted use of the unappropriated parts of the oceans for their navigation. In places where no local authority exists, where the subjects of all States meet upon a footing of entire equality and independence, no

permitted. On the contrary, international law has recognised since the inception and consolidation of *mare liberum* certain instances where interference is permissible. Piracy, slave trade and illegal fishing are a few examples of cases, which have involved the exercise of the right of visit of foreign vessels on the high seas in peacetime, while it is undisputed that belligerent states may exercise this right against enemy and neutral merchant vessels in wartime.

Recently, the number of cases in which this right is exercised has significantly increased, with the result that the negative concept of the freedom of the high seas is, arguably, challenged. Besides the unexpected rise of piratical acts off the coast of Somalia since 2008 and more recently in the Gulf of Guinea,[5] states have become increasingly involved in intercepting vessels on the high seas to counter threats, such as smuggling of migrants, drug trafficking, and the proliferation of weapons of mass destruction (WMD) at sea. Several partnerships in various forms have been established to this end, such as the Proliferation Security Initiative (PSI)[6] or the Agency for the Management of Operational Cooperation at the External Borders of the European Union (FRONTEX),[7] as well as numerous agreements concluded concerning the interdiction of suspect vessels in this regard. The 2005 SUA Protocol,[8] the 2000 Smuggling Protocol[9] and the 2008 CARICOM Maritime

---

one State, or any of its subjects, has a right to assume or exercise authority over the subjects of another', *Le Louis,* 2 Dods, 210, 243, 165 *Eng Rep* (1817), 1464, 1475. On the other side of the Atlantic, Justice Story held in *The Marianna Flora* case that 'Upon the ocean, in time of peace, all possess an entire equality. It is the common highway of all, appropriated to the use of all; and no one can vindicate to himself a superior or exclusive prerogative there', *The Marianna Flora,* 24 US (11 Wheat) (1826) 1, 42. See also *Lotus Case (France v Turkey),* judgment, PCIJ, Ser A, No 10 (1927) 25.

[5] See SC Res 2018/2011 and SC Res 2039/2012 and discussion below, Ch 6.

[6] PSI is described on the website of the US Department of State as 'a global effort that aims to stop trafficking of weapons of mass destruction (WMD), their delivery systems, and related materials to and from states and non-state actors of proliferation concern': see www.state.gov/t/isn/c10390.htm.

[7] For further information regarding FRONTEX, see its website: www.frontex.europa.eu. See also generally R Weinzierl and U Lisson, *Border Management and Human Rights: A Study of EU Law and the Law of the Sea* (Berlin: German Institute for Human Rights, 2007) (hereinafter: Weinzierl and Lisson) and E Papastavridis, 'Fortress Europe and FRONTEX: Within or Without International Law?' 79 *Nordic Journal of International Law* (2010) 75.

[8] Protocol of 2005 to the Convention for the Suppression of Unlawful Acts against the Safety of Maritime Navigation, IMO Doc LEG/CONF.15/21 (2005), available on the website of the US Department of State at www.state.gov/t/isn/trty/81727.htm (hereinafter: 2005 SUA Protocol). The 2005 SUA Protocol entered into force on 28 July 2010 and as at 31 October 2012 it had 22 parties; see the list of states parties available at www.imo.org/About/Conventions/StatusOfConventions/Documents/Status%20-%202012.pdf.

[9] 2000 Protocol against the Smuggling of Migrants by Land, Sea and Air, supplementing the United Nations Convention against Transnational Organized Crime, 2241 UNTS 507 (entered into force 28 January 2004) (hereinafter: Smuggling Protocol). As at 25 November 2012, the Smuggling Protocol had 135 parties: see http://treaties.un.org/Pages/ViewDetails.aspx?src=TREATY&mtdsg_no=XVIII-12-b&chapter=18&lang=en .

and Airspace Security Agreement[10] are the principal examples of such multilateral treaties. Concurrently, the notion of *mare clausum*, namely that the high seas are subject to the appropriation of states, seems to have been reinvigorated, not in the traditional sense of claims for maritime dominion, but rather in the sense of claims for more functional jurisdiction on the high seas[11] or in the sense of a common 'responsibility for the seas' in an era of *mare crisium*.[12]

In essence, this book examines some of the legal issues that the relevant state practice has brought to the fore and thus aims at contributing to the current legal discourse on maritime interception on the high seas.[13] Its principal theoretical question is: how can the various grounds of interference with foreign vessels on the high seas, especially the foregoing regarding WMD, illicit migration and drug trafficking, be theoretically conceptualised and legally justified under a coherent regulatory order of the oceans? Given that none of these issues, but for privacy, are addressed by the pertinent provision of LOSC (article 110), it is questioned to what extent the legal order of the oceans, which is predicated upon the principle of non-interference on the high seas, can accommodate such claims for enforcement jurisdiction on the high seas. It is the purpose of this book to respond, inter alia, to this question and ascertain the role and the significance of these interception activities for the contemporary legal order of the oceans. In addition, it will endeavour to delineate the legal contours of interception operations on the high seas and address the question whether a new 'law of interdiction or interception' is emerging. Furthermore, it will provide a detailed appraisal of contemporary maritime interception operations against the background of both the law of the sea and general international law.

The overarching tenet of the present enquiry is that the oceans are subject to a certain organisational and regulatory scheme premised upon both negative and positive legal principles, which can aptly be designated as a

[10] CARICOM Maritime and Airspace Security Cooperation Agreement, signed at Bolans, Antigua and Barbuda on 4 July 2008; available at www.caricom.org/jsp/secretariat/legal_instruments/agreement_maritime_airspace_security_cooperation.pdf (hereinafter: CARICOM Agreement).

[11] On the issue of functional jurisdiction in the maritime domain and its contemporary challenges see M Gavouneli, *Functional Jurisdiction in the Law of the Sea* (Leiden: Martinus Nijhoff Publishers, 2007).

[12] See D Vidas, 'Responsibility for the Seas', in Vidas D (ed) *Law, Technology and Science for Oceans in Globalisation: IUU Fishing, Oil Pollution, Bioprospecting, Outer Continental Shelf* (Leiden: Martinus Nijhoff, 2010) 3, 35.

[13] The authors that have more recently contributed to this discourse are inter alia D Guilfoyle, *Shipping Interdiction and International Law of the Sea* (Cambridge: Cambridge University Press, 2009) (hereinafter: Guilfoyle, *Shipping Interdiction*), N Klein, *Maritime Security and the Law of the Sea* (Oxford: Oxford University Press, 2011) (hereinafter: Klein, *Maritime Security*) and C Allen, *Maritime Counterproliferation Operations and the Rule of Law* (Westport, London: Praeger Security International, 2007) (hereinafter: Allen, *Counterproliferation*).

'legal order of the oceans'.[14] The latter term resembles the original conception of Myres McDougal and William Burke of 'public order of the oceans'; however, it is neither coterminous in substance, nor does it bring along the public policy considerations enshrined in these authors' work.[15] On the other hand, it shares some characteristics without, however, being identical to the notion of 'ocean governance',[16] which is premised more upon concepts, such as 'common heritage', 'public trusteeship', 'global commons' or 'public interest', rather than fundamental norms, such as the principle of non-interference, the nationality of vessels, the conservation and management of the marine living resources, and the protection of the marine environment.[17] These norms constitute the 'Grundnormen' of this legal order, in the sense that they are the cornerstones, against which any relevant legal development is assessed and further elaborated.[18] In addition to the above principles pertaining to the law of the sea, the legal order of the oceans consists also of norms of general international law, such as the prohibition of unnecessary and disproportionate use of force and the protection of fundamental human rights and of humanitarian law.[19]

II. CONTEMPORARY CHALLENGES TO THE FREEDOM OF THE HIGH SEAS AND MARITIME INTERCEPTION

A. Terrorism and WMD

In general, most instances of interference on the high seas pertain to the following issues: first, to the threats posed by international terrorism and

---

[14] *cf UN Memorandum*, para 26. The term 'legal order of the oceans', along with the Wolffian term *'civitas maxima* of the oceans' will be used interchangeably in the present thesis.

[15] See M McDougal, W Burke, *The Public Order of the Oceans* (New Haven, CT: Yale University Press, 1962) (hereinafter: McDougal and Burke).

[16] See inter alia Y Tanaka, *A Dual Approach to Ocean Governance: the Cases of Zonal and Integrated Management in International Law* (Farnham: Ashgate, 2008) and the contributions by various authors in 'International Ocean Governance in the 21st Century' 23 *International Journal of Marine and Coastal Law* (2008).

[17] See in general R Churchill, AV Lowe, *The Law of the Sea*, 3rd edn (Manchester: Manchester University Press, 1999) (hereinafter: Churchill and Lowe) and on the particular principles see inter alia: D Nelson, 'The Development of the Legal Regime of High Seas Fisheries' in A Boyle, D Freestone (eds), *International Law and Sustainable Development* (Oxford: Oxford University Press, 2001), 119; C Redgwell, 'From Permission to Prohibition: The 1982 Convention on the Law of the Sea and the Protection of the Marine Environment', in D Freestone, R Barnes (eds), *The Law of the Sea: Progress and Prospects* (Oxford: OUP, 2006), 180.

[18] On the notion of 'Grundnorm' see H Kelsen, *Pure Theory of Law* (transl and ed M Knight) (Berkeley: University of California Press, 1970).

[19] See inter alia L Sohn, 'Peacetime Use of Force on the High Seas' in H Robertson (ed), *The Law of Naval Operations* (Newport: Naval War College Press, 1991) 39; and B Oxman, 'Human Rights and the UNCLOS' 36 *Columbia Journal of Transnational Law* (1998) 399.

by the proliferation of WMD,[20] which have been the object of much public and academic concern as well as of numerous unilateral or multilateral efforts by individual states and by international organisations.[21] The PSI has a pivotal role in this regard. Initially conceived as a 'collection of interdiction partnerships' among 11 core members,[22] it has subsequently expanded to a multifaceted international effort to combat the transfer of banned weapons and weapons technology, receiving the support of another 80 states.[23] In addition, reference should be made to UN Security Council Resolutions 1373 (2001)[24] and 1540 (2004),[25] the IMO SOLAS Amendments[26] and the 2005 SUA Protocol, the NATO Operation Active Endeavour[27] and a plethora of other unilateral and bilateral measures in this regard.[28] In terms of the number of interdictions, suffice to note that in the course of NATO's 'Operation Active Endeavour' alone, 'NATO forces . . . hailed more than 100,000 merchant vessels, boarding some 155 suspect ships'.[29]

The so-called 'War on Terror', triggered by the shattering event of '9/11', has also led to operations involving the use of force, such as the armed intervention in Afghanistan in October 2001.[30] In the course of the latter

[20] eg the 2004 UN High-Level Panel Report emphasised that preventing the proliferation of nuclear, chemical, and biological weapons materials and their potential use must remain an urgent priority for collective security; see Report of the UN Secretary-General's High-level Panel on Threats, Challenges and Change, (2004), 39. See also Allen, *Counterproliferation,* 11.

[21] The possible use of WMD by 'rogue states' and by terrorists has been identified as a major security threat, for example, in NATO's New Strategy Concept, approved by heads of state and government participating in the meeting of NATO in Washington DC, on 23 and 24 April, 1999; available at www.nato.int/docu/pr/1999/p99-065e.htm. *Cf* inter alia the European Strategy in respect of WMD in J Littlewood, 'The EU Strategy against Proliferation of WMD' 1 *Journal of European Affairs* (2003) 1.

[22] See J Garvey, 'The International Institutional Imperative for Countering the Spread of WMD' 10 *Journal of Conflict and Security Law* (2005) 125, 129.

[23] See US Department of State, Proliferation Security Initiative Participants (as of 10 September 2011), available at www.state.gov/t/isn/c27732.htm.

[24] SC Res 1373 (28 September 2001) UN Doc S/RES/1373. See M Happold, 'Security Council Resolution 1373 and the Constitution of the UN' 16 *Leiden Journal of International Law* (2003) 593.

[25] SC Res 1540 (27 April, 2004) UN Doc. S/RES/1540. See also S Sur, 'La Resolution 1540 du Conseil de Securité (28 Avril 2004)' 104 *Revue Générale de Droit International Public* (2004) 855.

[26] The new Chapter XI-2 and the ISPS Code, which came into force in July 2004, introduced far-reaching measures to improve the security of ships and port facilities. See inter alia G Hesse, 'Maritime Security in a Multilateral Context' 18 IJMCL (2003) 327; F Odier, 'La Sûreté Maritime ou les Lacunes du Droit International', in *Mélanges Offerts à Laurent Lucchini et Jean-Pierre Quéneudec* (Paris: Pedone, 2003) 455.

[27] See relevant information at www.nato.int/cps/en/natolive/topics_7932.htm.

[28] See AJ Roach, 'Initiatives to Enhance Maritime Security at Sea' 28 *Marine Policy* (2004) 41.

[29] See above n 27.

[30] See from the vast bibliography on the use of force in Afghanistan, E Myjer, N White, 'The Twin Towers Attack: An Unlimited Right of Self-defence?' 7 *JCSL* (2002) 5; O Corten, F Dubuisson, 'Operation *Liberté Immuable*' 106 *Revue Générale de Droit International Public* (2002) 51.

campaign, named 'Operation Enduring Freedom' the states involved were considerably engaged in visitations of suspect vessels on the high seas, similar to interceptions in the course of NATO's 'Operation Active Endeavour' in the Mediterranean Sea.[31] There is, however, an important legal difference between these operations, which lies in the fact that the states parties to the armed conflict in the territory of Afghanistan enjoyed *ipso facto* the belligerent right of visit and search on the high seas. Suffice it also to include in this category the Israeli operation off Gaza Strip in 2010[32] which involved interdiction measures on the high seas justified under the rules of the law of war, as well as Operation Unified Protector in Libya in 2011.[33]

B. Drug Trafficking

Similar enforcement measures on the high seas are often exercised in the context of drug trafficking.[34] Although a wide variety of methods are utilised by drug traffickers in plying their trade, the use of private and commercial vessels has long been significant. This is particularly the case with drugs such as cocaine, opium and its derivatives, and cannabis, all regulated by the Single Convention on Narcotics Drugs, as amended,[35] where transportation from source to consumer country frequently involves passage over ocean areas.[36] For example, given its relative widespread availability and low cost, the vast majority of marijuana and cocaine entering the US from abroad is said to be transported by private vessels.[37] As is reported by the UN Office on Drugs and Crime (UNODOC),

> For the North American market, cocaine is typically transported from Colombia to Mexico or Central America by sea and then onwards by land to the United States and Canada. Cocaine is trafficked to Europe mostly by sea, often in container shipments. Colombia remains the main source of the cocaine found in

---

[31] See P Jimenez-Kwast, 'Maritime Interdiction of WMD in an International Legal Perspective' 38 *Netherlands Yearbook of International Law* (2007) 163, 235 (hereinafter: Jimenez-Kwast).

[32] See Report of the Secretary-General's Panel of Inquiry on the 31 May 2010 Flotilla Incident (September 2011), available at www.un.org/News/dh/infocus/middle_east/Gaza_Flotilla_Panel_Report.pdf and comments by D Guilfoyle at www.ejiltalk.org/the-palmer-report-on-the-mavi-marmara-incident-and-the-legality-of-israel%E2%80%99s-blockade-of-the-gaza-strip/.

[33] On Libya see inter alia SC Resolutions 1970 (2011), 1973 (2011) and 2009 (2011), and on the Operation see www.nato.int/cps/en/SID-D936FE09-8BE07838/natolive/topics_71652.htm.

[34] See in general Guilfoyle, *Shipping Interdiction*, 69–85 and P Van der Kruit, *Maritime Drug Interdiction in International Law* (Utrecht: Druk OBT/TDS, 2007).

[35] See Single Convention on Narcotic Drugs (1961) 520 UNTS 151; as amended by the 1972 Protocol 976 UNTS 3.

[36] See P Van der Kruit, above n 34, 21.

[37] See W Gilmore, 'Narcotics Interdiction at Sea, US-UK Cooperation' (1989) *MP* 218.

Europe, but direct shipments from Peru and the Plurinational State of Bolivia are far more common than in the United States market.[38]

Also, the means employed by the drug-traffickers in Central America have become highly sophisticated: apart from 'go-fast' vessels,[39] they use semi-submersible vessels, which are almost impossible to be properly stopped and visited.[40] Such vessels are 'both difficult for the Coast Guard to detect and easy for crewmembers, who often prefer losing their cargo to being caught, to sink. At the first sign of the Coast Guard, drug traffickers can quickly sink the vessel and jump into the ocean, which destroys the evidence necessary to prosecute them for a drug offense . . .'.[41]

This traffic by sea has led to various initiatives taken by those states most affected, such as the US and European countries. Central to this has been the policy of interception of vessels not only in the territorial waters of the consumer states, but also on the high seas and even further in the territorial waters of the source or transit States. This policy has been effectuated either through informal means, ie ad hoc consent of the flag state or of the vessel's master (consensual boarding), or through bilateral and multilateral treaties, such as the Caribbean ship rider agreements[42] and

[38] See at www.unodc.org/unodc/en/drug-trafficking/index.html. The latest World Drugs Report-Executive Summary (2011) issued by the UN Office on Drugs and Crime, recorded that 'since 2006 seizures have shifted towards the source areas in South America and away from the consumer markets in North America and West and Central Europe. The role of West Africa in cocaine trafficking from South America to Europe might have decreased if judged from seizures only, but there are other indications that traffickers may have changed their tactics, and the area remains vulnerable to a resurgence in trafficking of cocaine'; see www.unodc.org/documents/data-and-analysis/WDR2011/WDR2011-ExSum.pdf

[39] These are typically 25–50 ft open boats, powered by twin outbound engines and capable of sustaining speed of 20–40 knots in 1–3 ft seas. Such boats present significant detection problems and their high speed enables them to escape into foreign territorial waters when confronted by the possibility of interdiction on the high seas; see W Gilmore, *Agreement Concerning Co-operation in Suppressing Illicit Maritime and Air Trafficking in Narcotic Drugs and Psychotropic Substances in the Caribbean Area* (London: The Stationery Office, 2005) 2 (hereinafter: Gilmore, Caribbean).

[40] Drug submarines, which can be made for as little as $500,000 each and assembled in fewer than three months, are thought to carry almost thirty percent of Colombia's cocaine exports; see David Kushner, *Drug-Sub Culture,* NY TIMES, April 23, 2009, 30, available at <http://www.nytimes.com/2009/04/26/magazine/26drugs-t.html.> It is reported that 'One self-propelled semi-submersible vessel intercepted by the Coast Guard, for example, contained seven tons of cocaine, worth $187 million'; see A Bennett, 'The Sinking Feeling: Stateless Ships, Universal Jurisdiction, and the Drug Trafficking Vessel interdiction Act' (2012) 37 *Yale Journal of International Law* 433, 434.

[41] Ibid, 434.

[42] The problem of maritime illicit traffic of narcotic drugs is particularly acute in the Caribbean region, where there are a number of contiguous nations separated by relatively narrow bodies of water which serve, for the smugglers, as natural 'stepping stones' between source and consumer states. These nations provide the 'quintessential drug trafficking havens due to their sparse populations and limited enforcement capability'; see K Rattray, 'Caribbean Drug Challenges', in M Nordquist and JN Moore (eds), *Ocean Policy: New Institutions, Challenges and Opportunities* (The Hague: Nijhoff, 1999) 179, 185.

the 1988 UN Convention against Illicit Traffic in Narcotic Drugs and Psychotropic Substances, respectively.[43]

C. Illicit Migration

Another realm, where the interception of vessels on the high seas looms large, pertains to illicit migration and asylum. It is a truism that the high seas have always furnished a way to safety for potential asylum-seekers or forced migrants. In the last century alone, the world witnessed the plight of Jewish refugees fleeing Nazi persecution before World War II,[44] the 'boat people' from Indochina during the 1970s[45] and, more recently, the thousands of Haitians and Cubans travelling to the United States[46] and many of diverse nationalities heading to southern Europe across the Mediterranean Sea.[47] Episodes like the *Tampa*[48] and the *Monica*,[49] which involved asylum-seekers at sea, have attracted notable media coverage

---

[43] See UN Convention against Illicit Traffic in Narcotic Drugs and Psychotropic Substances (Vienna, 19 December 1988) 21 *International Legal Materials* (1988) 1261 (hereinafter: 1988 Vienna Convention). As at 25 November 2012, the Convention had 188 state parties; see treaties.un.org/Pages/ViewDetails.aspx?src=TREATY&mtdsg_no=VI-19&chapter=6&lang=en. For commentary see inter alia UN Economic and Social Council, *Commentary on the UN Convention against Illicit Traffic in Narcotic Drugs and Psychotropic Substances 1988* (1998) (hereinafter: Vienna Commentary).

[44] See G Thomas, M-M Witts, *The Voyage of the Damned* (New York: Stein and Day, 1974). Famous was the *St Luis* episode, where over 900 Jews fleeing Nazi Germany en route to Cuba were not allowed to disembark in that country and were summarily rejected by a number of the Latin American governments and the US and Canada; see J van Selm and B Cooper, *The New 'Boat People': Ensuring Safety and Determining Status* (Washington DC: Migration Policy Institute, 2006) 91 (hereinafter: Van Selm and Cooper).

[45] See inter alia B Grant, *The Boat People* (London: Penguin, 1980).

[46] For the last quarter of century, the US shores have been the target destination of thousands of undocumented migrants or asylum-seekers coming mostly from Cuba, Haiti and Dominican Republic. In response to discrete episodes of mass irregular migration, the US government has authorised various maritime interdiction programmes, which have evolved into standing boarder enforcement. See Van Selm and Cooper, 79.

[47] Migrant and refugee flows have long been a challenge to the states bordering the Mediterranean Sea. These maritime movements to a greater or lesser degree affect all Mediterranean states. See for further information: Meeting of State Representatives on Rescue at Sea and Maritime Interception in the Mediterranean (Madrid, 23–24 May 2006), available at *www.unhcr.org/refworld/pdfid/45b8d8b44.pdf*.

[48] In August 2001, the Norwegian-flag cargo vessel M/V *Tampa* rescued 440 people from an Indonesian ferry that was sinking about 75 nm north-west of Christmas Island, Australia. When Tampa sought to offload its passengers in Australia, the latter, concerned with an influx of immigrants, refused to accept them. Following lengthy negotiations, New Zealand and Nauru eventually accepted the refugees. For the facts, see D Rothwell, 'The Law of the Sea and the M/V Tampa Incident' 13 *Public Law Review* (2002) 118.

[49] On 17 March 2002, the merchant vessel *Monica*, a 75-metre long cargo ship, flying the flag of Tonga and with more than 900 Kurdish refugees on board, was detected and subsequently intercepted in the Eastern Mediterranean by the French Navy, which proceeded to verify the identity of the ship, after a signal from the Italian authorities. See I Thomas, 'L'affaire du "*Monica*"' 106 *RGDIP* (2002) 391.

and triggered serious academic and political debate.[50] Given that the prime concern of these people is to flee from their country of origin, rather than to flee to any particular place, it is not surprising that they flee by whatever means possible, including overcrowded and unseaworthy vessels.[51] Such vessels will often be at risk of sinking and indeed many do sink, with the result that thousands of lives are lost every year.[52] This has been particularly noticeable in the period since January 2011, which has seen an increase in departures of migrant boats from North Africa and, allegedly, at least 1,500 persons have lost their lives while trying to cross the Mediterranean.[53] Currently, there is a mass exodus of Syrian nationals fleeing from their country often by boats due to the deteriorating security situation in Syria.[54]

It is evident that in the contemporary era the focus of most, especially developed, states has predominantly shifted to preventing asylum-seekers or illicit migrants from reaching their territory.[55] Amongst the 'non-arrival' policies employed to this end,[56] a primary role is attributed to interception, which has attained even more vigour recently in the light of the adoption of the Smuggling Protocol, as well as of the relevant

[50] See inter alia: X Hinrichs, 'Measures against Smuggling of Migrants at Sea: A Law of the Sea Related Perspective' 36 *Revue Belge de Droit International* (2003) 413 (hereinafter: Hinrichs), P Mathew, 'Australian Refugee Protection in the Wake of *Tampa*' 96 *American Journal of International Law* (2002) 661.

[51] Reports to IMO recount almost unimaginable means of transportation, such as a small inflated raft for children of two metres length, carrying two migrants, a windsurfer with two migrants, an improvised raft (a wooden door with plastic bottles tied to it) with two migrants etc; see Second Biannual Report, IMO doc MSC3/Circ 2 (October 31, 2001); available at www.imo.org.

[52] See information and reports of dead or missing people up to 2011 in the UNHCR's website on asylum and migration, entitled 'All in the same boat: the challenges of mixed migration'; available at www.unhcr.org/pages/4a1d406060.html.

[53] See inter alia Report by T Hammarberg, Commissioner for Human Rights of the Council of Europe (Strasbourg, 7 September 2011) – CommDH (2011) 26, available at https://wcd.coe.int/wcd/ViewDoc.jsp?id=1826921. See also the recent allegations with respect to NATO vessels leaving people to die off the coast of Libya at www.guardian.co.uk/world/2011/may/08/nato-ship-libyan-migrants (8 May 2011), and commentary in S Trevisanut's and E Papastavridis' posts at EJILTALK, available at www.ejiltalk.org.

[54] According to UNHCR, there are 'more than 280,000 people registered or in need of humanitarian assistance and protection as of end of September [2012]; see UN, Syrian Regional Response Plan, Second Revision (September 2012); available at http://data.unhcr.org/syrianrefugees/uploads/SyriaRRP.pdf.

[55] In terms of immigration and refugee matters, it is submitted that the current debate is premised on a rather stark dichotomy between protection and control as ways of regulating migration in a globalised world. This is more apposite now than ever, in the aftermath of 9/11; see G Loescher, 'Refugee Protection and State Security: towards a Greater Convergence' in RM Price and MW Zacker (eds), *The UN and Global Security* (New York: Palgrave Macmillan, 2004) 161.

[56] The usual measures employed in order to tackle this problem, besides interception, are inter alia pre-inspection, visa requirements, carrier sanctions, 'safe third country' concepts, security zones, and international zones; see G Goodwin-Gill and J McAdam, *The Refugee in International Law* 3rd edn (Oxford: Oxford University Press, 2007) 374 (hereinafter: Goodwin-Gill and McAdam).

practice of states, like Australia,[57] the US[58] and various European states.[59] The latest example is manifestly the 2009 'push-back' operations conducted by Italy in cooperation with Libya in the central Mediterranean Sea.[60]

A central role in the interception of asylum-seekers or illicit migrants has been ascribed to FRONTEX, which was established in 2004 to help EU Member States in implementing community legislation on the surveillance of the EU borders, including maritime borders, and to coordinate their operational cooperation.[61]

> While considering that the responsibility for the control and surveillance of external borders lies with the Member States, the Agency, as a body of the Union . . . shall facilitate and render more effective the application of existing and future Union measures relating to the management of external borders, in particular the Schengen Borders Code . . . It shall do so by ensuring the coordination of the actions of the Member States in the implementation of those measures, thereby contributing to an efficient, high and uniform level of control on persons and of surveillance of the external borders of the Member States.[62]

As officially stated by FRONTEX, the Agency 'plans, coordinates, implements and evaluates joint operations conducted using Member States' staff and equipment at the external borders (sea, land and air)'.[63] Truly, many joint interception operations have been executed by EU

---

[57] Following the *Tampa* incident in 2001, the then Howard Government passed a series of laws –commonly referred to as 'Pacific Strategy' (previously, 'Solution') – 'excising' various islands and coastal ports from the migration zone. See in this regard A Schloenhardt (ed), *Migrant Smuggling, Illegal Migration and Organized Crime in Australia and Asia Pacific Region* (Leiden: Martinus Nijhoff, 2003). Instrumental to the implementation of the Pacific Strategy were maritime interception operations; see P Mathew, 'Address: Legal Issues Concerning Interception', 17 *Georgetown Immigration Law Journal* (2003) 221, 227.

[58] For interception operations recently launched in relation to Haiti see B Frelick, 'Abundantly Clear: *Refoulement*' 19 *Georgetown International Law Journal* (2005) 245.

[59] From time to time, European states such as Italy or Spain have engaged in interception at sea; see UNHCR, Selected Reference Materials, Rescue at Sea, Maritime Interception and Stowaways (November 2006), available at www.unhcr.bg/other/law_of_the_sea.pdf.

[60] According to the Italian authorities, from 6 May to 6 November 2009, a total of nine operations were carried out, returning a total of 834 persons to Libya; see further information at http://migrantsatsea.wordpress.com/2010/03/18/unhcr-files-ecthr-third-party-intervention-in-hirsi-v-italy/ and also V Moreno-Lax, 'Seeking Asylum in the Mediterranean: against a Fragmentary Reading of EU Member States' Obligations Accruing at Sea' 23 *International Journal of Refugee Law* (2011) 174, 185 and M Giuffré, 'State Responsibility beyond Borders: What Legal Basis for Italy's Push-backs to Libya?' (2012) 24 *International Journal of Refugee Law* (forthcoming) [on file with the author].

[61] See above n 7.

[62] See art 1 of Regulation (EU) No 1168/2011 of the European Parliament and of the Council amending Council Regulation (EC) No 2007/2004 establishing a European Agency for the Management of Operational Co-operation at the External Borders of the Member States of the European Union (FRONTEX) (25/10/2011), OJ L 304 (hereinafter: 2011 FRONTEX Regulation).

[63] See at http://frontex.europa.eu/about/mission-and-tasks.

Member States at sea.[64] Currently, there are five joint operations coordinated by FRONTEX, namely *Operation Hera* in the Canary Islands, *Operations Indalo and Minerva* in the south coast of Spain, *Operation Hermes* in the central Mediterranean, *Operation Aeneas* in South Italy and the Adriatic Sea and finally *Operation Poseidon* in the Aegean Sea.[65] Moreover, the operation capabilities of FRONTEX have been significantly enhanced by the very recent Regulation (EU) No 1168/2011, which amended the Council Regulation (EC) No 2007/2004 establishing FRONTEX. Under this Regulation, the Agency, inter alia, has the authority to plan, on its own, joint operations or pilot projects, while Member States should contribute with an appropriate number of skilled border guards and make them available for deployment on a semi-permanent basis.[66]

D. Piracy and Armed Robbery at Sea

Besides international peace and security, drug trafficking and illicit migration, which have recently come at the centre of the focus of international community, the most hotly debated relevant issue lately is piracy in Africa. While piracy *jure gentium* had been considered almost obsolete until 2008, it has forcefully come to the fore since then. The extraordinary growth in piracy off the coast of Somalia has attracted unprecedented media coverage and has led the international community to take many measures to suppress and to prevent this scourge.[67] NATO as well as the European Union have launched maritime operations to protect international shipping from such attacks and the UN Security Council has made a series of Resolutions under Chapter VII authorising entry into the territorial waters or even into the mainland of Somalia for the purpose of arresting the suspect pirates.[68] Lately, the theatre of many pirate attacks

---

[64] Examples of recently accomplished operations include inter alia: Operation EPN-Hermes, from 20 February 2011 to 31 March 2012, which aimed to implement coordinated sea border activities to control illegal migration flows from Tunisia towards south of Italy (mainly Lampedusa and Sardinia); JO EPN Hera 2009 (extended in 2010), on tackling illegal immigration coming from West African countries disembarking in Canary Islands; JO Operation POSEIDON 2009 (extended in 2010) in the Eastern Mediterranean Sea; see http://frontex.europa.eu/operations/archive-of-accomplished-operations.

[65] Information provided in a personal communication with the author under conditions of anonymity (12.11.2012).

[66] See inter alia 2011 FRONTEX Regulation, art 1(5) amending art 3 of Regulation No 2007/2004.

[67] See inter alia www.imo.org/MediaCentre/resources/Pages/Piracy-and-armed-robbery-against-ships.asp.

[68] On piracy off Somalia see inter alia R Geiss, A Petrig, *Piracy and Armed Robbery at Sea. The Legal Framework for Counter-Piracy Operations in Somalia and the Gulf of Aden* (Oxford: OUP, 2011) (hereinafter: Geiss and Petrig); D Guilfoyle, 'Combating Piracy: Executive Measures on the High Seas' 53 *Japanese Yearbook of International Law* (2010) 149; E Papastavridis, 'Piracy off Somalia: The Emperors and the Thieves of the Oceans in the 21st Century', in A Abass (ed),

has shifted to West Africa, in particular the Gulf of Guinea, which has been condemned by the Security Council.[69] Closely related to the uprising of piracy *jure gentium* is the novel crime of armed robbery at sea, which describes those piratical acts that take place within a coastal state's jurisdiction.[70] Often, such incidents of armed robbery at sea are closely intertwined with *acta pirata* off the Somali coast and other African states.

E. IUU Fishing

Lastly, it should not be omitted that one of the most long-standing and recurrent grounds for interference with foreign vessels on the high seas is illegal fishing, or, as currently labelled, illegal, unreported, unregulated (IUU) fishing.[71] Combating IUU fishing has been one of the main issues on the international fisheries agenda for the past decade, as it has been recognised as a major threat to fisheries conservation and marine biodiversity.[72] It is reported that 'in case of fisheries, more than 75 per cent of the world's fish stocks are reported as already fully exploited or overexploited and increasing numbers of marine species are considered threatened or endangered'.[73] Numbers regarding IUU fishing are telling: 'the 2008 estimates for the total value of IUU losses worldwide are between USD 10 and 23 billion annually'.[74] The international community has endeavoured

Protecting Human Security in Africa (Oxford: Oxford University Press, 2010) 122 (hereinafter: Papastavridis, *Somalia*).

[69] See above n 5.

[70] IMO, Code of Practice for the Investigation of the Crimes of Piracy and Armed Robbery against Ships, adopted 29 November 2001, Res A922(22), art 2(2), www.pmaesa.org/Maritime/Res%20A.922(22).doc. *Cf* also art 1 of the Regional Cooperation Agreement on Combating Piracy and Armed Robbery against Ships in Asia (28 April 2005), *International Legal Materials* (2005) 829.

[71] See 2005 Rome Declaration on Illegal, Unreported and Unregulated Fishing adopted by the FAO Ministerial Meeting on Fisheries, Rome, 12 March 2005, available at ftp://ftp.fao.org/fi/document/ministerial/2005/iuu/declaration.pdf. See also Closing the Net: Stopping Illiegal Fishing on the High Seas, Final Report of the Ministerially-led Task Force on IUU Fishing on the High Seas, 2006, available at www.high-seas.org and M Palma et al, *Promoting Sustainable Fisheries: The International Legal and Policy Framework to Combat Illegal, Unreported and Unregulated Fishing* (Leiden: Martinus Nijhoff, 2010) 245 (hereinafter: Palma, *Fisheries*).

[72] See T Lobach, 'Combating IUU Fishing: Interaction of Global and Regional Initiatives', in Vidas D (ed), *Law, Technology and Science for Oceans in Globalisation: IUU Fishing, Oil Pollution, Bioprospecting, Outer Continental Shelf* (Leiden: Martinus Nijhoff, 2010) 109, 109.

[73] R Rayfuse, 'Moving Beyond the Tragedy of Global Commons: The Grotian Legacy and the Future of Sustainable Management of the Biodiversity of the High Seas', in Leary D and Pisupati B (eds), *The Future of International Environmental Law* (Tokyo: United Nations University Press, 2010) 201, 204.

[74] K Gjerde, 'High Seas Fisheries Governance: Prospects and Challenges in the 21st Century', in Vidas D and Schei J (eds), *The World Ocean in Globalisation: Climate Change, Sustainable Fisheries, Biodiversity, Shipping, Regional Issues* (Leiden: Martinus Nijhoff, 2011) 221, 224.

to address this particular problem either globally by adopting multilateral instruments, such as the UN Fish Stocks Agreement (1995)[75] and the FAO Compliance Agreement (1993),[76] or regionally by the action of an array of regional fisheries management organisations (RFMOs).[77] To this end, joint enforcement operations and inspection schemes have been extensively employed both in areas under national jurisdiction and on the high seas.[78]

In conclusion, there are certain international problems that have given rise to extensive interception activities on the high seas, which, arguably, challenge the fundamental principle of the freedom of the high seas. Such activities concern not only long-standing matters, such as piracy or fisheries, but also contemporary challenges, in the form of maritime terrorism, proliferation of WMD, drug trafficking and illicit migration.

F. Are They All 'Threats to Maritime Security'?

Having said that, it is fitting to note here that there is a trend to include all these challenges under the generic and all-encompassing heading 'maritime security'. While there is a lack of any specific mention to 'maritime security' in LOSC or in the relevant IMO instruments, many authors speak of 'maritime threats' or of 'threats to maritime security'.[79] The latter term is also employed by the UN Secretary General in his 2008 *Report on Oceans and the Law of the Sea*, which has identified seven specific 'threats to maritime security': 1) piracy and armed robbery against ships, 2) terrorist acts against shipping, offshore installations and other maritime interests, 3) illicit trafficking in arms and weapons of mass destruction, 4) illicit trafficking in narcotic drugs and psychotropic substances, 5) smuggling

---

[75] UN Agreement for the Implementation of the Provisions of the UNCLOS of 10 December 1982 relating to the Conservation and Management of Straddling Fish Stocks and Highly Migratory Fish Stocks 1995, 2167 UNTS 88. The Agreement was opened for signature on 4 December 1995 and entered into force on 11 December 2001 (hereinafter: Straddling Stocks Agreement). As of 7 November 2012 , there were 80 parties; see www.un.org/Depts/los/reference_files/chronological_lists_of_ratifications.htm#Agreement for the implementation of the provisions of the Convention relating to the conservation and management of straddling fish stocks and highly migratory fish stocks.

[76] Agreement to Promote Compliance with International Conservation and Management Measures by Fishing Vessels on the High Seas (1994) 2221 UNTS 91. The FAO Compliance Agreement was approved on 24 November 1993 by Resolution 15/93 of the Twenty-Seventh Session of the FAO Conference and entered in force on 24 April 2003 (hereinafter: FAO Compliance Agreement).

[77] See eg M Lodge, 'Developing a Model for Improved Governance by Regional Fisheries Management Organizations', in Vidas D (ed), *Law, Technology and Science for Oceans in Globalisation: IUU Fishing, Oil Pollution, Bioprospecting, Outer Continental Shelf* (Leiden: Martinus Nijhoff, 2010) 157–74.

[78] See inter alia R Rayfuse, *Non-Flag State Enforcement in High Seas Fisheries* (Leiden: Brill Academic Publishers, 2004).

[79] See eg JA Roach, 'Initiatives to Enhance Maritime Security at Sea', above n 28, 41.

and trafficking of persons by sea, 6) IUU fishing, and 7) intentional and unlawful damage to the marine environment.[80]

Such activities are also included in the first comprehensive multilateral treaty concerning maritime security, the CARICOM Agreement (2008), which refers in article 1 para 2 to activities 'likely to compromise the security of a State party or the Region if it involves trafficking in drugs, arms or people, terrorism, smuggling, illegal immigration, serious marine pollution, injury to off-shore installations, piracy, hijacking and other serious crimes'. Besides this Agreement, there are also various shipboarding and shiprider agreements that the US has concluded with states in Africa or in the Pacific, which aim to suppress 'illicit transnational maritime activity' in general.[81]

As N Klein observes, 'while "maritime security" is widely used and understood in the day-to-day workings of naval and law enforcement officials, other government officials, vessel owners and operators, as well as in the academic literature, it is rarely defined in a categorical way, and instead tends to have a context-specific meaning'.[82] Apparently, this lack of precise definition manifests that the identification of what is threat to maritime security is not free from complexity.[83] More importantly, it is argued that each alleged 'threat to maritime security', which gives rise to maritime interception on the high seas, requires different legal treatment, as it is premised upon a different rationale. Hence, the inclusion of all such 'threats' under the same heading is a pragmatic, yet an oversimplified approach to contemporary challenges to the freedom of the high seas.

This notwithstanding, there are many cases, in which organised criminal groups would be associated with more than one illicit activity at sea, for example illegal fishing with smuggling of migrants.[84] This poses significant hurdles both in respect of the prevention of such crimes and in respect of the applicable legal framework. In any event and as far as inter-

---

[80] UNGA, 'Oceans and the Law of the Sea: Report of the Secretary-General' (10 March 2008), UN Doc A/63/63, paras 54, 63, 72, 82, 89, 98, 107–8. In the 2010 Report, the Secretary-General mentions only 'threats to maritime security, including piracy, armed robbery at sea, terrorist acts against shipping, offshore installations and other maritime interests'; UNGA, 'Oceans and the Law of the Sea: Report of the Secretary-General' (17 March 2011), UN Doc A/65/37, para 82.

[81] A list of such agreements is included in A Roach and R Smith, *Excessive Maritime Claims*, 3rd edn (Leiden: Martinus Nijhoff, 2012), Appendix 16 (on file with the author) (hereinafter: Roach, Appendix).

[82] Klein, *Maritime Security*, 11.

[83] For example, at the 2008 meeting of the United Nations Open-Ended Informal Consultative Process on Oceans and the Law of the Sea (UNICPOLOS), State representatives contested the inclusion of IUU fishing as a threat to maritime security; see Letter dated 25 July 2008 from the Co-Chairpersons of the Consultative Process addressed to the President of the General Assembly, UN Doc A/63/174 Part B, paras 70–71.

[84] For numerous of such examples see eg UNODC, Transnational Organized Crime in the Fishing Industry. Focus on Trafficking in Persons, Smuggling of Migrants and Illicit Drugs Trafficking (Vienna, 2011).

ception is concerned, it must be stressed that each illicit activity or 'threat to maritime security' is subject to a different set of rules and a different legal basis for interception at sea.

III. THE OUTLINE OF THE BOOK

The book will proceed as follows: Chapter 2 will be devoted to discussion of the theoretical framework of the right of visit on the high seas. In this chapter, the historical claims to the freedom of the seas and the celebrated controversy between *mare liberum* and *mare clausum* will be canvassed. Drawing valuable insights from this historical survey, it will be possible to revisit this controversy and ascertain the role of interception on the high seas in the legal order of the oceans of the twenty-first century. It is posited that the rationales behind the contemporary interception operations reflect the old-fashioned *mare clausum* arguments and they fall under three general categories, namely, the maintenance of international peace and security, the protection of the *bon usage* of the oceans and the maintenance of welfare and *ordre public* of the states and of international society. These categories, far from being hermetically sealed or isolated, are interconnected and leave considerable room for permeation by the various grounds for interference. They also inform the content of the following chapters, in the sense that the various interception activities will be explored in the light of this categorisation.

Before turning to the detailed analysis of these activities, it is necessary to have a thorough discussion over the 'law of maritime interception or interdiction', ie the legal framework of interception activities on the high seas. Accordingly, in Chapter 3 the classical belligerent right of visit and search, but, more importantly, its peacetime counterpart, the right of visit under article 110 of LOSC, will be canvassed. In more detail, questions such as its *modus operandi*, the requirement for the existence of 'reasonable suspicions', as well as its restrictions under the law of the sea and general international law, will be adequately addressed and analysed. As far as the latter are concerned, reference will be made to question of the use of force in the course of interception operation and whether it constitutes another exception to article 2(4) of the UN Charter. In addition, the restrictions posed by human rights and humanitarian law as well as other considerations, such as the protection of marine environment or of commercial interests will be discussed in this regard. Finally, particular reference will be made to the assertion of prescriptive and enforcement jurisdiction over these criminal acts at sea. Attention will be also drawn to questions, such as whether and to what extent technological developments have altered the traditional conception of the right of visit on the high seas. It will be argued that to a certain extent this has occurred. Nonetheless, it will be submitted that there is no such thing as a distinct 'law of interdiction', albeit an array of international legal rules delineating the contours of interception activities on the high seas.

Chapter 4 will be devoted to the first theoretical category, namely, the interference on the high seas for the maintenance of international peace and security and more specifically, to the issues of the belligerent right of visit and search as it applies today and of the maritime enforcement of SC Resolutions. It will scrutinise the belligerent right of visit and search as has been exercised in the past, but also in more recent international and internal armed conflicts. It will be submitted that there is certainly merit in considering it relevant in the twenty-first century. In addition, all the maritime interdiction operations authorised by the UN Security Council will be discussed.

Chapter 5 will be a canvass of the novel threats of terrorism and of proliferation of WMD. The latter threats will be assessed against the background of the initiatives taken by international organisations, namely the UN, NATO and IMO, as well as by states individually and collectively, such as the PSI, and unilaterally. This assessment will include analysis of the possible legal justifications for unilateral interdiction measures under international law. Finally, there will be a brief consideration of the legal restrictions involved in the exercise of the right of visit in that context, mainly of the issue of enforcement jurisdiction over terrorism and WMD on the high seas.

In Chapter 6, the focus will shift to maritime interception activities to safeguard the fundamental freedoms of the high seas, namely interception activities to counter piracy *jure gentium* and IUU fishing. It is not surprising that more emphasis will be placed on the revival of piracy in the Gulf of Aden and the West Indian Ocean and recently in East Africa. In this regard, there will be a thorough analysis of the legal bases for the operations taking place both on the high seas and in the territorial seas of the African states concerned as well as of the various challenges posed by the non-assertion of jurisdiction over piracy and armed robbery by the intercepting states. Also, the question of the applicability of human rights in these operations will be addressed. The chapter will close by a short reference to the threats posed by IUU fishing and to the measures, including interception on the high seas, which states and the RFMOs concerned have taken in this respect.

Chapter 7 will revolve around the problem of drug trafficking on the high seas. The relevant discussion will consider both the treaty-law bases for interference with drug smuggling on the high seas, such as the 1988 Vienna Convention against Illicit Trafficking in Narcotic Drugs and the customary law bases, such as the consent of the flag State. It will also scrutinise the relevant international legal restrictions governing such interference including the question of the use of force and the question of jurisdiction over the relevant offences.

A similar structure will be followed in respect of the third current problem and source of interception activities on the high seas, namely, illicit migration and human trafficking. Accordingly, the analysis in Chapter 8 will commence with a legal characterisation of the relevant issues, and then will assess both the treaty and the customary law justifications for such interference on the high seas. The chapter will end with a brief canvass of the pertinent international legal restrictions, including the rules on the use of force and the prohibition of *non-refoulement* under refugee and human rights law.

What is left out of the scope of the book? From the alleged 'threats to maritime security' or from the grounds of interference included in article 110, only the issue of the pollution of the marine environment and that of 'unauthorised broadcasting', respectively, are left out. The former is excluded, because it has never involved significant interception activities on the high seas, notwithstanding the recent CARICOM Security Agreement (2008),[85] and the latter, as it seems to have fallen in desuetude. For reasons of space and because it has extensively been analysed elsewhere, the issue of state responsibility arising from the exercise of the right of visit is also excluded.[86]

The present enquiry will close with some concluding remarks in Chapter 9 assessing the impact of these challenges on the existing legal order of the oceans.

---

[85] Art 1(2) of the 2008 CARICOM Agreement designates 'a serious or potentially serious pollution of the environment' as 'an activity likely to compromise the security of a State Party' and thus the right of visit is accorded under art 9 of the Agreement. To the knowledge of the author, there is no relevant practice in this regard.

[86] On this issue, see the excellent treatises of P Wendel, *State Responsibility for Interferences with the Freedom of Navigation in International Law* (Berlin: Springer, 2007) (hereinafter: Wendel) and of D Guilfoyle, *Shipping Interdiction*, Ch 12.

2

The Theoretical Framework of the Right of Visit on the High Seas: Mare Liberum v Mare Clausum Revisited

I. THE HISTORICAL CLAIMS TO FREEDOM OF THE SEAS

A. From Antiquity to the Middle Ages

T HE ORIGINS OF the principle of the freedom of the seas, as well as the seeds of its controversy with the claims of maritime dominion, can be traced back to the Greek and Roman periods. While in the former period, the practice and doctrine regarding the sea dwelt predominantly upon maritime dominion, rather than maritime liberty,[1] in the age of Rome, a more conscious and articulate recognition of the problem of maritime freedom and dominion is observed. For instance, in the *Institutes* of Justinian, it is famously stated: 'By the law of nature, the following things are common to all men: the air, flowing water, the sea, and consequently the shores of the sea.'[2] However, turning to state practice, there were phenomena almost identical to those observed among the Greek states.[3] As Potter explains,

> as in the case of Athens, much of the Roman claim to maritime dominion rested upon her activities to piracy . . . piracy was an official state activity and its suppression a matter of interstate war . . . accordingly; success in that direction might naturally produce maritime dominion between state and state.[4]

---

[1] On the freedom of the seas in antiquity see P Potter, *The Freedom of the Seas in History, Law and Politics* (New York, London: Longmans, 1924) 11–35 and further material therein (hereinafter: Potter).

[2] Justinian, *Institutes*, II, 1, 1; cited in Potter, 25.

[3] Carthage, the Italian states preceding Rome, and Rome herself, all attempted to secure and definitely claimed maritime dominion; see Potter, 27.

[4] Potter, 34. On the ancient history of piracy see V Pella, 'La répression de la piraterie' 15 *Recueil de Cours de l'Académie de la Haye de Droit International* (1926-V) 149, 151. See also generally P Gosse, *The History of Piracy* (New York: Tudor, 1946).

After the disintegration of the Roman Empire, the absolute lawlessness and insecurity at sea led merchants to form associations for mutual protection. By the thirteenth century, nation states came to discharge this right of exercising jurisdiction on the neighbouring sea and protection of navigation, which soon turned into assertions of exclusive dominion and sovereignty.[5] Thus, in the Middle Ages, an institution of national maritime dominion was recognised and accepted as part of the principles of inter-state relations or even international law and custom.[6] In the fifteenth and sixteenth centuries, while the struggle for sovereignty over closed and geographically restricted seas continued unabated,[7] there were novel claims to dominion over the open oceans of the world by Spain and Portugal, which had earlier been the leading seafarer nations of the Age of Discovery.[8] The main rival against the Spanish claims for dominion of the oceans was England, which under the reign of Queen Elizabeth, took over the leading role in the struggle for freedom of the seas,[9] not only against the Spaniards[10] but also against Danish claims in the Baltic Sea.[11] This period for England, however, ended with the ascendance to the throne of James I, first of the Stuart kings.[12]

[5] See R Anand, *Origin and Development of the Law of the Sea: the History of International Law Revisited* (The Hague: Martinus Nijhoff, 1983) 84 (hereinafter: Anand) and T Fulton, *The Sovereignty of the Sea* (London: W Blackwood Pub, 1911) 30 (hereinafter: Fulton).

[6] See Potter, 41.

[7] For example, the British expanded their rule into the '*Oceanus Britannicus*' and they gradually established the celebrated sea ceremonial. This refers to the obligation of foreign vessels to salute the British flag in the North Sea. As Colombos states, 'the right to a salute assumed a considerable importance in the sixteenth and seventeenth centuries as establishing the rank and precedency due to England and the consequent recognition by the other States of the King's right of sovereignty in the British Seas. Numerous instances are recorded of foreign warships being forced to salute the British flag in the North Sea': C Colombos, *International Law of the Sea* (London: Longmans, 1967) 52 (hereinafter: Colombos); J Verzijl, *International Law in Historical Perspective*, Vol IV (Leiden: Sijthoff, 1971) 10. It is also significant to note that the British became actively involved with the question of maritime warfare; see L Hautefeuille, *Historie des origines, des progrès et des variations du droit maritime international* (Paris: Guillaumin et Aug. Durand, 1858) 124.

[8] See W Grewe, *The Epochs of International Law* (Berlin: De Gruyter, 2000) 257 (hereinafter: Grewe).

[9] The words of Sir Walter Raleigh encapsulated perfectly British interests in this period: 'whosoever commands the seas, commands the trade; whosoever commands the trade of the world, commands the riches of the world and consequently the world itself'; cited in Fulton, 136.

[10] The reply of Elizabeth to Mendoza, the Spanish Envoy to London in 1580, is often quoted in this regard: 'the use of sea and air is common to all; neither can any title to ocean belong to any people or private men'; cited in TA Walker, *A History of the Law of Nations*, Vol I (Cambridge: Cambridge University Press, 1899) 161.

[11] The practical effect of these claims consisted mainly in the prohibition against fishing in these waters, which was issued by the Danish kings; see Fulton, 108–11.

[12] It was a particularly Scottish interest which provided the impetus for an abrupt change in policy of the freedom of the seas at the beginning of the Stuart reign; see Grewe, 265. As Fulton points out, 'it was with respect to the right of fishery on the British coast that the claim to maritime sovereignty was revived in the 17th century, and with which it was chiefly concerned', at 57.

Contrary to the Hispano-Portuguese claims were also doctrinal works, which, surprisingly, came mainly from Spain.[13] Ferdinard Vasquez (1509–66), for example, refuted the juristic value of the claims to maritime dominion of not only the Venetians and of the Genoese, but even of the Spanish Crown. He maintained that to make the seas and the waves into private national property was contrary to the law of nature and the elementary principles of international relations.[14] An important, yet less credited work in this respect is of Alberto Gentilis, who, albeit starting from the premise that the sea was *'res communis omnium'*, made a sharp distinction between the high seas and coastal waters, as well as between the concepts of maritime dominion and maritime jurisdiction.[15] Under the latter heading, he asserted that restrictions of imports, of immigration and exports are justified for the sake of the safety and morals of people.[16]

B. The 'Battle of the Books'

It is widely assumed that it was Hugo Grotius who first propounded the doctrine of the freedom of the seas, and heralded the dawn of a new epoch for the world's oceans.[17] The truth, however, is that the concept of the freedom of the seas had been enunciated by Spanish theologians and publicists in the previous century. It is well known that Grotius presented and elaborated his thesis relating to freedom of the high seas in his famous book *Mare Liberum*, published anonymously in 1609.[18] In fact, *Mare Liberum* was merely one chapter (Chapter XII) of a bigger work, *De Jurae Praedae* (1613),[19] which as an advocate of the Dutch East India Company Grotius had prepared as a legal brief to defend the seizure of the *Sta*

---

[13] The most important Spanish writers on the law of nations of the sixteenth century belonged to the camp which defended the freedom of the seas; see comments by Grewe, 259.

[14] See Vasquez de Menchaca, *Illustrium Controversarium, Libri Tres* (Barcelona: Edition Princeps 1563). Along the same lines was Alfonso de Castro in *De Potestate Legis Penalis*, Vol I; see E Nys, *Les Origines de Droit International* (Bruxelles: Castaigne, 1894) 382.

[15] The coastal waters, in his view, stretched over 100 miles from the coast and were subject to the jurisdiction of the littoral state; see Grewe, 264.

[16] See A Gentilis, *De Jure Belli Libri tres* (1588) and his *Hispanicae Advocationis Libri duo* (1605), as cited in Potter, 54.

[17] See R Anand, 'Freedom of the Seas: Past, Present and Future', in R Gutiérrez Girardot et al (eds), *Essays in Honour of Wolfgang Abendroth* (Frankfurt: Campus Verlag, 1982) 215, 216. As C Meurer dramatically put it, 'Up to modern times the freedom of the seas slumbered the sleep of the Sleeping Beauty, until there appeared from Netherlands the knight whose kiss awakened her once more': *The Program of the Freedom of the Sea* (Washington, 1919) 7.

[18] See H Grotius, *The Free Sea* (ed D Armitage) (Indianapolis, IN: Liberty Fund, 2004) (hereinafter: Grotius). As it is stated in the introduction to this edition, 'few works of such brevity have caused arguments of such global extent and striking longevity as *Mare Liberum*'; at xi.

[19] See H Grotius, *De Jure Praede Commentarius* (ed H Hamaker) (Hagae Comitum: Nijhoff, 1868).

Katharina in the East Indian Seas in February 1603.[20] The principal aim of Grotius in *Mare Liberum* was to defend his country's right to navigate in the Indian Ocean and other Eastern Seas and trade with the neighbouring states, over which Spain and Portugal asserted a commercial monopoly as well as political domination. His main argument was that freedom of navigation and trade, whether applied to particular communities or to the universal society of humanity, reflected primary natural laws, with which the Portuguese claims of exclusive access to the East Indies were in discord. *Mare Liberum*, even if it was not consistently defended by its own author,[21] elicited polemics and aroused a celebrated doctrinal controversy in the seventeenth century, commonly referred to as the 'Battle of the Books'.[22] Many renowned jurists of that time, such as Welwood,[23] Selden[24] and Freitas[25] participated in this debate; nevertheless, it is a commonplace that the names of Grotius and Selden marked its high point.[26]

[20] Grotius defended the Dutch seizure of the *Sta Catherina* on the basis of a set of natural laws, self-defence and self-preservation, which he derived originally from the principle of divine will. As he contended in the Chapter XII, 'even if the war were private war, it would be just, and the prize would be justly acquired by the Dutch East India Company'; at 216. See also P Borschberg, 'The Seizure of *Sta Katarina* Revisited' 33 *Journal of South Asian Studies* (2002) 31.

[21] Grotius conveniently forgot his freedom of the seas principle, which he propounded with such fervour, and went to England in 1613 with a Dutch delegation to argue in favour of the Dutch monopoly of trade with the Spice Islands. He was allegedly surprised that his own book, published anonymously, was being quoted by the British against him. See G Clark, 'Grotius' East Indian Mission to England' 20 *Transactions of the Grotius Society* (1934) 15, 79.

[22] See inter alia: G Gidel, *Le Droit de la Mer*, Vol I (Paris: Etablissements Mellottee Chateauroux, 1932) (hereinafter Gidel), 4; Ortolan, 128; and W Knight, *The Life and Works of Hugo Grotius* in the Grotius Society Publications Vol. IV (London: Sweet and Maxwell, 1925) 36. Potter rightly observes that 'the works of Grotius, Selden and their coadjutors were products of personal and national desires rather than works of pure and unbiased juristic science'; at 61.

[23] W Welwood, *An Abridgement of All Sea Laws* (1613) ch XXVI and *De Dominio Maris* (1615). Welwood had understood *Mare Liberum's* alleged East Indian context as a cover for the work's 'real purpose', namely to reinforce the claims of the Dutch herring fleet to fish in British (in particular Scottish) territorial waters. Yet Welwood stressed only the argument about fishing and ignored the broader questions of trade and navigation. Nonetheless, it was actually the only work to which Grotius replied; see Grotius, *In Defensio capiti quinti Maris Liberi* (*c* 1615).

[24] Shortly after the publication of *Mare Liberum*, James I asked John Selden to write a counter-thesis, which was published much later, titled as *Mare Clausum seu de dominio maris libri duo* (1635). Selden's *Mare Clausum* was divided into two books. In the first, he attempted to refute Grotius' thesis arguing that it is demonstrated that sea, according to the law of nature and nations, is not common to all, but can be subject to jurisdiction and domain of individuals in the same way as land can be. In the second, Selden sought to prove that dominion over the British Seas was part of this insular realm; see Grewe, 268.

[25] JS Freitas, *De Justo Imperio Lusitanorum Asiatico* (1635). Freitas wrote this treatise for the King of Spain, who was at the time also the King of Portugal. According to Freitas, the King of Spain had full sovereign rights over the sea, by virtue of which he dispatched his fleets to rid the sea of pirates and of other enemies. See Grewe, 259 and also C Alexandrowicz, 'Freitas *versus* Grotius' 35 *British Yearbook of International Law* (1959) 162.

[26] See Grewe, 266.

C. The Era of Consolidation and Codification of *Mare Liberum*

While Grotius' thesis was focused on the Hispano-Portuguese monopoly in the East Indies, it was mainly the British, who, in view of the ongoing Anglo-Dutch dispute over the '*Oceanus Britannicus*', challenged his theory.[27] However, British claims for sovereignty of the sea shrank in parallel to the increase in power of their fleet and the decline in power of the rival Spanish and Dutch fleets at the end of the seventeenth century. Concomitantly, an interest in the idea of freedom of the seas reappeared in the English policy after the end of the Anglo-Dutch disputes.[28] The deciding factors were, on the one hand, the consolidation of Britain's de facto dominion over the oceans and on the other, the colonial and commercial conceptions of mercantilism.[29] In the course of the eighteenth century, the freedom of the seas, in the traditional sense, garnered wide acceptance in the practice of European states due to colonialism and the European imperial expansion, and most writers shared the view that no state had exclusive dominion over the open seas, excepting the waters contiguous to its own coastal territory.[30]

In the nineteenth century the world saw, on the one hand, the freedom of the seas attaining even more importance, due to the growing needs and demands of the industrial revolution in Europe,[31] while, on the other, the British fleet came to 'rule the waves' and adopt the role of an international maritime police. The twentieth century was the era of the codification of the freedom of the high seas, first, in the 1958 Geneva Convention, and then in LOSC. *Mare liberum* was taken to mean that the high seas were common to all states and that no state may purport to subject any part of them to its territorial sovereignty. However, it was *ratione loci* limited to 'all parts of the sea that are not included in the exclusive economic zone, in the territorial sea or in the internal waters of a State, or in the archipelagic waters of an archipelagic State' (article 86 of LOSC).

[27] The Anglo-Dutch dispute occupied three-quarters of the seventeenth century and gave rise to three wars. On the history and legal consequences of this rivalry, see Fulton, 346.

[28] See Grewe, 273.

[29] It is of interest that as early as 1689 a book which was published by Sir Philipp Meadows criticised sharply the English claims for sovereignty of sea in the extended maritime zone of the *Oceanus Britannicus*; see Meadows, *Observations concerning the Dominion and Sovereignty of the Seas* (1689). See Fulton, 524.

[30] See eg C Bynkershoek, *De Dominio Maris Dissertatio* (1703); E de Vattel, *Le droit des gens*, Liv I 279–95. These texts are also referred to by Potter, 94.

[31] See Anand, 127. As McFee points out, 'there was so much trading and it could be done so much cheaper with a complete free and open sea, that the very idea of owning the sea vanished': *The Law of the Sea* (Philadelphia: Lippincott, 1950) 142.

D. The Legal Nature of the High Seas

Whilst no serious dispute existed in the last century on the freedom of the seas, international jurists had not agreed as to the legal basis on which the doctrine was founded. On the one hand, it was said that the high seas belong to nobody (*res nullius*) while, on the other, it was said that the high seas belong to everybody (*res communis*).[32] 'In favour of the first view, it is urged that sovereignty is absent on the high seas; in favour of the second view, it is contended that the sea is common because it is a necessary instrument to international navigation and trade.'[33] Conversely, Fauchille criticised the employment of both the Latin terms, and opined that the usage of the sea remains eternally open to all nations,[34] while Nicolas Politis was of the view that the '*res communis*' characterisation of the open sea is more in accord with the positive conception of the solidarity on which all modern international relations are grounded.[35]

Although the open sea is *res extra commercium*,[36] it is, nevertheless, subject to the *corpus juris gentium* (or, in the words of Gidel, the principle of *la juridicité de haute mer*).[37] The legal order of the high seas is predicated primarily on the rule of international law, which requires every vessel to possess the nationality of one state, which is, thus, responsible to maintain the minimum public order of the oceans.[38] Under the LOSC, the freedom of the high seas includes the freedom of navigation, the freedom of over-flight, the freedom to lay submarine cables, to construct artificial islands and other installations, the freedom of fishing and lastly, the freedom of scientific research.[39] 'All high seas freedoms, whether expressly stated in the Convention or not, are enjoyed subject to the qualification that they shall be exercised by all States *with due regard for the interests of other States* in their exercise of the freedom of the high seas'.[40]

---

[32] R Bierzanek, 'La nature juridique de la hautemer' 65 RGDIP (1961) 233, 234.

[33] Colombos, 65.

[34] P Fauchille, *Traité de droit international public*, Vol I (Paris: Rousseau, 1925) 14–15.

[35] N Politis, quoted in the minutes of the meeting of the Institut de droit international held on 1 August 1925, extracted in (1925) 32 *Annuaire de l'Institut de droit international*, 526.

[36] On the legal nature of the high seas; see Colombos, 62–67.

[37] Gidel was the first to elaborate this principle extensively: Gidel, 225. As Gidel refers, however, it was, previously posited by Meurer as follows: 'das Meer ist frei von der Gebietshoheit aber nichts von der Rechtshoheit'; Meurer *Das Programm der Meeresfreiheit* (Tubingen: Mohr Siebeck, 1918). See also O'Connell, 798.

[38] McDougal and Burke write that 'the major function served by the attribution by States of national character to ships has been in establishing the basic organisational principle by which States have sought to maintain public order in the oceans . . .': ibid, 86 and Ch 8. See also generally H Meyer, *The Nationality of Ships* (The Hague: Martinus Nijhoff, 1967).

[39] See art 87 of LOSC. This list of freedoms as the wording clearly indicates is not restrictive; see Oppenheim's *International Law*, 729.

[40] LOSC art 87(2) (emphasis added).

E. Concluding Observations

In conclusion, it is readily apparent that the history of the law of the sea has been marked by the doctrinal controversy and the tensions between the two phenomenically divergent regimes of *mare clausum* and *mare liberum*.[41] It was in the end the socio-economic needs of international society to have free access to the markets of the world and to freely communicate and trade at sea that marked the triumph of *mare liberum* over *mare clausum* claims. As stated by McDougal and Burke:

> By appropriate accommodation and compromise, a public order of the sea has been maintained to permit States to send their argosies to all the four corners of the world and to take adequate account of both the general security interest of the community of States and the special security interest of particular states . . . The historic process of decision has similarly achieved a very wide sharing in the allocation of resources and in access to the oceans and markets of the world. Though coastal states have been given a reasonable measure of protection in control of protection in control of immediately adjacent activities and resources, the larger expanses of oceans have been mostly preserved as accessible to all.[42]

However, was there ever such a stark dichotomy between *mare liberum* and *mare clausum*? Were Selden, Grotius and the other jurists in real disagreement over the regime of the 'vast and expanded oceans of the world'? Furthermore, what was the role of interference on the high seas in this historical context, and what conclusions should be drawn from it? Is there any room for the historical claims for *mare clausum* in the contemporary legal order of the high seas?

II. THE CONTEMPORARY RIGHT OF VISIT: LESSONS FROM THE HISTORICAL AND THEORETICAL FRAMEWORK OF *MARE LIBERUM*

A. *Mare Liberum v Mare Clausum*: Antithetical or Complementary Concepts?

Drawing insights from the works of Grotius, Selden and the other authors in the celebrated era of the 'Battle of the Books', it is possible to make the following observations: first, Grotius never propounded a theory of absolute negative freedom of the high seas, in the sense of Gidel, ie of an

---

[41] In the words of Rayfuse and Warner, 'the entire history of international law of the sea has been one of oscillation between freedom and restriction': Rayfuse and Warner, 'Securing a Sustainable Future for the Oceans beyond National Jurisdiction' 23 *IJMCL* (2008) 399, 400.

[42] McDougal and Burke, 55–56. In the same vein, DP O'Connell wrote: 'One common thread running through the formulation of the various jurisdictional zones in the contemporary law of the sea is the idea of accommodation of interests, or a balancing of rights and duties, which can be summed up in the concept of "reasonable use"': O'Connell, 57.

absolute prohibition of interference with foreign vessels in the oceans. On the contrary, *Mare Liberum* itself was initially written as a defence of an interference with a foreign vessel, namely *Sta Catarina* in the Straits of Singapore, which according to the Dutch East India Company was a lawful booty in a just war. Thus, Grotius consciously excluded *bellum justum* and *jus praedae*, including measures such as visit of foreign vessels on the high seas, from the scope of *mare liberum*.

In addition, Grotius acknowledged that the crux of the matter was not the status of the coastal waters but of the open sea. In his words,

> the question at issue is not one that concerns an inner sea, one which is surrounded on all sides by the land, and at some places does not even exceed a river in breadth. The question concerns the whole ocean, which antiquity called it immeasurable and infinite . . . and in this ocean the controversy is not of a bay or a narrow strait or concerning *all that may be seen from the shore*.[43]

Hence, it readily appears that Grotius never intended to dispute the sovereignty of the coastal state in *mare proximum* – now termed the territorial sea – and he was mainly concerned with the legal regime of the 'infinite ocean' – nowadays, the high seas.[44] Surprisingly, a similar view was shared by his traditional opponents. For example, Welwood accepted that the liberty of navigation was beyond all controversy, and agreed to the principle of the complete freedom of the seas, so far as concerned the 'main Sea or great Ocean',[45] as well as Selden, who admitted that 'as to the free use of the sea . . . to prohibit innocent navigation would be contrary to the dictates of humanity'.[46] It is clear that both Grotius and his adversaries agreed on the basic premise that the open seas are free to navigate and to economically exploit, subject to various restrictions, such as measures in just war and against piracy,[47] whereas the sea belt adjacent to the coast – according to Grotius, the sea 'visible from the shore' – was susceptible to the coastal state's sovereignty or jurisdiction. Consequently, serious doubts may rise

---

[43] Grotius, 32–33 (emphasis added).

[44] It is true that Grotius departed from this position in the *Defence of Mare Liberum*, where 'in his enthusiasm to demolish Welwood's thesis . . . he said that whatever [*mare liberum*] applied to the whole sea, applied to all its parts and he allowed no exception for a sea washing a coast'; Anand, 102. However, by 1625, he had come to agree with Welwood that territorial waters could be possessed; Grotius, *De Jure Belli ac Pacis*, II (1625) 3.13–15.

[45] Later, he argued that it was incontestable that the vast and boundless waters beyond the *mare proximum* were open to all nations indifferently for all uses; see Welwood, *De Dominio Maris*, as cited by Fulton, 353–54.

[46] He held, however, that 'the permitting of such innocent navigation does not derogate from the dominion of the sea': at Lib i cap xx, cited by Fulton, 371. Along the same lines was Freitas, who, according to Alexandrowicz, did not deny in principle the freedom of the high seas, but instead contended that it could be limited and reduced by the claims to sovereignty of coastal states; see above n 25, 173.

[47] It must be recalled here that Freitas asserted that by virtue of his sovereign rights, the King of Spain dispatched his fleets to rid the sea of pirates and of other enemies. His jurisdiction extended over all seas, the supervision and protection of which he had undertaken; see Grewe, 259.

on the actual extent of the theoretical dichotomy between *mare liberum* and *mare clausum*.[48]

It is also significant to consider the grounds that the proponents of *mare clausum* put forward in order to justify their claims. Welwood, for example, enunciated that the usufruct of the adjacent sea belonged to the inhabitants of the coastal state; and that 'one of the main reasons why that portion of the sea should pertain to the neighbouring state was the risk of the exhaustion of its fisheries from promiscuous use'.[49] In the same vein, Selden denied that the sea was inexhaustible from promiscuous use; on the contrary, 'the sea may be made worse for him that owns it by reason of other men's fishing, navigation and commerce and less profit accrue from it'.[50] On a different footing, Freitas spoke of limitations to *mare liberum* dictated by the principle of effectiveness and of rights in the sea which can be acquired in relation to the purpose of the preservation of the security on particular sea routes.[51] It is also generally observed that the basis of coastal states exclusive control over a belt of the sea was the principle of protection.[52] Vattel, writing in 1758, explained the grounds for exclusive rights in the coastal sea as follows: the uses of the sea near the coast render it very susceptible of appropriation, because it supplies fish, shells, pearls and other things and with respect to all these its use is not inexhaustible; in addition, another reason for the extension of territorial dominion over the adjoining seas is the security and welfare of the state as well as the exercise of territorial jurisdiction.[53]

In summary, the grounds invoked for assertion of sovereignty and of jurisdiction in *mare proximum* were, mainly, the protection and the non-exhaustion of fisheries, as well as the security and the welfare of the state. Interestingly, similar reasons existed for the interference with vessels on the high seas, ie the protection of international commerce and the preservation of order at seas with regard to piracy,[54] as well as the maintenance of security of states with the invocation of the principles of self-defence and self-help for *justa causa* seizures of vessels.

It is submitted that these grounds for *mare clausum* and for interference with freedom of navigation on the high seas still reflect the main grounds

---

[48] *cf* the discussion in Potter, 77. See also K Zemanek, who notes that 'the dispute was primarily about free trade *versus* monopoly, and only [inter alia] also about the sovereignty over the High Seas'; Zemanek, 'Was Hugo Grotius Really in Favour of the Freedom of the High Seas?' 1 *Journal of the History of International Law* (1999) 48, 58.

[49] Fulton, 355.

[50] ibid, 372.

[51] See Alexandrowicz, above n 25, 173–75.

[52] Anand, 138.

[53] See Fulton, 560–61.

[54] Writing the account of Pompey's war against the pirates in 67 BC, Plutarch states: 'this power [of the pirates] extended . . . over the whole of our sea, making it . . . closed to all commerce. This inclined the Romans to send out Pompey with a commission to take the sea away from pirates'; Plutarch, *Pompey* XXV-XXVI, cited in Potter, 29–30.

for such interference in present times. The protection of fisheries, the security and welfare of the coastal state and the need to exercise territorial jurisdiction in a maritime zone adjacent to the shores were the main underpinnings of the gradual extension of this zone to three nautical miles and further to 12 nautical miles, of the recognition of police powers in the contiguous zone, as well as of the establishment of exclusive fishing zones and of the Exclusive Economic Zone (EEZ).[55] The same grounds are also behind the adoption of the numerous boarding agreements since the nineteenth century: suffice to note the various treaties regarding high seas fisheries (protection of fisheries), the US bilateral treaties for counter-smuggling purposes (social welfare) and the Nyon Agreement of 1937 (piracy).

This does not mean, however, that, in stark contrast to the common conviction, it was *mare clausum* eventually that prevailed over *mare liberum*; rather, as was previously implied, these two theories have never been in real discord, but have co-existed and complemented each other. This is even more patent in relation to the freedom of navigation and to the principle of non-interference on the high seas: on the one hand, the theory of *mare liberum* recognised, since its inception, exceptions to these principles, such as the right to interfere with vessels in wartime and in self-defence, as well as the right to seize vessels engaged in piracy. Thus, an 'absolutely negative' freedom of the high seas never existed, but it was a priori qualified and limited by similar policy grounds to those that underpinned the *mare clausum* claims. On the other hand, *mare clausum* never contested the thrust of the freedom of the seas, namely the navigation on the high seas; they only purported to convey the coastal states' legitimate concerns for the control of the adjacent maritime zones. These concerns, however, were never defined in strict geographical terms, but being of a more general nature, they were gradually acknowledged as legitimate grounds for the coastal state jurisdictional extension to the open seas as well as for the establishment of the right of visit.

B. *Mare Clausum* Concerns and the Contemporary Right of Visit on the High Seas

Building on the foregoing insights, it is thus possible to contend that the various treaty and customary exceptions to the principle of non-interference on the high seas find their rationales in the above *mare clausum* concerns. The sole difference is that, when these concerns were advanced then, they mostly expressed individualistic, or, to adopt the

---

[55] See the discussion of the extension of the territorial sea in Fulton, at Section II, Chs I, II and V. See also Anand, 135.

terminology of McDougal and Burke, 'exclusive claims' of states to maritime dominion.[56] In the last century, these claims were 'internationalised', ie they came to be perceived as 'essentially inclusive'[57] by international society, in the sense of legitimate concerns shared not only by the states individually but also by the international society as a whole, consisting of both States and of other participants in the law-making process of the oceans.[58]

It is apt here to refer to the authoritative *UN Memorandum* (1950), where Gidel acknowledged that the predominant negative principle of the freedom of the seas could be modified:

> dans deux directions: d'une part, 'la conception positive de la solidarité qui à la base des relations internationales modernes'[59] substitute à l'idée de l'utilisation individualiste de la haute mer, l'idée que l'intérêt général exige au contraire une utilisation concertée.[60]

He linked the adoption of the conventions permitting the right to visit on the high seas with this notion of general interest for the rational use of the high seas.[61] Accordingly, he asserted that these conventions constitute an embryonic organisation of the high seas, which reflects the common interest of states to utilise the high seas in conditions 'excluant le scandale, le désordre, le gaspillage'.[62]

These threats to the rudimentary organisation of the oceans, ie 'scandal, disorder and wastage', give substance to the corresponding claims to *ordre public*, social welfare and good use of the seas in peacetime. In addition, the claim to the security of states and of the international society reflects the ground for interference with enemy and neutral merchant vessels in wartime. Accordingly, it is maintained that international society, having espoused these traditional state *mare clausum* concerns, has transformed

---

[56] On the definition of exclusive claims see McDougal and Burke, 1.

[57] McDougal and Burke write in respect of the right of visit: 'the claim to apply policy on the high seas is also essentially inclusive as each state usually claims to exercise authority only over its own vessels. The claims to apply policy to foreign vessels relate mainly to maintenance of minimum order and to prevention of widely condemned practices'; at 34.

[58] The term 'international society' will be generally preferred to the term 'international community', especially when the discussion pertains to the decision-making process in the law of the sea. It is submitted that the participants in the process of interaction and in the policy-making in the oceans are not only states or intergovernmental organisations, but also non-state actors, such as the shipping industry. This is reflected also in the decision-making process of the IMO. See E Roucounas, 'Facteurs Privés et Droit International Public' 299 RCADI (2002) 9, 23. Conversely, the term 'international community' will be employed in its usual context, for example, in relation to *jus cogens* or to the UN Charter. On 'international community' see G Abi-Saab, 'Whither the International Community?' 9 *European Journal of International Law* (1998) 249. On the concept of 'international society' see H Mosler, 'The International Society as a Legal Community' 140 RCADI (1974-IV) 17.

[59] N Politis, above n 35, 526

[60] *UN Memorandum*, para 32.

[61] This 'general interest' point is taken also up by R Barnes; see below n 64.

[62] *UN Memorandum*, para 26.

them to positive assertions of '*l'intérêt général*' in the contemporary legal order of the oceans.

In conclusion, the various cases of interferences on the high seas, both historical and contemporary, could be conceptualised and categorised as follows: at a first level, there are the cases of interference, which find their justification in the need to maintain the peace and security of states and of international society. At a second level, there are the cases of interference which aim to maintain a *bon usage* or the 'internal order' of the oceans, in the sense of a reasonable and non-abusive use of the freedoms of the seas without detriment to the 'usufruct' itself. Lastly, at a third level stand the interferences that pertain to the general welfare and the *ordre public* of states and of international society, which aim thus to maintain the 'external order' of the oceans. Each will be considered in turn in the ensuing paragraphs. Finally, it should be mentioned that these levels or categories are not hermetically sealed nor isolated, in the sense that each case of interference reflects solely the legitimate concerns of the respective category. On the contrary, there is patently a degree of permeation between these categories, which, however, does not repeal the above classification, based on the *ratio juris* of each claim.

Finally, it is apt to note here that this is not the first effort to categorise the grounds for interference on the high seas: apparently drawing inspiration from the work of Gidel, Olivier de Ferron put forward an analogous, but far from identical, classification, which, however, was neither historically substantiated nor comprehensive, since he limited his analysis to the peacetime conventional exceptions to the exclusivity principle.[63] In addition, R Barnes furnishes a very insightful threefold classification of public-interest orders in the construction of an account of the public function of property.[64] In his theory, first-order interests are all accounts of property seeking to guarantee a minimal level of subsistence, such as certain basic goods, namely air, water, food, and shelter. Second-order interests are those interests that secure social order per se, while third-order interests are those interests that are particular to a given society and reflect its collective aims or its fundamental values. It is apparent that the third-order public interests reflect the third category of the present thesis's claims to interference on the high seas; however, the general scope of this work considerably differs from the present thesis.

Last but not least, Rosemary Rayfuse makes a similar tripartite categorisation of restrictions to the Grotian ideal of a *mare liberum*, as she posits them: 'Today, the freedom [of the seas] is not unfettered; an ever-increasing range of restrictions, embodied in numerous treaties and rules of customary international law, exist on the freedom. These restrictions can broadly be

---

[63] See O de Ferron, *Le droit international de la mer* (Paris: Librairie Minard, 1958) 118.
[64] See R Barnes, *Property Rights and Natural Resources* (Oxford: Hart, 2009) 113.

grouped into three categories: geographical restrictions; participant restrictions; and activity restrictions.'[65] However, she falls short of linking any of these restrictions with interference of vessels on the high seas.[66]

C. The Claims for Maintenance of International Peace and Security

As was observed, the principle of non-interference was never absolute, according to Grotius; on the contrary, the right to interfere with foreign vessels in the oceans in the course of a just war between nations or even in the course of a 'private just war' in the case of self-help was never disputed.[67] It is beyond the scope of the present enquiry to have regard to the parameters of 'just war' and 'self-help' in the time of Grotius. It is significant, however, that the intercourse of war at sea and the taking of lawful prizes were not the subject-matter of warships or public vessels, but rather of duly commissioned privateers, whose only distinctive trait from pirates was the possession of letters of marque or letters of reprisal.[68] In the centuries to follow, both the belligerent right of visit and search on the high seas and the notion of maritime neutrality were gradually accepted and regulated not only by customary law but also by various treaties, all of which have been predicated on the existence of war. In addition, it was always acknowledged that states had the right to visit and seize vessel in peacetime as a lawful exercise of the right of self-defence.[69]

Moreover, states concluded international agreements providing for police measures on the high seas to control the trade in arms in certain regions. Reference is made to the 1919 St Germain Convention[70] and to the 1925 Geneva Convention,[71] whose *ratio juris* was claimed to be, as cited by Gidel,

> d'empêcher que les quantités considérables de munitions de guerre qui étaient accumulées dans les divers pays anciennement belligérants et qui étaient devenues tout a coup sans emploi, ne soient dispersées dans le monde et ne constituent un *grand danger pour la paix générale.*[72]

[65] R Rayfuse, 'Moving Beyond the Tragedy of Global Commons: The Grotian Legacy and the Future of Sustainable Management of the Biodiversity of the High Seas', in Leary D and Pisupati B (eds), *The Future of International Environmental Law* (Tokyo: United Nations University Press, 2010) 201, 202.

[66] The sole exception is the 'participant restriction' relating to stateless vessels, which are not afforded the same privileges and protections as the vessels flying the flag of a state: ibid, 203.

[67] See eg H Grotius, *De Jure Belli ac Pacis, Libri Tres.*

[68] On the history of privateering and its relationship with piracy see F Stark, *The Abolition of Privateering and the Declaration of Paris* (New York: Columbia University, 1897), 49.

[69] See extended discussion in Gidel, 248.

[70] St Germain Convention on the Control of Trade in Arms and Ammunition, signed at 10 September 1919, 7 *League of Nations Treaty Series* 331.

[71] Geneva Convention on the International Commerce of Arms, signed 17 June 1925.

[72] Gidel, quoting Admiral Surie, 410–11 (emphasis added)

These agreements provided for the right of visit by the state parties of vessels less than 500 tonnes in certain maritime zones in Africa, such as the Red Sea, the Gulf of Aden, the Persian Gulf, in order to supervise the application of the prohibition in trade, but they never entered into force.[73]

In the post-World War II era, the advent of the UN Charter and of the system of collective security has enabled the Security Council to 'internationalise' the right of visit and search, in the sense that the Council has the power to authorise such measures not only in cases of existing armed conflicts, but also in cases of threats to international peace and security.[74] Under this authority, the Security Council has identified various such threats, the averting of which may also engage the right of visit on the high seas. Of particular importance for the present enquiry are the threats of international terrorism and of WMD, which have already given rise to coercive measures, including interdiction of foreign shipping on the high seas. Hence, in discharging its principal function under the UN Charter to address breaches and threats to international peace and security, the Council has effectively transformed exclusive claims for security at sea to 'essentially inclusive ones'.[75]

It is submitted that both the interference with foreign shipping by states in an armed conflict or 'short of an armed conflict proper (eg off the Gaza Strip, by Israel), and by states under the auspices of the Security Council, correspond to the need to maintain the peace and security of the legal order of the oceans. The common denominator or the common purpose in all the above instances is the maintenance of peace and security of the international community and *a majore ad minus* of the *civitas maxima* of the oceans. In view of that, it is not unlikely that the Council will, in the future, identify further threats to international peace and security, which might involve the adoption of coercive measures on the high seas. A potential candidate, in this vein, could be the scourge of the illicit trafficking in small arms, especially in the African continent.[76]

---

[73] See ibid, 414 and also G Politakis, *Modern Aspects of the Laws of Naval Warfare and Maritime Neutrality* (London: Keagan Paul International, 1998) 424 (hereinafter: Politakis).

[74] See eg the cases of Iraq, Former Republic of Yugoslavia et al.

[75] This function can also be attributed to the drafters of the St Germain and Geneva Conventions, who expressly designated the trade in arms in Africa as a 'serious danger to general peace'; above n 68.

[76] On this issue see Protocol against the Illicit Manufacturing and Trafficking in Firearms, Their Parts and Components and Ammunition, supplementing the UN Convention against Transnational Organized Crime (2000) and L Arabian, 'Combating the Illicit Manufacturing of and Trafficking in Small Arms and Weapons' 7 *Mediterranean Journal of Human Rights* (2003) 5.

D. The Claims for Protection of the *Bon Usage* of the High Seas

Mare liberum, as was eventually codified in the Geneva Convention and in
LOSC, encompassed various different freedoms, such as the freedoms to
navigate on the high seas, to fish and to lay submarine cables. Each freedom, however, is susceptible to over-exploitation or abuse, which might
eventually endanger the existence of the freedom itself or destabilise the
internal order of the high seas. It is worth recalling that both Welwood's
and Selden's *mare clausum* arguments rested in part upon the premise that
the wealth of the seas, mainly fisheries, was not inexhaustible, and thus
surveillance and control of the coastal state was required.[77] Thus, fisheries
were considered as 'common property natural resource',[78] subject to
property rights only once it is removed from the sea.[79] In the nineteenth
century, even though the sovereignty of the coastal states to the *mare proximum* had already been firmly established, there were claims regarding
the need to manage diminishing fish stocks. These claims took two forms:
first, coastal state authority to regulate fisheries has been extended
seaward, and secondly, the first multilateral and bilateral treaties on the
protection of high seas fisheries were concluded, which provided for the
right to interfere with delinquent fishing vessels on the high seas.[80] This
trend continued also in the last century, even though an Exclusive
Economic Zone (EEZ) of 200 nautical miles was recognised.[81] Indeed, as
was mentioned in the previous chapter, a variety of RFMOs were established to cooperate in managing the high seas fishery for certain stocks in
a defined area by prescribing management and conservation measures.

There have also been claims for control and surveillance in the oceans
in order to protect the other fundamental freedom of the high seas, namely
the freedom of navigation, which is intertwined with *jus communicationis*,
ie the right to communicate and a fortiori with the right to trade freely
with other nations using the high seas routes.[82] The major threat to these
freedoms historically has been piracy. Suffice to reiterate here Plutarch's
comments on Pompey's expedition against the pirate states,[83] or to refer to
the historical grounds for the English maritime ceremonial, which accord-

---

[77] See above n 49 and corresponding text.

[78] Churchill and Lowe, 281.

[79] For a very interesting analysis of fisheries from the perspective of property rights, see
Barnes, above n 65, esp Ch 3.

[80] See eg the International Convention for the Purpose of Regulating the Police of the
Fisheries in the North Sea outside Territorial Waters, 6 May 1882. For a detailed analysis of
these treaties and generally the problem of the protection of the high seas fisheries see Gidel,
Livre V, Ch III, IV, Livre V, Chs I–IV. See also P Jessup, 'L'exploitation des Richesses de la
Mer', 29 RCADI (1929-IV) 403.

[81] See Part V of LOSC and also Churchill and Lowe, Ch 9. See also Straddling Stocks
Agreement (1995).

[82] See Grotius, *Mare Liberum*.

[83] See above n 56.

ing to Fulton was to 'enable the King's officers, who were there to maintain the security of navigation, to ascertain the true nature of the vessel, which they challenged, whether it was a peaceful trader or a pirate'.[84]

It is a truism that the right to visit and seize a pirate vessel on the high seas was never contested as such. The thorny question has always been the definition of piracy and the propensity in international thought and practice to blur and extend its *ratione materiae* limits. As a result, it has often been associated with privateering, insurgency and national liberation movements or it has been used to justify suppression of other delinquent acts on the high seas, such as the slave trade.[85]

In general, the concept of piracy is the most characteristic paradigm of the permeation between the three categories of the present theoretical framework, since it, arguably, fits also in the next category of the *ordre public* of states as well as in the previous of the threats to international peace and security. Nonetheless, it is submitted that it fits better in the present category for the following reasons: first, the rationale behind its suppression was never the heinousness or the *contra bona mores* character of the *acta pirata,* but the pragmatic consideration of the protection of navigation and commerce on the high seas.[86] Furthermore, with the fall of the Barbary Pirates states and with the abolition of privateering in the nineteenth century, the oldest crime at sea ceased to bear the hallmark, inter alia, of a threat to the peace and security of states and be conflated with just war or self-help measures. It continued to be, principally, *crimen juris gentium,* whose suppression purported to protect freedom of navigation and commerce in the oceans.

Recently, the dividing line with the category of peace and security has been blurred again, due to the involvement of the Security Council in the repression of piracy and armed robbery off Somalia. Suffice to underscore in this respect that the SC in all its relevant Resolutions refrained from qualifying piracy as a 'threat to the peace and security', but it linked it with the already existing 'threat to the peace' in Somalia.[87] Also, those SC Resolutions that concern piracy and armed robbery at sea in the Gulf of Guinea are under Chapter VI of the UN Charter.[88]

In addition, there is the freedom of laying submarine cables, which has been conceived by states and the international society as in need of

[84] Fulton, 7.
[85] See in respect of piracy and '*piraterie par analogie'*, as the author qualified these trends, Gidel, Livre III, Ch III, Sect I. See also Zwanenberg, 788.
[86] See in this regard, E Kontorovich, 'The Piracy Analogy: Modern Universal Jurisdiction's Hollow Foundation', 45 *Harvard International Law Journal* (2004)183 (hereinafter Kontorovich).
[87] All SC Resolutions adopted in respect of piracy included the following caveat: 'Determining that the incidents of piracy and armed robbery against vessels in the territorial waters of Somalia and the high seas off the coast of Somalia exacerbate the situation in Somalia which continues to constitute a threat to international peace and security in the region' see inter alia SC Resolutions 1816 (2008), 1838 (2008), 1851 (2008).
[88] See Ch 1.

protection. The freedom of laying submarine cables as such was firstly enunciated in the Geneva Convention, but there had already been agreements between states regulating this activity since the nineteenth century.[89] The basic multilateral treaty in this respect, which is still in force, namely the 1884 Paris Convention, stipulated that warships of all signatory powers have a right to stop and verify the nationality of merchant ships of all nations, which are suspected of having infringed the regulations of the treaty.[90] As it was drafted to apply also vis-à-vis third states, the interference on the high seas was limited to the right of approach and *d'enquête du pavilion,* which, however, involved the right to board, but not to search the vessel.[91]

Further, there is certainly merit in discussing also the question of the protection of marine environment in the present framework.[92] As was noted also in respect of piracy, this issue could equally be classified under the next heading qua an inclusive claim for the maintenance of the *ordre public* of international society. However, it is argued that, even though there is no such freedom on the high seas, the protection and preservation of the marine environment fits neatly in the current discourse concerning the *bon usage* of the oceans, since the pollution of oceans may have deleterious effects in the usufruct of the high seas and may thwart states and international society from the *bon usage* of the oceans.

On the other hand, it should be recalled that there are authorities that classify serious pollution of the marine environment as a 'threat to the maritime security'; consequently, it may regarded as falling under the previous category. For instance, the 2008 CARICOM Agreement designates 'a serious or potentially serious pollution of the environment' as 'an activity likely to compromise the security of a State Party'. It is submitted that the pollution of the environment, however serious may be, is not equivalent to the threat posed by terrorism or WMD and thus such overly broad approach to the notion of international peace and security should be rejected.

It is true that there have been increasing claims for interference with vessels that intentionally and severely pollute the marine environment not only in the coastal states' jurisdictional zones, but also on the high seas. In the aftermath of the *Torrey Canyon* incident in 1967,[93] the 1969

---

[89]   See AP Higgins, 'Submarine Cables and International Law' *BYIL* (1921–22) 27.

[90]   art 10(2) of the Convention for the Protection of Submarine Cables, signed at Paris 14 March, 1884. *Cf* also arts 112–15 of LOSC.

[91]   See Gidel, 420. On contemporary issues concerning submarine cables see E Wagner, 'Submarine Cables and Protections provided by the Law of the Sea' 19 *MP* (1995) 127 and M Green, 'Security of International Submarine Cable Infrastructure: Time to Rethink?' in M Nordquist (ed), *Legal Challenges in Maritime Security* (Leiden: Martinus Nijhoff, 2008) 557.

[92]   See C Redgwell, above Introduction (n 8) and Churchill and Lowe, Ch 15.

[93]   The Torrey Canyon was a supertanker, which was shipwrecked off the western coast of Cornwall, England in March 1967, causing an environmental disaster. The UK decided to send the Royal Air force to drop cans of aviation fuel to make the oil blaze, in order to avoid

Brussels Convention was adopted, which granted to state parties, subject to consultation with other affected states, the right to 'take such measures on the high seas as may be necessary to prevent, mitigate or eliminate grave and imminent danger to their coastline or related interests from pollution or threat of pollution of the sea by oil, following upon a maritime casualty . . . which may reasonably be expected to result in a major harmful consequences'.[94] This, of course, entails that in case of such casualty on the high seas, the affected states may interfere with the vessel concerned without the consent of the flag state. It is argued that the legal basis for such interference lies not only with the primary rule of the above provision, but also with the secondary rule of state of necessity.

In addition, there could hypothetically be cases of interference with the freedom of navigation in the context of Marine Protected Areas and especially in the context of the recently promulgated 'Particularly Sensitive Seas Areas'.[95] Currently, however, there is only one treaty that provides for the interception on the high seas in case of serious pollution of the environment and that is the 2008 CARICOM Agreement. Since it is a novel instrument, there has been no relevant State practice to attract further comments.

A final remark would be that it is in the present category that the 'stateless vessels' ground for interference should be included.[96] The reason for this is simply that the maintenance of a minimum public order on the oceans, including the protection of the high seas freedoms as well as the preservation of a *bon usage* of the oceans is postulated on the principle that all the vessels navigating on the high seas have the nationality of a state, which is, in principle, responsible for this function. In the absence of a flag state, this function cannot be discharged and a fortiori the internal order of the high seas is in jeopardy; therefore, the public vessels of all states have the authority to visit such vessels.

In conclusion, there has been a consistent practice of states to criminalise and suppress practices on the high seas, which have as a consequence the '*gaspillage*' or the abuse of the wealth of the oceans as well as the endangerment of the freedoms themselves and thus of the 'internal' order of the oceans. The latter is also closely linked to the idea of 'ocean governance'; as Rayfuse and Warner note, 'building on the underlying concept of "international public trusteeship" it is possible to identify a range of mechanisms and tools that might be adopted by the international community to address

further catastrophe. See detailed commentary in P Quénedec, 'Les Incidences de l'Affaire du *Torrey Canyon* sur le Droit de la Mer', 14 *Annuaire Français de Droit International* (1968) 701.

[94] art 1 of the Brussels International Convention Relating to Intervention on the High Seas in Cases of Oil Pollution Casualties; 970 UNTS 211.

[95] See T Scovazzi, 'Marine Protected Areas on the High Seas. Some Legal and Policy Considerations' 19 *IJMCL* (2004) 1; M Gavouneli, 71.

[96] See LOSC art 110(1).

the shortcomings that have been identified in high seas governance'.[97] In similar vein, Vidas advocates the following thesis:

> [T]he emerging consciousness of a probable new epoch, the Anthropocene – the first geological time unit in the history of earth that we humans have created – must give rise to a new pragmatism.[98] . . . Given our technological development and abilities, that would lead us to only one certain feature: to *mare crisium*, the 'sea of crisis' . . . The need of our time is responsibility for the seas and the key segment that is fundamentally needed today relates to enabling us to deal with human impacts on the marine component of the Earth System.[99]

Against this background, the problems of irregular fishing, piracy *jure gentium*, the protection of submarine cables as well as marine pollution were canvassed. It is submitted that, even though they could also fit in the other two categories, they do share the common *ratio juris* of the present category, ie the protection of the freedoms of the high seas and hence of the internal order of the oceans. This was also reflected by the famous caveat introduced in the relevant article 87 of LOSC: 'all the freedoms shall be exercised by all States *with due regard for the interests of other States* in their exercise of the freedom of the high seas' (emphasis added). In this vein, there could be other freedoms of the high seas, which would be in need of protection, such as the freedom to construct artificial islands or the freedom of marine scientific research. Finally, in the future, there might be more comprehensive regulations for the protection of the Area and its resources,[100] including the right of visit in this regard.

E. The Claims for Maintenance of the '*Ordre Public*' of States and of International Society

The last category of the traditional *mare clausum* claims and of the grounds for interference with vessels on the high seas pertains to the maintenance of the social welfare and the *ordre public* of states and of international society. Gentillis was the first to posit, very perceptively, that restrictions of imports, of immigration and exports in a zone up to 100 nautical miles, in which the coastal state exerts jurisdiction, are justified for the sake of the safety and morals of people.[101] Later, Vattel based the extension of coastal

---

[97]   R Rayfuse and R Warner, above n 41, 411.

[98]   D. Vidas, Responsibility for the Seas', in Vidas D (ed), *Law, Technology and Science for Oceans in Globalisation: IUU Fishing, Oil Pollution, Bioprospecting, Outer Continental Shelf* (Leiden: Martinus Nijhoff, 2010) 3, 33.

[99]   ibid, 35. See also V Golitsyn, 'Major Challenges of Globalisation for Seas and Oceans: Legal Aspects', in Vidas D (ed), ibid, 59.

[100]   On the Area and its regulation see 1994 Agreement relating to the Implementation of Part XI of UNCLOS 33 ILM (1994) 1309 and M Lodge, 'The International Sea Bed Authority and article 82 of UNCLOS' 21 *IJMCL* (2006) 323.

[101]   See above n 16.

state authority on the need to protect the 'social welfare' of that state and to exert territorial jurisdiction over certain harmful activities.[102] These claims gained currency in international thought and practice and eventually led to the genesis of another maritime zone, adjacent to the territorial waters, the contiguous zone, where the coastal states enjoyed certain police powers for the prevention and punishment of the infringement of their customs, fiscal, sanitary and immigration regulations.[103]

Simultaneously, they gave rise to assertions for interference with foreign navigation on the high seas for similar reasons, such as the enforcement of customs and anti-smuggling regulations and of prohibitions relating to socially and politically unsound activities. An example of the former was the series of bilateral agreements that the US concluded in order to enforce the 1922 Volstead Act, referred to as the 'Liquor Treaties',[104] while of the latter was the British efforts towards the abolition of the slave trade,[105] leading to the adoption of numerous boarding agreements.[106] With the gradual development of international society, these claims were, accordingly, 'internationalised' and were given the imprimatur of international regulations for the maintenance of the *ordre public* and the '*bones mores*' of international society. Multilateral treaties were concluded which elevated some of these prescriptions to the apex of the normative pyramid, qua peremptory norms of the international legal order.[107] Thus, for example, the prohibition of slave trade was characterised as a rule of *jus cogens* and the warships of all states could visit vessels engaged in such activity and free the persons on board.[108]

In similar vein, the 1988 Vienna Convention proscribed the illicit trafficking of narcotic drugs and other psychotropic substances, and accorded the right to visit suspect vessels to the state parties. The Vienna Convention was the first of a series of regional and bilateral boarding agreements which were subsequently concluded with a view to protecting the public health and social welfare of states and of international society from the

---

[102] See above n 30.

[103] On the history of the contiguous zone, see Anand, 141. See also art 33 of LOSC and O'Connell, Ch 27.

[104] See inter alia Colombos, 143.

[105] In analysing the grounds for the British decision to take a leading role in the abolition of slave trade, Grewe cites the declaration of Wilberforce before the House of Commons in 1791: 'the abolition is indispensable required not only by religion and morality but by every principle of *sound policy*' (emphasis added). According to Grewe, the sound policy related to the economic and political background of that period, which provided the impetus for the British campaign, rather than sheer considerations of morality; Grewe, 555.

[106] See in this respect J Allain, 'The Nineteenth Century Law of the Sea and the British Abolition of the Slave Trade' 78 BYIL (2007) 343.

[107] On peremptory norms of international see A Orakhelasvili, *Peremptory Norms in International Law* (Oxford: OUP, 2006); R Kolb, *Théorie du ius cogens international* (Paris: Presses Universitaires de France, 2001).

[108] See *ILC Articles Commentary*, 112 and also *Barcelona Traction Case* (*Belgium v Spain*) ICJ Reports (1970) para 34.

scourge of narcotic drugs. In addition, a novel problem which has come forcefully to the forefront, and which directly challenges the social fabric and the *ordre public* of states is the smuggling of illicit migrants from underdeveloped and developing countries mainly to Europe, the US and Australia. In response, it has been already stated that states and the international society have adopted various anti-smuggling measures, including 'interception' on the high seas.[109] It is also clear that the visit of vessels for 'unauthorised broadcasting' under art 110 of LOSC fits neatly in the present category.

The interferences with foreign shipping in the present context follow a similar pattern: in the nineteenth century and in the early twentieth century, there was interference against the smuggling of alcohol and of other products and for the abolition of the trade of slaves, while, currently, such interference is accorded against the smuggling of narcotic drugs and for the abolition of the transfer of illicit migrants, respectively. It is very characteristic that both the assertions in relation to slave trade and with regard to the smuggling of migrants were phenominically premised upon moral and humanitarian considerations; however, as it was observed in relation to slave trade and will be demonstrated in respect of smuggling of migrants, the rationale behind these assertions were sheer public policy considerations. Therefore, it is suggested that in relation to the interception of human beings, a subtle distinction should be made between interference for 'negative' purposes, ie for the prevention of influx of migrants and for 'positive' purposes, namely for setting free people under various manifestations of exploitation.

Behind the above treaties proscribing such activities and providing for the right of visit stand the fundamental rationales of the social welfare and of the *ordre public* of states and of international society in general;[110] the latter notions may, however, vary, according to the perceptions of these values in each epoch.[111] This entails that the classification of the relevant cases of interference under the present heading is not permanent but evolutionary and dynamic; thus, this classification may alter, since it is contingent upon the changing values of each epoch and of each society. For example, the traffic of narcotic drugs may be considered as less deleterious and thus be de-classified as a threat to the *ordre public* of international society, whereas the protection of marine environment may attain a greater prominence for

---

[109] See eg art 8 of the Smuggling Protocol and the recent interception operations organised by FRONTEX.

[110] *cf* also the opinion of Gidel concerning '*le scandale et le disodre*' as threats to the 'general interest' of states and thus as grounds for positive assertions on the high seas; *UN Memorandum*, para 26.

[111] *cf* the analysis of McDougal and Burke with respect to the various 'manifold changing' objectives, which the process of interaction, ie the making of claims and the authoritative decision-making will take into account. They include inter alia solidarity, well-being, rectitude, wealth, enlightenment; at 17.

the maintenance of the welfare of international society. The decisive factor would be how the latter would perceive the relevant concerns of the states individually and whether it would 'internationalise' them by proscribing the respective activity in a universal treaty and more importantly by providing for the right of visit in this regard. Again, it bears reiterating that whilst each category of interests is conceptually discreet, it is yet closely related to the other.

This notwithstanding, the *fundamentum divisionis* of the present category from the previous relating to the international peace and security and to the protection of the freedoms of the seas lies with the fact that the present claims are extrinsically imposed to the organisation of the oceans, reflecting thus external order considerations that do not emanate from ocean activities as such. On the contrary, the previous category pertains exclusively to such activities and thus purports to maintain the internal order of the oceans. In the theory of Martti Koskenniemi, the present claims would reflect 'descending' or 'utopian' international legal arguments, while the previous two would convey rather 'ascending' or 'apologetic' arguments in the formulation of the *civitas maxima* of the oceans.[112]

III. INTERFERENCE IN THE CONTEMPORARY LEGAL ORDER OF THE HIGH SEAS: CONCLUDING REMARKS

As the history of the freedom of the seas well attests, the theories of *mare liberum* and of *mare clausum* were never antithetical or mutually exclusive, especially as far as the freedom of navigation on the high seas was concerned. On the contrary, there was consensus on the freedom of vessels to navigate in the vast and immense oceans, subject to certain restrictions, as well as consensus on the grounds that dictated the sovereignty or jurisdiction of the coastal state over the *mare proximum*. In the subsequent centuries, the claims to *mare clausum*, advanced in the height of the 'Battle of the Books', also gave substance to the claims for further jurisdiction on the high seas, not in the sense of sovereign rights, but of the right of visit for certain purposes. Thus, more instances of interference with foreign vessels on the high seas were gradually recognised in order to accommodate these *mare clausum* claims. In addition, the latter claims were legally transformed, ie from purely national claims to their acknowledgment as claims of the nascent international society. Eventually, they became the positive underpinnings of the predominantly negative legal order of the oceans, in the Gidelian sense of non-interference and of the exclusivity of flag state jurisdiction. This exclusivity principle was positively qualified in a three-fold

---

[112] See M Koskenniemi, *From Apology to Utopia* (Cambridge: Cambridge University Press, 2005) 59.

sense: to accommodate claims for the maintenance of international peace and security, for the protection of the *bon usage* of the oceans and for the maintenance of the *ordre public* of international society.

This classification has the obvious merit that it conceptualises, categorises the various ostensibly independent grounds for interference on the high seas, and thus conduces to the configuration of a coherent legal order of the oceans in the twenty-first century. It is a rather intuitive tool to comprehend the interrelationship between these grounds.

Finally, has the current extensive practice of interference with foreign shipping on the high seas destabilised or eroded *mare liberum* in the twenty-first century? The reply to this question flows easily from the foregoing analysis: the freedom of the high seas was never an absolute principle; it has always been qualified by '*mare clausum*' claims for jurisdiction and for police powers on the high seas, which served certain firmly established and coherent purposes, namely the maintenance of peace and security, the protection of the freedoms of the high seas and the maintenance of the *ordre public* of international society. Contemporary practices and interferences do not deviate from this scheme; on the contrary, they share the same purposes and they put forward similar legal justifications. Indeed, it may be concluded that the recent practice has not brought about substantial changes to the legal order of the oceans, in the sense of curtailing the fundamental tenet of the exclusivity of flag-state jurisdiction.[113] It is also doubtful whether such change will occur in the near future, since these rationales are well embedded in the legal order of the oceans.

---

[113]   *cf* however, the different opinion of N Klein, who contends that 'although the predominant emphasis in the law of the sea has been that common interest is achieved through maintaining the freedoms of the high seas and respecting flag State authority in these areas, these central motivations may no longer be completely appropriate given the recent claims to undertake various measures for the enhancement of maritime security'; see Klein, *Maritime Security*, 16–17.

3

The Law of Maritime Interception on the High Seas

I. INTRODUCTORY REMARKS

T
HE PREVIOUS CHAPTER examined the historical and theoretical framework of maritime interception on the high seas, and addressed questions such as to what extent the traditional paradigm of *mare liberum* has been eroded and how can all these numerous interception activities be justified under a coherent legal order of the oceans. Chapter 3 will focus upon the legal framework of interception on the high seas, or, as officially pronounced, the right of visit. First, it will have regard to the classical belligerent right of visit and search and will discuss its basic parameters. Then, it will examine the right of visit in peacetime, delineating its legal contours under both the relevant treaty and customary law. In more detail, it will explore the following issues: i) the right of approach and the right of visit per se, as they were customarily framed and as they are currently practised by states; ii) the influence of recent technological advents to the right of approach (eg LRIT, doctrines of maritime domain awareness, maritime identification zones); iii) the prerequisite of 'reasonable suspicions' and how this has been recently addressed, in view, also, of intelligence-gathering; iv) the modus operandi, ie the operational rules generally applicable in interception operations, and v) in particular, the issue of the use of force in the course of such operations.

In addition, the discussion of the legal framework of interception operations on the high seas will inevitably include references to the relevant restrictions imposed by general international law. These will mainly be restrictions under international human rights law or humanitarian law, which address the fundamental question of 'how persons intercepted on the high seas should be treated under international law'. Closely linked is another question: who is competent to exercise jurisdiction over the alleged delinquent act, and on what basis under international law.

Having said that, it is apt to underscore that the relevant obligations of states intercepting foreign vessels on the high seas fall under different rubrics according to international law: on the one hand, the right of visit as such, including the existence of 'reasonable suspicions', falls under article 110 of LOSC and on the other, human rights or humanitarian law considerations as well as the assertion of jurisdiction are regulated by the respective treaties and customary international law. As a result, maritime interception on the high seas is subject to various international legal norms, all constituents of the legal order of the oceans, which, nevertheless, require different treatment and entail different legal consequences; thus, for example, the intercepting State may incur responsibility for more than one internationally wrongful acts.

Concluding, the present chapter will be confined to the aforementioned parameters of the legal framework of interception and will not extend to the secondary, yet very significant issues of state responsibility for internationally wrongful acts committed in the course of interception operations. Also, the question of the applicable national law and the issue of immunities during interdictions will not be addressed.[1] These issues have found an excellent treatment elsewhere and will be dealt with here only in passing.[2]

II. THE RIGHT OF VISIT ON THE HIGH SEAS IN WARTIME

The primary distinction to be drawn is between the right of visit and search in peacetime and in wartime. Even if this traditional dichotomy has lost a considerable part of its force in the contemporary era, it retains its validity. 'The right of visit and search, during war, of all merchant ships upon the high seas, whatever be the ships, whatever be the cargoes, and whatever be the destinations is an incontestable right of lawfully commissioned cruisers of a belligerent nation.'[3] This right finds its legal justification in the basic premise of sea warfare, according to which private property, enemy but also neutral under certain conditions, can be confiscated.[4] Capture is only conceivable through the modalities of visit and search.[5]

---

[1] The question of immunities has been at the centre of a recent incident in which Italian marines, embarked aboard an oil tanker to protect it, appear to have killed two Indian fishermen, mistaking them for pirates; see further comments in D Guilfoyle's post at www.ejiltalk.org/shooting-fishermen-mistaken-for-pirates-jurisdiction-immunity-and-state-responsibility/.

[2] On the issue of state responsibility, see Wendel and Guilfoyle, *Shipping Interdiction*, Ch 12. On the question of national jurisdiction and immunities, see Guilfoyle, *Shipping Interdiction*, Ch 11.

[3] *The Maria* [1799] 1 C *Robinson's Admiralty Reports* 340, 360, cited in Colombos, 753.

[4] Among the leading treatises on this issue see AP Higgins, 'Le Droit de Visite et Capture dans la Guerre Maritime' 11 *RCADI* (1926) 65; W Heinegg, 'Visit, Search, Diversion and Capture in Naval Warfare: Part II' 30 *Canadian Yearbook of International Law* (1992) 89.

[5] In the words of Emmerich de Vattel, 'on ne peut empêcher le transport des effets de contrabande, si l'on ne visite pas les vaisseaux neuters, que l'on rencontre en mer. On est donc en droit de les visiter'; de Vattel, *Le Droit des Gens*, Tome II (1758) chap VII, para 148; cited in Politakis, 530.

A. The Law of Naval Warfare in the Past and in the Present

The historic origins of such practice can be traced back to the collection of maritime usages known as the *Consolato del Mare*, first published at Barcelona in 1494, and to a number of earlier treaty provisions, which explicitly recognised the right of visit for the purposes of verifying the neutral character of encountered merchantmen.[6] Also prescribed in certain treaties and national enactments was the right to capture all ships which resist visit and search.[7] According to the 1907 Hague Regulations, the belligerent right of visit and search may be conducted only in those sea areas where a belligerent can lawfully engage his enemy, that is to say, everywhere beyond neutral waters.[8]

There have been considerable doubts as to whether the traditional law of naval warfare, and concomitantly the belligerent right of visit and search, remains intact in the post-Charter era.[9] This is mainly because the legal framework governing armed hostilities at sea, ie the law of naval warfare, dates back to the 1907 Hague Regulations and has not recently been revisited.[10] Other relevant international instruments are equally dated: the Paris Declaration of 1856,[11] the Declaration of London of 1909,[12]

---

[6] An early instance is the Treaty of Tournai in 1407 between the plenipotentiaries of Charles IV, King of France, and of William, King of Holland; see AP Higgins, above n 4, 74.

[7] See eg the Treaty of Pyrenees, concluded in 1659 between France and Spain as well as the French Ordinance of 1681. On the early history of visit and search, see inter alia T Ortolan, *Règles Internationales et Diplomatie de la Mer*, Tome II (1864) 248 (hereinafter: Ortolan); C Dupuis, *Le Droit de la Guerre Maritime d'àpres les Doctrines Anglaises Contemporaines* (Paris: Pedoner, 1899) 296.

[8] See art 2 of 1907 Convention XIII Concerning the Rights and Duties of Neutral Powers in Naval Warfare; see below n 10.

[9] See eg AV Lowe, 'The Commander's Handbook on the Law of Naval Operations and the Contemporary Law of the Sea', in H Robertson (ed), *The Law of Naval Operations* (Newport: Naval War College Press 1991) 109, 130.

[10] The relevant Hague Regulations are the following: The Hague Convention for the Pacific Settlement of International Disputes (1907); The Hague Convention VI Relating to the Status of Enemy Merchant Ships at the Outbreak of Hostilities (1907); The Hague Convention VII Relating to the Conversion of Merchant Ships into Warships (1907); The Hague Convention VIII Relative to the Laying of Automatic Submarine Contact Mines (1907); The Hague Convention IX Concerning Bombardment by Naval Forces in Time of War (1907); The Hague Convention XI Relative to Certain Restrictions With Regard to the Exercise of the Right of Capture in Naval War (1907); The Hague Convention XIII Concerning the Rights and Duties of Neutral Powers in Naval War (1907). These conventions are compiled in N Ronzitti (ed), *The Law of Naval Warfare: A Collection of Agreements and Documents with Commentaries* (Dordrecht: Martinus Nijhoff, 1988).

[11] The Declaration of Paris represented the first codification of the rules of maritime war to be generally accepted among maritime states; see Declaration Respecting Maritime Law, 16 April 1856, 1 AJIL (Supp 1907) 89. The Paris Declaration is given an exhaustive treatment in F Piggot, *The Declaration of Paris, 1856* (London, 1919).

[12] The London Declaration Concerning the Laws of Naval Warfare (1909) was the first and only exhaustive, yet ill-fated compilation and codification of all the aspects of maritime warfare. See JB Scott, 'The Declaration of London of February 26, 1909' 8 *AJIL* (1914) 274.

and the London Protocol relating to the Rules of Submarine Warfare of 1936.[13] In view of the considerable age of the Hague Regulations and of the other instruments, it is obvious that they might be ill-suited to meeting the realities of modern weaponry and contemporary methods and means of naval warfare.[14] Nonetheless, the basic principles, such as the right of visit in wartime, are still generally recognised as reflecting customary international law.[15]

Recently, two texts have been produced by private bodies, namely the San Remo Institute[16] and the International Law Association,[17] which even though they have no formal status, are both widely considered, in the most part, as restatements of the contemporary customary law applicable to armed conflicts at sea.[18] Green has commented in respect of the San Remo Manual that 'although it is an unofficial statement, it is generally regarded as expressive of accepted customary law'.[19] Moreover, the US has submitted before the International Court of Justice that 'most of [the San Remo Manual's] provisions reflect customary international law'.[20] Finally, of further authoritative value are the military manuals of some states from among the most influential naval powers, which have been revised in order to encapsulate the current status of the relevant customary law, as perceived or practised by them.[21]

---

[13] See E Nwogugu, 'Commentary on the 1936 London Procès Verbal', in N Ronzitti (ed), above n 10, 353.

[14] See relevant discussion in Politakis, 643–44.

[15] See W Heinegg, 'The UNCLOS and Maritime Security Operations' 48 *German Yearbook of International Law* (2006) 151, 154.

[16] See International Institute of International Humanitarian Law, San Remo Manual on International Law Applicable at Armed Conflicts at Sea, para 118 (hereinafter: San Remo Manual). See for the text of the manual and commentary: L Doswald-Beck (ed), *San Remo Manual on International Law Applicable at Armed Conflicts at Sea* (Cambridge: Cambridge University Press, 1995).

[17] See ILA, Helsinki Principles on the Law of Maritime Neutrality (1998) (hereinafter: Helsinki Principles).

[18] See eg Y Dinstein, 'Sea Warfare', in R Bernhardt (ed), *Encyclopedia of Public International Law* (Amsterdam: North-Holland, 1994) (1998–V) 340, 350. See also generally W Heinegg, 'The Law of Military Operations at Sea', in TD Gill and D Fleck (eds), *The Handbook of the International Law of Military Operations* (Oxford: Oxford University Press, 2010) 325–74.

[19] LC Green, *The Contemporary Law of Armed Conflict*, 3rd edn (Manchester: Manchester University Press, 2008) 45.

[20] *Oil Platforms (Islamic Republic of Iran v United States of America)* (Counter-Memorial and Counter-Claim Submitted by the United States of America) 23 June 1997, 130 fn 2925; available at www.icjcij.org/icjwww/idocket/iop/ioppleadings/iop_ipleadings_19970623_countermem_us_04.pdf4.

[21] See eg US Navy, *Commander's Handbook on the Law of Naval Operations* (US Navy, NWP 1–14M) (edition of July 2007), available at www.usnwc.edu/getattachment/a9b8e92d-2c8d-4779-9925-0defea933 25c/1-14M_%28Jul_2007%29_%28NWP%29 (hereinafter: US Commander's Handbook); German Commander's Handbook, in W Heinegg, H-J Unbehau, *Kommandanten-Handbuch* (2002) (hereinafter: German Manual) and UK Ministry of Defence, *The Manual of the Law of Armed Conflict* (2004) Ch 13 (hereinafter: UK Manual). See also the commentary of the latter in W Heinneg, 'Manoeuvring in Rough Waters: The UK Manual of the Law of Armed Conflict', in A Fischer-Lescano et al (eds), *Frieden in Freiheit: Festschrift für Michael Bothe zum 70 Geburstag* (Baden-Baden: Nomos, 2008), 427.

B. The Role of the UN Charter in the Contemporary Law of Naval Warfare

Two preliminary issues merit attention: the first involves the status of the law of armed conflict at sea – especially maritime neutrality – within the international legal framework established by the UN Charter. There is the argument that since the outlawing of the use of force by the UN Charter,[22] no 'state of' war' can lawfully arise. Accordingly, 'the criterion for the applicability of the Laws of the War cannot be met, the legality of all uses of force henceforth being judged by reference to the terms of the Charter'.[23] Nevertheless, 'other scholars maintain that the much-acclaimed prohibition of resort to the force in Article 2 (4) or *jus ad bellum*, is basically unconnected with the laws of war properly so called, or *jus in bello,* and therefore the traditional laws remain unaltered by the Charter limitations on the use of force.'[24] The merits of these opposing arguments have been canvassed *in extenso* elsewhere and this task will not be repeated here;[25] nonetheless, it is submitted that, in principle, a state's use of force at sea is subject to the basic rules governing naval hostilities, as amended and qualified by the collective security system of the Charter.[26]

In any event, from the moment armed force is used between two or more states, the customary international law of armed conflict at sea applies to all the parties to the conflict, irrespective of who was the aggressor and who is acting in self-defence.[27] As M Bothe rightly stresses,

> once an armed conflict has started because aggression has occurred, it is not possible to ask the question, whether there is an armed attack or a situation of self-defence, for each individual shot fired. Within the framework of an armed conflict, the legal yardstick for the individual act of violence is the law of war only and not the *ius contra bellum*.[28]

Equally, the San Remo Manual stipulates that 'the parties to an armed conflict at sea are bound by the principles and rules of international humanitarian law *from the moment armed force is used*'.[29]

---

[22] See art 2(4) of the UN Charter.

[23] See AV Lowe, above n 9, 130 *in fine.*

[24] Politakis, 7.

[25] See the general debate in N Ronzitti, 'Le Droit Humanitaire Applicable aux Conflits Armès en Mer', 242 *RCADI* (1993) 138–39.

[26] See also Doswald-Beck, 'The San Remo Manual of International Law Applicable to Armed Conflicts at Sea' 89 *AJIL* (1995) 192, 197.

[27] See in this regard San Remo Manual, 73.

[28] See M Bothe, 'Neutrality in Naval Warfare – What is Left of Traditional International Law?' in A Delissen and G Tanja (eds), *'Humanitarian Law of Armed Conflict* (Dordrecht: Martinus Nijhoff, 1991) 393.

[29] San Remo Manual, para 1 (emphasis added).

When the resort to force is the outcome of a decision of the Security Council under Chapter VII, the UN Member States are obliged to abide by the terms of the decision and support a United Nations action at the expense of their pure maritime neutrality.[30]

Significant in these modern restatements of the law of naval warfare is the lack of any reference to the traditional distinction between international armed conflicts and non-international armed conflicts. The San Remo Manual speaks mainly of international armed conflicts, although it leaves open the possibility for the application of its principles to non-international armed conflicts, as in para 1, it refers vaguely to the 'parties to an armed conflict', without further distinction. According to the Commentary to the Manual,

> although the provisions of the Manual are primarily meant to apply to international armed conflicts at sea, this has intentionally not been expressly indicated in paragraph 1 in order to dissuade the implementation of these rules in non-international armed conflicts involving naval operations.[31]

Hence, it is assumed that the law of naval warfare applies *in toto* to armed conflicts, regardless of whether the conflict is international or non-international.

C. The Applicability of LOSC in the Law of Naval Warfare

The second preliminary question is the impact of the LOSC on the laws of naval warfare. As Natalie Klein reports:

> the arguments have varied from one extreme to the other – from considering that UNCLOS is not applicable during the armed conflict,[32] to UNCLOS being applicable because the laws of naval warfare are no longer relevant with the changes in laws relating to when States may lawfully resort to force.[33] As may be expected, a more moderate position whereby "the maritime rights and duties States enjoy in peacetime continue to exist, with minor exceptions, during armed conflict' is the most tenable view.[34]

Indeed, although it is common ground that the LOSC does not directly bear on the law of naval warfare,[35] it has an extensive impact on the rules

---

[30] See ibid, paras 7–9 and US Commander's Handbook, 7.2.1.

[31] L Doswald-Beck (ed), above n 16, 73.

[32] See inter alia B Wilson and J Kraska, 'American Security and the Law of the Sea' 40 *Ocean Development and International Law* (2009) 268, 277.

[33] See AV Lowe, above n 9, 130–33.

[34] Klein, *Maritime Security*, 259. See also GK Walker, 'Self-defence, The Law of Armed Conflict and Port Security' 5 *South Carolina Journal of International Law and Business* (2009) 347.

[35] While none of the 1958 Geneva Conventions expressly so provide, it is true that the International Law Commission, which prepared draft articles on the subject, intended the

defining the 'regions' of naval operations, and especially the extent of these regions. Belligerent measures may be exercised on the high seas or in the territorial seas of belligerents, but not in areas under the sovereignty of neutral states.[36]

Despite allegations to the contrary,[37] neither the LOSC provisions concerning the peaceful use of the sea nor international state practice have contributed to the emergence of a rule of international law restricting the parties to an international armed conflict at sea to their respective internal waters and territorial seas. However, in view of the special legal status of the high seas and of the rights that neutral states continue to enjoy on them, belligerents are obliged to pay due regard to these aspects and refrain from interference therein.[38] The same considerations apply if belligerent measures are taken in the EEZ or the continental shelf areas of neutral countries.[39]

D. The Belligerent Right of Visit and Search: Rules and Procedures

Turning to the substantive laws governing in the contemporary era the right of visit and search of merchant vessels, the San Remo Manual sets forth that,

> In exercising their legal rights in an international armed conflict at sea, belligerent warships and military aircraft have a right to visit and search merchant vessels outside neutral waters where there are reasonable grounds for suspecting that they are subject to capture.[40]

As an alternative, they may be diverted to a specific sea area or port in order to be visited and searched there for the purpose of verifying whether they are liable to capture or verifying their neutral character.[41]

Noteworthy is that the San Remo Manual takes the view that any such right of visit and search can only be exercised upon 'reasonable grounds'

articles to apply in time of peace; see YbILC (1956-II) 256. The LOSC is similarly silent, although here, too, it was understood that the Conference was concerned with the peacetime law of the sea; see AV Lowe, above n 9, 132.

[36] See W Heinegg (ed), *Regions of Operations of Naval Warfare* (Bochum: Brockmeyer, 1995) 19–29.

[37] It is asserted that the combined effect of art 88 of LOSC, which reserves the high seas for peaceful purposes, and of art 301, which reiterates the prohibition on the use of force in international relations is entirely to outlaw armed conflicts in common maritime areas; see AV Lowe, above n 9, 131. *Cf* also, O Connell who, in particular, took the position that belligerents are restricted to their respective territorial sea areas; Connell, 'International Law and Contemporary Naval Operations' 44 *BYIL* (1970) 19.

[38] See San Remo Manual para 10(b) and para 36. See also Helsinki Principles para 3.1.

[39] See Hague Convention XIII arts 2 and 5, San Remo Manual para 14 and Helsinki Principles para 2.1.

[40] San Remo Manual para 118.

[41] See also RW Tucker, *The Law of War and Neutrality at Sea* (1957) 340.

for suspecting the vessel is subject to capture.[42] The UK Manual is in accord with this,[43] while the German Manual does not require the existence of 'reasonable grounds. It provides *simpliciter* that 'Warships of a party to a conflict are entitled to stop, visit, and search merchant ships flying the flag of a neutral state on the high seas and control the contents and destination of their cargo.'[44] Finally, the US asserts a similarly wide right of visit.[45]

As regards the traditional procedure of visit, 'on approaching a merchant ship for the purpose of visit, the commander of the visiting cruiser must summon her to stop.'[46] This signal may be given in different ways, either by raising the international flag signal, by siren or by radio communication. Frequent also is the practice of hoisting the flag and firing a blank charge, or affirming gun (*coup de semonce* or *coup d'assurance*): 'If the merchant vessel refuses to take heed, the warship may fire across the bows and, if necessary, disable the ship's steering gear.'[47] As the US Commander's Handbook states, 'Neutral vessels attempting to resist proper capture lay themselves open to forcible measures by belligerent warships and military aircraft and assume all risk of resulting damage.'[48] After the vessel has stopped, a boarding party is sent to examine the ship's papers in order to verify its flag of registry, its provenance and next port of call, and the character of its cargo. Should suspicion remain as regards the nationality of the ship or the nature of the cargo, the visiting officers may also interrogate the crew and search the ship's holds. If the enquiry shows nothing irregular, the boarding party should cause no more delay and release the vessel, after having signed an entry to the vessel's logbook.[49]

Further, a distinction should be made between enemy merchant vessels, which under certain circumstances could be characterised as military objectives and a fortiori attacked, and neutral merchant vessels, which are only susceptible to capture under traditional prize law. While the right to capture enemy merchant vessels is accepted without demur,[50] the principle that any merchant ship could be lawfully attacked on sight, if it could be established that its commercial activity is in reality promoting the war

---

[42] See the remarks of D Guilfoyle, 'The *Mavi Marmara* Incident and Blockade in Armed Conflict' 81 *BYIL* (2011) 171, 208.

[43] UK Manual paras 13.47, 13.91; see also Guilfoyle, ibid.

[44] German Manual para 1138.

[45] US Commander's Handbook para 7.6.

[46] Colombos, 765.

[47] Politakis, 533.

[48] US Commander's Handbook para 7.10.

[49] See Ortolan, 220 and AP Higgins, above n 4, 114. *Cf* also US Commander's Handbook para 7.6.1.

[50] According to the San Remo Manual, 'enemy vessels whether merchant or otherwise, and goods on board such vessels may be captured outside neutral waters. Prior exercise of visit and search is not required'; see para 135 and commentary, 205.

effort of the enemy, is not free of controversy. In light of the fundamental principle that 'attacks shall be limited strictly to military objectives', enshrined in article 52(2) of the 1977 First Additional Protocol, it is asserted that the destruction of enemy merchant vessels would be lawful only if it definitely made an effective contribution to military action and offered a definite military advantage.[51]

The latter instrument as well as the relevant customary law regulate also the degree of force that is permitted to be employed in the course of a belligerent right of visit. In this regard, of particular importance is the principle of proportionality, which requires commanders to conduct a balancing test to determine if the incidental injury, including death to civilians and damage to civilian objects, is excessive in relation to the anticipated concrete and direct military advantage.[52] In addition, the law of naval warfare and more specifically the law of prize set forth the relevant procedures in relation to the contraband and the captured vessel itself.[53] With regard to the officers and crews of captured neutral merchant vessels who are nationals of a neutral nation, it is accepted that they do not become prisoners of war, and must be repatriated as soon as circumstances reasonably permit. This rule applies equally to the officers and crews of neutral vessels that assumed the character of enemy merchant vessels or aircraft by operating under enemy control or resisting visit and search. If, however, the neutral vessels or aircraft have taken a direct part in the hostilities on the side of the enemy, they thereby assumed the character of enemy warships and, upon capture, their officers and crew may be interned as prisoners of war.[54]

E. Concluding Thoughts

To conclude, it is submitted that the customary belligerent right of visit and search, as has been restated in the San Remo Manual and in various military manuals, is still relevant. Even though the legal contours of naval warfare have been modified by the contemporary *jus contra bellum* and the law of the sea, there is still room for the application of the right of visit and search in the course of an international and, arguably, of a non-international

---

[51] As Politakis stresses, 'there is nothing in law to warrant the unprovoked instant destruction of unarmed merchant vessels whether enemy or neutral for the single reason of being engaged in enemy commerce'; Politakis, 639.

[52] 'An attack shall be cancelled or suspended if it becomes apparent that the objective is not a military one or is subject to special protection or that the attack may be expected to cause incidental loss of civilian life, injury to civilians, damage to civilian objects, or a combination thereof, which would be excessive in relation to the concrete and direct military advantage anticipated'; see art 57(2)(b) 1977 Additional Protocol.

[53] On the continuing validity of prize law, see W Heinneg, above n 21, 441.

[54] See eg US Commander's Handbook para 7.10.2.

armed conflict. The *modus operandi* of this right has been customarily set out, but it is also subject to the various provisions of contemporary military manuals as well as to the rules of engagement (RoEs) of each multinational naval operation. Nevertheless, the overall legal framework of such naval operations on the high seas, involving the right of visit of merchant vessels, is the *lex specialis* of international humanitarian law, complemented by the law of human rights.

III. THE RIGHT OF VISIT ON THE HIGH SEAS IN PEACETIME

This part will canvass the legal parameters of the right of visit on the high seas in peacetime and it will address the question whether there is a separate law of maritime interception on the high seas. It will first describe the general legal framework of this right, as has been created by customary and treaty law; it will then shift its attention to more special and contemporary issues, such as the influence of technology on the classical right of approach or the practice of states with regard to the requirement of 'reasonable suspicions'. In addition, there will be discussion of 'consent' as basis of maritime interception. Reference will be also made to the modus operandi of maritime interception on the high seas, as envisaged by LOSC and as applied by states. In this regard, special emphasis should be given to the use of force in the course of these operations. Finally, separate questions concerning the assertion of jurisdiction and the applicability of human rights will be addressed.

A. Treaty and Customary Law Framework of the Right of Visit

In peacetime and under the regime of the freedom of the high seas, it is generally accepted that no state can interfere with the shipping of another state unless the interfering state possesses an exceptional right clearly vested by customary law or pursuant to a particular treaty regime. Although the nature of this interference varies, justifiable acts of interference fall under two general rubrics: the right of approach (*droit de reconnaissance*) and the right of visit (*droit de visite*). On the one hand, 'it is a universally recognised customary rule of international law that warships of all nations, in order to maintain the safety of the high seas, have the power to require suspicious private vessels on the high seas to show their flag'.[55] The right to approach,

---

[55] Oppenheim's *International Law*, 737. The origins of the right of approach may be found in the old tradition of the maritime ceremonial, or the lowering of the flags of all vessels which encountered a British vessel. Although it is now considered as corresponding to courtesy at sea, rather than to a legal obligation, it is believed that it was used to ascertain whether a vessel was piratical; see Fulton, 7.

or *reconnaissance*, is limited to the right to approach a ship to identify her.[56] An approaching warship may request an encountered vessel to show her colours, which are prima facie evidence of her nationality.[57] Without evidence to counter this showing of nationality or further suspicions, a warship may not board the encountered vessel and, a fortiori, may not proceed to examine her papers or perform a search.[58] The exercise of this right, consequently, is not dependent on the existence of an exception to the exclusivity rule of flag state jurisdiction. Any public vessel may inquire the nationality of a foreign ship on the high seas, regardless of whether there is reason to suspect the ship of having committed an international delict, since no physical interference with the freedom of navigation is involved.[59]

On the other hand, 'under extreme circumstances, the public ships of a state are competent to visit and search the vessel of another State'.[60] The acceptance of the peacetime right of visit (*droit de visite*) has been gradual and controversial, since it was originally conceived as a belligerent right which did not apply in time of peace, unless provided for under a customary or conventional exception to the general rule of non-interference.[61] The traditional non-conventional exceptions were piracy and the right of self-defence, while the conventional exceptions in the nineteenth and early twentieth centuries pertained to fisheries, the protection of submarine cables, the slave trade and anti-smuggling measures.[62]

---

[56] The US Supreme Court has held: 'In respect to ships of war . . . there is no reason why they may not approach any vessels descried at sea, for ascertaining their real characters. Such a right seems indispensable for the fair and discreet exercise of their authority.' See *Marianna Flora,* 43.

[57] See O de Ferron, *Le Droit International de la Mer* (1958) 108–9; Y Van der Mensbrugghe, 'Le Pouvoir de Police des Etats en Haute Mer' 11 *RBDI* (1975) 56, 61.

[58] See G Gidel, *Le Droit de la Mer*, 289; François, *Regime of the High Seas,* UN Doc A CN A/17, reprinted in YbILC (1950-II) 36, 41; R Reuland, 'Interference with Non-National Ships on the High Seas' 22 *Vanderbilt Journal of Transnational Law* (1989) 1161, 1170 (hereinafter: Reuland).

[59] See H Smith, *The Law and Custom of the Sea* (London: Steven & Sons, 1959) 64. Both Colombos, at 311 and Oppenheim's *International Law*, 736 seem reluctant to disassociate the right of reconnaissance from the existence of suspicions . Gidel designates the right of *reconnaissance* as measures of 'police générale'. In his words, 'Les mesures de police générale peuvent être prises independamment de conventions et résultent purement et simplement de la coutoume elles sont générales, enfin, en ce qu'elles ne sont pas relatives à un ordre d'activité déterminé'; Gidel, 289.

[60] Reuland, 1170.

[61] Gidel wrote that 'le droit de visite en temps de paix n'existe pas, sauf exceptions strictement limitées et resultant d'accords conventionnels'; Gidel, 292. See also C Hyde, *International Law,* 2nd edn, Vol I (Boston: Little, Brown & Co, 1947) 764.

[62] See extensive discussion of these exceptions in Gidel, 301. He coins them as 'les mesures de police spéciale', [which] 'n'existent qu'en vertu de conventions: elles ne peuvent donc s'appliquer qu'entre les Etats parties à ses conventions; elles sont spéciales également en ce qu'elle rapportent à des activités déterminées', at 289. See also H Halleck, *International Law,* 3rd edn, Vol II (London: Kegan Paul, 1893) 240.

The right of visit is composed of two distinct operations: the *droit d'enquête du pavillon*, ie the right of boarding the vessel and of investigation of the flag, and the right of search (*perquisition*).[63]

> A warship may employ the *droit d'enquête du pavillon* – the first element of the comprehensive *droit de visite* – to ascertain or verify the true nationality of a vessel she encounters upon the high seas. She may exercise her *droit d'enquête* against only those vessels she reasonably suspects of having engaged in some proscribed activity, which, under customary or conventional law, would permit the warship to proceed against the suspect vessel.[64]

To effect a stoppage, of course, the warship will hail the suspect vessel or, if this is impossible or ineffectual, fire across its bow.[65] Similar to the corresponding belligerent right, the actual verification of the flag takes place aboard the suspect vessel, which requires that the warship will send a party under the command of an officer to the suspect vessel, who will examine the papers and documentation of the suspect vessel.[66]

> Only circumstances of extreme suspicion, however, will justify the search of the vessel, which may include a detailed inspection of all parts of the ship and its cargo and the questioning of the crew.[67] In the words of the ILC,

> the examination must in no circumstances be used for purposes other than those which warranted stopping the vessel . . . the boarding party must be under the command of an officer responsible for the conduct of his men. He has to watch that they do not go beyond the mission's purpose, do not interfere with the work of the captain or crew, or behave improperly with respect to persons or property on board the ship.[68]

[63] There is a certain discrepancy between the Anglo-Saxon and the French doctrines in the use of the relevant terms; for example, the former tend to speak only of a 'right of visit and search' and they employ the terms '*reconnaissance*' and '*enquête du pavillon*' to designate what was called 'the right of approach'; see inter alia Oppenheim's *International Law*, 737; Ortolan, 233.

[64] Reuland, 1172. He further notes: 'one can imagine how the exercise of the normally benign right of simple reconnaissance could easily ripen into a proper visitation and search. For example, a warship approaches a ship on the high seas and requests that she identify herself. The ship responds in suspicious manner, taking evasive action or refusing to fly a flag'; Reuland, 1172 (fn 27). Then, according to Colombos, 312 'she becomes at once suspect'. In the prevailing view, it is assimilated *ipso facto* to stateless vessel and thus boarding is permitted. However, as Smith rightly avers, 'if the vessel approached shows a foreign flag, even suspicious conduct will not justify active interference except in those cases . . . where it is authorised by treaty'; above n 59, 64–65.

[65] See Ortolan, 252 and R-J Dupuy, D Vignes, *Traité du nouveau droit de lamer* (Paris: Economica 1985) 371.

[66] In the ILC discussions of the High Seas Convention, G Scelle opined that the verification of the merchant vessel's flag should take place on board the investigating warship. This, however, encountered piercing criticism from François, see *Regime of the High Seas*, Draft Articles, A/CN4/79, section II, reprinted in YbILC (1955-I) 27. See also LB Sohn, 'International Law of the Sea and Human Rights Issues' in Clingan (ed), *The Law of the Sea: What Lies Ahead?* (1988) 56 (hereinafter: Sohn, Human Rights).

[67] See Oppenheim's *International Law*, 738.

[68] See Report of the ILC to the GA, 11 GAOR Supp (No 9) 21, reprinted in YbILC (1956-II) 29.

According to Reuland,

> If the search yields sufficient evidence that the vessel has indeed engaged in proscribed activity, the warship may arrest the vessel or otherwise bring the vessel to account. If however, the search proves fruitless, the flag-state of the warship may be liable for any loss or damages sustained by the vessel as a result of the visit and search.[69]

The 1958 High Seas Convention adopted virtually unchanged article 46 of the ILC's Draft Articles of 1956 and thereby codified for the first time in a treaty the peacetime right of visit.[70] Article 22 of the High Seas Convention maintained the above distinction between the right of visit or *'droit d'enquête du pavillon'* and the right of search,[71] whereas it remained silent on the question of the customary right of approach. This did not entail, however, that the right of approach ceased to exist, as it was clear that the ILC intended only to codify the right of visit as such. It is apt to note here that, in the process of the drafting by the ILC, G Scelle called for a separate provision setting forth the right of verification of the flag, as a general police measure, accorded to all warships. He warned that 'the omission of a general article concerning the general policing of the high seas, as distinct from provisions concerning the special cases of piracy and slavery, would be not only serious, but also incomprehensible, because in the absence of any international body with police powers, order must be protected if anarchy was to be averted'.[72]

As far as the right of visit (*droit de visite*) as such is concerned, article 22 of High Seas Convention, and later article 110 of LOSC, which was primarily based on the former provision,[73] set forth that it is accorded to warships against only those vessels reasonably suspected of having engaged in certain proscribed activities. These activities are: a) piracy, b) slave trading, c) unauthorised broadcasting d) absence of nationality of the ship, or e) though flying a foreign flag or refusing to show its flag, the ship is in reality of the same nationality as the warship.[74] It is true that not all of the above circumstances are relevant in the contemporary era; for example,

---

[69] Reuland, 1176. The liability for an unjustified visit and search is well established; see inter alia art 110(3) of LOSC; Gidel, 298.
[70] See Report of the ILC covering the work of its 8th session (A/3159), art 46, YbILC (1956-II) 283 and M Nordquist (ed) *UNCLOS 1982: A Commentary* (1993-II) 239 (hereinafter: Nordquist, *Commentary*).
[71] See art 22 of the 1958 Geneva Convention on the High Seas, 450 UNTS 52 (hereinafter: High Seas Convention).
[72] See *Regime of the High Seas*, above n 66, 28.
[73] The only substantial changes were the inclusion in the grounds of interference of the 'vessel without nationality' and unauthorised broadcasting. On the Third UN Conference on the Law of the Sea (UNCLOS III) in general see R Platzöder, *Third United Nations Conference on the Law of the Sea* (London: Oceana Publications, 1982–7) and on art 110, in particular, see Nordquist, *Commentary*, 239–44.
[74] See Churchill and Lowe, 203; Nordquist, *Commentary*, 237.

both the 'unauthorised broadcasting'[75] and the 'slave trade'[76] provisions have minimal application, whereas, 'piracy', once almost obsolete, has attained greater prominence lately, in view of the recent piratical activity off the coast of Somalia. As regards (d) 'absence of nationality of the ship', it denotes stateless vessels, ie vessels lacking any any claim to nationality under article 91 of LOSC on the basis either of state registration or some other right to fly a state's flag. Under article 92 (2) LOSC, vessels flying two or more flags according to convenience may also be assimilated to stateless vessels. It needs to be stressed here that in light of the wording of article 91 (1),[77] vessels may hold nationality independent of registration. For example, 'national legal systems commonly only require vessels of certain size to register, and smaller vessels may be entitled to fly the flag of their owner state's nationality without registration'.[78] This is important especially in relation to any exercise of enforcement jurisdiction over the vessel or the persons on board, in the sense that the lack of registration would not mean *ipso facto* that no State exercises jurisdiction over the vessel or the persons.

Furthermore, by virtue of article 110(1), other forms of interference can by conferred by treaty on a variety of subjects.[79] Accordingly, states have concluded numerous multilateral and bilateral agreements that provide for the right of visit on the high seas with a view to addressing various challenges or suppressing illegal activities, such as illegal fishing, drug trafficking, maritime terrorism and WMD. The above-mentioned circumstances and challenges that have given rise to boarding agreements will be discussed in detail in subsequent chapters.

B. Contemporary Challenges to the Customary Right of Approach

It is submitted that the customary right of approach has, in principle, remained intact in the twenty-first century, albeit its implementation has been significantly modified in light of the technological changes. As a contemporary commentator has described it,

> In its exercise of the customary 'right of approach', a warship may intercept a
> vessel, inspect it from a safe distance to determine its name, flag, and home

---

[75] For a contemporary overview of the 'unauthorized broadcasting' see Guilfoyle, *Shipping Interdiction*, 161–71.

[76] Nevertheless, it is argued that the relevant provision should be reinvigorated to suppress certain forms of human trafficking; see the extensive discussion below.

[77] 'Every State shall fix the conditions for the grant of its nationality to ships, for the registration of ships in its territory, and for the right to fly its flag. Ships have the nationality of the State whose flag they are entitled to fly.' Article 91 (1) LOSC.

[78] Guilfoyle, *Shipping Interdiction*, 95 with further references.

[79] Both the High Seas Convention and LOSC contain the exception 'where acts of interference derive from powers conferred by treaty'; see arts 22(1) and 110(1) respectively.

port, receive and review any data the vessel may be emitting from its automatic identification system (AIS) or long range identification and tracking (LRIT) equipment, perhaps scan other electromagnetic emissions if so equipped, and finally hail it on the radio.[80]

i. AIS and LRIT

Truly, the advent of the AIS and LRIT systems has significantly changed the customary right of approach. In more detail, AIS was adopted in 2000 by IMO as part of a revised new chapter V of SOLAS Convention. It requires ships to carry an automatic identification system (AIS) capable of providing information about the vessel, such as her identity, location, course, and speed, to other vessels and to coastal authorities automatically. The regulation requires AIS to be fitted aboard all ships of 300 gross tonnage and upwards engaged on international voyages, cargo ships of 500 gross tonnage and upwards not engaged on international voyages, and all passenger ships, irrespective of size.[81] However, it is reported that AIS has various shortcomings, besides not applying to vessels of less than 300 gross tonnage, such as, for example, that 'the ship to ship communications is usually 20 miles and for ship to shore communications only 40 miles or that broadcasts may be accessed by anyone with the appropriate AIS equipment and so potentially be accessible by criminal organizations (e.g. pirates)'.[82]

In light of these shortcomings of AIS, the IMO revised further the SOLAS Convention in order to increase the tools available to states to learn about vessels in the surrounding waters. Regulation 19-1 on LRIT, which was adopted under Chapter V of SOLAS in 2006 and entered into force in July 2009, requires ships to automatically transmit information, through a satellite-based system, as to the identity of the ship, her position (longitude and latitude), and the date and time of the position.[83] This information is to be received for 'security and other purposes as agreed' by the IMO,[84] such as for safety and marine environment protection purposes.[85] Similar to AIS, it applies to vessels engaged on international voyages and encompasses passenger ships, cargo ships of 300 gross tonnage and upwards, and mobile offshore drilling units.[86]

---

[80] Allen, *Counterproliferation*, 82–83.
[81] See the International Convention for the Safety of Life at Sea (SOLAS), Ch. V, as amended in June 2001. The requirement became effective for all ships on 31 December 2004. See more information at www.imo.org/OurWork/Safety/Navigation/Pages/AIS.aspx.
[82] See Klein, *Maritime Security*, 228–29.
[83] See the relevant documents and further information at www.imo.org/OurWork/Safety/Navigation/Pages/LRIT.aspx.
[84] reg 19-1 para 8.1.
[85] See IMO Res MSC 243 (83) (12 October 2007) IMO Doc MSC 83/28/Add 2 (Annex 6).
[86] See reg 19-1 para 2.1.

The LRIT information may be received by the flag state of the vessel regardless of where the vessel is located.[87] A port state may also receive information once a foreign flagged vessel has indicated its intention to enter that port, except when the vessel is on the landward side of the baselines of another state.[88] Finally, a coastal state may receive the information from a foreign flagged vessel when it is 'navigating within a distance not exceeding 1000 nautical miles of its coast, but again with the same exception with regard to vessels on the landward side of the baselines of another state.[89] Each state must bear the cost of any information requested and received.[90] Moreover, regulation 19-1 stipulates that LRIT information will not be sent to a coastal state from the territorial sea of the state to which the vessel is flagged.[91] Another general limitation is that a state may decide that vessels flying its flag will not provide information to coastal states 'in order to meet security or other concerns'.[92]

In parallel to AIS and LRIT systems, there are also vessel monitoring systems (VMS), which have been developed and installed by some states and shipping companies and are used in marine accidental investigations, search and rescue, as well as safety and pollution prevention.[93] The type of information collected may include the course of the vessel, its speed, draft and estimated time of arrival and departure from various positions. The use of VMS has also become an important means of deriving information about the location of fishing vessels, to which, for example, LRIT regulation does not usually apply, because of their smaller size; thus, many regional fisheries organisations have introduced VMS as a means of enhancing surveillance and enforcement.[94]

It becomes readily apparent that information as to the vessel's identity, cargo, position and destination, which has traditionally been the *sedes materiae* of the right of approach, can be collected today through other means by the coastal states. Warships or other duly authorised vessels of the latter states, which, hypothetically, would have an interest in knowing more about a vessel on the high seas, approaching their sovereign waters, could obtain the relevant information through the use of AIS or LRIT, rather than requesting her to hoist her flag. Other flag states may receive information through the AIS or the VMS. Hence, the customary right of approach on the high seas acquires more practical significance vis-à-vis

---

[87] ibid, para 8.1.1.
[88] ibid, para 8.1.2.
[89] ibid, para 8.1.3.
[90] ibid, para 8.11.
[91] ibid, para 8.4.
[92] ibid, para 9.1. See further comments in Klein, *Maritime Security*, 233.
[93] See ibid, 227–28.
[94] See eg *Volga Case (Russia v Australia) (Prompt Release)* ITLOS Case No 11; 42 ILM (2003) 159 and R Rayfuse, *Non-Flag State Enforcement in High Seas Fisheries* (Leiden: Brill Academic Publishers, 2004) 269.

vessels less than 300 gross tonnage, which are not obliged to be equipped with LRIT or AIS instruments, or to vessels that, for one or another reason, have switched off their LRIT data transmitters. In any event, it is submitted that the advent of all these identification and monitoring systems has not rendered the customary right of approach obsolete; rather, it has decreased its utility as well as altered its modus operandi.

ii. Maritime Domain Awareness and Intelligence-Gathering on the High Seas

The need for intelligence-gathering on the high seas ranks high in the maritime security policy of many states.[95] For example, one of the main US policy initiatives in relation to intelligence-gathering since 9/11 has been the creation of a system of Maritime Domain Awareness (MDA), which seeks to generate and use information concerning vessels, crews and cargos.[96] According to the US National Plan to Achieve Maritime Domain Awareness, 'MDA is the effective understanding of anything associated with the maritime domain that could impact the security, safety, economy, or environment of the US'.[97] To this end, MDA should include, inter alia, the institution of worldwide standards for broadcast of vessel position and identification, and automated tools to discern patterns of suspicious behaviour and potential threats.[98]

Other states or regional organisations have developed their own strategies in handling information on maritime security. Suffice it to refer to Australia and New Zealand, which have adopted similar MDA policies in light of their large expanses of EEZs and search and rescue regions.[99] The Western Pacific Naval Symposium created a Regional Maritime Information Exchange to share non-sensitive information on maritime

[95] On intelligence-gathering on the high seas see inter alia N Klein, 'Intelligence Gathering and Information Sharing for Maritime Security Purposes under International Law', in N Klein et al (eds), *Maritime Security: International Law and Policy Perspectives from Australia and New Zealand* (Abingdon: Routledge, 2010) 224; P Liakouras, 'Intelligence Gathering on the High Seas', in A Strati, M Gavouneli, N Skourtos (eds), *Unresolved Issues and New Challenges to the Law of the Sea* (Leiden: Nijhoff, 2006) 123–48; S Kaye, 'Freedom of Navigation, Surveillance and Security: Legal Issues Surrounding the Collection of Intelligence from beyond the Littoral' 24 *Australian Yearbook of International Law* (2003) 95.
[96] On the concept of MDA see DA Goward, 'Maritime Domain Awareness: The Key to Maritime Security', in M Nordquist et al (eds), *Legal Challenges in Maritime Security* (Leiden: Martinus Nijhoff, 2008) 513.
[97] US National Plan to Achieve Maritime Domain Awareness for the National Strategy for Maritime Security (October 2005) ii; available at www.dhs.gov/xlibrary/assets/HSPD_MDAPlan.pdf.
[98] See US Navy, 'Navy Maritime Domain Awareness Concept' (May 2007); available at www.navy.mil/navydata/cno/Navy_Maritime_Domain_Awareness_Concept_FINAL_2007.pdf.
[99] See eg D Rothwell and N Klein, 'Maritime Security and the Law of the Sea', in N Klein et al (eds), *Maritime Security: International Law and Policy Perspectives from Australia and New Zealand* (Abingdon: Routledge, 2010) 22.

security threats.[100] In the context of the EU, a *Common Information Sharing Environment* (CISE) is currently being developed jointly by the European Commission and EU/EEA Member States. This will integrate existing surveillance systems and networks and give all concerned authorities access to the information they need for their missions at sea.[101] In addition, NATO has adopted the 'Maritime Situational Awareness Tools' scheme in order to collect and share valuable information of threats to maritime security.[102]

Closely linked to this MDA concept is the Australian Maritime Identification System (AMIS). On 14 December 2004, the then Australian Prime Minister Howard promulgated the 'Maritime Identification Zone' (MIZ), as part of Australia's effort to strengthen its offshore maritime security.[103] The creation of this zone, extending 1000 nautical miles from Australia's coastline, was to enable the Australian authorities to identify vessels, including their crew, cargo and course of journey, seeking to enter Australian ports. As the MIZ was initially envisaged, vessels not complying with the request of Australia to give information would be subject to interdiction measures on the high seas.

Without dwelling much upon this, it is clear that, even though Australia would be entitled to request information from vessels seeking to enter its ports under customary international law (right of approach) and in accordance with the SOLAS amendments and the adoption of ISPS Code, 'there is no exception to flag State authority on the high seas that would permit the right of visit to enforce a coastal State requirement to provide information in pursuit of that State's maritime security policies'.[104] It was no surprise that Australia's claim to such interdiction authority raised serious concerns as to the legality of the MIZ under international law. Eventually, Australia reformulated it into the AMIS, so that ships would be requested to provide information on a wholly voluntary basis and the new system would be premised upon cooperative international arrangements, particularly with neighbouring states.[105]

As N Klein observes, 'the need to collect, process and share information is fundamental to the range of law enforcement and military activities

---

[100] See PA Pedrozo, 'Maritime Information Sharing in the Asia-Pacific Region', in M Nordquist et al (eds), above n 94, 527, 535–36.

[101] See Council of the European Union, 'Council Conclusions on integration of maritime surveillance' (Brussels, 23 May 2011); available at www.consilium.europa.eu/uedocs/cms_data/docs/pressdata/EN/genaff/122177.pdf.

[102] See further information at https://transnet.act.nato.int/WISE/BRITE/Trifoldsfo/MaritimeSi/file/_WFS/MSA%20Tri-fold.pdf.

[103] See relevant information in N Klein, 'Legal Implications of Australia's Maritime Identification System' 55 *International and Comparative Law Quarterly* (2006) 337, 337.

[104] Klein, *Maritime Security*, 226. See also N Klein, ibid, 345–50 and 352–57.

[105] Klein, *Maritime Security*, 227.

that are likely to be needed to ensure maritime security'.[106] For the purposes of maritime interception on the high seas, intelligence-gathering
and MDA policies have repercussions as to the contemporary relevance of
the right of approach and the requirement of 'relevant suspicions' predicated by the relevant texts. As regards the right of approach, it is inevitable that it loses part of its relevance, since the information collected and
shared by various law enforcement agencies, in conjunction with the
operation of vessel identification and monitoring systems makes the need
to visually identify the suspect vessel less imperative. Warships or coastguard cutters are still entitled to approach a suspect vessel on the high
seas under customary international law and to request her to identify herself; nonetheless, in the majority of the cases, this would be unnecessary,
as concrete information concerning the identity or the cargo of the suspect
vessel would be already available to states concerned. Approaching the
vessel in such cases and asking questions might even jeopardise the outcome of the interception operation, as the vessel could, in the meantime,
discharge its illicit cargo, or even flee.

iii. Rules of Engagement of NATO and EU

It is important also to note that there have been certain recent rules of
engagements, promulgated by NATO and the European Union in the context of the EUNAVFOR Somalia/Operation Atalanta, which seem to blur
the lines between the right of approach and the right of visit. Suffice it to
say that in the context of the latter operation, reference is made to the right
of 'peaceful approach', ie a preliminary stage of the actual boarding, or *le
droit d'enquête du pavillon*. This may involve the consensual 'informal'
boarding of the vessel for maritime security awareness reasons without
engaging in actual search of the vessel or in any hostile action, and without being considered as an official visit on the high seas.[107] It is obvious
that this right of 'peaceful approach' deviates from the traditional right of

---

[106]   ibid, 218. A more conservative approach on the utility of MDA is taken by MN Murphy,
'Lifeline or Pipedream? Origins, Purposes and Benefits of Automatic Identification System,
Long-Range Identification Tracking and Maritime Domain Awareness', in R Burns et al
(eds), *Lloyds' MIU Handbook of Maritime Security* (Baton Rouge, LA: CRC Press, 2009) 13, 14.

[107]   According to the OPORDER (Operational Order) of Operation Atalanta, 'an approach
is defined as a de-escalatory low key interaction. *This may include visits on board if invited but
does not include "boarding exploitation" of the vessel* (crew checks, searching cargo/crew) . . . the
approach is an informal means of engaging with the maritime population and is crucial
means of promoting information exchanges . . . Approaching a vessel with the sole intent of
engaging in dialogue may result in an *invitation of the master of the vessel to continue the conversation on board his vessel . . . this is not considered as a boarding in the legal sense.* Embarkation by
EUNAVFOR personnel is limited to continuing the conversation and does not include any
further investigation'. Information provided in a personal communication with the author
under conditions of anonymity (20.4.2009) (emphasis added). On the NATO RoEs regarding
'consensual boarding', see below.

approach under customary international law and resembles more a right of visit proper, or *'le droit d'enquête du pavillon'*. Thus, there must be a different basis under international law that would justify such interference; in the context of EUNAVFOR Operation Atalanta, such basis is apparently afforded by piracy *jure gentium*.

In conclusion, it has been argued that even though the customary right of approach is heavily challenged from technological advents, such as the AIS or the LRIT, as well as from intelligence gathering and information sharing policies, it still retains its relevance in the twenty-first century legal order of the oceans. No matter if its utility may have decreased or its modus operandi may have changed, the right of approach is still an intrinsic part of the general policing of the high seas. Probably more apposite today than ever is the call of G Scelle for the adoption of a provision regarding general policing of the high seas;[108] such provision may have not been adopted by the ILC back in 1956, yet it is almost in place, in light of concepts such as MDA or the application of vessel monitoring systems.

C. The Right of Visit: The Contemporary Practice of Interception on the High Seas

i. Some Questions of Terminology

It is apt to refer, at the outset, to the various terms employed to denote physical interference with foreign vessels on the high seas. The most common is the term 'interception' or 'interdiction', or in more general, 'maritime interception operation' (MIO), which were originally used by the US in a narrow sense to refer only to naval operations taken to enforce UN Security Council Resolutions.[109] Over the years the MIO concept has expanded in response to the growing array of peacekeeping and peace enforcement measures. The US Navy defines 'maritime interception operations as the legitimate action of denying suspect vessels access to specific ports for import or export of prohibited goods to or from a specified nation or nations, for purposes of peacekeeping or to enforce imposed sanctions'.[110]

Similarly, states participating in the Proliferation Security Initiative (PSI) have adopted the term 'interdiction' in their Statement of Interdiction Principles.[111] In addition, the term 'interception' is very commonly used to denote the stopping and diversion of 'boat-people', in the framework of

---

[108] See above n 72 and corresponding text.
[109] See Allen, *Counterproliferation*, 84.
[110] ibid, 85. See also US Commander's Handbook para 4.4.4.
[111] See PSI: Statement of Interdiction Principles (4 September 2003); available at www.state.gov/t/np/rls/fs/23764.htm.

counter-migrant smuggling operations. According to the Executive Committee of UN High Commissioner for Refugees (UNHCR),

> interception or interdiction occurs when mandated authorities representing a State: i) prevent embarkation of persons on an international journey, ii) prevent further onward international travel by persons, who have commenced their journey; or iii) assert control of vessels where there are reasonable grounds to believe the vessel is transporting persons contrary to international or national maritime law.[112]

Patricia Mallia suggests that 'the process of "interception" (or interdiction), the ordinary meaning of which is to prevent something from proceeding or arriving, is not limited solely to the migrant smuggling context, but is a tool used in the suppression of other threats'.[113] On the other hand, in the words of Ronzitti, 'as a rule, naval interdiction does not imply the arrest and visit of the interdicted vessel, but only harassment by navigational means and warning shots aimed at diverting the ship from its route'.[114]

Whatever designation is used to describe the practice of interference with vessels on the high seas, the incontrovertible fact is that under LOSC the only exception to the rule of non-interference is the right of visit. Nowhere in the Convention is there any reference to interception or inter-diction *eo nomine*; thus any physical interference with vessels on the high seas should come under the customary and conventional rubric of the right of visit.[115] This notwithstanding, there will be cases where the interference in question will be justified under other rules of international law; for example under other international agreements or on the basis of the ad hoc consent of the flag state; not to mention the invocation of 'secondary' rules of international law, namely circumstances precluding wrongfulness under the law of state responsibility, such as 'consent', 'state of necessity' and 'countermeasures'.[116]

For the purposes of this book, the generic and commonly used term 'interception' is preferred, in order to encompass all cases of interference with foreign vessels on the high seas and not only these excused under

---

[112] See Conclusion on Protection Safeguards in Interception measures No 97 (LIV), adopted by the Executive Committee on International Protection of Refugees, available at www.unhcr.org/excom/EXCOM/3f 93b2894.html.

[113] P Mallia, *Migrant Smuggling by Sea: Combating a Current Threat to Maritime Security through the Creation of a Cooperative Framework* (Leiden: Martinus Nijhoff, 2010) 21 (hereinafter: Mallia).

[114] See N Ronzitti, 'Coastal State Jurisdiction over Refugees and Migrants at Sea', in N Ando et al (eds), *Liber Amicorum Judge Shigeru Oda* (2002) 1271, 1278 (hereinafter: Ronzitti).

[115] Notwithstanding their legal irrelevance, both terms 'interception' and 'interdiction' will be used interchangeably in the present thesis to denote the physical interference with foreign vessels on the high seas.

[116] See eg the *CMS Gas Transmission Company v Argentina*, Decision on application for annulment of 25 September 2007, ICSID Case No ARB/01/8 (2007), paras 133–34.

article 110 of LOSC. Nonetheless, the terms 'right of visit' or 'interdiction' may be used interchangeably.

ii. The Existence of 'Reasonable Suspicions'

Under LOSC, the sole requirement for states to board a foreign vessel on the high seas is the existence of 'reasonable suspicions' that the vessel is engaged in one of the activities listed in article 110. A similar requirement is included in other multilateral boarding agreements (eg article 8 para 2 of Smuggling Protocol). However, neither LOSC nor the other treaties clarify this criterion of 'reasonableness', ie what kind of suspicions would amount to 'reasonable suspicions' so as to trigger the right of visit. Apparently, being an abstract legal concept, it is very difficult to be a priori defined, and it will be always assessed on an ad hoc basis.

In any case, due to the exceptional character of the right to visit to the fundamental principle of the freedom of navigation on the high seas, it is submitted that 'reasonable suspicions' must be construed as amounting to more than a mere suspicion. Moreover, this suspicion has to be assessed as objectively as possible, and not left to the complete discretion of the commander of the warship or of the officer in command of the boarding party, as they might be prone to abuse of the right to visit.[117] According to another view, however, less than actual evidence is required and sufficient cause for suspicion is the yardstick for this provision.[118] Such suspicion might also extend to the master or the crew of the vessel; not to mention that any suspicion involving one or more crew members would justify a request for authorisation.

Besides these general remarks, there are cases where the criterion of 'reasonable suspicions' would be easily satisfied; for instance, the vessels that are engaged in piracy off the coast of Somalia have certain common features, and thus suspicions over their illicit activities would easily arise. Furthermore, the establishment of 'reasonable suspicions' is today significantly facilitated by intelligence-gathering and information-sharing between states. The purpose of MDA concepts is, to a great extent, this: to collect and disseminate information on potential threats to maritime security. Should such information be credible enough, they will obviously constitute 'reasonable suspicions' that could trigger the right of visit on the high seas. The key question, however, is credibility; suffice it to refer to the *MV Nisha* incident, which attracted much media attention in 2001. The *MV Nisha* was a cargo ship carrying 26,000 tonnes of raw sugar to London. It picked up the sugar in Mauritius, but also called at Djibouti.

---

[117] In contemplation of this, both the 1958 and 1982 Conventions provide that the ship boarded shall be 'compensated for any loss or damage . . . in all cases the suspicion proves unfounded'. See also Sohn, Human Rights, 57.

[118] See eg Hinrichs, 434.

En route to London, it was interdicted by British authorities on the basis of intelligence that it was carrying terrorist material. As it turned out that information was incorrect, and after a five-day search the vessel was allowed to complete its journey.[119] While the *MV Nisha's* owners publicly stated that they would consider suing British authorities, there was no report that court proceedings were ever initiated.[120]

iii. Ad Hoc Consent to Interception on the High Seas

Article 110 of LOSC sets out the circumstances, in which the right of visit is lawfully exercised as well as provides that such right could be accorded by the means of a treaty. In this respect, there has been an array of treaties that provide for maritime interception on the high seas. Nevertheless, in the everyday practice, interception of foreign vessels on the high seas takes place on the basis of more informal or ad hoc arrangements, namely either with the consent of the flag state authorities or even with the consent of the master of the vessel (the so-called 'consensual boarding').

On the one hand, the practice of requesting the ad hoc consent of the flag state of the suspect vessel could be legally characterised under the veil of both primary rules of international law, namely qua informal treaties, and of secondary rules of state responsibility, namely qua 'consent' (article 20 of the ILC Articles).[121] With regard to the former option, it can be argued that the request to board a suspect vessel, which is addressed by the administrative agency of the boarding state to the respective agency of the flag state, and the positive reply of the latter state to this request create a bilateral relationship, which can aptly be designated as an informal or administrative agreement.[122] These agreements, as long as they obtain an oral form, do not come under the scope of the VCLT, which requires an agreement in written form;[123] however, the fact remains that they will still be subject to important parts of the law of treaties, for example relating to invalidity and termination, as provisions of customary law.[124] These informal agreements operate only on ad hoc basis and they must be assessed on their own merit and against the background of the relevant principles of international law. This was raised very recently in the *Medvedyev* case

---

[119] See House of Commons Select Committee on Defence, Sixth Report (24 July 2002); available at www.parliament.the-stationery-office.co.uk/pa/cm200102/cmselect/cmdfence/518/51806.htm.

[120] See Guilfoyle, *Shipping Interdiction*, 254.

[121] See ILC Articles Commentary, 72.

[122] *Cf United States v Gonzalez* case.

[123] See art 2(1) of VCLT (1969).

[124] *Cf* art 3 of VCLT, which stipulates that the limitation of art 2, ie that VCLT applies only to agreements 'in written form', is without prejudice to the legal force of agreements not 'in written form'. See also M Fitzmaurice and O Elias, *Contemporary Issues in the Law of Treaties* (Utrecht: Eleven International Publishing, 2005) 10.

before the European Court of Human Rights, where the basis for the interdiction of the Cambodian-flagged *Winner* had been a *note verbale* from the Cambodian Minister of Foreign Affairs after a request of authorisation by France, namely an ad hoc *accord* according to the court.[125]

Extremely pertinent is the question very astutely posed by Sohn, which is whether these informal arrangements fall under the scope of the exception of article 110(1), which requires that the relevant 'acts of interference derive from powers conferred by treaty', since they are not treaties in the sense of the VCLT.[126] On the face of the latter provision and based on a literal interpretation of the relevant term, the answer must be negative. However, these agreements do not operate only in the level of primary (permissive) rules of international law (article 110(1) of LOSC), they also have a parallel secondary exculpating effect, since the consent that they encapsulate falls under the ambit of article 20 of the ILC Articles. Hence, it is rather this attribute of them, ie the circumstance precluding the wrongfulness of the interference with the freedom of the high seas that brings the interdiction in consonance with international law. Ergo, the arrangements under scrutiny do not assume only the legal cloth of an informal agreement, but also operate as an act of consent in accordance with the relevant rules of state responsibility, in particular article 20 of the ILC Articles.

On the other hand, the practice of 'consensual boarding' raises serious questions under international law. In more detail, it denotes the practice, mainly of the US, of obtaining, first, the consent of the master of the vessel and later of the flag State in order to interdict the suspect vessels and subsequently exert enforcement jurisdiction, for example, seize the illicit cargo and arrest the suspects. This has also been practised in the context of both Operation Enduring Freedom and Operation Active Endeavour.[127] According to the US Commander's Handbook,

> a consensual boarding is conducted at the invitation of the master (or person in charge) of a vessel that is not otherwise subject to the jurisdiction of the boarding officer. The plenary authority of the master over all activities related to the operation of his vessel while in international waters . . . includes the authority to allow anyone to come aboard his vessel as his guest, including foreign law enforcement officials.[128]

---

[125] See *Medvedyev et al v France* App No 3394/03 (ECtHR, Grand Chamber judgment of 29 March 2010) and commentary in E Papastavridis, 'Case Comment: ECHR, *Medvedyev v France*' 59 *ICLQ* (2010) 867–82.

[126] In his words, 'Is such informal consent valid under international law? Recall Articles 92 and 110 of the Law of the Sea Convention, which provide that acts of interference with a flag State's jurisdiction must be authorised by treaty, if not otherwise specifically approved in the Convention. What reasons support this treaty requirement? Could a flag State by treaty provide for informal ways to grant its consent?' See Sohn, *Human Rights*, 209. In accord is also Stieb, 142.

[127] See also S Hodgkinson, 'Challenges to Maritime Interception Operations in the War on Terror' 22 *American University International Law Review* (2007) 583, 589.

[128] US Commander's Handbook paras 3-11–5-2.

The US Coast Guard *Guide to the Law of Boarding Operations* adds:

> During a consensual boarding, the boarding team may only examine spaces with the voluntary consent of the master or individual controlling them. The consent may be limited in scope and may be revoked at any time. No suspicion is required, and there is no prohibition against the Boarding Officer actively requesting consent to inspect or search in areas that might otherwise be inaccessible to the boarding team . . . master's consent is generally not sufficient for the United States to exercise jurisdiction over criminal acts conducted aboard the vessel extraterritorially.[129]

A vexed question in this regard is: who is supposed to give its consent for the boarding and in particular, is the flag state's authorities' consent required, or is the consent of the master of the vessel sufficient? The ILC's Commentary sheds some light upon this issue, stating that

> Whether consent has been validly given is a matter addressed by international law rules outside the framework of State responsibility. Issues include whether the agent or person who gave the consent was authorized to do so on behalf of the State (and if not, whether the lack of that authority was known or ought to have been known to the acting State).[130]

In the light of the foregoing, it will primarily be an issue of the internal law of the flag state whether the master is endowed with the power to give his consent for an exercise of enforcement jurisdiction on the part of a third state. Ted McDorman writes in this regard that another perspective to justify 'consensual boarding' is that 'a vessel master is an agent of the flag State and, as such, the consent of the master is the consent of the flag State'.[131] However, he refutes this perspective due to 'the loose relationship that can exist between a vessel and its flag'.[132] Even more significant in this respect is another comment of the ILC, ie 'who has authority to consent to a departure from a particular rule may depend on the rule' itself.[133] The rule *in casu* is the freedom of navigation (art 87 LOSC) and the exclusivity of the jurisdiction on the high seas (art 92 LOSC). This brings to the fore the question of to whom the respective rights are ascribed: to the vessel or to the flag state? On the face of these provisions, it is evident that they are to the flag state. Therefore, the latter has the sole responsibility to decide whether it will waive its right and will give its assent to a

---

[129] See the USCG, *Guide to the Law of Boarding Operations* (June 2008) (on file with the author). *Cf* 46 USC § 70502 (not including master's consent within the definition of 'vessels subject to the jurisdiction of the United States') (ibid, 21). Courts have upheld jurisdiction where the USCG boarded first with master's consent and obtained flag state consent later; see eg *United States v Khan* 35 F 3d 426, 430 (9th Cir 1994).

[130] See ILC Articles Commentary, at 176.

[131] T McDorman, 'Maritime Terrorism and the International Law of Boarding of Vessels at Sea: A Brief Assessment of the New Developments', in D Caron and HN Scheiber (eds), *The Oceans in the Nuclear Age: Legacies and Risks* (Leiden: Martinus Nijhoff, 2010) 239, 251.

[132] ibid.

[133] See ILC Articles Commentary, 177.

boarding both on an a priori basis and ad hoc. This means that the rebuttable presumption is in favour of the flag state consent rather than of the master's consent in this regard and the boarding state has the *onus probandi*.[134] In any event, the master's consent might suffice for the assertion of the right of boarding by a third state, as a valid alternative where flag state consent is not possible or practical,[135] yet it will ring hollow as far the exercise of the right of search, not to mention arrest and detention, is concerned. In the latter cases, even the fervent proponents of the right of master's consensual boarding would agree that the flag state's assent is required.[136]

iv. The Modus Operandi *of the Interception on the High Seas.*

a. The LOSC

Without deviating significantly from the customary law framework, paragraphs 2 and 3 of article 110 of LOSC set out the modus operandi, ie the procedure of the right of visit and search, as well as establishing the obligation of the flag state to compensate the visited vessel for any loss or damages.[137] In more detail, article 110(2) stipulates that

> [T]he warship may proceed to verify the ship's right to fly its flag. To this end, it may send a boat under the command of an officer to the suspected ship. If suspicion remains after the documents have been checked, it may proceed to a further examination on board the ship, which must be carried out with all possible consideration.

In addition, article 110, paragraphs 4 and 5, provide, respectively, that, apart from warships, military aircrafts, or other ships and aircrafts clearly marked and identifiable as being on government service and duly authorised, may engage in the right of visit.[138] It must be stressed that all these provisions are widely accepted as reflective of customary international law.[139] Furthermore, by virtue of article 58(1) of LOSC, the right of visit applies not only on the high seas, but also in the EEZ, subject to the coastal state rights therein.[140]

---

[134] *Contra*: SL Hodgkinson, above n 125, 604.

[135] See also D Wilson, 'Interdiction on the High Seas: The Role and Authority of a Master in the Boarding and Searching of his Ships by Foreign Warships' 55 *Naval Law Review* (2008) 157, 185.

[136] This is also accepted in the US Commander's Handbook, where it is provided that 'the voluntary consent of the master permits the boarding, but it does not allow the assertion of law enforcement authority. A consensual boarding is not, therefore, an exercise of maritime law enforcement jurisdiction per se; at 3–11–2–5.

[137] See art 110(2) and (3) of LOSC.

[138] See art 110(4) and (5) of LOSC. *Cf* also arts 107 and 111 of LOSC.

[139] This is also countenanced by states not party to LOSC, such as the US. See eg US Commander's Handbook paras 1–2.

[140] See arts 58, 56 and 60(4), (6) of LOSC; and also Nordquist, *Commentary*, 537.

b. Military Manuals and Relevant State Practice

The military manuals of naval states as well as the manuals of coast guard authorities usually include detailed rules of engagement governing the right of visit on the high seas. For example, the US Commander's Handbook stipulates in detail the relevant procedure of the right of visit, consisting in 'the right to approach the vessel, stop it, board it and examine the vessel's documents'.[141] Under the Handbook, once the investigation is completed, the boarding party must either depart the vessel, obtain the master's consent to stay on board, or, if criminal or unusual activity is discovered, the enforcement officials must notify and ask their operational commander for guidance.[142]

In practice, according to most standing RoEs, there are various different types of boarding on the high seas depending on the level of cooperation of the suspect vessel. In more detail, the various types of boardings can be designated as follows:[143]

i)   **Compliant or consensual boardings:** obviously, situations of 'compliant boarding', namely when both the flag state and the master of the vessel consent to the interception, present no considerable problems. When the flag state has not replied to the request of the boarding state and the latter boards the suspect vessel on the basis of the consent of the master, this is a typical case of 'consensual boarding', whose legal merits have been already addressed above. When the flag state consents to boarding, but the master refuses to permit boarding by enforcement officials of another vessel, this is termed '**flag state-authorised non-consensual boarding**'. 'Graduated measures are usually employed in order to stop a vessel, including attempting to hail the vessel by radio and loud-hailer, flashing signal lights, spraying water across the vessel's decks, firing warning shots across the bow, and firing small-calibre rounds at the vessel's engines in order to disable, but not sink, it'.[144]

ii) **Unopposed boardings:** if the master of the vessel is co-operative, a boarding party should be dispatched to the vessel. If found or it is suspected to be in violation, for example, of sanctions, the master should be given direction on where and when to proceed.

iii) **Non-compliant or non-cooperative boardings:** when the commanding officer is satisfied his orders have been understood and a reasonable time has been followed for those orders to be complied with, albeit

---

[141] US Commander's Handbook para 7.6.1.

[142] ibid. See also US Coast Guard, 'Model Maritime Operations Guide' (April 21, 2003), 2–17.

[143] Personal communication with the author under conditions of anonymity (20.4.2009). See also Allen, *Counterproliferation*, 80–82.

[144] P Mallia, above n 112, 20.

there is no compliance with orders; or the master does not acknow-ledge communications or cooperate in establishing his purpose in the area; or the master continuously refuses to cooperate in allowing the boarding to take place (including stating he will attempt to prevent the boarding party gaining access to the vessel) by manoeuvre or non-provision of means of access, or when physical barriers/non-kinetic means can be expected to be employed against the boarding, then the boarding is to be regarded as non-cooperative.

iv) **Opposed boardings:** if the master actively refuses to allow the board-ing to take place, then any subsequent boarding is to be regarded as opposed and appropriate measures, consistent with authorised ROE, may be taken.

v. The Question of the Use of Force in the Course of Interception Operations

Central to every legal discussion of interception on the high seas is the question of the permissibility of the use of force in the course of such operations.[145] At the outset, it is evident from the face of article 110 of LOSC that the pertinent provision of LOSC fails to provide a concrete answer to this question. According to Shearer, 'the sole reference to the degree of force to be used in enforcement measures under the 1982 Convention appears in Article 225, which states:

> In the exercise under this Convention of their powers of enforcement against foreign vessels, States shall not endanger the safety of navigation or otherwise create any hazard to a vessel, or bring it to an unsafe port or anchorage, or expose the marine environment to an unreasonable risk.[146]

With regard to the relevant multilateral or bilateral treaties, they have scarcely addressed the topic of the use of force. Article 22, paragraph 1(f) of the Straddling Stocks Agreement, for example, states:

> 1. The inspecting State shall ensure that its duly authorized inspectors:
>
>   . . .
>
>   (f) avoid the use of force except when and to the degree necessary to ensure the safety of the inspectors and where the inspectors are obstructed in the execution of their duties. The degree of force used shall not exceed that rea-sonably required in the circumstances.

The 2003 Caribbean Agreement includes a final savings clause providing, inter alia, that nothing in the treaty impairs the exercise of the inherent right of self-defence and requiring that the discharge of firearms against

---

[145] See eg the extensive and thoughtful analysis of Guilfoyle, *Shipping Interdiction*, 271–98.
[146] IA Shearer, 'Problems of Jurisdiction and Law Enforcement against Delinquent Vessels' 35 *ICLQ* (1986) 320, 342. See also WJ Fenwick, 'Legal Limits on the Use of Force by Canadian Warships engaged in Law Enforcement' 18 *CYIL* (1980) 113–45.

or on a suspect vessel is to be reported as soon as possible to the flag state (article 22),[147] while a similar provision is included in the 2008 CARICOM Agreement. Article XIV stipulates that 'the use of force pursuant to this Agreement shall in all cases be (a) in strict accordance with the applicable national laws and policies and (b) the minimum reasonably necessary under the circumstances'. Only the reference to the use of force in these treaties entails that it should not be disallowed *ipso jure*.

According to the preponderant view, the intercepting state may, in principle, use force but in extreme moderation and in strict accordance with the requirements of necessity and proportionality.[148] This is not without resonance in the jurisprudence of international courts and tribunals. In the *I'm Alone* arbitration, the incidental sinking of a vessel in the course of efforts to board, search and seize a suspect vessel was considered acceptable, but the intentional sinking of such vessel was not justified.[149] The *Red Crusader* incident also considered the legitimate use of force to stop a vessel. There, a Commission of Inquiry considered that firing without warning of solid (as opposed to blank) gunshot and creating danger to human life on board was in excess of what was necessary in pursuit of a fishing vessel fleeing arrest.[150]

However, the *locus classicus* in this regard has been the judgment of the International Tribunal for the Law of the Sea (ITLOS) in the *M/V Saiga (No 2)* case (1999). The Tribunal expressed the view that

'international law requires that the use of force must be avoided as far as possible and, where force is unavoidable, it must not go beyond what is reasonable and necessary in the circumstances. Considerations of humanity must apply in the law of the sea, as they do in other areas of international law'.[151]

The Tribunal also set out the applicable modus operandi:

The normal practice used to stop a ship at sea is first to give an auditory or visual signal to stop, using internationally recognized signals. Where this does not succeed, a variety of actions may be taken, including the firing of shots across the bows of the ship. It is only after the appropriate actions fail that the pursuing vessel may, as a last resort, use force. Even then, appropriate warning must

---

[147] See Agreement Concerning Co-operation in Suppressing Illicit Maritime and Air Trafficking in Narcotic Drugs and Psychotropic Substances in the Caribbean Area, concluded on 10 April 2003, at San José, Costa Rica and entered into force on 18 September 2008; available in Gilmore, *Caribbean Agreement*.

[148] See inter alia AV Lowe, 'National Security and the Law of the Sea' 17 *Thesaurus Acroasium*, (1991) 133, 162. On the principle of proportionality in law enforcement operations see K-C Fu, 'Policing the Sea and the Proportionality Principle', in M Nordquist et al (eds), *The Law of the Sea Convention: US Accession and Globalization* (Leiden: Martinus Nijhoff, 2012) 371–81.

[149] See *I'm Alone* case 3 *Reports of International Arbitral Awards* (1949) 1609.

[150] See *The Red Crusader (Commission of Enquiry Denmark v United Kingdom)* 35 ILR (1962) 485.

[151] *M/V SAIGA II* case, para 155.

be issued to the ship and all efforts should be made to ensure that life is not endangered.[152]

Reference to the threat of use of force at sea was made also in the very recent arbitration between *Guyana and Suriname* (2007).[153] The ad hoc arbitral tribunal had to consider whether acts of Surinamese gunboats seeking to prevent drilling activities in a disputed maritime area could be viewed as law enforcement activities. The Tribunal accepted

> the argument that in international law force may be used in law enforcement activities provided that such force is unavoidable, reasonable and necessary. However in the circumstances of the present case, this Tribunal is of the view that the action mounted by Suriname on 3 June 2000 seemed more akin to a threat of military action rather than a mere law enforcement activity.[154]

Suriname had significantly relied on the judgment of the ICJ in the *Fisheries Jurisdiction* case (*Spain v Canada*). In rejecting Spain's argument, the ICJ had stated that the

> Court finds that the use of force authorized by the Canadian legislation and regulation falls within the ambit of what is commonly understood as enforcement of conservation and management measures . . . *Boarding, inspection, arrest and minimum use of force for those purposes are all contained within the concept of enforcement of conservation and management measures* according to a 'natural and reasonable' interpretation of the concept.[155]

It follows from the foregoing case law that the use of force in the context of law enforcement operations on the high seas should be considered as a *lex specialis* case, and not falling within the ambit of the generic prohibition of the use of force under article 2(4) of the UN Charter.[156] The only case that regards such use or threat of use force as within the remit of article 2(4) of the UN Charter seems to be the *Guyana v Suriname* case; however, this case is not relevant to the present discussion, as it pertains to the assertion of sovereign rights in disputed areas of EEZ/continental shelf and the 'threat of the use of force' was, arguably, in order to protect such sovereign rights. Such assertion fundamentally differs from the right of visit of a foreign

---

[152] ibid, para 156.
[153] See *Guyana-Suriname Award* 47 ILM (2008) 164, and also P Jimenez-Kwast, 'Maritime Law Enforcement and the Use of Force: Reflections on the Categorisation of Forcible Action at Sea in the Light of Guyana/Suriname Award' 13 *JCSL* (2008) 49.
[154] ibid, para 445.
[155] See *Fisheries Jurisdiction* (*Spain v Canada*) Jurisdiction of the Court, Judgment, ICJ Reports 1998, 432 (emphasis added).
[156] In particular, it is averred that 'Although the terms "territorial integrity" and "political independence" are generally not intended to restrict the scope of the prohibition of the use of force they lend an argument in favour of the widely accepted view that certain cases of the threat or use of force within the law of the sea are not comprised by article 2(4)'; see Randelzhofer, 'Art 2(4)', in Simma (ed), *The United Nations Charter. A Commentary* 2nd edn (Oxford: Oxford University Press, 2002) 124. Concurring is also D Joyner, *International Law and the Proliferation of WMD* (Oxford: Oxford University Press, 2009) 325.

vessel on the high seas, which is a 'policing' right ascribed to flag states by the law of the sea and not a 'sovereign' right, in close connection with the 'territorial integrity and political independence' of a coastal state. In other words, the distinction between cases like *Guyana/Suriname* and cases of interception on the high seas lies in the rationale behind the resort to the use of force: in the former case, it is the protection of 'sovereign rights' and in the latter, the advancement of the interests of international community.

In any event, as Milano and Papanicolopulu, in commenting on the *Guyana/Suriname case*, assert,

> the limited use of force that may be needed in order to enforce the legislation of the coastal State in maritime areas claimed by it is conceptually different from the use of force in international relations prohibited by Art. 2 para. 4 UN Charter. While in the latter case the use of force is the content and the end of the action by the State, in the former case the use of force is instrumental to another activity, consisting in applying the legislation of the coastal State.[157]

Moreover, the explicit reference to the exercise of a minimum use of force in the above-mentioned treaties lends credence to the view that such use of force is a *lex specialis* to article 2 para 4 of the UN Charter; otherwise, such reference would have amounted to a flagrant violation of the said provision, which reflects a peremptory norm of international law,[158] and, as a result, the relevant treaties would have been null and void pursuant to article 53 of VCLT.[159]

Another line of argumentation to the same end could be based upon the premise that article 2(4) of UN Charter purports to regulate or proscribe the use of force, which is not provided for or sanctioned by a 'primary' rule of international law. Such rule, however, exists in the present context, ie a minimum use of force is positively permitted in law enforcement operations by warships. Thus, it is submitted that the use of force in such cases does not fall within the scope of the 'secondary' negative scope of article 2(4), but rather it is intrinsic to the primary rule permitting the right of visit on the high seas (article 110 of LOSC).

In a similar vein, D Guilfoyle, even though he does not disassociate the use of force in interception operations with the prohibition of article 2(4), avers that

---

[157] E Milano and I Papanicolopulu, 'State Responsibility in Disputed Areas on Land and at Sea' 71 *Zeitschrift für ausländisches öffentliches Recht und Völkerrecht* (2011) 587, 622–23. Against the expanding of the scope of article 2 (4) of the UN Charter in such cases is also C DeFrancia, Enforcing the Nuclear Nonproliferation Regime: The Legality of Preventive Measures' 45 *Vanderbilt Journal of Transnational Law* (2012) 704, 770.

[158] See per this view A Orakhelashvili, 'The Impact of Peremptory Norms on the Interpretation and Application of United Nations Security Council Resolutions' 16 *EJIL* (2005) 59, 63. Cf the dictum of the ICJ in the *Nicaragua* case, which states that 'the law of the Charter as concerning the prohibition of the use of force in itself constitutes a conspicuous example of a rule on international law having the character of *jus cogens*', para 190.

[159] Art 53 of VCLT provides that 'A treaty is void if, at the time of its conclusion, it conflicts with a peremptory norm of general international law.'

Article 110 represents the prior consent of States to their vessels being interdicted in certain cases, not a non-exhaustive list of police powers. A 'police action' is not something other than a use of force; consent may simply render it not a *prohibited* use of force.[160]

With regard to the circumstances precluding wrongfulness applicable in the present context, it is evident that they have to abide by the provision of article 26 of the ILC Articles. According to this article, when the internationally wrongful act of the State, otherwise excused under the plea of the above circumstances, involves the violation of *jus cogens*, like here the use of force,[161] the excuses in question cannot be invoked.[162] This prima facie encumbrance to the use of force in such operations on the high seas premised upon consent, necessity or countermeasures might be superseded on account of the thesis advanced by Roberto Ago, one of the former special rapporteurs on the issue of state responsibility, who distinguished between the most serious uses of force and others less grave. Although the latter are still prohibited by article 2(4), Ago was doubtful whether they fell under the scope of the *jus cogens* prohibition.[163] He questioned therefore the *ratione materiae* concordance of the prohibition of article 2(4) with the corresponding prohibition under *jus cogens*.

In conclusion, the *sedes materiae* for the assessment of the legality of the use of force in the course of interception operations are the rules governing law enforcement at sea, as set forth by the previous jurisprudence and as provided in each state's RoEs, and not the rules under the *jus ad bellum*. Instructive would also be certain soft law instruments that apply in relevant cases, such as the Code of Conduct for Law Enforcement Officials or the UN Basic Principles on the Use of Force and Firearms by Law Enforcement Officials. The former was adopted in December 1979 by the UN General Assembly and consists of eight articles, which reiterate the fundamental principles of proportionality (force to be used only to the extent required) and necessity (force to be used only when strictly necessary).[164] The latter were adopted by the Eighth UN Congress on the Prevention of Crime and the Treatment of Offenders (1990) and embodied 26 principles concerning the use of force by law enforcers.[165]

---

[160] Guilfoyle, *Shipping Interdiction*, 276.

[161] See above n 155.

[162] See art 26 of ILC Articles and the Commentary, 206.

[163] See Addendum to the Eighth Report on State Responsibility by Mr Roberto Ago, YbILC (1980-II), 40.

[164] See Code of Conduct for Law Enforcement Officials; UNGA Resolution 34/69; 106th pl mtg (17 December 1979) and R Crawshaw et al, *Human Rights and Policing: Standards for Good Behaviour and a Strategy for Change* (The Hague: Kluwer Law International, 1998), 108.

[165] See the UN Basic Principles on the Use of Force and Firearms by Law Enforcement Officials; adopted by the 8th UN Congress on the Prevention of Crime and the Treatment of Officers adopted in Havana, Cuba (27 August–7 September 1990); available at www2.ohchr.org/english/law/firearms.htm.

D. Other Legal Considerations in Maritime Interception Operations

As Guilfoyle states,

> Under the primary rules of police action applicable to all interdictions, the boarding State must take due account of the safety of life at sea, the ship and its cargo and the need not to prejudice the commercial or legal interests of the flag State. In addition, boarding parties must comply with relevant human rights law.[166]

The rules of international law governing interception on the high seas are not only rules belonging to the law of the sea, including the permissibility of the use of force as corollary of the right of visit, but also other rules of general international law, which form the 'legal order of the oceans'. Of paramount importance would be rules of international human rights law or refugee law as well as rules concerning the assertion of jurisdiction in international law. These two categories of general international law will be briefly discussed in this section; however, there are other legal parameters that should be taken into consideration in maritime interception, yet they will not be addressed in the present enquiry. For example, the commercial interests of the vessels and their owners, issues of international environmental law, the question of immunities of state officials and, last but not least, the responsibility of states for internationally wrongful acts in the course of an interception on the high seas.

i. Application of International Human Rights Law

Maritime interception operations should be in keeping with fundamental human rights, such as the right to life, the prohibition of torture or of the arbitrary deprivation of liberty. This has recently been corroborated by a series of European Court of Human Rights' judgments concerning the assertion of enforcement powers on the high seas.[167] Also, of paramount importance especially with regard to the interception of refugees on the high seas is the prohibition of non-refoulement under article 33 of the Refugee Convention (1951) and customary law. It is the purpose of this part of the chapter, first, to explore the preliminary, yet essential issue of extraterritorial application of international human rights law and then to set out the basic human rights that are in need of protection in the course of maritime interception operations on the high seas.

---

[166] Guilfoyle, *Shipping Interdiction*, 343.
[167] See, inter alia, *Medvedyev ao v France* App no 3394/03 (ECtHR, 10 July 2008), confirmed by the Grand Chamber in its judgment of 29 March 2010 (hereinafter: *Medvedyev* case); *Hirsi Jamaa ao v Italy* App no 27765/09 (EctHR, Grand Chamber Judgment of 23 February 2012) (hereinafter: *Hirsi* case). On the *Hirsi* case see M Giuffre, 'Waterdown Rights on the High Seas: Hirsi Jamaa and others v Italy (2012)' 61 *ICLQ* (2012) 728–50.

a. The Extraterritorial Application of Human Rights Law

It is trite knowledge that the protection of human rights extends to persons under the jurisdiction of the State parties to the pertinent treaties. It is, however, this concept of 'jurisdiction' that has aroused considerable controversy in international legal discourse. The main international human rights treaties on civil and political rights, including the ECHR and its Protocols, conceive state responsibility for securing the rights they contain essentially in terms of the state's 'jurisdiction'. Thus, it is necessary to establish whether a situation falls within the state's 'jurisdiction' before the obligations in these instruments are in play.[168]

On the one hand, in the celebrated *Bankovic* case, the ECtHR proceeded from the assumption that the concept of 'jurisdiction' in these treaties is the same concept of jurisdiction which exists in general international law.[169] In the words of the Court, 'Article 1 of the Convention must be considered to reflect this ordinary and essentially territorial notion of jurisdiction, other bases of jurisdiction being exceptional and requiring special justification in the particular circumstances of each case'.[170] Amongst these exceptional bases are, however, 'the activities . . . on board . . . vessels flying the flag of that State'.[171] The Court also noted that the European Convention applies 'in the legal space [*espace juridique*] of the Contracting States' and it was not designed to be applied throughout the world, even in respect of the conduct of the contracting states.[172]

According to another strand of legal doctrine, there is a second notion of jurisdiction, which is found, inter alia, in human rights treaties and in various decisions of human right bodies, and denotes a certain kind of power that a state exercises over territory or persons. This notion of jurisdiction 'relates essentially to a question of fact, of actual authority and control that a State has over a given territory or person. "Jurisdiction", in this context, simply means actual power, whether exercised lawfully or not, nothing more, and nothing less'.[173] 'Factivity' in this regard 'creates normativity'[174] or in the recent words of the European Court of Human Rights, 'de facto control gives rise to de jure responsibilities'.[175]

---

[168] See R Wilde, 'Triggering State Responsibility Extraterritorially: The Spatial Test in Certain Human Rights Treaties', 40 *Israel Law Review* (2007) 503, 506.

[169] On jurisdiction in general international law see inter alia V Lowe and C Starker, 'Jurisdiction', in M Evans (ed), *International Law*, 3rd edn (Oxford: OUP, 2010) 315 and M Akehurst, 'Jurisdiction in International Law' 46 *BYIL* (1972–1973) 145.

[170] *Bankovic and Others v Belgium and Others* 2001-XII 333; 44 EHRR (2007) para 57.

[171] ibid para 73.

[172] ibid para 80.

[173] M Milanović, 'From Compromise to Principle: Clarifying the Concept of State Jurisdiction in Human Rights Treaties' 8 *Human Rights Law Review* (2008) 411, 429.

[174] M Sheinin, 'Extraterritorial Effect of the International Covenant on Civil and Political Rights', in F Coomans et al (eds), *Extraterritorial Application of Human Rights* (Antwerp: Intersentia, 2004) 73, 81.

[175] *Al-Saadoon and Mufdhi v United Kingdom* App no 61498/08 (EctHR, 30 June 2009) para 88.

What follows therefrom is that whenever states exert factual control over territory or persons, they exercise 'jurisdiction', insofar the application of human rights treaties is concerned. The consistent jurisprudence of the relevant human rights bodies and the International Court of Justice (ICJ) as well as international doctrine construe 'jurisdiction' as operating extraterritorially in certain circumstances.[176] 'The term has been understood in the extraterritorial context as a connection between the State, on the one hand, and either the territory in which the relevant acts took place – referred to as a *spatial or territorial* connection – or the individual affected by them – referred to as a *personal individual* or because of the type of State action involved, *State-agent-authority* connection.'[177]

In the maritime context, and in particular on the high seas, the situation is rather unambiguous in light of the jurisprudence of the Strasbourg Court: the Convention applies on the high seas, in so far as control, and therefore, jurisdiction is exerted by organs of the states parties, usually warships or other duly authorised vessels. This assertion is supported by the *Xhavara v Albania and Italy* case,[178] involving the sinking of an Albanian vessel by an Italian warship on the high seas, and by the *Rigopoulos v Spain* case,[179] involving the arrest of a drug-trafficking vessel on the high seas, in which cases the jurisdiction *ratione loci* of the Court was never contested. In the *Medvedyev v France* case (2010), the Grand Chamber addressed this issue succinctly and held that 'as this was a case of France having exercised full and exclusive control over the *Winner* and its crew, at least de facto, from the time of its interception, in a continuous and uninterrupted manner until they were tried in France, the applicants were effectively within France's jurisdiction for the purposes of article 1 of the Convention'.[180]

Most recently, in the *Hirsi* case (2012), which concerned Somalian and Eritrean migrants who had been intercepted on the high seas by the Italian authorities and sent back to Libya, the Grand Chamber held that

---

[176] From the very rich and recent jurisprudence on extraterritorial jurisdiction and human rights, see inter alia G Goodwin-Gill, 'The Extra-Territorial Reach of Human Rights Obligations: A Brief Perspective on the Link to Jurisdiction' in L Boisson de Chazournes and M Kohen (eds), *International Law and the Quest for its Implementation. Liber Amicorum Vera Gowlland-Debbas* (Leiden: Martinus Nijhoff, 2010) 293; E Lagrange, 'L' Application de la Convention de Rome à des Actes Accomplis par les Etats Parties en dehors du Territoire National' 112 *RGDIP* (2008) 521; M Gondek, *The Reach of Human Rights Treaties in a Globalizing World: Extraterritorial Application of Human Rights Treaties* (Antwerp: Intersentia, 2009); and M Milanović, *Extraterritorial Application of Human Rights Treaties: Law, Principles and Policy* (Oxford: Oxford University Press, 2011).

[177] R Wilde, 'Compliance with Human Rights Norms Extraterritorially: Human Rights Imperialism?', in L Boisson de Chazournes (ed), ibid, 319, 324.

[178] See *Xhavara and Others v Italy and Albania* App no 39473/98 (ECtHR Admissibility Decision of 11 January 2001) (hereinafter: *Xhavara* case).

[179] See *Rigopoulos v Spain* App no 37388/97 EHRR 1999–II (hereinafter: *Rigopoulos case*).

[180] See *Medvedyev* case, para 67.

the events took place entirely on board ships of the Italian armed forces, the crews of which were composed exclusively of Italian military personnel. In the Court's opinion, in the period between boarding the ships of the Italian armed forces and being handed over to the Libyan authorities, the applicants were under the continuous and exclusive de jure and de facto control of the Italian authorities . . . Accordingly, the events giving rise to the alleged violations had fallen within Italy's jurisdiction within the meaning of Article 1.[181]

Hence, the *Hirsi* case comes to complement the above decisions and provide potency to the argument that the Convention applies on the high seas.

The application of the Convention on the high seas presupposes a certain degree of factual control over the vessel or over the persons that are to come under the jurisdiction of the boarding state. Such degree of control would be satisfied in cases of boarding and search of the vessel, let alone when the suspects are detained and transferred to the judicial authorities of the state party to the Convention, such as in the *Medvedyev* case, or when they are transferred to a third state on the intercepting vessels, such as in the *Hirsi* case. It may also be satisfied in cases when there is a ship-to-ship operation prior to boarding, which involves limited use of force to bring the 'delinquent' vessel to a halt. For example, in the *Andreou v Turkey* case, the ECtHR stated that 'the opening of fire on the crowd from close range . . . was such that the applicant must be regarded as within the jurisdiction of Turkey'.[182] In a similar vein, in *Women in Waves v Portugal*, the Court regarded the Convention applicable simply on the basis that the Portuguese warship intercepted *Borndiep*, seemingly without even boarding.[183]

Nonetheless, there are certain scholarly opinions that seem to suggest that the 'shadowing' or surveillance of a vessel on the high seas, even prior to its interception, suffices to bring the latter vessel under the jurisdiction of the European flag state involved.[184] More prudently, Petrig and Geiss advocate the thesis that 'shifting the perspective from the operational radius of an individual military ship, when considered cumulatively and viewed as a whole, the various vessels involved in the multinational enforcement operations in the Gulf of Aden could arguably be said to have establish a net of effective overall control over their joint operational area'.[185] It is highly unlikely that, in view of the 'exceptional'

---

[181] *Hirsi* case, paras 81 and 82.

[182] *Andreou v Turkey* App no 45653/99 (ECtHR, 3 June 2008) para A3c.

[183] See *Women on Waves and Others v Portugal* App no 31276/05 (ECtHR, 3 May 2009) para 23.

[184] See S Piedimonte Bodini, 'Fighting Maritime Piracy under the European Convention on Human Rights' 22 *EJIL* (2011) 829, 835.

[185] R Geiss, A Petrig, *Piracy and Armed Robbery at Sea. The Legal Framework for Counter-Piracy Operations in Somalia and the Gulf of Aden* (Oxford: OUP, 2011) 108 (hereinafter: Geiss and Petrig).

character of extraterritorial jurisdiction under international law, measures such as surveillance or even the approach of the vessel, can trigger the jurisdiction of the state under the ECHR and thus of the Court. This derives support from the recent judgment in the *Al-Skeini* case, in which the Grand Chamber held that state jurisdiction does not arise solely from the control exercised by a state agent over a physical space (eg buildings, ships), but requires the 'exercise of physical power and control over the person in question'.[186] On the face of this judgment, it seems difficult to sustain that anything less than actual physical interference or control of the vessel in question, either by intercepting or by boarding, would trigger the extraterritorial application of the ECHR.[187]

The next question is whether the full gamut of human rights comes into play in the case of the exercise of jurisdiction on the high seas. In the *Bankovic* case, the applicants proposed the idea of 'sliding scale' or 'cause and effect' jurisdiction: Obligations apply insofar as control is exercised; their nature and scope is set in direct proportional relation to the level of control.[188] The European Court rejected this argument; for it, the concept of jurisdiction could not be 'divided and tailored in accordance with the particular circumstances of the extraterritorial act in question.'[189] Nevertheless, there is room for a contrary assertion, namely that 'control entails responsibility', ie the extent to which contracting parties must secure the rights and freedoms of individuals outside their borders is commensurate with the extent of their control over these individuals, is on a stronger legal footing.[190] This proposition was corroborated very recently in the *Al-Skeini* case, in which the European Court held, in stark contrast to its previous dictum in the *Bankovič* case, that

> it is clear that whenever the State through its agents exercises control and authority over an individual, and thus jurisdiction, the State is under an obligation under article 1 to secure to that individual the rights and freedoms under Section 1 of the Convention that are relevant to the situation of that individual. In this sense, therefore the Convention rights can be 'divided and tailored'.[191]

b. The Basic Human Rights in Need of Protection

Having ascertained, in principle, their extraterritorial application, it is apt at this point to determine which human rights are relevant in the present

---

[186] See *Al-Skeini v UK* App no 55721/07 (ECtHR, Grand Chamber Judgment of 7 July 2011) para 136 (hereinafter: *Al-Skeini* case).

[187] In accord seems to be D Guilfoyle, 'Human Rights Issues and Non-Flag State Boarding of Suspect Ships in International Waters', in C Symmons (ed), *Selected Contemporary Issues in the Law of the Sea* (Leiden: Nijhoff, 2011) 83, 89.

[188] See *Bankovic v Belgium,* above n 24, para 75.

[189] ibid, para 76.

[190] See R Lawson, 'Life after Bankovic: On the Extraterritorial Application of the European Convention on Human Rights', in F Coomans et al (eds), above n 28, 120.

[191] See *Al-Skeini* case, para 137.

context, ie in the course of an interception operation on the high seas and describe their legal content.

The first right that is in need of protection in the course of maritime interception operations, in which force is used in order to interdict a vessel and arrest the suspects on board the vessel, is undoubtedly the right to life. All universal and regional human rights treaties provide for the protection of the right to life, which is considered as customary international law; for example, article 6 para 1 of the International Covenant on Civil and Political Rights (ICCPR, 1966) declares that 'Every human being has the inherent right to life. This right shall be protected by law. No one shall be arbitrarily deprived of his life.'[192]

The fundamental tenets of necessity and proportionality are the cornerstones on which each and every case of lethal force would be assessed. As held before the ECtHR in the landmark case of *McCann and others v United Kingdom* (1995),[193] deprivations of life must be subject to the most careful scrutiny, particularly where deliberate lethal force is used, taking into consideration not only the actions of the agents of the State who actually administer the force but also all the surrounding circumstances.

In addition, the prohibition of torture or inhuman or degrading treatment, and more specifically the prohibition of non-refoulement, loom large in all discussions of the application of human rights treaties to maritime interception operations on the high seas, either such operations are to counter illicit immigration or in the fight against piracy.[194] The legal principle of non-refoulement is primarily enshrined in article 33(1) of the Refugee Convention (1951),[195] which prescribes, broadly, that no refugee should be returned to any country where he or she is likely to face persecution, other ill-treatment or torture.[196] It is an unassailable fact that the principle of non-refoulement is a fundamental component of the treaty as

[192] See art 6 of the International Covenant on Civil and Political Rights, 19 Dec 1966, 999 UNTS 171. See also art 2 of ECHR.

[193] See *McCann and others v United Kingdom* (1995) EHHR Series A No 324.

[194] See eg G Goodwin-Gill, 'The Right to Seek Asylum: Interception at Sea and the Principle of Non-Refoulement' 23 *IJRL* (2011) 443; M den Heijer, 'Europe beyond its Borders: Refugee and Human Rights Protection in Extraterritorial Immigration Control', in B Ryan and V Mitsilegas (eds) *Extraterritorial Immigration Control* (The Hague: Brill, 2010) 169; E Papastavridis, 'Interception of Human Beings on the High Seas: A Contemporary Analysis under International Law' 36 *Syracuse Journal of International Law and Commerce* (2009) 145.

[195] art 33(1) reads as follows: '1. No Contracting State shall expel or return (*"refouler"*) a refugee in any manner whatsoever to the frontiers of territories where his life or freedom would be threatened on account of his race, religion, nationality, membership of a particular social group or political opinion'; see Convention Relating to the Status of Refugees (adopted 28 July 1951, entered into force 22 April 1954) 189 UNTS 137.

[196] On this principle see the excellent treatise on the issue by Sir E Lauterpacht and D Bethlehem, 'The Scope and Content of the Principle of *Non-Refoulement*: Opinion' in E Feller et al (eds), *Refugee Protection in International Law* (Cambridge: Cambridge University Press, 2001) 87 (hereinafter: Lauterpacht and Bethlehem) and C Wooters, *International Legal Standards for the Protection from Refoulement* (Antwerp: Intersentia, 2009) (hereinafter: Wooters).

well as customary prohibition of torture, cruel, inhumane, and degrading treatment or punishment.[197] Apart from the express prohibition of refoulement in article 3 of the Convention against Torture,[198] this principle has been construed as implicit in the pertinent prohibition of torture or cruel, inhuman, or degrading treatment enshrined in various human right treaties, including the ECHR (article 3).[199]

The principle of non-refoulement in the human rights context is absolute and non-derogable, preventing extradition, expulsion, or removal in any manner whatsoever.[200] Moreover, in contrast to the principle in the refugee context, which is focused on asylum-seekers, non-refoulement in the human rights context is not predicated on any given status of the individuals at risk.[201] Therefore, it applies to all persons compelled to remain or return in a territory where substantial grounds can be shown for believing that they would face a real risk of being subjected to torture or cruel, inhuman, or degrading treatment. Depending on the specific situation of the persons concerned, states may have negative or positive obligations.[202] Negative obligations are those obligations by which a state is obliged to refrain from acting, such as the prohibition of expulsion, deportation, transfer, extradition, or in general the forced removal of the persons concerned, whereas the positive obligations refer to obligations whereby the state is required to take certain action, such as the obligation to install procedural safeguards or the obligation for a Refugee Status Determination (RSD).[203]

Another fundamental right that should be safeguarded by both the flag state intercepting illicit migrants, drug traffickers or pirates on the high seas as well as by the coastal state, in whose territory these persons may be are transferred, or by the state that exerts jurisdiction over these persons, is the right to liberty and security. It is true that in many cases involving maritime interception operations, there are several issues regarding

---

[197] See Lauterpacht and Bethlehem, 144. Very recently the prohibition of torture was pronounced as a peremptory norm of international law (*jus cogens*); see ICJ, *Questions relating to the Obligation to Prosecute or Extradite* (*Belgium v Senegal*), Judgment of 20 July 2012, para 99.

[198] Convention against Torture and Other Cruel, Inhuman or Degrading Treatment or Punishment, 10 Dec 1984, 1465 UNTS 85, art 3 (hereinafter CAT).

[199] See, inter alia, *Soering v UK* (1989) 98 ILR 270, para 88; *Ahmed v Austria* (1997) 24 EHHR 278, paras 39–40; and *Saadi v Italy* App no 37201/06 (ECtHR, 28 February 2008) para 125. See also the recent judgment of the Grand Chamber of the European Court of Human Rights in the case of *MSS v Belgium and Greece* (21 Jan 2011), where it held inter alia that Belgium violated the prohibition of inhuman and degrading treatment by transferring an Afghan asylum-seeker to Greece, from where he was likely to be sent back to his country without examination of the merits of his case; see *MSS v Belgium and Greece* App no 30696/09 (ECtHR, Grand Chamber Judgment of 21 January 2011) para 344 *et seq.*

[200] See Lauterpacht and Bethlehem, 162.

[201] ibid, 158.

[202] See relevant discussion in Wouters, 133 *et seq.*

[203] See R Marx, 'Non-Refoulement, Access to Procedures and Responsibility for Determining Refugee Claims' 7 *IJRL* (1995) 393.

the quality of legal standards surrounding the detention of the suspects both onboard the vessel and in the territory of the state of disembarkation. Under, for example, article 5 of the ECHR, any detention must be in accordance with a procedure prescribed by law, which must be accessible, foreseeable and must afford legal protection to prevent arbitrary interferences of the right to liberty. Safeguards relating to the right to liberty include: informing the persons detained of their rights, allowing them to contact a lawyer and bringing them before an appropriate judicial authority within a reasonable time.

As the ECtHR has consistently upheld,

> where deprivation of liberty is concerned, it is particularly important that the general principle of legal certainty be satisfied. It is therefore essential that the conditions for deprivation of liberty under domestic and/or international law be clearly defined and that the law itself be foreseeable in its application . . . a standard which requires that all law be sufficiently precise to avoid all risk of arbitrariness.[204]

ii. The Assertion of Jurisdiction by the Intercepting State

It is often assumed that the exercise of the right of visit on the high seas *ipso facto* entails the full extension of the jurisdictional powers of the boarding states.[205] On the contrary, the right to visit on the high seas as an exception to the freedom of the high seas and the assertion of enforcement jurisdiction in relation to persons or property on board the vessel are two distinct legal issues that fall under different legal frameworks. For example, the right to board a suspect pirate vessel on the high seas is provided by LOSC article 110, whereas the jurisdictional basis for its seizure is accorded by LOSC article 105. The LOSC and other treaty and customary law regulate the interference with the vessel on the high seas, while the question of jurisdiction is contingent upon the prior establishment of legislative jurisdiction, which would enable the boarding state to arrest and try the offenders, as well as to confiscate the vessel and the illicit cargo.

In general, jurisdiction is 'the term that describes the limits of the legal competence of a State or other regulatory authority (such as the European Community) to make, apply and enforce rules of conduct upon persons'.[206] A common distinction is between legislative jurisdiction, ie, the jurisdiction to prescribe rules, which presupposes the existence of one or more bases or principles of jurisdiction and enforcement jurisdiction, ie,

---

[204] See *Medvedyev* case, para 80 and *Malone v UK* Series A No 82 (ECtHR, 2 August 1984) para 67.

[205] See also relevant discussion in E Papastavridis, 'Enforcement Jurisdiction in the Mediterranean Sea: Illicit Activities and the Rule of Law on the High Seas' 25 *IJMCL* (2010) 569, 577–83.

[206] *Oppenheim's International Law*, 456.

'the power to take executive action in pursuance of or consequent on the making of decisions or rules'.[207] It is submitted that enforcement jurisdiction includes both the authority to compel compliance, ie to enforce laws, as well as adjudicative or curial jurisdiction, which defines the authority of national courts to adjudicate a case.[208]

On the high seas, ie in areas beyond national jurisdiction, it is essential to have either a treaty provision, analogous to LOSC article 105, or a customary rule, in the form of a jurisdictional principle, such as the protective[209] or the universality principle,[210] which would provide the necessary legal basis for the establishment of prescriptive jurisdiction. As acknowledged by Lowe and Starker, 'the best view is that it is necessary for there to be some clear connecting factor, of a kind whose use is approved by international law, between the legislating State and the conduct that it seeks to regulate'.[211] On the other hand, the fundamental principle governing enforcement jurisdiction on the high seas is that it may not be exercised without the consent of the flag state. This consent may be granted either by a pre-existing international agreement or on an ad hoc basis. It is usually included in the agreements that they grant the right of visit as such, or it may be requested by the boarding state after the visit and search of the delinquent foreign-flagged vessel. If the flag state accords its consent for the exercise of enforcement jurisdiction, this would entail measures such as bringing the vessel to a port of the boarding state, arrest of the suspects on board, initiation of criminal proceedings and confiscation of the illicit cargo and of the vessel itself.

E. Concluding Remarks: Is there a Law of Maritime Interception?

Guilfoyle concludes his excellent treatise on shipping interdiction and the law of the sea as follows:

---

[207] I Brownlie, *Principles of Public International Law,* 7th edn (Oxford: Oxford University Press, 2008) 297 (hereinafter: Brownlie).

[208] See R Rayfuse, 'Regulation and Enforcement in the Law of the Sea' 24 *AYIL* (2005) 181–200, 182.

[209] Under the protective principle, a state claims jurisdiction over crimes which are injurious to its national security. Hence, the nexus for this base of jurisdiction is the nature of its interest that has suffered harm. This jurisdiction allows a state to claim jurisdiction over offences directed against the security or vital interests, or other offences threatening the integrity of governmental functions that are generally recognised as crimes; see, inter alia, I Cameron, *The Protective Jurisdiction of International Criminal Jurisdiction* (Aldershot: Dartmouth, 1994).

[210] On universal jurisdiction see, inter alia, M Inazumi, *Universal Jurisdiction in Modern International Law* (Antwerpen: Intersentia, 2005); R O'Keefe, 'Universal Jurisdiction' 2 *Journal of International Criminal Justice* (2004) 735.

[211] Lowe and Starker, above n 166, 320.

> What this book has demonstrated . . . is that there may be a law that is generally applicable to how interdictions are conducted and to the consequences of wrongfully conducted interdictions before national tribunals.[212]

This chapter has extensively discussed the general rules applicable to the interception on the high seas, especially interception in times of peace, as compared to the belligerent right of visit and search during armed conflict. It has examined the legal content of the right of visit on the high seas, including its legal basis and its modus operandi, as has been framed in the contemporary practice of states. In addition, it has identified certain legal considerations that delineate the contours of interception on the high seas, such as international human rights law and rules concerning the assertion of a state's jurisdiction.

In concluding, it is submitted that even though there are certain common rules of international law governing every case of interception on the high seas, it is difficult to sustain the argument that there is a separate category of international law, a 'self-contained regime', entitled 'law of interception or interdiction'. Rather, interception on the high seas is subject to various rules of international law, which all form part of the 'legal order of the oceans'.

---

[212] Guilfoyle, *Shipping Interdiction*, 344.

4

Interception on the High Seas in the Context of Peace and Security: The Right of Visit in Cases of Armed Conflict and Security Council's Action

I. INTRODUCTORY REMARKS

THE PRESENT CHAPTER will address the practice of interference with vessels under the first heading of the proposed theoretical structure, ie the maintenance of peace and security of states and of international society. In more detail, the enquiry will start from the application of the belligerent right of visit and search in the contemporary era. Accordingly, a series of recent cases will be discussed, where either the belligerent right of visit was applied or the interdiction operations were mandated by the UN Security Council. The underlying idea will be that it is legally more justifiable to classify such interdiction operations under the rubric of the law of naval warfare, rather than under the *jus ad bellum* and the right of self-defence, this being more congruent with the basic tenet of *'la juridicité'* of the high seas, as well as with the fundamental principle of legal certainty under general international law. To be more specific, the law of naval warfare provides the 'boarding' states with an uncontested legal basis for the relevant action, while, very importantly, it opens up the possibility for the capture and the confiscation of the 'contraband' cargo. In addition, the rules of engagement as well as the recourse to force in the course of the belligerent right of visit is apparently permitted under less rigid conditions than in the case of law enforcement operations.

It is beyond the scope of the present thesis to have regard to all the maritime interdiction operations (MIOs) carried out in the course of recent armed conflicts. Suffice it, for the present purposes, to refer to some of the cases in which the right of visit of foreign vessels finds legal justification under the rubric of the law of naval warfare. The first part will take note of MIOs in international conflicts, which were mainly justified by states as self-defence, while the second part will discuss the maritime enforcement of UN Security Council Resolutions, as, for example, against Libya in

2011. Reference will also be made to the sui generis situation of Gaza, which has been at the centre of the international attention lately.

The focus then shifts to the threats to international peace and security, namely, international terrorism and WMD proliferation, which have engendered a series of maritime interdiction measures. These two closely linked issues will be assessed against the background of the initiatives taken by international organisations, namely the UN, NATO and IMO, and by states collectively as well as individually. In this regard, a series of possible legal justifications for the exercise of the right of visit will be scrutinised, such as multilateral and bilateral agreements as well as customary rules of international law. Finally, there will be a short reference to certain legal restrictions of the right of visit in this regard, as set out in the previous chapter, such as the question of enforcement jurisdiction.

II. THE BELLIGERENT RIGHT OF VISIT AND SEARCH AND ITS CONTEMPORARY APPLICATION IN THE LEGAL ORDER OF THE OCEANS

A. The Right of Visit in Cases of Armed Conflict

It is a commonplace that the majority of the post-World War II international armed conflicts have been conducted *extra muros* of the collective security edifice of the UN Charter, and have mostly been premised on the right of self-defence. This entails that, in principle, all the parties to the ensuing conflicts were bound by the fundamental tenets of *jus in bello* and more specifically by the laws of naval warfare. Accordingly, on the one hand, the belligerent states have enjoyed *ipso facto* the right of capture of enemy merchant vessels and of visit, search and diversion of neutral vessels on the high seas, while, on the other hand, all neutral flag states have been under a duty to acquiesce in the legitimate exercise of these measures as long as the conflict lasts, the only exception being the right to convoying.[1]

i. The Iran-Iraq War

There are abundant examples of conflicts where the belligerent right of visit has been employed under the guise of self-defence, while very few where it has been invoked *eo nomine*. Reportedly, the latter did occur during the war between Iran and Iraq (1980–88), where there was an

---

[1] It has long been recognised that neutral warships are entitled to convoy merchant vessels of their home flag or even another neutral state's flag in order to eschew belligerent search and possible diversion; see Politakis, 575. See also Helsinki Principles, Principle 6(1).

extensive exercise of the belligerent right of visit on the high seas.[2] Neutral vessels were systematically stopped and boarded, mainly by Iranian forces at the entrance of the Persian Gulf, and eventually diverted and detained in Iranian ports.[3] It is of importance to note that several foreign governments, amongst them, the US, Italy, the Netherlands, France and the Soviet Union, through various statements, acknowledged the belligerent right of visit and search, as well as the doctrine of convoy.[4] Moreover, most legal commentators were of the view that the Iranian practice of boarding and diverting neutral vessels was in keeping with the customary law of naval warfare, and reaffirmed the continued validity of established principles on the subject.[5]

ii. Algeria

The Algerian crisis of 1956–62 was a case of armed conflict involving a plethora of visitations, and which was controversially labelled as self-defence. During that period, the French government relied on the right of self-defence as the basis for the action, in which the French naval and customs authorities undertook to patrol vast areas of the high seas in an attempt to control weapons and ammunition infiltration to the Algerian rebels.[6] The French action gave rise to numerous unsuccessful judicial proceedings before French courts as well as to protestations by several flag states.[7] An interesting case is that of the Italian vessel *Duizar*, in which the applicants unsuccessfully sought compensation for damage sustained to their ship because of a visit and search conducted by the French in 1966. The *Conseil d'Etat* on 30 March 1966 declined to quash the decision of the *Tribunal Administratif*, not specifically on the ground that the visit and search constituted an 'act of government', but on the ground that it was a measure taken in the course of military operations, which of their nature

---

[2] See, inter alia, D Momtaz, 'Commentary on the Iranian Practice', in A De Guttry, N Ronzitti (eds), *The Iran-Iraq War and the Law of Naval Warfare* (Dordrecht: Martinus Nijhoff, 1993) 24.

[3] ibid.

[4] See relevant references in Politakis, 544 and D Guilfoyle, 'The Proliferation Security Initiative: Interdicting Vessels in the International Waters to Prevent the Spread of Weapons of Mass Destruction' 29 *Melbourne University Law Review* (2007) 733, 744.

[5] See eg A Goia, N Ronzitti, 'The Law of Neutrality: Third States' Commercial Rights and Duties' in F Dekker, H Post (eds), *The Gulf War of 1980-8* (Dordrecht: Martinus Nijhoff, 1992) 232; B Boczek, 'Law of Warfare at Sea and Neutrality: Lessons from the Gulf War' 20 *ODIL* (1989) 261.

[6] See in general Ch Rousseau, 'Chronique des faits internationaux' 70 *RGDIP* (1966) 1062 and L Lucchini, 'Actes de contrainte exercés par la France en Haute Mer au cours d'opération en Algérie' 12 *AFDI* (1966) 803.

[7] The cases failed either because the preliminary issue of visit was held not to be within the competence of a court trying the question of seizure of cargo, or because police measures taken in pursuit of national self-defence were a matter of an 'act of government', in respect of which the administrative tribunals were not competent: *Splosna-Plovba Ship-owners v Customs Authorities*, cited in O'Connell, 805 (fn 63). See also Zwanenberg, 791.

did not engage the responsibilities of the state, in the absence of a specific law.[8]

The Algerian conflict is exceptional, for it falls within the category of internal rather than international armed conflicts. The question arises whether the laws of naval warfare traditionally applied in the context of international conflicts can also apply *mutatis mutandis* in cases such as the Algerian insurgency. Should the response be in the affirmative, there is no doubt that the acts of France were in full conformity with the belligerent right of visit and search and hence, in principle, lawful. Conversely, should the answer be that there is no corresponding law of 'internal' naval warfare, this means that the acts of both France and of the Algerian insurgents were unlawfully extended to the high seas, and should have been confined *ratione loci* to the respective internal and territorial waters.[9]

The problem, in general, lies in the fact that there is no conventional regulation of internal armed conflict at sea, and the customary law, if existent, is very obscure. For example, according to Brownlie, 'Ships controlled by insurgents may not, without recognition of belligerency by third States, exercise belligerent rights against the shipping of other States.'[10] *A contrario argumentum*, it would be lawful for the insurgents to visit and search enemy vessels and, once they are recognised as belligerents, they could lawfully engage in interception of neutral vessels. The San Remo Manual itself refers mainly to international armed conflicts, although it leaves open the possibility for the application of its principles to non-international armed conflicts.[11]

Accordingly, there is room for the view, based also upon the widespread practice of both colonial states and insurgents in the nineteenth century,[12] that when there is a recognised insurgency[13] or a war of national liberation, the basic tenets of the customary law of naval warfare are applicable

---

[8] See *Ignazio Messina et Cie v L'Etat (Ministre des Armees)*, cited in O'Connell, ibid.

[9] See per this view Heinegg, who contends that 'In cases of inner disturbances and of internal armed conflicts the parties may not, beyond the territorial sea, interfere with foreign shipping and aviation, unless the measures taken are in conformity with the law of the sea or other rules of international law'; W Heinegg, 'The Legality of MIOs within the Framework of Operation Enduring Freedom', in WP Heere (ed), *Terrorism and the Military* (The Hague: TM Asser Press, 2003) 43, 46.

[10] See Brownlie, 231.

[11] See Ch 3, n 33 and accompanying text.

[12] See eg *The Virginius* case (1876), in which a ship flying the American flag captured on the high seas by a Spanish warship while running men and arms from Jamaica to insurgents in Cuba. Persons on board were tried by court-martial and shot, as in wartime. See Moore, *Digest of International Law* (1906-II), 895.

[13] The requirements for insurgents to be considered belligerents under the traditional *jus in bello* are the following: a) a base of operations in the territory which the insurgents were liberating; b) an organised force with a command structure capable of taking responsibility for wrongful acts; and c) a flag of its own. See Goldie, 'Terrorism, Piracy and the Nyon Agreements', in Y Dinstein (ed) *International Law in Times of Perplexity* (Dordrecht: Nijhoff, 1989) 225, 232. See also *Republic of Bolivia v Indemnity Mutual Marine Insurance Co* [1909] 1 KB 785, 797 (AC).

mutatis mutandis.[14] This is not without support in international legal doctrine[15] and would definitely be in more harmony with international law than the labelling of each case of visitation as an act of self-defence. What may be different in practical terms is the fact that the theatre of maritime operations as well as the volume of vessels visited on the high seas in case if a non-international armed conflict will be limited in comparison with the case of an international armed conflict. Nevertheless, it must be noted that in the present case the problem lay in the fact that the Algerian rebels were not recognised as insurgents even by France and other nations such as the UK.[16] Arguably, the relevant rules of customary law of naval warfare may also apply in cases of de facto insurgency.[17]

iii. The Falklands

Another armed conflict in which the belligerent right of visit was not recognised as such, albeit the right of self-defence was invoked, was the Falklands Islands / Islas Malvinas conflict (1982).[18] Every single episode of the conflict, as well as the establishment of the relevant war zones, namely the Maritime Exclusion Zone and the later Total Exclusion Zone (TEZ),[19] was justified by the British exclusively in terms of self-defence.[20] This was also the reason given for the sinking of the *General Belgrano* while it was steaming south-west and well outside the 200 nautical mile exclusion zone.[21] It is beyond the scope of the present enquiry to have regard to the legal merits of this incident. Suffice to note, however, that the *Belgrano* incident, assessed against the background of the classical laws of naval warfare, would pose no legal problem; it involved nothing more than a warship being spotted and sunk on sight by an enemy vessel on the high seas. However, 'when an unprovoked attack, even against hostile warships, comes to be appraised with self-defense standards, it is no longer free of legal objections'.[22] In other words, it would be more consistent with

---

[14] See also H Lauterpacht 46 *RGDIP* (1939) 513.
[15] See Colombos, 455 and US Supreme Court, *The Three Friends* [1897] 166 US 1, 63.
[16] See Zwanenberg, 791.
[17] Lauterpacht urges that recognition of insurgency is a duty dependent on factual situations, and not on the whim of a government; see ibid, *Recognition in International Law* (Cambridge: Cambridge University Press, 1947) 270.
[18] See in respect of this conflict A Coll and A Arend, *The Falklands War: Lessons for Strategy, Diplomacy and International Law* (Boston: Allen & Unwin 1985).
[19] In the course of the two-month conflict, the UK established four different types of war zone in succession; see Politakis, 77.
[20] See eg the statement of the UK Representative, A Parsons, in the course of the UN Security Council debate of 22 May 1982, 53 *BYIL* (1982) 551–53.
[21] On 12 May 1982, the Argentine cruiser *General Belgrano* was torpedoed and sunk while steaming some 36 nautical miles outside of the Total Exclusion Zone. See more information in S Woodward and P Robinson, *One Hundred Days – The Memoirs of the Falklands Battle Group Commander* (London: Harper Press, 1992).
[22] Politakis, 85.

both the *jus ad bellum* and *jus in bello* to avoid the claim of self-defence in this regard, as well as to abstain from imposing self-limitations upon the theatre of war. This serves as an illustration of the unnecessary legal problems created by the conflation of these two normative categories.

iv. The Gulf War

Similarly, in the first period of the Gulf War and prior to the adoption of Resolution 678 (1990), it could be argued that the maritime enforcement of the UN embargo against Iraq was based upon the belligerent right of visit and search. The events surrounding this conflict are too extensively discussed elsewhere to warrant detailed repetition.[23] Simply put, following the adoption of Resolution 661 (1990) and the establishment of an almost complete embargo of all imports and exports from Iraq,[24] the US, exercising the right of collective self-defence, officially announced that US forces 'will intercept ships carrying products and commodities that are bound to and from Iraq'.[25] In fact, according to an official 'Diversion Summary', only two ships were diverted by US warships between the latter proclamation of the US (16 August) and Security Council Resolution 665 (25 August).[26] The latter Resolution officially authorised 'those Member States co-operating with the Government of Kuwait which are deploying maritime forces to the area to use such measures commensurate to the specific circumstances as may be necessary under the authority of the Security Council to halt all inward and outward maritime shipping'.[27] It thus put an end to the objections to the legality of the aforementioned US interception programme.[28] It was followed in the next year by famous SC Resolution 678 (1990), which triggered Operation Desert Storm.[29] During the seven months of this conflict 'more than 165 ships from 19 Coalition navies challenged more than 7,500 merchant vessels, boarded 964 ships to inspect manifests and cargo holds, and diverted 51 ships carrying more than one million tons of cargo in violation of UN sanctions'.[30]

---

[23] A comprehensive chronology of the events is provided in P Rowe (ed), *The Gulf War 1990-1 in International and English* Law (London: Routledge, 1993), 3.

[24] UN SC Res 661 (6 August 1990), UN Doc S/RES/661 (1990).

[25] See Secretary of Defense, Public Affairs Guidance message 170205Z, cited in H Robertson, 'Interdiction of the Iraqi Maritime Commerce' 22 *ODIL* (1991) 294, 295. See also L Fielding, *Maritime Interception and United Nations Sanctions* (London: Austin & Winfield, 1997) 47.

[26] See Robertson, ibid, 295.

[27] UN SC Res 665 (25 August 1990), UN Doc S/RES/665 (1990).

[28] See R Morabito, 'Maritime Interdiction: Evolution of a Strategy' 22 *ODIL* (1991) 301, 307.

[29] SC Res 678 (1990) and the resultant use of force by the Coalition prompted dissonant views over the legal basis of the Operation. For a good overview of the opposing arguments, see D Sarooshi, *The United Nations and the Development of Collective Security* (Oxford: Oxford University Press, 1999) 174 (hereinafter: Sarooshi).

[30] US Department of Defense, *Conduct of the Persian Gulf War, Final Report to the Congress* (1992) 76.

It is submitted that the US-led interception operation was in full accord with the right of visit and search under the law of naval warfare. Upon deciding to exercise their right of collective self-defence in support of Kuwait,[31] the US and other Coalition states became parties to the international armed conflict triggered by Iraq's invasion of 2 August 1990.[32] Therefore, they were fully entitled, even if they opted to invoke self-defence instead, to visit or divert and search neutral vessels on the high seas or in the belligerent waters in order to control contraband material destined for Iraq.[33] This right was not suspended or replaced by a different right on 25 August 1990, the date Resolution 665 was adopted, or even later with Resolution 678; it only changed legal foundation then, as far as the *jus ad bellum* component was concerned, ie from the ambit of collective self-defence to the collective security system of the UN Security Council. As regards the *jus in bello*, however, the belligerent right of visit and search continued unabated, until the official cease-fire and end of the armed conflict promulgated by Resolution 687 (1991).[34] This notwithstanding, the adoption of SC Resolution 661 and then 665 had inescapable repercussions on the applicability of other rules of law of naval warfare, such as the law of maritime neutrality. No state could claim the latter rules and not enforce the embargo against Iraq as well as engage in convoying and other measures in order to avoid the right of visit.[35]

v. Operation Enduring Freedom

In the twenty-first century, the most important armed conflict with significant naval dimensions was the military campaign of the US against Al Qaeda and the Taliban in Afghanistan. Following the refusal of the Taliban to surrender the Al Qaeda leaders held responsible for the 9/11 attacks, on 7 October 2001 the US launched a military operation, later named Operation Enduring Freedom.[36] A component of the Operation was, as announced by Pentagon officials in November 2001, the visit of cargo ships suspected of carrying or providing support to Al Qaeda. Subsequently, Coalition forces

---

[31] See eg Letter from the *Chargé d'affaires* of the United States Mission to the UN, UN Doc S/12537 (1990), reprinted in E Lauterpacht (ed), *The Kuwait Crisis: Basic Documents* (Cambridge: Grotius Publications, 1991) 247.

[32] See also A Soons, 'A New Exception to the Freedom of the High Seas' in T Gill, W Heere (eds), *Reflections on Principles and Practices of International Law: Essays in Honour of Leo J Bouchez* (The Hague: Martinus Nijhoff, 2000) 205, 212 (hereinafter: Soons).

[33] In the present case as well as in all cases in which an embargo has been set forth by the Security Council, the lists of contraband is actually provided by the Resolution itself; see also general discussion about contraband in the UN era in Politakis, 433.

[34] SC Res 687 (3 April, 1991), reprinted in 30 ILM (1991) 846. See also L Fielding, above n 25, 93l; *contra* Sarooshi, 201.

[35] *cf* arts 25 and 103 of the UN Charter and also San Remo Manual, 80.

[36] See the general discussion of this Operation in C Gray, *International Law and the Use of Force*, 3rd edn (Oxford: Oxford University Press, 2008) 203 (hereinafter: Gray).

started to board vessels, amongst others, in the Indian Ocean, the Red Sea and the Straits of Hormuz. 'Despite the large scale and geographic reach of the MIOs within this framework, for obvious reasons, little data on specific interdiction is available.'[37] Operation Enduring Freedom has continued to operate long after the overthrow of the Taliban regime, with the goal of quelling any resistance by the remaining Taliban forces and of furthering the needs of the 'Global War on Terrorism', and there has not been an official termination of the Operation by the US.[38]

The modus operandi involved the monitoring and hailing by radio of all passing merchant vessels. The answers were transmitted to a command centre where they were checked against a database, and if suspicions arose or if the vessel declined to answer, a boarding team was sent to search the ship. 'It seems that allied forces were more aggressive towards local tiny fishing boats (known as "dhows"). Teams of sailors boarded them and searched the cargo and passengers. On the contrary, the allied forces were much more cautious with international shipping.'[39] Interestingly, all the Coalition forces, save for the US, first attempted to obtain the consent of the ship's master and then boarded and searched the vessel.[40] Moreover, it is reported that 'Weapons, ammunition and other military equipment destined for international terrorists or supply goods as well as everything serving for the financing of international terrorism, including drugs or other prohibited goods, may be captured and seized.'[41]

A detailed examination of the interdiction measures during Operation Enduring Freedom is not only a thorny task due to the paucity of relevant information, but is also beyond the scope of the present enquiry. However, as far as the legal basis of the Operation is concerned, the following remarks are in order: the use of force by the US and other Coalition states against Afghanistan, be it a lawful exercise of the right of self-defence or not,[42]

---

[37] Jimenez-Kwast, 235. This author reports that in 'the period October 2001–October 2003 alone, over 1,100 ships were boarded by coalition forces while tens of thousands vessels were hailed'; ibid (fn 416). Allegedly, an operation involving four NATO members intercepted a ship in the Gulf of Oman in July 2002 that was transporting four suspect Al-Qaeda officials; see M Becker, 'The Shifting Public Order of the Oceans' 46 *Harvard ILJ* (2005) 131, 152 (hereinafter: Becker).

[38] It seems that the Operation will officially end with the withdrawal of the remaining US forces from Afghanistan. See the latest news in this regard www.state.gov/p/sca/ci/af/index.htm.

[39] A Syrigos, 'Developments on the Interdiction of Vessels on the High Seas', in A Strati et al (eds), *Unresolved Issues and New Challenges to the Law of the Sea* (The Hague: Martinus Nijhoff, 2006) 149, 181.

[40] See Jimenez-Kwast, 236. See also 'Le "Consensual Boarding" une Evolution Majeure de Droit de la Mer?' 7 *Annuaire du droit de la Mer* (2002) 556.

[41] W Heinegg, above n 8, 56.

[42] The prevailing view is that the *jus ad bellum* justification of the Operation was the right of self-defence, and not the authorisation of the UN Security Council pursuant to Res 1368; see relevant comments in E Papastavridis, 'Security Council Resolutions 1368 and 1373: Collective Security or the Right of Self-Defence?' 55 *Revue Hellénique de Droit International* (2002) 531.

triggered the laws of international armed conflict and thence the customary laws of naval warfare. Accordingly, the parties, for the duration of the conflict, were entitled to visit and search neutral vessels and capture enemy vessels on the high seas. Therefore, Operation Enduring Freedom at sea was, in principle, within the bounds of *jus in bello* for the period of the conflict and no other authority, but the law of naval warfare, was required.[43]

Nevertheless, the crucial matter here is the legality *ratione temporis* of the Operation, namely, the legality of the Operation since the fall of the Taliban government. With the cessation of hostilities and the political settlement in the Bonn Agreement in December 2001, an Afghan Transitional Administration was established and a UN-authorised force, ISAF, was sent to Afghanistan in January 2002 to assist the government of Afghanistan in the maintenance of security.[44] Arguably, these events marked the official end of the international armed conflict in Afghanistan.[45] Thus, it seems that the legal basis for the continuation of Operation Enduring Freedom in the territory of Afghanistan is the consent of the Kabul government.[46] As Gray observes, 'the longer Operation Enduring Freedom continues, the further is detached from its initial basis. It may be that awareness of this led to express reference to Operation in Security Council Resolutions'.[47] Indeed, starting from Resolution 1510 (2003), the Council has called in a series of Resolutions for 'closer operational synergy' between ISAF and 'Operation Enduring Freedom',[48] as well as between the Afghan government and the aforementioned international forces.[49] However, even though 'these Resolutions may

[43] See relevant discussion in Jumenez-Kwast, 237. *Contra* Heinegg, who avers that 'MIO conducted within the framework of Operation Enduring Freedom can be based upon the right of individual and collective self-defence and additionally, on Resolution 1373 of the UN Security Council'; above n 8, 58.

[44] See further information about NATO-ISAF at www.isaf.nato.int.

[45] This does not mean that peace or stability in Afghanistan have been accomplished; on the contrary, insurgent Taliban forces have engaged increasingly in conventional conflicts with Afghan government and international security forces; for example, on 17 May 2012, it was reported that 'suicide attackers with explosives stormed a governor's compound in southwestern Afghanistan on Thursday, killing themselves and seven people'; see www.cnn.com/2012/05/17/world/asia/afghanistan-violence/index.html. See also the latest Report of the UN Secretary-General, 'The Situation in Afghanistan and its Implications for International Peace and Security' (13 December 2011); available at http://daccess-dds-ny.un.org/doc/UNDOC/GEN/N11/622/56/PDF/N1162256.pdf?OpenElement.

[46] Concurring is W Heinegg, 'Terrorism, NATO, Rules of Engagement' in D Karpen et al (eds), *Maritime Security – Current Problems in the Baltic Sea* (Baden-Baden: Nomos, 2005) 103, 111.

[47] Gray, 206.

[48] See SC Res 2069 of 9 October 2012 which extended the authorisation of ISAF for a period of 12 months until 13 October 2013 welcomed, '. . . the continued coordination between ISAF and the OEF coalition, and in-theatre cooperation established between ISAF and the EU presence in Afghanistan'. See also SC Resolutions 1659 (2006), 1707 (2006), 1746 (2007), 1833 (2008), 1868 (2009), 2011 (2011).

[49] For example, in its recent Resolution on Afghanistan of 22 March 2012, the Council 'calls upon the Afghan Government, with the assistance of the international community, *including ISAF and the Operation Enduring Freedom coalition*, in accordance with their respective designated responsibilities as they evolve, to continue to address the threat to the security

be seen as implicit acceptance of the legality of Operation Enduring Freedom',[50] they fall short of authorising the latter Operation or even of containing anything express on its legal basis.

Similarly, the legal basis for the maritime operations conducted as part of Operation Enduring Freedom after the end of the international armed conflict should be sought in another legal framework, and not in the law of naval warfare, triggered by the right of self-defence to the '9/11' attack or by an express Security Council authorisation. Although first Resolution 1776 (2007) and then Resolution 1833 (2008) made express reference to the latter maritime operations, 'expressing its appreciation for . . . the contribution of many nations to ISAF and to OEF [Operation Enduring Freedom], *including its maritime interdiction component within the framework of the counter-terrorism operations in Afghanistan and in accordance with the applicable rules of international law*',[51] it is readily apparent that no authorisation per se was given for such operations.[52] Noteworthy is that there is no such reference to maritime operations in the following Resolutions concerning Afghanistan.

Accordingly, there is room for the following propositions: first, it is submitted that the conflict was transformed from an international to a non-international armed conflict, in light of the insurgent activities of the Taliban forces.[53] As a result, and similarly to the case of the Algerian crisis, the belligerent right of visit of neutral vessels can be lawfully exercised by the Government of Afghanistan in cooperation with its international partners, ie ISAF and Operation Enduring Freedom. This seems to derive support from the continuous references of the Council to the ongoing 'conflict' in Afghanistan.[54] Another, less convincing, argument in this respect could be that from March 2003 and until the end of Operation Iraqi Freedom,

and stability of Afghanistan posed by the Taliban, Al-Qaida and other violent and extremist groups, illegal armed groups, criminals and those involved in the production, trafficking or trade of illicit drugs'; SC Res 2041/2012 para 23 (emphasis added). See also SC Res 2069 (2012), para. 4.

[50] Gray, 206.

[51] SC Res 1833 (2008), preamble (emphasis added). It is of interest to note that SC Res 1776 (2007) did not contain the part 'within the framework of the counter-terrorism operations in Afghanistan and in accordance with the applicable rules of international law'.

[52] As Gray notes in relation to SC Res 1776, there was an unwillingness to accept the legality of all aspects of the activities in question; see the statements of Russia and China in SC 5744th meeting (2007) and Gray, 207.

[53] See above n 44.

[54] See eg SC Resolution (2041/2012), 'Recalling its resolutions 1674 (2006), 1738 (2006) and 1894 (2009) on the protection of civilians in *armed conflict*, expressing its serious concern with the increased high number of civilian casualties in Afghanistan, in particular women and children, the increasingly large majority of which are caused by the Taliban, Al-Qaida and other violent and extremist groups and illegal armed groups, reaffirming that all parties to *armed conflict* must take all feasible steps to ensure the protection of civilians, calling for all parties to comply with their obligations under international law including international humanitarian and human rights law' (emphasis added).

Operation Enduring Freedom assisted the Coalition forces in the war against Iraq and thus the interdiction operations in that period drew their legality from the laws applicable to the latter armed conflict at sea.[55] Finally, and perhaps more tenably, it could be argued that the widespread practice of the states involved to seek the assent of the master of the vessel or of the flag state prior to boarding indicates that the interception operations in question are exclusively based on the peacetime right of visit and its relevant legal justifications,[56] since in the context of the belligerent right of visit the consent of the flag state is not required. In this vein, it is noteworthy that the most famous episode of interception in the context of the Operation Enduring Freedom, namely the *So San* incident (2002), was conducted on the legal basis of the statelessness of the vessel.

vi. Operation Iraqi Freedom

In addition to Operation Enduring Freedom, the US and its allies launched Operation Iraqi Freedom in March 2003, against the Iraqi government. According to N Klein, 'the US asserted a belligerent right of boarding, seizing, disabling or destroying maritime vessels considered a threat to coalition naval forces at the outset of the 2003 war in Iraq'.[57] She cites M Valencia, who reports that

> on 21 March 2003, as the war on Iraq began, the US Navy's Liaison Office issued a notice to all shipping in the Eastern Mediterranean, Red Sea, Arabian Sea, Gulf of Oman, and Arabian Gulf that warned 'all maritime vessels or activities that are determined to be threats to coalition naval forces will be subject to defensive measures, including boarding, seizure, disabling or destruction, without regard to registry or location'.[58]

There is no further information on actual interdiction and seizure of vessels in the course of Operation Iraqi Freedom; however, on the face of the US Navy's statement, it seems that the US conflated the 'belligerent right of visit' with 'acts of self-defence', which is common in the post-Charter era (eg Algeria, Falklands). Interestingly enough, the US reserved the right to take such measures 'without regard to registry or location'. To

---

[55] See in this respect, Syrigos, who reports that 'During the war in Iraq, the naval forces participating in Operation Enduring Freedom continued tracking merchant vessels and conducting maritime interdiction operations'; see above n 38, 182. It goes without saying that a claim for the applicability of laws of naval warfare in the politically and not legally characterised 'Global War against Terror' is a *non sequitur*; see inter alia W Heinneg, 'Security at Sea: Legal Restrains or Lack of Political Will?', in M Nordquist et al (eds), *Legal Challenges in Maritime Security* (Leiden: Martinus Nijhoff, 2008) 133, 143 and Gray, 207.

[56] Such legal bases are, in principle, the statelessness of the vessel, the consent of the flag state or the right of self-defence in response to a terrorist attack.

[57] Klein, *Maritime Security*, 289.

[58] M Valencia, *The Proliferation Security Initiative*, Adelphi Paper 376 (The International Institute for Strategic Studies, 2005), 34, citing *Lloyd's List*, 21 March 2003.

reiterate, in the course of law of naval warfare, a belligerent state cannot take forcible measures in neutral waters or destroy neutral vessels on the high seas. Hence, the above statement appears more an anticipatory warning regarding 'acts of self-defence', rather than an announcement of the exercise of the belligerent right of visit and search.

vii. Gaza Strip

Finally, reference could be made to the operations of the Israeli forces off the Gaza Strip in December 2008 and, more recently, in May 2010, which have raised some perplexing questions of international law. Following the taking of power in Gaza by Hamas (2007), the Israeli Naval Forces established a controversial exclusion zone off the Gaza Strip.[59] On 3 January 2009, the government of Israel officially declared a 'naval blockade on the coast of the Gaza Strip, in order to prevent weapons, terrorists and money from entering or exiting the Gaza Strip by sea'.[60] Arguably, this has provided the legal basis for the interception since then of many vessels trying to approach this region.[61] For example, on 30 December 2008, even prior to the official proclamation of a naval blockade, a Gibraltar-registered vessel, *Dignity,* which was carrying medical volunteers and supplies, was forcefully interdicted by an Israeli patrol boat 90 miles off Gaza. The official justification provided by the Israeli forces was that the vessel was 'warned not to proceed to Gaza because it is a closed military area'.[62]

Much publicity attached to the incident of the *MV Mavi Marmara* off Gaza Strip in 2010. On 31 May 2010 a flotilla of six vessels was boarded and taken over by the Israeli Defense Force, 72 nautical miles from land. The vessels were carrying people and humanitarian supplies. The flotilla had been directed to change course by the Israeli forces, who stated that the coast of Gaza was under a naval blockade. Nine passengers lost their lives and many others were wounded as a result of the use of force during the take-over operation by Israeli forces. The incident caused considerable controversy between Israel and Turkey as to the legality of the boarding.

---

[59]   The relevant NAVTEX was transmitted to the author under conditions of anonymity, and reads as follows: 'in light of the security situation, all foreign vessels are advised to remain clear of area bound by . . . Vessels approaching the maritime zone off the coast of Gaza Strip are requested to maintain radio contact with Israel Naval Forces and will be subject to supervision and inspection' (on file with the author).

[60]   See *Public Commission to Examine the Maritime Incident of 31 May 2010 – The Turkel Commission*, 36; available at www.turkel-committee.gov.il/files/wordocs/8808report-eng.pdf.

[61]   See ibid, 33. Most recently, Israel intercepted the *Victoria*, a vessel on its way from Syria to Egypt, which carried 25 tonnes of weapons and ammunition suspected to be destined for Gaza; see Briefing by Mr Oscar Fernandez-Taranco, Assistant Secretary-General for Political Affairs, to the Security Council on the situation in the Middle East, including the Palestinian question, UN SCOR, 66th Sess, 6501st mtg at 4, UN Doc S/PV 6501 (22 March 2011).

[62]   See 'Gaza Relief Boat Damaged in Encounter with Israeli Vessel' (30 December 2008); available at www.cnn.com/2008/WORLD/meast/12/30/gaza.aid.boat/index.html.

On 2 August 2010, the UN Secretary-General established a Panel of Inquiry on the 31 May 2010 Flotilla Incident, which issued its Report in September 2011.[63] The Report took the view that the blockade of Gaza was legal; however, Israel was found to have used 'excessive and unreasonable' measures in boarding the *Mavi Marmara,* resulting in 'unacceptable' loss of life; and to have subsequently engaged in 'significant mistreatment' of those detained.[64]

It is beyond the scope of the present enquiry to address extensively the merits of the Palmer Report or whether Israel had the lawful right to declare and enforce a naval blockade.[65] The Report itself, based on 'the facts as they exist on the ground',[66] considered that 'the conflict should be treated as an international one for the purposes of the law of blockade. This takes foremost into account Israel's right to self-defence against armed attacks from outside its territory'.[67] In the Appendix of the Report, its authors laid down the 'Applicable International Legal Principles', in which it was argued that, even if the conflict in Gaza is not designated an international one,[68] 'the law of blockade would also be applicable in non-international armed conflicts in which the parties and/or neutral countries recognize each other as belligerents'.[69] This assertion was premised, on the one hand, upon the *Prize* cases during the US Civil War[70] and was inferred, on the other, from the silence of the San Remo Manual on the question of the applicability of the law of naval warfare in non-international armed conflicts.[71]

Notwithstanding that this assertion was heavily criticised,[72] what is of significance for present purposes is that there is considerable support for the argument that certain parts of the law of naval warfare may apply in cases of non-international armed conflict, such as, for example, the

[63] See Report of the Secretary-General's Panel of Inquiry on 31 May 2010 (September 2011) (hereinafter: Palmer Report) and commentary by D Guilfoyle, www.ejiltalk.org/the-palmer-report-on-the-mavi-marmara-incident-and-the-legality-of-israel%E2%80%99s-blockade-of-the-gaza-strip/ (6 Sept 2011).

[64] See Palmer Report, paras 117, 134, 145.

[65] See in this regard the excellent analysis of D Guilfoyle, 'The *Mavi Marmara* Incident and Blockade in Armed Conflict' 81 *BYIL* (2011) 171–223.

[66] Palmer Report, para 73.

[67] ibid.

[68] Nonetheless, it is also argued that a conflict becomes international 'if it takes place between an Occupying Power and rebel or insurgent groups—whether or not they are terrorist in character—in occupied territory', such as in the Palestinian Occupied Territories'; see Palmer Report, Appendix I, para 20. Authors per this view are A Cassese, *International Law*, 2nd edn (Oxford: Oxford University Press, 2005) 420 and A Zimmermann, 'Article 8, War Crimes –Preliminary Remarks on para 2(c)-(f) and para 3' in O Triffterer (ed), *Commentary on the Rome Statute of the International Criminal Court*, 2nd edn (Oxford: Oxford University Press, 2008) 484.

[69] Palmer Report, Appendix I, para 23.

[70] See The Prize cases 67 US (1863) 635, 666–69.

[71] See Palmer Report, Appendix I, para 24.

[72] See D Guilfoyle, above n 64.

belligerent right of visit and search. Moreover, the legality of the interference with foreign vessels in such cases is inevitably assessed on an ad
hoc basis, as occurred in the *MV Mavi Marmara* case, which was found
unlawful. As far as the case of the *Dignity* is concerned, it is argued that
the proclamation of a 'war zone', prior to the official blockade, does not
'significantly alter the rights of the belligerents and the neutrals within
that zone'.[73] Thus, even if the *Dignity* could not qualify as a 'hospital ship'
under international humanitarian law,[74] a vessel carrying humanitarian
support can never be considered a legitimate military target and, hence,
the interception and the damage to the vessel were markedly beyond the
bounds of international law.[75]

viii. Concluding Remarks

As the foregoing survey has demonstrated, the belligerent right of visit
and search is still relevant and may furnish the necessary legal justification for any interdiction operation on the high seas in the course of an
armed conflict, whether international or non-international. The most
important prerequisites in this regard are, first, to legally designate a conflict as an 'armed conflict', which would trigger the law of naval warfare
and the right in question, and second, to decipher its *ratione temporis*
parameters. Subsequently, the exercise of the right of visit would be
legally assessed against the relevant background of the law of naval warfare and against international humanitarian law in general, especially the
principles of distinction and proportionality. Finally, it is apt to reiterate
that it is more consistent with the principle of *'la juridicité'* of the high seas
and generally with the legal order of the oceans to invoke and apply the
belligerent right of visit in such cases rather than the right of self-defence.

B. Maritime Enforcement of UN Security Resolutions

With the advent of the UN Charter, a potential new exception to the freedom of the high seas was created: the authority of the UN Security Council
under Chapter VII to order the interception of vessels in situations of

---

[73] See C Michaelsen, 'Maritime Exclusion Zones in Time of Armed Conflict at Sea' 8 *JCSL*
(2003) 363, 385.
[74] *cf* Convention No X adopted at the Hague Conference 1907 and the 1949 Red Cross
Convention on the Amelioration of the Condition of the Wounded Sick and Shipwrecked
Members of the Armed Forces at Sea (75 UNTS 85). See also O'Connell, 1119.
[75] Such vessels could be included in the exception of 'ships engaged in Scientific, Religious
and Philanthropic Missions', which was adopted by the 1907 Hague Convention No XI; see:
O'Connell, 1123. Generally, on vessels under protection under the law of naval warfare see
L Doswald-Beck, 'Vessels, Aircrafts and Persons Entitled to Protection during Armed
Conflict at Sea' 65 *BYIL* (1994) 211.

'threat to the peace, breach of the peace or act of aggression' (article 39 of the UN Charter). Once the Security Council determines that a situation falls under the scope of article 39 of the UN Charter, it can activate the collective security system under Chapter VII. It can make recommendations or adopt binding decisions, including the use of force, as well as authorise Member States or international organisations to take 'all necessary means to restore international peace and security'.[76] Although until the end of the Cold War the Security Council had only imposed economic sanctions twice,[77] since the 1991 Gulf War, it has recurrently relied on the option of establishing embargoes pursuant to article 41 of the Charter.[78] On a number of occasions, the Council has explicitly authorised maritime interdiction in order to enforce these embargoes. Maritime interdiction has also been part of the enforcement action that Member States and other international organisations have been authorised to take in many cases of threats and breaches of international peace and security.

i. The Legal Basis of Maritime Interdiction Operations

There is no doubt that the legal basis for the UN-mandated naval operations in peacetime lies with the relevant Security Council Resolutions under article 41 and/or article 42 of the Charter.[79] 'In order for the Council's authorization to confer legality on States' actions when carrying out a naval interdiction, the authorization will either have to override the State's treaty law obligations or constitute a valid exception to both Article 2(4) of the Charter and Article 87 of the 1982 UNCLOS.'[80] In respect of the latter provision and the freedom of the high seas in general, it must be

---

[76] These are the standard terms used in authorisation-delegation of Chapter VII powers to Member States; see eg SC Res 678 (1991). On Chapter VII in general, its historical origin and the evolution of the Council's practice see: Frowein/Krisch, 'Introduction to Chapter VII' in Simma (ed), *The Charter of the United Nations. A Commentary*, 2nd edn (Oxford: Oxford University Press, 2002) 702, as well as the bibliography contained therein. On the issue of authorisation of Chapter VII powers, the benchmark work is of D Sarooshi, who scrutinises the collective security system through the prism of the theory of delegation of powers in international organisations; see D Sarooshi, *The United Nations and the Development of Collective Security* (Oxford: Oxford University Press, 1999) (hereinafter: Sarooshi). See also L-A Sicilianos, 'Entre multilatéralisme et unilatéralisme: l'autorisation par le Conseil de sécurité de recourir à la force' 339 *Recueil des Cours* (2008) 9–436 and ibid, 'L'Autorisation par le Conseil de Sécurité de recourir a la force: une tentative d'évaluation' 106 *RGDIP* (2002) 1–50.

[77] The first use of the tool of economic sanctions under Chapter VII was against Southern Rhodesia (SC Res 232 of 16 December 1966) and the second was in 1977 against South Africa (SC Res 418 of 4 November 1977).

[78] *cf* inter alia embargoes against Iraq, the territory of the former Yugoslavia, Somalia, Liberia, Angola and Sierra Leone. See in general V Gowland-Debbas (ed), *United Nations Sanctions and International Law* (The Hague: Kluwer Law International, 2001) and D Cortright et al, 'The Sanctions Era: Themes and Trends in UN Security Council Sanctions since 1990' in AV Lowe *et al* (ed), *The United Nations Security Council and War* (Oxford: Oxford University Press, 2008) 205.

[79] See also Politakis, 546.

[80] Sarooshi, 194–95.

recalled that article 110 of LOSC relating to the right of visit contains the famous caveat 'Except where acts of interference derive from powers conferred by treaty'. As R Churchill notes, 'international treaties in article 92 and "treaties" in article 110 appear to include the UN Charter as well as legally binding acts adopted thereunder such as UNSCR under Chapter VII'.[81] Thus, it is contended that States implementing a Council authorised naval interdiction are exercising powers which have been delegated by the Council under the Charter and therefore fall within this exception.[82] Therefore, a valid or intra vires Resolution of the Security Council suffices to afford the legal basis for the boarding of foreign vessels on the high seas in the context of UN sanctions.[83]

A different question, however, is whether the states interdicting the suspect vessels have also the authority, pursuant to SC Resolutions, to exert further enforcement powers, such as the seizure of the prohibited cargo. This will, of course, be contingent upon the terms of the Resolution itself; nonetheless, the legal basis for the deviation from the principle of the exclusive jurisdiction of the flag state on the high seas lies with the SC Resolution setting forth the relevant embargo. The terms of the latter Resolution have ascendancy over all the conflicting treaty obligations of the Member States, such as article 92 of LOSC, in view of the application of article 103 of the UN Charter.[84] In establishing the primacy of the Charter, article 103 provides that 'in the event of a conflict between the obligations of the Members of the United Nations under the present Charter and their obligations under any other international agreement, their obligations under the present Charter shall prevail'.[85] It is questioned, in this respect, whether the authorisations-delegations by the UN Security Council have the same overriding effect as the binding decisions under article 41 of the Charter. According to the prevailing view, 'the implementation of UN sanctioned collective measures, even if nonmandatory should not be obstructed by treaty obligations'.[86]

---

[81]   R Churchill, 'Conflicts between UN Security Council Resolutions and the UNCLOS' 38 *IYHR* (2008) 185, 189.

[82]   See also J Fawcett, 'Security Council Resolutions on Rhodesia' 41 *BYIL* (1965–66) 103, 120.

[83]   It is argued that solely intra vires acts of UN Security Council, namely Resolutions that have been adopted according to the Charter, will be considered lawful 'treaty exceptions' of the freedom of the high seas. See on the issue of intra/ultra vires Resolutions *Namibia* Advisory Opinion, 12, and also C Doehring, 'Unlawful Resolutions of the Security Council', 1 *Max Planck Yearbook of United Nations Law* (1997) 98.

[84]   To furnish an example from the Iraq-Kuwait war (1990–91), SC Res 665 authorised the interdiction of suspect vessels 'to ensure the strict implementation of the provisions related to such shipping laid down in resolution 661 (1990)'; in other words, the authority for the implementation of further measures and for the seizure of the vessel laid not with SC Res 665 but with SC Res 661 (1990), which, on the face of article 103 UN Charter, prevailed over all conflicting obligations of the Member States.

[85]   'This article represents the partial suspension of the basic international law maxim *pacta sunt servanda*'; see R Bernhardt, 'Article 103' in B Simma (ed); above n 77, 1296.

[86]   Sarooshi, 151. *Cf* also LA Sicilianos, above n 77, 5.

In the case of an existing armed conflict, in which the Security Council intervenes, the legal basis for the interdiction operations is different. While the parties to the conflict have a priori the belligerent right of visit and search of all neutral vessels, it is submitted that the involvement of the Council alters, on the one hand, the *jus ad bellum* rubric of the conflict, ie from the right of self-defence, for example, to a UN enforcement operation, and on the other, its *jus in bello* contours.[87] Accordingly, the aforementioned right remains, in principle, still in force during the conflict, albeit it is qualified and tailored to the legal framework of the UN collective security system. In other words, the Security Council action retains the right of visit and search, because, 'otherwise, belligerents would be unable effectively to control and enforce the prohibition of carriage of contraband or the institution of a blockade'.[88] However, from the moment, and as long as, the Council is involved in the conflict under its Chapter VII powers, the customary right of visit is subordinated to the legal framework of the UN Charter. To explicate this, suffice to mention that the contraband lists are actually established by the relevant SC Resolutions and not by the belligerents, whereas the notion of neutrality provides no justification for not enforcing the imposed sanctions.

It must be accepted with no demur that the customary right of visit revives in case the Security Council ceases its action before the conflict is resolved. An interesting question is whether this right retains its autonomous validity for the belligerent state, which is the target of the UN enforcement action. In view of the fact that the law of armed conflict at sea applies to all the belligerents, it is arguable that the target state still enjoys the customary right to engage in visits and searches of enemy and neutral vessels.

ii. Southern Rhodesia

The first experience of maritime enforcement of UN sanctions, which there was not in the course of an armed conflict, was in Southern Rhodesia under the terms of SC Resolution 221 (1966).[89] Pursuant to the latter Resolution, the Royal Navy was empowered to stop and divert a Greek vessel, *Manuela* and inspect the *Joanna V*, actions which, before the adoption of the Resolution, were thwarted because of the refusal of consent by

---

[87] It is worth quoting here the relevant comments by the San Remo Manual, 'the Member States not involved in the conflict are subject to certain duties which override the law of neutrality, namely that they must not give assistance to the State or States identified by the Security Council as responsible for resorting to force in violation of international law'; ibid, 79.

[88] ibid, 196.

[89] See the comprehensive study of V Gowland-Debbas, *Collective Responses to Illegal Acts under International Law: UN Action in the Case of Southern Rhodesia* (Dordrecht: Martinus Nijhoff, 1990).

the flag state, Greece.[90] Regardless of debate on its precise legal foundation under the Charter,[91] Resolution 221 provided a sufficient legal basis for the so-called 'Beira Patrol' conducted by the United Kingdom until the sanctions were lifted in 1979.[92]

iii. The 1991/First Gulf War

The next maritime enforcement operation under the auspices of the UN was in the Iraq-Kuwait War. As was discussed previously in detail, the blockade by the US, UK and other Coalition states preceded the adoption of Resolution 665 (1990), which authorised 'member States cooperating with the Government of Kuwait to use such measures commensurate to the specific circumstances as may be necessary . . . to halt all inward and outward maritime shipping'. Whatever its exact legal basis,[93] it is submitted that Resolution 665 did nothing more than reaffirm that the law of maritime neutrality was significantly changed by the adoption of Resolution 661. It set forth *expressis verbis* that all states should respect the embargo established by the latter Resolution; otherwise they would be susceptible to the belligerent right of visit and search already exercised by the Coalition states, pursuant to the principle of collective self-defence.[94] The situation in the Kuwait crisis was markedly different than in the Southern Rhodesia case, as the right of visit on the high seas existed *ipso jure* in accordance with the law of naval warfare. As Soons points out, 'After the ending of the hostilities in April 1991, Article 51 ceased to be a basis for enforcing the embargo. From then on, only Resolution 665 based on Article 41 remained.'[95]

iv. The Case of Former Yugoslavia

The phrase used in Resolution 665 quoted above became standard language for cases where the SC wanted explicitly to authorise states to enforce an embargo at sea. It was used subsequently in Resolutions covering the arms embargo against former Yugoslavia, and against Haiti. Turning first to the war in the former Yugoslavia,[96] the possibility of boarding and searching

---

[90] See: *Keesings* (1965–66), 214–17.

[91] See eg the discussion in Sarooshi, 197–98.

[92] See also R McLaughlin, 'UN Mandated Naval Interdiction Operations in the Territorial Sea?' 51 *ICLQ* (2002) 249, 257.

[93] See: inter alia R Lavalle, 'The Law of the UN and the Use of Force under the Relevant Security Council Resolutions of 1990 and 1991' 23 *NYIL* (1992) 16; R Zacklin, 'Les Nations-Unies et la Crise du Golfe' in B Stern (ed), *Les Aspects Juridiques de la Crise et de la Guerre du Golfe* (Paris: Montchrestien, 1991) 67.

[94] In contrast to SC Res 665 (1990), SC Res 678 (1990) was more significant since it conduced the legal metamorphosis of the *jus ad bellum* to the contours of the armed conflict.

[95] Soons, 213.

[96] See in general L Silber and A Little, *Yugoslavia: Death of a Nation* (London: Penguin, 1997).

suspect vessels was provided by SC Resolution 787 (16 November 1992), which aimed at further tightening the economic sanctions and preventing the infringements of the trade embargo established by Security Council Resolutions 713 (1991) and Security Council 757 (1992).[97] Paragraph 12 reiterated verbatim the phrase used in 665, with the sole difference that it called upon 'States acting nationally or through regional agencies or arrangements' and not upon a coalition of states cooperating with one party of the conflict. Pursuant to Resolution 787 (1992), the naval forces of NATO and Western European Union present in the Adriatic were authorised to intercept merchant vessels, board them in order to verify the cargo and divert them or take them into custody for inspection to a neighbouring port.[98]

On 17 April 1993, Security Council adopted Resolution 820, which tightened further the economic isolation of the Federal Republic of Yugoslavia (FRY) and provided inter alia for the seizure, detention and confiscation of vessels violating the embargoes. It reaffirmed the authority of states acting under paragraph 12 of Resolution 787 (1992) and very interestingly, in stark contrast to Resolution 665, it explicitly permitted the maritime forces there to enforce the embargo in the territorial waters of Serbia and Montenegro.[99] Pursuant to Resolution 820, Operation Sharp Guard began in June 1993 with the view to preventing all unauthorised shipping from entering the territorial waters of FRY.[100]

The permission to enter the territorial waters of FRY and interdict foreign shipping was not the sole difference with the case of Iraq;[101] more importantly, the states involved were not officially parties to the armed conflict and thus they were not entitled to the belligerent right of visit and search. The legal basis for the maritime interdiction and for the blockade that they were called upon to enforce lay exclusively with the relevant SC Resolutions.[102] This is also reflected by the fact that the entities authorised

[97] See detailed discussion of these Resolutions in Fielding, above n 25, 228. It is reported that by November 1992, NATO and WEU forces, deployed in the Adriatic, had followed the movement of some 3,469 ships of which 71 were suspected of violating the UN embargo; see UN Doc S/24847, 25 November 1992.

[98] See Politakis, 549.

[99] See para 29 of SC Res 820 (1993). Before the adoption of this resolution, this was not allowed and enforcement of the arms embargo in the territorial sea of Slovenia and Croatia remained permissible only with the consent of the coastal states; see comments in Soons, 219.

[100] From 22 November 1992 to 15 June 1993, over 12,000 ships had been challenged, of which 803 were stopped and 176 diverted for cargo inspection; among these nine violations were detected; see J Kriendler, 'NATO's Changing Role-Opportunities and Constraints for Peacekeeping' 41 *NATO Review* (1993) 19.

[101] It is not the purpose of this enquiry to address the international legal issues raised by interdiction of vessels in the territorial waters of the FRY; see, however, the interesting treatment of SC Res 820 in R McLaughlin, 'UN Mandated Naval Interdiction Operations in the Territorial Sea?' 51 *ICLQ* (2002) 249, 264.

[102] In accord is Soons, writing that 'in these cases, there was no situation of armed conflict between the enforcing States and the target State and there was no alternative for article 41 as the basis for these resolutions'; Soons, 220.

to enforce the UN sanctions against FRY were all Member States 'acting nationally or through regional agencies or arrangements', such as NATO and WEU, and not only the Coalition states, as in the case of Iraq.[103]

v. Haiti

The maritime interception in the Haitian constitutional crisis was unlike both the Iraqi and Yugoslavian cases.[104] In Haiti, there was no armed conflict, and thus no right of interception could have been based on the laws of naval warfare. By Resolution 841 (1993), Resolution 861 (1993) and Resolution 873 (1993), the Security Council, acting under Chapter VII, imposed, lifted and reimposed respectively a selective oil and arms embargo against Haiti, while Resolution 875 (1993) called upon Member States to 'halt inward maritime shipping as necessary in order to inspect and verify their cargoes and destinations'. Similar authorisation was given by para 10 of Resolution 917 (6 May 1994), which set up a total trade embargo and prohibited all maritime traffic from entering or leaving the territory or territorial sea of Haiti with some exceptions (para 9). As in the case of Yugoslavia, all Member States, 'acting nationally or through regional arrangements' were called upon to proceed to interdiction operations, which were to took place on the high seas. However, US vessels also operated within the territorial sea of Haiti with the permission of the legitimate government of Haiti.[105]

vi. Sierra Leone

The conflict in Sierra Leone (1997) resembles prima facie the case of Haiti, in the sense of being another episode of forcible action to restore a democratically elected government. Nevertheless, this is not accurate, as far as the present analysis is concerned, since, in stark contrast to the case of Haiti, the maritime embargo and the interdiction operations had started months before the adoption of the relevant SC Resolution 1132 (1997).[106] In more detail, from the time of the coup, in May 1997, ECOMOG forces had imposed a de facto embargo on Sierra Leone through interception of ships and aircrafts. This was formalised in the June meeting of ECOWAS[107] but

---

[103] *cf* the different wording of SC Res 665.

[104] On the Haitian crisis see Y Daudet (ed), *La Crise d'Haïti* (Paris: Montchrestien, 1996) and R Falk, 'The Haiti Intervention', 36 *Harvard ILJ* (1995) 58.

[105] See Soons, 220.

[106] In short, the government in Sierra Leone that had been elected under UN supervision after a prolonged civil war was overthrown by a coup in May 1997. Nigeria, acting in the name of ECOWAS, used force to restore the legitimate government. The basis for the legality of ECOWAS was the express consent of the democratically elected President both before and after the coup in May 1997. The presence of ECOMOG was legitimised *a posteriori* by the Conakry Peace Agreement in October 1997; see Gray, 414.

[107] See Decision of the ECOWAS of 29 August 1997, UN Doc S/1997/695, 8.9.1997 Annex II.

it was not until October 1997 that ECOWAS sought Security Council support for its efforts. On 8 October 1997, the Security Council passed Resolution 1132 and, acting under Chapters VII and VIII, authorised ECOWAS to ensure the strict implementation of an oil and arms embargo on Sierra Leone by halting inward shipping. The authorisation was not to UN Member States acting nationally or through regional agencies or arrangements, but only to ECOWAS itself.[108] 'The language of Resolution 1132 was cautious and it did not amount to an authorisation for enforcement action apart from that needed to implement the sanctions. However, the reference to ECOWAS could be taken as endorsement of Nigeria's claim to be acting through regional organization and not unilaterally.'[109]

It is patent from the face of the Resolution that its purpose was both *ex post facto* to approve and *ex nunc* to authorise the embargo and the enforcement measures already in place. Hence, a similar distinction, as in the case of Iraq, should be made between the interception measures before the adoption of SC Resolution 1132 and the conclusion of the Peace Treaty and the measures after its adoption on 8 October 1997. Accordingly, it should be maintained, firstly, that the interception measures *ante* SC Resolution 1132 were based on the belligerent right of visit and search accruing from the armed conflict between ECOMOG forces and Sierra Leone, under its new Government. Secondly, the adoption of SC Res. 1132 altered, arguably, the *jus ad bellum* justification of the ECOMOG Operation and qualified the *jus in bello* right of visit.[110] Lastly, when the belligerency officially ceased with the Peace Agreement a few days later, all the subsequent interception measures were based on the authority of SC Resolution 1132.[111]

This Resolution deviated from the standard construction of the archetypal Resolution 665 not only in respect of the entity to enforce the interception operation, namely ECOWAS and not the Member States, but also with the reference to applicable international standards rather than to commensurate measures. According to Soons, two interpretations are possible here: 'One is that the applicable international standards include the same measures that have become international standards through the practice of implementing the previous Security Council resolutions on maritime enforcement of embargoes. Another interpretation would be that this phrase was intended to exclude measures of coercion against foreign ships'.[112] In the light of the foregoing analysis, it is submitted that the

---

[108] UN Member States could only provide technical and logistical support to ECOWAS to carry out these responsibilities.

[109] Gray, 413.

[110] It is beyond the compass of the present enquiry to discuss the basis of the initial intervention of Nigeria and ECOMOG, which most probably was founded on the controversial right of intervention upon invitation by the legitimate government and on the right of self-defence.

[111] For the next stages of the Sierra Leone conflict, see Gray, 416.

[112] Soons, 218.

reference to 'applicable international standards' includes both the *acquis* of previous maritime enforcement operations and the measures already adopted by ECOMOG forces against Sierra Leone.

vii. Lebanon

In addition, a passing mention should be made to the atypical situation of the Lebanese crisis, in 2006.[113] Following the clashes between Israeli forces and Hezbollah armed groups in the territory of Lebanon in July 2006, the Security Council passed Resolution 1701, on 11 August 2006, under Chapter VII, and imposed an embargo on arms destined for Hezbollah forces as well as enhancing the UN Interim Force in Lebanon (UNIFIL) in numbers, equipment, mandate and scope of operations.[114] More pertinently, in paragraph 12, it called upon 'the Government of Lebanon to secure its borders . . . and to prevent the entry in Lebanon without its consent of arms or related material'. In accordance with this paragraph, the Prime Minister of Lebanon requested in September 2006 the UN Secretary-General to provide a naval task force that would help prevent the unauthorised entry of arms or related material by sea into Lebanon.[115] Such a naval force was deployed shortly after this request and assisted the Lebanese forces in boardings and searches of vessels within the six-mile territorial sea of Lebanon.

It is readily apparent that the legal basis for the deployment of this multinational force and for the right of visit of vessels in the territorial waters of Lebanon lay with the consent of the latter state and not with the relevant Security Council Resolution. It can further be questioned whether the legal basis for the interference with the right of innocent passage of the foreign vessels in the Lebanese territorial waters was laid in para 14 of the SC Res 1701 or was premised on the coastal state authority to suspend passage which is not 'innocent' per se (see art 25 of LOSC). It is submitted that both arguments reinforce each other, in the sense that the Resolution called upon Lebanon to enforce its already existing right to control vessels engaged in a non-innocent passage in its territorial waters, such as is the carrying of arms to Hezbollah. In practice, however, 'the scope of UNIFIL's authority has not been a matter of practical challenge; the vessels whose identity the Maritime Task Force has checked and confirmed, have complied with orders diverting them to Lebanese ports'.[116]

---

[113] See N Ronzitti, 'The 2006 Conflict in Lebanon and International Law' 16 *Italian Yearbook of International Law* (2007) 3; MN Schmitt, 'Change Direction 2006: Israeli Operations in Lebanon and the International Law of Self-Defence' 29 *Michigan Journal of International Law* (2008) 127.

[114] See in particular paras 11 and 12 of SC Res 170, UN Doc S/RES/1701 (11 Aug 2006).

[115] See Letter of PM Fouad Siniora to the UN Secretary-General, dated 6 September 2006 (on file with the author).

[116] U Häussler, Crisis Response Operations in Maritime Environments', in M Odello and R Piotrowicz (eds), *International Military Missions and International Law* (Leiden: Martinus Nijhoff, 2012) 161, 178.

Lebanon was also primarily responsible for any inspection of the vessels therein and thus responsible for any violation of international law in the course of the operations.[117] Notwithstanding the perplexity of the legal status of the conflict as such, it is argued that the states involved had the belligerent right of visit and search both in their territorial waters and on the high seas as well as the right to establish a blockade in the region. A naval blockade was actually enforced by Israel in the first days of the war,[118] and this characterisation could have equally been ascribed to the above-mentioned 'blockade' by Lebanon and the international naval force, had the armed hostilities continued long after the ceasefire on 14 August, 2006. On that date, the belligerent right to blockade ceased to exist and thus the legality of the presence of such forces could be based solely on the consent of the coastal state.

viii. Libya

Finally, the most recent conflict in which an authorisation to inspect vessels on the high seas was conferred upon states by the UN Security Council, was in Libya. As is well-known, on 26 February 2011 the UN Security Council adopted Resolution 1970, which imposed a series of sanctions upon Colonel Gaddafi's regime pursuant to article 41 of the UN Charter, including an arms embargo.[119] In view of the rapid escalation of the internal armed conflict in Libya, the Security Council very soon adopted another Resolution, namely Resolution 1973 (2011), which authorised Member States inter alia to use all necessary means to 'protect civilians and civilian populated areas under threat of attack in the Libyan Arab Jamahiriya, including Benghazi' (para 4) and 'to enforce compliance with the ban on flights' (para 8) imposed in the airspace of Libya in order to help protect civilians.[120] SC Resolution 1973 afforded the necessary legal basis for NATO's Operation 'Unified Protector', which resulted to the overthrowing of Gaddafi's regime and the official end of war on 23 October 2011.[121]

As regards the enforcement of these Resolutions in the marine context, it must be noted that while SC Resolution 1970 failed to provide for any

---

[117] In the decision taken by the Council of Ministers of Lebanon on 4 September 2006, it was set forth, inter alia, that 'Inspection and towing will be under the supervision of the LAF and in coordination with UNIFIL command'; see above n 102.

[118] See MN Schmitt, above n 114, 128.

[119] See S/RES/1970 (2011), paras 9–11.

[120] See S/RES/1973, adopted 17 March 2011. On SC Resolution 1973 and the operation in Libya see C Antonopoulos, '"The Legitimacy to Legitimise": The Security Action in Libya under Resolutuion 1973 (2011)' 14 *International Community Law Review* (2012) 35–79.

[121] On NATO's Operation see www.nato.int/cps/en/natolive/71679.htm. On various international legal questions arising out of the Operation and the armed conflict in Libya, including the death of Muammar Gaddafi and the killing of civilians, see the various contributions to www.ejiltalk.org/tag/libya/.

inspection regime on the high seas,[122] SC Resolution 1973, besides the aforesaid authorisations, determined 'that paragraph 11 of resolution 1970 (2011) shall be replaced by the following paragraph:

> Calls upon all Member States, in particular States of the region, acting nationally or through regional organisations or arrangements, in order to ensure strict implementation of the arms embargo established by paragraphs 9 and 10 of resolution 1970 (2011), to inspect in their territory, including seaports and airports, and on the high seas, vessels and aircraft bound to or from the Libyan Arab Jamahiriya, if the State concerned has information that provides reasonable grounds to believe that the cargo contains items the supply, sale, transfer or export of which is prohibited by paragraphs 9 or 10 of resolution 1970 (2011) as modified by this resolution, including the provision of armed mercenary personnel, calls upon all flag States of such vessels and aircraft to cooperate with such inspections and *authorises Member States to use all measures commensurate to the specific circumstances to carry out such inspections.*

The case of Libya is quite different from the previous cases of maritime enforcement of SC Resolutions, as the authorisation for inspections on the high seas was granted, for the first time, simultaneously with the general authorisation to use force to protect civilians. In all other cases of maritime enforcement of SC Resolutions, the relevant authorisation was given either prior to the general authorisation to use force (*cf* Resolutions 665/1990 and 678/1990) or independently and not to Member States directly but to regional organisations or international arrangements (*cf* Resolutions 917/1994 or 1132/1997). Instead, in the case of Libya, the Council preferred to include both the authorisation for a limited military intervention against Libya and the authorisation for maritime enforcement of the already imposed arms embargo in the same Resolution. Needless to say that, in terms of the law of naval warfare, there was no need for such authorisation, since from the moment that Operation Unified Protector commenced, the belligerent right of visit came into play. However, SC Resolution 1973 served as the legal basis for the military intervention in the ongoing conflict in Libya and at the same time qualified the *jus in bello* right of visit.

C. Unilateral Enforcement of UN Security Council Resolutions

The final, yet very subtle, question to be addressed with regard to the enforcement of UN Security Council Resolution is whether the absence of an explicit authorisation to 'halt inward maritime shipping' in a Resolution,

---

[122] In para 11, the Council called upon 'all States, in particular States neighbouring the Libyan Arab Jamahiriya, to inspect, in accordance with their national authorities and legislation *and consistent with international law, in particular the law of the sea* and relevant international civil aviation agreements, all cargo to and from the Libyan Arab Jamahiriya, in their territory, including seaports and airports' (emphasis added).

which establishes an embargo against a state, prohibits the unilateral adoption of enforcement measures on the high seas. This question is of considerable import, since the Security Council has in numerous cases imposed embargoes without, however, 'giving teeth' to the Member States to forcefully implement them against recalcitrant flag states.[123] To furnish an example, in the case of Somalia, SC Resolution 733 (1992) and more recently Resolution 1844 (2008) called upon all states to take all necessary measures to ensure the strict application of the arms embargo against Somalia but did not refer explicitly to halting maritime trafficking.[124] Similarly, there are recent Security Council Resolutions concerning the nuclear proliferation activities of North Korea and Iran, which imposed a selective embargo against nuclear or other relevant materials, albeit they steered clear from authorising *expressis verbis* maritime interdictions.[125]

Opposing views have been put forward with regard to the legality of the adoption of such unilateral interdiction measures. In relation to Somalia, one commentator asserted that 'If a State complies with this obligation by controlling the sea and air traffic to Somalia, it is allowed to stop and search any vessel or aircraft that it is reasonably suspected of being engaged in the transport of arms etc. because only by such control can a "general" embargo be effectively implemented.'[126] Others have raised a more cautious voice in this regard and have contended that 'the practice of adopting specific authorisations, in combination with the persistent abstention of member States to enforce mandatory embargoes against foreign ships at sea where the Security Council has not adopted specific authorisations . . . could lead to the conclusion that enforcement actions against foreign ships at sea, without the consent of the flag State, are only allowed with explicit Security Council authorisation'.[127] However, according to the same author, it would be very difficult for the Security Council

---

[123] See in general K Zou, 'Maritime Enforcement of United Nations Security Council Resolutions: Use of Force and Coercive Measures' 26 *IJMCL* (2011) 235

[124] In January 1992 the Security Council passed Res 733 imposing an embargo on all deliveries of weapons and military equipment to Somalia. Since then, there have been numerous Resolutions on Somalia, elaborating and amending the arms embargo, including SC Resolutions 1356 (2001), 1425 (2002), 1725 (2006), 1744 (2007), 1844 (2008) and most recently 1853 (2008) and 1863 (2009).

[125] On North Korea see SC Resolutions 1695 (2006), 1718 (2006) and 1874 (2009) and also A Paulus and J Müller, 'Security Council Resolution 1718 on North Korea's Nuclear Test', ASIL Insights (3 Nov 2006); available at www.asil.org/insights061103.cfm. On Iran see inter alia SC Resolutions 1696 (2006), 1737 (2006), 1747 (2007), 1803 (2008) and 1929 (2010).

[126] W Heinegg, 'The United Nations Convention on the Law of the Sea and Maritime Security Operations' 48 *GYIL* (2006) 151, 155. See also ibid, 'The Legality of Maritime Interception/Interdiction Operations within the Framework of Operation Enduring Freedom' 79 *International Law Studies* (2003) 255, 263.

[127] Soons, 214. He reports with regard to Somalia that 'when in February 1993 the Greek vessel *Bana I* with a cargo of arms destined for Somalia, approached the area, the American authorities, when they became aware of the voyage, did not intervene but requested the assistance of the flag State and the port State'; Soons 214 (fn 32). See also per this view: Becker, 218 and Klein, *Maritime Security*, 278.

to disapprove an ad hoc or incidental interdiction of a foreign vessel on the high seas, which is violating the embargo, if there is no time to ask the permission of the flag state, or the latter declines it.[128]

There seem to be sound reasons for concluding that such unilateral enforcement would be contrary to the normative and interpretative framework of Security Council Resolutions.[129] First, it is asserted that, in general, SC Resolutions under Chapter VII should be construed *stricto sensu* and any unilateral action involving the use or threat of force should not lightly be presumed.[130] More importantly, to interpret the relevant Resolution as allowing the Member States to take interdiction measures without any explicit authorisation would run counter to the text of the Resolution itself, as well as not finding any warrant in the common practices of the Council. In addition, an important presumption in the hermeneutics of Security Council Resolutions is the use of certain phrases or formulas which reflect the collective will and the shared understandings of the interpretive community of the Council.[131] Such is the formula used in Resolution 665 (1990), which has, almost ritually, been reiterated in all the other cases of maritime enforcement operations. Hence, it is reasonable to infer from its absence in the Resolution in question that the Council had no intention to authorise such operations. This becomes even more evident when in the same Resolution the Council positively requests the Member States to take the necessary measures only vis-à-vis their flag vessels and not vis-à-vis the vessels of third states.[132]

To provide a pertinent example, in a recent Resolution on Iran, the Council expressly

> called upon all States, in accordance with their national legal authorities and legislation and *consistent with international law, in particular the law of the sea* . . . to inspect the cargoes to and from Iran, of aircraft and vessels, at their *airports and seaports,* owned or operated by Iran Air Cargo and provided that there are reasonable grounds to believe that the aircraft or vessel is transporting goods prohibited under this resolution or resolution 1737 (2006) and 1747 (2007).[133]

A contrario argumentum, vessels on the high seas which are not owned by the Islamic Republic of Iran Shipping Line are exempt from any interception measure pursuant to this Resolution. More importantly, the Council emphasises that all the inspection measures should be consistent

---

[128] See Soons, 215.

[129] On the interpretation of Security Council Resolutions see M Wood, 'The Interpretation of Security Council Resolutions', 2 *Max Planck YBIL* (1998) 73 and E Papastavridis, 'Interpretation of Security Council Resolutions under Chapter VII in the Aftermath of the Iraqi Crisis' 56 *ICLQ* (2007) 83.

[130] See in this respect Papastavridis, ibid, 107

[131] See ibid, 101.

[132] *cf* eg para 15 of SC Res 1701 (2006) that 'all States shall take the necessary measures to prevent, by their nationals or from their territories or using their flag vessels'.

[133] See UN SC Res 1803 (2008); para 11 (emphasis added).

with the law of the sea, ie, amongst others, the freedom of the high seas. It is true that by virtue of article 103 of the UN Charter, a Security Council Resolution could trump this freedom, if the Resolution in question grants the relevant authorisation to Member States or international organisations to interfere with foreign shipping on the high seas. Absent such authorisation, the latter interference is beyond the scope of application of Article 103 and, hence, the Member States would be permitted to suspend their trade relationships with the target state pursuant to the relevant Resolution. However, they would not be permitted to suspend the freedom of navigation on the high seas enjoyed by the latter state and, of course, by third states, without incurring international responsibility.[134]

This notwithstanding, there have been reports of two incidents of interdiction on the high seas of foreign vessels without the explicit consent of the flag states, which were shipping arms in violation of SC Resolution 1747 (2007).[135] In more detail, first there was the case of *Hansa India*, flying the German flag, attempting to transport arms from Iran to Hezbollah in Lebanon. On 3 October 2009, the US proceeded to intercept the vessel with the consent of its master and without the formal permission of Germany, which was however informed through the US Embassy in Berlin. After discussions the ship was permitted to continue its voyage to Malta, where some of the cargo was confiscated. It eventually ended up in Germany, for investigation by the German police and customs. At no stage did Germany protest about the boarding on the high seas.

The second case concerned the *Francop*, a ship owned by a Germany company but flying the flag of Antigua and Barbuda, which was interdicted by the Israeli Navy and brought to Israel before reaching Cyprus. The cargo of the ship consisted of 300 tons of armaments, which 'apparently had their origin in Iran'.[136] They were loaded in Egypt with final destination the Hezbollah in Syria. Neither Germany nor Antigua and Barbuda protested.

In commenting on these two cases, J. Frowein asserts that apparently the shipments were in violation of SC Resolutions 1747 (2007) and thus the confiscation of the cargo was in accordance with international law;[137] the legal basis for the interdiction as such on the part of the US and Israel was either the acquiescence of the flag states, Germany and Antigua and

---

[134] *cf* the opinion of Gowlland-Debbas, who stresses that the authorisations of Security Council serve a very important function, ensuring, inter alia, that states would not thereby incur international responsibility, operating thus a 'circumstance precluding wrongfulness' in the context of the law of state responsibility; ibid, 'The Limits of Unilateral Enforcement of Community Objectives in the Framework of UN Peace Maintenance' 11 *EJIL* (2000) 361, 370. *Cf* art 59 of ILC Articles.

[135] See the discussion of the cases and further relevant references in J Frowein, 'The Security Council and the Security on the Seas', in H Hestermeyer et al (eds), *Law of the Sea in Dialogue* (Berlin: Springer, 2011) 179.

[136] ibid, 188.

[137] ibid, 186.

Barbuda respectively, or the right of self-defence.[138] With regard to the latter point, it is highly unlikely whether Israel has the individual or the US the collective right of self-defence against Hezbollah; in respect of the argument of acquiescence, it cannot serve as the legal basis proper, since under the law of state responsibility, 'acquiescence' is tantamount to the loss of the right of the injured state to invoke the responsibility.[139] In the present case, the lack of protestation by Germany or Antigua and Barbuda entailed the loss of their right to invoke the responsibility of the US and Israel respectively, which had arisen from the unlawful interdiction of the vessels concerned. In conclusion, the interdiction of these vessels was beyond the bounds of international law, whereas the subsequent confiscation of the cargoes seems to have been in accord with the relevant SC Resolution. In any event, it is important to stress that no one claimed the right to unilaterally enforce the SC Resolution 1747 (2007).

Thus, it follows that UN Member States have no authority to interdict foreign vessels on the high seas in order to enforce a UN embargo, without the explicit authorisation of the Council. As long as the latter remains seized of the matter, Member States are obliged to refer to the Council any possible infraction of the embargo and the Council will be entitled to authorise a general interdiction operation, such as in the case of Resolution 665 (1990) or more ad hoc and targeted measures, such as in Resolution 221 (1966). As regards the type of situation described by Soons, of an isolated and incidental visit of a vessel on the high seas, the pertinent justification, if any, should be sought in other legal frameworks, such as the circumstances precluding wrongfulness in the law of state responsibility, and not to the framework of the UN Charter.

Finally, special mention should be made to Resolution 1874 (2009) on North Korea, which very subtly postulates another way of controlling illegitimate cargoes from and to the latter state.[140] First, in paragraph 12, the Council calls upon all 'Member States to inspect vessels, with the *consent of the flag State*, on the high seas, if they have information that provides reasonable grounds to believe that the cargo of such vessels contains [proscribed] items'.[141] More importantly, in the next paragraph, the Council affirms that 'if the flag State does not consent to inspection on the high seas, *the flag State shall direct the vessel to proceed to an appropriate and convenient port for the required inspection* by the local authorities pursuant to paragraph 11'.[142]

The former paragraph sets forth the already existing right under general international law of the flag state consent to the right of visit and thus

---

[138] ibid, 188.
[139] See art 45(2) of ILC Articles and ILC Articles Commentary, 122.
[140] SC Res 1874 (12 June 2009) S/RES/1874 (2009).
[141] ibid, para 12 (emphasis added).
[142] ibid, para 13 (emphasis added).

does not hold any special legal merit; however, the latter paragraph is exceptional, in the sense that even though it falls short of authorising the high seas inspection, it attempts to attain the same result in case of suspect vessels on the high seas by providing for a compulsory port state control by the UN Member States. The flag state is obliged either to assent to the interdiction and inspection of the suspect vessel or to direct the latter to a Member State's port, where the required inspection will proceed under the legal authority of port state jurisdiction as well as of paragraph 11 of Resolution 1874.[143] Thus, the purpose of interdicting proscribed cargoes from and to North Korea is served either directly, on the high seas, with the consent of the flag state, or indirectly, in the port of a third state, regardless of the former state's consent. This is the first time that the Security Council has employed such a formula; as N Klein observes, 'The action authorized by the Security Council against North Korea deviates from earlier practice in that the grant of power to conduct interdictions is moderated by the requirement of flag State consent in the first instance and then allowing the flag State some say in where and by whom an inspection should occur.'[144]

However, this kind of inspection regime was not followed in the subsequent Resolutions concerning either Iran or North Korea. In SC Resolution 1929 (2010) concerning the situation in Iran, the Council sets out that

> States, consistent with international law, in particular the law of the sea, *may request inspections of vessels on the high seas with the consent of the flag State,* and calls upon all States to cooperate in such inspections if there is information that provides reasonable grounds to believe the vessel is carrying items the supply, sale, transfer, or export of which is prohibited by . . . for the purpose of ensuring strict implementation of those provisions.[145]

Evident from the face of the Resolution is that there is no additional obligation on the flag states to divert the vessels to ports in order for an inspection to take place.

III. CONCLUSIONS

These remarks with regard to the question of unilateral enforcement of SC Resolutions concludes the discussion of the right of visit of foreign vessels

---

[143] ibid, para 11 'calls upon all States to inspect, in accordance with their national authorities and legislation, and consistent with international law, all cargo to and from the DPRK, in their territory, including seaports and airports, if the State concerned has information that provides reasonable grounds to believe the cargo contains items'.

[144] Klein, *Maritime Security,* 279. See also R Beckman and T Davenport, 'Maritime Terrorism and the Law of the Sea', in M Nordquist et al (eds), *The Law of the Sea Convention: US Accession and Globalization* (Leiden: Martinus Nijhoff, 2012) 229, 249.

[145] UN SC Res 1929, adopted on 9 June 2010, para 15 (emphasis added).

on the high seas in cases either of armed conflict or of activation of the collective security mechanism of the Charter. The purpose of this section was
to analyse the multifaceted interception operations undertaken in the context of armed conflicts, whether or not the Council has been involved. It
demonstrated that the belligerent right of visit and search retains its relevance in the contemporary law of armed conflict and provides in many
instances the more arguable justification for such interceptions on the
high seas. Equally, the legal basis for these interceptions can be found in
the text of a Security Council Resolution under Chapter VII, which would
authorise the Member States or an international organisation to enforce
an embargo by 'halting all inward shipping' to the sanctioned state. As
the foregoing survey showed, however, the authorisation to use force to
enforce a maritime embargo should not be lightly presumed and it should
always be explicitly granted by the Council. In any case, the relevant
authorisation should be in accordance with the legal framework of the
Charter and in conformity with general international law.[146]

---

[146] See on the consequences of 'unlawful' SC Resolutions the excellent treatise by A
Tzanakopoulos, *Disobeying Security Council: Countermeasures against Wrongful Sanctions*
(Oxford: Oxford University Press, 2011).

5

Contemporary Challenges to International Peace and Security: International Terrorism and the Proliferation of Weapons of Mass Destruction

I. INTRODUCTION

B Y WAY OF preface, let us have regard to certain incidents concerning terrorist acts and WMD at sea that have occurred in the twenty-first century.[1] First, on 30 October 2001, the Liberation Tigers of Tamil Eelam claimed responsibility for suicide bombers destroying the oil tanker *Silk Pride,* 12 nautical miles north of Point Pedro off Sri Lanka.[2] Just under a year later, on 6 October 2002, a kamikaze speedboat attacked the French supertanker *Limburg* near the port of Al Mukalla, Yemen.[3] The collision resulted in a massive explosion and fire, killing the speedboat crew and one member of the *Limburg's* crew. A terrorist organisation linked to Al Qaeda claimed responsibility for the incident.[4]

Two months later, the most celebrated episode occurred: on 10 December 2002, Spanish naval forces patrolling the Arabian Sea were alerted by US intelligence to the presence of a suspicious cargo vessel in the Indian Ocean en route from North Korea. While the suspect vessel, which displayed no flag, had initially undertaken evasive manoeuvres, Spanish forces succeeded in intercepting and boarding the vessel 600 miles from the coast of Yemen. Upon searching the vessel, the inspecting team discovered a cache

[1] For a comprehensive chronology of recent interdiction of WMD material, either by coastal states or on the high seas, see Jimenez-Kwast, 223. See also generally on this topic R Beckman and T Davenport, 'Maritime Terrorism and the Law of the Sea', in M Nordquist et al (eds), *The Law of the Sea Convention: US Accession and Globalization* (Leiden: Martinus Nijhoff, 2012) 229–57.

[2] The incident is reported in A Syrigos, 'Developments on the Interdiction of Vessels on the High Seas', in Strati A, Gavouneli M, Skourtos N (eds), *Unresolved Issues and New Challenges to the Law of the Sea* (Antwerp: Martinus Nijhoff, 2006) 149, 182.

[3] See 'Bomb Blast Fallout Starts To Hit Yemen', *Lloyd's List Int'l,* 17 Oct 2002, 7.

[4] See A Marcopoulos, 'Flags of Terror: An Argument for Rethinking Maritime Security Policy Regarding Flags of Convenience', 32 *Tulane Maritime Law Journal* (2007) 277, 292.

of 15 Scud missiles, although only a cargo of cement was listed on the ship's manifest. Because the vessel, which was later determined to be registered in Cambodia as the *So San*, was not flying any flag, the Spanish authorities had acted lawfully under the LOSC in boarding the ship. On the next day, however, the vessel was released with its cargo and was allowed to continue to Yemen. The US acknowledged the lack of authority for seizing the missiles, since the sale between North Korea and Yemen, as well as the transport of ballistic missiles by sea, was not prohibited under any international instrument.[5] As Byers observes, 'Stopping and searching the *So San* was probably legal . . . but seizing the cargo from a properly registered vessel was an entirely different matter.'[6]

This incident was instructive for another interception under the PSI, that of the *BBC China*, a German-owned vessel (flagged in Antigua and Barbuda) that the UK and the US suspected was carrying uranium centrifuge parts to Libya. In early October 2003, the German government ordered the owner to dock at the Italian port of Taranto, where centrifuge parts were removed by Italian customs before permitting the ship to continue. Some suggest that the *BBC China* interdiction contributed to Libya's decision in late 2003 to abandon its WMD programme.[7] On 27 February 2004, an explosive device was detonated on the Philippine *Superferry 14*, killing over 100 passengers and sinking the ferry. Abu Sayyaf, a known terrorist group, claimed responsibility for the attack.[8]

This admittedly non-comprehensive account of recent incidents highlights the potential threats to international peace and security posed by the asymmetrical dangers of terrorism and WMD. The protection of international shipping from such threats has attained great prominence, given that it is commonly estimated that over 90 per cent of the world's goods are transported by sea. An attack that successfully closed a mega-port or vital waterway would likely cause major economic disruption around the world. As a result, states have generally recognised that there is a shared interest in addressing such threats.[9]

The focus of the present chapter will be on these threats to international peace and security, and the series of maritime interdiction measures which they have engendered. These two closely linked issues will be assessed

---

[5] See F Kirgis, 'Boarding of North Korean Vessel on the High Seas', ASIL Insights, www.asil.org/insights/insigh94.htm and A Nascimento, 'El Episodio del So Sane' 55 *Revista Española de Derecho Internacional* (2003) 267. See also the detailed legal assessment in D Guilfoyle, 'The PSI: Interdicting Vessels in International Waters to Prevent the Spread of WMD?' 29 *Melbourne University Law Review* (2005) 733, 735.

[6] M Byers, 'Policing the High Seas: The PSI' 98 *AJIL* (2004) 526 (hereinafter: Byers).

[7] See D Guilfoyle, above n 5, 739 and Allen, 67.

[8] See A Marcopoulos, 'Flags of Terror: An Argument for Rethinking Maritime Security Policy Regarding Flags of Convenience' 32 *Tulane Maritime Law Journal* (2007) 277, 292 and J Bradford, 'The Growing Prospects for Maritime Security Cooperation in Southeast Asia' 58 *Naval War College Review* (2005) 63, 67.

[9] See also Klein, *Maritime Security*, 151.

against the background of the initiatives taken by international organisations, namely the UN, NATO and IMO, and by states collectively as well as individually. In this regard, a series of possible legal justifications for the exercise of the right of visit will be scrutinised, such as multilateral and bilateral agreements, as well as customary rules of international law. Finally, there will be a short reference to certain legal restrictions of the right of visit in this regard, as under the question of enforcement jurisdiction.

Having said this, it should be clarified from the outset that it is not the purpose of the present enquiry either to address comprehensively all the questions raised by terrorism and WMD, or to normatively equate them. Rather, the purpose is to analyse both problems of international terrorism and proliferation of WMD through the prism of the international legal order of the oceans, ie to pinpoint the available legal bases for such visits on the high seas as well as to substantiate that even if these issues are widely perceived as novel, *ergo* in need of new rules, the *corpus juris gentium* provides the requisite normative framework. This follows from the basic premise of the present theory that even if these threats appear to be new, the nature of the claims or the pertinent legal solutions is not.

II. THE CHALLENGES OF TERRORISM AND WMD PROLIFERATION

It is a truism that a definition of terrorism generally accepted by governments and legal scholars has proven difficult, if not impossible.[10] However, very recently, the Appeals Chamber of the Special Tribunal for Lebanon declared that the 'customary international law definition of terrorism' consists of the following three key elements: (i) the perpetration of a criminal act (such as murder, kidnapping, hostage-taking, arson, and so on), or threatening such an act; (ii) the intent to spread fear among the population (which would generally entail the creation of public danger) or directly or indirectly coerce a national or international authority to take some action, or to refrain from taking it; (iii) when the act involves a transnational element.[11]

Not surprisingly, the holding by the Tribunal that these elements are part of customary law has been already criticised.[12] Nevertheless, there is

---

[10] See H Neuhold, 'Post-Cold War Terrorism: Systemic Background, Phenomenology and Definitions', in *New Threats to International Peace and Security* (2004) 13, 18. On the controversial issue of the definition of terrorism, see B Saul, *Defining Terrorism in International Law* (Oxford: Oxford University Press, 2006).

[11] See Interlocutory Decision on the Applicable Law: Terrorism, Conspiracy, Homicide, Perpetration, Cumulative Charging, Case No STL-11-01/I (16 Feb 2011), para 147; *available at* www.stl.org/x/file/TheRegistry/Library/CaseFiles/chambers/20110216_STL-1101_R176bis_F0010_AC_Interlocutory_Decision_Filed_EN.pdf.

[12] See eg MP Scharf, 'Special Tribunal for Lebanon Issues Landmark Ruling on Definition of Terrorism and Modes of Participation', *ASIL Insights* (4 March 2011); available at www.asil.org/insights110304.cfm.

no doubt that there is a general consensus on its essence, namely that terrorism should be understood as the unlawful use or threat of physical violence, which is committed 'to intimidate a population, or to compel a Government or an international organization to do or to abstain from doing any act'.[13]

Until the seminal date of 9/11, the international community followed a pragmatic, sectoral approach in combating transboundary terrorism.[14] Conventions on specific forms and aspects of terrorism were concluded which required no general definition.[15] The key element of the mechanism provided in these conventions was the principle *aut dedere aut judicare*, which obliged the state where the offender took refuge either to extradite him to another state that had established its jurisdiction, or to submit the case immediately to its competent authorities for the purpose of prosecution.[16]

In the aftermath of 9/11, all the relevant conventions and declarations seem to have adopted the teleological approach of the definition in the 1999 Terrorism Financing Convention, namely the serious intimidation of a population and compelling a government or international organisation to perform or abstain from performing an act.[17] Another ramification of 9/11 is that the approach to the phenomenon of terrorism became more multi-faceted: from the traditional repression by criminal law, to the combating of the financing of terrorism and the use of force against non-state actors involved in terrorist acts.[18] Also, the protagonists increased; today not only are more states involved, but also numerous international organisations and more importantly the UN Security Council within the framework of Chapter VII.[19] With respect to 'maritime terrorism' in particular, it is evident that there is no broadly accepted definition of the term; the only pertinent treaties, which, however, does not contain any specific definition is the SUA Convention and its 2005 Protocol. They rather adhere to the sectoral pattern, while the latter Protocol includes the teleological approach of the Terrorism Financing Convention.

---

[13]   *cf* art 3*bis*(1)(a) of the 2005 SUA Protocol.

[14]   For this 'sectoral' approach, see J Lambert, *Terrorism and Hostages in International Law* (Cambridge: Grotius Publications, 1990) 29–45, and for the international response to terrorism see R Higgins, 'The General International Law of Terrorism', in R Higgins, M Flory (eds), *Terrorism and International Law* (London: Routledge, 1997) 23.

[15]   UN Conventions on Terrorism are also available online at http://untreaty.un.org/English/Terrorism.asp. See also B Saul (ed), *Terrorism* (Oxford: Hart Publishing, 2012).

[16]   See for the customary nature of this principle M Plachta, 'The Lockerbie case: The Role of the SC in Enforcing the Principle *Aut Dedere Aut Judicare*' 12 *EJIL* (2001) 125.

[17]   See UN Convention for the Suppression of Financing of Terrorism adopted by GA Resolution of December 9, 1999, 39 ILM (2000) 270. See also the definition adopted by the EU Council on 13 June 2002, [2002] OJ L164/03.

[18]   See M Bothe, 'The International Community and Terrorism', in *Les nouvelles menaces contre la paix et la sécurité internationals* (Paris: Pedone, 2004) 48. See also generally C Walter et al (eds), *Terrorism as a Challenge for National and International Law* (Berlin: Springer, 2004).

[19]   *cf* UN SC Resolutions 1267/ 2000, 1373 (2001), 1566 (2004) et al. See also the *Kadi* case.

The proliferation of WMD by non-state actors is inextricably linked to the phenomenon of international terrorism.[20] Nevertheless, counter-proliferation or non-proliferation of WMD[21] has its own legal history, which is entwined with international arms control.[22] As used in this chapter, the term 'weapons of mass destruction' means all nuclear, chemical and biological-toxin weapons, together with their delivery systems[23] and related materials.[24] Needless to say the problem for the international community is not the existence of WMD as such, but the fear that WMD will end up in 'the wrong hands', however this is construed.[25] The responses to this danger include mainly the non-proliferation treaties and regimes system, ie the 'web of hard and soft international law normative frameworks regulating the proliferation of WMD';[26] domestic and multilateral export controls and UN Security Council Resolutions.[27] In general, international arms control and the non-proliferation security regime seek to limit the kind and number of available WMD and to deter states from using them, by, for example, imposing limits on weapon testing and

[20] See P van Ham and O Bosch, 'Global Non-Proliferation and Counter-Terrorism: The Role of Resolution 1540 and its Implications', in O Bosch, P Van Ham (eds), *Global Non-Proliferation and Counter-Terrorism: The Impact of UNSCR 1540* (2007) 3, 8 (hereinafter: Van Ham and Bosch). See also C Schaller, 'Keeping Weapons of Mass Destruction from Terrorists – An International Law Perspective', in Giegerich T (ed), *A Wiser Century?: Judicial Dispute Settlement, Disarmament and the Laws of War 100 Years after the Second Hague Peace Conference* (Berlin: Duncker & Humblot, 2009) 121.

[21] In contrast to non-proliferation, counter-proliferation generally refers to the more robust efforts to prevent the movement of WMD materials, technology and expertise from states that fail to conform to non-proliferation norms to hostile states and terrorist organisations. For the distinction between non-proliferation and counter-proliferation, see: D Joyner, 'The PSI: Non-proliferation, Counter-proliferation, and International Law', 30 *Yale Journal of International Law* (2005) 507, 519.

[22] On WMD generally, see O Fidler, 'International Law and WMD: End of Arms Control Approach?' 14 *Duke Journal of Comparative and International Law* (2004) 39; A O'Day, *WMD and Terrorism* (Place: Publisher, 2004); B Schneider, J Davis (eds), *Avoiding the Abyss Progress, Shortfalls and the Way Ahead in Combating the WMD Threat* (Westport: Praeger Security International, 2006); Busch N, Joyner D (eds), *Combating Weapons of Mass Destruction: the Future of International Non-Proliferation Policy* (Athens, GA: University of Georgia Press, 2009).

[23] The UNSC defines the term to include 'missiles, rockets and other unmanned systems capable of delivering nuclear, chemical, or biological weapons, that are specially designed for such use'; see SC Res 1540.

[24] As defined by the Security Council, the term includes 'materials, equipment and technology covered by relevant multilateral treaties and arrangements, or included on national control lists, which could be used for the design, development, production or use of nuclear, chemical and biological weapons and their means of delivery'; ibid.

[25] See eg US State Dept., *Nuclear Weapons and Rogue States: Challenge and Response* (2003); available at www.state.gov/t/us/rm/26786pf.htm. See also L Goldstein, *Preventive Attack and WMD* (Stanford, MA: Stanford University Press, 2006) 13.

[26] Joyner, xxi.

[27] See inter alia C Allen, 'A Primer on the Non-Proliferation Regime for Maritime Security Operations Forces' 54 *Naval LR* (2007) 51, 53; I Antony, 'Arms Control and Non-proliferation: the Role of International Organizations' in *SIPRI Yearbook (2005): Armaments, Disarmament and International Security* (Oxford: Oxford University Press, 2006), 529.

prohibiting the emplacement of nuclear weapons in the global commons, such as outer space and the seabed.[28] Additionally, they seek to 'halt and even reverse the proliferation of WMD and their delivery systems, with the long term goal of a complete, irreversible and verifiable disarmament of all WMD'.[29]

These non-proliferation measures are pursued through multilateral treaties and other export control regimes, which, while vital, only restrict exports of WMD materials from Member States, and only to the extent that those members choose to implement them.[30] The relevant treaties include, inter alia, the Nuclear Non-Proliferation Treaty of 1968 (NPT), which seeks to restrict the application of nuclear technology to peaceful purposes;[31] the International Convention for the Suppression of Acts of Nuclear Terrorism (2005),[32] which, plainly, embraces a law enforcement approach to the threat posed by nuclear and radiological weapons in the hands of terrorists and extends the criminal regime applicable to proliferation-related offences in several important respects.[33] In addition, the Chemical Weapons Convention (1993)[34] prohibits state parties from developing, producing, stockpiling or using chemical weapons. Another pertinent treaty is the Biological Weapons Convention (1972), which aims at banning the production, acquisition or stockpiling of biological agents or toxins (BTW agents).[35]

[28] See Treaty on the Prohibition of the Emplacement of Nuclear and Other Weapons of Mass Destruction on the Seabed and the Ocean Floor and in the Subsoil Thereof (1971); Treaty on Principles Governing the Activities of States in the Exploration and Use of Outer Space, Including the Moon and Other Celestial Bodies (1967).

[29] Allen, above n 27, 53.

[30] Multilateral export control regimes by supplier states include the Nuclear Suppliers' Group, the Australia Group and the Missile Technology Control Regime. Each is primarily a political commitment based on a non-binding agreement by responsible supplier states to restrict and regulate exports of specified WMD materials and delivery systems and does little to address the actual transport of such materials. See D Joyner, 'Restructuring the Multilateral Export Control Regime System' 9 *JCSL* (2004) 181.

[31] The NPT defines proliferation in art 1 as 'the transfer of nuclear weapons, other nuclear devices or control over such devices, from a nuclear weapon State Party to ay recipient whatsoever or to non-nuclear weapon State Party from any transferor whatsoever'. On the NPT in general see D Joyner, *Interpreting the Nuclear Non-Proliferation Treaty* (Oxford: Oxford University Press, 2011).

[32] International Convention for the Suppression of Acts of Nuclear Terrorism, annexed to GA Res 59/240, UN Doc A/RES/59/240, reprinted in 44 ILM (2005) 815. The Convention entered into force on 7 July 2007, and as at 29 August 2012, it had 79 parties; see http://treaties.un.org/Pages/ViewDetailsIII.aspx?&src=IND&mtdsg_no=XVIII-15&chapter=18&Temp=mtdsg3&lang=en.

[33] See: Allen, above n 27, 57.

[34] See: also W Krutzsch and R Trapp, *A Commentary to the Chemical Weapons Convention* (Dordrecht: Martinus Nijhoff, 1994).

[35] Although the Biological Weapons Convention includes a provision for reporting violations to the UN Security Council for possible action, in contrast to the Chemical Weapons Convention, it does not yet include provisions for verification and challenge inspections. See also M-I Chevrier (ed), *The Implementation of Legally Binding Measures to Strengthen the Biological and Toxin Weapons Convention* (Dordrecht: Kluwer Academic Publishers, 2004).

The non-proliferation and arms control regimes have long struggled with the problems posed by the dual-use of WMD technologies.[36] The dual use character of many WMD and related equipment and precursors significantly complicates compliance verification and monitoring.[37] Indeed, although the above-mentioned treaties restrict the transfer of WMD, the transport of the relevant materials is not necessarily a violation of their provisions,[38] with the treaties establishing the right to transfer dual-use material for peaceful purposes.[39] National implementing measures for export control regimes often limit their application to sellers, exporters and buyers, and typically exclude from their coverage transporters. As a result, those aboard a vessel engaged in transporting illicit WMD or related materials might not be in violation of any laws, even though the actual export of those materials infringed the source nation's export control regime. It is also true that, despite the fact that the UN Security Council has concluded that the proliferation of missile delivery systems for WMD constitutes a threat to international peace and security, international law does not presently prohibit the sale or transfer of missiles or missile technology. For that reason, the non-proliferation regime for missiles is the weakest of the four considered, as the *M/V So San* incident demonstrated.

III. RESPONSES AND INTERDICTION OPERATIONS WITHIN AN INSTITUTIONAL FRAMEWORK

A. The UN Security Council

The United Nations has had a long history of engagement with the issue of WMD proliferation, beginning with the very first GA Resolution on 24 January 1946.[40] On several occasions, the Security Council, in particular, has categorised the proliferation of missiles and WMD as a threat to international peace and security. For example, in Resolution 687 (1991), it

---

[36] Dual-use materials are those that have both legitimate (peaceful) and illegitimate (weapons) application. For example, a DNA synthesiser has any number of legitimate biotechnology applications, but might also be used to produce BTW agents. See also discussion in Joyner, Ch 3.

[37] Approximately 95 per cent of WMD elements are of a dual use nature; see Jimenez-Kwast, 165.

[38] See also ibid, 192.

[39] As Ahlström observes, 'State parties in fact may participate in the widest possible sharing of such goods so long as they are intended for peaceful purposes'; ibid, 'The PSI: International Law Aspects of the Statement of Interdiction Principles', in *SIPRI Yearbook (2005): Armaments, Disarmament and International Security* (Oxford: Oxford University Press, 2006) 741, 755.

[40] See D Joyner, 'Non-Proliferation Law and the UN System: Resolution 1540 and the Limits of the Power of SC' 20 *LJIL* (2007) 489, 494.

stated that WMD posed a threat to 'peace and security' in the Middle East, and imposed a stringent disarmament regime in Iraq. Also, in Resolution 1172 (1998), it condemned nuclear tests conducted by India and affirmed 'that the proliferation of all weapons of mass destruction constitutes a threat to international peace and security'.[41] Similarly, the Council has consistently since 1992 and the Lockerbie incident designated international terrorism as a threat to international peace and security.[42]

i. SC Resolution 1373 (2001)

However, the adoption of Resolutions 1373 (2001) and 1540 (2004) on terrorism and WMD respectively marked a significant departure from the traditional understanding of the Council's role and powers under Chapter VII and the beginning of a new chapter of quasi-legislative action of the Council in these areas.[43] In more detail and in chronological order, the Security Council passed Resolution 1373 on 28 September 2001, only 17 days after the terrorist attacks on New York and Washington DC. The Resolution commences by 'reconfirming that such acts, like any act of international terrorism, constitute a threat to international peace and security.' It thus clearly grounds the jurisdiction of the Security Council over international terrorism on its powers of determination under Article 39 and Chapter VII of the Charter. In its operative paragraphs, Resolution 1373 determines that all states shall prevent and suppress the financing of terrorist acts, including by criminalizing terrorist fundraising and donation activities, and by freezing assets of known terrorist individuals or entities. It continues that all states shall take necessary steps to prevent the commission of terrorist acts, deny safe haven to those who finance, plan or support terrorist acts, and ensure that any person who participates in terrorist acts is brought to justice.[44]

---

[41] SC Res 1172, UN Doc S/RES/1172 (1998). Also, the proliferation of WMD in general was presented as a threat to international peace and security at the heads of the state summit of the Security Council in 31 January, 1992, but this was presented in a Presidential Statement and not in a binding Resolution. See in general Joyner, Ch 4.

[42] See SC Res 748 UN Doc S/RES/748 (1992) and also the ICJ *Lockerbie* cases. See also SC Resolutions 1044/1996, 1189/1998, 1267/1999 and 1269/1999.

[43] With respect to SC Res 1540, it was very pertinently stated that 'one could argue that Resolution 1540 creates the foundation of a new system of global governance for dealing with the nexus of WMD proliferation, terrorism and illicit trafficking'; see Van Ham and Bosch, 5.

[44] See also S Szurek, 'La Lutte Internationale contre le Terrorisme' 109 *RGDIP* (2005) 5. The Council has reaffirmed that international terrorism constitutes a threat to international peace and security in numerous subsequent Resolutions, including, inter alia, SC Resolutions 1452 (2002), 1455 (2003), 1526 (2004), 1617 (2005), 1699 (2006), 1822 (2008), 1904 (2009) and 1989 (2011).

ii. SC Resolution 1540 (2004)

In para 4 of Resolution 1373, the Council 'noted with concern' the close connection between international terrorism and inter alia 'the illegal movement of nuclear, chemical, biological and other potentially deadly materials'. This phrase paved the way for a separate Resolution in this regard and thus, on 28 April 2004 the Security Council passed Resolution 1540. This Resolution was passed, not coincidentally, shortly after the revelation in February 2004 of the existence of a long-standing clandestine nuclear materials smuggling ring, headed by the father of Pakistan's gas centrifuge programme, Dr Abdul Qadeer Khan.[45] In this Resolution, the Council undertook to address a number of fundamental loopholes in the existing non-proliferation treaties and regimes system. First, it centred its focus on non-state actors. Existing treaties and regimes assume that only states have the intention and capabilities to develop WMD.[46] Thus, at the international level, there is no substantive restriction on private parties, including business entities as well as other non-state actors, engaging in any of these activities. The Resolution addresses this non-state actor problem in paragraph 1, in which it provides that 'all States shall refrain from providing any form of support to non-state actors that attempt to develop, acquire, manufacture, possess, transport, transfer or use nuclear, chemical or biological weapons and their means of delivery'. The Resolution defines a non-state actor in a footnote as 'an individual or entity, not acting under the lawful authority of any State in conducting activities, which come within the scope of this Resolution.' The definition is very broad and it does not limit its scope as to the nature, sector or type of the non-state actor.

This Resolution is also the only instrument to date that explicitly integrates proliferation concerns about delivery means with those about nuclear, chemical and biological weapons.[47] In addition, the Resolution is significant in requiring measures beyond the obligation laid out in the respective treaties. These are specified in its operative paragraphs 2 and 3 and concern financial security and accountability, physical protection, border and export controls. As in Resolution 1373, Resolution 1540 in paragraph 4 establishes a Committee of the Security Council to monitor the implementation by states of the obligations imposed by the Resolution.[48]

---

[45] See SG Ong, 'The PSI and Counter-Proliferation: A View from Asia', in Van Ham and Bosch, above, 154 and Joyner, xviii.

[46] See: Van Ham and Bosch, 9.

[47] See: ibid, 10.

[48] The 1540 Committee, initially mandated for a maximum of two years but renewed for two years, on 27 April, 2006, with SC Res 1673, and, for three years, on 25 April 2008, with SC Res 1810, comprises representatives of all fifteen Security Council members.

iii. The Implementation of SC Resolutions 1373 and 1540 on the High Seas

It is beyond the ambit of the present enquiry to address whether these Resolutions are ultra vires the powers of the Security Council. Suffice it to note here that there have been many voices of concern, not only with regard to their constitutionality, but also with regard to their practical utility in addressing the present problems.[49] The question, however, which is of relevance in the present context, is whether these 'generic' or legislative Resolutions[50] may afford the requisite legal basis for interdiction operations in order to suppress non-state actors engaged in terrorist acts and/ or in the proliferation of WMD. It is obvious that on the footing of the actual words used in the Resolutions, such a proposition finds no warrant. There is no explicit authorisation for any interdiction operations on the high seas for the present purposes. Moreover, it is important to stress that in the drafting of what is now operative paragraph 10 of the SC Resolution 1540, China was adamant in rejecting any reference to the word 'interdiction', included in the tabled drafts.[51] In its final version, paragraph 10 calls upon all states, in accordance with national and international law, to 'take cooperative action to prevent illicit trafficking in nuclear, chemical or biological weapons, their means of delivery and related materials'. The exhortatory nature of the latter provision in conjunction with, on the one hand, the deletion of the word 'interdiction' from the final draft and on the other, the explicit reference to international law, reflects the collective will of the Security Council in the Resolution not to authorise any such operation.[52] It bears also reiterating that, in general, SC Resolutions under Chapter VII should be construed *stricto sensu*, and any unilateral action involving the use or threat of force should not lightly be presumed.

It follows that there is no carte blanche for Member States to resort to coercive measures in order to enforce the Resolutions. Nonetheless, the mandatory character of both Resolutions implies that the Security Council

---

[49] See, inter alia, M Happold, 'Security Council Resolution 1373 and the Constitution of the United States' 16 *LJIL* (2003) 593; E Rosand, 'The Security Council as "Global Legislator": *Ultra Vires* or Ultra Innovative?' 28 *Fordham International Law Journal* (2005) 542.

[50] See also Talmon, 'The Security Council as World Legislature' 99 *AJIL* (2005) 175, 190 and G Abi-Saab, 'The Security Council as Legislator and as Executive in its Fight against Terrorism and against Proliferation of Weapons of Mass Destruction: the Question of Legitimacy' in R Wolfrum and V Röben (eds), *Legitimacy in International Law* (Berlin: Springer, 2008), 109.

[51] See UNSC Verbatim Record (22 Apr 2004), UN Doc S/PV 4950 (Resumption 1), 6 and also comments in Van Ham and Bosch, 6; S Logan, 'The PSI Navigating the Legal Challenges' 14 *Journal of Transnational Law and Policy* (2005) 253, 270 and Becker, 167.

[52] See per this view Byers, 532; Joyner, 321; Klein, *Maritime Security*, 283. It is noteworthy that the President of the Council emphasised that the Resolution does not authorise unilateral enforcement measures if a given state fails to take effective and appropriate measures. Any such action would be the subject of further decisions of the Council, which remains seized of the matter. See Allen, n 27, 45.

could pursue both military and non-military sanctions in accordance with further decisions. This presupposes that any breach of the Resolutions should be reported to the Council and the latter, qua the sole responsible authority, will impose non-military or military sanctions against the recalcitrant state. This becomes even more evident from the reading, for example, of paragraphs 12 and 13 of SC Res 1540, which set forth explicitly that the Council remains seized of the matter and will monitor closely the implementation of this Resolution, expressing its intention to take further decision, which may be required to this end.[53]

Nevertheless, there is also the contrary view, namely that Security Council Resolutions 1373 and 1540 both can provide sufficient legal justification for maritime interdiction operations. In respect of the former Resolution, Professor Heinegg has consistently argued that the legal basis for Operation Enduring Freedom 'is to be found in Resolution 1373 and in the right of individual and collective self-defence'.[54] The reference to the right of self-defence as a legal basis in this regard flows from the reaffirmation of this right by the Council in both Resolutions 1368 and 1373 in the aftermath of '9/11', which, according to Professor Heinegg, entails that the self-defence is admissible in all cases of armed force against a state from outside its borders even if that use of force cannot be attributed to another state.[55] Thus, this reaffirmation provides a continuing authority to Member States to label counter-terrorist operations, *in casu*, on the high seas, as a legitimate exercise of self-defence pursuant to Resolutions 1368 and 1373. In the same vein, the flag states, which willingly abstain from suppressing 'the transport of terrorists and goods that are designed to further acts of international terrorism' 'may also become legitimate targets of self-defence measures', if 'this abstention amounts to an attribution of the activities concerned'.[56]

It is submitted that these arguments encounter real difficulties if they are assessed against the normative background of SC Resolutions under Chapter VII and of general international law. Suffice to underscore here that the right of self-defence is not unlimited *ratione temporis,* and it ceases to exist when the attack has stopped and the peace has been restored.[57] In addition, the SC has not the authority to sanction the right of self-defence indefinitely and without a causal link with an existing attack, such as was

---

[53] See paras 11 and 12 of SC Res 1540 (2004) and *cf* the respective paras 8 and 9 of SC Res 1373.

[54] W Heinegg, 'Maritime Interception/Interdiction Operations within the Framework of Operation Enduring Freedom', in *Les Nouvelles Menaces contre la Paix et la Sécurité Internationales* (Paris: Pedone, 2004) 149, 158.

[55] See ibid, 156 and also T Bruha and M Bortfeld, ,Terrorismus and Selbstverteidigung' 5 *Vereinte Nationen* (1001), 165.

[56] Heinegg, ibid, 153.

[57] See: inter alia DW Greig, 'Self-defence and the Security Council: What does Art.51 Require?' 40 *ICLQ* (1991) 366, 396.

then 9/11.[58] It must also be recalled that the SC is not *legibus solutus*[59] and that by virtue of article 24 of the Charter, the Security Council is, in general, bound by the purposes and principles of the Charter, which by and large constitute the outer limits of the authority of Security Council,[60] as well as by the peremptory norms of international community (*jus cogens*), such as the prohibition to use force.[61] Therefore, the assertion of a continuing right of self-defence based solely on the above Resolutions is a non sequitur.

It has been further argued that

> even if such private acts may not be attributed to another State or if the flag State is unable to take the necessary measures according to Resolution 1373 an abstention or inactivity would still have to be considered as being in breach of international law. In any event, in such cases, third States are entitled to take necessary measures in order to fulfil the obligations of Resolution 1373 instead of the State that would be primarily responsible.[62]

This brings to the fore the previous discussion about the possibility of unilateral enforcement of SC Resolutions. To reiterate, the preponderant view is that such unilateral enforcement is not permitted; additionally, *in casu*, the Security Council itself as well as through its Counter-Terrorism Committee 'remains seized of the matter'[63] and it has the sole responsibility to decide the consequences of a violation of the provisions of SC Resolution 1373 (2001).[64]

---

[58] See E Papastavridis, 'Security Council Resolutions 1368 and 1373: Collective Security or the Right of Self-Defence?' 55 *RHDI* (2002) 531, 538.

[59] As the Appeals Chamber of the ICTY held in the *Tadić case*: 'neither the text nor the spirit of the Charter conceives of the Security Council as *legibus solutus* (unbound by law)'; para 28.

[60] See in this regard inter alia S Lamb, 'Legal Limits to UN Security Council Powers', in Goodwin-Gill and Talmon (eds), *The Reality in International Law: Essays in Honour of Ian Brownlie* (Oxford: Clarendon Press, 1999) 361; G Nolte, 'The Limits of the Security Council's Powers and its Functions in the International Legal System', in M Byers (ed), *The Role of Law in International Politics* (Oxford: Oxford University Press, 2000) 315.

[61] Acts *contra juris gestionis* are beyond the powers of an institution, *in casu* the Security Council and therefore the provisions of the UN Charter on the latter's powers have to be interpreted and executed in a way that is compatible with peremptory norms. See also the recent *Al-Jedda v UK* case (2011), in which the Grand Chamber of the ECtHR held that 'in interpreting its resolutions, there must be a presumption that the Security Council does not intend to impose any obligation on Member States to breach fundamental principles of human rights. In the event of any ambiguity in the terms of a Security Council Resolution, the Court must therefore choose the interpretation which is most in harmony with the requirements of the Convention and which avoids any conflict of obligations'; para 102. See also A Orakhelashvili, 'The Impact of Peremptory Norms on the Interpretation and Application of UNSC Resolutions' 16 *EJIL* (2005) 59, 69.

[62] Heinegg, above n 54, 153.

[63] See para 9 of SC Res 1373.

[64] *cf* also the relevant discussion with regard to the unilateral enforcement of SC Res 1441 (2002) in E Papastavridis, 'Interpretation of Security Council Resolutions under Chapter VII in the Aftermath of the Iraqi Crisis' 56 *ICLQ* (2007) 83, 111. See also C Denis, 'La Résolution 678 (1990) peut-elle légitimer les actions armées menées contre l'Iraq postérieurement à l'adoption de la résolution 687 (1991)?' 31 *RBDI* (1998) 485.

Similarly, with regard to SC Resolution 1540 (2004), the same author contends that 'non-compliance with the obligation laid down in Resolution 1540 will constitute a violation of international law and will entitle the injured States to take appropriate countermeasures, including counter-measures short of self-defence'.[65] This certainly constitutes a more subtle argument, forming part of a broader question, namely whether the law of countermeasures may permit unilateral boarding and arrest of foreign vessels at sea in order to secure compliance with obligations furthering the collective interest.[66] In other words, the argument runs that the duty to respect the exclusive jurisdiction of a flag state over its own vessels on the high seas could be suspended as a countermeasure, thus making it per-missible to board and arrest the vessel or persons on board and seize, for example, the WMD *in casu*. As Guilfoyle notes,

> these arguments encounter . . . critical and common difficulties. The first is whether, and in what circumstances, a State may take unilateral action regard-ing a wrongdoing State's breach of an obligation owed to a group of States or the international community as a whole (countermeasures in the collective interest). In particular, can a State invoke countermeasures in the collective interest when it has not itself suffered any direct injury?[67]

There are compelling reasons to conclude that the law of countermeas-ures fails to provide a tenable justification for the interdiction of vessels of states acting in defiance of SC Resolution 1540 (2004).[68] Countermeasures are ordinarily available to an injured state when another state has breached an obligation owed to it.[69] The requirement of an injured state is crucial, for it is this criterion that identifies who is permitted to take action that would otherwise be unlawful in response to a state's prior illegal con-duct.[70] According to the relevant provision of the ILC Articles, 'a State is

---

[65] See W Heinegg, 'The Proliferation Security Initiative: Security v. Freedom of Navigation?' 35 *IYHR* (2005) 181, 183. See also on responsibility of states for violations of non-proliferation agreements, P Rubenstein, 'State Responsibility for Failure to Control the Export of WMD' 23 *California Western International Law Journal* (1992–93) 351.

[66] For example, it has been suggested that a Member State could be justified, in some cir-cumstances, in enforcing compliance with regional fisheries organisation (RFO) manage-ment and conservation measures against other members through non-consensual at-sea boarding and arrest of their vessels as a countermeasure; see R Rayfuse, 'Countermeasures and High Seas Fisheries Enforcement' 51 *Netherlands International Law Review* (2004) 41, 63. *Cf* also S Kaye, 'The PSI in the Maritime Domain' 35 *IYHR* (2005) 205, 223.

[67] D Guilfoyle, 'Interdicting Vessels to Enforce the Common Interest: Maritime Countermeasures and the Use of Force on the High Seas' 56 *ICLQ* (2007) 69, 71 (hereinafter: Guilfoyle, *Countermeasures*).

[68] Concurring are also R Lavalle, 'A Novel, if Awkward Exercise in International Law Making: Security Resolution 1540 (2004)' 51 *NYIL* (2004) 411, 424; A Zimmermann, B Elberling, 'Grenzen der Legislativbefugnisse des Seicherheitsrats' 52 *VN* (2004) 71, 76.

[69] See art 49 of the ILC Articles and J Crawford, *The International Law Commission's Articles on State Responsibility: Introduction, Text, and Commentaries* (Cambridge: Cambridge University Press, 2002) 281.

[70] See Guilfoyle, *Countermeasures*, 72.

entitled as an injured State to invoke the responsibility of another State if the obligation breached is owed to: (*a*) that State individually; or (*b*) a group of States including that State, or the international community as a whole, and the breach of the obligation: . . . (i) specially affects that State'.[71] A state which is injured in the sense of article 42 is also entitled to resort to countermeasures in accordance with the rules laid down in the relevant Chapter of the ILC Articles.[72]

In light of the foregoing, it must be established that either SC Resolution 1540 creates obligations owed to the boarding state individually, or the latter state is specially affected by the relevant violation. As Guilfoyle rightly points out,

> it is not self-evident that a Security Council Resolution creates obligations owed to the members of the United Nations individually and collectively, as opposed to obligations owed to the Security Council itself. Further . . . UNSCR 1540 does not on its face establish a network of bilateral or reciprocal obligations between all States . . . Transporting WMD in breach of UNSCR 1540 will simply be a breach of the obligations in Articles 25 or 48 of the UN Charter to implement Security Council decisions. The only obvious obligation- holder is the Security Council.[73]

It is readily apparent that no individual state can claim either to be an injured or a specially affected state in order to resort to countermeasures for violations of SC Resolution 1540; therefore, the extension of the label of 'injured states' to all UN Member States lacks legal merit. Notwithstanding this, it could be maintained that the obligations under scrutiny are *erga omnes partes,* ie owed to all UN Member States or *erga onmes,* ie owed to the international community as a whole, and therefore collective counter-measures could arguably be plausible.[74] This supposition, however, is on unstable legal ground, since, according to the preponderant view, collective

---

[71] art 42 of the ILC Articles and Commentary, 117. The exact legal nature of this article and in general of the provisions of this Part of the ILC Articles, ie whether they codify customary rules or they reflect 'progressive development of international law', remains ambiguous. However, it is true that the distinction between a state that is 'injured' and a state 'other than an injured State' departs significantly from earlier drafts on this subject. See further comments in L-A Sicilianos, 'The Classification of Obligations and the Multilateral Dimensions of the Relations of International Responsibility' 13 *EJIL* (2003) 1127, 1138.

[72] See Chapter 2 of Part III of ILC Articles and Commentary, 128. On the issue of proportionality in countermeasures, see T Franck, 'On Proportionality of Countermeasures in International Law' 102 *AJIL* (2008) 715.

[73] He further notes that 'even presuming that UNSCR 1540 creates obligations owed to the UN membership as a whole, it would remain difficult to find States injured by their breach . . . It is also hard to see that any one given transfer of WMD radically alters the position of all parties to the UN Charter. None of the categories of States entitled to take counter-measures appears to be met.' Guilfoyle, Countermeasures, 76. In accord is Gavouneli, 177.

[74] *cf* in this regard art 48 of ILC Articles. See also D Alland, 'Countermeasures of General Interest' 13 *EJIL* (2002) 1211; B Simma, 'From Bilateralism to Community Interest in International Law' 250 *RCADI* (1994-IV) 217.

countermeasures are not permitted under customary international law.[75] Besides that, it could never reasonably be held that the SC Resolution under scrutiny is an integral treaty, creating obligations *erga omnes partes*, as well as that it sets forth obligations owed to the international community as a whole. It should be stated in this respect that even after the adoption of SC Resolution 1540, not even the mere transportation of WMD between sovereign states is considered unlawful.[76] It is thus difficult to sustain the argument that this transportation between states and non-state actors is currently prohibited by a peremptory norm of international law.

In conclusion, it is submitted that the infringement of the obligations laid down in SC Resolutions 1373 and 1540 falls short of triggering interdiction measures on the high seas, either in the form of unilateral enforcement of the SC Resolutions or in the form of collective countermeasures. This, however, does not mean that there will not be isolated cases, where vessels transporting terrorists or WMD for non-state actors will be lawfully boarded on the high seas;[77] the argument put forward here is that there is no such unilateral right, in general, not that the interdiction of suspect vessels is prohibited under all circumstances.[78] It goes without saying, of course, that the Security Council can always mandate such interdiction measures in case of breach of the pertinent Resolutions,[79] as well as ad hoc in respect of particular vessels suspected of involvement in transit of WMD-related materials.[80]

B. NATO and Operation Active Endeavour

In response to the 9/11 attacks, on 4 October 2001, for the first time in its history, NATO invoked the collective self-defence provision (article 5 of

---

[75] As the ILC Articles Commentary expressly states, 'At present, there appears to be no clearly recognised entitlement of States referred to in article 48 to take countermeasures in the collective interest'; ibid, 301. It is disputed whether the right to visit and arrest of the vessel would be considered 'lawful measures', under art 54 of the ILC Articles; see Sicilianos, who contends that these 'lawful measures' include, in principle, collective countermeasures in 'La Codification des contre-measures par la Commission du Droit International' 38 *RBDI* (2005) 447, 494.

[76] It is argued, for example, that the passing of SC Res 1540 would not alter the legal regime of incidents such as the *MV So San*, as it was a legal transaction between sovereign states.

[77] Such interdiction can arguably be based upon the consent of the flag state, the state of necessity or self-defence.

[78] *cf* the remarks made above by Soons with regard to incidental or ad hoc interdiction of vessels in order to enforce UN embargoes.

[79] See also R Wolfrum, 'Fighting Terrorism at Sea: Options and Limitations under International Law', in M Nordquist et al (eds), *Legal Challenges in Maritime Security* (Leiden: Martinus Nijhoff, 2009), 30.

[80] See Joyner, 320. However, in the same author's view, this possibility is fraught with practical difficulties, such as time efficiency and intelligence-sharing.

the North Atlantic Treaty).[81] One of the eight measures agreed upon by the Allies was the deployment of its Standing Naval Forces to the Eastern Mediterranean to serve in a naval operation focusing on the interdiction of ships transporting Al Qaida terrorists, associated persons and materials. The deployment, which was formally named Operation Active Endeavour, was also extended, in March 2003, to the western area of the Mediterranean Sea. Within another month, the mandate of the naval operation was expanded from surveillance to include systematic boarding and searching of suspect ships in the entire Mediterranean.[82]

> NATO forces have hailed over 100,000 merchant vessels and boarded some 155 suspect ships . . . Since April 2003, NATO has been systematically boarding suspect ships. These boardings take place with the compliance of the ships' masters and flag states in accordance with international law.[83]

According to NATO,

> What happens in practice is that merchant ships passing through the Eastern Mediterranean are hailed by patrolling NATO naval units and asked to identify themselves and their activity. This information is then reported to both NATO's Allied Maritime Component Commander in Naples, Italy, and the NATO Shipping Centre in Northwood, the United Kingdom. If anything appears unusual or suspicious, teams of between 15 and 20 of the ships' crew may board vessels to inspect documentation and cargo. NATO personnel may otherwise convey this information to the appropriate law-enforcement agency at the vessel's next port of call. The suspect vessel is then shadowed until action is taken by a responsible agency/ authority, or until it enters a country's territorial waters.[84]

It is evident that Operation Active Endeavour entails a considerable degree of policing of the Mediterranean Sea, due to the increased number of vessels involved and monitored. What is significant for present purposes is the legal justification put forward for the interceptions, which is the consent of the flag state or ship's master. Notwithstanding that the Operation was initially perceived as a collective self-defence measure to redress the 9/11 attack, NATO has not subsequently made use of the belligerent rights of visit and search, but has returned to the peacetime law of the sea framework through reliance on flag state consent[85] as well

---

[81] In the relevant press release, NATO officials stated that '[9/11] shall be regarded as an action covered by Article 5 of the Washington Treaty, which states that an armed attack against one or more of the Allies in Europe or North America shall be considered an attack against them all'; see NATO Press Release No 124 (12 Sept2001), http://nato.int.

[82] See NATO to Expand Operation Active Endeavour to the whole Mediterranean, NATO Press Release (2004) 039, 16 March 2004 and Jimemez-Kwast, 233.

[83] See www.nato.int/cps/en/natolive/topics_7932.htm.

[84] ibid.

[85] Jimenez-Kwast reports two incidents, as examples: 'on 29 and 30 April 2003, the merchant vessels *Nino Star* and the *M/V Dimo* respectively both flying a Comorian flag, were boarded by NATO naval forces in international waters near Cyprus. Both cases involved a

as the practice of 'consensual visit', ie the boarding of the vessel upon the invitation of the master.[86] This reflects the legal conviction of the participating states that they are not in a state of armed conflict and thus they are not exercising their right of collective self-defence, as was initially stated to be the case in 2001.

More importantly, the reliance on flag state consent leaves no doubt as to the lawfulness of the adopted interdiction policy.[87] On the contrary, it is contestable whether the continuing invocation of article 5 as the legal basis for the deployment of the Operation is tenable, since it is clear that there is no actual or imminent threat of armed attack at present. However, this is more an internal institutional legal issue, rather than a question pertaining to the legality of the interception on the high seas.[88] On the latter issue, it suffices that the states involved seek for the flag state's consent.

C. International Maritime Organisation (IMO)

i. The ISPS Code

Following the attacks of 11 September 2001, the IMO Assembly resolved to review existing legal and technical measures to prevent and suppress terrorist acts against ships both at port and at sea, and to improve security aboard and ashore. One of the key developments in addressing ship and port security was the adoption of the International Code for the Security of Ships and of Port Facilities (ISPS). The code was developed as an amendment to the SOLAS Convention and came into force in July 2004.[89]

compliant-boarding in which the cargo was found to be in accordance with the manifests and the vessels were subsequently allowed to continue their journey'; ibid, 234.

[86] ATP (Allied Tactical Publication) 71 of NATO states that 'A consensual visit is conducted at the invitation of the master (or person-in-charge) of a vessel, which is not otherwise subject to the jurisdiction of the boarding officer. The voluntary consent of the master permits the boarding, but it does not allow the assertion of law enforcement authority, such as arrest or seizure. A consensual visit is not, therefore, an exercise of maritime law enforcement jurisdiction *per se*' at 1-4 (on file with the author). Albeit that, according to NATO, this is not tantamount to 'boarding' as such, it is submitted that it actually constitutes the 'droit d'enquête du pavillon' and the boarding state bears responsibility accordingly.

[87] In accord is also Jimemez-Kwast, 234.

[88] In this vein, it is also of interest to question whether NATO bears responsibility for any wrongful act in the course of the interception operations. Nevertheless, the issue of responsibility is beyond the scope of the present enquiry. See some relevant remarks in N Ronzitti, 'The PSI and International Law', in A Fischer-Lescano et al (eds), *Frieden in Freiheit: Festschrift fur Michael Bothe zum 70 Geburtstag* (Baden-Baden: Nomos, 2008) 269, 282.

[89] Amendments to the Annex to the International Convention for the Safety of Life at Sea, opened for signature 12 December 2002 and entered into force 1 July 2004, International Code for the Security of Ships and of Port Facilities; available also at www.imo.org/About/mainframe.asp?topic_ id=5838&doc_ id=2689 (hereinafter: ISPS Code). The ISPS Code was passed as an amendment to SOLAS Convention. A new chapter XI-2 was adopted, entitled 'Special Measures to Enhance Maritime Security', which required that states comply with the ISPS.

In essence, the new SOLAS chapter XI-2 and the ISPS Code take the approach that ensuring the security of ships and port facilities is a risk management activity, and that in order to determine what security measures are appropriate, an assessment of the risk must be made in each particular case. The Code covers both passenger ships and cargo ships (including tankers) of 500 gross tonnes or more, as well as port facilities serving ships on international voyages and mobile offshore drilling units.[90] It is divided into two parts. Part A, which is mandatory, contains detailed security-related requirements for governments, ports, and shipping companies, while Part B contains non-mandatory guidelines that basically describe 'how-to' implement Part A requirements.[91]

ii. The Revision of the SUA Convention

Another major initiative of the IMO in the field of maritime security was the revision of the 1988 SUA Convention and its Protocol.[92] The IMO Legal Committee completed its work on the draft protocols at its eighty-third session in April 2005, and these protocols were adopted at a diplomatic conference in October 2005.[93] The 2005 SUA Protocol entered into force on 28 July 2010, and as at 31 October 2012, it had 22 contracting states.[94] The SUA Convention and its Protocol in their revised forms should be seen as complementary to the practical measures put in place by chapter XI-2 of the SOLAS Convention and the ISPS Code. Whereas the latter instruments provide the technical framework for ensuring that ships and port facilities are rendered as safe as possible from terrorist attacks, the 2005 SUA Protocol provides the necessary legal framework to allow states to take prompt and effective action against alleged offenders in the event of such an attack.[95]

[90] See reg 2(1), ibid.
[91] See a detailed analysis of the ISPS code from a practical viewpoint in S Jones, *Maritime Security: A Practical Guide* (London: The Nautical Institute, 2006).
[92] See Convention for the Suppression of Unlawful Acts against the Safety of Maritime Navigation, IMO Doc SUA/CONF/15, reprinted in 27 ILM (1988) 672 (hereinafter: SUA Convention) and Protocol for the Suppression of Unlawful Acts against the Safety of Fixed Platforms Located on the Continental Shelf, also reprinted in 27 ILM (1988) 680 (hereinafter SUA Protocol).
[93] On that day, the IMO Conference adopted also the 2005 Protocol to the SUA Protocol of 1998, which reflects the amendments in the 2005 Protocol. By decision of the Conference, the original 1988 SUA Convention and Protocol, as respectively amended by the 2005 SUA Protocols, were deemed to constitute single instruments. On the drafting history of 2005 SUA Protocol, see K Mbiah, 'The Revision of the SUA Convention, 1988', in *Maritime Violence and Other Security Issues at Sea*, (Malmo: WMU, 2002) 193, 216; C Young, 'Balancing Maritime Security and Freedom of Navigation on the High Seas' 24 *University of Queensland Law Review* (2005) 355 and C Tiribelli, 'Time to Update the 1998 SUA Convention' 18 *Sri Lanka JIL* (2006) 149.
[94] See above Introduction (fn 9).
[95] See also R Balkin, 'The International Maritime Organisation and Maritime Security' 30 *Tulane Maritime Law Journal* (2006) 1, 22.

While the original 1988 SUA Convention and Protocol provided for the arrest, detention and extradition of alleged offenders with respect to certain categories of acts of violence committed on board or against unlawful shipping, it lacked an effective means to apprehend offenders.[96] 'The inclusion of a procedure in the 2005 Protocol to allow states to board ships marks a shift from merely providing lawful bases to establish jurisdiction to creating the means to exercise jurisdiction'.[97] Indeed, the 2005 SUA Protocol sets out in article 8*bis* procedures by which states parties may request flag states of suspect vessels to permit boarding outside the territorial sea of any state and thus it represents the latest exception to the traditional rules relating to the exclusive jurisdiction of the flag state over its vessels when those vessels are on the high seas[98] Noteworthy also is that the 2005 Protocol and the above SC Resolutions complement each other, in the sense that while Resolution 1540 proscribes the manufacture, possession, transport of WMD by non-state actors, the Protocol comes to criminalise the use of the latter weapons for terrorist purposes.

The first remark in respect of 2005 SUA Protocol is that while it primarily establishes a regime to combat maritime terrorism, there is no explicit reference to the term 'terrorism' in the body of the Protocol, nor, of course, any definition of this term.[99] There is only a terrorist-purposes or *mens rea* provision in article 3*bis*(1)a, based on the definition found in the 1999 Terrorism Financing Convention.[100] Besides article 8*bis*, the most salient amendments included in the new instrument pertain to the offences covered by it. Article 3*bis* of the 2005 Protocol, along with articles 3*ter* and 3*quater*, expands the list of offences covered by article 3 of the SUA

[96] As Halberstam notes, 'its operative provisions deal not so much with the suppression of such acts, as with the apprehension, conviction and punishment of those who commit them'; ibid, 'Terrorism on the High Seas' 82 *AJIL* (1988) 269, 292. On SUA Convention and Protocol see also G Plant, 'The Convention for the Suppression of Unlawful Acts against the Safety of Maritime Navigation' 39 *ICLQ* (1990) 27.

[97] N Klein, 'The Right of Visit and the 2005 SUA Protocol' 35 *Denver Journal of International Law and Policy* (2007) 287, 288 (hereinafter: Klein).

[98] The 2005 SUA Protocol has attracted considerable commentary from the academic doctrine; see inter alia M Mejia, P Mukherjee, 'The SUA Convention 2005: Critical Evaluation of its Effectiveness in Suppressing Maritime Criminal Acts' 12 *Journal of International Maritime Law* (2005) 170; H Tuerk, 'Combating Terrorism at Sea: The Suppression of Unlawful Acts against the Safety of Maritime Navigation', in M Nordquist, above n 79, 41; C Harrington, 'Heightened Security: The Need to Incorporate Article 3*bis*(1)(a) and 8*bis*(5)(e) of the 2005 Draft SUA Protocol into Part VII of the UNCLOS' 16 *Pacific Rim Law and Policy Journal* (2007) 107.

[99] Nevertheless, the terms 'terrorism' and 'terrorist acts' are used numerous times in the Preamble of 2005 SUA Protocol; see: Mejia, Mukherjee, ibid, 174.

[100] As R Balkin, Director of the IMO's Legal Affairs Division, reports, 'one debate that took place fairly early on during discussions in the legal committee was whether the titles of the SUA Convention and Protocol should be amended to include the term "terrorist acts". However, whilst there was no disagreement as to the objective of the revision, to deal with terrorist activities directed against international shipping, it was ultimately decided that such an amendment would not be appropriate since the amending instruments were merely protocols to an existing convention and protocol'; see above n 95, 24.

Convention, widening significantly its prescriptive scope.[101] Terrorist actions prohibited by article 3*bis* span a wide range of activities from the use of a ship as a weapon to the use of a ship as a mode of transport of terrorist material to the targeting of a ship in a terrorist attack. Under article 3*ter*, a person also commits an offence within the meaning of the Convention if that person unlawfully or intentionally transports another person on board a ship knowing that the person has violated the above provisions or any offence set forth in any treaty listed in the Annex of the 2005 Draft Protocol. This provision considerably broadens the ambit of the Convention, bringing on board all the anti-terrorist conventions signed heretofore.[102] Finally, article 3*quater* criminalises attempts, accomplice, liability and organising or directing others to commit the aforementioned offences.[103]

This comprehensive list of offences enshrined in the new article 3 of the 2005 SUA Protocol would be ineffective without the reciprocal framework for interdiction of state parties' vessels suspected of such offences on the high seas stipulated in article 8*bis*. This article is essentially derived from article 17(1) of the 1988 Vienna Convention and article 7 of the Smuggling Protocol. These provisions, if read together, mould a new type of broad multilateral treaty exception to the freedom of the high seas, similar to article 110 of LOSC.[104] It is in this particular light that article 8*bis* should be read and assessed. From the viewpoint of treaty law technique, however, the introduction of the boarding provisions contained in article 8*bis* can best be described as atypical. Article 8*bis* is an extremely long article, which reads like a treaty within a treaty: it has its own preamble principles and detailed procedural prescriptions. 'It really looks like a symbol of the irruption of new times into an old treaty.'[105]

In substance, article 8*bis* is premised on the scenario of a state party wishing to board a vessel that either flies the flag or displays marks of registry of another state party[106] and is 'located seaward of any State's ter-

---

[101] It is important to note that the 2005 Protocol is only open to parties to the SUA Convention.

[102] Nevertheless, if a state is not party to a treaty listed in the Annex, it may when adhering to the Protocol declare that the treaty in question shall be deemed not to be included in that provision; see further comments in H Tuerk, above n 98, 70.

[103] See in this respect Mejia, Mukherjee, above n 98, 175.

[104] There are, of course, other bilateral and regional treaties providing exceptions to the freedom of the high seas, but these Conventions, along with the Straddling Stocks Agreement, have a universal perspective.

[105] Blanco-Bazán, 725.

[106] The drafting of the 2005 Protocol considered how the nationality of vessels was to be described. A number of delegates supported inclusion of reference to a ship 'claiming its nationality', but the compromise text settled on was 'displaying marks of registry', which provided greater precision than a claim to nationality. See IMO Review Working Group, 1st Sess, Agenda item 2, Review of SUA Convention and Protocol: US Submissions, IMO Doc LEG/SUA/WG.1/2/6 (July 12, 2004), 32.

ritorial sea', ie on the high seas or in the EEZ.[107] Even though there is no explicit reference to these maritime zones and hence no overt recognition of how the rights of states may vary within these different areas, the Protocol explicitly obliges a state party to take 'due account of the need not to interfere with or affect 'the rights and obligations and the exercise of jurisdiction of coastal States in accordance with the international law of the sea'.[108] Hence, this provision seems to strike a balance between the broad *ratione loci* scope of the Convention and the requirement to safeguard coastal states' rights under the law of the sea.

According to article 8*bis*(5), a state party wishing to board a ship flying the flag of another state party should proceed via the following two requests: the first is simply the confirmation of nationality; only upon confirmation of nationality will the requesting party ask for authorisation to board and take appropriate measures, including stopping, boarding or searching of the ship and the searching and questioning of persons on board. Such request must follow certain formalities: it should if possible contain the name of the suspect ship, the IMO ship identification number, the port of registry, the ports of origin and destination, and any other relevant information.[109] If a request is made orally, a confirmation in writing should follow as soon as possible.[110] The latter provision is commendable, since it recognises the practical exigencies and time constraints of interdiction operations on the high seas,[111] but also requires the subsequent confirmation in writing for reasons of legal certainty and due process.[112]

The Convention regulates the duty of the first party to acknowledge receipt of any written or oral request. Acknowledgment does not mean the provision of the information requested, let alone, authorisation to board the vessel. A proposal to regulate the consequences of lack of acknowledgment of request did not find enough support at the IMO Legal Committee.[113] This does not mean, however, that 'lack of acknowledgment or lack of confirmation of nationality, may lead to actions governed by the law of piracy'.[114] On the contrary, the lack of confirmation of nationality coupled with the corresponding inability of the vessel in question to

---

[107] See art 8*bis*(5).

[108] art 8*bis*(10)(c)(i). It would appear that boarding must therefore take account of the right of coastal states in exercising sovereign rights and jurisdiction in the EEZ so as not to interfere with those rights; see Klein, 320.

[109] The innovation here in comparison with the other relevant treaties is that the request in question should include, if possible, the IMO ship identification number.

[110] art 8*bis*(2).

[111] In view of the danger that the suspect ship will evade boarding and seizure, it is of cardinal importance that the requesting state communicates with the flag state and receives the confirmation of nationality in an expeditious fashion.

[112] Suffice it to note here the *R v Charrington* case before UK courts, involving drug trafficking on the high seas, which is discussed *in extenso* below, Ch 7.

[113] See Young, above n 93, 362, 365.

[114] Blanco-Bazán, 726.

validly claim a nationality may lead to consideration of the vessels as stateless, which suffices for the boarding of the vessel under article 110 of LOSC and customary law.

Confirmation of nationality by the first party becomes the source of an ample set of rights and obligations. It is only after confirming nationality that, in accordance with para 5(b), the first party formally becomes the flag state, and assumes its rights and obligations as such. The request for authorisation to board and take consequential measures can be answered by the flag state in different ways: it can simply refuse to authorise boarding without further ado, or indicate that it will conduct the boarding and search with its own law enforcement officials. It can also propose to conduct boarding and search together with the requesting party, or authorise the requesting party to do so on its behalf.[115] As is clearly expressed in para 8, the flag state retains the right to exercise jurisdiction throughout the whole process of boarding and search, as well as, subsequently, over the detained ship, cargo or over the arrested persons. Thus, the 2005 SUA Protocol follows an approach similar to the other relevant treaties, ie it fully adheres to the principle of preferential flag state jurisdiction, with the sole exception of the consensual conferment of the jurisdiction to the requesting state or another party.[116] This conferment, however, is contingent upon the establishment of jurisdiction by the requesting or the other parties pursuant to article 6 of the SUA Convention. This highlights one potential drawback of the Protocol, ie while it obliges state parties to establish jurisdiction based upon the territorial, flag state or active nationality principle, it eschews doing the same for the case of an authorisation to visit a foreign vessel on the high seas.[117] Nevertheless, if the boarding state takes the alleged offenders in its territory, then it is obliged either to establish the requisite jurisdiction or extradite them (*aut dedere aut judicare* principle).[118] In addition, the 2005 SUA Protocol falls short of addressing the question of concurring jurisdictional claims by more than one state, in the event that the flag state decides not to exert jurisdiction in this regard.[119] This omission, which is noticeable in all the relevant treaties,[120] may lead to problems of conflicting jurisdictions, since, besides the absence of a *lex specialis* in these treaties, there is no customary rule to resolve such issues.

Another potential shortcoming of the Protocol, which, however, reflects

---

[115] See art 8*bis*(5)(c).

[116] See art 8*bis*(8).

[117] art 6 of the SUA Convention is divided into two paragraphs: the first one defines the conditions under which a state is obliged to establish jurisdiction over the offenders, whereas the second sets criteria by which a state party may also establish that jurisdiction. See further comments in C Joyner, 'The 1988 SUA Convention' 31 *GYIL* (1988) 230, 248.

[118] See art 6(4) of the SUA Convention. See potential application of this provision in the context of the counter-piracy campaign off the coast of Somalia, below Chapter 6.

[119] See discussion in respect of 2005 Protocol in C Young, above n 93, 374 and A Blanco-Bazán, 728–31.

[120] See eg the remarks with respect to the 1988 Vienna Convention, below Ch 7.

the consensus during the negotiations at the IMO in favour of the pre-eminence of the flag state's jurisdiction, is the absence of an obligation on the part of the flag state to take measures against one of its vessels when there are reasonable grounds to suspect the involvement of that vessel in the commission of an offence under the SUA Convention or the 2005 Protocol. The flag state may simply refuse to authorise the boarding and abstain from any enforcement action against the suspect vessel. It is argued that 'this possibility of flag state inaction would appear to be a regrettable gap in the 2005 Protocol's enforcement regime'.[121] Nevertheless, it is important to stress that the flag state will incur responsibility and will be violating mandatory provisions of SC Resolutions 1373 and 1540, in case the suspicions are substantiated and the vessel in question transports WMD for terrorist purposes.

In stark contrast to the other relevant multilateral treaties, the Protocol is considerably more innovative in respect of the alternatives to the general regime of ad hoc authorisation.[122] In earlier formulations of article 8*bis* the US had proposed that requesting states could imply authorisation if a flag state did not respond to the request to board after four hours.[123] Concerns about authorising boarding through implicit consent during negotiations resulted in a proposal that states could opt out of such a situation by notifying the Secretary-General that boarding would only be authorised by express consent.[124] Ultimately, the need for express consent to be afforded on an ad hoc basis prevailed and implied consent after four hours was re-configured as an 'opt-in' clause. This implicit authorisation after a four-hour wait therefore constitutes an alternative avenue for states parties. Paragraph (d) of Article 8*bis* permits a boarding to proceed in these circumstances provided the flag state had previously notified the Secretary-General to this effect. [125] A third alternative is that a flag state may notify the Secretary-General that a requesting state is 'authorized to board and search a ship, its cargo and persons on board, and to question the persons on board in order to determine is an offence set forth . . . has been, is being or is about to be committed'. The supremacy of the flag

---

[121] Klein, 324. See also relevant discussion in T McDorman, 'Maritime Terrorism and the International Law of Boarding of Vessels at Sea: A Brief Assessment of the New Developments', in D Caron and HN Scheiber (eds), *The Oceans in the Nuclear Age: Legacies and Risks* (Leiden: Martinus Nijhoff, 2010) 239, 254–56.

[122] This rule was modelled on the Caribbean Drugs Agreement (2003) and in particular art 16(3) thereof. The same rule, albeit adapted, can be found in the bilateral ship boarding agreements concluded by the US from 2004 onwards.

[123] Review of SUA Convention and Protocol: Draft amendments to the SUA Convention and SUA Protocol, submitted by the US (2003), Annex 1, 23.

[124] See also C Young, above n 93, 370. It is not yet known whether any states have opted for any of these alternatives.

[125] While this approach is more deferential to flag states, it does not overcome a number of the difficulties described by those opposing any form of implicit authorisation. The four-hour time limit was criticised as impractical due to the problem of time zones and public holidays. See IMO Legal Committee, 88th Sess, Agenda item 3 (19 March 2004), para 4.

state is further affirmed by the fact that the notifications relating to either form of implicit authorisation may be withdrawn at any time.

Finally, article 8*bis* subjects the application of the boarding provisions to a comprehensive set of conditions and safeguards. Most of them are simply guidelines, although some could have a decisive weight in the consideration of whether an authorisation for boarding would be granted.[126] They substantially follow the respective provisions of the Vienna Convention and of the Smuggling Protocol and set forth duties such as the protection of the persons on board, the safety and security of the ship and its cargo, and, not prejudicing the commercial or legal interests of the flag state.[127] The conduct of the boarding must also be consistent with international law requirements relating to the use of force.[128]

This examination of the 2005 SUA Protocol concludes the discussion of the initiatives taken within an institutional setting in order to suppress international terrorism and WMD, which also included the relevant SC Resolutions 1373 and 1540 as well as Operation Enduring Freedom in the context of NATO. In the following paragraphs, the respective initiatives taken beyond international institutions will be canvassed. In addition, all the possible legal justifications for unilateral measures in the present context will be addressed. It must be stressed that such justifications may also have applicability in cases where, for example, no explicit authorisation is given under the 2005 SUA Protocol.

D. CARICOM

The most recent development concerning the fight against the threats of maritime terrorism and the proliferation of WMD comes from the Caribbean Community of States (CARICOM).[129] In 2008, the Member States of CARICOM signed in Antigua and Barbuda the CARICOM Maritime and Airspace Security Cooperation Agreement, which, according to article 2, had as objectives:

> to promote cooperation among the State Parties to enable them to conduct such law enforcement operations as may be necessary to address more effectively their own security as well as the security of the Region, consistent with their available law enforcement resources and related priorities, and in conformity with international law and applicable agreements.

---

[126] See: Blanco-Bazán, 727.

[127] *cf* eg art 17(5) of the Vienna Convention.

[128] See Klein, *Maritime Security*, 182.

[129] The Caribbean Community, also known as CARICOM, consisting at present of 15 countries, mostly English-speaking and mostly island states. It was essentially a regional trade agreement creating a common market with a common external tariff (CET) but has been deepened in the last 10 or so years with a view to forming a single market and economy; see further information at www.caricom.org/.

For the purposes of the latter paragraph, it was explicitly acknowledged that 'law-enforcement operations may relate to, inter alia (b) combating terrorism and other threats to national security' (article 2, para 2). As at 3 December 2010, six states had signed the Agreement,[130] two of which had deposited an instrument of ratification[131] and thus the Agreement was not yet in force.[132]

It is evident from the face of the Agreement that it does not set forth a loose cooperative mechanism to counter threats to the maritime security of the CARICOM; on the contrary, the Agreement provides for very close cooperation of the contracting states, including routine security patrols (article VII), operations in waters of another state party (article VIII), airspace operations (article X), exchange of information and notification of results (article XII). Suffice to mention in this regard that each state party may designate under article VI Security Force Officials, which would have the authority to conduct routine patrols and law enforcement operations in the territorial waters of another state party, either on a Security Force vessel of their own nationality or on board another state party's security vessel.[133] These vessels would also fly the CARICOM flag and they would be under the authority of the Security Force official (Article VI para 4). Such enhanced collaboration is deemed necessary in the region due to 'its geographical dispersion and the porosity of shorelines open to an extensive maritime space' as well as feasible in view of the commitment of the CARICOM Member States to create a Regional Security System.[134]

As far as the interception operations on the high seas are concerned, it is not surprising that the relevant provision of the CARICOM Agreement departs from the scheme of article 8*bis* of 2005 SUA Protocol and resembles more the bilateral PSI Agreements or the 2003 Caribbean Agreement on drug trafficking, that both will be discussed later. In more detail, article IX of the Agreement provides:

> Where the Security Force Officials of a State Party ('requesting State party') encounter a suspect vessel claiming nationality of another State party ('requested State party') located seaward of any State's territorial sea, the requesting State party may request the competent authority of the requested State party to (a) verify the claim of nationality by the suspect vessel; and (b) where such claim is verified, (i) to authorize the boarding and search of the

---

[130] Antigua and Barbuda (4 July 2008), St Kitts and Nevis (13 March 2009), St Lucia (13 March 2009), St Vincent and the Grenadines (4 July 2008), Suriname (4 July 2008), Trinidad and Tobago (4 July 2008); see at www.caricomlaw.org/Details.aspx?EntryId=91.

[131] St Vincent and the Grenadines (13 October 2008) Trinidad and Tobago (23 May 2009); ibid.

[132] According to art XXVII, 'this Agreement shall enter into force 60 days after the deposit of the third instrument of ratification'.

[133] See also arts VII and VIII of the CARICOM Agreement.

[134] *cf* the Preamble of the CARICOM Agreement.

suspect vessel . . .; and (ii) if evidence of any activity likely to compromise the security of the region or of any State party is found, authorize the Security Force Officials of the requesting State party to detain the vessel, cargo and persons on board pending instructions from the competent authority of the requested State party as to the exercise of jurisdiction.

Noteworthy is the fact that the requested state party reserves the right to deny permission to board and search the vessel or to decide to conduct the interception operation with its own Security Force officials or jointly with the requesting state (article IX, para 2). Of importance are the following paragraphs of this article, which set out the 'presumptive or provisional flag State authorisation' model, ie 'if the nationality is not verified within two hours, the requested State party may, notwithstanding, authorize Security Force Officials of the requesting State party to board and search the vessel' (para 3) and the 'deemed or tacit authorisation' model, that is 'when there is no response from the requested State party to within two hours of its receipt of the request, the requested State party shall be deemed to have refuted the claim of the suspect vessel to nationality and the requesting State party shall be deemed to have been authorised to board the suspect vessel' (para 4). Neither the 'presumptive flag state consent' nor 'deemed or tacit consent' are novel mechanisms, as they have been included in other relevant treaties. The difference between them is solely that in the former case it is the requested state party who authorises the boarding, whereas in the latter case, it is the requesting party who is presumed to have been authorised to proceed to the interception of the suspect vessel. In both cases, the CARICOM Agreement provides for a short time frame, ie two hours after the initial request, in comparison with four hours, which is the rule in the most PSI bilateral agreements.

The CARICOM Agreement will also be referred to in other parts of this book; it is probably the most comprehensive and collaborative instrument in the fight against threats to maritime security and this is due to its *ratione personae* scope, namely its participants. In other words, this Agreement aims at the strengthening of law enforcement at sea between the Member States of a 'closed' regional international organisation, who have already attained an integrated level of inter-state cooperation. It is very unlikely that such provisions could have ever been included in a 'global' treaty, like the 2005 SUA Protocol, or in a respective regional treaty, like the 1995 Council of Europe Agreement on drug trafficking. It is characteristic that the only multilateral agreement with similar arrangements comes from the same region, ie the 2003 Caribbean Agreement.

IV. RESPONSES AND INTERDICTION OPERATIONS BEYOND INTERNATIONAL ORGANISATIONS

It is true that the states mostly concerned with the threats of maritime terrorism or WMD proliferation have opted to counter them both within international organisations as well as beyond such institutions, namely either unilaterally, ie with purely unilateral measures, or collectively, ie with bilateral arrangements and collective enterprises, such as the PSI. The appraisal of the relevant collective and unilateral measures will commence with the PSI and an assessment of potential interdiction measures on the high seas. The focus will then turn to the bilateral boarding agreements most relevant for present purposes, principally between the US and various other States.

A. The Proliferation Security Initiative (PSI)

The frustrating experience with the North Korean vessel, *M/V So San*, in November 2002 is widely believed[135] to have led US President GW Bush to announce on 31 May 2003 a new counter-proliferation initiative, the PSI.[136] The latter 'seeks to develop partnerships of States working together, employing their national capabilities to develop a broad range of legal, diplomatic, economic and other tools to interdict threatening shipments of WMD and missile-related equipment and technologies via air, land and sea'.[137] In agreeing on a non-binding Statement of Interdiction Principles, the participants committed themselves to establishing 'a more coordinated and effective basis through which to impede and stop shipments of [weapons of mass destruction], delivery systems, and related materials flowing to and from states and non-state actors of proliferation concern, consistent with national legal authorities and relevant international law and frameworks, including the UN Security Council'.[138]

---

[135] See inter alia Byers, 528 and T Perry, 'Blurring the Ocean Zones: The Effect of the PSI on the Customary International Law of the Sea' 37 *ODIL* (2006) 33. However, according to Allen, the roots of the PSI date back more than a decade, more specifically, to 7 December 1993, when the Clinton Administration announced the Defence Counter-proliferation Initiative; ibid, 47.

[136] On PSI generally see www.state.gov/t/isn/c10390.htm. The PSI has triggered significant academic concern; see: inter alia J Doolin, 'The PSI: Cornerstone of a New International Norm' 59 *Naval WCR* (2006) 29; T Lehrman, 'Enhancing the PSI: The Case for a Decentralised Non-proliferation Architecture' 45 *VJIL* (2004) 223; M Valencia, *The Proliferation Security Initiative*, Adelphi Paper 376 (Washington, DC: The International Institute for Strategic Studies, 2005); JR Holmes and A Winner, 'The Proliferation Security Initiative', in N Busch and D Joyner (eds), *Combating Weapons of Mass Destruction: the Future of International Nonproliferation Policy* (Athens, GA: Georgia University Press, 2009) 139.

[137] A Bergin, 'The PSI: Implications for the Indian Ocean', 20 *IJMCL* (2005) 85, 86. See also S Logan, 'The PSI Navigating the Legal Challenges' 14 *JTLP* (2005) 253, 255.

[138] US Dep't of State, Office of the Press Secretary, 'PSI: Statement of Interdiction Principles' (4 September 2003); available at www.state.gov/t/isn/c27726.htm.

The PSI has evolved through a series of regular meetings,[139] while many interdiction exercises have been coordinated and conducted jointly by PSI members.[140] At the regional level, the PSI has led to the development of a similar programme, the Regional Maritime Security Initiative (RMSI), which applies to the Asia-Pacific area. The idea behind the RMSI is to 'develop a partnership of willing nations to enhance their capabilities through unity of effort to identify, monitor, and intercept trans-national maritime threats consistent with existing international and domestic laws'.[141]

While there are many international legal issues involved in the PSI which call for comments a detailed analysis of them is beyond the compass of the present enquiry. Rather, the focus here is on whether this initiative affords a tenable legal basis for interdiction operations on the high seas and, if so, what are their legal contours of such operations. As regards the exact legal nature of the PSI, its authors have consistently characterised it as 'an activity, not organization' and as 'a collection of interdiction partnerships',[142] while academic doctrine share the same view designating it as an 'international partnership of countries',[143] or a 'loose alliance'.[144] Furthermore, according to Spadi, 'the language used in the Statement and the nature of the commitments clearly reveals that it is a gentlemen's agreement, i.e. an instrument falling in the realm of soft law. As such, it is not legally binding and its violation would not entail international responsibility but "only" the subsequent political fallout'.[145] In conclusion, it is evident that the PSI per se is not an international organisation and that the Interdiction Principles Statement is merely a non-binding political instrument or a non-legal agreement[146] which falls short

---

[139] Further information is available at www.state.gov/t/isn/c27700.htm. It is reported that the Operational Experts Group (OEG), consisting of 20 PSI-countries, meets two to three times a year in order to take the Initiative further; see T Winkler, 'PSI: Application in the Baltic Sea', in U Karpen, *Maritime Safety: Current Problems of Use of the Baltic Sea* (2005) 65. It is stated that 'high-level meetings of representatives . . . are the only recognizable structure within the PSI'; M Malirsch and F Prill, 'The PSI and the 2005 Protocol to the SUA Convention' 67 *ZaöRV* (2007) 229, 234.

[140] ibid.

[141] See www.pacom.mil/rmsi and F Spadi, 'Bolstering the PSI: A Comparative Analysis of Ship-Boarding as a Bilateral and Multilateral Implementing Mechanism' 75 *Nordic JIL* (2006) 249, 254 (hereinafter: Spadi) and C Ahlstrom, 'The Proliferation Security Initiative: International Law Aspects of the Statement of Interdiction Principles', in *SIPRI Yearbook (2005): Armaments, Disarmament and International Security* (Oxford: Oxford University Press, 2006) 741, 756.

[142] Bureau of Non proliferation, US Department of State, *PSI (continued) Frequently Asked Questions (FAQ)*, 11 January 2005; available at www.state.gov/t/np/rls/fs/32725.htm.

[143] J Garvey, The International Institutional Imperative for Countering the Spread of Weapons of Mass Destruction: Assessing the Proliferation Security Initiative' 10 *JCSL* (2005) 125, 129.

[144] S Logan, above n 137, 255.

[145] Spadi, 259 (emphasis added).

[146] See Malirsch and Prill, above n 139, 233.

of enumerating any legal obligations or rights and thus is not a treaty or a binding agreement in the broad sense.[147]

It is important also to examine the *ratione personae* scope of the PSI; it specifically targets 'States or non-state actors of proliferation concern'.[148] States of proliferation concern are not defined collectively. Rather, it is up to those involved in the interdiction effort to determine which states are of concern. 'Non-state actors' is clearly meant to refer to various terrorist organisations around the world that cannot be unequivocally identified with a particular state.[149] Furthermore, the formulation 'to and from' would seem to limit PSI activities to cases in which both the exporter and the recipient are States of proliferation concern.[150]

Finally, as far as the *ratione materiae* scope of the application of the PSI is concerned, it also appears ambiguous, since there is no specific definition of 'WMD, their delivery systems, and related materials'. It can be argued that these definitions are more or less imported by SC Resolution 1540 (2004), which, however, does not completely resolve the problem, since, irrespective of its intrinsic ambiguities, Resolution 1540 pertains solely to the transfer of WMD to non-state actors.[151] More importantly, the PSI does not seem to take into account the fact that the treaty obligations of the states involved pertain to the transfer of weapons themselves, but not the transfer of related materials, ie dual-use goods.[152]

In respect of the interdiction of suspect vessels on the high seas, it is submitted that the PSI does not afford by itself any legal basis for such interdiction operations. Despite concerns and assertions to the contrary,[153] the PSI never purported to establish an autonomous legal authority for

---

[147] On the international plane, it is possible to have three categories of instruments: i) treaties within the strict definition of the VCLT, ii) other binding agreements, such as informal or oral agreements and iii) non-binding instruments, such as political accords or gentlemen's agreements. See: generally on what constitutes a treaty under international law, M Fitzmaurice, 'The Identification and Character of Treaties and Treaty Obligations between States in International Law' 73 *BYIL* (2002) 141. *Cf* also art 2(1) of Vienna Convention on the Law of Treaties (1969) 1155 UNTS 331 (hereinafter: VCLT).

[148] Defined in the Statement of Interdiction Principles as 'those countries or entities that the PSI participants involved establish should be subject to interdiction activities because they are engaged in proliferation through: (1) efforts to develop or acquire chemical, biological, or nuclear weapons and associated delivery systems; or (2) transfers (either selling, receiving, or facilitating) of WMD, their delivery systems, or related materials'.

[149] Logan, above n 137, 256.

[150] See also Ahlstrom, above n 141, 758.

[151] In addition, an important source of legal authority will be the 2005 SUA Protocol, when it enters into force and provided that it will be broadly ratified by members of the international community.

[152] Concurring is also Ahlstrom, above n 141, 758 and Y-H Song 'The US-Led PSI and UNCLOS: Legality, Implementation and an Assessment' 38 *ODIL* (2007) 101, 114.

[153] See in this respect Bergin above n 137, 87 and Garvey, above n 143, 132. See also the relevant discussion in T Thomas, 'The Proliferation Security Initiative: Towards Relegation of Navigational Freedoms in UNCLOS? An Indian Perspective' 8 *Chinese Journal of International Law* (2009) 657.

the interception of WMD shipments on the high seas, and this was emphatically stated in the Statement of Interdiction Principles.[154] On the contrary, the Statement enunciated that the PSI participant flag States commit to 'seriously consider providing consent . . . to the boarding and searching of its own flag vessels by other States, and to the seizure of such WMD-related cargoes'.[155] Accordingly, the requisite legal basis for such interdictions would be sought in the consent of the flag state.[156] Moreover, the latter states, which are participants in the Initiative, are under a political but not a legal commitment to give their consent.

In any event, it would be difficult to hold that a Statement, which is of a political rather than of a legal nature, and an Initiative, which lacks any institutional mantle, could create as such any legal authority for interdiction purposes. It is rather the individual practice of states in the context of the PSI that bears legal significance. However, due to the secrecy and the lack of sufficient information concerning actual interdiction cases,[157] it is not certain whether this practice is consistent with international law, in particular with article 110 of LOSC.[158] As N Klein rightly observes, 'the extent that the PSI is likely to achieve changes in international law appears to be limited by the very nature of the activity'.[159] She notes further 'the absence of information about the precise operation, and consequent interpretation or application of the Statement of Interdiction Principles tends to deny the potential for existing laws to be altered'.[160]

Furthermore, what is important to underline is that the responsibility for any act or omission during the interception on the high seas lies exclusively with the boarding state. Similarly, any jurisdictional question should be resolved in accordance with the law of that state as well as with the principle of the exclusive jurisdiction of the flag state. For all these reasons, 'it is more likely for practical reasons that the really core aspect of PSI [will be] the consistent use of port state controls and information

[154] It must be recalled that all the relevant efforts should be 'consistent with national legal authorities and relevant international law and frameworks'; see PSI Statement of Interdiction Principles (4 September 2003); above n 138. See also JA Roach, 'PSI and SUA: An Update', in M Nordquist above n 79, 287 and D Rothwell, 'The Proliferation Security Initiative: Amending the Convention on the Law of the Sea by Stealth?', in D Caron and HN Scheiber (eds), *The Oceans in the Nuclear Age: Legacies and Risks* (Leiden: Martinus Nijhoff, 2010) 285, 287.
[155] Principle 4(c); ibid.
[156] There could be individual cases, where other legal justifications could be available, such as self-defence or the state of necessity. See also S Kaye, 'The Proliferation Security Initiative in the Maritime Domain' 35 *IYHR* (2005) 205, 210.
[157] The Bush Administration cited intelligence concerns as the main reason for not providing detailed accounts of PSI interdictions; see Song, above n 152, 132. See also Klein, *Maritime Security*, 206.
[158] For example, in the highly advertised search of *BBC China*, the diversion to the Taranto port in Italy happened with the consent of Germany, the ship owner's country of nationality. Cf also the *Baltic Sky* (2003) and *Be Gae Hung* (2003) incidents, where the relevant search for WMD occurred at ports of PSI participants states; see: Y-H Song, ibid, 121.
[159] Klein, *Maritime Security*, 205.
[160] ibid, 206.

exchange between PSI countries'.[161] Closely linked to this policy are various US supply chain security initiatives, such as the Container Security Initiative[162] and the Customs-Trade Partnership against Terrorism.[163]

In conclusion, it is readily apparent that the principle of '*la juridicité*' of the high seas remains intact and the rule of law seems to prevail in the present context. Thus, the '*mare clausum*' claims for interference with navigation on the high seas in order to address the threat of proliferation of WMD finds only legal expression through the classical paradigm of the right of visit, ie in full accordance with the legal order of the oceans. Such expression is found, amongst others, through the conclusion of bilateral treaties, which is permitted under article 110(1) of LOSC.

B. Bilateral Boarding Agreements

In view of the fact that the PSI falls short of providing a sufficient legal basis for interdictions on the high seas, the US shifted their attention to concluding bilateral agreements that put in place a framework for consensual boardings of vessels flying the flag of the respective parties on the high seas.[164] Accordingly, the US has signed agreements with 11 major flag states, namely Liberia, Panama, the Marshall Islands, Croatia, Cyprus, Malta, Belize, Mongolia and Bahamas, St Vincent and the Grenadines, and Antigua and Barbuda.[165] Arguably, these agreements fall within the rubric of 'specific actions' under paragraph 4c of the Statement of Interdiction Principles and thus they are considered an intrinsic part of the PSI.[166] However, they mostly mirror the bilateral agreements already in place for

---

[161] Bergin, above n 137, 90. As was confidentially reported to the author, this was the thrust of the most recent OEG meetings, ie the shift of the emphasis predominantly to port state control. *Cf* also the port state control alternative inserted in SC Res 1874 (2009) on North Korea.

[162] The former US Customs Service launched the Container Security Initiative (CSI) in February 2002 to enhance the security of shipping containers destined for the US. In essence, the CSI allows US Customs officials to identify and examine high-risk maritime containerised cargo at foreign ports, before they are loaded on board vessels destined for the US; see further information at www.cbp.gov/linkhandler/cgov/border_security/international_ activities/csi/csi_fact_sheet.ctt and commentary in J Romero, 'Prevention of Maritime Terrorism: the Container Security Initiative', 4 *Chicago Journal of International Law* (2003) 597 and Klein, *Maritime Security*, 163–68.

[163] See in this regard C Allen, 'The International Supply Chain Security Regime', in M Nordquist (ed), above n 79, 232.

[164] Apparently, the US is the only PSI state so far that has concluded such agreements. While Belize has reported to the Security Council that it is 'actively considering' entering such an arrangement with the UK, the UK has not concluded any such arrangements yet; see: D Guilfoyle, 'Maritime Interdiction of Weapons of Mass Destruction' 12 *JCSL* (2007) 1, 23 (hereinafter: Guilfoyle, *WMD*).

[165] The text of all these agreements is available at www.state.gov/t/isn/c27733.htm.

[166] At the 2003 London meeting of the PSI participating states, the US presented a proposal to the other participants to negotiate standing agreements with key flag states to put in place a framework for consensual boardings of vessels flying their flag; see Allen, 53.

counter-narcotics interdiction operations. Therefore, they are not legally a novel institution akin only to the PSI, albeit they reflect a common and pragmatic approach to problems requiring the extended policing of the high seas. With regard to the legality of these agreements against the background of the law of the sea, they are in accord with article 110 of LOSC, which provides that acts of interference may also derive from powers conferred by treaty.

In summary, all these ship-boarding agreements refer to suspect vessels, defined as ships 'used for commercial or private purposes in respect of which there are reasonable grounds to suspect it is engaged in proliferation by sea', the latter being described as the 'transportation by ship of WMD, their delivery systems and related materials to and from States or non-State actors of proliferation concern'. They all work within the framework of flag-state consent, upholding the requirement of flag-state permission to board a vessel on the high seas and the primacy of its jurisdiction to prosecute any offences discovered aboard. The agreements define the vessels flagged by either party that will be subject to interdiction, provide a procedure for obtaining consent to boarding a flag vessel on high seas and contain clauses on 'safeguards' to be observed by boarding states and claims for loss or damage arising from an interdiction. A detailed analysis of all their provisions is beyond the spatial confines of the present thesis;[167] nevertheless, it would be apposite to have a closer look at some points which are of particular interest:[168]

First, it is important to stress that the above states are mostly flag-of-convenience states[169] and thus represent the majority of the world's commercial shipping dead-weight tonnage. This, according to Guilfoyle,

> gives these agreements considerable reach and indicates US use of its comparative advantage in diplomatic and legal resources to build a negotiated framework for WMD materiel interdictions.[170]

On the contrary, it is has been argued that any interdiction occurring under these arrangements will simply reflect the US's 'inordinate

---

[167] For a detailed commentary on these ship-boarding agreements see: Guilfoyle, *WMD*, 23, Spadi, 256 and JA Roach, 'PSI: Countering Proliferation by Sea', in M Nordquist et al (eds), *Recent Developments in the Law of the Sea and China* (Leiden: Martinus Nijhoff, 2006) 351, 360.

[168] The following remarks should also be juxtaposed with the respective analysis below on the counter-narcotics bilateral agreements.

[169] A flag of convenience is just a device that shipowners use to obtain low registration fees, avoid taxes and employ cheap labour. There is no genuine link between the real owner of a vessel and the flag the vessel flies. Indeed, in many cases the flag-of-convenience registry is not even run from the country concerned; see more in E Anderson, 'The Nationality of Ships and Flags of Convenience: Economics, Politics and Alternatives' 21 *Tulane Maritime Law Journal* (1996) 139.

[170] Guilfoyle, *WMD*, 23.

leverage'.[171] In any case, the result remains the same, ie by virtue of these treaties, the US is in the position to control and inspect the bulk of the world shipping, which would be difficult to achieve through the complex and rather cumbersome procedures of multilateral treaty making, such as in the IMO. Notwithstanding that the application of the treaties in question is based on the principle of reciprocity, they are de facto 'unequal treaties'.[172] It is unlikely that many of these treaty partners would decline a US request to board and inspect a vessel; a fortiori, it is improbable that, say, Liberia or the Marshall Islands would ever seek to exercise the bilateral provisions to attempt to interdict a US vessel.[173]

As far as the modus operandi of the boarding is concerned, where one party ('the requesting state') encounters a suspect vessel on the high seas which is flying the flag or bearing marks of nationality of the other party ('the requested state'), it may request that it confirm the vessel's nationality, and if confirmed, request permission to board.[174] It is significant to note that all the agreements refer to obtaining consent from the state of *nationality*, not *registry*.[175] This language reflects experience in other fields, since when it is required that the flag state is requested to confirm *registry* before authorising boarding, this can be 'a significant cause of delay' if the competent authority lacks 'round-the-clock access to their national register of shipping'.[176] If the requested state refutes the claim of nationality, the vessel will be rendered constructively stateless, and will be subject to boarding in any event.

Furthermore, the majority of the agreements under scrutiny, with the exception of those with the Bahamas, Belize and Croatia, set forth that, if the nationality is not verified within a certain timeframe, usually two hours or four hours, the requested party may, through its competent authority, nevertheless, authorise the boarding and search, or refute the claim of the suspect vessel to its nationality.[177] This reflects the concept of 'presumptive or provisional flag state authorisation', which is found mostly in the treaties under scrutiny as well as in the aforementioned CARICOM Agreement,

---

[171] According to Garvey, 'the reality is that because the flag of convenience has no bearing on the actual ownership of ships and cargo, flag-of-convenience jurisdiction, although providing legal justification and therefore some degree of legitimacy, is largely irrelevant to the political interests ignited by an interdiction; above n 143, 133.

[172] On 'unequal treaties' see below.

[173] See also Guilfoyle, *WMD*, 23.

[174] See eg art 4(1) of the US-Belize Agreement; art 4(1) of the US-Cyprus Agreement.

[175] Nonetheless, the definition of 'suspect vessels' extends to include vessels 'registered under the law of one of the Parties under a bareboat charter, notwithstanding an underlying registration in another State not Party to this Agreement'; *cf* art 3(c) of the US-Cyprus Agreement and art 3(1)(b) of the US-Malta Agreement.

[176] See Guilfoyle, *WMD*, 23.

[177] See eg art 4(3)(c) of the US-Cyprus Agreement; art 4(3)(c) of the US-Liberia Agreement; art 5(3)(c) of the US-Malta Agreement. The most recent agreements with Antigua and Barbuda and with St Vincent and the Grenadines provide for two hours.

and not in the 2005 SUA Protocol. Under this concept, completion of the registry check is not a prerequisite for the flag state to grant permission to take appropriate actions based on the vessel's claim of nationality. Because the status of a vessel claiming the protection of a state can only be either that of a vessel of a claimed flag state or a stateless vessel, the presumed flag state has the right, if not the responsibility, to determine if a vessel claiming its protection is entitled to it.[178] Conversely, the vessel that claims a certain nationality is under the discretionary power of its flag state and is prone to face the consequences, if the claim is unfounded.

A different provision is often included to address those situations in which the requested party has acknowledged receipt of a request, but does not respond within a reasonable time, usually two or four hours, of the request to board the vessel. In such cases, the requesting party will be deemed to have been authorised to board the suspect vessels for searching the vessel to determine whether it is engaged in proliferation by sea. This tacit or deemed authorisation model is shared with the counter-narcotics agreements as well as an option in the 2005 SUA Protocol. However, there is no common formula in all the proliferation treaties; for instance, the US-Marshall Islands agreement grants deemed consent after four hours,[179] the US-Mongolia agreement and the US-Antigua and Barbuda agreements after two hours,[180] while the US-Belize as well as the US-St Vincent and the Grenadines treaties require a response two hours after a boarding request is acknowledged, albeit they provide for another attempt to contact the flag state.[181] Notably, the US-Croatia agreement contains no deemed consent provision. While it obliges the requested state to reply within four hours, no consequences follow from exceeding this time limit as it expressly provides 'the requesting Party shall not board the vessel without the [flag state's] express written authorization'.[182]

Similar to the 2005 SUA Protocol, 'each request shall contain the basis for the suspicion, the geographic position of the vessel and if possible the name

---

[178] It is, however, acknowledged that while the granting of permission to board and search on the basis of presumptive flag state authority provides a useful means of expediting the authorisation process. It does not negate the need for actual registry check, nor does it prevent a boarding state from making the relevant determination; see JA Roach, above n 167, 389.

[179] See art 4.

[180] See US-Mongolia, art 4(3)(d) and US-Antigua and Barbuda, art 4(3)(d).

[181] If a response is not received within two hours, the requesting state must attempt to contact the requested state once more. If at that stage no contact can be made, the requesting state may board the suspect vessel and inspect its documents to verify its nationality. If the vessel is confirmed as having the nationality of the requested party, there is deemed consent 'to question persons on board and to search the vessel to determine if it is so engaged in proliferation by sea'; see US-Belize art 4(3)(e). See also US-St Vincent and the Grenadines, art 4(3)(d).

[182] See article 4(3)(b) and (c) of the US-Croatia Agreement. Neither is such provision in the most recent agreement with the Bahamas. See further comments in relation to the tacit consent model in Guilfoyle, WMD, 23.

of the suspect vessel, the registration number, the IMO number, home port, port of origin and destination[183] . . . if a request is conveyed orally, the requesting Party shall confirm the request in writing.'[104] In addition, the recent agreements contain the same four options for the requested party, as under the 2005 Protocol, namely, the latter party may: i) decide to conduct the boarding and search with its own Security Force officials, ii) authorise the boarding and search by the respective officials of the requesting party, iii) decide to conduct the boarding together with officials of the requesting party, or iv) deny permission to board and search.[185]

Finally, as regards jurisdiction over any proliferation activities discovered on board, all these bilateral treaties retain the primacy of flag-state enforcement jurisdiction ('including seizure, forfeiture, arrest, and prosecution'), but allow the flag state either to 'waive its right to exercise jurisdiction' or to 'consent to the exercise of jurisdiction by the other [boarding] Party'.[186] This concept of preferential enforcement jurisdiction is quite common in drug interdiction treaties and was also included in the 2005 SUA Protocol. However, the latter treaties as well as the Protocol require that parties establish legislative jurisdiction over the relevant offences in order to be able to exert jurisdiction if the flag state relinquishes it. The bilateral arrangements under scrutiny contain no such provision;[187] this omission attains more significance if it is contemplated that the SUA Protocol, which criminalises such activities, is not yet in force, as well as that the SC Resolution 1540 concerns exclusively non-state actors, while its requirement for adoption of relevant domestic legislation has not yet fully materialised. Not to mention, of course, the problem with the trade and transport of dual-use materials; this is not proscribed by the relevant treaties.

The foregoing analysis has been centred on the multilateral or bilateral treaties that provide for such interdiction operations as well as on the relevant SC Resolutions that might furnish the requisite legal justification. In this context, it was discussed whether UN Member States may proceed to countermeasures involving visitations on the high seas in order to induce flag states to adhere to the above Resolutions. In addition, collective or unilateral initiatives to tackle the threats of terrorism and WMD were scrutinised, such as the NATO Operation Enduring Freedom and the PSI.

---

[183] As Roach mentions, 'the US views the proposed content of the request to be sufficient information upon which the flag State may conduct a timely registered check and take a decision with respect to authorising a boarding'; see above n 167, 387.

[184] See eg art 4(2) of the US-Mongolia Agreement. According to Roach, 'competent authorities may make and receive initial requests and responses via telephone, or in person, followed up by appropriate written confirmation using available technology, including fax or email'; ibid, 387.

[185] See eg ibid art 4(3); art 4(3) of the US-Bahamas Agreement.

[186] See eg art 5 of the US-Cyprus Agreement.

[187] See also the relevant comments of Guilfoyle, *WMD*, 26.

However, it is apt now to address the question that was raised in all the previous contemplations, namely what unilateral legal justifications are available for such visits on the high seas. These justifications may be found in general international law, more specifically, in the pertinent rules of the law of the sea, as enshrined in the LOSC, in the *jus contra bellum* and lastly in the secondary rules of state responsibility.

V. LEGAL JUSTIFICATIONS FOR UNILATERAL INTERDICTION MEASURES UNDER GENERAL INTERNATIONAL LAW

A. Law of the Sea

The point of departure for the discussion of the legal bases for the interception of vessels on the high seas for the present purposes will be article 110 of LOSC, which, as was stated above, is considered as to be reflective of customary law. On the face of this provision, it is evident that international terrorism and the proliferation of WMD are not contemplated by the Convention as specific grounds for the right to visit of a foreign vessel. As a result, the requisite legal basis should be either extrapolated from the grounds for interference that are enshrined in the above provision, or be sought in another legal framework. Before examining the latter option, it is apt to consider first whether article 110 can provide any justification for the boarding in question.

First, it is clear that the unauthorised broadcasting and the slave-trade grounds are completely irrelevant to the present survey. Moreover, the 'same nationality' ground seems not to raise any particular problems, since in this case the vessel will be susceptible to the full jurisdiction of the flag state pursuant to article 92 of LOSC. The grounds of 'the absence of nationality' as well as 'piracy', however, merit a scrutiny. As far as the former ground is concerned, it is very often the case that the transportation of persons involved in terrorist actions or of WMD and related materials is carried out using non-registered vessels, without name or flag, ie stateless vessels. To exemplify this, suffice to mention the *M/V So San* incident, in which the boarding was premised on the fact that it was not flying any flag and thus was considered stateless. By virtue of article 110(1) (d) of LOSC, warships or other duly authorised vessels of any state may exercise the right of visit on stateless vessels; hence, the boarding and search of *M/V So San* by the Spanish frigates was lawful.

This incident highlights also the jurisdictional deficit of the above provision, ie the right to visit stateless vessels does not *ipso facto* entail the full extension of the jurisdictional powers of the boarding states. This runs counter to a significant strand of legal doctrine, which supports that the boarding states may also completely subject stateless vessels to their laws.[188] Nevertheless, as was demonstrated in the *M/V So San* episode, article 110 LOSC does not accord any further jurisdictional powers vis-à-vis stateless vessels than the right of visit. In the present case, the transport of ballistic missiles by sea is not prohibited under any international instrument and thus there was no legal justification for the confiscation of the cargo and the arrest of the crew. This notwithstanding, there will be cases involving international terrorism where the visit of a stateless vessel will be followed by the arrest of the suspects pursuant to principles such as the passive nationality[189] or the protective principle.[190]

With regard to piracy and whether it could be employed as justification for the visit of vessels involved in international terrorism, suffice to refer to the extended debate following the *Achille Lauro* incident,[191] where the rules of piracy were arguably considered as the best legal vehicle to address the problem of maritime terrorism.[192] Nevertheless, as it will be demonstrated later, the question of maritime terrorism, especially in cases like the *Achille Lauro*, where the two-ship requirement is missing, falls beyond the scope of piracy *jure gentium*. Nevertheless, there will be situations in which specific terrorist acts on the high seas involving two ships could be identified as *acta pirata*.[193] Consequently, states could rest on the customary law, codified in article 110 of LOSC, and exercise the right of visit vis-à-vis the vessel engaged in terrorist activities on the high seas.

B. The Right of Self-defence

It is a widely shared view that in many cases the right of self-defence is the most appropriate legal justification for the interdiction of vessels engaged in terrorist activities.[194] In this view, 'the target State, or the potential target

---

[188] This is in accord with the practice by the UK and US, that a stateless vessel may be seized by any state, as it enjoys the protection of none; see O'Connell, 756 and also the US Commander's Handbook, para 3.11.2.3.

[189] *cf* the case of Leo Klinghoffer, the US citizen who was murdered in the *Achille Lauro* incident, which was the reason for the US to assert the passive nationality principle in their domestic legislation. See *United States v Yunis* 681 F Supp 896, 902 (DDC 1988), aff'd, 924 F 2d 1086 (DC Cir 1991); see also M Halberstam, 'Terrorism on the High Seas' 82 *AJIL* (1988) 269, 297–98.

[190] See above Ch 3 (n 209).

[191] See also the *Santa Maria* (1961), which involved a politically motivated seizure in 1961 of the Portuguese passenger ship *Santa Maria* by Enrique Galvao, intended to draw world attention to the fascist regime in Portugal; see C Fenwick, 'Piracy in the Caribbean' 55 *AJIL* (1961) 426.

[192] Characteristically, Dinstein proclaimed that 'The terrorist has replaced the pirate as the *hostis humani generis par excellence*': see Y Dinstein, 'Terrorism and War of Liberation', in Bassiouni C, (ed), *International Terrorism and Political Crimes* (Springfield: Charles C Thomas, 1975) 164.

[193] See discussion below.

[194] See inter alia W Heinegg, 'The Proliferation Security Initiative: Security v Freedom of Navigation?' 35 *IYHR* (2005) 181, 196; Allen, 140.

State, and its allies, do not have to adopt a wait-and-see policy but may take all measures necessary to prevent future attacks as early and as efficiently as possible . . . In the maritime context such preventive measures may comprise of . . . visit, search and capture.'[195] Similarly, 'if the proliferation of WMD by non-State actors is sufficiently linked to a given threat of armed attack . . . under the rules of self-defence, the coastal State will certainly be entitled to take all necessary measures, including the capture of the vessel'.[196]

It is a commonplace that following 9/11, the legal contours of the right of self-defence have been blurred, especially with regard to the threat posed by non-state actors and international terrorism.[197] It is beyond the ambit of the present enquiry to address *in extenso* the perplexing issues of self-defence and the contemporary law on use of force;[198] rather, its purpose is to highlight certain instances where the law of self-defence could provide the requisite justification for interdiction measures on the high seas. In general, it is significant to pay due regard, as a matter of principle, to the circumstances of each case and its legal parameters; first, a clear distinction should be made between the suppression and the prevention of maritime terrorism, or in other words, between interdiction *a priori* or *a posteriori* a terrorist attack. As far as the first is concerned, it presupposes logically that the terrorist attack has already taken place and *arguendo* the interdiction on the high seas is employed *ex post facto* as a defensive measure. The cardinal question to be addressed in such cases is whether the terrorist act qualifies as an 'armed attack' under article 51 of the UN Charter and customary law, as well as, whether the interdiction on the high seas is in line with the principles of necessity and proportionality.[199] It is at this juncture that the whole academic discourse on the permissibility of self-defence in response to terrorist acts comes to the fore.[200] Before

[195] W Heinegg, 'The United Nations Convention on the Law of the Sea and Maritime Security Operations' 48 *GYIL* (2006) 151, 170.

[196] W Heinneg, above n 194, 183. See also Byers, 532 and S Kaye, 'The PSI in the Maritime Domain' 35 *IYHR* (2005) 205, 218.

[197] See the excellent Report of E Roucounas, Rapporteur on Self-Defence of the 10th Commission of the Institut de Droit International (on file with the author) and the Resolution adopted at the Santiago Session (27 October 2007); available at www.idi-iil.org/idiF/resolutionsF/2007_san_02_fr.pdf.

[198] For the most recent works in this regard see inter alia T Gazzini, *The Changing Rules on the Use of Force in International Law* (Manchester: Manchester University Press, 2006); C Antonopoulos, 'Force by Armed Groups as Armed Attack and the Broadening of Self-Defence' 5 *NILR* (2008) 159; K Trapp, 'Back to Basics: Necessity, Proportionality and the Right of Self-Defence against Non-State Actors'; 56 *ICLQ* (2007) 141 and ibid, *State Responsibility for International Terrorism: Problems and Prospects* (Oxford: Oxford University Press, 2011).

[199] On the right of self-defence in general see Y Dinstein, *War, Aggression and Self-Defence*, 5th edn (Cambridge: Cambridge University Press, 2005).

[200] On the issue of the use of force in response to international terrorism pre-9/11, see inter alia N Lubell, *Extraterritorial Use of Force against Non-State Actors* (Oxford: Oxford University Press, 2010); O Schachter, 'The Lawful Use of Force by a State against Terrorists in Another Country' 19 *IYHR* (1989) 209; post-9/11, C Stahn, 'International law at a Crossroads?' 62 *ZaöRV* (2002) 183; C Tams, 'The Use of Force against Terrorists' 20 *EJIL* (2009) 359.

addressing this, let us quote the pertinent paragraph of the recent Resolution of the Institut de Droit International:

> In the event of an armed attack against a State by non-State actors, Article 51 of the Charter as supplemented by customary international law applies as a matter of principle. A number of situations of armed attack by non-State actors have been raised, and some preliminary responses to the complex problems arising out of them may be as follows:
>
> (i) If non-State actors launch an armed attack at the instructions, direction or control of a State, the latter can become the object of action in self-defence by the target State.
> (ii) If an armed attack by non-State actors is launched from an area beyond the jurisdiction of any State, the target State may exercise its right of self-defence in that area against those non-State actors.[201]

It is submitted, therefore, that the interdiction of a vessel on the high seas, which is suspected has been engaged in a terrorist act, would come under the scope of self-defence, provided that this act was imputable to a state,[202] it had the requisite 'scale and effects' to qualify as armed attack,[203] and the response was in line with the strict requirements of necessity and proportionality.[204] In this last regard, the action of the state should be immediate *ratione temporis* and limited to the necessity of apprehending the perpetrators and eliminating the danger emanating from the vessel concerned. Moreover, it should always be reported to the Security Council, in accordance with the pertinent requirement of article 51.

In addition, by virtue of para 10(ii) of the above Resolution, there is the possibility of an armed attack from an area beyond the jurisdiction of any state, ie the high seas. It is true that, according to the judgment in the *Oil Platforms* case,[205] the right of self-defence could be merely triggered by a

---

[201] para 10; above n 195.

[202] See L Condorelli, 'The Imputability to States of Acts of International Terrorism' 19 *IYHR* (1989) 240. It should be mentioned here in relation to the question of attributability that a possible modification of the pertinent rules in the aftermath of 9/11 would be the shift of the threshold required from 'effective control' to the more lax one of 'overall control', while acts like giving shelter or abetting terrorists *ex post facto* would be very likely to come under the same criterion of attribution. See in this respect the remarks of Randelzhofer 'Art 51', in B Simma (ed), *The Charter of the United Nations. A Commentary* (Oxford: Oxford University Press, 2002) 802. See also C Stahn, 'Nicaragua is Dead, Long Live Nicaragua', in C Walter et al (eds), above n 18, 850; T Gazzini, 'The Rules on the Use of Force at the Beginning of the XXI Century' 11 *JCSL* (2006) 319, 333 and Tams, above n 200, 386.

[203] See the wording at para 51 of the judgment in the *Nicaragua* case (the *locus classicus* on the use of force), which laid down the criteria for the existence of an indirect armed attack.

[204] See the opinion of T Shah, 'Self-defence, Anticipatory Self-Defence and Pre-emption' 12 *JCSL* (2007) 95, 110.

[205] 'The Court does not exclude the possibility that the mining of a single military vessel might be sufficient to bring into play the "inherent right of self-defence"'; *Oil Platforms* case, para 72. See also commentary in W Taft, 'Self-defence and the *Oil Platforms* Decision' 29 Yale JIL (2004) 295. See also AV Lowe, 'Self-Defence at Sea' in Butler (ed), *The Non-Use of Force in International Law*, (Dordrecht: Martinus Nijhoff, 1989) 185, 188.

hostile act against a single military vessel (unit self-defence);[206] thus, as a response to such an attack from a vessel on the high seas, the victim flag state or other states could exercise the right of individual or collective self-defence and interdict the terrorist vessel on the high seas. The next question is what happens when either the terrorist attack is without a link to any state, or the level of force used was *de minimis*.[207] In such cases, it is apt to consider the remarks by Judge Simma in his Separate Opinion in the *Oil Platforms* case. Building on the ambivalent dictum of the *Nicaragua* case concerning the permissibility of forcible counter-measures in case of armed intervention,[208] he propounds the thesis that a distinction should be drawn between full-scale self-defence against an 'armed attack' within the meaning of article 51 of the Charter, on the one hand and, on the other, the case of hostile action below the level of article 51, 'justifying proportionate defensive measures on the part of the victim, equally short of the quantity and quality of action in self-defence expressly reserved in the United Nations Charter'.[209]

Turning now to the question of the legality of interdiction measures on the high seas for the prevention of maritime terrorism, or, in other words, the recourse to these measures prior to the terrorist attack, the following illustration is instructive: at one end of the spectrum, one could picture the situation in which there is a sufficiently established nexus between a vessel which is transporting terrorists or/and WMD material and the threat of an attack. In such cases, the answer in favour or against the legality of the forcible interdiction of the vessel is contingent upon the acceptance of the right of anticipatory self-defence, namely, the right to respond by force to the imminent threat of an armed attack. Having its origins in the *locus classicus* of self-defence, the *Caroline* case,[210] this right has a bearing on every legal discussion with regard to self-defence in general.[211]

---

[206] This is the relevant terminology used by the US Navy to designate such cases of self-defence. See US Commander's Handbook, 4.4.3.

[207] This is without prejudice to the theory of accumulation of events, which is normally used to qualitatively transform a series of acts which, taken individually, would be considered as mere violation of the rules on the use of force, into an armed attack. *Cf* in this regard the *Oil Platforms* case, para 64.

[208] See *Nicaragua* case, para 249.

[209] See Separate Opinion of Judge Simma, para 12. See also *Armed Activities case (Congo v Uganda)*, paras 126–27 and C Antonopoulos, above n 198, 166.

[210] The *Caroline* case (1837) is regarded by many authorities to set out the criteria of the legality of anticipatory self-defence, namely, 'a necessity of self-defence, instant, overwhelming, leaving no choice of means, and no moment for deliberation'. For the *Caroline* case and the celebrated correspondence between the Secretary of State D Webster and the British Minister Fox (1841): see inter alia Moore, *Digest of International Law*, Vol II (Washington, DC: Government printing office, 1906) 412; J Kearly, 'Raising the *Caroline*' 17 *Wisconsin International Law Journal* (1999) 325.

[211] Per the right of anticipatory self-defence is, inter alia, C Waldock, 'The Regulation of the Use of Force by Individual States in International Law' 81 *RCADI* (1952-II) 451, 496; *contra*: I Brownlie, *International Law and the Use of Force by States* (Oxford: Clarendon Press, 1963), 269.

There is no clear answer in the academic doctrine on this issue; nonetheless, the tendency in the aftermath of 9/11 has been to accept the customary right of anticipatory self-defence in case of an imminent threat.[212] It is argued that present-day terrorist and proliferation-security realities demonstrate a need to develop 'the concept of what constitutes an "imminent" armed attack to meet new circumstances and new threats'.[213] 'In this connection, although a high threshold should be placed on the required degree of certainty as to the suspicion of the ship trafficking WMD, at the same time the temporal element in the formula should not be construed unduly narrowly.'[214] It follows, therefore, that if this sufficient nexus with an imminent threat exists, the boarding of the vessel in question would be lawful and most probably in keeping with the principles of necessity and proportionality.[215]

At the other end of the spectrum, however, are situations where the threats involved, although potentially grave, will be uncertain, distant and diffuse, rather than *ante portas*, ie imminent. Here, the legal assessment of a potential interdiction operation would be against the realm of the right of 'pre-emptive' or 'preventive' self-defence, namely, the right to recourse to armed force as a response to inchoate, merely foreseeable or even just conceivable threats.[216] Suffice it to stress that this theory is firmly disallowed by the overwhelming majority of international legal doctrine[217] and thus the boarding of vessels on this basis would be manifestly illegal.

In conclusion, it is difficult to escape the conclusion that the prevention of terrorism on the high seas on the basis of self-defence will depend on the level of the imminence of the threat, ie on whether 'the necessity of self-defence is instant, overwhelming, leaving no choice of means and no moment of deliberation'.[218] Furthermore, the interdiction in question should abide by the requirements of necessity and proportionality, namely it must be based upon sound evidence of the terrorist purpose of the vessel and effected only after a request has been made to the flag state, to no

[212] *cf* the Resolution of the IDI, which states that 'the right of self-defence arises for the target State in case of an actual or *manifestly imminent armed attack*'; above n 195 (emphasis added) as well as Report of the Secretary-General, 'In Larger Freedom', UN doc A/59/2005, 21 March 2005, para 124.
[213] AV Lowe, *International Law* (Oxford: Oxford University Press, 2007) 278.
[214] Jimenez-Kwast, 202. See also AV Lowe, noting that 'There is much to be said for interpreting the requirement of imminence to mean that action to avert the threat, even if some cases that opportunity arises a considerable time before the actual attack is expected to occur'; ibid, 278, and ibid, 'Clear and Present Danger: Responses to Terrorism' 54 *ICLQ* (2005) 191.
[215] See Jimenez-Kwast, 202.
[216] See N Shah, above n 202, 126; T Franck, 'Pre-emption, Prevention and Anticipatory Self-Defence', 27 *Hastings International and Comparative Law Review* (2004) 425.
[217] See inter alia M Bothe, 'Terrorism and the Legality of Pre-emptive Force' 14 *EJIL* (2003) 227, 230; N Jackson, 'New Frontiers, Old Problems: The War on Terror and the Notion of Anticipating the Enemy' 51 *NILR* (2004) 1.
[218] See above n 208.

avail. In addition, the force employed was the minimum necessary required to stop it and apprehend the terrorists or seize the WMD cargo.[219] As far as state practice is concerned, there is hardly any substantive practice of the invocation of anticipatory self-defence as a ground for the interdiction of a vessel suspected of trafficking WMD, besides the already discussed case of *Francop*, which was more convincingly based on the UN SC sanctions against Iran.[220]

C. Other Circumstances Precluding the Wrongfulness of Interdiction under the Law of State Responsibility

Finally, it is apt to consider the application of the law of state responsibility in the present enquiry, which sets forth a whole framework of possible legal justifications.[221] In accordance with the ILC Articles, a State may plead certain circumstances as, in the words of the ILC, 'a shield against an otherwise well-founded claim for the breach of an international obligation', *in casu*, a defence against the infringement of the exclusivity of the flag State jurisdiction on the high seas or of the coastal State's sovereignty. The six circumstances precluding wrongfulness are: consent (article 20), self-defence (article 21), countermeasures (article 22), *force majeure* (article 23), distress (article 24) and necessity (article 25).[222]

The circumstances of self-defence and counter-measures have already been extensively discussed, while it is readily apparent that the circumstances of *force majeure* or distress are of no relevance to the present context, since it is highly unlikely to be invoked by the intercepting States.[223] Nevertheless, there might be room for the application of the state of necessity, which, in general, is used to denote those exceptional cases where the

---

[219] *cf* also the opinion of Shah, namely that 'the proportionality requirement entails two main conditions. First, the degree of force exercised would have to be proportional in terms of intensity and magnitude. Second, the duration of the anticipatory attack would have to be strictly limited to the removal of the threat'; above n 202, 123.

[220] See above Ch 4 (n 137 and corresponding text). *Cf* also Operation Noah's Ark on 3 January 2002. This episode involved the Israeli interdiction of the Tongan-flagged vessel *Karine A* in the Red Sea about 300 nm from the Israeli coast; see discussion in JM Van Dyke, 'The Disappearing Right to Navigational Freedom in the EEZ' 29 *MP* (2005) 118.

[221] On 6 December 2007, the General Assembly in Res 62/61 (UN Doc A/RES/62/61) commended the Articles to the attention of all states and established a working group to consider the question of a Convention or other appropriate action on the basis of the Articles. On the customary nature of the majority of its provisions, see inter alia *Application of the Genocide Convention Case*, paras 173, 385, and 388. *Cf* also relevant remarks by Ronzitti in relation to the application of such justification in the context of WMD; ibid 'The Proliferation Security Initiative and International Law', in A Fischer-Lescano et al (eds), *Frieden in Freiheit: Festschrift für Michael Bothe zum 70 Geburtstag* (Baden-Baden: Nomos, 2008), 269, 275.

[222] See ILC Articles Commentary, 169. For a very insightful critique of the 'exculpation' approach undertaken by the ILC, see AV Lowe, 'Precluding Wrongfulness or Responsibility: A Plea for Excuses' 10 *EJIL* (1999) 405.

[223] See: arts 23 and 24 of the ILC Articles correspondingly.

only way a State can safeguard an essential interest threatened by a grave and imminent peril is, for the time being, not to perform some other international obligation of lesser weight or urgency.[224] This is reflected in the ILC and in its work on the codification of the State Responsibility, which set out a number of strictly defined conditions under which the state of necessity could be invoked.[225] It is not inconceivable that all the conditions of the state of necessity could be satisfied in certain highly exceptional cases requiring the interdiction of a ship suspected of trafficking WMD or involved in terrorist activities.[226] However, it should be noted that the plea of necessity is subject to strict limitations as well as that it has always been construed and applied in *stricto sensu* by international jurisprudence.[227]

Accordingly, in order for a situation to justify an invocation of necessity, there must be 'a grave danger either to the essential interests of the State or of the international community as a whole'; this could arguably be supported in relation to terrorism and proliferation of WMD, in light of the importance ascribed to these threats by the international community. Moreover, article 25(1)(b) requires that 'the interest relied on must outweigh all other considerations, not merely from the point of view of the acting State, but on reasonable assessment of the competing interests, whether these are individual or collective'.[228] As it is rightly observed, 'this condition sets a high threshold. It requires the balancing of the security interest of the interdicting State with its obligation to respect the exclusivity of the flag State jurisdiction, taking into account the global interests in freedom of navigation'.[229] In addition, the course of action taken must be the 'only way' available to safeguard that interest. According to the ILC, 'the plea is excluded if there are other (otherwise lawful) means available, even if they may be more costly or less convenient'.[230] In light of the foregoing, the acting state should establish that interdiction is the only way to avert the threat and safeguard its interests, which presupposes contacting the flag state prior to the interdiction. In conclusion, the invocation of a state of necessity in this regard should

---

[224] See *Gabćikovo-Nagymaros* case, para 51 and *M/V Saiga II*, paras 132–36.

[225] Under art 25 of the ILC Articles, necessity can preclude the wrongfulness of an act if it cumulatively '(a) is the only way for a State to safeguard an essential interest against a grave and imminent peril; and b) does not seriously impair an essential interest of the State or of the international community as a whole'.

[226] See also D Nelson, 'The *Virginius* Revisited', in *Maritime Violence and Other Security Issues at Sea* (Malmo: WMU, 2002) 1, 4.

[227] See inter alia S Heathcote, 'Circumstances Precluding Wrongfulness in the ILC Articles on State Responsibility', in J Crawford et al (eds), *The Law of International Responsibility* (Oxford: Oxford University Press, 2010) 491; A Laursen, 'The Use of Force and (the State of) Necessity' 37 *Vanderbilt JTL* (2004) 485; I Johnstone, 'The Plea of Necessity in International Legal Discourse' 43 *Columbia JTL* (2005) 337.

[228] See ILC Articles Commentary, 84. In the *Gabcikovo-Nagymaros* case, the ICJ affirmed the need to take into account any countervailing interest of the other state concerned; para 58.

[229] Jimenez-Kwast, 200.

[230] See ILC Articles Commentary, 84. See also the *GabcNkovo-Nagymaros* case, para 55.

be neither lightly presumed, nor, in principle, rejected.[231] All will depend on the factual circumstances of each individual case;[232] however, the fact remains that it is another legal tool for unilateral responses to maritime terrorism and to proliferation of WMD by sea.

Furthermore, a common practice of many states involved in interdiction on the high seas in the context of counter-narcotics or counter-migrant smuggling operations is to request authorisation by the flag states. Therefore, it could also apply in respect of vessels suspected of transporting WMD or having terrorists on board. In more detail, this practice could be legally characterised under the veil of both primary rules of international law, namely qua informal agreements, and of secondary rules of state responsibility, namely qua 'consent' (article 20 of ILC Articles).[233]

To recapitulate, this perusal of the circumstances precluding wrongfulness under the law of state responsibility revealed enough legal avenues for states to interfere with the freedom of navigation on the high seas for counter-terrorist and counter-proliferation purposes. Briefly, the case of consent as well as the case of self-defence was the most relevant for the present enquiry. Conversely, while the circumstances of counter-measures and state of necessity could not, in principle, be disallowed, they are not free from perplexity and therefore they should not be lightly presumed.

Having considered all legal justifications for unilateral action in this regard, it is of interest to take note of M Byers' argument, which addresses the possibility that the US, in particular, 'may simply choose to violate the law rather than seek to modify it'.[234] Building on the Kosovo intervention, he posits this approach as 'exceptional illegality' and continues in his argument, saying that 'by doing so, they allow their action to be assessed subsequently, but in terms of its political and moral legitimacy, with a view to mitigating their responsibility rather than exculpating themselves.'[235] In the present context, if the US 'interdicted a North Korean vessel on the high seas and seized its cargo without claiming their legal right to do so, it would be opening itself up to a requirement of reparation', which however, it would be mitigated, since 'in this era of global terrorism, there is an argument to be made that trafficking in missiles and WMD, even if not illegal, involves a degree of negligence on the part of the trafficking State'.[236]

In conclusion, it is of significance to stress that international law has furnished enough legal justifications for the unilateral interference with foreign navigation in the context of international terrorism and WMD

---

[231] Very reticent in accepting this plea is Allen, 173. See also S Kaye, above n 156, 221.

[232] This is without prejudice to the application of the provision of art 26 of the ILC Articles.

[233] See relevant discussion above, Ch 3.

[234] Byers, 543.

[235] ibid.

[236] ibid. *Cf* also art 39 of the ILC Articles, stating that any determination of reparations must take into account any contributory 'wilful or negligent action or omission of the injured State'.

proliferation. Besides the possibility of treaty conclusion to this end, it is submitted that there are also the arguments of 'piracy' and of self-defence; as well as the circumstances precluding wrongfulness, namely 'consent', 'state of necessity' and arguably 'countermeasures' available to states concerned. Hence, the legal order of the oceans is able to accommodate the relevant concerns of states and of international society and to subject them to the rule of law. In this vein, it does also impose certain legal restrictions to the exercise of the right of visit and to the assertion of further enforcement measures on the high seas.

VI. ADDITIONAL INTERNATIONAL LEGAL ISSUES: USE OF FORCE, ENFORCEMENT JURISDICTION AND HUMAN RIGHTS

There are various international legal restrictions to the exercise of the peacetime right of visit on the high seas in cases of international terrorism and of the proliferation of WMD. The principal distinction to be made is between treaty-based interferences with foreign navigation and custom-based visitations on the high seas. In the former case, it is submitted that there must first be recourse to the *lex specialis*, ie the relevant treaties and then to the *lex generalis*, namely general international law. Such *lex specialis* is certain provisions of LOSC regarding piracy[237] and the exercise of the right of visit,[238] as well as the relevant safeguards of the 2005 SUA Protocol,[239] and the provision for preferential jurisdiction of the flag state in this regard.[240] Similar provisions are included in the respective bilateral boarding agreements.[241] In these treaties and in the 2005 SUA Protocol reference is made also to the question of the use of force in the course of the relevant operations; the use of force is, in principle, allowed subject, however, to the strict requirements of the principles of necessity and proportionality.

With regard to *lex generalis*, ie the relevant limitations imposed to the right of visit on the high seas by general international law, it can tenably be argued that, first, the use of force should be the minimum necessary to intercept the suspect vessel and to conduct the lawful right of boarding and searching the vessel.[242] However, in the case of the exercise of the right of self-defence, it is submitted that the relevant legal framework is furnished by *jus ad bellum,* rather than that of law enforcement at sea. Moreover, it is of paramount importance to address the question of the jurisdiction over the vessel and over the alleged offenders. It is rightly

---

[237] *cf* arts 101–107 of LOSC.
[238] See: art 110(2)(3) of LOSC.
[239] See: art 8*bis*(10) of 2005 SUA Protocol.
[240] See: art 8*bis*(8) of 2005 SUA Protocol.
[241] See eg US-Bahamas Treaty (art 4) and US-Cyprus Treaty (art 5).
[242] *cf* art 8*bis*(9) of 2005 SUA Protocol.

observed in this regard that 'even though [for example] flag State jurisdiction clearly permits the right of visit, there is nothing inherent in flag State jurisdiction alone that provides the legal authority to seize the ship's cargo. The seizure component of any flag State jurisdiction intended to block the transfer of WMD-related materials would require authorisation from some other source of law.'[243] It is true that the visit of a vessel on the high seas, regardless of the legal justification, does not *ipso facto* entail the delegation of authority to seize the cargo and arrest and try the offenders. The boarding states should have already established jurisdiction over such offences, which will enable their law enforcement agencies to apprehend the offenders and their courts to try them in accordance with due process of law.[244]

In the context of the present survey, it is true that, in principle, there is no rule of customary international law, but only treaty law, such as the aforementioned treaties, prohibiting states from holding weapons.[245] In addition, few states have adopted legislation concerning the transfer of WMD materials on the high seas,[246] let alone conferring universal jurisdiction upon their courts to adjudicate cases, where there is no link between the alleged offences and the forum state.[247] Similarly, even though there are numerous anti-terrorist conventions providing for establishment of legislative jurisdiction in respect of the relevant offences, there are no provisions, such as article 105 of LOSC, to furnish universal jurisdiction. Moreover, it is highly contested whether international terrorism has attained the status of a crime of universal jurisdiction under international law.[248] With respect to the proliferation of WMD by non-state actors, SC Resolution 1540 clearly provides for the establishment of relevant laws; nevertheless, besides the fact that the majority of UN Member States has not implemented them, these laws will be premised upon the principle of territoriality and the flag state jurisdiction, and thus will not establish universal jurisdiction proper. However, the situation will certainly be improved when the 2005 SUA Protocol, as well as the Convention on

---

[243] Becker, 185. On the disposition of seized vessel and materials, see Allen, 177.

[244] See also E Papastavridis, 'Enforcement Jurisdiction in the Mediterranean Sea: Illicit Activities and the Rule of Law on the High Seas' 25 *IJMCL* (2010) 569, 596.

[245] *cf Nicaragua* case, 135 and N Ronzitti, 'The Proliferation Security Initiative and International Law', in A Fischer-Lescano, M Bothe (eds), *Frieden in Freiheit: Festschrift fur Michael Bothe zum 70 Geburtstag* (Baden-Baden: Nomos, 2008) 269–84, 272.

[246] Suffice to note that the US did not enact the relevant domestic laws until 2006; see 18 USCA § 2283 (West 2006), prohibiting the transportation of biological, chemical or radioactive or nuclear materials aboard any vessel within the United States and on waters subject to the jurisdiction of the United States or any vessel outside the United States and on the high seas or having United States nationality. See also Allen, 17.

[247] On universality see above, Ch 3.

[248] See inter alia A Cassese, 'Terrorism is Also Disrupting Some Crucial Legal Categories of International Law' 12 *EJIL* (2001) 994 and M Morris, 'Prosecuting Terrorism: The Quandaries of Criminal Jurisdiction and International Relations', in Heere (ed), *Terrorism and the Military: International Legal Implications* (The Hague: Asser Press, 2003) 133, 145.

Nuclear Terrorism attract further contracting states, since all parties are obliged to enact domestic legislation over WMD-related offences.

To conclude, whenever a state interdicts a vessel suspected of transporting WMD or involved in terrorist activities on the high seas, a very important yet intricate matter is the establishment of enforcement jurisdiction, which presupposes the corresponding prescriptive jurisdiction, in the form of domestic legislation. The enforcement jurisdiction could be either conferred by a treaty, such as the SUA Convention, in accordance with the principle *aut dedere aut judicare*, or by a relevant bilateral agreement, postulating the possibility of a waiver of the jurisdiction by the flag state.[249] In the alternative, there could be an *ad hoc* delegation of the jurisdictional authority by the flag state; otherwise, the boarding state will not be able to enforce its jurisdiction over the persons and shipment involved, without being in violation of the principle of exclusive jurisdiction of the flag state on the high seas.

All these contemplations, however, will be devoid of any legal merit if the boarding states have not established prior prescriptive jurisdiction in this regard. Such jurisdiction will be the corollary of the domestic application of the relevant counter-terrorist treaties, like the SUA Convention, as well as of the SC Resolutions 1373 and 1540. Nevertheless, in the absence of such domestic legislation or of any jurisdictional link with the suspect vessel and the persons on board, the boarding state will not have any legal authority to seize the cargo and try the alleged offenders.

Needless to say that the states involved should, in any event, respect the fundamental human rights of the persons on board, especially their rights not to be arbitrarily deprived of their liberty and not to face any torture or inhumane and degrading treatment.[250] In relation to terrorism in general, it is indicative to note that during the CoE's High-Level Meeting on Protecting Human Rights while Fighting Terrorism (2005), the following minimum standards, amongst others, were suggested: the need for enhanced control over, and transparency of, the detention of suspects during the interrogation; the issue of access to lawyer; the need to elaborate guidelines on the prohibition of torture and the problem of so-called administrative detention, ie detention only under article 5 of the ECHR.[251] Regarding the EU counter-terrorism actions pursuant to the various SC

---

[249] *cf* art 5 of the US-Mongolia Agreement.

[250] See arts 3 and 5 of ECHR. *Cf Chahal v UK* (ECtHR, judgment of 25 October 1996) para 79 and *Aksoy v Turkey* (ECtHR, judgment of 18 December 1996) para 61 and generally J Hedigan, 'The European Convention on Human Rights and Counter-Terrorism' 28 *Fordham ILJ* (2005) 392.

[251] Human Rights and the Fight against Terrorism: The Council of Europe Guidelines (Strasbourg, 2005), cited and commented by E Myjer, 'The ECHR, the Fight against Terrorism and the Ticking Bomb Situation', in M Kohen (ed), *Promoting Justice, Human Rights and Conflict Resolution through International Law, Liber Amicorum Lucius Caflisch* (Leiden: Martinus Nijhoff, 2007) 379, 383.

Resolutions,[252] suffice it to make reference to the *Kadi* case, in which the ECJ upheld that since the EC Regulation at issue provides no procedure for communicating the evidence justifying the inclusion of the names of the persons concerned in the list, either at the same time as, or after, that inclusion, it violated the right to be heard and the right to an effective remedy. These rights constitute fundamental principles of the international legal order that not even the Security Council can just ignore.[253]

VII. CONCLUDING REMARKS

This chapter has canvassed in detail the contemporary claims for interference on the high seas in order to counter the threats of maritime terrorism and WMD proliferation. Its purpose was to demonstrate that international law is in a position to scrutinise all the relevant claims and refute those that may jeopardise the legal order of the oceans, premised upon the coexistence of *mare liberum* and *mare clausum* and upon the principle of *'la juridicité'* of the high seas. Thus, only claims that can be justified by either the primary or the secondary rules of international law pertaining to the right of visit are accepted as legitimate *mare clausum* claims under the *civitas maxima* of the oceans.

Accordingly, all the possible legal bases afforded by international law were examined, including the right of visit under the LOSC, the relevant multilateral and bilateral accords, the right of self-defence and the circumstances precluding wrongfulness under the law of state responsibility. Finally, there was a brief discussion of the additional legal restrictions to the exercise of the right of visit in the present context posed by the relevant treaties and general international law, such as the prohibition of unnecessary use of force and the requirements of enforcement jurisdiction.

---

[252] See in this regard M Sossai, 'EU Counter-Terrorism Action and Due Process Guarantees', in K Chainoglou et al (eds), *International Terrorism and Changes in International Law* (Cizur Menor: Thomson/Aranzadi, 2007) 227.

[253] See *Kadi* case and commentary by G Barker et al in 58 *ICLQ* (2009) 229. See also M Bothe, 'Security Council's Targeted Sanctions against Presumed Terrorists: the Need to Comply with Human Rights Standards' 6 *JICL* (2008) 541.

6

Maritime Interception to Safeguard the Fundamental Freedoms of the High Seas

I. INTRODUCTION

IN CHAPTER 3 it was stated that historically, claims for control and surveillance in the oceans have derived from the need to protect the fundamental freedoms of the high seas, namely the freedom of fishing and the freedom of navigation. The dangers to be protected against include the over-exploitation or abuse of the freedom of fishing – qualified as illegal, unreported and unlawful fishing (IUU fishing) – which eventually endangers the existence of the freedom itself and destabilises the internal order of the high seas. The freedom of navigation has historically been threatened by piracy *jure gentium* (recently reinvigorated in Africa).

There are also other freedoms, such as the freedom of laying submarine cables, which have been conceived by states and international society as in need of protection.

In the present chapter, the discussion will mainly revolve around the threat of piracy on the high seas, which has almost monopolised the interest of the international community in recent years due to the increase of piratical attacks in African waters. A short reference is also made to the threat of IUU fishing, which has given rise to numerous interception measures, albeit in a rather regional context. The reason that no particular emphasis will be placed on this issue is because the measures taken internationally to counter IUU fishing go well beyond the classical models of visitation on the high seas, involving complex inspection schemes, port state control, licensing and other measures. Finally, questions concerning enforcement measures on the high seas for the protection of marine environment or for the protection of submarine cables fall outside the ambit of the present chapter, since they seldom involve interceptions on the high seas.[1]

---

[1] A notable exception is the 2008 CARICOM Agreement, which designates 'a serious or potentially serious pollution of the environment' as 'an activity likely to compromise the security of a State Party'; see relevant analysis in Chs 2 and 5.

II. THE CASE OF PIRACY JURE GENTIUM AS A THREAT TO THE FREEDOM OF NAVIGATION AND COMMERCE

Piracy *jure gentium* and its contemporary manifestations off the coast of Somalia and more recently in the Gulf of Guinea obviously merit discussion especially as far as the relevant interception operations are concerned. Accordingly, the present enquiry will proceed as follows: first, reference will be made to the definition of piracy under international law and the controversial issue of the distinction between 'private' and 'political ends', as well as to the connected crime of armed robbery at sea. Then, the discussion will focus on the relevant interception measures on the high seas under LOSC and general international law. Next, the assertion of jurisdiction over pirates under LOSC and general international law will be addressed.

This general framework will be made more concrete in the next part, when the recent outbreak of piracy off the coasts of Africa, mainly off the Somalian coast and very recently off the Gulf of Guinea, will be discussed. In this regard, reference will be made to the traditional mechanisms employed in the region, such as patrolling and interdiction operations on the high seas, as well as to alternative ones, which are currently in place off the coasts of Africa, namely the use of shipriders, vessel protection detachments (VPDs) and private armed guards. Closely linked to the use of shipriders is the thorny question of the assertion of jurisdiction over the Somali pirates, which has proved a very significant obstacle to the efficient suppression of piracy in the region. Lastly, the limitations posed by international human rights law to the relevant interception measures will be scrutinised.

A. The Definition of Piracy under International Law

i. Treaty and Customary Definition

Piracy *jure gentium* has been described as 'every unauthorized act of violence by a private vessel on the open sea with the intent to plunder (*animo furandi*).[2] English jurisprudence historically treated the crime of piracy as felony or robbery carried out on the high seas. In 1934 the British Privy Council concluded that piracy had evolved as a crime, from one of 'acts of robbery and depredations upon the high seas which, if committed

---

[2] L Oppenheim, 'Disputes, War and Neutrality', in H Lauterpacht (ed), *International Law: A Treatise*, 8th edn (London: Longmans, 1955) 608. The qualification *jure gentium* serves as the distinguishing trait between piracy under international law, and piracy under national law.

upon land, would have amounted to felony there', to 'any armed violence at sea which is not a lawful act of war'.[3] However, this broad concept[1] was narrowed down by the conventional definitions of the 1958
Geneva Convention on the High Seas and the LOSC, which should be
considered, on this point, as declaratory of customary international law.[5]
Article 101 of LOSC defines piracy as consisting of any of the following
acts:

> Any illegal acts of violence or detention, or any act of depredation, committed
> for private ends by the crew or passengers of a private ship . . . and directed:
> (a) on the high seas, against another ship . . . (b) against a ship, aircraft, persons
> or property in a place outside the jurisdiction of any State.

This reiterates the definition furnished by the relevant provision of the
Geneva Convention, which, in turn, relied heavily on the 1932 Harvard
Research Draft.[6]

Noteworthy is, first, the two-ship requirement contemplated in the relevant provisions, which entails that situations in which only one vessel is
involved, such as the crew seizure or passenger takeover of their own vessel, are explicitly excluded from the definition of international sea piracy.[7]
Also, it is stipulated that the crime of piracy *jure gentium* should take place
on the high seas, or in the Exclusive Economic Zone (EEZ), in which the
relevant provisions apply subject to the coastal state rights therein. Last
but not at all least, there is the criterion of 'private ends', ie the requirement that acts must be committed for 'private ends', as opposed to 'public
ends', which has aroused considerable doctrinal controversy.[8]

ii. 'Private v Political Ends' Revisited

In more detail, the concept of 'private ends' may not necessarily denote
the classic element of *animus furandi*, which is no longer considered as

---

[3] *Re Piracy Jure Gentium* 49 Lloyd's List L Repts (1934) 411. Piracy was similarly treated in
the USA, see A Van Zwanenberg, 'Interference with Ships on the High Seas' 10 *ICLQ* (1961)
785, 802.

[4] A very informative perusal of the case law concerning piracy is offered by R Constantinople,
'Towards a New Definition of Piracy: The *Achille Lauro* Incident' 26 *Virginia Journal of
International Law* (1986) 723, 727.

[5] On the provisions of LOSC concerning piracy see Nordquist, Commentary, 182. On
piracy in general see H Dubner, *The Law of International Sea Piracy*, 2nd edn (The Hague:
Martinus Nijhoff, 1988); A Rubin, *The Law of Piracy*, 2nd edn (New York: Transnational, 1998).

[6] Harvard Research in International Law, Draft Convention on Piracy, reprinted in 26 *AJIL
Supp* (1932) 743 (hereinafter: 'Harvard Research).

[7] cf art 101(a)(ii), which alludes to acts of piracy directed against a ship, aircraft, person, or
property in a place outside the jurisdiction of any state, ie *terra nullius*.

[8] See in this regard S Davidson, 'International Law and the Suppression of Maritime
Violence', in R Burchill et al (eds), *International Conflict and Security Law* (Cambridge: Cambridge
University Press, 2005) 265, 271.

sine qua non,[9] albeit, arguably, it still excludes purely politically motivated acts.[10] According to the Harvard Research,

> [it] excludes from its definition of piracy all case of wrongful attacks on person or property for political ends, whether they are made on behalf of states or of recognised belligerent organisations or of unrecognised revolutionary bands.[11]

Historically, the requirement that a pirate act had to be committed for 'private ends' had its origin in the distinction between piracy and privateering.[12] The Declaration of Paris abolished privateering in 1856,[13] but

> the distinction between private and public ends was maintained because courts and states wanted to differentiate between piracy and acts of maritime depredation carried out by insurgents or rebels.[14]

Consequently,

> it is regretted that the League of Nations Committee and its successors chose this formulation and not the one that stems most logically from the pirate-privateer distinction, that is to say piracy is an act undertaken without *due authority*. After all, the insurgents that customary law and in turn the Committee and then the Group sought to protect were bodies that that had won some form of recognition or whose acts would have been legal if they had been recognized, and who directed their depredations solely against the vessels of the country whose government they sought to overthrow.[15]

In accord also is Guilfoyle, writing that

> the words 'for private ends' . . . were originally included to acknowledge the historic exception for civil-war insurgencies who attacked only the vessels of the government they sought to overthrow.[16]

---

[9] See the Commentary of the International Law Commission to Draft Article 39, reprinted in YbILC (1956-II) 282. See also M McDougal and W Burke, 810.

[10] For relevant arguments per and *contra* this view see, inter alia, B Bornick, 'Bounty Hunters and Pirates: Filling in the Gaps of the 1982 UNCLOS' 17 *Florida Journal of International Law* (2005) 259; T Garmon, 'International Law of the Sea: Reconciling the Law of Piracy and Terrorism in the Wake of September 11th' 27 *Tulane MLJ* (2002) 257.

[11] Harvard Research, 786. On the historical debate over the belligerent naval rights of insurgencies see L Moir, *The Law of Internal Armed Conflict* (Cambridge: Cambridge University Press, 2002) Ch 1.

[12] On privateering see D Petrie, *The Prize Game: Lawful Looting on the High Seas in the Days of Fighting Sail* (Anapolis: Naval Institute Press, 1999) and F Stark, *The Abolition of Privateering and the Declaration of Paris* (New York: Columbia University Press, 1897).

[13] See Declaration Respecting Maritime Law, 16 April 1856, published in 1 *AJIL* (Supp 1907) 89. The Paris Declaration is given an exhaustive treatment in F Piggot, *The Declaration of Paris 1856* (London, 1919).

[14] M Murphy, 'Piracy and UNCLOS' in P Lehr (ed), *Violence at Sea: Piracy in the Age of Global Terrorism* (London: Routledge, 2007) 155, 160.

[15] ibid, 160 (emphasis added).

[16] D Guilfoyle, 'Piracy off Somalia: UN Security Council Resolution 1816 and IMO Regional Counter-Piracy Efforts' 57 *ICLQ* (2008) 690, 693. See also Harvard Draft, 798 and 857.

Drawing from this insight, it is submitted that there will be cases of maritime violence, where, despite the political ends involved, the lack of 'a due authority' and 'legitimate targets' will be decisive for the designation of the acts concerned as *acta pirata* under customary law. For example, any such act by a recognised belligerent or rebel group against vessels of third states and not of the state towards which they are in revolt, regardless of its motive, would not fall within the 'political ends' exception and thus if the other requirements of article 101 of LOSC exist, it could be considered piracy.[17] Accordingly, the words 'for private ends' must be construed broadly, and all acts of violence lacking 'due authority' and legitimacy, according to international law, are acts undertaken 'for private ends'.

Probably, this was the *ratio decidendi* in the case of *Castle John* before the Belgian Cour de Cassation, concerning Belgian Greenpeace protestors who took violent action against a Dutch vessel on the high seas to draw attention to its polluting activities.[18] The Belgian Court found that the protestors' political motivation provided no defence, and by committing acts of violence in support of a personal point of view, Greenpeace members had committed an act of piracy.[19]

iii. Piracy v Armed Robbery at Sea

From the face of the definition of piracy, it is evident that acts of violence that occur in the territorial or internal waters of the coastal state fall beyond the ambit of the international regulation of piracy *jure gentium*. This raises significant problems, since the majority of the relevant incidents at the beginning of the twenty-first century occurred in territorial waters or ports of States, while the ships were at anchor or berthed. Accordingly, acts of piracy committed, for example, in the territorial waters of states littoral to the Malacca Straits[20] as well as in the territorial sea of Somalia cannot be designated as piracy *jure gentium*. In view of this, the international community, and in particular IMO, created a separate

---

[17] See also Colombos, 450: 'if a warship rebels and confines her attentions to solely political ends done for political ends against the State towards which she is in revolt, principle and practice require such ships to be left unmolested by the ships of war of other States'. See also, inter alia, the *Huascar* case (1877) and *Montezuma* case (1887) in WP Cobbett, *Leading Cases on International Law* (London: Sweet & Maxwell, 1922) 299, 301.

[18] See *Castle John and Nederlandse Stichting Sirius v Nv Marjlo and Nv Parfin* (1986) 77 ILR 537 and commentary in SP Menefee, 'The Case of the Castle John or Green beard the Pirate?' 24 *California Western International Law Journal* (1993) 1.

[19] *Castle John and Nederlandse Stichting Sirius v Nv Marjlo and Nv Parfin* 540. See also Guilfoyle, *Shipping Interdiction*, 38.

[20] On the attacks in the Malacca Straits, see inter alia JN Mak, 'Pirates, Renegades and Fishermen: The Politics of "Sustainable" in the Strait of Malacca', in Lehr P (ed), *Violence at Sea: Piracy in the Age of Global Terrorism* (London: Routledge, 2007) 199; JS Burnett, *Dangerous Waters: Modern Piracy and Terror on the High Seas* (New York: Plume, 2003) 9.

crime in the Draft Code for the Investigation of the Crimes of Piracy and Armed Robbery against Ships, that of 'armed robbery against ships':

> any unlawful act of violence or detention or any act of depredation or threat thereof, other than an act of piracy, directed against a ship or against persons or property on board such a ship, within a state's jurisdiction over such offences.[21]

Evident from the face of this definition is that neither the 'two-ship requirement' nor the 'private ends' one is necessary for the crime of armed robbery at sea. It is highly unlikely that this crime has entered the corpus of international customary law, and in any event, it falls upon each coastal state to enact the relevant legislation.

In light of the foregoing, 'it is claimed that the definition of piracy is too narrow and that this constitutes one of the major deficiencies of the international legal regime concerning the suppression of piracy'.[22] Indeed, the *Institut de Droit International* acknowledged in its Naples Declaration in 2009 that 'the existing international law on piracy, as reflected in the 1982 United Nations Convention on the Law of the Sea, which is restricted to proscribing acts of violence committed for private ends on the high seas and undertaken by one ship against another, does not fully cover all acts of violence endangering the safety of international navigation'.[23] Nonetheless, there is considerable merit in keeping the present definition, for it still reflects what States perceive of the international crime of piracy and more importantly what States are ready to accept as such. For example, it seems highly unlikely that States would succumb to the *ratione loci* extension of the crime of piracy within their territorial waters. In any event, there is neither a serious proposition for the amendment of LOSC to this end nor any sufficient practice and *opinio juris* for a broader definition of piracy under customary law.

B. The Interception of Pirate Vessels under International Law

As far as the interception of pirate vessel is concerned, it is uncontested that according to article 110 of LOSC, all warships are entitled to board and search vessels suspected of being engaged in such activity. The only requirement that article 110 sets out is that there are 'reasonable grounds'

---

[21] IMO, Code of Practice for the Investigation of the Crimes of Piracy and Armed Robbery against Ships, adopted 29 November 2001, Res A922(22), art 2(2), www.pmaesa.org/Maritime/Res%20A.922(22).doc. *Cf* also art 1 of the Regional Cooperation Agreement on Combating Piracy and Armed Robbery against Ships in Asia (28 April 2005) ILM (2005) 829.

[22] V Golitsyn, 'Maritime Security (Case of Piracy)', in H Hestermeyer et al (eds), *Coexistence, Cooperation and Solidarity: liber amicorum Rüdiger Wolfrum* (Leiden: Nijhoff, 2012) 1157, 1162.

[23] Institut de Droit International, Naples Declaration on Piracy, 10 September 2009, Session de Naples-2009, 73 *Annuaire de l'Institut de droit international* (2009), 584.

to suspect that the vessel has been engaged in the proscribed activity, as well as that the boarding warship or the other 'duly authorized state vessel' should abide by the modus operandi laid down in article 110(2) (3) of LOSC. It goes without saying that the visit itself presupposes that the vessel is suspected for being engaged in piracy *jure gentium*, as it is defined in article 101.

Article 110 applies in respect of vessels suspected of being engaged in piracy; it is submitted that for pirate vessels or for vessels under the control of pirates, the legal basis for the interception shifts from article 110 to article 105 of LOSC. The latter stipulates that

> On the high seas, or in any other place outside the jurisdiction of any State, every State may seize a pirate ship or aircraft, or a ship or aircraft taken by piracy and under the control of pirates, and arrest the persons and seize the property on board.

The definition of a 'pirate ship' is provided by article 103, which sets out that

A ship or aircraft is considered a pirate ship or aircraft if it is intended by the persons in dominant control to be used for the purpose of committing one of the acts referred to in article 101. The same applies if the ship or aircraft has been used to commit any such act, so long as it remains under the control of the persons guilty of that act.

It follows from the foregoing provisions that as long as there are only 'reasonable suspicions' that a vessel is engaged in piracy, the interception will be carried out on the basis of article 110. However, as soon as this is considered a 'pirate' vessel, namely a vessel definitely under the control of pirates, the interception will be carried out under the authority of article 105 of LOSC and subject to the general rules applicable to all interception operations. The latter provision will also afford the requisite basis for the boarding of a vessel undertaken by pirates. It is true that article 105 provides, in addition, for the subsequent assertion of jurisdiction over the pirates, but this does not mean that the first step towards the arrest of the pirates, that is the interception of the pirate vessel, does not fall under the *ratione materiae* scope of article 105 (see also *argumentum a majore a minus*).

Finally, it should be noted that the visit of pirate vessels under article 110 constitutes a right and not an obligation of the flag states under international law.[24] Thus, should states abstain from taking enforcement measures against piracy, they would, arguably, not incur state responsibility, notwithstanding the provision of LOSC, which requires states to cooperate in the

---

[24] *cf* the hortatory and not mandatory wording used in both arts 105 and 110 of LOSC. See eg Kontorovich, 183.

repression of piracy 'to the fullest possible extent' (article 100).[25] It is submitted that this provision sets forth a general obligation of cooperation, ie an obligation of conduct and not of result, which entails that it would be difficult to substantiate a breach of international law.[26] Moreover, as Guilfoyle very astutely asserts,

> In the face of such limited State practice it is difficult to conclude that there is a duty of national criminalization and harder still to conclude that there is a duty to either prosecute suspected pirates or to send them to a State that will. If there were such duties, many States would be continually in breach of them. Thus Article 100 embodies a duty to cooperate, but a discretion to prosecute.[27]

C. The Assertion of Jurisdiction Over Pirates

As far as the suppression of the international crime of piracy is concerned, it has customarily been recognised and codified under LOSC that those on board a pirate vessel may be arrested by the seizing vessel and may be subsequently tried by any state before whose courts they are brought and be subject to penalties imposed by its laws (article 105 LOSC). It is common knowledge that for as long as sovereignty-based jurisdictional principles have existed (that is, at least since the early seventeenth century), any nation could try any pirates it caught, regardless of the pirates' nationality or where on the high seas they were apprehended.[28] The legitimacy of universal jurisdiction over piracy throughout the past several hundred years has been recognised by jurists and scholars of every major maritime nation.[29] Universal jurisdiction over pirates applies to both civil

[25] The ILC in its commentary on the equivalent provision in the 1958 High Seas Convention noted: 'any State having an opportunity of taking measures against piracy, and neglecting to do so, would be failing in a duty laid upon it by international law. Obviously, the State must be allowed certain latitude as to the measures it should take . . . in any individual case'; see YbILC (1956-2) 282.

[26] According to the first reading of the ILC's Draft Articles on State Responsibility (1977), 'obligations of conduct' were defined as obligations that must be implemented through conduct, ie means specifically determined by the international obligation itself, whereas 'obligations of result' were those that require the state to ensure the obtainment of a particular situation – a specified result – and leave for that state to achieve such situation or result by means of its own choice; see arts 20 and 21 Draft Articles in ILC Yearbook (1977-II) 8. This distinction was not reflected in the final version of the ILC Articles on State Responsibility. See also R Wolfrum, 'Obligation of Result versus Obligation of Conduct: Some Thoughts about the Implementation of International Obligations' in M Arsanjani et al (eds), *Looking to the Future: Essays on International Law in Honor of W Michael Reisman* (The Hague: Brill, 2011) 363.

[27] D Guilfoyle, 'Combating Piracy: Executive Measures on the High Seas', 53 *Japanese Yearbook of International Law* (2011) 149, 161.

[28] The law of nations also permitted any nation that caught a pirate to summarily execute him at sea; see J Kent, *Commentaries* in P Kurland and R Lerner (eds), The *Founders' Constitution* (Chicago: University of Chicago Press, 1987) 87, cited by Kontorovich, 190.

[29] See eg A Van Zwanenberg, 'Interference with Ships on the High Seas' 10 *ICLQ* (1961) 785, 805.

and criminal proceedings. For example, when a pirate ship was captured and brought into port, where the ship and its accoutrements would be sold in a prize proceeding, those robbed by pirates could bring suit in admiralty court requesting compensation from the proceeds of the sale.[30]

Thus, while the establishment of jurisdiction over piracy *jure gentium* would seem rather unproblematic to a law student reading the provisions of article 105,[31] the truth off the waters of Somalia is markedly different. States have been reticent to prosecute pirates and try them before their courts, mostly because of the anticipated difficulty, expense or the fear of asylum claims.[32]

According to an empirical study by E Kontorovich and S Art,

> of all clear cases of piracy punishable under universal jurisdiction, international prosecution occurred in no more than 1.47 percent. This figure includes the unprecedented international response to the Somali piracy surge that began in 2008, which accounts for the vast majority of prosecutions. Prior to 2008, nations invoked universal jurisdiction, a doctrine that arose precisely to deal with piracy, in a negligible fraction of cases (just 0.53 percent, a total of four cases).[33]

It is readily apparent that states scarcely invoke article 105 and the universality principle in order to try pirates, which brings into question the relevance of this provision in the twenty-first century. Another issue at hand is that there is no hierarchy of jurisdictions in international law.[34] As Guilfoyle aptly explains,

> A capturing state is neither obliged to prosecute a suspect pirate nor to offer a right of first prosecution to the pirate's State of nationality, the State of nationality of any victims or the flag State of the attacked vessel (although as a practical matter it may). Nor is a State exercising universal jurisdiction after the event required to secure the consent of other states or satisfy itself that no other state could, or is willing to, prosecute the case first . . . On the other side of the equation, no state has a duty under the law of piracy to receive a captured pirate

---

[30] Kontorovich, 192.

[31] 'The courts of the State which carried out the seizure may decide upon the penalties to be imposed, and may also determine the action to be taken with regard to the ships, aircraft or property, subject to the rights of third parties acting in good faith': art 105 LOSC.

[32] In the words of E Kontorovich, 'Proving that a group of undocumented men in a boat are pirates could be difficult. Concerns include logistical difficulties, the possibility that pirates could request asylum from the prosecuting state, the possibility that they would invoke the Geneva Conventions, the difficulties of proving a criminal case when the arrest was made by military personnel, and other problems reminiscent of the Guantanamo debate', 'Introductory Note to Exchange of Letters between the European Union and the Government of Kenya' 48 ILM (2009) 747.

[33] E Kontorovich and S Art, 'An Empirical Examination of Universal Jurisdiction over Piracy',104 *AJIL* (2010) 436. Professor Rubin has shown in his authoritative history of piracy law that very few criminal prosecutions for piracy can be found that depended on universal jurisdiction. He enumerates fewer than five cases in the past 300 years; see A Rubin, above n 5, 302, 348.

[34] See eg R Cryer et al, *An Introduction to International Criminal Law and Procedure* (Cambridge: Cambridge University Press, 2007) 37.

from a seizing warship and to prosecute them: all could do so, but none must do so.[35]

D. The Extraordinary Case of Piracy in Africa

i. The International Response to Piracy in the Region

The crime of piracy remains at the centre of international concern, particularly in view of its upsurge off the coast of Somalia and more recently in the Gulf of Guinea, in recent years.[36] The extraordinary growth in piracy in the region has attracted unprecedented media coverage and has led to a multipronged international response. According to IMO,

> In the first eight months of 2012 there were 84 attacks against ships in the waters off the coast of Somalia, resulting in the hijacking of 13 ships. The majority of attacks leading to vessels being hijacked during 2012 took place in the western Indian Ocean. This compares with 234 reported attacks and 29 ships hijacked during the same period in 2011. As of 31 August 2012, 224 people and 17 vessels (including three fishing vessels and eight dhows) were being held hostage. This compares with 378 people and 18 vessels (including 4 fishing vessels, 1 dhow and 1 yacht) held at the end of August 2011.[37]

It follows that while there is a remarkable decrease in piratical attacks in 2012; piracy in the West Indian Ocean still looms large. It is true that by 2007 the International Maritime Organization was calling directly for international action.[38] It took the hijacking of a French yacht, *Le Ponant*, in April 2008 to prompt Security Council action with Resolution 1816 of 2 June 2008.[39] Moreover, several nations as well as NATO and the European Union have started sending naval assets to patrol the Gulf of Aden in an effort to protect international commercial shipping. In addition, a Contact Group on Piracy off the Coast of Somalia has been created since 14 January 2009 pursuant to Security Council Resolution 1851 (2008). This is a voluntary ad hoc international forum meeting quarterly at the UN with the view to 'coordi-

---

[35] D Guilfoyle, 'Legal Challenges in Fighting Piracy', in B Van Gingel and F-P Van der Putten (eds), *The International Response to Somali Piracy: Challenges and Opportunities* (Leiden: Martinus Nijhoff, 2010) 127, 130–31.

[36] The grounds for the increase of the piratical acts off the Somali coast are explained inter alia in Papastavridis, Somalia, 124–25 and Guilfoyle, above n 25, 150–54. See also the Report of the International Expert Group on Piracy off the Somali Coast commissioned by the Special Representative of the S-G of the UN to Somalia, 15; available at www.imcsnet.org/imcs/docs/somalia_piracy_intl_experts_report_consolidated.pdf.

[37] IMO source (on file with the author). For an updated list of cases of piracy and armed robbery see at <http://gisis.imo.org/Public/PAR/Default.aspx>

[38] See IMO Doc A 25/Res 1002 (6 December 2007) para 6.

[39] See inter alia D Guilfoyle, 'Piracy off Somalia: UN Security Council Resolution 1816 and IMO Regional Counter-Piracy Efforts' 57 *ICLQ* (2008) 690; T Treves, 'Piracy, Law of the Sea, and Use of Force: Developments off the Coast of Somalia' 20 *EJIL* (2009) 404.

nating political, military, and other efforts to bring an end to piracy off the coast of Somalia and to ensure that pirates are brought to justice'.[40]

By 30 November 2009, less than 18 months after Resolution 1816, the Security Council could refer in Resolution 1897's preamble to:

> the efforts of the EU [Naval Force] operation Atalanta . . . North Atlantic Treaty Organization operations Allied Protector and Ocean Shield, Combined Maritime Forces' Combined Task Force 151, and other States acting in a national capacity in cooperation with the TFG and each other, to suppress piracy and to protect vulnerable ships transiting through the waters off the coast of Somalia.[41]

As described by Guilfoyle,

> their efforts are coordinated in three ways. First, in August 2008 Operation Enduring Freedom's combined forces established 'a maritime security patrol area ["MPSA"] in international waters off the Somali coast.' The MPSA is a defined area within the Gulf of Aden, providing a common system of reference which allows naval forces to 'de-conflict' their activities. De-confliction aims at mutual awareness and avoiding duplication without implying any unitary command. Second, building on the MPSA there is a Shared Awareness and Deconfliction process ('SHADE') among those States with naval assets in the Gulf, essentially a process of meetings and information sharing. Third, running through the MPSA is an internationally recognised transit corridor (the 'IRTC'), established in August 2008 by the United Kingdom Maritime Trade Organization. Information for shipping using the IRTC is available through a website run by the Maritime Security Centre (Horn of Africa), itself part of EU Operation Atalanta. Vessels are grouped for transit through the IRTC in order that they arrive at the most vulnerable times for pirate attacks (dawn and dusk) in areas with a heavier naval presence; such 'area protection' does not involve escorting convoys.[42]

In the meantime, states have taken up a series of initiatives in order to effectively address the thorny question of jurisdiction over pirates. As was mentioned above, states are markedly reticent to prosecute the arrested pirates.[43] As an alternative, states such as the US[44] and the UK[45] as well as

---

[40] '45 countries and seven international organizations (the African Union, the League of Arab States, the European Union, INTERPOL, International Maritime Organization, NATO, and UN Secretariat) now participate in the Contact Group, along with two major maritime industry groups, BIMCO and INTERTANKO, who take part as Observers'; available at www.state.gov/t/pm/ppa/piracy/contactgroup/index.htm.

[41] UNSC Resolution 1897 (2009) Preamble.

[42] Guilfoyle, above n 25, 155.

[43] See also in this regard E Kontorovich, 'A Guantanamo on the Sea: The Difficulty of Prosecuting Pirates and Terrorists' 98 *California Law Review* (2010) 243–76.

[44] See Memorandum of Understanding between the United States of America and the Republic of the Seychelles concerning the conditions of transfer of suspected pirates and armed robbers and seized property in the western Indian Ocean, the Gulf of Aden, and the Red Sea, signed at Victoria July 14, 2010. There had also been a US-Kenya Agreement on transferring pirates for trial (January 2009), see relevant practice at: www.reuters.com/article/worldNews/idUSTRE52480N20090305.

[45] Reportedly, the UK has signed relevant agreements with Kenya, Seychelles, Tanzania and more recently with Mauritius. See eg 'Republic of Kenya and the United Kingdom Sign

the European Union[46] have opted for entering into Memoranda of Understanding with countries in the region, for example Kenya, Seychelles, Tanzania and Mauritius, and transferring the suspects to the latter states. In addition, the international community had been contemplating of another solution, namely 'the establishment of specialized Somali courts to try suspected pirates both in Somalia and in the region, including an extraterritorial Somali specialized anti-piracy court'.[47]

Nonetheless, in light of the strong opposition by the Somali authorities, the current focus has been on strengthening the capability of the piracy prosecution centres in Kenya, the Seychelles and Mauritius, as well as on facilitating the post-trial international transfer of pirates to Somali prisons. Indeed, the UNODC counter-piracy program has made considerable efforts build judicial capacity in the region and to improve prison conditions. This has included assistance in the establishment of Piracy Prosecution Centers in Kenya, Seychelles and Mauritius, as well as the refurbishment or building of prisons in Mombasa, Kenya and in Somalia (Hargeisa in Somaliland and Bossaso and Garowe in Puntland *et al*) and training of personnel.[48]

UNODC has also been supporting transfer arrangements with third states prosecuting Somali nationals in order to assist these states to return Somali nationals to Somali's prisons. The benefits of this approach are that the Somali nationals are closer to their homes and this alleviates the burden on the (third party) states involved. Accordingly, in 2011 Seychelles signed relevant MOUs with the Transitional Federal Government, with

A Memorandum Of Understanding On Piracy Along the Coast Of Somalia', available at www.mfa.go.ke/mfacms/index.php?option=com_content&task=view&id=305&Itemid=62 and 'Signing of Piracy Agreement with Mauritius' (8 June 2012); available at www.number10.gov.uk/news/piracy-agreement-mauritius/.

[46] See Exchange of Letters between the EU and the Government of Kenya on the conditions and modalities for the transfer of persons suspected of having committed acts of piracy (6 March 2009); Exchange of Letters between the European Union and the Republic of Seychelles on the Conditions and Modalities for the Transfer of Suspected Pirates and Armed Robbers (2 December 2009) and Agreement between the European Union and the Republic of Mauritius on the Conditions and Modalities for the Transfer of Suspected Pirates and Associate Seized Property from the European-led Naval Force to the Republic of Mauritius and on the Conditions of Suspected Pirates after Transfer' (14 July 2011). The text of the agreements and all relevant information are available at www.consilium.europa.eu/eeas/security-defence/eu-operations/eunavfor-somalia/legal-basis.aspx?lang=en.

[47] See UNSC Res 1976 (2011), para 26 and the Report of the Special Adviser to the Secretary-General General on Legal Issues Related to Piracy off the Coast of Somalia Mr Jack Lang (annex to document S/2011/30). See also Report of the Secretary-General on the modalities for the establishment of specialised Somali anti-piracy court, S/2011/360/15 June 2011. A commentary of the recent developments is provided in C Massarella, 'UN Security Council Resolution 1976 (2011) and Efforts to Support Piracy Prosecutions' 26 *IJMCL* (2011) 679–85.

[48] See further information UNODC Counter-Piracy Programme Brochure, Issue 8 (February 2012); available at <http://www.unodc.org/documents/easternafrica//piracy/20120206-UNODC_Brochure_Issue_8.1.pdf.>

Puntland and with Somaliland. These MOUs enable such transfers to be considered on a case-by-case basis. This means requests are required to be made by Seychelles for each proposed transfer of a convicted person and consent must be obtained from the TFG, Puntland or Somaliland authorities. The consent of the person proposed for transfer is also required. In the event of a transfer, TFG, Puntland or Somaliland is required to enforce the sentence as if it had been imposed in the latter. The transferred person must be treated in accordance with applicable international human rights obligations, and Seychelles has the right to monitor that those obligations are complied with.[49]

It should be noted that on 26 January 2009, a high-level meeting of 17 states from the Western Indian Ocean, Gulf of Aden, and Red Sea areas was convened by the International Maritime Organization (IMO) in Djibouti to help address the present problem. The meeting has adopted a Code of Conduct concerning the Repression of Piracy and Armed Robbery against Ships in the Western Indian Ocean and the Gulf of Aden on 29 January 2009 (the Djibouti Code).[50] It was not concluded in legally binding form (article 15),[51] and it is to apply only between the participants.[52]

Furthermore, it is worth mentioning that revised guidance on combating piracy and armed robbery against ships was agreed by IMO's Maritime Safety Committee (MSC) in its 86th session from 27 May to 5 June 2009. In more detail, the MSC produced updated Recommendations to Governments for preventing and suppressing piracy and armed robbery against ships and Guidance to ship owners and ship operators, shipmasters and crews on preventing and suppressing acts of piracy and armed robbery against ships. The guidance to shipmasters and crew includes a new annex aimed at seafarers, fishermen, and other mariners who may be kidnapped or held hostage for ransom. An MSC circular on piracy and armed robbery against ships in waters off the coast of Somalia was also adopted, to include best management practices to deter piracy in the Gulf of Aden and off the Coast of Somalia.[53]

The most controversial recent initiative of IMO in this respect, however, was the Interim Recommendations for Flag States Regarding the Use of

---

[49] UN SC Report of the S-G (20 January 2012), at paras 22–24.

[50] See Code of Conduct concerning the Repression of Piracy and Armed Robbery against Ships in the Western Indian Ocean and the Gulf of Aden, adopted in Djibouti on 29 January 2009, available at www.fco.gov.uk/resources/en/pdf/pdf9/piracy-djibouti-meeting.

[51] The choice of a non-binding instrument followed some participants' concerns that 'it would take significantly longer . . . to gain parliamentary support for entering a binding agreement'; see D Guilfoyle, above n 25, 169.

[52] The Djibouti Code is open for signature only by the 21 states referred to as 'Participants' in the Preamble of the Code. The list includes, inter alia, Comoros, Djibouti, Egypt, Eritrea, Ethiopia, France, Kenya, Madagascar, Oman et al.

[53] See MSC 1/Circ 1339, Best Management Practices for Protection against Somalia-Based Piracy (BMP 4) (revokes MSC 1/Circ 1337), available at www.imo.org/OurWork/Security/SecDocs/Documents/Piracy/MSC.1-Circ.1339.pdf.

Privately Contracted Armed Security Personnel on Board Ships in the High Risk Area, which were approved by the Maritime Safety Committee, at its eighty-ninth session (11 to 20 May 2011).[54] The IMO succumbed to the calls of shipowners, who, in an increasing number of cases, employ private armed guards to augment shipboard security arrangements when transiting the area of the Gulf of Aden and West Indian Ocean. As was noted in the Revised Interim Guidance to Shipowners, Ship Operators, and Shipmasters on the Use of Privately Contracted Armed Security Personnel on board Ships in the High Risk Area, flag State jurisdiction and thus any laws and regulations imposed by the flag State concerning the use of PMSC and PCASP apply to their ships. Furthermore it is also important to note that port and coastal States' laws may also apply to such ships.[55]

An important distinction must be drawn between these 'private armed guards' and the 'Vessel Protection Detachments' (VPDs), ie navy detachments deployed either on board a foreign warship in the context of EUNAVFOR Operation Atalanta[56] or on board a merchant vessel flying the same flag with the VPD unit. The latter option has been under serious consideration by the international community lately, but, to the knowledge of the author, there has been no official instrument adopting or regulating such measure.[57] Nonetheless, VPDs have been apparently employed by a few states, such as Italy, in view of the recent incident of two marines on board an Italian oil tanker off southern India, who mistook two Indian fishermen as pirates and killed them.[58] This incident

---

[54] See MSC 1/Circ 1406 (23 May 2011). On the use of private armed guards see C Spearin, 'Private Military and Security Companies v International Naval Endeavours v Somali Pirates' 10 *Journal of International Criminal Justice* (2012) 823–37.

[55] See MSC.1/Circ.1405/Rev.2 (25 May 2012), available at www.imo.org/OurWork/Security/SecDocs/Documents/Piracy/MSC.1-Circ.1405-Rev2.pdf. See also Revised Interim Recommendations for Flag States Regarding the Use of Privately Contracted Armed Security Personnel on Board Ships in the High Risk Area'; MSC.1/Circ.1406/Rev.2 (25 May 2012) and Revised Interim Recommendations for Port and Coastal States Regarding the Use of Privately Contracted Armed Security Personnel on Board Ships in the High Risk Area; MSC.1/Circ.1408/Rev.1 (25 May 2012).
For example, Greece very recently enacted legislation concerning the use of Private Armed Guards by Greek-flagged vessels; see Law No 4058/63 A' (22 March 2012). For further information see at www.hellenicparliament.gr/Nomothetiko-Ergo/Anazitisi-NomothetikouErgou?law_id=e70e53fd-b089-4c28-a30f-9ee1c61d8798 (in Greek).

[56] See eg the Estonian VPD deployed on a French frigate taking part in Operation Atalanta; further information available at www.eunavfor.eu/2011/05/french-naval-ship-embarks-an-estonian-vessel-protection-detachment/.

[57] The only exception seems to be the following reference in the latest SC Resolution on piracy off Somalia, which '*notes* the importance of securing the safe delivery of World Food Programme (WFP) assistance by sea, *welcomes* the ongoing work by WFP, EU operation Atalanta and Flag States with regard to Vessel Protection Detachments on WFP vessels'; SC Resolution 2020 (22 November 2011); para 27.

[58] BBC, 'Italy Marines to Face Indian Law, says Minister' (22 February 2012); available at www.bbc.co.uk/news/world-asia-india-17123240.

raises several questions regarding immunities of such officers on board private vessels, as well as questions concerning state responsibility.[59]

A final comment in respect of the surge of piracy in Africa is that there has been a significant increase of piratical attacks since 2011 in the Gulf of Guinea. Reportedly, 'in 2011, incidents in the Gulf of Guinea hit a four-year high, with 64 attacks on ships, compared to 45 in 2010. The number of attacks continues to climb, with 13 vessels reportedly attacked in January and February of 2012'.[60]

The international community has not remained idle in the face of this unprecedented wave of piracy and armed robbery in the African continent. The Security Council issued, first, a Press Statement on 30 August 2011 expressing its concern over the increase in piracy, maritime armed robbery and reports of hostage-taking in the Gulf of Guinea and calling States and the regional organisations to take measures in order to counter this threat. Then, on 31 October 2011 it adopted Resolution 2018, which, inter alia, '*condemns* all acts of piracy and armed robbery at sea committed off the coast of the States of the Gulf of Guinea' (para. 1) [and] *encourages* States of ECOWAS, ECCAS and the GGC, through concerted action, to counter piracy and armed robbery at sea in the Gulf of Guinea through the conduct of bilateral or regional maritime patrols consistent with relevant international law' (para 3).

On 29 February 2012, the Council adopted Resolution 2039, which, *inter alia*,

> *Urges* States of the region of the Gulf of Guinea to take prompt action, at national and regional levels with the support of the international community where able, and by mutual agreement, to develop and implement national maritime security strategies, including for the establishment of a legal framework for the prevention, and repression of piracy and armed robbery at sea and as well as prosecution of persons engaging in those crimes, and punishment of those convicted of those crimes and encourages regional cooperation in this regard; (para. 5) [and] *Encourages* Benin and Nigeria to extend their joint patrols beyond March 2012. (para 6).

Indeed, since September 2011, Benin and Nigeria commenced joint naval patrols in the region with the view of countering these attacks.[61] It is not yet known how these joint patrols are conducted, and whether has been any official agreement between these two states delineating their corresponding responsibilities. As regards the aforementioned Resolutions, it

[59] See brief discussion of this by D Guilfoyle, 'Shooting Fishermen Mistaken for Pirates: Jurisdiction, Immunity and State Responsibility' (2 Mar 2012); available at www.ejiltalk.org/shooting-fishermen-mistaken-for-pirates-jurisdiction-immunity-and-state-responsibility/.

[60] See B Rinehard, 'In Focus: Piracy and Armed Robbery in the Gulf of Guinea' (2 April 2012); available at www.cimicweb.org/cmo/medbasin/Holder/Documents/i009%20CFC%20Med%20Basin%20Review%20-%20INFOCUS%20(03-Apr-12).pdf.

[61] See BBC, 'Nigeria and Benin Mount Patrols as Piracy Soars' (28 September 2011); available at www.bbc.co.uk/news/world-africa-15085313.

is noteworthy that neither of them has been adopted under Chapter VII, which indicates that piracy as such is not considered as a 'threat to international peace and security'. Also, both Resolutions included the caveat that 'the provisions of this resolution apply only with respect to the situation in the Gulf of Guinea', so as not to create a relevant precedent.

ii. The Legality of Interdiction of Pirates in Africa

In the case of Somalia, it is submitted that the requirements of LOSC are in the majority of the cases well satisfied. Indeed, most piratical incidents occur on the high seas and involve two vessels, while the ends pursued by the pirates are predominantly private rather than political. Further, the warships of the international forces present in the region comply in general terms with the relevant modus operandi, that is, they first board the vessel to suppress an ongoing *actum piratum*, or to identify the vessel's character, and if suspicions remain, they thoroughly search the vessel and collect the necessary evidence.[62] According to the EU Guidance on the Collection of Evidence and Transfer of Suspected Pirates, Armed Robbers and Seized Property from EUNAVFOR to Kenya,

> the primary objective on boarding a suspect dhow or coming alongside a suspect skiff is to complete a security sweep of the vessel to ensure there is no threat to own personnel . . . If following the securing of the vessel suspicions still remain that persons onboard are engaged in piracy or armed robbery at sea, the boarding team should take appropriate steps to preserve the scene until the evidence 'collection' team can be transferred from the warship to the dhow / skiff.[63]

It is also accepted that if no grounds exists to continue with search of the vessel, the latter and its crew are released.

Notwithstanding this prima facie legality of such interdiction operations, the following comments are in order: first, pursuant to the EUNAVFOR Rules of Engagement (RoE), there are certain types of boarding, namely cooperative boarding or unopposed boarding and non-cooperative boarding.[64] It is the view of the author that there is no need for such distinctions in the case of piracy, since the visit of a suspected pirate vessel constitutes a customary right of warships of all states, regardless of the consent of the flag state or of the master of the suspect vessel. This right, however, presupposes that there exist a priori 'reasonable grounds' to suspect the vessel concerned. Thus, in cases in which the attack on the merchant vessel has not

---

[62] *cf* the Flow Chart of the EU NAVFOR, ANNEX C TO OP ATALANTA EU OHQ SOP LEGAL 001, dated 26 March 2009 (on file with the author; hereinafter 'EU Flow Chart').

[63] See ANNEX C TO OP ATALANTA EU OHQ SOP LEGAL 001 dated 26 March 2009, para 6.2 (on file with the author; hereinafter 'Guidance to EUNAVFOR').

[64] See EU Flow Chart.

yet materialised, it is apt to question the applicable standard of 'reasonableness of the grounds' to board a suspect vessel.

To reiterate, it is asserted, in general, that due to the exceptional character of the right to visit to the fundamental principle of the freedom of navigation on the high seas, this phrase must be construed as amounting to more than a mere suspicion. However, *in casu* and more particularly in the context of EUNAVFOR *Operation Atalanta*, even more flexible criteria apply: the relevant RoE have set out certain presumptions that may furnish the legal basis not only of the right of visit but also of the detention and the transfer to Kenya of the suspects. For example, in the case of an unaccompanied skiff , the most likely factors, according to the Guidance to EUNAVFOR, to indicate whether there is sufficient evidence are, inter alia, the skiff contains firearms with ammunition. In particular, the number and type of weapons are such that they are in excess of that required for personal self-defence (for example, RPGs); the skiff is located on the high seas in areas known to be used by pirates or in the territorial waters of Somalia; there is no compelling evidence that the skiff is engaged in lawful activity such as fishing (for example, no nets on board, or recently caught fish).[65]

It is submitted that such factors or such circumstantial evidence would not suffice to support the prosecution of the persons on board; however, insofar as the right of visit as such, it is suggested that there is room for a different reading of the 'reasonable grounds' *in casu* in comparison to the other law enforcement cases of article 110. In more detail, due to the high number of piratical incidents in the region carried out almost exclusively by such skiff s or dhows, it can be maintained that the flexible criterion of 'reasonableness' has been adjusted to the exigencies of the suppression of piracy in the region. Thus, such evidence or *indicia* of piratical activity may suffice to allow the boarding of the vessels in question. This does not deprive the boarding vessels of the obligation to abide by the relevant requirements of international law as well as to compensate the suspect vessel in accordance with articles 110(3) and 106 of LOSC. In addition, such factors or evidence are not required in cases of an ongoing piracy or in cases of the interception of a vessel already under piracy, since for such cases the relevant legal basis is, arguably, afforded by article 105 of LOSC.

Lastly, in respect of the 'private ends' requirement of article 101 of LOSC, it could have been questioned whether there is room for the contention that certain acts of the Somali pirates might have a political character and thus might fall beyond the scope of the relevant provision. As was explained above, the words 'for private ends' must be construed broadly and all acts of violence lacking 'due authority' and legitimacy, according to international law, are acts undertaken 'for private ends'. It

---

[65] See Guidance to EUNAVFOR, para 4.1.

follows from the foregoing that even if it is conceded that certain acts of Somali pirates have 'political ends', the simple fact that they target third states' vessel suffice to designate these acts as piratical.[66] In addition, as Guilfoyle asserts,

> there can be no international armed conflict as pirates are not State forces. There can be no NIAC [non-international armed conflict] as pirates do not satisfy any of the usual definitions of 'armed groups': they are not organised in any manner analogous to military discipline, they control no territory, they conduct no hostilities *within* Somalia and their attacks are not *directed against* other armed bands or government forces. Their attacks are directed against private merchant and passenger vessels. Pirate activity thus seems closest to 'situations . . . such as riots, [and] isolated and sporadic acts of violence' falling below the threshold for the existence of any armed conflict.[67]

Moving now to the possibility of interdiction of pirates in the territorial waters of Somalia or of the states littoral to the Gulf of Guinea, it should be reiterated that acts of violence and depredation committed exclusively in the coastal states' territorial waters do not constitute piracy under international law. They might be legally classified as piracy under the national law of the coastal state, or, according to the IMO, armed robbery at sea. In addition, vessels committing piracy on the high seas and fleeing to the territorial waters, *in casu* of Somalia or of Benin and Nigeria, cannot be visited therein. Nor is there a right of reverse hot pursuit or land pursuit.[68]

All these were considered significant obstacles to the effective suppression of piracy mainly off Somalia until the adoption of a series of Security Council Resolutions under Chapter VII of the UN Charter. The most significant for the present purposes was, first, Security Council Resolution 1816 (2008), which in paragraph 7 *decided* that:

> For a period of six months from the date of this resolution, States *cooperating with the TFG* [Transitional Federal Government of Somalia] in the fight against piracy and armed robbery at sea off the coast of Somalia, for which advance notification has been provided by the TFG to the Secretary-General, may:
>
> (a) Enter the territorial waters of Somalia for the purpose of repressing acts of piracy and armed robbery at sea, in a manner consistent with such action permitted on the high seas with respect to piracy under relevant international law; and
>
> (b) Use, within the territorial waters of Somalia, in a manner consistent with action permitted on the high seas with respect to piracy under relevant

---

[66] See also Papastavridis, *Somalia*, 135.

[67] Guilfoyle, above n 25, 159.

[68] Reverse hot pursuit is considered the hot pursuit of delinquent vessels from the high seas to the territorial waters, while land pursuit refers to the continuation of such pursuit in the land of the coastal state; see on these notions in the context of drug trafficking, J Kramek, 'Bilateral Maritime Counter-Drug and Immigrant Interdiction Agreements: Is this the World of the Future?' 31 *University of Miami Inter-American Law Review* (2000) 121.

international law, all necessary means to repress acts of piracy and armed robbery.

It is apparent from this paragraph that an ad hoc authorisation was given to states to visit vessels engaged in armed robbery and piracy in the territorial waters of Somalia, regardless of the *locus delicti*.[69] The sole requirements posed in this regard were the general obligation to comply with relevant international law as well as the 'cooperation' and the 'advance notification provided by the TFG to the Secretary-General'. This has also been affirmed in paragraph 9, namely that

> this authorisation has been provided only following receipt of the letter from the Permanent Representative of the Somalia Republic to the United Nations . . . conveying the consent of that State.

Given the latter stipulation, it is rightly observed that

> the Security Council Resolutions were not strictly necessary, since the Transitional Government could have granted permission for foreign States to conduct law enforcement operations within its waters . . . without them.[70]

Notably, the Council underscored that this authorisation shall not be considered as establishing customary international law and this authorisation applies only with respect to the situation in Somalia.[71]

Furthermore, as Judge Treves states,

> The Security Council has framed the relevant resolutions very cautiously. It has introduced a number of limitations which make the provisions adopted less revolutionary than they might appear, and seem aimed, in particular, at fending off possible criticism of the Council acting as a 'legislator'.[72]

In Resolution 1851 (2008), the Council went even further and authorised the 'land pursuit' of the pirates in Somalia; more specifically, it decided that the member states cooperating with the TFG

> may undertake all necessary measures that are appropriate *in Somalia*, for the purpose of suppressing acts of piracy and armed robbery at sea, pursuant to the request of TFG.[73]

---

[69] The SC has renewed this authorisation for periods of 12 months by SC Res 1846 (2008), para 10, SC Res 1851 (2008), para 6, SC Res 1897 (2009), para 7 and SC Res 1950 (2010), para 7. The last renewal of the authorisation for 12 months (until November 2012) was by SC Res 2020 (2011), para 9.

[70] See Chatham House, Briefing Note, 'Pirates and How to Deal with them', Africa Programme and International Law Discussion Group, 22 April 2009, 3; available at www.chathamhouse.org.uk/files/13845_220409pirates_law.pdf. In accord is also T Treves, above n 37, 406.

[71] See inter alia SC Res 1816 (2008), para 9. *Cf* also SC Res (1851), para 10.

[72] T Treves, above n 37, 404. See also Dalton, Roach, and Daley, 'Introductory Note to United Nations Security Council: Piracy and Armed Robbery at Sea: Resolutions 1816, 1846 and 1851' 48 *ILM* (2009) 129.

[73] SC Res 1851 (2008), para 6 (emphasis added). It is reported that concerns raised by other Council members led the US to withdraw draft language referring to operations in Somali

Similar to Resolution 1816 (2008), the Council stresses that 'the measures undertaken shall be undertaken consistent with applicable international humanitarian and human rights law'. The remark made above with respect to the legal necessity of Resolution 1816 applies equally here, namely the consent of Somalia would suffice for states to enter the territorial waters as well as the land of Somalia and arrest the pirates in cooperation with TFG, pursuant to article 20 of the ILC Articles on State Responsibility. The latter sets forth that

> consent by a State to particular conduct by another State precludes the wrongfulness of that act in relation to the consenting State, provided the consent is valid and to the extent that the conduct remains within the limits of the consent given.[74]

The consent of Somalia conveyed by the letter of 9 December 2008 to the UN, prior to the adoption of the Resolution in question, functions not only as a circumstance precluding the wrongfulness of the infringement of the sovereignty, which the coastal State enjoys in its territorial waters and in its territory, but also as a circumstance precluding wrongfulness for the exercise of enforcement jurisdiction therein. With respect to the question of jurisdiction over pirates, it is patent from the face of the Resolution that it does not create any new jurisdictional basis aside from Chapter VII powers. Hence, there are sound reasons to conclude that the authorisation provided by Resolution 1851 as well as by previous relevant Resolutions was not legally necessary for the exercise of the right to visit and seize vessels engaged in piracy off Somalia.

Insofar as the problem of piracy and armed robbery in the Gulf of Guinea is concerned, it is true that the Security Council has not taken up such robust action, as the political situation in that region is different than in Somalia; it has only called upon the states and the regional organisations concerned to coordinate their action and to set up joint patrols. It goes without saying that in cases of piracy on the high seas off the Gulf of Guinea, the authority to interdict the suspect vessels or the vessels actually engaged in piracy derives from articles 110 and 105 of LOSC respectively. In cases of armed robbery, ie acts of maritime violence within the coastal states' waters, then it is up to these coastal states to suppress the armed robbery. It is in this regard that the relevant SC Resolutions call upon Nigeria and Benin to conduct joint patrols; should, for example, the suspect vessel be within Nigerian territorial waters, the authorisation of the competent Nigerian officer would suffice for the interception of that

---

'airspace', although the US argues that the effect of the Resolution remains the same, and that use of Somali airspace is permitted; see E Kontorovich, 'International Legal Responses to Piracy off the Coast of Somalia' *ASIL Insights*, 6 February 2009, 3, available at www.asil.org/insights090206.cfm.

[74] See ILC Articles, 173.

vessel by a joint patrol vessel. It is obvious that such joint patrols require an appropriate legal basis, in the form of a bilateral arrangement, which would address questions of immunities, applicable Rules of Engagement and international responsibility.

Finally, the question of the use of force in the course of repression of piracy in the present context merits certain discussion. In respect of the current operations in Somalia concerning piracy and armed robbery at sea, it is true that there have been several cases of use of lethal force against pirates on the high seas.[75] Nevertheless, in the majority of the cases, it is not evident from the relevant reports whether the use of force was in exercise of self defence or a necessary and proportionate measure to apprehend the pirates. Given the fact that the pirates are always armed with light weapons and do not hesitate to open fire to achieve their purposes, it should generally be accepted that prima facie the use of deadly force, where it is unavoidable, is within the bounds of international law. Reportedly, an exception to this was the case of the Indian warship *Tabar*, which attacked a suspected pirate vessel, sank the ship, and caused loss of life. However, it was later reported that the ship that was attacked was identified as a recently hijacked fishing vessel with hostages on board, not a pirate ship.[76] It goes without saying that India incurred international responsibility in accordance with articles 106, 110(3) of LOSC as well as with the relevant general international law.

Besides the general regime of the law of the sea, it is of particular interest to have regard to the *lex specialis*, that is, the relevant resolutions as well as the rules of engagement promulgated by the international organisations and the nations taking part in counter-piracy operations. It is patent from the face of the resolutions in question that they are silent on the permissible degree of force to be employed as such; Resolution 1816, however, expressly urges states to 'use all necessary means . . . in a manner consistent with such action permitted on the high seas with respect to piracy under the relevant international law'. Even though this Resolution is adopted under Chapter VII and it employs the'magic formula' of the usual authorisation, that is, 'to use all necessary means',[77] it is asserted that the explicit reference to the regime of 'piracy under the relevant international law' entails that the counter-piracy operations in question are not subject to the *jus ad bellum*, but to the peacetime law enforcement at sea. This would be in harmony with the textual interpretation of the relevant

---

[75] See, eg, BBC News, 'French Warship Captures Pirates', 15 April 2009, http://news.bbc.co.uk/2/hi/africa/8000447.stm

[76] See Chatham House, *Piracy*, above n 70, 4. *Cf*, however, the opinion of the Indian navy that it attacked a pirate's mother ship, www.nytimes.com/2008/11/19/world/asia/19iht 20pirate.17953692.html. Another case that involved the deadly use of force against pirates was the Ariya case; information on file with the author.

[77] *cf* SC Res 678 (1990), para 2.

Resolution as well as with the 'object and purpose' of the latter, which is the repression of the crime of piracy and armed robbery in the region. Resolution 1851, on the other hand, authorises the land pursuit of the pirates and thus it is not relevant to the issue of the use of force at sea; it does, however, makes reference to the 'applicable international humanitarian and human rights law', which has consequences concerning the detention of these persons.[78]

As far as the RoEs of the multinational operations involved in Somalia are concerned, it is reported that in the context of EUNAVOR Operation Atalanta, the decision to use deadly force is the prerogative of the Force Commander, according to the applicable RoE, and thus the Commanding Officer is obliged to request the relevant authorisation prior to the engagement.[79] In addition, the Guidance to EUNAVFOR sets forth that any incident during a counter-piracy operation in which shots are fired by EUNAVFOR personnel resulting in the death or injury of any person or where death or injury is believed to have occurred, should be reported, recorded, reviewed and investigated in accordance with the TCN's (troop contributing nation's) national shooting incident review procedures.[80]

In conclusion, it must be noted that as far as the piracy off the Somali coast is concerned, the international community came up with certain solutions in order to minimise the *acta pirata* and the incidents of armed robbery in the region. This notwithstanding, piracy and armed robbery still flourishes in the region, and thus states are considering alternative methods of preventive action, such as the placement of private armed guards or VPDs on board merchant vessels. As regards the interception operations as such, it is no doubt commendable that they are generally in compliance with international law; however, there are certain legal issues that merit closer scrutiny, such as the 'reasonable grounds' of article 110(1) of LOSC or the permissibility of use of force and the implementation of the relevant Security Council Resolutions.

iii. The Complexities of the Assertion of Enforcement Jurisdiction

It is sad but true that the prosecutions of the arrested pirates are proportionally low in comparison to the volume of piratical attacks since 2006.

As reported by the IMO,

> 'As at 24 September 2012, 1179 suspected pirates had been prosecuted or were awaiting prosecution in 21 States: Belgium; Comoros; France; Germany; India; Japan; Kenya; Madagascar; Malaysia; Maldives; Netherlands; Oman; Seychelles; Somalia; Republic of Korea; Spain; United Arab Emirates; United Republic of

---

[78] See relevant remarks in E Kontorovich, above n 73, 4.
[79] See Flow Chart and personal communication with anonymous source (25.5.2009).
[80] Guidance to EUNAVFOR, 5.3.

Tanzania; United States and Yemen. Of the 1179 individuals, 614 have been convicted, 26 have been acquitted and 539 are awaiting trial.'[81]

It is readily apparent that the above-mentioned numbers are far from satisfactory or sufficient to quell piracy in the region. The difficulties in prosecuting suspected pirates have been extensively analysed in the academic literature.[82] More specifically, as was mentioned in the latest Secretary-General's Report, there have been many instances where pirates have been apprehended by naval forces which subsequently were forced to release them due to lack of sufficient evidence.[83] In other cases this was due to the non-existence of relevant laws and in others due to the peculiarities of the laws of the capturing state. For example, Denmark and Germany can prosecute pirates only if their actions threaten national interests or harm their citizens. Under French law, a captain may apprehend and hold pirates, but only a judicial authority can arrest and detain them.[84] In addition, even the states that have enacted such laws, often prefer to abstain from prosecuting and trying pirates before their courts. Therefore, the dominant approach had been to avoid capturing pirates in the first place, or, if captured, releasing the pirates without charging them with a crime or transferring them to third states.

As a consequence, it is the regional piracy prosecution centres, established in Kenya as well as the Seychelles and Mauritius, that have assumed the burden of receiving and trying the majority of suspected Somali pirates. It is first, questioned whether transferring suspects to these states is in compliance with the relevant international law. As far as the law of the sea is concerned, it should be underscored that article 105 of LOSC provides that the prosecution should be by 'the courts of the state *which carried out the seizure*'. The drafting history and more specifically the pertinent Report of the International Law Commission reveals that this provision was intended to preclude transfers to third-party states. It follows that prima facie the assertion of enforcement jurisdiction by Kenya or the

---

[81] IMO source, (on file with the author).

[82] See *inter alia* E Kontorovich, 'A Guantanamo on the Sea: The Difficulty of Prosecuting Pirates and Terrorists' 98 *California Law Review* (2010) 243–76; J Ademun-Okeke, 'Jurisdiction over Foreign Pirates in Domestic Courts and Third States under International Law', 17 *Journal of International Maritime Law* (2011) 121, at 124–26; S Hodgkinson, 'International Law in Crisis: Seeking the Best Prosecution Model for Somali Pirates' 44 *Case Western Reserve Journal of International Law* (2011), 303–16 and J Landsidle, 'Enhancing International Efforts to Prosecute Suspected Pirates' 44 *Case Western Reserve Journal of International Law* (2011) 317–23. See also the various contributions to Symposium: Testing the Waters: Assessing International Responses to Somali Piracy' 10 (4) *Journal of International Criminal Justice* (2012).

[83] See UN Security Council, Report of Secretary-General on Specialized Anti-Piracy Courts in Somalia and other States in the Region', S/2012/50, 20 January 2012. It is reported also that 'over 60% of the pirates apprehended under *Operation Atalanta* are released, which illustrates the impunity of the pirates'; see H Tuerk, *Reflections on the Contemporary Law of the Sea* (Leiden: Martinus Nijhoff, 2012) 95.

[84] See Chatham House, Piracy, 4.

Seychelles, ie not the boarding states, is in dissonance with article 105 of LOSC.

However, there is contrary view, namely that

> the limited reference in UNCLOS Article 105 to the seizing State's adjudicative/ curial jurisdiction does not preclude the existence of other valid jurisdictions nor prevent transfers between them. Nothing, for example, precludes a 'receiving' State exercising its own jurisdiction which has an independent basis in customary international law once a suspect is within its territory.[85]

It is true that the relevant state practice in the Gulf of Aden certainly supports such a power of transfer, which, in any event, must be permitted, due to the application of the broader universality principle under article 105 and customary law (*argumentum a majore ad minus*). Accordingly, the conclusion to be drawn is that the transfer of suspected pirates to neighbouring states is not prohibited under international law; however, it is contingent upon the prior assertion of prescriptive jurisdiction over piracy by the latter states, such as Kenya, Seychelles or Tanzania, as well as upon the existence of a relevant agreement, such as that already existing between the EU and Kenya, which would set out all the necessary details.

Even if the latter states have established prior legislation concerning piracy on the basis of the universality principle, it is questioned whether they could also try suspects engaged in armed robbery against vessels in the Somali territorial waters? It bears repeating that while piracy *jure gentium* attracts universal jurisdiction pursuant to article 105 of LOSC, the phenomenon of armed robbery falls upon the coastal state, within which it is committed, to proscribe and exert enforcement jurisdiction. As a result, states such as Kenya or the Seychelles are not, in principle, competent to try acts of armed robbery within Somalia. It is rather unfortunate that the Guidance to EUNAVFOR and the EU-Kenya Exchange of Letters have not addressed this issue.

In contemplation of possible legal solutions to this problem, Resolution 1816

> *calls upon* all States, and in particular flag, port and coastal States, States of the nationality of victims and perpetrators or piracy and armed robbery, and other States with relevant jurisdiction under international law and national legislation, to cooperate in determining jurisdiction, and in the investigation and prosecution of persons responsible for [these] acts. (para 11)

---

[85] D Guilfoyle, above n 25, 164. In accord are E Kontorovich, above n 30, 747–79, and T Treves, who asserts that 'the rule in Article 105 does not, however, establish the exclusive jurisdiction of the seizing state's courts. Courts of other states are not precluded from exercising jurisdiction under conditions which they establish'; above n 37, 402 and Y Dinstein, 'Piracy *Jure Gentium*', in H Hestermeyer et al (eds), *Coexistence, Cooperation and Solidarity: liber amicorum Rüdiger Wolfrum* (Leiden: Martinus Nijhofff, 2012) 1125, 1141.

This paragraph obviously recognises that there must be cooperation amongst states for jurisdictional purposes, in the sense that whoever state can establish jurisdiction on any of the five headings of international jurisdiction should accept to try the suspect persons. However, as far as armed robbery is concerned, the problem again lies in the fact that there is no universal jurisdiction and hence any prosecution of such criminal act should be conducted on another jurisdictional basis, namely the territoriality or the nationality principles.

On the other hand, Resolution 1851 seems to have acknowledged that the crux of the matter is the establishment of jurisdiction and offered some additional legal bases in this regard, such as the SUA Convention (1988) and the UN Convention against Transnational Organised Crime (2000).[86]

More pertinent is the SUA Convention, the application of which could facilitate States, such as Kenya, to surmount the obstacles of the lack of universal jurisdiction. This treaty adopts the key element of the mechanism provided in the terrorist conventions, namely the principle *aut dedere aut judicare*.[87] Consequently, it obliges the state party where the offender is found either to extradite him to another state that has established its jurisdiction or to submit the case without delay to its competent authorities for the purpose of prosecution. Given in the present context that, for example, Kenya is party to the SUA Convention,[88] it can prosecute the alleged offenders in accordance with the latter Convention.

It is very instructive that in the first transfer of pirates from EUNAVFOR to Kenya pursuant to the relevant agreement, in the case of *Mohamed Hashi and 8 others, t*he Kenyan High Court *held that 'Kenyan Courts are not conferred with or given jurisdiction to deal with any matters arising or which have taken place outside Kenya'.*[89] *As the crime concerned was not committed in territorial waters within the jurisdiction of Kenya under Section 5 of Kenyan Penal Code,*[90] *the Court ordered immediate and unconditional release of the applicants from custody.*[91] *This decision was appealed by the Prosecutor and* on 12 November 2010, the High Court of Kenya decided not to release the prisoners until further notice. Very recently, the Court of Appeal overruled this judgment and convicted Hashi and others to imprisonment on the count of piracy.

---

[86] UN Convention against Transnational Organised Crime (2001) annexed to UNGAR 55/25 (8 January 2001) 40 ILM 353.

[87] See art 6(4) of the SUA Convention.

[88] See: www.imo.org/includes/blastDataOnly.asp/data_id%3D25670/status-x.xls.

[89] See *Re Muhamud Hashi and 8 Others v Republic,* [2009] KLR Miscellaneous Application No 434 of 2009; available also at Lloyd's List (8 November 2010) 17.

[90] The section provides: '[t]he jurisdiction of the courts of Kenya for the purposes of this Code extends to every place within Kenya, including territorial waters'; see http://www.kenyalaw.org/kenyalaw/klr_app/frames.php.

[91] See above n 95, at 33. See also Ademun-Odeke, above n 84, at 139.

With regard to the SUA Convention, it must be observed, first, that it has been scarcely employed in state practice.[92] In addition, the party concerned, eg Kenya, is entitled to prosecute the relevant offences only if they are committed against or on board a ship flying a Kenyan flag,[93] or in Kenyan territory or territorial waters[94] or by a Kenyan national[95] and, alternatively, if committed against a Kenyan national, provided that it has notified the Secretary-General of the IMO.[96] As of July 2012, Kenya has not given any such notification to the IMO.[97] Therefore, it seems that the use of the SUA Convention as the jurisdictional nexus to prosecute acts of piracy or armed robbery in the region is limited.[98]

However, the trigger for the assertion of jurisdiction on the part of the states parties to the SUA, to which the suspect pirates are transferred,[99] lies in the application of article 4(2), in conjunction with the already-referred obligation of *aut dedere aut judicare* in article 6 para 4. In more detail, article 4(2) sets out that

> In cases where the Convention does not apply pursuant to paragraph 1, it nevertheless applies when the offender or the alleged offender is found in the territory of a State party other than the State referred to in paragraph 1.

According to a commentator, 'this provision embraces the drafters' intent to enhance prospects for bringing alleged offenders to trial through extradition means if necessary'.[100] Thus, Kenya, which would hold custody of the transferred suspects, is obliged either to extradite them to a state having appropriate jurisdiction under article 6 paras 1–3 of the Convention or prosecute the case under its own municipal laws, *in casu*, the 2009 Merchant Shipping Act,[101] regardless of the fact that Somalia is not party

---

[92] A notable exception is the *United States v Shi* case (2008), in which the US Court of Appeals for the Ninth Circuit upheld the conviction of a Chinese national for acts of violence on board a Taiwanese-owned, Seychelles-flagged, Chinese-crewed vessel in the middle of the Pacific Ocean. This remarkable case is the first prosecution brought under the statute codifying US obligations under the SUA Convention. See *United States v Shi* 525 F 3d 709, cert denied, 129 SCt 324 (2008) and commentary in E Kontorovich 103 *AJIL* (2009) 734.

[93] art 6(1)(a) of SUA Convention.

[94] art 6(1)(b), ibid.

[95] art 6(1)(c), ibid.

[96] art 6(3), ibid.

[97] See relevant statements at www.imo.org/About/Conventions/StatusOfConventions/Documents/Status%20-%202012.pdf. See also in this regard P Musili Wambua, 'The Jurisdictional Challenges to the Prosecution of Piracy Cases in Kenya: Mixed Fortunes for a Perfect Model in the Global War against Piracy' 11 *WMU Journal of Maritime Affairs* (2012) 95, 103.

[98] See relevant discussion in Geiss and Petrig, 156–64.

[99] Besides Kenya, also Mauritius and Seychelles, ie the states with which the EU has signed transfer agreements, are parties to the SUA Convention; see at www.imo.org/About/Conventions/StatusOfConventions/Documents/Status%20-%202012.pdf, pp 406–7.

[100] C Joyner, 'The 1988 IMO Convention on the Safety of Maritime Navigation: Towards a Legal Remedy for Terrorism at Sea' 31 *GYIL* (1988) 230, 248.

[101] Available at www.kenyalaw.org/Downloads/ Acts/The_Merchant_Shipping_Act_2009.pdf and see comments in Musili Wambua, above n 103, 134 *et seq*.

to SUA or that Kenya itself may have no other jurisdictional nexus with the offence concerned. It goes without saying that extradition requests would be very rare in the case of piracy off Somalia; in such cases, as well as in cases of competing claims of jurisdiction, it must be observed that article 11(5) seems to give priority to the interest of the flag state.[102]

Besides the SUA Convention, an apposite mechanism to surmount jurisdictional obstacles is the employment of 'shipriders'. Indeed, article 7 of the Djibouti Code concerns 'embarked officers' – often called 'shipriders' in other instruments. There are various forms of shiprider agreement, which involve the hosting of law enforcement officers from one state (the 'sending state') aboard another state's government vessel (the 'host state'). They usually aim at broadening the law enforcement powers that may be exercised by a warship or other government vessel within a third state's territorial waters. The embarked officials may lawfully take action in the territorial waters of their sending state or, alternatively, can authorise on-spot enforcement action vis-à-vis a vessel flying the flag of the sending state on the high seas. The 'shiprider' model has been employed extensively to counter illicit drug-trafficking, especially in the Caribbean Sea.[103]

Having that as precedent, it was contemplated that such a model could prove instrumental to the suppression of piracy in the Gulf of Aden, and especially to the assertion of jurisdiction over armed robbery within Somalian territorial waters. In more detail, any State willing to exercise its jurisdiction over such offences, would embark an officer on a foreign warship, taking part, for example, in Operation Ocean Shield or in EUNAVFOR Operation Atalanta. The warship would proceed to the interdiction of the vessel engaged in piracy or armed robbery, while the embarked officer would make the relevant arrest under the laws of the sending state. Obviously, the purpose here would not be to enlarge enforcement powers as such, but rather to enable the exercise of adjudicative jurisdiction over pirates and armed robbers at sea.[104]

The use of 'shipriders', in this sense, was also encouraged under Security Council Resolutions 1851 and 1897. Both Security Council Resolutions invited states 'to conclude special agreements or arrangements with countries willing to take custody of pirates in order to embark law enforcement officials ("shipriders") from the latter countries, in particular countries in the region, to facilitate the investigation and prosecution of persons detained as a result of operations conducted under this resolution'.[105]

---

[102] See per this view F Francioni, 'Maritime Terrorism and International Law: The Rome Convention of 1988' 31 *GYIL* (1988) 263, 278; *contra* M Halberstam, 'Terrorism on the High Seas: The *Achille Lauro*, Piracy and the IMO Convention on Maritime Security' 82 *AJIL* (1988) 269, 302.

[103] See for further remarks on the shiprider institution and on the relevant questions of responsibility below Ch 7.

[104] See Geiss and Petrig, 88.

[105] UN SC Res 1851, para 3 and UN SC Res 1897, para 6.

In more detail, the shiprider agreements called for in Security Council Resolutions 1851 and 1897 and envisaged in the Djibouti Code are markedly different from previous joint policing model.

> Whereas a 'common' shiprider agreement would have foreseen the embarkation of Somali law enforcement officials who could undertake or authorize law enforcement operations within Somalia's territorial waters, paragraph 3 of the Security Council Resolution 1851 and paragraph 6 of Security Council Resolution 1897 refer to the embarkation of shipriders from 'countries willing to take custody of pirates'. This defies the common rationale for embarking shipriders, which is the authorization of law enforcement measures in the territorial waters of the coastal State.[106]

It is to be recalled that such authorisation has already been granted pursuant to Security Council Resolution 1846 (para 10b). In any case, such agreements would not negate the requirement of the 'advance consent of the TFG' for the 'exercise of third State jurisdiction by shipriders in the Somalia waters' (SC Res 1851, para 3).

It is obvious that the rationale for the use of shipriders in counter-piracy operations had been to facilitate the exercise of adjudicative jurisdiction over pirates and armed robbers at sea by bringing the latter directly within the jurisdiction of the shiprider's home state. In the words of UNODC, 'shiprider agreements . . . would enable a law enforcement official from, for example, Djibouti, Kenya, Tanzania or Yemen to join a warship off the coast of Somalia as a "shiprider", arrest the pirates in the name of their country and then have them sent to their national court for trial.'[107]

It follows that shiprider agreements in the traditional form could be of relevance only in cases of piracy or armed robbery in the waters of third states in the region, in which cases the embarked officers would be of the nationality of the latter states. Such agreements may be concluded in order to repress the increasing incidents of armed robbery in the Gulf of Guinea. The use of shipriders in the traditional form would be particularly useful in this regard and this is most probably the form in which the joint patrols between Nigeria and Benin are conducted.

It is true that shiprider agreements attain even more significance in the present context as far as the crime of armed robbery at sea is concerned. Under a shiprider agreement, Tanzania, for example, could exercise jurisdiction over a suspect who commits armed robbery within Somalia's territorial waters. This however, would require the prior establishment of prescriptive jurisdiction on the part of the sending state, ie Tanzania, which is not always the case, as well as the prior consent of TFG in accordance with SC Resolution 1851.

---

[106] Geiss and Petrig, 87.
[107] UN, UNODC, Annual Report 2009, available at www.unodc.org/documents/about-unodc/AR09_LORES.pdf>, at 17.

While shiprider arrangements appear highly desirable, they have not yet been implemented in the Gulf of Aden under the Djibouti Code or as a result of Security Council Resolutions. As Guilfoyle mentions, 'There are a number of potentially formidable obstacles in practice, not the least of which is national law'.[108] In more detail, the regional law enforcement officials require appropriate national legal authority in order to board a third state's vessel and conduct piracy-related arrests and evidence-gathering.[109] There is also the question of less-developed states' capacity to spare personnel to act as shipriders.

'Finally, there are a range of practical issues for the State "hosting" a ship-rider. These include: storage of the ship-rider's weapons and ammunition (if any), cabin-space, laundry costs, who will have tactical control during interdictions, and the extent of the shiprider's authority to authorize warning shots or disabling fire.'[110]

Nonetheless, such an arrangement has definitely been concluded in the framework of the Southern African Development Community (SADC).[111] More specifically, South Africa signed a Memorandum of Understanding with Mozambique on 1 June 2011, which provides for joint patrols in the area, including the embarkation of law enforcement agents on South African warships, with a view to repressing piratical activities in the region.[112] Similar arrangement, as has been mentioned, would seem to be already in place in the Gulf of Guinea; however, no further details in this regard are available.

In addition, a more integrated mechanism to counter piracy as a 'threat to maritime security' has been included in the 2008 CARICOM Agreement. Even though the threat of piracy in the region is marginal,[113] the drafters of the Agreement included 'piracy' in its *ratione materiae* scope, without providing any different definition or further qualification.[114] The Agreement provides for routine security patrols and operations to the territorial waters of state parties to prevent threats to maritime security, including piracy, by designation of 'Security Force Officials' and 'Security Force Vessels' by all states. The permission for such patrols and operations is granted by the

---

[108] See Guilfoyle, above n 25, 172.

[109] For example, Kenyan police have no powers at Kenyan law outside the territorial sea; see ibid, at 172.

[110] ibid.

[111] See further information on SADC at http://www.sadc.int/.

[112] See Memorandum of Understanding on Piracy and Trans-Border Crime between South Africa and Mozambique, signed on 1 June 2011. For more information see www.info.gov.za/speech/DynamicAction?pageid=461&sid=18794&tid=34350.

[113] In 2011, only one attempted attack was reported in the Caribbean basin; see C Mody, 'Maritime Piracy, the Reality Around the Globe' 2011 WMU International Conference on Piracy at Sea (on file with the author).

[114] Under art 1(2) of the 2008 CARICOM Agreement, 'An activity is likely to endanger the security of a State Party or the region if it involves: . . . h) piracy, hijacking and other serious crimes'.

Agreement *ipso facto* and there is no need for separate request. Needless to say that the provision of the Agreement concerning the interdiction of suspect vessels on the high seas is not necessary for piracy, in light of articles 105 and 110 of LOSC. It is questionable, however, whether incidents of armed robbery in the territorial waters of the states concerned would fall under *ratione materiae* scope of the Agreement. In any event, it is unlikely that such incidents would not fall within the ambit of the other crimes referred to in conjunction with piracy, ie 'hijacking and other serious crimes'.

iv. Human Rights Considerations

It is true that the application of international human rights law in the context of counter-piracy operations off the coast of Somalia has attracted particular academic interest.[115] This has been fuelled, mainly, by a series of judgments of the ECtHR, which concerned matters directly relating to the law of the sea and which might be the forerunner of relevant judgments against the European states participating in these operations. The preliminary, yet paramount question of the extraterritorial application of human rights as well as the basic human rights applicable in maritime interception operations have been already discussed in Chapter 3; thus, it is the purpose of this section to have regard to the particular issues involved in the counter-piracy context and to those particular rights, which are in need of protection in counter-piracy operations.

Given that the ECHR or the ICCPR may have application in interdiction operations on the high seas as well as in third states' territorial seas, and provided that the states concerned exert sufficient de jure or de facto control over the alleged pirates, it is, first, questioned whether there is truly such control in the present realm and when does it start. In the context of Operation Atalanta, the responsibility to transfer or to release suspected pirates lies with the EUNAVFOR and the Member States pursuant to the EU Flow Chart. Hence, it can be argued that from the moment that the commanding officer (CO) of the vessel decides to detain the suspects and until the detainees are either transferred to Kenya or the Seychelles or to the national authorities, or are released, due to the refusal of these states to try them, the pirates fall under the jurisdiction of the boarding state and therefore under the jurisdiction of the ECHR.

---

[115] See inter alia S Piedimonte Bodini, 'Fighting Maritime Piracy under the European Convention on Human Rights' 22 *EJIL* (2011) 829; D Guilfoyle, 'Counter-piracy Law Enforcement and Human Rights' 59 *ICLQ* (2010) 141; C Laly-Chevalier, 'Lutte contre le Piraterie Maritime et Droits de l'Homme' 42 *RBDI* (2009) 5; A Fischer-Lescano, L Kreck, 'Piracy and Human Rights: Legal Issues in the Fight Against Piracy Within the Context of the European "Operation Atalanta"' 52 *GYBIL* (2010) 525.

Two issues call for specific comments: first, it is observed that, accord-ing to the RoEs of EUNAVFOR, a considerable amount of time might pass between the decision of the CO to search the vessels and arrest the sus pects, which might also involve the transfer of the latter to the warship, and the decision of the CO to release or detain them. Does the Convention apply also during this period?

Neither the Flow Chart nor the Guidance to EUNAVFOR make any ref-erence to the legal status of the suspected pirates in this particular time period; they only set forth a few elementary safeguards for the protection of their life and dignity. Nonetheless, it is submitted that it would be more in harmony with international law to assert that these persons do come under the jurisdiction of the interdicting states and ergo within the pur-view of ECHR. The reason for this is merely that there is no need for the formal detainment of the persons concerned to be considered as subject to the protection of the Convention, since the cornerstone criterion is the existence of sufficient control of these persons by the organs of a state party to the Convention.

Similarly, it is disputed whether the Convention applies in the situation

'where the pirates are not taken on board the naval vessel, especially in cases where there are no naval officers aboard the pirate vessel (for example, where it has been surrounded and subdued)'.[116] 'Most EU countries would regard such a degree of control to be covered by the Convention. But some would not.'[117]

The aforementioned criterion applies equally here; in other words, it would be contingent upon whether the persons concerned are deprived of their freedom to such an extent so as to be considered under the de facto control of the state agents. This seems the case here and hence it is asserted that these persons fall under the jurisdiction of the capturing state.

Having determined that the suspect pirates are entitled to the basic pro-tection of the ECHR and of the ICCPR, it is apt to refer to particular provi-sions that might accordingly apply. Taking for example the ECHR, it is readily apparent that the most significant human rights in need of protec-tion are the right to life (article 2), the prohibition of torture and of degrad-ing and inhumane treatment (article 3), and the prohibition of arbitrary deprivation of liberty (article 5). It should be noted, from the outset, that the EU Guidance to EUNAVFOR set out a number of general principles

[116] See Guidance to EUNAVFOR, Enclosure 8 to Annex B. It has anonymously been reported to the author that the persons under the present circumstances are not considered to enjoy the full protection of human right treaties; on the contrary, they are perceived to be *persones extra judicates* (communication with the author, 25 April 2009).
[117] Chatham House, *Piracy*, 5.

for the treatment of detainees, which by and large reflect the above-mentioned provisions.[118]

With regard to the right of life, in particular, it is expressly provided in the above instrument that Operation Atalanta's RoEs prohibit the use of deadly force to prevent the escape of detainees'. Only when it is necessary and reasonable, force may be used to restrain detainees 'in accordance with national law on self-defence and Op Atalanta ROEs'.[119] To the knowledge of the author, there is no recorded incident of deaths of detainees by EU forces. On the other hand, there is no doubt that cases, such as the *Tabar*, in which the Indian warship attacked a suspected pirate vessel, sank the ship, and caused loss of life,[120] would definitely engage the responsibility of the states concerned for the violation of the right to life. In similar vein, it could be questioned whether Italy incurs responsibility for the killing of Indian fishermen by two Italian marines on board a merchant vessel.[121] Given that these two mariners were *de jure* organs of the Italian State, it is hard to see why they would not engage the latter State's responsibility for the violation of article 2 of the Convention. Nonetheless, it would not engage similar responsibility under the law of the sea, more specifically under articles 106 and 110 of LOSC, since there was no 'warship or other duly authorized vessel' involved.

Another relevant question that might be raised in the context of counter-piracy operations is whether a state party to the Convention is under the positive obligation to rescue its nationals that have been taken as hostages by pirates or terrorists at sea and there is a real and imminent risk of their lives. As questioned by Piedimonte Bodini, 'what if Somali pirates capture some passengers on a Danish or Italian cruise ship and given the Government's inaction, the hostages are taken to Somalia where they ... die from some other cause. Do Denmark and Italy where the ships are registered ... have an obligation to rescue the hostages?'[122] Piedimonte Bodini refers to two cases concerning hostage-taking, one of which, namely *Finogenov v Russia*,[123] may lead to the conclusion that had the relevant authorities known about a real and imminent risk of a life-threatening hostage-taking, their positive obligations, amongst others, under article 2,

---

[118] In its words, detainees 'are to be treated humanely and are entitled [inter alia] to respect for their person, honour, convictions and religious practices. In particular they are not to be subject to: a. Violence, b. Punishments c. Humiliating and degrading treatment, d. Reprisals, e. Threats of any of the above. Detainees are entitled to: a. Shelter, food and drinking water; b. Health and hygiene safeguards, c. Practice their religion and, if requested, appropriate and possible, to receive spiritual assistance from chaplains or similar persons'; Annex A to Operation Atalanta EU OHQ SOP Legal OO1, dated 26 March 2009.
[119] ibid, Section 3.
[120] See above n 74.
[121] See above n 56.
[122] See Piedimonte Bodini, above n 110, 838.
[123] See *Finogenov and others v Russia* (Application No 18299/03) Decision on Admissibility of 18 March 2010.

would have been triggered.[124] Whilst there is certainly merit in this argument in light of the positive nature of the obligations under article 2, on equal legal footing stands the assertion that the state is under a negative obligation to abstain from the use of force which may seriously risk the hostages' lives. It is readily apparent that, as was held in the *MacCann case*, a most careful scrutiny is needed in this regard, taking into account all surrounding circumstances.[125]

As far as the prohibition of non-refoulement is concerned, it comes to the fore,[126] on the one hand, in the event of the release of the detainee after the decline of Kenya or the Seychelles to initiate judicial proceedings or after the Operational Commander decides that the evidence is not sufficient. Both the EU Flow Chart and the Guidance to EUNAVFOR are silent regarding non-refoulement; on the contrary, they stipulate that arrangements should be made for their safe repatriation. It is readily apparent that this practice fails to take into consideration the prohibition under scrutiny and thus it might be in violation of article 3 of ECHR, should the returned suspect face torture or inhumane, and degrading treatment in Somalia or in another state. In addition, it might run counter to the Refugee Convention as such, which arguably applies on the high seas and protects potential refugees from such refoulement practices. Hence, it is submitted that there must always be a screening process of the detainees for the purpose of determining whether there is a substantial fear for persecution or torture in Somalia or in another country, for example in Kenya or Yemen, where they might be sent. In the latter case, the principle of non-refoulement should be fully respected.

For example, this was not respected in the case reported by Judge Treves of the Danish Navy ship *Absalon,* which on 17 September 2008 captured 10 pirates in the waters off Somalia. After six days of detention, the Danish government decided to free the pirates by putting them ashore on a Somalian beach, for they 'had come to the conclusion that the pirates risked torture and the death penalty if surrendered to (whatever) Somali authorities'.[127] However, the prohibition of non-refoulement not only protects the official repatriation but, in general, the return by any means of the persons concerned.

On the other hand, the said prohibition is significant in the process of transfer of individuals to states, such as Kenya and the Seychelles, with questionable human rights record, or when surrendering a suspect for

---

[124] See Piedimonte Bodini, above n 110, 839.

[125] *cf* the *Andronicou and Constantinou v Cyprus* (1997), where the Court found that a police operation which resulted in the death of a hostage, a young woman, and the hostage-taker did not breach art 2; see EHHR (1997-VI).

[126] Another discussion is the possibility of a suspect pirate to claim the refugee status before eg US national courts; see T Syring, 'A Pirate and a Refugee: Reservations and Responses in the Fight against Piracy' 17 *ILSA JICL* (2011) 437, 455.

[127] See Treves, above n 66, 408.

prosecution to the flag state of the boarded vessel itself. Once the suspect's disposition is within the de facto control of the boarding state, non-refoulement obligations may arise. As Guilfoyle notes,

> the starting position under both the ECHR and the CAT would then appear congruent: mere words of assurance are insufficient to discharge the obligation. The question is whether assurances can provide 'in their practical application [in individual cases], a sufficient guarantee that [a transferee] would be protected against the risk of [prohibited] treatment'.[128] This involves a wide-ranging contextual assessment, including any monitoring mechanisms established under assurances given.[129]

It is true that both the EU-Kenya Exchange of Letters and the EU-Seychelles Exchange of Letters seem to have taken this into consideration. For example, the EU-Kenya agreement refers expressly to the ICCPR and the CAT, and the parties undertake to:

> treat persons transferred . . . both prior to and following transfer, humanely and in accordance with international human rights obligations, including the prohibition against torture and cruel, inhumane and degrading treatment or punishment, the prohibition of arbitrary detention and in accordance with the requirement to have a fair trial.[130]

Further provisions deal, inter alia, with record-keeping, reporting requirements as to detainee health, access for humanitarian agencies and the exclusion of the death penalty. However, it was evident that there was also need for substantive prison reform assistance, to bring those prisons, to which piracy suspects are being transferred, up to international minimum standards.[131]

Having referred to prisons in Kenya, it is apt to note that the situation in the latter gave rise to the first case before European courts in relation to the legality of transfer of suspected pirates. In *Mohamed Hashi and 8 others*, the applicants initiated proceedings in Germany complaining that their arrest and their transfer of the applicants had been in violation of the German Constitution, the European Convention of Human Rights and the International Covenant on Civil and Political Rights (ICCPR). On 11 November 2011, the administrative court of Cologne ruled that Germany had violated the prohibition of torture, inhuman and degrading treatment (Articles 3 ECHR and 7 ICCPR) by transferring them to Kenya.[132] Interestingly, the Government claimed that the decision for the transfer was

---

[128] See *Saadi v Italy* App no 37201/06 (EctHR, 28 February 2008) para 148.

[129] D Guilfoyle, 'Human Rights Issues and Non-Flag State Boarding of Suspect Ships in the High Seas', in CR Symmons (ed), *Selected Contemporary Issues in the Law of the Sea* (Leiden: Martinus Nijhoff, 2011) 83, 97.

[130] EU-Kenya Agreement para 2(c).

[131] See Guilfoyle, above n 115, 100.

[132] See summary of the case at <http://www.justiz.nrw.de/nrwe/ovgs/vg_koeln/j2011/25_K_4280_09urteil20111111.html> (in German).

made under the authority of the EUNAVFOR Operational Commander and thus Germany was under no responsibility for any potential violation of human rights law; however, the Court held that 'the decision to hand over suspected pirates to Kenya had been taken by German authorities, since the latter had the option to transfer the suspected pirates to Kenya or any other third country or to leave prosecution to the public prosecutor in Hamburg'.[133] On the other hand, the German court rejected two other claims by the plaintiffs that the capture and detention on the 'Rheinland-Pfalz' were in violation of international and German constitutional law.[134]

Evidently, the above-mentioned decision brings to the fore the cardinal issue of the allocation of responsibility between EU and its Member States, as Germany in casu, for the transfer of suspected pirates to third states with questionable human rights record. It is beyond the ambit of the present book to address this delicate question; suffice it to say that, arguably, the Member State, namely Germany had the 'effective control' in terms of article 7 of ILC Articles on the Responsibility of International Organizations over the decision to send these people to Kenya.[135] This, along the lines of the very recent *Dutchbat case*, Germany had the 'ability to prevent' the commission of the wrongful conduct on part of Kenyan authorities and thus it incurred responsibility.[136]

Insofar as the right to liberty and security goes, the European nations contributing to EUNAVFOR bear responsibility for any acts or omissions which infringe article 5 of the Convention, even if they occur on the high seas or in the territorial sea of Somalia. Accordingly, it is asserted that, on the one hand, any arrest or detention should have a legal basis in domestic law, which 'must be sufficiently accessible and precise, in order to avoid all risk of arbitrariness'. On the other hand, there is the obligation of

---

[133] *Ibid* (translation by the author).

[134] *Ibid.*

[135] Article 7 reads as follows: 'The conduct of an organ of a State or an organ or agent of an international organization that is placed at the disposal of another international organization shall be considered under international law an act of the latter organization if the organization exercises effective control over that conduct'; see Draft Articles on the Responsibility of International Organizations (2011); *ILC Report, Sixty-Third Session*, UN Doc. A/66/10 (2011); available at <http://untreaty.un.org/ilc/texts/instruments/english/draft%20articles/9_11_2011.pdf>

[136] The Dutchbat case concerns the attribution of the conduct of the Dutch contingent in the United Nations Protection Force (UNPROFOR) in relation to the massacre in Srebrenica. The District Court of The Hague applied the criterion of 'effective control' to the circumstances of the case and reached the conclusion that the respondent State was responsible for its involvement in the events at Srebrenica which had led to the killing of three Bosnian Muslim men after they had been evicted from the compound of Dutchbat; see Judgment of 5 July 2011, http://zoeken.rechtspraak.nl, especially paras 5.8 and 5.9. When giving a wide meaning to the concept of 'effective control' so as to include also the ability to prevent, the Court followed the approach taken by T Dannenbaum, 'Translating the Standard of Effective Control into a System of Effective Accountability: How Liability Should Be Apportioned for Violations of Human Rights by Member State Troops Contingents as United Nations Peacekeepers' 51 *Harvard International Law Review* (2010) 113, 157.

the state concerned promptly to bring the suspect pirates before a judge or other officer authorised by law to exercise judicial powers.

The *Medvedyev* case is more than instructive in this regard. This case will be discussed further in the next chapter; yet suffice it to say that the Court concluded that the applicants had not been deprived of their liberty in accordance with a procedure prescribed by law, and consequently held that there had been a violation of article 5(1). However, considering that the length of that deprivation of liberty had been justified by the 'wholly exceptional circumstances' of the case, in particular, the inevitable delay entailed by having the drug-smuggling vessel *Winner* tugged to France, the Court concluded that there had been no violation of article 5(3).

Accordingly, it is submitted that the European states which apprehend pirates in the course of Operation Atalanta and initiate judicial proceedings before their courts should have in place prior established, precise, and foreseeable national laws concerning the offences in question; otherwise, in view of the *Medvedyev* case, they will be in violation of article 5(1) of the ECHR. It is observed in this regard that not all European states have such precise and non-arbitrary laws, and this might be one of the reasons why they prefer to transfer the alleged offenders to third states. With regard to the 'promptness' of the transfer to the forum state, when there are objective reasons for the delay to bring the detainees before 'a judge or other officer authorised by law to exercise judicial power', the Court is lenient concerning the application of article 5(3) of the Convention. It is apt to reiterate here that the EU has instructed states participating in Operation Atalanta to make a decision either to transfer or to release the suspects within 48 hours after the CO's decision to detain. In addition, it has made an agreement with Djibouti to facilitate the air transfer of suspects.

E. Conclusions

It is certain that the problem of piracy and more recently of the crime of armed robbery at sea restricts the enjoyment of the freedoms of the high seas, mainly the freedom of navigation. Since time immemorial, pirates have attacked commercial shipping to loot, and this is still unfortunately the case today. The law of the sea had developed certain rules concerning piracy and had codified them in both the 1958 Geneva Convention and the LOSC. In short, 'piracy' would be any act of violence directed by a vessel against another vessel on the high seas for private purposes, while all states have the right to seize the pirate vessel and arrest the pirates on the count of universal jurisdiction as well as exercise the right of visit for such suspect vessels.

These rules, considered as part of customary law, came across new challenges on the face of the unprecedented growth of pirate attacks and acts of armed robbery off Somalia, and lately in the Gulf of Guinea. It is true that the international community had to look very deep in its arsenal to find weapons to address not only the problem of the suppression of piracy off Somalia, but also of the exercise of jurisdiction over these pirates. The activation of the Security Council, the use of shipriders, of private armed guards and the call for 'pirate chambers' in third states are only few of these.

In terms of the interdiction operations as such, the relevant practice seems to be in keeping with international law; however, there are some points of ambivalence, such as the 'reasonable grounds' asserted by the EUNAVFOR or some instances of the use of force, like the *Tabar* incident. Also, questions may arise in respect of the consistency of the action of EUNAVFOR in Operation Atalanta and of other states with international human rights law, as, for example, with the prohibition of non-refoulement.

III. IUU FISHING AS A THREAT TO THE FREEDOM OF FISHING

A. Introduction: The Problem of IUU Fishing

The maintenance of fish stocks has been at the centre of focus of states and subsequently of the international community since the time of Selden and Gentilis. Currently, the factor that has proved to be most detrimental to global fisheries resources is illegal, unreported and unregulated fishing (IUU fishing), a term coined by the 2001 FAO International Plan of Action to Prevent, Deter and Eliminate Illegal, Unreported and Unregulated Fishing (IPOA-IUU).[137] The concept of IUU fishing may be new; however, its components, ie 'illegal fishing', 'unreported fishing and 'unregulated fishing', are not.

> Collectively, IUU fishing encompasses a wide range of fishing activities which can be considered in violation of or without regard to applicable international, regional or national fisheries regulations and standards.[138]

In more detail, 'illegal fishing' includes all fishing activities conducted in contravention of national and international laws, as well as agreed regional fisheries management and conservation measures.[139] Such fishing may include fishing beyond allowable catch limits, the taking of juvenile fish, the taking of prohibited fish species, fishing during closed

---

[137] FAO, International Plan of Action to Prevent, Deter and Eliminate Illegal, Unreported and Unregulated Fishing, adopted at the Twenty-fourth Session of CDOFI, Rome Italy (23 June 2001) (hereinafter: IPOA-IUU).

[138] Palma, *Fisheries*, 37.

[139] See para 3.1 of the IPOA-IUU.

seasons or fishing in closed areas.[140] On the high seas, the illegal nature of fishing pertains to non-compliance with the agreed standards of RFMOs. For example, under the FAO Compliance Agreement, vessels fishing on the high seas are required not to engage in any activity that undermines the effectiveness of international conservation measures.[141]

On the other hand, according to IPOA-IUU, 'unreported fishing' can be categorised as non-reporting, misreporting, or under-reporting of fisheries data that a state or an RFMO requires under its laws, regulations or adopted conservation and management measures.[142] It is true that 'unreported fishing' significantly overlaps with both 'illegal' and 'unregulated' fishing, as the common denominator of all is the contravention with national laws, regulations and conservation measures.[143] As regards 'unregulated fishing', it is reported that its

> main characteristic is the lack of regulations governing a particular area, fish stock or type of vessel. Thus the cause of unregulated fishing can either be the failure of governance by States and RFMOs or the failure by flag States to discharge their flag State duties to control the activities of their vessels on the high seas, such as through high seas fishing authorisation or permits.[144]

Needless to say, the extent and impacts of IUU fishing described above requires the adoption and implementation of adequate legal and policy measures by states and regional organisations. The contemporary international legal framework regulating fisheries can be divided into two categories: legally binding multilateral agreements and non-binding instruments. As regards the former, there are four major global agreements directly related to fisheries: the LOSC, the Straddling Stocks Agreement, the FAO Compliance Agreement and the Port State Measures Agreement.[145] The latter include the FAO Code of Conduct as well as many other international instruments adopted after IPOA-IUU, such as various UN Resolutions on sustainable fisheries, the Rome Declaration on IUU Fishing[146] and the FAO Model Scheme on Port State Measures,[147] which address directly the problem at hand.

---

[140]   *cf* art 62 of LOSC and FAO Code of Conduct for Responsible Fisheries, adopted at the 28th session of the FAO Conference, Rome, Italy, 31 October 1995, para 8.2.2 (hereinafter: FAO Code of Conduct).

[141]   ibid, arts III(1), V(1) and V(2).

[142]   See para 3.2 of the IPOA-IUU.

[143]   See Palma, *Fisheries*, 44–45.

[144]   ibid, 48.

[145]   Agreement on Port State Measures to Prevent, Deter and Eliminate Illegal, Unreported and Unregulated Fishing, adopted in November 2009, Appendix V of the FAO Council 137th session, Rome, 28 September–2 October 2009.

[146]   2005 Rome Declaration on Illegal, Unreported and Unregulated Fishing, adopted by the FAO Ministerial Meeting on Fisheries, Rome, 12 March 2005.

[147]   FAO, Model Scheme on Port State Measures to Combat Illegal, Unreported and Unregulated Fishing (Rome: FAO, 2007).

A central role in the fight against IUU fishing has been ascribed to the RFMOs, which have taken numerous measures against delinquent vessels, usually flying the flag of a third state. For example, the Inter-American Tropical Tuna Commission (IATTC) has procedures to identify vessels flying the flag of non-members that diminish the effectiveness of their conservation measures.[148] Other RFMOs have a number of catch-reporting requirement for fishing vessels, such as the maintenance of fishing logbooks containing detailed record of catches and other information.[149]

The measures to combat IUU fishing on the high seas are closely intertwined with the measures that are taken by coastal and port states and thus fall beyond the ambit of the present enquiry. Nevertheless, it certainly merits discussing tersely the relevant measures on the high seas, especially the interception operations, which purport to eliminate this scourge. The discussion will commence with the LOSC and the Straddling Stocks Agreement and will shift briefly to the RFMOs.

B. The LOSC and the 1995 Straddling Stocks Agreement

LOSC devotes articles 116–20 to the regulation of high seas fisheries.[150] Flag states have the primary responsibility to exercise enforcement jurisdiction over their vessels for unlawful fishing activities wherever they occur. In addition, article 117 refers to states taking measures for their 'respective nationals as may be necessary for the conservation of the living resources of the high seas'. This provision affords the legal basis for states to take action against their nationals who engage in IUU fishing even if the national is on a vessel flagged to another state.[151]

As regards enforcement on the high seas, LOSC falls short of providing for interception powers against foreign-flagged vessels on the high seas. The only ground under LOSC that may be invoked in order to board and inspect a fishing vessel on the high seas is the statelessness of vessels (article 110(1)(d) of LOSC).[152] Besides this, there must be a treaty granting such powers to contracting states, such as the Straddling Stocks Agreement. This lacuna under the LOSC became evident in the famous *Estai* case, that is, the dispute between Canada and Spain before the ICJ concerning fishing immediately outside Canada's EEZ. Canada sought to extend its enforcement powers to these vessels on the basis, inter alia, of an ecological emergency,

---

[148] See IATTC, Resolution C-04-03, Resolution on a System of Notification of Sightings and Identification of Vessels Operating in the Convention Area.

[149] See more information Palma, Fisheries, 46.

[150] See in general E Hey, 'The Fisheries Provisions of the LOS Convention', in E Hey (ed), *Developments in International Fisheries Law* (Hague: Kluwer Law International, 1999) 20.

[151] See Guilfoyle, *Shipping Interdiction*, 101.

[152] See inter alia T McDorman, 'Stateless Fishing Vessels, International Law and the UN High Seas Fisheries Conference' 25 *Journal of Maritime Law and Commerce* (1994) 531.

whereas Spain argued that Canada had to respect the principle of exclusive flag state jurisdiction on the high seas. At the end, the Court held that it lacked jurisdiction to resolve the dispute and thus the merits of the case were never discussed.[153]

The global treaty that allows for enforcement action against foreign vessels on the high seas is the 1995 Straddling Stocks Agreement.[154] In general, the Agreement establishes a general framework and principles and rules within which particular straddling and highly migratory fish stocks may be better managed at the regional level. One of the most significant aspects is the emphasis on cooperation among states to conserve and manage these stocks through appropriate regional or sub-regional fisheries management organisations and arrangements.[155] Cooperation in the conservation and management of resources on the high seas is not only an obligation of RFMO members but it is also extended to non-members of or non-participants in such organisations. Article 8(3) stipulates that states fishing for these stocks on the high seas may choose not to join in the respective RFMO, yet they are obliged not to undermine the conservation and management measures adopted by the latter organisation. In addition, under article 17(1), non-member states of RFMOs are not discharged from the obligation to cooperate in the conservation and management of such fish stocks.

With regard to enforcement on the high seas, considerable deference is accorded to the flag state's authority;[156] for example, under article 18, state parties are only to authorise their vessels to fish on the high seas where those states are able to exercise effectively their responsibilities, including controlling fishing through licences, authorisations or permits, undertaking monitoring, control and surveillance of their fishing vessels. However, the Straddling Stocks Agreement anticipates also a role for third states in enforcing conservation and management requirements through inspection. State parties to the said Agreement must permit access to duly authorised inspectors from other states consistent with sub-regional and regional schemes of cooperation. The interception and inspection regime is laid down in articles 21 and 22 and applies in the absence of boarding and inspection procedures being developed within an RFMO. The innovation of the Agreement is that this inspection regime applies to vessels within high seas areas under the competence of an RFMO, irrespective of whether the flag state of those vessels is a member of the organisation or

---

[153] *Fisheries Jurisdiction* case (*Spain v Canada*) Preliminary Objections (1998) ICJ Rep 432. For commentary see R Churchill in 12 *LJIL* (1999) 597–611.

[154] See above Introduction (n 72). See also M Hayashi, 'The 1995 Agreement on the Conservation and Management of Straddling and Highly Migratory Fish Stocks: Significance for the Law of the Sea Convention' 29 *Ocean & Coastal Management* (1995) 51–69.

[155] art 8 of Straddling Stocks Agreement.

[156] See Klein, *Maritime Security*, 138.

the arrangement; suffice it that the flag state is bound by the Straddling Stocks Agreement.

In more detail, article 21 provides that

1. In any high seas area covered by a subregional or regional fisheries manage-ment organization or arrangement, a State Party which is a member of such organization or a participant in such arrangement may, through its duly author-ized inspectors, board and inspect, in accordance with paragraph 2, fishing ves-sels flying the flag of another State Party to this Agreement, whether or not such State Party is also a member of the organization or a participant in the arrange-ment, for the purpose of ensuring compliance with conservation and manage-ment measures for straddling fish stocks and highly migratory fish stocks established by that organization or arrangement.

2. States shall establish, through subregional or regional fisheries management organizations or arrangements, procedures for boarding and inspection pursuant to paragraph 1, as well as procedures to implement other provisions of this arti-cle. Such procedures shall be consistent with this article and then basic proce-dures set out in article 22 . . . Boarding and inspection as well as any subsequent enforcement action shall be conducted in accordance with such procedures.

According to article 22, in the process of boarding and inspecting a ves-sel, the duly authorised inspectors must present credentials to the master and a copy of text setting out the conservation and management measures in force in the high seas area. The flag state is to be given notice at the time of the boarding and inspection (article 22(1)(b)) and a copy of the report from the boarding and inspection is to be provided the flag state (article 22(1)(d)). When there are clear grounds for believing that a vessel has engaged in any activity in contravention to conservation and manage-ment measures applicable in the area, the inspecting state must promptly notify the flag state. Should the latter remain idle, the inspectors may remain on board the vessel and secure evidence, which may include the vessel going in to the nearest appropriate port (article 21 para 8). However, as noted by Klein,

at each stage, the flag State's authority to conduct enforcement action holds sway over the actions of the inspecting State . . . Moreover, a core weakness of this regime ultimately rests in the fact that is only available in relation to vessels registered to state parties to the treaty. The ability of vessels to re-flag to avoid such obligations will thereby reduce the effectiveness of enforcement measures designed to improve the conservation and management of fish resources.[157]

In any case, the Straddling Stocks Agreement is a very interesting treaty in terms of treaty law, in the sense that even though it recognises and anti-cipates the adoption of specific measures and boarding procedures in the context of RFMOs as *lex specialis*, it still provides for inspection of vessels

---

[157] ibid, 139–40.

flying the flag of states that are not members of these organisations. Hence, it obliges them to cooperate in the conservation and management of certain fish stocks and to abide by measures adopted under the authority of an instrument that is *res inter alios acta* for them.[158] However, the Agreement is very careful to set forth that any enforcement measures against delinquent vessels pursuant to the Agreement are contingent upon a 'serious violation' of the provision of the Agreement, and not of the RFMO's measures as such (article 21 para 11). The Agreement has had significant impact since it was adopted in 1995. Several treaties establishing new RFMOs have incorporated principles of the Agreement, such as the treaty establishing the South East Atlantic Fisheries Organisation.[159]

C. The RFMOs

The most advanced and efficient initiative to manage fisheries on the high seas has been the establishment of regional fisheries management organisations (RFMOs).[160] Such organisations have the competence to prescribe fishery conservation and management measures, including total allowable catches (TACs) for some fish stocks, as well as to take various steps to promote compliance with these measures.[161] These enforcement mechanisms applicable between the contracting states include what may be characterised as more traditional maritime enforcement measures, such as intercepting, boarding, inspecting and potentially arresting a vessel.

To provide an example, the North Pacific Anadromous Fish Commission, which was established in 1993 with a treaty between Japan, the US, Canada and Russia,[162] aims to prevent directed fishing for certain salmon species within the management area. The said Convention sets forth a reciprocal boarding and inspection scheme: duly authorised officials of any state party may board any other party's fishing vessel upon reasonable suspicion that it is in violation of the Convention and inspect the vessel and question persons aboard. The inspecting state may arrest a person or the vessel, should it reasonably believe that it has breached the Convention, and conduct further investigations if necessary. However,

---

[158] See arts 34–38 of VCLT.

[159] Convention on the Conservation and Management of Fishery Resources in the South-East Atlantic Ocean (2001), 2221 UNTS 189.

[160] On RFMOs in general see inter alia R Barston, 'The Law of the Sea and Regional Fisheries Organisations' 14 *IJMCL* (1999) 333; T Henriksen et al, *Law and Politics in Ocean Governance: the UN Fish Stocks Agreement and Regional Fisheries Management Regimes* (Leiden: Martinus Nijhoff, 2006).

[161] For a list of the principal RFMOs see A Sydnes, 'Regional Fishery Organizations: How and Why Organizational Diversity Matters' 32 *ODIL* (2001) 349, 353.

[162] See Convention for the Conservation of Anadromous Stocks in the North Pacific Ocean, TIAS 11465.

only the flag State may try violations and impose penalties upon the delinquent vessel.[163]

It is true that further enforcement measures have been considered necessary in order to eliminate or mitigate the harm caused by IUU fishing.[164] For example, RFMOs have established catch documentation schemes, which track landings of fish and the trade flow of particular species.[165] Also, vessel monitoring schemes have been put forward as a means of tracking the location of vessels.[166] In addition, RFMOs have relied on 'blacklisting' of vessels and flag states that have systematically violated conservation and management measures.[167] Finally, it is observed that the most effective means of addressing this threat to the conservation of high seas fisheries is the enhancement of port-state control, and the adoption of the 2009 Port State Measures Agreement is towards this direction.[168]

D. Concluding Remarks

In concluding, it merits referring to certain arguments that R Rayfuse has made in relation to fisheries enforcement on the high seas. First, she has averred that there may be a customary law obligation to grant consent to boarding and inspection by a non-flag state vessel in an RFMO context. In the alternative, she argues that refusing such consent may constitute a breach of an international obligation allowing countermeasures to be taken. Also, RFMO members could use the law of countermeasures to justify boarding the fishing vessels of RFMO parties or even non-parties, where they are acting in violation of RFMO measures.[169]

Many arguments can be put forward with equal fervour to counter the aforementioned assertions;[170] suffice it to mention that the obligation of cooperation under article 117 of LOSC and the Straddling Stocks Agreement is very diffuse, which makes extremely difficult to identify the injured state, which could claim countermeasures. In addition, the practice of third states

---

[163] See ibid, art 5(2).

[164] A thorough analysis of the inspection schemes of numerous RFMOs is furnished by Guilfoyle, Shipping Interdiction, 112–60.

[165] See inter alia M Haward, 'IUU Fishing: Contemporary Practice' in A Oude Elfernik and D Rothwell (eds), *Ocean Management in the 21st Century: Institutional Frameworks and Responses* (Leiden: Martinus Nijhoff, 2004) 87, 93–98.

[166] See R Rayfuse, *Non-Flag State Enforcement in High Seas Fisheries* (Leiden: Brill Academic Publishers, 2004) 269–70.

[167] ibid, 271–72.

[168] *cf* also the new EC Regulation (EC) No 1005/2008 establishing a Community system to prevent, deter and eliminate illegal, unreported and unregulated (IUU) fishing. See also commentary in M Tsamenyi et al, 'The European Council Regulation on Illegal, Unreported and Unregulated Fishing: An International Fisheries Law Perspective' 25 *IJMCL* (2010) 5–31.

[169] See for these arguments ibid, 344 and ibid, 'Countermeasures and High Seas Fisheries Enforcement' 51 *NILR* (2004) 41–76.

[170] See arguments by Guilfoyle, *Shipping Interdiction*, 161–68.

in granting their consent to boarding and inspection schemes in the context of RFMOs and the concomitant *opinio juris* are not conclusive of an emerging customary law.

As Guilfoyle rightly concludes,

On the present state of RFMO law and practice, there is no general international law of boarding and inspection applicable to all high seas fisheries. The minimum rules in FSA [Straddling Stocks Agreement] Articles 21 and 22 have not proved operationally capable of implementation without further agreement on significant practical details.[171]

---

[171] ibid, 168.

7

Interception on the High Seas to Counter Drug Trafficking

I. INTRODUCTION

I LLICIT TRAFFIC IN narcotic drugs and psychotropic substances attained great prominence in the last decades of the twentieth century and has been the subject of various international legislative and enforcement measures. The most important UN Conventions that are in force concerning the fight against drugs are the following: first, the 1961 Single Convention on Narcotics Drugs, which replaced all the previous conventions on this matter.[1] This Convention improved the system of international control through strict limitation of manufacture, exports and imports of a broad list of drugs, including opium, poppy, coca leaf and cannabis,[2] and it was amended by the 1972 Protocol.[3] Secondly, the 1971 Convention on Psychotropic Substances was established as a companion instrument of the 1961 Convention, since it deals with psychotropic substances next to narcotic drugs.[4] Lastly, there is the 1988 Vienna Convention, intended to deal specifically with the growing problem of international trafficking, which the earlier instruments only tackled in a marginal fashion.[5] This Convention also included provisions allowing the interception

---

[1] As early as 1912, the problems associated with the use of certain types of drugs were recognised as a matter of international concern, which led to the adoption of the first international instrument in this regard, the 1912 International Opium Convention, 8 LNTS 187. This was followed by a plethora of relevant treaties, such as the Second Opium Convention (1925), the Convention for Limiting the Manufacture and Regulating the Distribution of Narcotic Drugs (1931) and the Convention for the Suppression of the Illicit Traffic in Dangerous Drugs (1936). For an overview of these treaties see B Renborg, *International Drug Control: A Study of International Administration by and through the League of Nations* (Carnegie Endowment for International Peace, 1992).

[2] The state parties to the Convention agreed to cooperate closely in a coordinated campaign against illicit traffic in narcotic drugs, and to assist each other in the campaign.

[3] The 1972 Protocol amending the latter Convention made several improvements in the implementing and monitoring mechanisms, extradition provisions, technical assistance, and treatment and preventative measures; 976 UNTS 3.

[4] See Convention on Psychotropic Substances (New York, 21 February 1971) 1019 UNT, 176. For a comparison of the Single Convention with the Psychotropic Convention, see also CH Vignes, 'La Convention sur les substances psychotropes' 17 *AFDI* (1971) 641.

[5] As Gilmore, who is a leading commentator on the issue at hand, observes, 'while these Conventions focused primarily on controlling the production of licit drugs and the prevention

on the high seas of ships suspected of illicit trafficking by a state party other than the flag state.

The 1988 Vienna Convention was followed by other similar agreements in a regional context: first, the 1995 Council of Europe Agreement on Illicit Traffic by Sea, then the 2003 Caribbean Agreement, and the last was the 2008 CARICOM Agreement. In addition there have been numerous bilateral accords providing for the interception of suspect vessels on the high seas or in the territorial waters of the consumer states in order to tackle the scourge of drug trafficking. In addition to this treaty-making policy, the states concerned have resorted to other less formal means, such as seeking the ad hoc consent of the flag state or of the master of the suspect vessel in order to exert the right to board and search the latter for counter-drug trafficking purposes.

This overall practice, as it was concluded in the relevant theoretical discussion, reflects these claims for interference which aim to maintain the social welfare and the public order of states and of international society. It is the purpose of this chapter to discuss this practice of interception operations to suppress illicit traffic in narcotic drugs within the framework of the legal order of the oceans. The latter has furnished the necessary legal justifications for interception activities in this regard as well as has placed certain international legal restrictions to this practice, in accordance with the principle of '*la juridicité*' of the high seas.

II. INTERNATIONAL LEGAL JUSTIFICATIONS FOR INTERCEPTION OF DRUG SMUGGLING VESSELS ON THE HIGH SEAS

A. Multilateral Treaty Law Bases for Interception

i. The LOSC

The point of departure for the following assessment is necessarily article 110 of LOSC. On the face of this provision, it is evident that drug trafficking is not contemplated by the Convention as a specific ground for the right to visit of a foreign vessel. The LOSC only refers to illicit drug trafficking on the high seas in article 108 and only asks that states cooperate in its suppression.[6] In more detail, paragraph 1 sets out a general obliga-

---

of their diversion into the illicit market place, they were widely seen as making insufficient provision for effective international cooperation in law enforcement'; see ibid, 'The 1988 UN Convention against Illicit Traffic in Narcotic Drugs and Psychotropic Substances' 15 *MP* (1991) 183 (hereinafter: Gilmore, *Vienna*).

[6] The provision in question was proposed for the first time by Malta at the 1971 session of the Sea-Bed Committee; see A/AC 183/53, art 16, reproduced in SBC Report 1971, pp 105, 123. See also Nordquist, *Commentary*, 224.

tion for all states to cooperate, when the illicit traffic is 'contrary to international conventions'. This obligation depends on the content of the above mentioned Drug Conventions as well as that it is an obligation of conduct rather than result.[7] On the other hand, paragraph 2 addresses the issue of providing assistance to suppress the traffic in question. Nevertheless, only the state 'which has reasonable grounds for believing that the ship flying *its* flag is engaged in illicit traffic' in such drugs or substances 'may request the co-operation of other States to suppress such traffic'.[8] As Sohn observes, 'The opposite case of a State asking for cooperation of a State whose ship is suspected of smuggling drugs to other countries is noticeably not mentioned.'[9] Consequently, article 108 falls short of providing any enforcement mechanism to complement the obligation to cooperate enshrined in paragraph 1. This, in conjunction with the absence of any explicit reference to drug trafficking in article 110 LOSC, entails that in principle the LOSC and the respective customary law fail to furnish any basis for boarding drug smuggling vessels on the high seas.[10]

During the negotiation of LOSC, there had been several proposals for the adoption of boarding provisions with respect to illicit drug trafficking.[11] First, at the second session of the Conference (1974), there was a proposal by nine West European states for a new article on narcotic drugs, which set forth in paragraph 2 the right of seizure of illicit cargos from ships of less than 500 tons.[12] Introducing this proposal, the representative of France explained that this provision was included 'to prevent ships of small tonnage from discharging illicit cargo before entering ports'.[13] However, when this article reappeared in the Informal Single Negotiating Text (ISNT, 1975), the paragraph authorising seizure of illicit drugs cargo

---

[7] *cf* Bellayer-Roille writing that 'Une obligation de coopération est donc bien inscrite dans cet article, mais il ne s'agit en réalité que d'une obligation d'une 'obligation théorique', reposant sur la bonne volonté des Etats et, a fortiori, sur leur capacité réelle de réaction'; ibid, 'La Lutte contre le Narcotrafic en Mer Caraïbe' 111 *RGDIP* (2007) 355, 365.

[8] Emphasis added; see Nordquist, *Commentary*, 224.

[9] See Sohn, *Human Rights*, 60.

[10] This was the reason that, for example, the boarding of the Honduran flagship *Fidelio*, loaded with several tonnes of hashish, by the Italian authorities on the high seas in 1986 was declared illegal by the Court of Appeal of Palermo in a judgment of 30 June 1992; see below.

[11] It should be mentioned that the High Seas Convention did not include a similar provision. However, illicit traffic in drugs is referred to in art 19(1)(d) of the Convention on the Territorial Sea and the Contiguous Zone (1958) as a case for the exercise of the criminal jurisdiction of the coastal state; 516 UNTS 205. See also O'Connell, 956 and YbILC (1956-II) 275.

[12] The proposal set out in para 2 that 'any State which has reasonable grounds for believing that a vessel is engaged in illicit traffic in narcotic drugs may, whatever the nationality of the vessel but provided that its tonnage is less than 500 tons, seize the illicit cargo. The State which carried out this seizure shall inform the State of nationality of the vessel in order that the latter State may institute proceedings against those responsible for the illicit traffic'; see A/CONF 62/C 2/L 54 (1974), art 21*bis*, III *Official Records* 230.

[13] See Second Committee, 42nd meeting (1974), para 2, II *Official Records* 292.

was not included.[14] The reason was that several delegations expressed concern about the effect that such language might have on the freedom of navigation, fearing that states might use it as a pretext for abuse or harassment.[15] In addition, analogous proposals were made in the context of the drafting of article 110, starting at the third session (1975), when the informal consultative group on the high seas included the illicit traffic in narcotic drugs as a ground for the exercise of the right to visit.[16] However, with the insertion in the ISNT of a separate article on illicit traffic of narcotic drugs the substance of this provision was changed to apply to unauthorised broadcasting.[17]

In consequence, it is submitted that the only relevant heading under article 110 of LOSC is the 'absence of nationality', since none of the other grounds, ie piracy, slave trade, unauthorised broadcasting and the same nationality, would be applicable. Many drug traffickers operate in unregistered, stateless vessels, in which case article 110(1)(d) of LOSC applies.[18] It is pursuant to this provision that warships or other duly authorised vessels of any state may exercise the right of visit on these vessels. However, it bears repeating that the right to visit stateless vessels does not *ipso jure* entail the right to seize the illicit cargo or exert any further enforcement jurisdiction over the persons on board the vessel. It is the view of the present author that the boarding states would have to rely on some positive basis of jurisdiction to exercise jurisdiction over persons and property on these vessels, since the statelessness itself would fall short of according them such jurisdiction.

However, there is a case, in which the statelessness of the vessel suffices not only for the boarding but also for the assertion of jurisdiction *per se*; this is the case of submersible or semi-submersible vessels according to the Drug Trafficking Vessel Interdiction Act (DTVIA), adopted by the US Congress in 2008.[19] The DTVIA purports to address the practical difficulties posed by the use of such vessels by criminalising the operation of a submersible or semi-submersible vessel without nationality and with the intent to evade detection. Unlike other relevant laws, the DTVIA does not use a vessel's statelessness solely as a jurisdictional hook, but makes the operation of a stateless vessel a key component of the substantive crime it

[14] See art 94 of the Informal Single Negotiating Text/Part II, a/conf 62/wp 8/Part II (ISNT, 1975) IV OR 166.

[15] See Nordquist, *Commentary*, 227.

[16] See Provision 174, Formula B of the Revised Text of the Informal Consultative Group on the High Seas; reprinted in R Platzöder, *Third United Nations Conference on the Law of the Sea, Vol IV* (Baden-Baden: Nomos, 1994) 329.

[17] See Nordquist, *Commentary*, at 242.

[18] Such vessels are of course, the semi-submersible vessels used for drug-trafficking purposes see *supra* Introduction (fn 40).

[19] 18 USCA § 2285 (West 2011).

proscribes.[20] In *United States v Ibarguen-Mosquera,* the Eleventh Circuit upheld the DTVIA without noting any significant difference between the jurisdictional requirements of the DTVIA and of previous laws; in the words of the Court, 'international law permits any nation to subject stateless vessels on the high seas to its jurisdiction . . . Jurisdiction exists solely as a consequence of the vessel's status as stateless'.[21] Notwithstanding this case, there is no warrant for such reading of statelessness as a separate and independent head of jurisdiction under international law.

The absence of nationality of a vessel is the only relevant legal justification under LOSC in general; nonetheless, it should be recalled that in accordance with articles 92 and 110 of LOSC, such interference may be authorised pursuant to a treaty. Indeed, there have been numerous bilateral agreements as well as a few multilateral treaties, which have granted such authorisation to state parties with respect to drug trafficking.

ii. Vienna Convention (1988)

a. The Boarding Provision

The most important multilateral instrument in this regard is the 1988 Vienna Convention, which contains provisions specifically directed to traffic at sea, including the right to board the vessels of other state parties engaged in illicit drug traffic.[22] The Vienna Convention was the outcome of protracted negotiations between states and various UN bodies from 1982.[23] It was then – just before the official adoption of the LOSC – that Canada for the first time raised the issue of 'arrangements for law enforcement authorities to board vessels flying foreign flags'.[24] Even though the relevant Expert Group rejected Canada's proposal, this was reinstated in 1986 by the UN Commission on Narcotic Drugs, and with certain modifications found its way through into the body of the Convention and in particular to article 17(3). This reads as follows:

> A Party which has reasonable grounds to suspect that a vessel exercising the freedom of navigation in accordance with international law and flying the flag

---

[20] A Bennett, 'The Sinking Feeling: Stateless Ships, Universal Jurisdiction, and the Drug Trafficking Vessel interdiction Act' 37 *Yale Journal of International Law* (2012) 433, 434.

[21] 634 F.3d 1370 (llth Cir 2011), at 1379 (quoting *Marino-Garcia* 6, 79 F.2d at 1382). The 11th Circuit also upheld the DTVIA in *United States v Saac*, 632 F.3d 1203, 1210- 1211 (11th Cir 2011).

[22] See above Introduction (n 42).

[23] See in this respect Gilmore, *Vienna*, 184 and F Rouchereau, 'La Convention des Nations Unies contre le Traffic Illicite de Stupéfiants et de substances psychotropes' 36 *AFDI* (1988) 601.

[24] See Review and Implementation of the Programme of Strategy and Policies for Drug Control: Report of the Expert Group to Study the Functioning, Adequacy and Enhancement of the Single Convention in Narcotic Drugs, UN Doc E/CN 7/ 1983/2/Add 1, para 3, cited also in Gilmore, ibid, 185.

or displaying marks of registry of another Party is engaged in illicit traffic may so notify the flag State, request confirmation of registry and, if confirmed, request authorisation from the flag State to take appropriate measures in regard to that vessel.

This provision should be scrutinised in relation both to article 17 as a whole, entitled 'illicit traffic by sea', and to other key provisions of the Vienna Convention, with which it is inextricably linked. For example, while the focus of article 17 is on facilitating the exercise of enforcement jurisdiction in relation to suspect vessels, the overall effectiveness of the scheme is contingent upon the possession by states of appropriate pre-scriptive jurisdiction, which is accorded by article 4.[25]

The first and most significant remark is that article 17(3) requires the explicit 'authorisation' of the flag state, a word which was included after lengthy informal consultations.[26] As is pointed out in the *travaux prépara-toires*, this word was deliberately used to 'stress the positive nature of the decision and of the action which the flag State in the exercise of its sover-eignty was to take with regard to the vessel. It is entirely within the discre-tion of that State to decide whether to allow another party to act against its vessel.'[27]

In more detail, article 17 reiterates in the first two paragraphs the gist of the provisions in article 108 LOSC, albeit in more imperative and enhanced tenor. Thus, paragraph 1 of article 17 requires, for the first time, coopera-tion 'to the fullest extent possible . . . in conformity with the international law of the sea' in order to suppress illicit traffic by sea.[28] Similarly, para-graph 2 builds upon article 108(2), with the significant contribution that it makes special reference to vessels without nationality. Hence, it expands the situations in which cooperation may be requested to include interdic-tion of stateless vessels. In doing this, it seems to assimilate such vessels to flag state vessels, since it gives the opportunity to all states to request the cooperation of other states in the suppression of drug smuggling by state-less vessels in the same way that they would do with regard to the vessels flying their flag. Nonetheless, while in the latter case, the source of this authority is obviously the exclusive jurisdiction, which the flag state exerts over its vessels, in the case of vessels of no nationality, the authority to request such cooperation is not so manifest. In any event, the provision in question is not imposing any relevant obligation, since it is framed in

---

[25] See Vienna Commentary, 323.

[26] This requirement for explicit authorisation is also reiterated in art 6 of the 1995 Council of Europe Agreement on Illicit Traffic by Sea, implementing art 17 of the UN Convention against Illicit Traffic in Narcotic Drugs and Psychotropic Substances, *European Treaty Series* No 156 (hereinafter: 1995 CoE Agreement), as well as in art 8 of the Smuggling Protocol, which was modelled after this Convention.

[27] See *Official Records of the Vienna Convention,* Summary Records of Committee II, 29th meeting, para 7.

[28] See art 17(1) Vienna Convention, and also Gilmore, *Vienna,* 187.

hortatory rather than mandatory terms and it fails to provide for the establishment of jurisdiction with regard to the illicit cargo and to the offenders.[29]

In addition, questions could arise with regard to the jurisdiction and the concomitant responsibility over the intercepted vessels when the flag state request another state to suppress the use of its own vessel for the purpose of illicit traffic. It is submitted that, while, in the case of article 17(3), the requesting state would have concurrent jurisdiction with the intervening State and the latter would bear the responsibility for its conduct, the situation envisaged in paragraph 2, ie the vessel of a state party coming to the assistance of the flag state resembles rather an 'organ placed at the disposal of another State' of article 6 of the ILC Articles.[30] Consequently, it would be on more stable legal ground to hold that the flag state should maintain its jurisdiction over the vessel, the persons and property on board, as well as that it would incur responsibility for any potential loss or damage, unless the latter is directly attributable to the conduct of the assisting state.[31]

As far as the right to visit other state parties' vessels is concerned, enshrined in paragraph 3, the triggering fact is, of course, the existence of 'reasonable grounds to suspect' the illicit traffic, an assessment which falls, nevertheless, with the flag state, who solely holds the authority to decide about the existence and gravity of these grounds.[32] Apart from the need for the explicit authorisation underlined above, the requesting party has, first, to notify the flag state, then request confirmation of the registry, and lastly request the authorisation. This provision should be read in conjunction with paragraph 4, which stipulates that 'the flag State *may* authorise the requesting State to *inter alia*: a) board the vessel, b) search the vessel and c) if evidence of involvement in illicit traffic is found, take appropriate action with respect to the vessel, persons and cargo on board'.[33] What logically flows from these provisions is that the consent of the flag state is necessary for any measure taken against the vessel and the authorisation by the latter state should exist with respect to each process individually, ie the boarding, search and detention of the vessel.

In addition, it is very significant that the drafters highlight the disjunctive nature of the various processes which the right of visit includes, ie the

---

[29] This has been rectified by the 1995 CoE Agreement (art 3 para 3), which expressly provides for the establishment of jurisdiction in this respect.

[30] See ILC Articles Commentary, 43.

[31] This same approach is taken also by the 1995 CoE Agreement (art 26 para 3). In the same vein, the flag state should share the burden of the costs for the interdiction operation with the assisting state; see Vienna Commentary, 342.

[32] Even if the flag state retains the final authority to assess the validity of these grounds, there were some concerns raised in the negotiation process with regard to the clarity and specificity of the phrase in question; see Summary Records of meetings of Committee II, above n 24, 269.

[33] See art 17(4) (emphasis added).

right to visit (boarding) and the right to search,[34] as well as that they disassociate the right of visit as an exception to the freedom of the high seas with the enforcement jurisdiction over the illicit cargo and the offenders.[35] This distinction is not so self-evident in the context of operations based on bilateral treaties or ad hoc arrangements. While the decision for the authorisation will always be at the discretion of the flag state, it will be within the spirit of the Convention and in harmony with the principle of effectiveness that denials of such requests should be given with moderation and be appropriately justified. In any event, the fact that the flag state will decline its authorisation for boarding does not divest itself of the obligation to cooperate in the suppression of illicit drug traffic, ie the obligation to take itself all necessary measures to suppress such traffic on board the suspect vessel.

The debate on paragraph 3 proved highly controversial and was centred not on whether provision should be made for the interdiction of foreign flag vessels, nor on whether such action should require the consent of the flag state, but rather on the *ratione loci* ambit of this provision, namely the maritime area to which it applied.[36] The reference to the 'exercise of the freedom of navigation in accordance with international law' in conjunction with the statement in paragraph 11 that any action 'must take due account of the need not to interfere with . . . the jurisdiction of coastal States' were the outcome of a difficult compromise. As a result, 'the suspected ship must be located beyond the outer limit of the territorial sea for an authorisation to be requested from the flag state to board the vessel'.[37]

In addition, article 17 addresses a number of issues, which are instrumental to the application of the provision in question. For example, there is the requirement for each party to designate an authority to receive and respond to requests (paragraph 7).[38] While it is for each state party to determine the appropriate location for the designated national authority

---

[34] As the Commentary stresses, 'the drafting of the paragraph was intended to make clear the disjunctive nature of the various processes which might be taken against the vessel concerned: boarding; search and only if evidence is found further appropriate action'; see Vienna Commentary, 330.

[35] The informal working group decided to delete any reference to seizure of the vessel in question. Nonetheless, this omission was balanced by the inclusion of the phrase 'inter alia', which indicates that the range of possible measures is not limited to those expressly mentioned; see ibid, 330 and Gilmore, *Vienna*, 190.

[36] See T Treves, 'Intervention en Haute Mer et Navires Etrangers' 41 *AFDI* (1995) 651, 656.

[37] Vienna Commentary, 326.

[38] As has been pointed out, 'this designation must be transmitted to the Secretary-General, who will notify all the participating States. This essential contact information, including addresses, telephone and facsimile numbers, and hours of operation, is published by the United Nations and updated on a periodic basis'; see Vienna Commentary, 335. See in this respect UN, *Competent National Authorities under the International Drug Control Treaties* (Geneva: United Nations, 1995) 89. It is also worth noting that a Practical Guide on this matter was published by UN Office on Drugs and Crime in 2003 (hereinafter: Practical Guide).

and the powers and functions to be entrusted, the need for it to be in a position to respond effectively and expeditiously to incoming requests is even more important here, in light of the often-difficult operational environment presented by open ocean areas. Notwithstanding this pragmatic need for flexibility and efficiency, there should always be certain guarantees that the process will not be abused and competent State agents will give the authorisation.

Article 17 is primarily concerned with making detailed provisions for procedures designed to allow state parties to exercise enforcement jurisdiction on the basis of flag state consent. Nevertheless, this article hinges its application and effectiveness upon the existence of the respective prescriptive jurisdiction, which is the function of article 4. This article, the scope of which is confined to the most serious international drug trafficking offences specified in article 3, commences by requiring state parties to establish jurisdiction over any such offences committed in its territory or on board its vessels. Interestingly, however, in spite of precedents,[39] the Vienna Convention fails to require the states to establish jurisdiction over offences committed by their nationals[40] as well as over the offences committed on board a vessel concerning which that state has been authorised to take appropriate measures pursuant to article 17(3). The assertion of legislative jurisdiction in these cases was made an option under article 4(1)(b)(i) and (ii) and it is reported that relatively few states have established such jurisdiction.[41]

As a result, there could be a case where a state party will be authorised to seize the suspect vessel on the high seas by the flag state, yet it will lack the requisite jurisdiction to seize the cargo and try the offenders in its courts. Undoubtedly, this lack of mandatory establishment of jurisdiction undermines the effective application of article 17.

In addition, neither the latter provision nor article 4 address the issue of which state's jurisdiction would apply in the case of the boarding of a vessel of another state party. What can logically be inferred from article 17(4), which requires the explicit authorisation of the flag state for all the relevant measures, is that it is the flag state which enjoys primary jurisdiction. Nevertheless, it may devolve the relevant jurisdictional competence to the intervening state, which assumes concurrent jurisdiction over the persons and the cargo onboard. It is regrettable, however, that while concurrent claims to jurisdiction will inevitably arise within this context, the Vienna Convention does not seek to solve the problem of what priority to give to such competing assertions.[42] It should be noted in this regard that in two

---

[39] See eg art 6(1)(c) of 1988 SUA Convention.
[40] The decision to make this ground optional stemmed from a fundamental difference between common law and civil law states about whether nationality should be a sufficient ground to establish jurisdiction; see UN Doc E/Conf 82/c1/SR18, 7–12. See also Sproule and St-Denis, 'The UN Drug Trafficking Convention: An Ambitious Step' 27 *CYIL* (1990) 263, 275.
[41] See Vienna Commentary, 107.
[42] See ibid, 101.

reported cases concerning boardings on the high seas on the basis of the Convention, such a problem has not in fact occurred.

b. Relevant Case Law

These cases could be of import to the present analysis as they involve many of the issues addressed in the previous paragraphs. First, reference should be made to the case of the vessel *Archangelos*, which provides a good example of an interdiction in full conformity with the provisions of the Vienna Convention.[43] In January 1995, the Central Investigating Court no 1 of Spain'sAudiencia Nacional was informed that the *Archangelos*, a vessel flying the Panamanian flag, was on the Atlantic Ocean sailing towards Europe with a cargo of cocaine. After obtaining verbal authorisation from the Panamanian embassy in Spain, in accordance with article 17 §§ 3 and 4 of the Vienna Convention, the investigating judge ordered that the vessel be boarded and searched while still on the high seas. On 23 January 1995 the crew of a Spanish vessel, the *Petrel I*, boarded the vessel. After an exchange of fire with several members of the crew who had barricaded themselves into the engine room, the 14-member crew surrendered. After searching the *Archangelos*, the customs officers seized 68 packets of cocaine weighing 2,713 kg in total.

The embassies of the states of which the detained crew members were nationals were informed of their detention and the relevant judicial procedures were initiated leading to the conviction and sentencing to a nine-year prison sentence for drug trafficking of the master of the vessel, Mr Rigopoulos, by the Audiencia Nacional on 13 October 1998. However, before this decision, Mr Rigopoulos lodged an appeal (*recurso de amparo*) with the Constitutional Court. He complained, inter alia, that he had been illegally detained and that he had not been brought promptly before a judicial authority. In a judgment of 10 February 1997, the Constitutional Court dismissed his appeal. The Court found that the measures taken by the Central Investigating Court had complied with all the requirements of the Convention in question and, therefore, the applicant had been detained in accordance with the law and the applicable international rules.

It is readily apparent that in this case, all the relevant measures were in conformity with the Convention and relevant international law. In more detail, a competent authority of the flag state gave an express authorisation, the boarding was consistent with the applicable rules and the use of force employed in the case was the minimum necessary to arrest the crew and seize the vessel. Furthermore, Spain had lawfully exerted jurisdiction

---

[43] See with regard to the *Archangelos* case the ensuing ECtHR Decision in *Rigopoulos v Spain* App no 37388/97 (12 January 1999) and the analysis therein, and V Gualde, 'Suppression of the Illicit Traffic in Narcotic Drugs and Psychotropic Substances on the High Seas: Spanish Case Law', 4 *Spanish Yearbook of International Law* (1996) 91, 102–03.

in this case, since it had already enacted legislation with regard to cases of drug trafficking by Spaniards or foreigners on the high seas, most probably based on universality.[44] In addition, no other state which could advance a jurisdictional claim, namely, either Panama, the flag state, or Greece, the state of the nationality of the applicant, did so.

Conversely, the second reported case involving the application of article 17 of the Vienna Convention, namely *R v Charrington and others* (1999), raised various contentious issues.[45] These related primarily to the manner in which the consent of Malta, the flag state of *Simon de Danser*, was obtained by the UK and the circumstances in which the boarding of the latter vessel was accomplished, on 5 May 1997.[46] In short, the British Crown Court granted a stay, because the boarding, search and seizure of the vessel in question were *mala fides*, thus unlawful, as was the subsequent taking of the boat to the United Kingdom.

This judgment raises the following issues of interest to the present enquiry: first, it was considered that the boarding was authorised by an inappropriate authority, since the British official who claimed to have telephoned the office of the Attorney-General of Malta, ie the designated authority under the laws of Malta for article 17(7) purposes, was unable to produce evidence to the satisfaction of the court that such contact had been made. It must be recalled in this regard, however, that, while, for example, in the context of the 1995 Agreement there is a specific requirement for the requests to be made in writing, this is not the case in respect of the Vienna Convention. Moreover, as Gilmore points out, the statutory rules in question neither were of fundamental importance, nor was their violation so manifest as to lead to the invalidation of the consent given by Malta, along the lines of article 46 of the VCLT.[47] He contends, rather

---

[44] 'The Constitutional Court reiterated that section 23(4) of the Judicature Act of 1 July 1985 gave the Spanish courts jurisdiction over acts committed by Spaniards or aliens outside Spanish territory if those acts constituted an offence like (as in the case in point) drug trafficking'. See *Rigopoulos*, 66.

[45] See report of the case and extensive commentary in W Gilmore, 'Drug Trafficking at Sea: The Case of *R. v. Charrington and Others*' 49 *ICLQ* (2000) 477 (hereinafter: Gilmore, *Regina*). The failure of the prosecution in this case prompted the Commissioners of Customs and Excise to commission an independent inquiry into this operation and its aftermath; see Inquiry into HM Customs and Excise Aspects of the *Simon de Danser* case: Report by Sir Gerald Hosker KCB QC (1999).

[46] The *Simon de Danser* was on the high seas, some 100 miles off the coast of Portugal, when it was approached in darkness by members of the Royal Marines Special Boat Squadron, accompanied by officers of HM Customs and Excise. The boarding party used rigid inflatable boats and was dispatched from a British warship, *HMS York*. Four tonnes of cannabis were found on board. A number of individuals were arrested and brought to the United Kingdom, and they were charged with offences relating to conspiracy to evade the prohibition on the importation of drugs.

[47] Under art 46 of the VCLT, a state may contest the validity of a treaty on the ground that it was concluded in violation of a provision of its internal law regarding competence to conclude treaties. However, this right is subject to the satisfaction of certain specified and exacting criteria; namely that the rule of internal law must be of fundamental importance and the violation

persuasively, that 'a safer conclusion would be that it was legally satisfactory for the UK to rely on the ostensible authority of the Malta Maritime Authority in providing consent'.[48] Even though this opinion appears to be praiseworthy in many respects, the judgment under scrutiny demonstrates how significant the written form of the authorisation is for reasons of legal certainty and due process.

In addition, considerable attention was devoted in the court proceedings to the content of the British request, which, as the court concluded, contained 'blatantly misleading information'.[49] In more detail, while the British request indicated that 'the vessel *Simon de Danser* is currently exercising freedom of navigation in accordance with international law off the coast of the United Kingdom', it later transpired that the vessel had been in Funchal harbour in Madeira. However, at no stage did the British authorities inform Malta of the facts concerning location when these became known. Hence, as was submitted by the counsel for defence, 'the boarding and subsequent acts of British authorities were unlawful because the consent of Malta was obtained through the provision of materially inaccurate information, which was, thereafter, deliberately left uncorrected'.[50]

In the appraisal of the case, it is of particular significance to stress that article 17 of the Vienna Convention says very little either about the manner in which a request is to be made or as to the contents of the request.[51] Therefore, parties to the Convention remain free to fashion their claims as they see fit, taking, of course, into account their obligation to apply as well as to interpret the treaty provision in question in good faith.[52] Nevertheless, it is for the requested party to determine the sufficiency and accuracy of the information with which it has been provided in any particular case. Further, as Gilmore stresses, 'the specification of the location of the vessel may properly be regarded by the requested State as relevant or even critical to its decision on whether or not to authorise action'.[53] Premised upon an analogy with the law of treaties, Gilmore contends that 'this misrepresentation of the *locus* of the vessel could qualify as error and thus as a basis for the invalidity of the authorisation pursuant to article 48 of the VCLT. Consequently, the agreement procured was voidable, yet at no stage of the legal proceedings did Malta invoke the original error as a

must be manifest. The latter condition is satisfied 'if it would be objectively evident to any State conducting itself in the matter in accordance with normal practice and in good faith'.

[48] Gilmore, *Regina*, 480. He relies also on the fact that both the Attorney-General and Executive Director of the Malta Maritime Authority appeared as witnesses for the Crown and argued that, as a matter of domestic law, valid authority had in fact been granted in this instance.

[49] See transcript, Day 18, p 1027, cited in Gilmore, *Regina*, 484.

[50] ibid.

[51] On the contrary, art 21 of the 1995 CoE Agreement as well as art 6(3) of the Caribbean Agreement deal in a detailed fashion with the contents of the requests to board.

[52] *cf* arts 26 and 31(1) of VCLT.

[53] Gilmore, *Regina*, 484.

basis for impeaching the validity of the agreement thus the Court erroneously did not consider this in its judgment.'[54] In the view of the author, it
would suffice to invoke the lacuna with regard to the content of the
request in the Vienna Convention in conjunction with the principle of
acquiescence on the part of Malta to this misrepresentation of the facts to
draw the same conclusion as above.[55]

Finally, it was submitted by the defence that the manner in which the
boarding was effected also constituted a violation of the agreement with
Malta and Article 17(10) of the Vienna Convention, which restricts the
action to be taken to 'warships . . . or other ships . . . clearly marked and
identifiable as being on government service and authorised to that effect'.
Here, the boarding had taken place, under cover of darkness, by unmarked
rigid inflatable boats. They had set off from *HMS York*, which was located
a considerable distance away from the target of the operation.[56] What is
evident from the face of the relevant provision is that the requirement that
a vessel be 'clearly marked and identifiable' does not apply only to warships but also to the other ships exercising the right to visit, such as *in casu*
the inflatable boats.[57] To controvert this, it could be asserted that this
requirement is satisfied by the mother ship or the 'platform', which here
was the *HMS York*,[58] as well as that there are clear practical law enforcement considerations, which may point toward the need for secret or cov-
ert boardings in circumstances where drug shipments are involved.[59]
While no clear conclusion appears in the judgment at hand on this matter,
its overall tenor and thrust suggests that it was more in favour of the
former argument. However, it is submitted that there is room for the contrary view, ie that it would be in harmony with the principle of effectiveness
to conclude that where unmarked boats set off from warships and subsequently do not violate other pertinent rules, such non-compliance with
the above-mentioned requirements should not be decisive.[60]

---

[54] ibid, 484. It is important to stress here that in accordance with art 48 of VCLT, an error of
this kind does not make an agreement automatically void; see also *Temple of Preah Vihear*
case, 26. On invalidity of treaties in general see Ch Rozakis, 'The Law of Invalidity of
Treaties', 16 *Archiv des Völkerrects* (1974) 150.

[55] On acquiescence qua unilateral act see Brownlie, 61.

[56] See transcript, Day 9, p 324, cited in Gilmore, *Regina*, 485.

[57] See on the treatment of the issue in general international law, Nordquist, *Commentary*, 221.

[58] In this regard, it could be also asserted that the law of the sea recognises in another
context, ie in 'hot pursuit', the principle of the 'constructive presence', which could also
apply in the case of warships and their boats; *cf* art 111 LOSC and N Poulantzas, *The Right of
Hot Pursuit in International Law*, 2nd edn (The Hague: Martinus Nijhoff, 2002).

[59] See Gilmore, *Regina* 487.

[60] Similar questions could be raised in respect of night boardings of vessels in circumstances
of secrecy. The US courts that have considered such cases have reached the conclusion that
night-boarding of a US vessel in order to conduct a safety and document check is permissible,
even without a founded suspicion of safety or documentary violations. See *US v Watson*, 678
F 2d 765 (9th Cir), *cert denied*, 459 US 1058 (1982). See also *US v Portocarrero-Reina* 2006 WL
1460277 (MD Fla May 23, 2006) (slip opinion).

iii. The Council of Europe Agreement (1995)

The shortcomings of the Vienna Convention were in the regional context to a certain extent mitigated by the 1995 Council of Europe Agreement.[61] As was mentioned above, article 17(9) of the Vienna Convention calls for the establishment of bilateral and regional arrangements to enhance the effectiveness of the provisions of article 17. Such an arrangement is the 1995 Agreement that supplements and strengthens the relevant treaty framework in the European context, consisting, besides the Vienna Convention, of few bilateral treaties.[62] The final Agreement is intimately connected to the 1988 Convention, since article 17 and other relevant provisions acted as a constant frame of reference for the drafters.[63]

As a result, following article 17, parties to the 1995 CoE Agreement undertake to cooperate to the fullest extent possible to interdict narcotics trafficking at sea. Action towards this end is envisaged in respect of private and commercial vessels located beyond the territorial sea of any state[64] and of course includes the right of visit of vessels flying the flag of another state party, which has given its explicit authorisation to this end. It was agreed from the outset that, as with the Vienna Convention, action of this kind would be firmly based on the concept of authorisation of the flag state,[65] as well as that there is no obligation for a flag state to respond affirmatively to a request for authorisation.[66] Nevertheless, in the preparatory stage, a number of alternative ways, which are prevalent in the context of bilateral interdiction agreements, were discussed, namely that

[61] The Agreement entered into force on 1 May 2000 and as at 29 August 2012 it had 13 states parties; see at www.conventions.coe.int/Treaty/Commun/ChercheSig.asp?NT=156&CM=8&DF=29/08/2012&CL=ENG. For the associated official Explanatory Report, see Council of Europe Document CDPC (94) 22, Addendum of 27 June 1994; also available at http://conventions.coe.int/Treaty/en/Reports/Html/156.htm (hereinafter: Explanatory Report).

[62] See for further information on the negotiation W Gilmore, 'Narcotics Interdiction at Sea: The 1995 CoE Agreement' 20 *MP* 3 (hereinafter: Gilmore, CoE) and Van der Kruit, *Maritime Drug Interdiction in International Law* (Utrecht: Druk OBT/TDS, 2007) 142.

[63] Because of the fact that this Agreement is implementing art 17 of the Vienna Convention, it was accepted from the outset that, for example, solutions which were contrary to the letter or spirit of the Vienna Convention would not be acceptable. In addition, it was decided to limit the possibility of becoming a party to the instrument to those Member States of the Council of Europe which have ratified the Vienna Convention (art 27).

[64] As the Explanatory Report notes: 'this would include the high seas, the contiguous zone and the EEZ within the meaning of the Montego Bay Convention and customary international law' ibid, 25.

[65] Art 6 reads as follows: 'Where the intervening State has reasonable grounds to suspect that a vessel, which is flying the flag or displaying the marks of registry of another Party or bears any other indications of nationality of the vessel, is engaged in or being used for the commission of a relevant offence, the intervening State may request the authorization of the flag State to stop and board the vessel in waters beyond the territorial sea of any Party, and to take some or all of the other actions specified in this Agreement. *No such actions may be taken by virtue of this Agreement, without the authorization of the flag State*' (emphasis added).

[66] See also art 17 of the 1995 Agreement.

prior authorisation to stop and board a vessel could be contained in the Treaty or that failure to respond to a request in a timely fashion would constitute tacit consent. After lengthy discussion, it was decided to give effect to the more conservative approach.[67] Noteworthy also is that the provision relates to vessels 'engaged in or *being used for*' the commission of a drug trafficking, with the words 'used for' being added with a view to addressing the situation where a mother ship has unloaded drugs to a smaller vessel to be transported to the coast.[68]

While the 1995 Agreement draws significantly from the paradigm of the Vienna Convention, its merit lies not only in that it addresses some of the already observed weaknesses of the latter Convention, but also in that it espouse practices, which are more prevalent in the realm of bilateral agreements. First, it is of great practical significance that it requires rather than merely permits, as does the Vienna Convention, the extension of pre-scriptive criminal jurisdiction to relevant offences taking place on board both the flag vessels of other parties and stateless ships.[69] Especially with respect to vessels without nationality, it is worth recalling that article 17(2) of the Vienna Convention only makes provision for states to request assistance in suppressing the use of such vessels in illicit traffic without making any allusion to legislative jurisdiction in this regard. Conversely, article 3(3) of the Agreement requires each participating state 'to take such measures as may be necessary to establish its jurisdiction over the rele-vant offences on board a vessel without nationality'.[70]

Furthermore, it is certainly noteworthy that while as a consequence of the approach adopted in article 3 the boarding state and the flag state will possess concurrent jurisdiction over the relevant offences, it was decided even within the Pompidou Group to follow the approach adopted in some bilateral treaties, that in such circumstances the rights of the flag state should be accorded priority.[71] Hence, so-called 'preferential jurisdiction' was recognised, which in the words of article 1(b) means that 'in relation to a flag State . . . the right to exercise its jurisdiction on a priority basis, to the exclusion of the exercise of the other State's jurisdiction over the offence'.[72]

Besides the 1995 Agreement, there had been another proposal for a regional counter-drug-trafficking agreement in the European context. Reportedly, in 2002, Spain submitted a proposal to the European Union for a maritime interdiction convention, drawn up on the basis of article 34

---

[67] See Gilmore, CoE, 7.
[68] See Explanatory Report, 11.
[69] See art 3 of the 1995 CoE Agreement and the Explanatory Report, ibid.
[70] See the pertinent remarks in W Gilmore, CoE, 5 and Vienna Commentary, 110.
[71] See eg the terms of the 1990 Agreement between Italy and Spain (art 4 para 2).
[72] See art 14 and Commentary in Explanatory Report, 34.

of the EU Treaty.[73] The objective of this initiative was to 'provide the Member States with a convention that strengthens cooperation between the EU's customs administrations in the fight against illicit drug trafficking, by extending the possibilities for immediate action on the high seas, with prior authorisation against a member state's vessel'.[74] However, to the knowledge of the author, there has been no other development since then.

In the European context, there is also is an inter-governmental working group or taskforce comprising seven EU Member States: Spain, France, Ireland, Italy, the Netherlands, Portugal and the UK, which is called Maritime Analysis and Operation Centre – Narcotics (MAOC-N) and aims to tackle maritime drug smuggling in Europe.[75] The mission of MAOC-N is to enhance intelligence and coordinate police action on the high seas, with a view to intercepting vessels carrying cocaine and cannabis. Naval and law-enforcement bodies (police, customs) participate in MAOC-N, although the latter leads the operations. This notwithstanding, there is no standing treaty giving boarding powers to Member States, while MAOC-N falls short of being an international organization *per se.*

iv. The Caribbean Agreement (2003)

Another regional arrangement to be regarded is the Agreement Concerning Co-operation in Suppressing Illicit Maritime and Air Trafficking in Narcotic Drugs and Psychotropic Substances in the Caribbean Area, concluded on 10 April 2003 at San José, Costa Rica and entered into force on 18 September 2008.[76] This agreement may be said to have emerged from the extensive practical experience of the states and territories of the region, which has also materialised in an extensive network of bilateral agreements in respect of drug trafficking. In addition, it has been significantly influenced by the special geographical circumstances of the Caribbean basin. As was observed in the Introduction, the existence, for example, of a series of navigational 'choke points' has a direct relevance to the increased drug trafficking in the

---

[73] See 2002 Draft Convention Established by the Council in Accordance with Article 34 of the Treaty on European Union on the Suppression by Customs Administrations of Illicit Drug Trafficking on the High Seas, Council of the EU, ENFOCUSTOM 2, 5382, Brussels, 4 February 2002. In 2004 the European Parliament submitted its position on the 2002 Draft Convention suggesting some amendments; see Van der Kruit, above n 59, 189.

[74] ibid, 190.

[75] See further information at <http://www.emcdda.europa.eu/about/partners/maoc>.

[76] The text and a short commentary is found in W Gilmore, *Agreement Concerning Co-operation in Suppressing Illicit Maritime and Air Trafficking in Narcotic Drugs and Psychotropic Substances in the Caribbean Area* (2005) (hereinafter: Caribbean Agreement). See also A Bellayer-Roille, above n 7, 369. As of 19 April 2011, parties to the Agreement were Belize, Costa Rica, Dominican Republic, France, Guatemala, Netherlands, Nicaragua and United States of America. Signatures subject to ratification were Haiti, Honduras, Jamaica, United Kingdom. See A Roach and R Smith, *Excessive Maritime Claims*, 3rd edn (Leiden: Martinus Nijhoff, 2012), Appendix 16 (on file with the author) (hereinafter: Roach, *Appendix*).

region as well as to the difficulties that law enforcement operations face therein.

This Agreement, like the 1995 CoE Agreement in the European region, purports to enhance the effectiveness of article 17 of the Vienna Convention in the Caribbean basin; however, it is far more innovative and ambitious than the latter, since it is based less on the Vienna Convention and more on the bilateral arrangements already in place in the region. Accordingly, this instrument contains detailed provisions concerning law enforcement operations of all state parties in and over the territorial waters of the con-tracting states (articles 11–15); a zone of coastal state sovereignty beyond the *ratione loci* reach both of the Vienna Convention and of the 1995 Agreement.[77] It directly addresses issues arising in illicit trafficking by air and regulates in some detail assistance by aircraft for the suppression of illicit traffic in zones of coastal state jurisdiction; issues on which the aforementioned treaties are largely silent. By virtue of articles 11 and 13(6), however, the previous authorisation of the coastal state is a prereq-uisite for such operations, which, in any event, are subject to the authority of the coastal state and should be carried out by, or under the direction of, its law enforcement authorities.[78]

Another innovative feature which has been directly drawn from the bilateral treaties is the already discussed 'shiprider', where each party is required to designate law enforcement officials to embark on the vessels of other parties in order to facilitate the timely provision of authorisations and the exercise of relevant national law enforcement powers within zones of jurisdiction of the former party (article 9). Under this provision, duly authorised law enforcement officials may enforce the laws of the designating party both in the waters of that party or seaward of such waters, 'in the exercise of the right of hot pursuit or otherwise in accord-ance with international law', such as in the proper exercise of contiguous zone jurisdiction. In addition, they may authorise the entry of the vessel on which they are embarked into the territorial sea of the designating party and authorise the conduct of counter-drug patrols and boarding of suspect vessels therein. Given the obvious complexity of such arrange-ments from a formal legal perspective, article 9(4) clarifies that when enforcement action is conducted pursuant to the authority of the embarked law enforcement officials, any search, seizure, detention or use of force shall be carried out by such officials.[79] Also, when the law enforcement

---

[77] art 1(h) of the Agreement defines 'waters of a Party' to mean the territorial sea and archipelagic waters of that party. Importantly Nonetheless, art 15 provides a party with the option of extending the application of the Agreement to some or all of its internal waters.

[78] See Gilmore, *Caribbean*, 23.

[79] See also ibid, 21. Provision is also made for the crew members of the vessel to assist in any such action, but only to the extent and in the manner requested. Such requests may only be made and acted upon if the action in question 'is consistent with the applicable laws and procedures of both Parties' (art 9(4)).

vessels and officials on board are in the territorial waters of another party, they shall 'respect the laws' and the relevant customs and traditions of the latter (article 8(1)).

It is questioned, however, in this respect whether the designated party, ie the flag state of the vessel on which the shipriders operate, bears any responsibility for the above acts. While the general question of responsibility for interdiction operations is beyond the scope of the present enquiry, some comments are in order:[80] first, it is possible that there will be a joint commission of an internationally wrongful act and the individual responsibility both of the sending state and of the host state will be engaged. There is no doubt that multiple states can incur responsibility under international law for a single incident. This is confirmed in article 47 of the ILC Articles, which articulates that where several states are responsible for the same internationally wrongful act, 'the responsibility of each State may be invoked in relation to that act'.[81] *In casu*, such joint responsibility between the boarding or the host state and the flag or designating state would be engaged, in the sense that the former exercises the right of visit per se and the latter the right of search and the further enforcement measures.[82]

A second option would be that the host or boarding state would be held responsible for aiding or assisting the commission of an ostensibly wrongful act (article 16 of ILC Articles).[83] The argument that the boarding state is completely at the disposal of the shiprider, in the sense of article 6 of ILC Articles, would seem less convincing. The application of this provision is contingent upon the degree of the control that the shiprider exercises on the boarding vessel, which, in turn, is a matter to be determined on a case-by-case basis.

Furthermore, even in relation to subject areas common to the 1995 Agreement or the Vienna Convention, namely the authorisation to visit suspect vessels on the high seas, the Caribbean Agreement significantly departs from the latter treaties. In stark contrast to the requirement of explicit

---

[80] See also the more extensive analysis in respect of responsibility of shipriders, below.

[81] According to the Commentary, in such cases, 'each State is separately responsible for the conduct attributable to it' and 'responsibility is not diminished or reduced by the fact that one or more States are also responsible for the same act'; see ILC Articles Commentary, 124. On the issue of joint commission of an internationally wrongful act, see, inter alia, ICJ, *Oil Platforms (Islamic Republic of Iran v USA)* (Merits) Judgment of 6 November 2003, Separate Opinion Judge Simma, para 74 and C Chinkin, 'The Continuing Occupation? Issues of Joint and Several Liability and Effective Control', in P Shiner and A Williams (eds), *The Iraq War and International Law* (Oxford: Hart, 2008) 161, 168 et seq.

[82] *cf* also relevant comments in Guilfoyle, *Interdiction*, 322.

[83] The general international standard for responsibility for aiding or assisting an internationally wrongful act is that the aid must have been given '(1) with a view to facilitating the commission of the specific act in question; (2) with an awareness of the circumstances making the act wrongful; and (3) the completed act must be such that it would have been wrongful had it been committed by the assisting State itself'; see ILC Articles Commentary, 66.

authorisation prior to the visit of a vessel of another state party, article 16 of the Agreement under scrutiny stipulates that 'when law enforcement officials of one Party encounter a suspect vessel claiming the nationality of another Party located seaward of any State's territorial sea, this Agreement constitutes the authorisation by the claimed flag State Party to board and search the suspect vessel, its cargo and question the persons found on board'.[84] In other words, the ratification by the flag state of the Agreement itself constitutes henceforth an a priori and *ipso facto* authorisation for every case of boarding on the high seas. This certainly enjoys the merit of expediency and efficiency, since the intervening state is divested of the need to contact the flag state and request authorisation prior to boarding, which might jeopardise the success of the operation in case of a delayed response, taking also into account the operational problems posed by the use of so-called 'go-fast' boats.[85] This is also in keeping with the overall philosophy of flexibility and practicality reflected in the text as a whole.[86]

Although this a priori authorisation is the rule, the parties, mindful of the fact that such a radical departure from past multilateral treaty might pose policy, legal or other difficulties for some states, provided in the Agreement for two additional alternatives: state parties can either opt for the express authorisation model of the Vienna Convention (article 16(2)), or the implied or tacit authorisation model (article 16(3)). Under the paragraph 3 option, authorisation is deemed to have been granted by the flag state if there is no response to an oral request for verification of the nationality or the requested party can neither confirm or deny nationality within the four-hour time frame envisaged in article 6(4).[87] Both options are available to state parties upon signing or ratifying the Agreement or any time thereafter by notifying the Depositary (Costa Rica); a notification that can be withdrawn at any time.[88] It is also of relevance to note here that the boarding and search of a suspect vessel under article 16 'is governed by the laws of the boarding Party' (paragraph 8).

Like the 1995 Agreement, article 24 makes clear that in all cases of vessels subject to law enforcement operations seaward of the territorial sea,

---

[84] See art 16(1). The term 'suspect vessel' is defined in art 1(l) as 'any vessel in respect of which there are reasonable grounds to suspect that it is engaged in illicit traffic', which is in conformity with the standards of art 110 of LOSC and art 17 of the Vienna Convention.

[85] For the same reasons of time efficiency, the states parties are requested in art 6 to respond within four hours to incoming requests with regard to the verification of nationality of a vessel. Moreover, each request could be conveyed orally and later confirmed by written communication; *cf* also 1995 CoE Agreement.

[86] See Gilmore, *Caribbean*, 28. It is noted that in art 22 of the initial draft of the Agreement (1997), there was an explicit mention of boarding undertaken 'with the consent of the master of the vessel', ie consensual boarding. However, 'due to the lack of unanimity of views among participating jurisdictions as to the consistency of the practice with the law of the sea, such a provision was not included in art 17, which deals with other boardings under international law'; ibid, 31.

[87] See also relevant comments in Klein, *Maritime Security*, 137.

[88] See art 16(2) and (3) and relevant analysis in Gilmore, *Caribbean*, 30.

the flag state retains what is designated as 'primary' or 'preferential' jurisdiction over the detained vessel, cargo and the persons on board. When,
however, the vessels are detained in the territorial waters of a state party,
the coastal state has primary jurisdiction. Given that it is preferential and
not exclusive, the flag or the coastal state respectively may waive the jurisdiction in favour of the intervening party. A prerequisite to this will be, of
course, that both states have prescriptive jurisdiction in respect of the relevant offences. In contemplation of this, article 23, similarly to the 1995
Agreement and contrary to the Vienna Convention, provides for the compulsory establishment of jurisdiction in respect of offences on own flag
vessels, on vessels without nationality and on board the vessels of other
parties when located seaward of the territorial sea of any state. Given
the mandatory nature of these jurisdictional provisions, all parties
should ensure that the relevant legislation would apply in all of the above
circumstances.

v. The 2008 CARICOM Maritime Agreement

In the same region that the aforementioned Agreement operates, namely
the Caribbean basin, the CARICOM Member States decided in 2008 to have
an all-encompassing maritime security agreement. The 2008 CARICOM
Agreement, which has already been discussed in relation to maritime terrorism and piracy, differs from the 2003 Caribbean Agreement in the scope
of both *ratione materiae* and *ratione personae*: on the one hand, it aims at
addressing a series of threats to maritime security, including drug trafficking, and it is not restricted to the latter activity and on the other, it is open
only to the Member States of the Caribbean Community and not to third
states, such as the US and the UK.[89] In any case, it is characteristic that the
first 'threat to the security of a State party or to the region' recognised by the
CARICOM Agreement is 'illicit trafficking in narcotic drugs, psychotropic
substances', which evidences how significant is the problem of drug trafficking in the region.

In terms of the measures that the parties to the CARICOM Agreement,
which at the time of the writing, had not been yet in force, may adopt to
counter drug trafficking, the following comments are in order: as far as
the interception operations on the high seas are concerned, article IX of
the CARICOM Agreement appears more conservative than the 2003
Agreement, in the sense that it permits the exercise of the right of visit and
search as well as the subsequent detention of the vessel, the cargo and the
crew only upon the flag state's authorisation (article IX paras 1 and 2).
This authorisation may be either express or tacit, ie if two hours after the

[89] None of the states that have signed or ratified the 2008 CARICOM Agreement are signatory states of the 2003 Caribbean Agreement.

initial request the flag state has not responded (para 3). Such request 'may be conveyed orally but shall later be confirmed by written communication' (article V). It also includes the 'presumptive or provisional flag state authorisation' model in para 3. Conversely, article 16 of the 2003 Caribbean Agreements sets forth the a priori authorisation model and only alternatively the express authorisation or the deemed or authorisation. Another difference between the two agreements lies in the fact that the CARICOM Agreement provides for a short time window, ie two hours after the initial request for the deemed authorisation, in comparison with four hours under the Caribbean Agreement.

With regard to the jurisdiction over the provisionally detained vessel, cargo and crew, article XI does not depart from the rule of the flag state's preferential jurisdiction; however, the flag state may decide to waive its primary right to exert jurisdiction and authorise the enforcement of another state party's law against the vessel, cargo or persons on board (article XI para 2). What seems as missing in the Convention is the lack of any requirement for parties to assert their legislative jurisdiction over the respective crimes. However, it is true that the object of this agreement is to facilitate the cooperation between the contracting states, rather than to criminalise certain behaviour.

As regards operations within coastal states' territorial waters, Article VIII provides expressly in paragraph 1 that

> This Agreement constitutes permission by each State party for any other State party to conduct law enforcement operations in the waters of the first-mentioned State party to address any activity likely to compromise the security of the Region or of any other State party, where a) on notification of the proposed operation, permission is granted; or b) authorized pursuant to paragraph 3(e) of Article XI.

In para 2, the said Article stipulates that:

> Notwithstanding paragraph 1, during the course of a routine patrol in the waters of a State party . . . the Security Force Officials engaged in the patrol may, in the waters of the State party, conduct such law enforcement operations as may be necessary to address any activity likely to compromise the security of the Region or of any State party, where a) a suspect vessel detected in international waters enters the waters of the State party and i) no Security Force Official of that State is embarked on the Security Force vessel . . . ii) no Security Force vessel of that State party is in the immediate vicinity to investigate and iii) notice is given to the competent authority of that Party . . . and b) a suspect vessel is detected within the waters of that State party.

While paragraph 1 of Article VIII seems innovative, providing that any state party may exercise interception operations against drug trafficking vessels within another party's waters, should the latter or one of its designated Security Force Official give their permission, this is not the case.

These interception operations would again be contingent upon the permission of the coastal state or its officials. On the contrary, paragraph 2 is far more interesting, since it incorporates both the reverse hot pursuit model and the entry-to-investigate model, which are common in numerous relevant bilateral treaties.

B. Bilateral Treaty-Law Bases for Interception

Indeed, there is an array of bilateral agreements, which also include the right to visit foreign-flagged vessels suspected of illicit traffic in narcotic drugs on the high seas as well as in the territorial seas of the state parties. The US and many states in Central and South America have concluded the majority of them. In general, they mirror rather the recent Caribbean Agreement or the CARICOM Agreement than the Vienna Convention or the 1995 CoE Agreement. They are noticeably flexible and practical, which, on the one hand, has considerable merits, while on the other, might create certain hazards for legal certainty and the rule of law in the oceans. This corresponds, of course, to their bilateral nature, that enables the negotiating parties to circumvent many of the procedural hurdles that unavoidably arise in a multilateral process when more than two jurisdictions are involved. A corollary of this, however, is that, as in the case of the migrant smuggling agreements, these treaties appear to be profoundly unequal or non-reciprocal.[90]

However, in view of the fundamental principle that the exceptions to a rule should always be construed strictly (*exceptiones sunt strictissimae interpetationes*),[91] it is submitted that the right to interfere on the high seas pursuant to these treaties should not be lightly presumed. This is also warranted by the arbitral award in the *Wanderer* case (1921), ie one of the few cases brought before an international tribunal where the flag State objected to the action of a foreign warship pursuant to an international agreement. The international arbitral tribunal held that any agreement containing an exception to the general international law rules prohibiting visitation and search of foreign vessels 'must be constructed *stricto jure*'.[92]

---

[90] The designation of a treaty as 'unequal' does not entail any legal consequence of invalidity, notwithstanding the arguments to the contrary put forward by the doctrine of international law in Communist states; see Brownlie, 91.

[91] 'Exceptions to a rule should always be construed narrowly'; see *Nationality Decrees* case, 25.

[92] The tribunal held that international regulations concerning fur-sealing contained only a prohibition of using firearms, not their mere possession; that an Act of Congress which authorised seizure of vessels having on board implements for taking seals went beyond the regulations; that a seizure of a British vessel pursuant to that Act was a contravention of the regulations; and that appropriate damages should be awarded. See the *Wanderer* (*US v Great Britain*, 1921), 6 RIAA (1955) 68, 71–73, cited also in LB Sohn, above n 7, 59.

i. US-UK Agreement (1981)

In 1981, the UK and the US signed an Exchange of Notes concerning Co-operation in the Suppression of Unlawful Importation of Narcotic Drugs into the United States.[93] This Exchange of Notes permits the United States authorities to board private British vessels on the high seas in the Gulf of Mexico, the Caribbean Sea, a portion of the Atlantic Ocean and all other areas within 150 miles of the Eastern seaboard to search for drugs destined for unlawful importation into the United States. If drugs are found on board, the vessel may be seized and taken to the US where the vessel is liable to forfeiture and the crew to stand trial.[94]

In more detail, it should be noted, from the outset that it is an 'unequal' or non-reciprocal agreement, since the right to visit is ascribed only to US vessels and not to both state parties.[95] To emphasise the unique character of such a treaty as well as the 'special relationship' between the two state parties in this regard, in a letter accompanying their Note, the UK Government asserted that 'they do not consider that this Exchange of Notes should be regarded as setting a precedent for the conclusion of any further agreement affecting the freedom of passage of British ships on the high seas'.[96]

Another unique feature of this treaty is that it restricts its *ratione loci* scope to a certain geographical area, by virtue of paragraph 9 of Note No 1. This is not found in other bilateral or multilateral treaties of this nature, which apply generally on the high seas; nevertheless, as it is rightly observed, the 'agreement gives the US Coast Guard a very wide amount of latitude in the performance of its tasks'.[97] It may be fitting to note here that there has been a case, where this *ratione loci* scope was expanded in dissonance with the text of the agreement, which reflects exactly what was underscored at the outset, namely the flexibility or practicality, yet also the legal uncertainty that surrounds such arrangements.[98] Another

---

[93] UKTS (1982); Cmnd 8470 (hereinafter: US-UK Agreement). For commentary see J Siddle, 'Anglo-American Cooperation in the Suppression of Drug Smuggling' 31 *ICLQ* (1982) 726. It must be noted here that the designation of the Agreement as 'Exchange of Letters' is irrelevant as far as the juridical nature of the Agreement is concerned; see eg *Qatar v Bahrain* case, 120–22.

[94] Noteworthy here is that this treaty is reminiscent of the old Convention between the UK and the US regarding the Regulation of the Liquor Traffic (1924), which dealt in a similar fashion with an exceptional situation; see UKTS (1924) 22.

[95] It is worth quoting Siddle in this respect, who observes: 'there is no *quid pro quo* for the new agreement, beyond the satisfaction for the British Government that it is protecting the good name of the British flag and cooperating in the suppression of a trade which is part of a universal problem'; above n 89, 726.

[96] See ibid, 740.

[97] ibid, 739.

[98] Reference is made to the arrest of the UK sailing vessel *The Myth of Ecurie* in June 1987 on the high seas off the coast of California whilst en route from Hong Kong to San Francisco, resulting in the case of *US v Biermann*. As Judge Legge pointed out 'in this case the Coast Guard did request the consent of the UK to board the vessel and in its reply telex the United Kingdom gave its consent under the terms and conditions of the 1981 Agreement'; see *US v*

interesting point in this regard is that neither in paragraph 1 nor in paragraph 9 is any mention made of the high seas or maritime zones of third states. Hence, the boardings can take place on the high seas and within the various EEZs and contiguous zones of third states in the region.[99]

The Agreement states that the UK 'will not object' to the exercise of the right of visit by the US on board the latter vessels, 'in any case in which those authorities reasonably believe that the vessel has on board a cargo of drugs for importation into the United States in violation of the laws of the United States'. In providing that the UK 'will not object' to the boarding, it actually signifies that there is no need for any prior positive permission or authorisation by the flag state, which is also found, for example, in the Caribbean Agreement, albeit not in such negative formulation. The condition is, of course, the existence of 'reasonable belief' that the vessel is engaged in illicit drug trafficking, which is in keeping with the pertinent provisions of the Vienna Convention and of the LOSC in general.[100]

Apart from 'reasonable belief', an additional requirement for the application of the relevant provision is that the US Coast Guard takes the necessary steps to establish that 'an offence against the law of the United States relative to the importation of narcotic drugs is being committed'. Accordingly, the Notes under scrutiny presuppose that the US has already asserted legislative jurisdiction in relation to such offences, which would enable the US courts to exert the corresponding enforcement jurisdiction. Assuming that all these requirements are satisfied, the US authorities are entitled to forfeit the vessel and its cargo as well as to prosecute the persons found on board having committed the relevant offences. The sole exception is that the UK may, within 14 days of a vessel's entry into port, object to the continued exercise of US jurisdiction over the vessel.[101] Lastly, it must be noted that the treaty in question was followed by another agreement between the same parties, which specifically pertained to the Caribbean and Bermuda waters and included provisions for aerial counter-narcotic operations.[102]

Biermann, 678 F Supp (1988), 1437. This arrest and the subsequent reply of the UK authorities were palpably beyond the area stipulated in paragraph 9. See also W Gilmore, 'Narcotics Interdiction at Sea: UK-US Cooperation' 13 *MP* (1989) 218, 226.

[99] It is put forward by Gilmore that, 'given the prior consent of the coastal State in question there would appear to be nothing to prevent the Agreement constituting a sufficient basis for the US boarding of a UK vessel within the territorial waters of a third State'; ibid, 224. Indeed, on the face of the agreement, that will not create any problem; however, the legal basis for the boarding here would not only be the US-UK Agreement, but also, concurrently, the consent of the coastal State granted ad hoc or prior with a relevant treaty.

[100] *cf* the case of *US v Reeh*, for example, which arose out of the seizure of the Cayman registered *Jim Hawkins* in January 1982. Circuit Judge Vance held that 'The agreements standard of "reasonable belief" appears quite similar, if not identical, to the "reasonable suspicion" standard of US law'; see *US v Reeh* 780 F 2d (1986) 1541.

[101] See also para 5 with respect to the corresponding right of the state of the nationality of the crewmembers; see J Siddle, above n 85, 743.

[102] See US-UK Caribbean Agreement; entered into force 30 October 2000 TIAS (on file with the author).

ii. Caribbean Bilateral Treaties

In addition to these US-UK Agreements, the US has concluded a number of bilateral agreements with the neighbouring states in the Caribbean region as well as generally in Central and South America.[103] According to the latest International Narcotics Control Strategy Report (March 2012), 'there are 44 maritime counterdrug bilateral agreements or operational procedures in place between the United States and partner nations'.[104] The US has concluded agreements with the following countries in the region: Antigua, Barbuda, the Bahamas, Barbados, Belize, Colombia, Costa Rica, Dominica, Dominican Republic, Grenada, Guatemala, Guyana, Haiti, Honduras, Jamaica, Nicaragua, Panama, St Kitts and Nevis, St Lucia, St Vincent and Grenadines, Suriname, Trinidad and Tobago, and Venezuela.[105] There is also an agreement with the UK, and eight MoUs and Operational Procedures with other states having overseas territories in the region, such as the Netherlands[106] However these 'operational procedures' or informal arrangements might be termed, as long as they provide the legal basis for cooperation and joint exercise of jurisdiction over drug trafficking offences, they should be considered as legally binding within the meaning of the *Qatar-Bahrain Admission* case.[107]

Moreover, the US has concluded a counter-narcotics agreement with Malta,[108] a major flag state, as well as three operational agreements for aerial counter-narcotic activities.[109] Finally, it must be mentioned that the US has entered into a series of ship-rider and ship-boarding agreements with States in Africa and the Pacific Ocean concerning cooperation to suppress illicit transnational maritime activity in general, including drug

---

[103] A list of United States Maritime Law Enforcement Agreements as of 21 May 2008 was kindly provided to the author by Mr Brad Kieserman, US Coast Guard (on file with the author) (hereinafter: USCG List). An updated version of this list is included in Roach, *Appendix*.

[104] See International Narcotics Control Strategy Report Vol I (2012), 52; www.state.gov/documents/organization/187109.pdf.

[105] See above n 103.

[106] See eg Memorandum of Understanding between the Government of the United States of America and the Government of the Kingdom of the Netherlands concerning the deployment of United States Coast Guard Law Enforcement Detachments on Royal Netherlands Navy Vessels and Aircraft in the waters of the Caribbean Area, signed at Washington, June 15, 2011; available at Roach, Appendix.

[107] In this case, ICJ prescribed the elements of a treaty according to international law. In its words, 'They enumerate the commitments to which Parties have consented. They thus create rights and obligations in international law for the Parties. They constitute an international agreement', para 25. *Mutatis mutandis* in *Cameroon and Nigeria* case, para 263.

[108] See Agreement between the Government of the United States of America and the Government of the Republic of Malta concerning cooperation to suppress illicit traffic in narcotic substances and psychotropic substances by sea, signed at Valletta 16 June 2004; entered into force 24 January 2008. TIAS 08-110, available at www.state.gov/documents/organization/108878.pdf and /178588.pdf.

[109] See USCG List and Table of Treaties.

trafficking.[110] It would go beyond the scope of the chapter to discuss in detail these agreements; suffice it to say that they are subject to the same legal framework applicable to all relevant bilateral arrangements.

The majority of the aforementioned bilateral treaties provide for 'shiprider' law enforcement personnel and for interdictions in either party's territorial waters. This bilateral network of counter-drug interdiction agreements has culminated, as was noted above, mainly in the 2003 Caribbean Agreement and, partially, in the 2008 CARICOM Agreement, which build upon these treaties and have adopted many of their common characteristics. Mindful of the fact that the previously mentioned Agreements have been thoroughly scrutinised in the relevant section of the present treatise, not all these bilateral agreements will be analysed in full detail, but only some issues of particular concern will be addressed.[111]

a. The Modalities of the US Maritime Agreements

First, and as far as the right of visit is concerned, the treaties in question include two of the three options set forth in the pertinent article of the Caribbean Agreement, namely, prior or automatic authorisation and tacit or implied authorisation.[112] On the one hand, the US-Haiti and US-Costa Rica Agreements exemplify the first model, ie they provide automatic consent to boarding where boarding officials act upon reasonable suspicion.[113] On the other hand, the US-Guatemala agreement is typical in providing for either actual or presumed consent to boarding flag vessels.[114] The same mechanism is contained in US agreements with Honduras,[115]

---

[110] See eg Agreement between the Government of the United States of America and the Government of the Republic of Senegal Concerning Operational Cooperation to Suppress Illicit Transnational Maritime Activity [shiprider and shipboarding], signed at Dakar 29 April 2011; entered into force 29 April 2011; TIAS 11-429; available at www.state.gov/documents/organization/169471.pdf and /184719.pdf, and Cooperative Shiprider Agreement between the Government of the United States of America and the Government of the Republic of Palau to support ongoing regional maritime security efforts, effected by an exchange of notes on 5 and 20 March 2008; entered into force 20 March 2008, TIAS 08-320, available at www.state.gov/documents/organization/108937.pdf and /177848.pdf.

[111] The following analysis will focus exclusively on the boarding agreements at sea and not on the aerial counter-narcotics arrangements.

[112] See art 16 of the Caribbean Agreement and relevant analysis. It should be mentioned that art 3 of the US-Jamaican Agreement of 1997, before being amended in 2004, provided for the express authorisation model. According to the 2004 Protocol, the authorisation may be presumed after three hours from the initial request.

[113] See art 5 of the US-Costa Rica Agreement and art 14 of the US-Haiti Agreement.

[114] While consent must be requested, 'If there is no response . . . within two (2) hours . . . the requesting Party will be deemed to have been authorized to board the suspect vessel for the purpose of inspecting . . . documents, questioning the persons on board, and searching the vessel to determine if it is engaged in illicit traffic'; see art 7(3)(d) of the US-Guatemala Agreement.

[115] See art 6(1) of the US-Honduras Agreement.

Nicaragua,[116] Panama[117] and Venezuela.[118] Under the agreements with Colombia,[119] Barbados[120] and Jamaica,[121] consent may be presumed after three hours. This deemed or tacit authorisation only arises, however, if there is no response to the request, while the flag state maintains, in principle, the right to refute the boarding. As regards the assertion of jurisdiction over the illicit cargo and the drug traffickers on board the interdicted vessel, there is also no uniform practice. Some agreements, such as the US-Haiti Agreement,[122] provide for the preferential jurisdiction of the flag state similarly to the 1995 Agreement.[123] Others reverse the presumption against the flag state jurisdiction, setting forth that only the US may waive its jurisdiction and authorise the enforcement of foreign law against its flag vessel.[124]

In general, the agreements under scrutiny usually take the form of a four-part or six-part model. The six-part model includes 'a) ship boarding, b) entry-to-investigate, c) over flight, d) ship rider, e) pursuit and f) order-to-land',[125] while the four-part model excludes airborne provisions.[126] Obviously, of paramount importance in the application of these agreements is the right to enter in territorial waters and the shiprider element. As was stated above, these are prevalent in this context mainly due to the geographic conditions of the area, which require very close cooperation between the interested parties in order to suppress effectively the drug smuggling.[127] Thus, for example, the Agreement between the US and Trinidad and Tobago stipulates that qualified authorised officers ('shipriders') of the latter state may board a US vessel for the purpose of authorising the US Coast Guard to pursue a vessel that is fleeing into Trinidad and Tobago waters as well as to conduct counter drug patrols in Trinidad and

---

[116] See art 9(1) of the US-Nicaragua Agreement.

[117] See art 10(6) of the US-Panama Supplementary Arrangement.

[118] See art 4 of the US-Venezuela Agreement.

[119] See art 8 of the US-Colombia Agreement and USCG-Colombia Operating Procedures.

[120] See art 14 of the US-Barbados Agreement.

[121] See above n 103

[122] The Agreement provides that where illicit traffic is uncovered US officials may detain persons and cargo 'pending expeditious disposition instructions; from Haiti, which retains 'the primary right to exercise jurisdiction' over detained vessels, cargoes and persons but may waive it to 'authorize the enforcement of US law against the vessel' (arts 14 and 16).

[123] Similar arrangements are made in art 6 of the US-Costa Rica Agreement, in art 7(1) of the US-Honduras Agreement and art 15 of the US-Barbados Agreement.

[124] See eg art 10 of the US-Nicaragua Agreement and art 16 of the US-Colombia Agreement.

[125] See J Kramek, 'Bilateral Maritime Counter-Drug and Immigrant Interdiction Agreements: Is this the World of the Future?' 31 *UMiami I-ALR* (2000) 121, 133.

[126] See relevant analysis and relevant chart (valid as of 1999) with the categorisation of the agreements to the respective models in J Kramek, ibid, 150. Also see L Davis-Mattis, 'International Drug Trafficking and the Law of the Sea' 14 *Ocean Yearbook* (2000) 381.

[127] According to J Kramek, 'the use of ship-riders is sometimes more attractive to nations that do not wish to grant the US Coast Guard blanket consent to enter their territorial seas or board their vessels on the high seas'; ibid, 134 (fn 81). See also M Williams, 'Caribbean Shiprider Agreements' 31 *UMiami I-ALR* (2000) 163.

Tobago waters.[128] They may also enforce the laws of Trinidad and Tobago within that state's waters or seaward in the exercise of the right of hot pursuit or otherwise in accordance with the international law.[129]

This Agreement contains also a very doctrinally interesting provision, namely that when a Trinidad and Tobago shiprider is unavailable to embark on a US vessel, the latter may still enter Trinidad and Tobago waters in order to investigate any suspect aircraft or board any suspect vessel other than a Trinidad and Tobago flag vessel.[130] This right to enter territorial waters and exercise enforcement jurisdiction is found in various forms in many of the treaties in question.[131] What this seemingly innocuous provision actually entails is that third States' vessels can be subjected to the right of visit in the territorial waters of Trinidad and Tobago by a US cutter without the presence of any officer from the coastal state. According to the provisions of VCLT, the bilateral agreement in question cannot entail any obligation for third states if it is not provided therein and the latter states have not assented to it in writing (the rule *pacta tertiis nec nocent nec prosunt*).[132] Hence, the USCG could not invoke the terms of this agreement as such in order to board third states' vessels; rather it should base its relevant authority upon the customary and treaty powers that the coastal state enjoys therein and which have been delegated to the US. Accordingly, the source of the relevant obligation for the third state would rather be the relevant provision of LOSC and the corresponding customary rule,[133] rather than the US-Barbados Agreement. In any case, this is no longer a question of flag state jurisdiction, but of a parallel jurisdiction in a foreign state by the territorial sovereign (which retains primary jurisdiction) and the enforcing state.[134] Conversely, due to the derivative nature of its authority, the US, as the enforcing state, is limited to its jurisdiction by not only the scope of the coastal state's consent

---

[128] In this Agreement, 'waters' mean the territorial sea, archipelagic waters and internal waters and the airspace over such waters; see para 3 of the US-Trinidad and Tobago Agreement. Interestingly, in the US-Barbados Agreement only the territorial waters are mentioned (art 1(b)).

[129] See also, inter alia, the Agreements with the eastern Caribbean states, Antigua and Barbuda, St Kitts and Nevis, Dominica, Grenada, St Lucia and St Vincent and the Grenadines. For analysis see Davis-Mattis, above n 120, 382. On the high seas, however, the authority is granted by the ship-boarding element rather than by the shiprider.

[130] See art 8(c) of the US-Trinidad and Tobago Agreement.

[131] See relevant analysis in MJ Williams, 'Bilateral Maritime Agreements', in M Nordquist and J Moore (eds), *Ocean Policy: New Institutions, Challenges and Opportunities* (The Hague: Martinus Nijhoff 1999) 179, 188 and Guilfoyle, *Shipping Interdiction*, 91–94.

[132] See art 35 of VCLT, which provides that 'an obligation arises for a third State from a provision of a treaty if the parties to the treaty intend the provision to be the means of establishing the obligation and the third State expressly accepts that obligation in writing'.

[133] See in particular art 27(1)(d) LOSC with regard to the suppression of illicit traffic in narcotic drugs, which should also be considered as reflective of customary law.

[134] See also Guilfoyle, *Shipping Interdiction*, 94.

but also by the innocent and transit passage doctrines, if applicable. The jurisdiction that is granted by the coastal state cannot be more than the latter a priori has in accordance with international law, in line with the Latin maxim '*nemo dat quam non habeat*'.

In a similar vein, complex issues of international law arise when a US Coast Guard law enforcement detachment (commonly referred to as LEDET), which is commonly used to vest authority to US warships, is deployed on board a third state vessel, usually British or Belgian warships, assigned to patrol off the coasts of their possessions in the West Indies, and boards a vessel flagged in a third state under the authority of a bilateral maritime agreement between the US and the third state.[135] This scenario highlights again the problematic position of third parties in international law. Usually, there would be an agreement between the US and the flag state of the boarding vessel, the UK for example, and another treaty between the US and the flag state of the suspect vessel. In such case, reference should be made to the terms of the former agreement with regard to the scope of the powers attributed to the US LEDET, which prima facie would have the power to enforce the provisions of the latter treaty regardless of the vehicle or the platform that it uses, namely the vessel of a third state. Absent a treaty between the US and the flag state of the boarding vessel, there could be other issues besides the legal basis for the interdiction,[136] such as the question of state responsibility in this regard, ie who would be liable for damage to the third state vessel, the US or the UK on whose vessel the LEDET is employed.

b. The Question of Responsibility of Shipriders

To respond to this, it is apposite to refer, in general, to the question of the responsibility of shipriders. First, when there is a shiprider agreement, it is acknowledged that 'a different liability regime might exist for interdiction undertaken under the common shiprider provision. Here the shiprider as agent of the flag State of the boarded vessel permits the interdiction on a case-by-case basis. The decision whether to board or not a certain vessel thus remains under the exclusive control of the flag State'.[137] Hence, in the view of Wendel, the sending state bears the international responsibility for any interdiction operation under a typical shiprider

---

[135] See eg Memorandum of Understanding between the Government of the United States of America and the Government of the Kingdom of Belgium concerning the deployment of United States Coast Guard Law Enforcement Detachments on Belgian Navy vessels in the waters of the Caribbean Sea, signed at Washington March 1, 2001. In addition, reference and analysis of such cases is furnished by J Kramek, above n 115, 139.

[136] In any case, the flag state of the intercepted vessel could give its ad hoc consent in this regard.

[137] Wendel, 223.

agreement.[138] He acknowledges, however, that the 'other State could be liable for its contribution as assisting State'.[139]

With regard to the responsibility for 'aiding or assisting', it is well worth observing that under the US Model Maritime Agreement, for example, which has informed many shiprider agreements, it is envisaged that crew members of the host vessel may assist the shiprider in carrying out enforcement actions, if the latter expressly requests such assistance.[140] The host state thus may become responsible for its own act in deliberately assisting the sending state to breach an international obligation by which they are both bound.[141] Under article 16 of ILC Articles, a state may be responsible for its 'aid or assistance', provided that the aid must have been given (1) 'with a view to facilitating the commission of the specific act in question; (2) with an awareness of the circumstances making the act wrongful; and (3) the completed act must be such that it would have been wrongful had it been committed by the assisting State itself'.[142] Accordingly, should a breach of an obligation incumbent upon states under the law of the sea or of human rights law occur, the 'host state' may also be held responsible for assisting in the commission of such breach, provided that it had knowledge of the breach in question and assisted the shiprider in this regard.

Nevertheless, it is submitted that the host state may be held responsible not only for 'complicity' under article 16, but also on an individual basis. It is possible that there will be a joint commission of an internationally wrongful act and the individual responsibility both of the sending state and of the host state will be engaged under article 47 of the ILC Articles.

This proposition runs counter to the view that the warship is placed at the disposal of the flag state of the shiprider's sending state. Under article 6 of the ILC Articles, the commission of the wrongful act will be attributed solely to the sending state, if the warship or coast guard vessel 'is acting in the exercise of elements of governmental authority of the State at whose disposal it is placed'. This would require that the home state of the warship leaves control or command over the vessel exclusively to the shiprider, and consequently to the sending state. It is highly unlikely that this is the case in shiprider operations; rather, states are separately respon-

---

[138] ibid.

[139] ibid.

[140] See art 7 of the US Model Maritime Agreement Concerning Cooperation to Suppress Illicit Traffic by Sea, reprinted in Kramek, above n 115, Appendix B. See also Geiss and Petrig, 91.

[141] See J Crawford, *The International Law Commission's Articles on State Responsibility* (Cambridge: Cambridge University Press, 2002) 151.

[142] See ILC Articles Commentary, 66. On complicity in international law in general, see also H Aust, *Complicity and the Law of State Responsibility* (Cambridge: Cambridge University Press, 2011) and J Quigley, 'Complicity in International Law: A New Direction in the Law of State Responsibility' 57 *BYIL* (1987) 57.

sible for the pertinent violations under general international law. In any event, the application of article 6 would be contingent upon the degree of the control that the shiprider exercises on the boarding vessel, which, in turn, is a matter to be determined on a case-by-case basis.

It is also possible that both the sending state and the host state will be responsible for different violations in the course of interdiction operations. *Ex hypothesis*, there might be a shiprider interdiction operation, in which, on the one hand, there would be a disproportionate use of force by the officers of the host state's warship in violation of the relevant legal framework and on the other, a subsequent human rights violation committed under the authority of the shiprider and under directions of the sending state. In such cases, the host state would incur responsibility for the violation of the relevant obligations under the law of the sea and the sending state would incur separate responsibility for the violation of the relevant obligation under international human rights law.

The potential of separate responsibility in the context of shiprider interdiction operations is evident also on the face of the relevant agreements, which provide for the non-displacement of the flag state's law police powers, while the vessel is under another state's effective control. They do not require that the interdicting state's officers act in accordance with anything other than their national law.[143] Telling is also the wording of the US Model Maritime Agreement, which sets forth that 'the requests for assistance may only be made, agreed and acted upon in accordance with the applicable laws and policies of both parties, except for the use of force in self-defense'.[144]

In conclusion, it is indisputable that the use of shipriders in maritime interdiction operations engenders a host of perplexing legal questions, especially in respect of the law of state responsibility. In addressing such questions, first, recourse should be made to the shiprider agreement, which may regulate the allocation of responsibility between the sending and the host state. In addition, the facts of each individual case should be carefully scrutinised in order to discern who had effective control over the conduct that, arguably, gave rise to the internationally wrongful act.

In the foregoing example and the question of who would be liable for damage to the third state vessel – the US or the UK on whose vessel the LEDET is employed – the answer would be dependent upon the degree of control exerted to the third state's vessel by the US LEDET.[145] If

[143] See eg art 5(1) Treaty between the Kingdom of Spain and the Italian Republic to Combat Illicit Drug Trafficking at Sea 1990, 1776 UNTS 229.
[144] See art 7 of US Model Maritime Agreement, above n 134.
[145] This is inferred from the ILC Articles Commentary, which specifically stipulates that 'not only must the organ be appointed to perform functions appertaining to the State at whose disposal it is placed, but in performing the functions entrusted to it by the beneficiary State, the organ must also act in conjunction with the machinery of that State and under its exclusive direction and control, rather than on instructions from the sending State'; ibid 44.

the warship of the third state retains a portion of its authority and apparently there is joint police activity for counter-drug purposes, then the logical conclusion would be that there exists joint or concurrent responsibility of both the flag state of the warship and of the US, or the former is ostensibly assisting the commission of the wrongful act.[146]

In summary, the agreements under scrutiny 'enable the Parties to maximise their cooperation by enabling them to make the most efficient use of their law enforcement resources. Scarce patrol units, which have high operating costs, are able to respond immediately, or as the tactical situation dictates, without the need to await authorisations sought on a case-by-case basis through lengthy diplomatic channels.'[147] These agreements, based upon the consent of the states involved, are designed to surmount the legal obstacles that state sovereignty usually places to such operations and guarantee the maximum effectiveness in suppressing drug trafficking. Nonetheless, on the one hand, they are conspicuously unequal, in the sense that they are drawn with the purpose mainly of facilitating the US counter-drug policy and on the other; they may appear problematic in relation to the position of third states. Lastly, what is patent on the face of these treaties is that they fail to place any strict constraints on the relevant law enforcement operations or even to provide in detail for the establishment of jurisdiction on the part of the Caribbean states over the relevant offences, as the respective multilateral instruments did.

iii. Spain-Italy Treaty

Finally, in the European region, there is also a relevant bilateral instrument, ie the Treaty between Spain and Italy on the Suppression of the Illicit Traffic in Drugs at Sea (23 March 1990).[148] In particular, this treaty includes mutual recognition of a right of intervention that is exercisable outside the territorial waters by each of the parties with respect to ships flying the other party's flag. There is no need for prior authorisation from the flag state; thus, the treaty itself operates as the requisite legal basis for the exercise of the right to visit on the high seas.[149] Furthermore, concerning the parties' jurisdiction in actions relating to the illicit traffic of drugs on board vessels, the treaty establishes the obligation of the state parties to make such offences punishable under their domestic laws, even though,

---

[146] See Guilfoyle's relevant remarks for the responsibility of ship-riders in ibid, *Shipping Interdiction*, 336–37.

[147] M Williams, above n 127, 195.

[148] The treaty is in force since 7 May 1994. See a short commentary in VC Gualde, 'Suppression of the Illicit Traffic in Narcotic Drugs and Psychotropic Substances on the High Seas: Spanish Case Law' 4 *SYIL* (1996) 91, 97 and also I Lirola Delgado, 'La Represión del Tráfico Ilícito de Drogas en Alta Mar. Cooperación internacional y Práctica Estatal' 12 *Anuario de Derecho Internacional* (1996) 523, 556.

[149] See art 5(1).

as in the 1995 Agreement, the preferential jurisdiction of the flag state is recognised. Nevertheless, the boarding party may request the flag state to renounce its preferential jurisdiction pursuant to article 6(1) of the Treaty. The latter provides in the next paragraph that the flag state shall 'take into consideration, among other criteria, the place of seizure, the conditions under which evidence was obtained, any correlation between proceedings, the nationality of those involved and their place of residence'.[150] Lastly, in 1994 Spain concluded a broadly similar treaty with Portugal, though it provides for reciprocal right of interdiction only where 'circumstances prevent . . . prior [flag state] authorization being obtained in a timely manner'.[151]

C. Customary Law Bases for Interference

In the previous section there was a thorough scrutiny of the treaty-based exceptions to the exclusivity of the flag-state jurisdiction on the high seas with regard to drug trafficking. The conclusion of such treaties is in full accord with article 110(1) LOSC, which stipulates that the right to visit is not justified, 'except where acts of interference derive from powers conferred by treaty'. Can general international law offer additional justifications for such operations?

i. Is There any Separate Customary Basis for Interception?

In more detail, this enquiry is twofold: firstly, is there any customary rule that permits the right to visit of drug smuggling vessels on the high seas, and secondly, can the secondary rules of state responsibility provide such basis? As far as the first question is concerned, it can be argued that there is a customary obligation to cooperate in the suppression of drug trafficking on the high seas, which is drawn from the relevant provision of LOSC (article 108) and of the Vienna Convention (article 17(1) and (2)). These conventions of universal participation may have crystallised or generated a posteriori a corresponding rule of customary law.[152] Nevertheless, this would be an obligation of conduct, ie to cooperate in this respect, which might entail the obligation not to unjustifiably refuse to correspond to the request for authorisation by another state, but it would be quite different from the obligation to grant permission to all other states to board suspect

---

[150] See art 6(2) of the Treaty. It may be fitting to note here that the flag state has a period of 60 days, instead of 14 days according to the 1995 Agreement, from receipt of the request to notify its decision, on the understanding that failure to answer within this period indicates waiver of the jurisdiction.

[151] See *Practical Guide*, 157. See also the MAOC-N above n 95.

[152] See the decision of the ICJ in the *North Sea Continental Shelf* case, para 71.

vessels on the high seas. Such an obligation or conversely, such a right to visit without the express consent of the flag state is not accorded even in the context of the Vienna Convention; a fortiori, it cannot be accorded respectively in the realm of customary international law.

Having said that, it has been questioned whether there could be a regional custom emanating from the network of the Caribbean agreements to this effect.[153] Guilfoyle rightly concludes that

> given the diversity of options and the language of individual treaties, it would clearly be a mistake to suggest that any regional custom has emerged. The treaties usually contain a provision formally requiring express consent but stating that such consent is provided by the treaty. This negates any claim that general rights exists, independent of treaty and absent express consent, to conduct such pursuits.[154]

It could be added that the treaties in question lack this norm-creating character that it would be requisite, according to the *North Sea Continental Shelf* cases, to generate such customary norm.

ii. Secondary Excuses for Interception

Furthermore, it is questioned whether secondary rules or circumstances precluding wrongfulness could be invoked *in ultima ratio* to justify the infringement of a primary rule of international law, such as the exclusivity of the flag state jurisdiction on the high seas.[155] It goes without saying that the circumstances of self-defence, *force majeure* or distress are of no relevance to the present context.[156] Similarly, the plea of necessity, which under certain circumstances could be invoked in the terrorism context, it seems to be devoid of any merit in respect of drug trafficking. It is not only that the boarding of suspect vessels on the high seas must be the 'only way' available to safeguard the protected interest, which might be identified as the public health and social order,[157] but also that it is only when this interest is threatened by a grave and imminent peril that this condition is satisfied.[158] It would be rather difficult for the interdiction of a vessel suspected of illicit traffic in narcotic drugs on the high seas to fulfil

---

[153] For regional custom see the *Right of Passage Case (Merits)* ICJ Reports 1960, 6, 39–43; *Asylum Case* ICJ Reports 1950, 266, 276–78.

[154] Guilfoyle, *Shipping Interdiction*, 94.

[155] *cf CMS Annulment* case and comments above, Introduction (n 94).

[156] See arts 21, 23 and 24 of the ILC Articles.

[157] The plea is excluded if there are other (otherwise lawful) means available, even if they may be more costly or less convenient. Thus, in the *Gabcikovo-Nagymaros* case, the court was not convinced that the unilateral suspension and abandonment of the project was the only course open in the circumstances, having regard in particular to the amount of work already done and the money expended on it, and the possibility of remedying any problems by other means; para 55.

[158] See ILC Articles Commentary, 83.

either of these requirements. First, the shipments of narcotic drugs would fall short of qualifying as an exceptional threat, since they do not usually run randomly and exceptionally, but rather have a regular and systematic pattern. Also, the relevant traffic could not be designated as an imminent peril to the interests of the state, as the effect on public health is not direct or automatic. In addition, it can be maintained that the interdiction of these shipments on the high seas is not the only way to safeguard the interest in questions, since they are other lawful means of achieving the same result, namely to interdict the shipments in the contiguous zone or in the territorial waters of the consumer state.[159]

The same conclusion can be drawn in relation to countermeasures, which are taken by the 'injured state' against the State responsible for the internationally wrongful act in question.[160] The vexed question in this regard is whether the rules concerning drug trafficking entail rights attributed individually to states, which can thus be considered qua 'injured states'. It is true that the rules under scrutiny purport, on the one hand, to regulate and criminalise the relevant offences[161] and on the other, as far as the law of the sea is concerned, to establish the cooperation of flag states in the suppression of this traffic on the high seas.[162] These rules set out only obligations of conduct rather than of result; ergo, to establish their breach becomes a difficult task. This could arise only exceptionally, when, arguably, the wrongdoer repetitively displayed behaviour of non-cooperation in this regard vis-à-vis a particular state, which was specifically affected by this behaviour. More importantly, however, they fall short of providing for a synallagmatic or reciprocal type of obligation against a particular state, and thus it is difficult to identify the injured state, which would be entitled to take countermeasures.

In theory, however, it could be maintained that the obligations under scrutiny are *erga omnes partes,* ie owed to all state parties of the LOSC or the Vienna Convention, or *erga onmes,* ie owed to the international community as a whole, and therefore collective countermeasures could arguably be plausible.[163] However, neither the LOSC nor the Vienna Convention is the classical type of 'integral' treaty, whose infringement would involve

---

[159] Nonetheless, it cannot be a priori excluded in a single and isolated case of great shipment of drugs when, under the circumstances prevailing at the time, their interdiction on the high seas would be the only available way to safeguard society from the destructive effects of the drugs.

[160] See arts 49 et seq of the ILC Articles.

[161] It should be noted here that there is no formal obligation to criminalise the use of drugs within the UN Conventions; rather the possession with the purpose of trafficking is to be criminalised; see B de Ruyver, *Multidisciplinary Drug Policies and the UN Drug Treaties* (Antwerpen: Maklu, 2002) 15.

[162] See art 108 of LOSC and art 17(1) of the Vienna Convention.

[163] *cf* in this regard art 48 of the ILC Articles.

the collective action of all the state parties.[164] In addition, as the law stands, it would be rather difficult to hold the argument that the prohibition of drug trafficking has attained the status of an obligation *erga omnes* or *jus cogens*, which, in international criminal law context, arguably reflects crimes of universal jurisdiction.[165] Drug trafficking is not widely recognised as a crime of such a nature. In any event, as the ILC Articles Commentary expressly states, 'At present, there appears to be no clearly recognised entitlement of States referred to in article 48 to take countermeasures in the collective interest.'[166] In the light of the foregoing, it seems unlikely that the plea of countermeasures could afford a legal justification for the interdiction of drug smuggling vessels on the high seas.

Contrary to the above-mentioned circumstances precluding wrongfulness, 'consent' is of relevance and of extreme practical importance. As far as US practice is concerned, it is noted that 'informal agreements by consent have been utilised by the US under statutes that allow boarding of foreign flagged vessels if the consent is obtained by special arrangement'.[167] Indeed, the practice of obtaining the consent of the master of the vessel ('consensual boarding') and later of the flag state in order to interdict the suspect vessels and subsequently exert enforcement jurisdiction, ie seize the illicit cargo and arrest the traffickers, has been very common, especially in the Caribbean region and before the network of bilateral agreements was developed.[168]

This practice was analysed *in extenso* in the respective section of Chapter 3; suffice it to reiterate here, that on the one hand, the ad hoc consent of the flag state could be legally characterised under the veil of both primary rules of international law, namely qua informal treaties, and of secondary rules of state responsibility, namely qua 'consent' (article 20 of the ILC

---

[164] The obligations *erga omnes partes* have to be 'collective obligations', ie they must apply between groups of states and have been established in some collective interest; see ILC Articles Commentary, 126. See also the recent use of the term 'obligations *erga omnes partes*' with regard to the prohibition against torture included in the 1984 Convention against Torture by the ICJ in *Questions relating to the Obligation to Prosecute or Extradite (Belgium v Senegal)* Judgment of 20 July 2012; para 69.

[165] See eg the ICTY Trial Chamber in *Furundžija*, Trial Chamber II, Judgment of 10 December 1998 (case No IT-95-17/1-T), para 156.

[166] See ILC Articles Commentary, 301.

[167] Davis-Mattis, above n 120, 380.

[168] See the USCG, *Guide to the Law of Boarding Operations* (June 2008) (on file with the author). The latter states in this regard: 'During a consensual boarding, the boarding team may only examine spaces with the voluntary consent of the master or individual controlling them. The consent may be limited in scope and may be revoked at any time. No suspicion is required, and there is no prohibition against the Boarding Officer actively requesting consent to inspect or search in areas that might otherwise be inaccessible to the boarding team . . . master's consent is generally not sufficient for the United States to exercise jurisdiction over criminal acts conducted aboard the vessel extraterritorially'. *Cf* 46 USC § 70502 (not including master's consent within the definition of 'vessels subject to the jurisdiction of the United States') (p 21). Courts have upheld jurisdiction where the USCG boarded first with master's consent and obtained flag state consent later; see eg *United States v Khan*, 35 F 3d 426, 430 (9th Cir 1994).

Articles).[169] Such was the case in the *Medvedyev* case before the ECtHR, where the basis for the interdiction of the Cambodian-flagged *Winner*, was a *Note Verbale* from the Cambodian Minister of Foreign Affairs after a request for authorisation by France, namely an ad hoc accord, according to the court. On the other hand, it is submitted that the consent of the Master of the vessel would not suffice under international law for any enforcement measures, besides, controversially, the boarding as such of the vessel.

In conclusion, the foregoing paragraphs were devoted to the discussion of all the possible treaty and customary law justifications for the interference of foreign vessels on the high seas for counter-drug trafficking purposes. It was readily apparent once again that while the legal order of the oceans provides the necessary legal bases for such interference, it does however subject the latter to the strict requirements of the principle of '*la juridicité*' of the high seas, ie of general international law. Thus, it requires that either a relevant treaty is in place which provides for the right to visit suspect vessels on the high seas, or the boarding states request the consent of the flag state. In addition, it imposes certain fundamental international legal restrictions of the exercise of the right of visit in the present context.

III. ADDITIONAL INTERNATIONAL LEGAL ISSUES IN THE COURSE OF INTERCEPTION OPERATIONS

Similar to the discussion in the context of international terrorism and WMD, the following enquiry will assess the practice of interdiction of vessels on high seas for counter-drugs trafficking purposes against the background of general international law. It is submitted that the latter impose various international legal restrictions on this practice, mainly in relation to the use of force, to the assertion of jurisdiction and to human rights. It is beyond the compass of the present book to discuss all these issues in detail; rather, it is suggested to make an epigrammatic reference to the questions of use of force and of human rights and to analyse more extensively the issue of jurisdiction over drug offences on the high seas. This is of particular significance in the present context, because not only there are a high number of narcotic drugs' seizures on the high seas every year, but also because the suppression of the drug trafficking heavily depends on the establishment of jurisdiction *ex ante* and *ex post* the actual visit on the high seas.

---

[169] See ILC Articles Commentary, 72.

A. The Question of the Use of Force

First, insofar as the use of force in interception operations at sea is concerned, suffice to take note of the *Archangelos*[170] and *Winner* cases,[171] in which the boarding teams employed lethal force to gain control of the smuggling vessels. The use of force in maritime interdiction operations has been already discussed in Chapter 3. In general, it is submitted that the boarding state may, in principle, use force but in extreme moderation and in strict accordance with the requirements of necessity and proportionality, since it is considered as a *lex specialis* case to the generic prohibition of the use of force.

In both cases before the ECtHR, it was not clear, on the basis of the evidence before the Court, whether the use of force on the part of the boarding team was in the exercise of the right of personal self-defence or was excessive and not necessitated by the circumstances of the cases. Assuming that the members of the boarding team were confronted by armed resistance by the crew, or they employed force to the minimum necessary in order to arrest the applicants and search the vessel, then the force in question was not beyond the permissible bounds of international law. Even so, the deadly injury of a person in the course of the seizure of *Winner* casts doubts on the proportionality of the use of force *in casu*, especially in contemplation of the 'elementary considerations of humanity' applicable in law enforcement operations.[172] What seems odd, however, is that neither the applicants nor the Court referred to this issue in either case. This could be construed as a *sub silentio* acknowledgment that the de minimis use of force in law enforcement operations at sea is in full accord with international law. In any event, the use of force in the present cases buttresses the view that such use of force is rather within the normative bounds of law enforcement at sea than within the purview of the prohibition of article 2(4) of the UN Charter.

B. Human Rights Restrictions

With regard to human rights, it is contended that, in general, the boarding states are under the obligation to take all necessary measures to protect the fundamental human rights of the persons on board the vessels on the high seas, which, according to the preponderant view, are under their

---

[170] To reiterate, on 23 January 1995 the crew of a Spanish vessel, the *Petrel I* boarded the vessel and exchanged fire with several members of the crew who had barricaded themselves into the engine room; see *Rigopoulos* case.
[171] See *Medvedyev* case.
[172] See *Corfu Channel* case, para 22.

jurisdiction.[173] Such fundamental human rights are inter alia the right to life, the prohibition of torture and of degrading and inhumane treatment and the right to liberty of the persons concerned.[174]

As to the right of life, the discussion will pick up from the point that it was left above, namely the *Rigopoulos v Spain* case, but, mainly, the *Medvedyev v France* case before the ECtHR. It was observed that it is surprising that especially in the *Medvedyev* case, in which lethal force was used, the applicants did not raise any complaint under article 2. In more detail, in the latter case, the French frigate had had to fire some warning shots across the bow of the *Winner* in order to make it stop. In addition, the boarding team exchanged shots with members of the crew, which caused an individual to be wounded, resulting in his death a week later. It was reported in this respect that the deadly injury of a crew member was an accident.[175] As was stated above, the firing of weapons into open doors as well as the firing of 'warning' shots against the crew cast doubt on the proportionality of the use of force *in casu*. This might have been a decisive criterion in the assessment of the Court in respect of the violation of the right of life, should the applicants have submitted any complaint under article 2 of the Convention.

The same holds true in the *Rigopoulos* case, in which there was an exchange of fire between a Spanish warship and several members of the crew of a drug smuggling vessel, the *Archangelos,* who had barricaded themselves into the engine room.[176] This could be construed as a *sub silentio* acknowledgment that the de minimis use of force in law enforcement operations at sea is an intrinsic part of the 'lawful arrest' under article 2.[177] Nevertheless, it is submitted that the legality of the use of lethal force in such cases should not be lightly presumed. It would have been interesting to see what the Court ruled, should the applicants in the *Medvedyev* case have brought up a complaint under article 2.

These two cases are instructive also with regard to the application of the right of liberty in the context of drug trafficking on the high seas. In the *Medvedyev* case, the French government had argued that the detention was properly sanctioned under various treaties combating illegal drug trafficking, which allowed for the boarding of vessels and for the taking of coercive measures. On the other hand, the applicants, who shared the analysis followed by the Chamber in its judgment, claimed before the

---

[173] *cf* the *Medvedyev* case, para 50.
[174] See eg arts 2, 3 and 5 of the ECHR.
[175] When they boarded the *Winner*, the French commando team used their weapons to open certain locked doors. When a crew member of the *Winner* refused to obey their commands, a 'warning shot' was fired at the deck, but the bullet ricocheted and the crew member was wounded; para 13.
[176] See *Rigopoulos* case.
[177] This might be the ground why the applicants in the *Rigopoulos v Spain* abstained from raising this issue.

Grand Chamber that the interception of the *Winner* and their arrest 'was not prescribed by law' ie it lacked the requisite legal basis in international and French law.

The Grand Chamber was of the same view with the 2008 Chamber Decision on the case, ie that article 5(1) of ECHR was violated on account of the detention not being in accordance with a procedure prescribed by law. The Court observed that the text of the diplomatic note between France and Cambodia mentioned only 'the ship *Winner*'; 'evidently, therefore, the fate of the crew was not covered sufficiently clearly by the note and so it is not established that their deprivation of liberty was the subject of an agreement between the two States that could be considered to represent a "clearly defined law" within the meaning of the Court's case-law'.[178] In addition, the Court considered that the diplomatic note did not meet the 'foreseeability' requirement either. '[T]the intervention of the French authorities on the basis of an *ad hoc* agreement cannot reasonably be said to have been "foreseeable" within the meaning of the Court's case-law'.[179]

The duration of the restriction on the liberty of persons under the jurisdiction of states parties to the ECHR has formed the basis of the second complaint before the Court in the *Medvedyev* case, ie whether it was compatible with article 5(3) of the ECHR for some of the applicants to be brought before a judge 48 hours and for others 72 hours after their arrival at Brest harbour, and in total 15 and 16 days respectively after their arrest at sea. The issue therefore was whether the period of 15 or 16 days without a judicial decision was in compliance with the requirement of 'promptness' laid down in the above provision.

In general, 'promptness has to be assessed in each case according to its special features';[180] however, 'the scope of flexibility in interpreting and applying the notion of promptness is very limited'.[181] In other words, 'the significance to be attached to those features can never be taken to the point of impairing the very essence of the right guaranteed by article 5(3), that is to the point effectively negating the State's obligation to ensure a prompt release or a prompt appearance before a judicial authority'.[182]

The most pertinent precedent in this regard was the *Rigopoulos v Spain* case, in which the Panamanian-flagged vessel *Archagelos* was boarded on 23 January 1995 on the high seas by a Spanish coastguard vessel. The Spanish authorities, after discovering more than 2 tonnes of cocaine on board the vessel, detained the crew and brought the vessel to Las Palmas after 16 days. The applicant, Mr Rigopoulos, filed a complaint based on the same ground as *Medvedyev*, ie the violation of article 5(3) of ECHR.

---

[178] ibid, para 99.
[179] ibid, para 100.
[180] See inter alia *De Jong, Baljet and van den Brink* Series A No 77 (1986) 8 EHHR 20, 25 para 52.
[181] See *TW v Malta* App no 25644/94 (1999) 29 EHRR 185 para 42.
[182] *Brogan v UK*, Series A No 145 (1988) 11 EHRR 117 para 59.

Nevertheless, the Court considered that even though 'a period of sixteen days does not at first sight appear to be compatible with the concept of "brought promptly" laid down in article 5(3) of the Convention', 'having regard to the wholly exceptional circumstances of the instant case, the time which elapsed between placing the applicant in detention and bringing him before the investigating judge cannot be said to have breached the requirement of promptness in paragraph 3 of Article 5'.[183]

Mindful of the *Rigopoulos* case, the Chamber in the 2008 judgment held that it had not been materially possible to bring the applicants 'physically' before a 'legal authority' any sooner. It also found that two or three days in police custody after 13 days at sea were justified under the circumstances. It considered that the duration of the deprivation of liberty suffered by the applicants was justified by 'wholly exceptional circumstances', in particular the time it inevitably took to get the *Winner* to France.[184] The Grand Chamber, after a few paragraphs setting out and discussing the basic characteristics of the protection afforded by article 5(3) of the Convention, such as the 'promptness', the 'automatic nature of the review' and the required 'powers of the judicial officer' and then applied these principles to the present case, drawing the same conclusion as the Chamber in 2008.[185]

The significance of the *Medvedyev* case lies in the fact that it resoundingly introduced human rights and the rule of law to contemporary discourse over the fight against drug trafficking on the high seas. It follows that the interdiction of foreign or stateless vessels on the high seas for counter-drug trafficking should be regulated not only by the LOSC or by other pertinent treaties, but also by human rights instruments. It is also praiseworthy for another reason: it stressed the importance of the establishment of jurisdiction over drug offences on the high seas, which presupposes the existence of foreseeable and sufficiently precise national laws. This *sine qua non* requirement of international law is not always evident in the present context; rather, the practice of many states appears to be in discord with this requirement.

C. Jurisdictional Issues Involved

The issue of jurisdiction certainly invites discussion and it is proposed, accordingly, to use the US practice as our principal example. It is not only that the US has significantly engaged in the interdiction of drug smuggling vessels or has enacted various statutes with a view to establishing the necessary jurisdiction, but also that there is abundant jurisprudence and academic commentary to supplement the relevant discourse. This

---

[183] See *Medvedyev* case, 9.
[184] See 2008 judgment, para 68.
[185] See *Medvedyev* case (2010), paras 127–28.

notwithstanding, it should be mentioned that similar problems or questions may rise in all cases of interdiction of vessels on the high seas and therefore the ensuing *'problématique'* and analysis should not be considered as confined only to the US context.

To start with the respective legislation of the US, the first series of statutes which proscribed various aspects of high seas narcotics smuggling were enacted as part of the Comprehensive Drug Abuse Protection and Control Act of 1970.[186] However, soon it was realised that these statutes were an inadequate means of punishing smugglers, with the most glaring deficiency being that, although the Act prohibited the possession of drugs within the US waters, it did not forbid possession on the high seas.[187] Thus, the most effective method of prosecution under the 1970 Act was to charge defendants with conspiracy to import illegal drugs into the US and obtain a conviction without showing that the relevant prohibited offences had occurred.[188] These prosecutions were limited; however, as they were only successful in instances where clear proof existed to support a finding of conspiracy to distribute narcotic drugs within the US.[189]

These jurisdictional deficiencies were partly addressed in 1980, when the US Congress enacted the Marijuana on the High Seas Act.[190] This Act amended the provisions of 1970 Statute by adding a new section, 21 USC § 995a, which explicitly prohibited any person on board 'c) any vessel in US customs waters and d) any vessel subject to the jurisdiction of the United States', which was further defined as any 'vessel without nationality or a vessel assimilated to a vessel without nationality' under article 6(2) of the High Seas Convention, to knowingly or intentionally manufacture or distribute or possess with intent to distribute a controlled substance.[191] Notwithstanding that this Act tackled the possession of narcotics on the high seas on board US or stateless vessels, it left a serious gap in Congress's efforts to reach 'all acts of drug trafficking'; for example, it did not cover the possession with intent to distribute by foreign nationals on board foreign vessels.

[186]   Pub L No 91-513, 84 Stat 1236 (codified in scattered sections throughout the USC).

[187]   This particular week point in the Comprehensive Act was brought to light in *United States v Hayes*, in which the First Circuit held that under the prevailing federal statute, the possession of marijuana aboard a US vessel on the high seas with the intent to distribute would not constitute a crime absent a proof of 'intent to distribute in the United States'; see 653 F 2d 15 (1st Cir 1981).

[188]   See eg *United States v Lee* 622 F 2d 787 (5th Cir 1980) cert denied, *United States v Ricardo* 619 F 2d 1124 (5th Cir 1980). See also Stieb, 120.

[189]   Such proof was found, for example, in *United States v Caicedo-Asprilla,* in which one of the crew-members of a 30-ft boat apprehended in Florida waters confessed that he had received marijuana from a mother ship anchored in the Gulf of Mexico; see 632 F 2d 1164 (5th Cir 1980). See also A Anderson, 'Jurisdiction over Stateless Vessels on the High Seas' 13 *JMLC* (1982) 326.

[190]   See Pub L No 96-350, 94 Stat 1159-60, which was codified at 21 USC §§ 955a–955d.

[191]   See Anderson, above n 183, 327.

Congress filled the gap in a paradoxical fashion: it enacted section 955a(c), which stated that 'it is unlawful for any person on board any vessel within the customs waters of the US . . . to possess with the intent to distribute a controlled substance', and on the other, with section 19 USC § 1401(j). The latter provision extended the notion of 'customs waters' to include, besides the contiguous zone, 'the waters within such distance of the coast of the United States' as identified by 'treaty or other arrangement' with a foreign government as an area within which the laws of the US may be enforced. Therefore, a bilateral agreement could automatically create 'customs waters' around the suspect vessel on the high seas, in which the US could exert jurisdiction over drug smugglers pursuant to section 955a(c).[192]

Even though this fictitious and rather odd construction of 'customs waters' was not verbatim replaced,[193] the gap was addressed in a more orthodox fashion by the Maritime Drug Law Enforcement Act (1986).[194] Additionally, it is true that 'the new prevalence of cocaine made the law appear too weak because possessing drugs on the high seas, in and of itself, was not a crime'.[195] The major difference with the 1980 Act was that it included in the definition of 'vessels subject to the jurisdiction of the United States' 'vessels registered in a foreign nation where the flag nation has consented or waived objection to the enforcement of US law by the US and vessels located in the territorial waters of another nation, where the nation consents to the enforcement of US law'.[196] Furthermore, this consent or waiver of objection by a foreign nation to the enforcement of US law 'could be obtained by radio, telephone, or similar oral or electronic means and conclusively proved by certification of the Secretary of State or the Secretary's designee'.[197]

On 6 October 2006, further legislation was passed by the US Congress, namely the 'new Jones Act', which codified all the previous relevant statutes without making any significant amendments.[198] Of specific interest is

---

[192] See inter alia *United States v Romero-Galue* 757 F 2d 1147 (11th Cir 1985); *United States v Molinares Charris,* where it was held that 'a foreign vessel can be constructively within customs waters, even though it is on high seas, if there is a treaty or other arrangement between a foreign government and the US' (822 F 2d 1213, 1216 (1st Cir 1987).

[193] Neither the 1986 Act, nor the subsequent codification by the Jones Act (2006), adopted any special definition of 'customs waters', and thus the aforesaid s 19 of the Tariff Act remains in force.

[194] See Pub L No 99-570, §§ 3201–02. The 1986 Act which was amended and transferred 21 USC §§ 955a–955d, is codified as amended at 46 App USC §§ 1901–04 (hereinafter: MDLEA). For commentary, see M Neymayr, 'Maritime Drug Law Enforcement Act: An Analysis', *Hastings ICLR* (1988) 493.

[195] Bennett, above n 20, 442. See also E Kontorovich, 'Beyond the Article I Horizon: Congress's Enumerated Powers and Universal Jurisdiction over Drug Crimes' 93 *Minnesota Law Review* (2009) 1191, 1198.

[196] See 46 App USC § 1903(c).

[197] ibid. See also Sohn, 198.

[198] See PL 109-304 (6 Oct 2006) (HR 1442), codified as 46 USCA s 100 et seq.

paragraph 70507, entitled 'prima facie evidence', which sets out that 'Practices commonly recognized as smuggling tactics may provide prima facie evidence of intent to use a vessel to commit, or to facilitate the commission of, an offence under section 70503 of this title, and may support seizure and forfeiture of the vessel, even in the absence of controlled substances on board the vessel.'[199] Finally, as mentioned above, in 2008, the Congress passed the Drug Trafficking Vessel Interdiction Act (DTVIA) to address the employment of submersible or semi-submersible vessels.[200] The DTVIA states that anyone who 'operates . . . or embarks in any submersible vessel or semi-submersible vessel that is without nationality and that is navigating or has navigated into, through, or from waters beyond the outer limit of the territorial sea of a single country . . . with the intent to evade detection' has committed a crime against the United States.[201] Violations are punishable by up to fifteen years in prison, a fine, or both.

In the appraisal of these statutes as well as of the relevant jurisprudence, it is submitted, first, that there is not clear whether the above statutes address both the question of prescriptive and enforcement jurisdiction and the exercise of the right of visit as such. For example the MDLEA makes reference to vessels 'subject to jurisdiction of the United States', namely stateless vessels or foreign vessels for which there is an arrangement with the flag State, without ascertaining whether this arrangement refers both to the right of visit and to the assertion of enforcement jurisdiction by the US. This is of particular importance, since while the jurisdiction to legislate could be premised upon the provisions of the Vienna Convention or an established principle of international jurisdiction, the jurisdiction to enforce on the high seas, especially vis-à-vis foreign vessels, needs another consensual basis in international law, like a treaty or an ad hoc agreement.

In so far as the case of stateless vessels is concerned, it true that the jurisprudence of the US courts has not been consistent. Under the 1970 Comprehensive Act, the US courts had to invoke either the objective territorial principle or the protective principle of international criminal jurisdiction in order to establish the conspiracy offences on the high seas. Thus, US courts were able to give extraterritorial ambit to the aforesaid statute, and to punish foreign crew members aboard stateless vessels by, first, reasoning that 'A conspiracy on the high seas to commit drug

---

[199] These are inter alia '(1) the construction or adaptation of the vessel in a manner that facilitates smuggling, including a) the configuration of the vessel to ride low in the water or present a low hull profile to avoid being detected visually or by radar; . . . (2) The presence or absence of equipment, personnel, or cargo inconsistent with the type or declared purpose of the vessel . . . (5) The failure of the vessel to stop or respond or heave to when hailed by government authority, especially where the vessel conducts evasive manoeuvring when hailed'; ibid.

[200] See above n 19.

[201] Ibid, § 2285(a).

offences which are intended to have an impact on the US falls within the objective territorial principle despite the absence of an overt act within the United States';[202] and, second, by invoking the protective principle on the ground that 'The unlawful importation of drugs bypasses the federal customs laws, and thus directly challenges a governmental function.'[203]

Moreover, even after the adoption of the 1980 Act, the courts initially recognised the necessity of establishing a nexus between the activity of foreign citizens on stateless vessels and the interests of the US. For example, in the *United States v Angola*, the court stated that it could legitimately invoke section 955a to assert extraterritorial jurisdiction under the circumstances of this particular case, since the vessel, which was loaded with marijuana, 'represented a real . . . potential for harm to the effective administration of the United States' customs and narcotics laws'.[204] Nevertheless, the court added that this 'was not a case where a stateless vessel was stopped half way around the world in the Gulf of Siam'.[205] More importantly, in the *United States v James Robinson*, in which the facts did not clearly show a potential threat or any other nexus to the United States, the court disagreed with the government's contention that the protective principle authorised United States courts to assume subject matter jurisdiction over cases involving 'drug arrests of citizens of foreign countries on stateless vessels found on the high seas anywhere in the world'. Rather the court noted that 'there must be at least a potentially adverse effect on the national security or governmental functions of the US before the protective principle will allow the assertion of jurisdiction'.[206]

---

[202] *United States v Egan* 501 F Supp (1980) 1252, 1257. Even before this case, in the *United States v Williams*, the Fifth Circuit rejected the defendant's argument that the district court lacked jurisdiction over the offence because no overt act had occurred within the United States, see 589 F 2d, 213 (5th Cir 1979). In the UK the most famous case was *DPP v Doot* [1972] AC 807, in which the House of Lords allowed the DPP's appeal to permit the prosecution of five Americans for conspiracy to smuggle cannabis into the USA, even though the conspiracy was occasioned overseas.

[203] *United States v Egan*, ibid, 1258. Other cases in which the protective jurisdiction was invoked were inter alia *US v Romero-Galue*, 1154 and *United States v Peterson* 812 F 2d 486 (9th Cir 1987), and more recently *United States v Sinisterra*, No. 06-15824, 2007 WL 1695698, at *3 (11th Cir 2007) ('Congress, under the "protective principle" of international law, may assert extraterritorial jurisdiction over vessels in the high seas that are engaged in conduct that has a potentially adverse effect and is generally recognized as a crime by nations that have reasonably developed legal systems'; *United States v Bravo*, 489 F.3d 1, 7 (1st Cir 2007) ('The extra-territorial jurisdiction authorized in the MDLEA is consistent with the "protective principle" of international law'); *United States v Rendon*, 354 F.3d 1320, 1325 (11th Cir 2003) (same).

[204] Although the immediate destination of the cargo may not have been the US, the court found that the vessel's activity 'had an inherent and necessary effect of threatening the United States with the eventual flow of illicit drugs into this country'; see *United States v Angola* 514 F Supp (1981) 933, 936.

[205] ibid.

[206] See *United States v James Robinson* 515 F Supp (1981) 1340, 1345. The court held that under the protective principle of jurisdiction, it lacked subject matter jurisdiction to hear charges against foreign nationals on a stateless vessel carrying narcotic drugs where the ship

The position of the US courts over stateless vessels changed dramatically in the landmark case of *United States v Marino Garcia*, where it was unequivocally held that 'jurisdiction exists solely as a consequence of the vessel's status as stateless'.[207] Thus, the court concluded that foreign crew members on stateless ships are unprotected and can be prosecuted by any nation for violating that nation's laws.[208] This line of argument has been upheld from that time forth by US courts in all the relevant cases[209] and was sanctioned by the subsequent statutes concerning drug trafficking at sea.[210] Accordingly, in every case where a stateless vessel is involved, its statelessness grants the relevant authorities *ipso facto* not only the right to approach and search the vessel but also the right to seize the cargo, apprehend and prosecute the smugglers before their courts. Nevertheless, it is argued that the *US v James Robinson* decision holds greater legal merit than this position, namely there should be some nexus between the drug trafficking and the US or any other country for the assertion of enforcement jurisdiction.[211]

Accordingly, it is submitted that, on the one hand, there should be an overt act in the coastal state in order to invoke the objective territorial principle. On the other, there should be a real potential danger for the security or public order of the state concerned to attract the protective principle, which ipso facto necessitates a certain nexus between the illicit cargo and that particular state. This nexus could be inferred from indirect evidence, as was demonstrated in *United States v James-Robinson,* 'such as the location and heading of a ship on the high seas, size of the shipment documents or inscriptions found on the vessel or other relevant evidence'.[212] Such evidence is also the proximity of the vessel to the coast[213]

was seized 400 miles from the US and the government did not allege intent to distribute or to cause any other effect on the US.

[207] See *United States v Marino-Garcia* 679 F 2d 1373, 1383 (11th Cir 1982).

[208] See ibid, 1373.

[209] See inter alia the pertinent judicial pronouncements in *United States v Alvarez-Mena*: 'no showing of nexus or knowledge or intent is required where jurisdiction is predicated on the stateless status of the vessel on the high seas' (765 F 2d 1259, 1265 (5th Cir 1985); See also *United States v Pinto Mejia* (720 F 2d 248 (2nd Circ 1983); *United States v Juda*, 46 F 3d 961 (9th Cir 1995). For analysis see R Curtis, 'The Outer Limits of Jurisdiction on the High Seas: *United States v Romero-Galue* and *United States v Alvarez-Mena*' 5 *Wisconsin ILJ* (1986) 222.

[210] See 46 App USC § 1903(c), as repealed by § 70502(c) and confirmed by *United States v Martinez* 202 Fed Appx 353, 355 (11th Cir 2006).

[211] In accord seems to be L Roos, who is very critical upon such unilateral extension of extraterritorial jurisdiction by the United States; see ibid, 'Stateless Vessels and the High Seas Narcotics Trade' 9 *ML* (1984) 273. See also other authorities per this view in Stieb, 128 (fn 53). *Contra* seems to be Anderson, above n 183, 338.

[212] See above n 197, 1347.

[213] In *US v Aikens*, the court stated that the Fourth Amendment required not only that the search and seizure be reasonable, but that the location of the seizure also be reasonable (685 F Supp 1988, 732), while in *US v Davis*, the Ninth Circuit easily found the required nexus for a vessel within 35 miles of the United States coastline (905 F 2d 1990, 245); see also WH Latham, '*United States v Davis*' 16 *North Carolina JILC* (1991) 641.

as well as the existence of 'mother ships' and smaller boats used for delivery off the US coast.[214] In view of the foregoing analysis, it is unlikely whether the 'prima facie evidence' provision included in the new Jones Act correspond satisfactorily to the nexus requirement.

In any event, it would be in keeping with both the statelessness of the vessel and with the nature of the illicit cargo aboard the delinquent vessel that the boarding state should have the right to escort the vessel to its ports and forfeit the vessel, provided, of course, that no other state makes any claim of nationality, as well as the illicit drugs cargo. If there is not any relevant provision or any jurisdictional nexus, which grants the forum state jurisdiction to punish the master or the crew members, it would be for the state of nationality of the offenders to punish them in accordance with the well-established principle of nationality.[215]

This distinction between jurisdiction over the vessel and the persons on board was also maintained before European national courts, more specifically before the Italian courts in the *Fidelio* case. In more detail, in 1986 Italian naval units seized the Honduran vessel *Fidelio* on the high seas about 80 nautical miles off the coast of Italy. Neither the captain nor any among the 11 members of the crew had Italian nationality, and the *Fidelio* had not entered Italian territorial waters in any phase of the pursuit. In the proceeding brought against the drug smugglers, both the Tribunal and the Court of Appeal of Palermo held that the Italian criminal jurisdiction could not apply with respect to actions taking place beyond the territorial sea, and declared the lack of jurisdiction of any Italian court on the matter.[216] The Court of Cassation (decision of 1 February 1993) confirmed this and as a result, the 12 accused persons were released, even though they had been smuggling 6 tonnes of cannabis. The drugs were confiscated and destroyed in application of the relevant provisions of the Italian legislation. The latter legislation was applied in respect of the cargo (in rem), but not in respect of the persons on board (in personam).[217]

The only other solution for the forum state to punish the alleged offenders in question would be to invoke the principle of universal jurisdiction, which does not require any nexus between the offence and the forum state. As the law stands, the preponderant view is that drug trafficking is not included in the list of the international crimes for which universal

---

[214] See eg *US v Angola* 936.
[215] The authority of the state of nationality of the master and crew to exert enforcement jurisdiction over these persons distinctively from the flag state is also recognised in art 97(1) of the LOSC. On the principle of nationality in general, see P Arnell, 'The Case of Nationality-Based Jurisdiction' 50 *ICLQ* (2001) 955.
[216] Reproduced in RDI (1992) 1081.
[217] See further analysis in T Scovazzi, 'The Evolution of International Law of the Sea: New Issues and New Challenges' 286 *RCADI* (2000-I) 39, 225.

jurisdiction is afforded.[218] In the words of Gavouneli, 'interestingly enough and contrary to popular belief, neither slavery and slave related practices nor drug trafficking are covered . . .' [219] Nonetheless, there has been a recent case that held that drug trafficking is a universal crime,[220] while there is certainly a trend towards this direction and the possibility that in the near future such argument would gain the acceptance of international doctrine.[221] This *de lege ferenda* is very positive and welcome, in the sense that it would dissipate all these uncertainties concerning enforcement jurisdiction over drug smugglers on the high seas and would contribute to the proper categorisation and clarification of the other principles of international jurisdiction in this regard. In other words, the states concerned would not need to prove any nexus with the offences in question and more importantly they would not overextend the other relevant principles beyond the permissible bounds of international law. On the contrary, however, due regard should be paid to the inherent limits of universal jurisdiction, which is a potentially fearsome power that should be exercised in extraordinary circumstances. This would require, for example, a careful consideration of the definition of drug trafficking for universal jurisdiction purposes.[222]

As far as the extraordinary case of semi-submersible vessels and the recent DTVIA Act is concerned, it is readily apparent that even though in *United States v Ibarguen-Mosquera*, the Eleventh Circuit upheld the validity of DTVIA, the latter Act blurs the lines between the statelessness of the vessel as a basis for the assertion of enforcement jurisdiction in cases of drug trafficking and as a separate crime as such. As Bennett mentions, 'under DTVIA, not only is a vessel's statelessness grounds for the exercise of prescriptive jurisdiction; it is also an essential component of the conduct that the law criminalizes'.[223] In practice, just the operation of such a

---

[218] For example, during the drafting of the ICC Statute, the participants debated but ultimately rejected a proposal to include drug trafficking in the Court's jurisdiction. See relevant analysis in A Geraghty 'Universal Jurisdiction and Drug Trafficking' 16 Florida JIL (2004) 371, 387.

[219] M Gavouneli, *Functional Jurisdiction in the Law of the Sea* (Leiden: Martinus Nijhoff, 2007) 27–28.

[220] See, eg, *United States v Salcedo-Ibarra*, 2009 WL 1953399 (M.D. Fla. July 6, 2009).

[221] Even in the *Marino-Garcia* decision, it was acknowledged that 'There is a growing consensus among nations to include drug trafficking as a universally prohibited crime'; at 1382. Also, in the recent Jones Act it is stressed that 'Congress finds and declares that trafficking in controlled substances aboard vessels is a serious international problem, is universally condemned, and presents a specific threat to the security and societal well-being of the United States'; see § 70501. See also the Princeton Principles of Universal Jurisdiction (2001), which even though they did not include drug trafficking in the list of relevant crimes, leave the door open for such development (Principle No 2). Per is also CE Sorensen, 'Drug Trafficking on the High Seas: A Move towards Universal Jurisdiction under International Law' 4 *Emory International Law Review* (1990) 225.

[222] See discussion in A Colangelo, 'The Legal Limits of Universal Jurisdiction' 47 *Virginia Journal of International Law* (2007) 149.

[223] Bennett, above n 20, 446.

vessel would suffice for prosecution purposes, even if no drugs were found on the vessel in question and no jurisdictional nexus with the US existed. Statelessness thus becomes a *crimen jure gentium*, something which, most probably, is not in harmony with international law.

With regard to foreign vessels, it is true that the MDLEA, codified now in the Jones Act, grants jurisdiction to US courts to forfeit the cargo and to prosecute the offenders on board a foreign-flagged vessel whenever this vessel is 'subject to the jurisdiction of the United States', ie whenever there is a treaty or any other arrangement between US and the flag state.[224] As was observed at the outset, it is not clear on the face of this provision whether these arrangements contain both the legal bases for the boarding of the vessel and for the assertion of enforcement jurisdiction. Usually, they would contain the requisite consent for the boarding in question and they would be silent over the matter of the jurisdiction over the vessel and over the offenders. Thus, if the US asserts further jurisdiction in this regard without making a relevant request to the flag state, it must be presumed that this constitutes a violation of the exclusivity of the flag state jurisdiction on the high seas, and therefore that the US incurs responsibility. Nevertheless, it would often be the case that the injured state would not react to this assertion of enforcement jurisdiction, which, in theory, would qualify as a unilateral act of waiver of rights or acquiescence.[225] It would also result in the loss of the right of the injured state to invoke responsibility, provided that it has 'validly acquiesced in the lapse of the claim'.[226]

There have been cases where the legality not of the enforcement jurisdiction itself but of the initial right of visit of the vessel has been contested. In many cases, US courts have held that an enforcement vessel may lawfully detain a foreign vessel on the high seas, while awaiting consent from the flag state to board.[227] For example, in *United States v Bario-Hernandez*, a US Coast Guard seizure of a Honduran vessel was upheld where consent was not obtained until two days after the initial boarding. The only restriction the court required was that consent occurs before the resulting trial.[228] Also, in the *United States v Bustos-Useche*, the Fifth Circuit found that because Panama's consent to the boarding and

---

[224] See 46 App USC § 1903(c), as repealed by § 70502(d).

[225] See Brownlie, 641.

[226] See art 45 of the ILC Arts and Commentary, 121. ICJ endorsed the principle that a state may by acquiescence lose its right to invoke responsibility in *Certain Phosphate case*; ibid para 32.

[227] Also, in the USCG Guide, it is admitted that 'although a defendant may challenge U.S. jurisdiction over a vessel on the basis that the flag State failed to consent before trial, they may not do so on the basis that the United States obtained the flag State's consent after the USCG boarded or searched the vessel'; ibid 20.

[228] See 655 F Supp (1987) 1069. See also *United States v Rasheed*, 802 F Supp 312, 321–23 (D Haw 1992) and *United States v Reeh* 780 F 2d 1541, 1547 (11th Cir 1986).

search of the vessel concerned was given prior to the trial, the district court had jurisdiction.[229] This consent might be valid as far as the exercise of enforcement jurisdiction over the offenders is concerned, but it is invalid in respect of the prior interdiction of the vessel concerned on the high seas, since, it should have been given prior to the wrongful act and not *ex post facto*. Hence, the consent of Honduras or of Panama respectively was, in principle, a valid 'consent' for the purposes of the trial of the offenders and also, at the same time, a waiver of the right to challenge the illegality of the boarding and invoke the responsibility.

Another contentious issue in this respect is the legal form of the consent given by the flag state. As has been upheld by various decisions[230] and confirmed by the provisions of MDLEA and recently by the Jones Act, such consent can be obtained by informal means.[231] Nevertheless, it is submitted that the requirements of legal certainty and due process as well as the rules on invalidity of treaties, which apply *mutatis mutandis* in the case of unilateral acts, entail that the consent should be obtained by the competent authority of the flag state after a specific request by the boarding State, both of which should be recorded in writing.

Moreover, it should be pointed that the previous discussion with regard to the requirement of a jurisdictional nexus is pertinent also in relation to the seizures of foreign-flagged vessels. It is significant, first, to draw the distinction between the types of jurisdiction for which this nexus is arguably required. In cases where the flag state has consented via a 'treaty or other arrangement' to the enforcement jurisdiction on part of the United States, the nexus in question is requisite for the assertion of prescriptive jurisdiction in this regard. Conversely, when the flag state has only given the consent to boarding itself and not to the further assertion of jurisdiction, then, in principle jurisdictional priority is afforded to the flag state and not to the boarding state. Consequently, the US should, for example, first, contact the flag state and inquire whether it is willing to enforce its jurisdiction and then, if the latter declines to do so, proceed to confiscate the cargo and prosecute the offenders. However, at this particular stage, it should be scrutinised whether there is any jurisdictional nexus between the alleged offences and the requesting state, which is a prerequisite for the assertion of both legislative and enforcement jurisdiction in this regard. Also, simultaneously, there might be valid jurisdictional claims by third states, such as from the states of the nationality of the offenders.[232]

[229] See 273 F 3d 622, 624 (5th Cir 2001).
[230] See eg *US v Gonzalez*.
[231] *cf United States v Bent-Santana,* which held that 'assent to board and search a foreign flag vessel by a duly authorised official of that foreign government, communicated verbally or in writing to the appropriate personnel, is adequate to meet the terms of section 1401(j)'; see 774 F 2d 1545 (11th Cir 1985).
[232] See for example, the *MV Hermann* case, below n 229.

Mindful of the fact that there is no rule in general international law, which provides for any hierarchy among relevant jurisdictional claims, it would be particularly helpful to have treaty provisions regulating such concur ring claims. In the absence of such provisions, any conflict could be resolved by the application of comity or through bona fide negotiations.[233]

In addition, in the *United States v Cardales case*, the First Circuit held, while deciding that no proof of a nexus with the United States was required, that 'in order to satisfy due process, our application of the MDLEA must not be arbitrary or fundamentally unfair. In determining whether due process is satisfied, we are guided by principles of international law.'[234] Upon this basis, the Court of Appeals for the Ninth Circuit has consistently held that the extraterritorial application of a criminal statute to those aboard a foreign flag vessel violates the Due Process Clause of the Constitution if the offence charged lacks an adequate nexus to the US.[235] This notwithstanding, it is regrettable that most other circuits, that have considered the question have rejected the Ninth Circuit's approach and have been very reluctant to recognise the need for a nexus requirement.[236]

Furthermore, there have been very far-fetched dicta by the Courts in this regard, such as in the *United States v Romero-Galue*, in which the Court stated that 'Even absent a treaty or arrangement, the US could, under the protective principle of international law, prosecute foreign nationals on foreign vessels on the high seas for possession of narcotics.'[237] In addition, in the *United States v Perez-Oviedo* case, the court, in rejecting the nexus requirement, reasoned that 'the MDLEA was supported by the requisite congressional intent to override international law if the latter were to require a nexus with the United States'.[238]

On the other hand, very recently, on 6 November 2012, the Court of Appeals (Eleventh Circuit) handed down a rather controversial decision in the *US v Bellaizac-Hurtado case*, which *prima facie* seems to overturn all the aforementioned case-law in this regard.[239] The case involved a drug smuggling vessel, apparently stateless, which was spotted by a US Coast

---

[233] See also Allen, 161.

[234] See *United States v Cardales* 168 F 3d 548, 553 (1st Cir 1999).

[235] See eg *United States v Klimavicius-Viloria*, in which the court reasoned that the nexus requirement of the MDLEA served the same purpose as the 'minimum contacts test in personal jurisdiction'; see 144 F 3d 1249, 1257 (9th Cir 1998). See also A Weisburd, 'Due Process Limits on Federal Extraterritorial Legislation?' 35 *Columbia JTL* (1997) 379.

[236] See inter alia *United States v Suerte*, 291 F 3d 366 (5th Cir. 2002) and a very well-structured commentary of the case in M Costa, 18 *Temple ICLJ* (2004) 131. *Contra* see *United States v Jousef* 327 F 3d 56, 1000 (2nd Cir 2003) (following 9th Cir).

[237] See above n 175, 1154. This statement was also reaffirmed in *United States v Alomia-Riascos* 825 F 2d 769 (4th Cir 1987).

[238] See 281 F 3d 400, 403 (3rd Cir 2002).

[239] *United States v Bellaizac-Hurtado and others*, Case: 11-14049 (11th Cir, 2012) and commentary by Guilfoyle at www.ejiltalk.org/drug-trafficking-at-sea-no-longer-a-crime-of-universal-jurisdiction-before-us-courts/#more-7000 (22 November 2012).

Guard vessel patrolling in the Panamanian territorial sea. The crew fled ashore, while 760 kg of cocaine was discovered aboard their vessel. Panama waived jurisdiction to allow the US to prosecute the case under Article IX(2) of the US-Panama Supplementary Agreement.[240] The federal grand jury indicted the applicants for conspiracy to possess with intent to distribute cocaine, and for actual possession with intent to distribute cocaine, on board a vessel subject to the jurisdiction of the United States. However, the Court vacated their convictions by concluding that drug trafficking is not an 'Offence[] against the Law of Nations' and that Congress cannot constitutionally proscribe the defendants' conduct under the Offences Clause.

In the words of the Court, 'drug trafficking is also not a violation of contemporary customary international law. Although a number of specially affected States—States that benefit financially from the drug trade—have ratified treaties that address drug trafficking, they have failed to comply with the requirements of those treaties, and the international community has not treated drug trafficking as a violation of contemporary customary international law. Scholars also agree that drug trafficking is not a violation of contemporary customary international law. The United States argues that the widespread ratification of the 1988 United Nations Convention Against Illicit Traffic in Narcotic Drugs and Psychotropic Substances establishes that drug trafficking violates a norm of customary international law, but we disagree'[241] The main ground, according to the Court, is that in light of the North Sea Continental Shelf case,[242] 'drug trade continues to flourish in many specially affected States despite their ratification of the Convention'.[243]

Leaving aside the constitutional dimension of the case, it seems to the author that the reasoning of the court is not in consistency with international law. For example, the court applies erroneously the *North Sea Continental Shelf case*, especially as regards the creation of custom through a treaty. In the present case, illicit trafficking in narcotic drugs is of 'fundamentally norm creating character',[244] it has been criminalised by the overwhelming majority of the members of international community, which have enforced such laws and therefore widespread practice does exist,

---

[240] See Supplementary Arrangement between the Government of the United States of America and the Government of Panama to the Arrangement between the Government of the United States and the Government of Panama for Support and Assistance from the U.S. Coast Guard for the National Maritime Service of the Ministry of Government and Justice, signed at Panama February 5, 2002; entered into force February 5, 2002. TIAS 02-205.1, 2002 U.S.T. LEXIS 51.

[241] See above n 239, at 18.

[242] See *North Sea Continental Shelf Cases (Germany v Denmark and Germany v Netherlands)* ICJ Rep (1969) 3, 43.

[243] Ibid, 20.

[244] Ibid, 44, para 72.

while there is certainly strong *opinio juris sive necessitatis*.[245] In addition, singling out 'specially affected States' in this regard is totally misleading, since all States may be affected by drug trafficking. Finally, the Court quotes eminent authors, such as Cassese[246] and Kontorovich,[247] to substantiate the argument that there is no international custom;[248] however, what these authors do is simply argue against the status of drug trafficking as a crime subject to universal jurisdiction and not as customary law. It remains to be seen whether this judgment will be upheld in other judgments of the same or other Circuits.

In conclusion, it is observed that, in general, , the practice of the USCG as well as the application of the relevant statutes by the US courts is not always in strict compliance with international law. In case of violation, the US would incur responsibility and there could be, inter alia, diplomatic protests by injured states. Indeed, there has been an instance where the legality of US practice in this regard has been challenged diplomatically. On 30 January 1990, the Coast Guard intercepted the *M/V Hermann*, a vessel registered in Panama, which was suspected of carrying narcotic drugs in the Gulf of Mexico. On the same day, Panama gave the US written permission to board and to inspect the vessel. Cuba, however, protested the US enforcement actions to the UN Security Council, noting that the *MV Hermann* had a Cuban crew and that the vessel was leased to a Cuban firm. The US replied that because Cuba was not the vessel's flag state, it had no standing.[249] Finally, it should be mentioned that although the defendants in drug smuggling cases are not able to successfully invoke the violation of international law, they are able to invoke the US Constitutional protections, namely the 'reasonable suspicion' standard for searches pursuant to the Fourth Amendment[250] as well as the requirements of 'due process' clause of the Fifth Amendment.[251]

The foregoing survey of United States legislation and its judicial interpretation reveals largely the problems concerning the assertion of jurisdiction over drug smuggling vessels on the high seas. In short, there has certainly been in some cases an abusive and erroneous application of

[245] On *opinio necessitatis*, which, arguably, does exist in relation to drug trafficking see ICTY, *Kupreškić* et al (IT-95-16), Trial Judgment, 14 January 2000, paras 527 and 530.
[246] See A Cassese, *International Criminal Law* (Oxford: Oxford University Press, 2003) 24.
[247] See E Kontorovich, above n 195, 1226.
[248] See above n 239, 23.
[249] See US Dep't of State, Digest of US Practice in International Law, 1989-90, 452–56 (2003) and reference of the case in Sohn, 212.
[250] A very recent case before the First Circuit is very instructive as to how the US Courts construe the 'reasonable suspicion' requirement of the Fourth Amendment: in the *United States v Vilches-Navarrete*, 2008 WL 1009432 (1st Cir, 10 Apr 2008) (slip op), USCG Guide, 41.
[251] The issue is beyond the compass of this paper; for a thorough discussion of the relevant issues see inter alia *United States v Villamonte-Marquez* 462 US 579 (1983) and also IP Stotzky, 'Interdiction at Sea and the Fourth Amendment' in Th Clingan (ed), *The Law of the Sea: What Lies Ahead?* (Hawaii: Law of the Sea Institute, 1988) 72.

international criminal jurisdiction principles on the part of the US courts. It is not the objective of suppressing drug trafficking, but it is the method of not respecting in these cases basic tenets of international law, such as the freedom of the high seas and the requirements of due process, legal certainty and foreseeability, which hardly merits general approbation. This was markedly evidenced also in the European context, in the *Medvedyev* case.

IV. CONCLUDING REMARKS

The problem of the illicit trade and use of narcotic drugs has aptly been considered as especially detrimental to the social fabric and to the public health of nations. The fact that the oceans are extensively used for drug trafficking has reasonably given rise to forceful claims for interference with such vessels on the high seas. The international society has endorsed and 'internationalised' these claims, in the sense of having transformed them to 'inclusive' *ordre public* considerations. In consequence, various treaties, such as the 1988 Vienna Convention and the Caribbean bilateral agreements, have provided for the right of visit in this respect. Furthermore, states may invoke further legal justifications for interference in the present context: besides the 'no-nationality' ground of article 110 of LOSC, the circumstances precluding wrongfulness may occasionally apply. In addition, it was observed that the legal order of the oceans has simultaneously subjected the present claims for interference to general international law, including rules, such as the prohibition of the use of force, the protection of human rights, but more importantly rules concerning the establishment of jurisdiction under international law.

8

Interception on the High Seas and Human Beings

I. INTRODUCTION

THE PRESENT DISCUSSION will revolve around the practice of interception of human beings on the high seas in the contemporary legal order of the oceans. The regulation of immigration has been considered since the time of Gentillis as a legitimate ground for the extension of the coastal state's authority seaward. Indeed, the proscription and abolition of the slave trade, ie of the commerce in human beings, traded like commodities from one country or continent to another, was one of the first cases where the right of visit in peacetime was sought by the British, and eventually acknowledged and codified under LOSC. As was observed in the Introduction, the problem of illicit migration and of human trafficking looms large in current world affairs. States and international organisations have resorted to various measures to address these problems, including the interception of vessels on the high seas. Suffice to note the interception of thousands of Haitians and Cubans travelling to the US, or the FRONTEX operations in the Mediterranean Sea.

The right to visit vessels carrying such categories of human beings has been at the centre of the focus of many nations in different historic periods of the last centuries. Common ground in all of these cases has undoubtedly been the need to protect values such as social coherence, the *ordre public* and the economical prosperity of the population of a particular nation from the unregulated import of non-nationals under various circumstances. Such claims to interfere with foreign shipping in order to regulate this import of human beings have gradually been recognised by the international society and thus these *mare clausum* grounds have positively qualified the freedom of the high seas in the contemporary *civitas maxima* of the oceans. It is further submitted that this policy has both 'negative' and 'positive' aspects in the following sense: it is negative when the interference aims at deterring people from entering States, while it is positive, when the interference aims at safeguarding lives at sea or saving people from scourges, such as slave trade and currently human trafficking.

The purpose of this chapter is to assess comprehensively the contemporary practice of interception of human beings on the high seas against the background of the law of the sea and of other relevant rules of international law. In addressing the legal questions raised by the issue at hand, it will propound, firstly that the current practice of interception should equally reflect its 'positive' aspect, ie the necessary measures to suppress human trafficking and other similar practices. Secondly, that even when it is faced with new challenges, the legal order of the oceans has in its arsenal adequate means to address novel challenges and lastly that the present *mare clausum* claims should be subordinated to the rule of international law. In the present context, it is the protection of human beings more than any other value that should be at the heart of any normative consideration. This can be called the need to profoundly 'humanise' the interception operations,[1] which would be in accord, firstly, with the nature of the target of such operations, ie human beings as such, and secondly and more generally with the overarching purpose of maintaining a *civitas maxima* of the oceans, founded not only on the relevant freedoms of the high seas but also on values, such as elementary principles of humanity and international ethos.

Accordingly, the following enquiry will assess the legal bases of this practice, ie the justifications furnished by *jus gentium* for such operations on the high seas, both by the law of the sea and by other international rules. This will include not only *de lege lata* considerations, but also a novel or a *de lege ferenda* proposition for the reinvigoration of the seemingly obsolete slave trade provision of LOSC. In addition, other possible bases derived from relevant multilateral and bilateral treaties as well as from customary law will be discussed. Finally, certain additional legal issues will be canvassed.[2]

However, a preliminary, yet significant question to be addressed is the 'classification' – to use the terminology of conflict of laws – or a legal characterisation of the categories of people being intercepted by states on the high seas. Notwithstanding that all human beings fall within the *ratione personae* purview of this enquiry, it is suggested that classifying them in different legal categories entails different possible legal bases for their interdiction as well as different legal consequences for these persons as well as for the states involved.

The first category to consider is refugees, the legal definition of which can be found in article 1A(2) of the Refugee Convention: a refugee is a

---

[1] This term is along the lines of the recent title by Theodor Meron, *The Humanization of International Law* (Leiden: Martinus Nijhoff, 2006).

[2] See also further comments in E Papastavridis, 'Interception of Human Beings on the High Seas: A Contemporary Analysis under International Law' 36 *Syracuse JILC* (2009) 145–228.

person who, 'owing to a well-founded fear of being persecuted for reasons of race, religion, nationality, or membership of a particular social group or political opinion, is outside the country of his nationality and is unable or, owing to such fear, unwilling to avail himself of the protection of that country'. Pursuant to the work of UNHCR,[3] the class of beneficiaries has gradually moved to a more generic class of refugees, including those often large groups or categories of persons who can be determined or presumed to be without or unable to avail themselves of the protection of the government of their state of origin. In principle, it is still essential that the persons in question should have crossed an international frontier and that the reasons for flight should be traceable to conflicts, human rights violations, or other serious harm resulting from radical political, social or economic changes in their own country or natural and environmental calamities.[4]

It is odd yet true that the term 'asylum' does not appear in any of the instruments relating to refugees.[5] Asylum aptly describes the status of a person accorded refugee status and permanent residence in a state other than that of his nationality; however, it is a wider notion embracing in addition protection for reasons other than those particular grounds set out in the Refugee Convention.[6] *A fortiori*, the term 'asylum-seekers', a term of art rather than of law, has come to denote a broader notion than 'refugees' *simpliciter* and to be used interchangeably for people in search of asylum.

The second category of people being intercepted on the high seas is migrants, and to be more precise, unauthorised or undocumented migrants,[7] ie people who migrate in search of a better life, hoping to find employment opportunities and economic prosperity abroad and who are travelling without the required documentation. The term 'migrant' has been defined by the Smuggling Protocol as a person who is not a national or permanent resident of the state party where the illegal entry takes place. Additionally, the *actus reus* itself, ie the criminal behaviour of the smuggling of migrant, is designated as 'the procurement, in order to

---

[3] For an overview of the work of the UNHCR, see BS Chimni (ed), *International Refugee Law* (New Delhi: Sage, 2000) 213.

[4] See Goodwin-Gill and McAdam, 32.

[5] The right to asylum was explicitly postulated in art 14(1) of the Universal Declaration of Human Rights (1948), yet it constituted an imperfect right, because no corresponding duty was laid on states to grant asylum, but only a right of each person to leave his country in search of asylum. See also UN Declaration on Territorial Asylum (1967) GA Res 2312, UN GAOR, 22nd sess, Supp No 16, 81. On asylum generally see A Grahl-Madsen, *Territorial Asylum* (Stockholm: Almqvist & Wiksell International, 1980).

[6] See IA Shearer, 'International Law and Refugees in South-East Asia' 13 *Thesaurus Acroasium* (1987) 437.

[7] In this paper, the term 'undocumented' persons refers to those who are not in possession of the required documentation for travel to and entry to the country of intended destination.

obtain, directly or indirectly, a financial or other material benefit, of the illegal entry of a person into a State Party'.[8]

Asylum-seekers and migrants are usually people who either have been compelled or have freely chosen to make this perilous journey to a better future, but they are not under any authority or control. Moreover, there are other cases of people, where neither their journey as such nor their fate in the destination country is in their own hands. Historically, this portrays slaves, ie persons 'over whom any or all of the powers of ownership are exercised'.[9] A more recent, yet diverse class of persons in a similar situation are the victims of human trafficking.[10] The latter means the recruitment, transportation, transfer of persons, either by the threat or use of abduction, force, fraud, deception or coercion for the purpose of exploitation (including at minimum, the exploitation of the prostitution of the others, or other forms of sexual exploitation, forced labour, slavery or practices similar to slavery, or servitude).[11] It goes without saying that it is only a small number of trafficked persons who enter their destination country legally and who would not be considered, prima facie, smuggled migrants. The elements distinguishing trafficking from migrant smuggling – force/coercion for purposes of exploitation – may at first glance seem obvious, but in many cases such distinctions are less clear on the ground and there is considerable movement and overlap between the two categories.[12]

Alternatively, people susceptible to interception can be classified differently on the basis of another yardstick, namely the *modus* of their journey. In other words, asylum-seekers or migrants will either choose to travel by their own means, for example, on their own small boat,[13] or they may opt for illicit methods of transportation and they will either be smuggled or

---

[8] art 3(a) of Smuggling Protocol. In addition, reference should be made to the Convention on the Protection of All Migrant Workers and Members of their Families (1990), in art 2(1) of which the term 'migrant worker' is defined as 'a person who is to be engaged, is engaged or has been engaged in a remunerated activity in a State of which he or she is not a national'; 30 ILM 1521. An excellent report of the various modalities of smuggling of migrants is found in the UNODC, Issue Paper, 'Smuggling of Migrants at Sea' (Vienna, 2011).

[9] art 1 of the Slavery Convention.

[10] Human trafficking is one of the most worrisome scourges of modern times. It is estimated that up to 800,000 people, especially women and children, are trafficked around the world annually, see T Obokata, 'Trafficking of Human Beings as a Crime against Humanity' 54 *ICLQ* (2005) 445.

[11] See art 3(a) of the Protocol to Prevent, Suppress and Punish Trafficking in persons, Especially Women and Children, supplementing the UN Convention on Transnational Organized Crime, UN Doc A/55/383 (2000), entered into force on 25 December 2003 (hereinafter: Human Trafficking Protocol). See A Gallacher, 'Human Rights and the New UN Protocol on Trafficking and Migrant Smuggling' 23 *HRQ* (2001) 975. See also the CoE Convention on Action against Trafficking in Human Beings, (Warsaw, 5 May 2005) CETS No 197.

[12] See Gallacher, ibid, 1001.

[13] See Introduction fn 52 above.

stowed away.[14] The latter methods are employed also in the case of victims of modern forms of slavery or human trafficking, who nevertheless are bereft of any choice. Apart from the stowaways, who are reported by the master of the vessel and cannot be 'intercepted', properly speaking, all the other intercepted persons cannot be a priori classified without a further determination process or further information regarding their status.

II. INTERNATIONAL LEGAL JUSTIFICATIONS FOR INTERCEPTION ON THE HIGH SEAS

A. Treaty Bases for Interception

i. The Law of the Sea Convention

The point of departure for the discussion of the legal bases for all the cases of interception on the high seas in the present enquiry is article 110 of LOSC. *In casu*, it is evident that on the face of this provision trafficking and transporting illegal migrants or refugees are not contemplated by the Convention as a specific ground for the right to visit of a foreign vessel. As a result, the requisite legal basis should either be extrapolated from the above-mentioned grounds for interference, or be sought in another legal framework. Before examining the latter option, it is apt to consider first whether article 110 can provide any justification for the boarding in question.

First, it goes without saying that the piracy and the unauthorised broadcasting grounds are completely irrelevant to the present survey. Moreover, the 'same nationality' ground seems not to raise any particular problems, since in this case the vessel will be susceptible to the full jurisdiction of the flag state pursuant to article 92 of LOSC. Contrary, the grounds of 'the absence of nationality' as well as the 'slave trade' merit a closer scrutiny. As far as the former ground is concerned, it is very often the case that the transportation of the persons in question is carried out using non-registered small vessels, without name or flag, ie stateless vessels. With regard to the latter ground, it is submitted that there is room for the application of the slave trade provision to certain cases of human trafficking by sea. In any event, it is generally regrettable that there is a considerable

---

[14] Stowing away is a form of irregular migration which is frequently encountered in practice. According to the most recent definition, a 'stowaway' is defined as 'a person who is secreted on a ship or in cargo, which is subsequently loaded on the ship, without the consent of the ship owner or the Master . . . and who is detected on board the ship after it has departed from a port . . . and is reported as a stowaway by the master to the appropriate authorities.' See Amendments to the Convention on Facilitation of International Maritime Traffic, as amended by Resolution FAL 7 (29); entered into force 1 May 2003.

paucity of information about the boarding of such vessels, especially with respect to the legal bases used by the states involved.[15]

a. The Question of 'Stateless Vessels'

Based on the few related reports and literature, the 'absence of nationality' seems to be the most relevant ground for intercepting vessels with migrants and asylum-seekers on board.[16] In a Study of the European Commission, it was noted that

> Illegal immigration via [small craft aiming to reach the coast clandestinely] accounts for most of the illegal immigration by sea (over 70%–80% of detected illegal immigration by sea). These crossings involve small craft or dinghies which are not usually seaworthy and which are therefore jeopardising the lives of their occupants.[17]

It goes without saying that such small craft or 'dinghies' would not be flying any flag.

Stateless vessels are vessels, which, as a matter of international law, have no nationality. To such ships are assimilated those that sail under two or more flags, using them according to convenience (art 92(2) LOSC).[18] By virtue of the provision of article 110(1)(d) of LOSC, warships or other duly authorised vessels of any state may exercise the right of visit on these vessels.[19] Furthermore, according to one strand of legal doctrine, the boarding states may also subject stateless vessels to their laws. Ships without nationality lose the protection of the law with respect to boarding and seizure on the high seas, because otherwise these ships would be immune from interference on the high seas.[20] Therefore, as *quasi res nullius*, they fall

[15] It should be mentioned, in this regard, that in Resolution A867(20) of 2000, the IMO Maritime Safety Committee established a biannual reporting procedure to keep track of incidents involving unsafe practices associated with the trafficking in or transport of migrants at sea. Nevertheless, the Member States have scarcely availed of this opportunity to record the relevant traffic of migrants. More information is available at www.imo.org.

[16] See eg, cases like the ones reported to the IMO, above n 13 and N Ronzitti, 'Coastal State Jurisdiction over Refugees and Migrants at Sea', in N Ando et al (eds), *Liber Amicorum Judge Shigeru Oda* (The Hague: Kluwer Law International, 2002) 1271, 1274.

[17] *Study on the International Law Instruments in Relation to Illegal Immigration by Sea*, SEC (2007) 691, 15 May 2007, Annex, para 1.1.2.

[18] See in general H Meyers, *The Nationality of Vessels* (The Hague: Martinus Nijhoff, 1967). In addition, according to the US Commander's Handbook, such vessels are inter alia those, which 'make contradictory or inconsistent claims of nationality, change flags during a voyage, and have removable signboards showing different vessel names and/or homeports', para 3.11.2.4.

[19] The relevant provision was inserted for the first time in 1976 in the Revised Single Negotiating Text (A/CONF 62/WP 8/Part II, art 96, IV *Official Records* 166), reprinted in IV Platzöder, 129. It should be noted that the insertion of the stateless vessels did not encounter any difficulties or objections; see also Nordquist, *Commentary*, 240.

[20] See Brownlie, 235. This was also the opinion of the Special Rapporteur of ILC, François, in his initial Report on the Regime of the High Seas; *Regime of the High Seas*, Draft Articles, A/CN.4/79, section II, reprinted in *YbILC* (1955-I), , 39.

under the full jurisdictional scope of the boarding states.[21] A number of judicial pronouncements concerning stateless vessels in general support this line of reasoning.[22] Similarly, in the only reported case of illicit migrants on board such vessels before a national court, the *Pamuk and others* case in 2001, the 'stateless vessel' ground was considered by an Italian court as sufficient for the arrest and trial of illegal migrants on the high seas bound for the coast of Italy.[23]

Notwithstanding these judicial opinions, on a stronger legal footing seems to be the contrary assertion, namely that, in general, the right to visit such vessels does not *ipso facto* entail the full extension of the jurisdictional powers of the boarding States.[24] This rests in part upon the simple contemplation that, on the face of the pertinent provision, the right of visit in question is not actually different from the right of visit accorded in all the other circumstances provided in article 110 of LOSC, ie the right of boarding for the purpose of verifying the 'no nationality' of the vessel and in case of further suspicion, the right of search of the vessel. Nowhere does the Convention provide for any further assertion of jurisdiction with regard to these vessels.[25]

Besides this grammatical interpretation, recourse to the purpose of the provision in question lends more credence to this view. The *ratio juris* of article 110(1)(d) of LOSC lies in the idea that the whole edifice of the legal order of the oceans is postulated in the nationality of the vessels navigating on the high seas; it is, hence, dangerous to have ships sailing on the high seas which are not subject to the jurisdiction of any state, and being law unto them, need not comply with any generally accepted international regulations to ensure the minimum public order at sea.[26] It follows logically that the powers conferred upon the warships of all states are, in a first level, similar to the general police measures recognised vis-à-vis all vessels on the high seas: *reconnaissance*, or the right of approach to identify

---

[21] See also A Watts, 'The Protection of Merchant Vessels' (1957) 33 BYIL 52–84. Since the nineteenth century it has been claimed that stateless vessels should be equated to pirate or slave vessels which are subject to universal jurisdiction; see, eg, C Testa, *Le Droit Public International Maritime* (Paris: Durand et Pedone-Lauriel, 1886) 91; or to pirate vessels, see A Limitone, *The Registration of Ships in International and Intergovernmental Organisations* (Miami, FL: University of Miami Sea Grant Program, Sea Grant Special Bulletin #2, 1971) 7.

[22] See eg the decision of the Privy Council in *Molvan v Attorney-General for Palestine* [1948] AC 351. In that case the Council found that no breach of international law resulted when a British destroyer intercepted a ship carrying illegal immigrants bound for Palestine on the high seas and escorted into port, where the vessel was forfeited.

[23] Italian customs officers had arrested on the high seas a flagless vessel transporting illegal immigrants who had been transferred, on the high seas, to another vessel directed to the Italian coast and had subsequently entered Italian territorial waters. See the decision of Tribunale di Crotone, 27 September 2001, *Pamuk et al* cited in RDI (2001) 1155 and for commentary: S Trevisanut, 'Droit de la Mer' 133 *Journal du droit international* (2006) 1035.

[24] Similar arguments were put forward in relation to maritime terrorism and drug trafficking.

[25] See Nordquist, *Commentary*, 127.

[26] See Sohn, *Human Rights*, 58.

the nationality of the encountered vessel. Moreover, since the stateless vessel, by definition, flies no flag, the right to board and verify the statelessness (*droit d'enquête du pavillon*) is further acknowledged.

At a second level, the purpose of the right of visit *in casu* is the maintenance of the necessary public order at sea, by ensuring that these vessels abide by those international regulations, which constitute this order and which can be mainly conceived as the duties enshrined in article 94 of LOSC.[27] To discharge this duty, it is proposed that stateless vessels can be brought to a port and be subjected to further investigation in this respect.[28] However, the jurisdiction exercised would be limited to the purpose of inquiring as to the status of the vessel and of the persons on board and would not substitute the full scope of the jurisdiction of the flag state. Furthermore, under no circumstances would the vessels in question be equated to *res nullius* and thus be susceptible to appropriation or other enforcement measures.

In the light of the foregoing, the arrest of potential migrants or asylum-seekers on the high seas, as, for example, in the *Pamuk* case, seems to beg the question that a crime has really been committed on the high seas. It may be fitting to stress here that the act of carrying migrants on the high seas is not an international crime as such; the only conduct that is criminalised is the 'smuggling of migrants' and solely for the states parties to the respective Protocol. Therefore, in the absence of a similar treaty provision to this effect or without the explicit assertion of any jurisdictional principle, it is submitted that these persons should not be subjected to any detention or arrest, so long as they have not entered the territorial or contiguous zone of the coastal state thus violating its immigration laws.[29]

Notwithstanding that the boarding states should abstain from arresting persons on board of stateless vessels on the high seas, it is true that the latter states would face a problem of the procedure to be followed in respect of these persons. In cases where the vessel is in distress, or the persons on board are seeking asylum, the answer would be easy: rescue and refugee status determination process, respectively. In all other cases, however, the solution advocated by François appears to be the most sound, namely, bringing the vessel to a port of the coastal state and detaining the persons on board until there is a full determination of their nationality and intentions without, however, arresting them and trying them for illicit immigration. In any event, it is apt to reiterate here that the persons

---

[27] See for the text and commentary on this provision Nordquist, *Commentary*, 135.

[28] See eg the opinion of François: 'les autres navires peuvent exercer à l'égard du navire sans nationalité le droit de visite et de perquisition, ils peuvent l'amener dans un de leurs ports. Par ailleurs les Etats peuvent refuser d'admettre de pareils navires dans leurs ports à des fins de commerce, mais ils n'auraient pas le droit de les traiter comme pirates. Cette dernière opinion nous semble justifiée'; see 'Regime of the High Seas, Draft Articles, A/CN 4/79, section II', in *ILC Yearbook* (1955-I), 26.

[29] *cf* art 33 LOSC.

on board the ship should be treated in accordance with the internationally recognised human rights and unless they are stateless, they may be entitled to the protection of the state of their nationality, regardless of the fact that they are travelling on a stateless vessel.[30]

b. The 'Slave Trade' Argument in a Modern Perspective

The other possible legal basis afforded by the LOSC for interception of human beings on the high seas is suppression of the slave trade. Before going into the merits of this argument, however, it must be noted that this constitutes a novel proposition premised upon an evolutionary interpretation of the relevant texts, especially the LOSC. While there is an evident tendency in international judicial practice and doctrine to broadly interpret the relevant slavery provisions in order to include contemporary manifestations of slavery, there is no actual state practice or any judicial decision to buttress a corresponding interpretation of the relevant provision of the LOSC. Nonetheless, it is worth pursuing this line of argument for several reasons: first, it purports to address the problem of contemporary 'slave trade', ie human trafficking, and secondly it does so without the need of new instruments. It also reflects the 'positive' and humanitarian face of 'interception', which is completely different than the current state practice of external immigration controls. Finally, it aims to fulfil the normative content of article 99 of LOSC, namely the suppression of slavery in the legal order of the oceans.[31]

1. The Applicable Treaty Law

According to article 110(1)(b) of LOSC, vessels engaged in the slave trade may be visited on the high seas[32] and by virtue of article 99 LOSC, any slave taking refuge on board a ship shall *ipso facto* be free. Evident on the face of LOSC is that neither slavery nor the slave trade is defined therein. Thus, absent any *de lege specialis* definition in LOSC, recourse should be made to the relevant international law, which is reflected, principally, in the 1926 Slavery Convention. The latter defines 'slavery' as 'the status or

---

[30] See Sohn, *Human Rights*, 58.

[31] This argument, in a different form, was been put forward in E Papastavridis, above n 2, 163 et seq.

[32] The first decision to include slave trade as a justification for the right to approach 'on the same footing as in the case of piracy' was made by the ILC in 1951; see ILC Report to the GA, UN Doc A/1858 (1951), reprinted in 2 *YbILC* (1951) 139–40. However, in 1955, the Commission restricted the boarding of ships suspected of slavery to 'maritime zones treated as suspect in the international conventions for the abolition of slave trade'; see above Introduction (n 65), 26–27. At the actual Conference the provision on the slave trade was hotly attacked by the USSR and the United Arab Republic, on the grounds that it was obsolete and discriminatory and was designed as a pretext for controlling maritime trade in certain areas. Nonetheless, in the plenary session, not only the provision was maintained but also the clause relating to certain areas was removed; see 2 UN [First] Conference on the Law of the Sea, *Official Records*, 22.

condition of a person over whom any or all of the powers attaching to the right of ownership are exercised' (art 1 para 1), and the 'slave trade' as any act 'involved in the capture, acquisition or disposal of a person with intent to reduce him to slavery . . . and, in general every act of trade and transport in slaves (art 1 para 2).[33]

These definitions were incorporated into article of the 1956 Supplementary Slavery Convention, which also extended to persons of 'servile status' the international protection against 'institutions and practices similar to slavery', such as debt bondage, serfdom, bride-purchase, inheritance or sale of wives, and child indenture (Preamble, articles 1 and 7(b)).[34]

It is a truism that these concepts of slavery or 'servile status', especially slaves *de jure* owned by their masters, do not correspond to the reality of the twenty-first century; thus, according to the preponderant view, it is not possible to equate victims of human trafficking to slaves, since the requisite element of *de jure* ownership is absent.[35] This notwithstanding, it has been argued that

> the locution of *'any or all* the[se] powers' implies that the definition in point covers not only situations where a perfect right of ownership exists, but also those human relationships characterized by the exercise by one person over another of only one of the two powers that compose the right of ownership itself.

In other words,

> all situations where an individual exercises the right of disposal or that of enjoyment of another person, in a way that it is reasonably suitable to withdraw personal freedom and the capacity of self-determination of the victim, entails a violation of the international prohibition of slavery.[36]

In the alternative, it could be argued that only one of the attributes of 'ownership', as for example the act of sale as such, would suffice to bring some victims of human trafficking today under the scope of the Slavery Convention.

Such arguments however, are not in accord with the literal interpretation of the terms of the Slavery Convention, as well as with the legal status of

---

[33] See Convention on Slavery (1927) 60 UNTS (1927), art 1.The first multilateral effort to call for suppression of the slave trade was the Declaration of the Eight Courts Relative to the Universal Abolition of Slave Trade, annexed as Act XV to the 1815 General Treaty of the Vienna Congress, done 8 February 1815, 63 CTS 473. It was followed by the Brussels Act of 2 July 1890, relative to the African Slave Trade. See also H Kern, 'Strategies of Legal Change: Great Britain, International Law and the Abolition of the Transatlantic Slave Trade' 6 *JHIL* (2004) 233 and P Morgan (ed), *Maritime Slavery* (London: Routledge, 2012).

[34] Supplementary Convention on the Abolition of Slavery, the Slave Trade, and Institutions and Practices Similar to Slavery; 266 UNTS (1957) 3 (hereinafter: Supplementary Slavery Convention). For academic commentary see M Schreiber, 'Convention supplémentaire des Nations Unies relative á l'abolition de l'esclavage' *AFDI* (1956) 555.

[35] See per this view G Bastid-Burdeau, 'Migrations Clandestines et Droit de la Mer', in *La Mer et Son Droit* (Paris: Pedone, 2003) 59. *Cf* also Guilfoyle, *Shipping Interdiction*, 76–77.

[36] F Lenzerini, 'Suppressing Slavery under Customary International Law' 10 *IYIL* (2000) 145, 160.

slaves prior to the adoption of the said Convention, which actually formed the raison d'être of the Convention. To sustain such arguments would presuppose that there are national legislations that allow or, at least, do not criminalise the 'ownership or the sale of human beings', which seems highly unlikely in contemporary legal orders.

In conclusion, it appears difficult to claim that today there is *de jure* ownership of persons, ie 'slavery' *stricto sensu* under the terms of the 1926 Slavery Convention. However, this is not the purpose of the present enquiry; the latter is rather to make the claim that amongst contemporary 'boat people' there are also victims of human trafficking, who might end up facing conditions of slavery.

2. An Evolutionary Interpretation of the Definition of Slavery

It may be questioned, in the first place, whether such persons can qualify as 'slaves' in a contemporary evolutionary perspective, and in the second, whether article 110(1)(b) of LOSC can lend itself to such interpretation so as to include also these persons.

On the first question, what will be contested is the argument that 'slavery' exists only within the legal parameters of the Slavery Convention, which is predominantly a matter of hermeneutics of the latter Convention. According to the pertinent canons of interpretation, the natural and ordinary meaning of 'ownership' will be the starting point, but it will be construed in the light of the context, the object and purposes of the treaty and a number of other considerations, like subsequent practice, treaties or relevant rules of international law.[37] In this vein, it is acknowledged that the object and purpose, which is, in any case, an essential element of treaty interpretation, attains even more importance in the case of treaties of a humanitarian character.[38] The Slavery Convention is a treaty of the latter character *par excellence* and hence its *ratio juris* that the drafters of the Convention sought to actualise, ie to abolish slavery and slave trade in all its manifestations in all parts of the world, should be primarily taken into account in its interpretation.

Furthermore, drawing insights from a theory of purposive interpretation, this must also reflect a more objective component, ie the social values prevalent at the time the treaty is interpreted, including values of morality and justice, social goals and human rights.[39] The latter are furnished by

[37] See arts 31–33 VCLT.

[38] The matter was addressed by the ICJ in *Reservations to the Convention on the Prevention and Punishment of the Crime of Genocide,* Advisory Opinion, ICJ Reports (1951) 23.

[39] According to its architect, A Barak, purposive interpretation is a general system of interpretation, whose goal is to achieve the purpose that the legal text is designed to achieve. It is based on three components: language, purpose and discretion. As far as the second is concerned, the purpose is the values, goals, interests, and policies and aims that the text is designed to actualise. See A Barak, *Purposive Interpretation in Law* (Princeton, NJ : Princeton University Press 2005).

subsequent developments as well as by the international legal environment at the time of the application of the treaty. The relevance of subsequent developments in treaty interpretation is also explicitly affirmed in article 31(3) of VCLT, which provides that any subsequent agreement or practice of the parties regarding the interpretation of the treaty must be taken into account, as well as any relevant rules of international law applicable in the relations between the parties. While a detailed examination of this issue is beyond the present compass, suffice it to refer to the relevant dictum of the ICJ in the *Namibia* case (1971), namely that 'an international instrument has to be interpreted and applied within the framework of the entire legal system prevailing at the time of the interpretation'.[40] This pronouncement in conjunction with other congruent judicial and scholar opinions[41] bolsters the thesis that the notion of slavery should not remain static, but, in contrast, is evolutionary and should be informed by the subsequent treaty and customary developments as well as by the exigencies of slavery in the twenty-first century.

3. Slavery and Slavery-like Practices Today

Although probably all states have outlawed 'slavery' and the 'slave trade', it is sad but true that chattel-slavery in the traditional sense still persists in isolated cases and regions of the world, for example in Mauritania and Sudan,[42] while slavery-like practices, including debt bondage,[43] forced labour,[44] trafficking in people for purposes of prostitution, exploitation of immigrant workers as domestic servants or slaves[45] are present in many

---

[40] *Legal Consequences for States of the Continued Presence of South Africa in Namibia (South West Africa) notwithstanding Security Council Resolution 276* (1970), Advisory Opinion, ICJ Reports (1971) para 53.

[41] See inter alia: the Dissenting Opinion of Judge Tanaka in the 1966 *South West Africa* cases, who observed that developments in customary international law were relevant to the interpretation of a treaty concluded 40 years previously, particularly in view of the ethical and humanitarian purposes of the instrument in question; at 293. See also H Thirlway, 'The Law and Procedure of ICJ, 1960-89, (Part Three)' 62 *BYIL* (1992) 47.

[42] See Report of the Working Group on Contemporary Forms of Slavery 1996, UN ESCOR (48th Session), paras 96–100 and S Menefee, 'The Maritime Slave Trade in 21st Century' 7 *ILSA Journal of International and Comparative Law* (2001) 508.

[43] Debt bondage is defined in art 1(b) of the Supplementary Slavery Convention as the 'status or condition arising from a pledge by a debtor of his personal services or of those of a person under his control as security for a debt'. It is practised more often in the Indian subcontinent and today it is the most common form of slavery in the world; see K Bales, *Disposable People: New Slavery in the Global Economy* (Berkeley, CA: University of California Press, 2004) 60.

[44] Forced labour is defined by the 1930 Forced Labour Convention and the 1957 Abolition of Forced Labour Convention as 'all work or service which is exacted from any person under the menace of any penalty and for which the said person has not offered himself voluntarily'.

[45] The Parliamentary Assembly of the CoE in its Recommendation No 1663 (adopted on 22 June 2004) described domestic slavery as follows: 'Today's slaves are predominantly female and usually work in private households, starting out as migrant domestic workers, au pairs or "mail-order brides".' See also Recommendation No 1523 (2001), adopted on

parts of the world.[46] Reflecting this reality, the UN established the Working Group on Contemporary Forms of Slavery in 1988 (Working Group), which included in its agenda all the aforementioned practices, qua 'manifestations of contemporary forms of slavery'.[47] In addition, it explicitly designated forced labour as a contemporary form of slavery.[48]

In September 2007, the Human Rights Council established a new mandate on contemporary forms of slavery, including its causes and consequences. This mandate provided for a Special Rapporteur on Contemporary Forms of Slavery who would replace the Working Group in order to better address the issue of contemporary forms of slavery within the United Nations system.[49] The mandate on contemporary forms of slavery, which was renewed on 5 December 2010,[50] includes, but is not limited to, issues such as: debt bondage, serfdom, forced labour, child slavery, sexual slavery, forced or early marriages and the sale of wives.[51] Until now, Special Rapporteur Gulnara Shahinian has issued various reports on her missions to countries, such as Mauritania and Peru,[52] and two annual thematic Reports, the first on Domestic Servitude (2010)[53] and the second on Child Slavery in the artisanal mining and quarrying sector (2011).[54]

In these Reports, she openly acknowledges that, on the one hand, 'children working in artisanal mines and quarries are subject to a series of

26 June 2001 available at www.echr.coe.int. Especially acute is the problem of children in domestic work. For example, the ILO reports that 175,000 children under 18 are employed in domestic service in Central America, more than 688,000 in Indonesia, 53,942 children under 15 in South Africa and 38,000 children between five and seven in Guatemala; see at www.ilo. org/ipec/areas/Childdomesticlabour/lang--en/index.htm.

[46] Estimations with regard to the numbers of people subject to contemporary forms of slavery differ from 27 million to 200 million. See with regard to the scourge of modern slavery K Bales, *Disposable People – New Slavery in the Global Economy* (Berkeley: University of California Press, 1999).

[47] See 'Contemporary Forms of Slavery', Commission on Human Rights, Res 1999/46, available at http://ap.ohchr.org/documents/E/CHR/resolutions/E-CN_4-RES-1999-46. doc and the last Report of the Working Group (2006), available at http://daccessdds.un. org/doc/UNDOC/GEN/G06/136/76/PDF/G0613676.pdf?OpenElement.

[48] See the first reference in 1994/5 Report of the Working, available at http://ap.ohchr.org/ documents/E/SUBCOM/resolutions/E-CN_4-SUB_2-RES-1994-5.doc. See also Y Rassam, above n 3, 341.

[49] UN Human Rights Council, Resolution 6/14 (28 September 2007); available at http:// ap.ohchr.org/documents/E/HRC/resolutions/A_HRC_RES_6_14.pdf.

[50] UN Human Rights Council, Resolution 15/2 (5 October 2010); available at http://daccess-dds-ny.un.org/doc/UNDOC/GEN/G10/165/77/PDF/G1016577.pdf?OpenElement.

[51] See further information at www.ohchr.org/EN/Issues/Slavery/SRSlavery/Pages/ SRSlaveryIndex.aspx.

[52] See further information at www.ohchr.org/EN/Issues/Slavery/SRSlavery/Pages/ CountryVisits.aspx.

[53] See Report of the Special Rapporteur on contemporary forms of slavery, including its causes and consequences, Gulnara Shahinian A/HRC/15/20 (18 June 2010); available at www.ohchr.org/Documents/Issues/Slavery/SR/A.HRC.15.20_en.pdf.

[54] See Report of the Special Rapporteur on contemporary forms of slavery, including its causes and consequences, Gulnara Shahinian A/HRC/18/30 (4 July 2011); available at www.ohchr.org/Documents/Issues/Slavery/SR/A-HRC-18-30_en.pdf.

violations of human rights and very often find themselves in conditions that amount to contemporary forms of slavery',[55] while on the other, 'domestic slavery, alongside other forms of slavery, still exists in parts of the world, notably in certain countries of the Sahel region of Western Africa'.[56] 'Although the victims are largely invisible, domestic servitude constitutes a global human rights concern. Every region in the world is affected. Domestic servitude takes many shape and forms, ranging from slavery as understood by the 1926 Slavery Convention to slavery-like practices, such as bonded domestic labour and child domestic labour.'[57] More importantly, she observes that 'slavery, practices similar to slavery and servitude are among the worst forms of exploitation that can result from trafficking'.[58] A similar statement is included in the Preamble of the 2005 Council of Europe Convention on Action against Trafficking in Human Beings, namely that 'trafficking in human beings may result in slavery for victims'.[59]

4. Other Treaty Prohibitions of Slavery and Slavery-like Practices

In addition to the Slavery Convention and its Supplementary Convention, prohibitions against slavery or against forcing people to such status, ie enslavement, can be found in numerous human rights treaties as well as in statutes of international criminal tribunals. These include inter alia article 8 of the ICCPR (1966),[60] article 4 of the ECHR (1950)[61] and article 6 of the ACHR (1969), which also proscribes traffic in women.[62] Furthermore, enslavement in general is explicitly prohibited and punished as crime against humanity, pursuant to article 5(c) of the Statute of the ICTY, article 3(c) of the Statute of the ICTR and last but not least article 7(2)(c) of the Rome Statute of ICC.[63] The majority of the above treaties provide for

---

[55] ibid, para 9.

[56] See above n 51, para 28.

[57] ibid, para 92.

[58] ibid, para 59.

[59] Council of Europe Convention on Action against Trafficking in Human Beings, Warsaw, 16 May 2005); Preamble; available at http://conventions.coe.int/Treaty/en/Treaties/Html/197.htm. The Explanatory Report accompanying this Convention states emphatically: 'Trafficking in human beings, with the entrapment of its victims, is the *modern form of the old worldwide slave trade*. It treats human beings as a commodity to be bought and sold, and to be put to forced labour, usually in the sex industry but also, for example, in the agricultural sector, declared or undeclared sweatshops, for a pittance or nothing at all' (emphasis added); available at www.coe.int/T/E/human_rights/trafficking/PDF_conv_197_trafficking_e.pdf.

[60] It sets forth that 'No one shall be held in slavery or servitude; slavery and the slave-trade in all their forms shall be prohibited; no one should be held in servitude. No one shall be required to perform forced and compulsory labour.'

[61] This provides that 'No one shall be held in slavery or servitude.'

[62] 'No one shall be subject to slavery or to involuntary servitude, which are prohibited in all their forms, as are the slave trade and traffic in women.'

[63] See art 7(2)(c) ICC Statute, A/CONF 183/9 (17 July 1998) (emphasis added). In addition, according to the relevant Elements of Crime, 'such deprivation of liberty may, in some circumstances, include exacting forced labour or otherwise reducing a person to a servile

supervisory mechanisms, which have occasionally addressed the present issue[64] and held that even if there is not *de jure* slavery in the post-World War era, there have certainly been many instances, in which people have been subject to conditions of servile status.

In the international criminal law context, reference should be made, first, to *Pohl and Others*, where a US Military Tribunal linked forced labour, even though it was not included in the Nuremberg Charter, to enslavement in the following statement: 'Slavery may exist without torture. Slaves may be well fed and well clothed and comfortably housed, but they are slaves if without lawful process they are deprived of their freedom by forceful restraint.'[65] More recently, the ICTY had the opportunity to pronounce on the issue of enslavement in the cases of *Kunarac* and *Foca*. In more detail, in the former, the Trial Chamber held that enslavement as a crime against humanity included trafficking of human beings,[66] while, in the latter, Stankovic and others were accused by the ICTY Prosecutor of enslavement for the detention of their victims in a house against their will.[67]

Moving to the human rights context, in the renowned case of *Siliadin v France* (2005), the ECtHR found that the applicant, a Togolese citizen, who had arrived in France in 1994 at the age of 15 and worked as a domestic servant for several years in a household in Paris under appalling working conditions, was held in servitude, which 'in the light of the case-law on this issue . . . means an obligation to provide one's services that is imposed by the use of coercion, and is *to be linked with the concept of* "slavery"'.[68]

status . . . It is also understood that the conduct described in this element includes trafficking in persons, in particular women and children'; see RS Lee (ed), *The ICC, Elements of Crimes and Rules of Procedure and Evidence* (Ardsley, NY: Transnational Publishers, 2001) 84. See also V Oosterveld, 'Sexual Slavery and the ICC' 25 Michigan JIL (2003) 605.

[64] It may be fitting to underline here that these courts or tribunals have treated 'slavery' and slavery-like practices within their own setting and not as a general matter of international law and thus there must be due regard to what conclusions are drawn from these pronouncements.

[65] *Trial of Oswald Pohl and Others*, US Military Tribunal, quoted in MM Whiteman, *Digest of International Law* (Washington, DC: Department of State publications, 1968) 905.

[66] The accused was convicted of enslavement for the detention of women for one to three months during which the women were forced to perform household chores, before some of them were sold to other Serb soldiers; see *Prosecutor v Kunarac* (trial judgment) IT-96-23 (22 Feb 2001) 542.

[67] See *Gagovic and Others*, Case No IT-96-23 (Indictment of 26 June 1996), paras 10.6–10.8. See also *Krnojelac*, ICTY Tr Ch, II 15.03.2002, paras 193–95.

[68] See *Siliadin v France* App no 73316/01 (ECtHR, 26 July 2005), para 124. In reaching this conclusion, the Court stressed that 'reference should be made to the relevant international conventions in this field . . . for identifying modern forms of slavery and servitude, which were closely linked to trafficking in human beings, and to the internationally recognised necessity of affording children special protection on account of their age and vulnerability; para 91.

Also, in another landmark judgment, *Rantsev v Cyprus and Russia (2010)*, the Strasbourg Court unanimously ruled that human trafficking fell within the scope of art 4 of the Convention.[69] In more detail, it held that

> trafficking in human beings, by its very nature and aim of exploitation, is based on the exercise of powers attaching to the right of ownership. It treats human beings as commodities to be bought and sold and put to forced labour, often for little or no payment, usually in the sex industry but also elsewhere . . . In view of its obligation to interpret the Convention in light of present-day conditions, the Court considers it unnecessary to identify whether the treatment about which the applicant complains constitutes 'slavery', 'servitude' or 'forced and compulsory labour'. Instead, the Court concludes that trafficking itself, within the meaning of Article 3(a) of the Palermo Protocol and Article 4(a) of the Anti-Trafficking Convention, falls within the scope of Article 4 of the Convention.[70]

In addition, the Court clarified the positive obligations upon states to investigate allegations of trafficking and to implement measures to prevent and protect people from human trafficking.

Reference should also be made to a 2008 judgment of the Economic Community of West African States Court of Justice ordering the Government of Niger to pay compensation to a former domestic 'slave' sold to her 'master' at the age of 12 and made to work for almost 10 years.[71] Although slavery in Niger is criminalised, national courts did not recognise the plaintiff's right to be free from her 'master' and marry another man.[72]

5. Conclusions: Contemporary Slavery and Human Trafficking

To conclude, it is evident from the foregoing that 'slavery' in its contemporary forms still persists in the world. The common denominator between the old and the new slavery is that people are enslaved by violence and held against their wills for purposes of exploitation. Even though modern slaves do not encounter a de jure control over their lives – not ownership in the classic sense, as this has been almost universally proscribed, they certainly do suffer a de facto control – a deprivation of part or all of their juridical personality, which very often engenders the same heinous result. It follows that at least certain severe aspects of practices, such as debt bondage, which was also included in the Supplementary Slavery Convention, domestic servitude and forced labour, as well as

---

[69] See *Rantsev v Cyprus and Russia* [2010] ECHR 25965/04 (7 January 2010) and commentary in J Allain, '*Rantsev v Cyprus and Russia*: the European Court of Human Rights and Trafficking as Slavery' 10 *Human Rights Law Review* (2010) 546.

[70] ibid, paras 281–82.

[71] *Hadijatou Mani Koraou v The Republic of Niger* App no ECW/CCJ/APP/08/08; Judgment no ECW/CCJ/JUD/06/08 (Economic Community of West African States, Community Court of Justice, 27 October 2008).

[72] See also above n 49, para 29.

child slavery, may qualify as 'slavery' in a contemporary perspective. In addition, the same holds true for the trafficking or even the smuggling of human beings, when the traffickers not only smuggle but also subsequently exploit their victims to the extent of forced labour or domestic servitude.[73] This does not mean, however, that human trafficking is equated to slavery, but that human trafficking may often result in slavery for its victims. As Jean Allain rightly underscores, 'where the elements of the definition of trafficking in persons overlap with the definition of slavery, then the act of trafficking will breach a *jus cogens* norm, but not because it is manifestly an act of trafficking in persons, but because it is slavery'.[74]

6. The Right of Visit in the Fight against Contemporary 'Slave Trade' on the High Seas

Having addressed the first and the most important question, that is, whether victims of human trafficking or of similar practices can become, under certain conditions, slaves, the next question is whether their traffic can come within the purview of the boarding provision of article 110(1)(b) of LOSC. To respond in the affirmative, it must be substantiated that the traffic in question is included in the interpretation of the term 'slave trade' in article 110. Such an interpretive approach, apart from the other requirements of article 31(1) VCLT, would inevitably have to take into account the 'relevant rules of international law applicable in the relations between the parties'. This means all the treaties and customary law that deal with slavery and slave trade, which, even though they are not part of the LOSC per se, are imported to its interpretation, in line with the provision of article 31(3)(c) VCLT.[75]

This also reflects the approach of the members of the ILC when they drafted the High Seas Convention and *in concreto* the article on the prohibition of slave trade.[76] Noteworthy in this regard is that the states involved

[73] This view is not without support in the academic literature; see C Brolan, 'An Analysis of the Human Smuggling Trade and the Smuggling Protocol' 14 *IJRL* (2002) 579; J Morrison and B Crosland, 'The Trafficking and Smuggling of Refugees', 62; available at www.unhcr.org/research/RESEARCH/3af66c9b4.pdf; M Jacobson, 'Maritime Security: an Individual or Collective Responsibility?', in J Petman and J Klabbers (eds) *Nordic Cosmopolitanism* (Leiden: Martinus Nijhoff, 2006) 391, 409. Silvia Scarpa has put forward the absolute thesis that trafficking in persons is a 'new form of slavery'; see ibid, *Trafficking in Human Beings: Modern Slavery* (Oxford: Oxford University Press, 2008). See also the following recent studies: J Quirk, *The Anti-Slavery Project: From the Slave Trade to Human Trafficking* (Philadelphia, PA: Pennsylvania University Press, 2011) and A Brysk and A Choi-Fitzpatrick (eds), *From Human Trafficking to Human Rights: Reframing Contemporary Slavery* (Philadelphia, PA: Pennsylvania University Press, 2012).
[74] J Allain, 'Book Review of S Scarpa, *Trafficking in Human Beings: Modern Slavery*' 20 *EJIL* (2009) 456.
[75] This is also the interpretation ascribed to by Nordquist, *Commentary*, 239.
[76] This reference to both the work of the ILC and to the First UNCLOS does not purport to equate them as the relevant *travaux préparatoires*. To the contrary, it is solely the work of the

espoused almost verbatim the draft article proposed by the Commission.[77] The latter made reference to an array of treaties prohibiting slavery and slave trade, in order to frame the pertinent provision.[78] In addition, during the meetings of ILC in 1956, the Special Rapporteur explicitly referred to the Commission's articles on the Supplementary Convention as 'in conformity with the relevant parts of the draft to be submitted to the Conference'.[79] Hence, the ILC was mindful of the existence of other institutions and practices analogous to slavery, whose trade might be subjected to the boarding powers of the parties to the Geneva Convention. Finally, a subtle yet very important detail is that in the final report, the Special Rapporteur mentioned only the 1890 Brussels Act, which granted boarding powers to the state parties, and not the Slavery Convention, which was silent on the latter point.[80] The conclusion to be drawn accordingly is that, as far as the ILC was concerned, all the 'relevant international law' and not only the Slavery Convention conduced to the elaboration of the provision in question; a fortiori this should also be the case in its interpretation.

On the other hand, it is true that the participating states in both UNCLOS I and III were not equally open to the broadening of the relevant definitions. In more detail, there was a proposal during UNCLOS I by Philippines to 'bring [draft] article 37 in line with the Convention on the Abolition of Forced Labour', since the latter reflected 'a very real danger at the present time'.[81] However, this isolated proposal was rejected. Furthermore, before UNCLOS III, there was a working paper by Malta at the 1971 session of the Sea-Bed Committee, which contained a new draft article, with a reference, among many others, to the presence of 'slaves or persons in conditions akin to slavery in the vessel'.[82] Nevertheless, this proposal was not accepted, perhaps due to the general reticence of the pertinent Committee to bring about many changes to the corpus of the 1958 High Seas Convention.[83]

Conference, which qualifies as *travaux* proper; however, the plain fact that the negotiating states took as a point of reference the proposed text of the ILC, to which they made slight modifications, gives an increased weight to the latter.

[77] The ILC addressed the prohibition of the transport of slaves in draft art 37. On the discussion at UNCLOS I, who brought about slight modifications to the above draft article, see Report of the Second Committee, A/CONF 13/L 17 (1958), paras 33 and 34.

[78] See eg the preliminary Report of the Special Rapporteur in 1950, which invoked the pertinent provisions of the 1890 Brussels Act, of the Convention of Saint-Germain (1919), as well as of the 1926 Convention; see *YbILC* (1950-II), 41.

[79] See Report of the International Law Commission to the GA, 11 GAOR Supp (No 9), 37.

[80] It is patent from both the 1926 and 1956 Conventions that neither of them contained a boarding provision, even though there were relevant proposals to this end, mainly by the crusader against slave trade, Great Britain. See the pertinent remarks by Sohn, above n 26, 56.

[81] See [First] UNCLOS *Official Records*, Vol IV, 21.

[82] See A/AC 138/53, art 25, reproduced in SBC Report 1971, 105, 125 (Malta).

[83] See Nordquist, *Commentary*, 239.

These cases notwithstanding, there is certainly room in legal doctrine for the proposition that the provisions of LOSC should be informed by the contemporary evolution of the terms in question. This drives also support from the application of article 31(3)(c) of VCLT in a number of recent judicial decisions,[84] with a view to advancing a systemic integration of international law rather than an unlimited fragmentation.[85] Suffice to note, for our purposes, the decision of the ICJ in the *Oil Platforms* case (2003), where it interpreted the provision of article XX of the 1955 Treaty of Amity, Economic Relations and Consular Rights between the United States and Iran in light of the law on use of force, as it has been currently moulded, ie almost 50 years after the latter treaty.[86]

It seems reasonable to infer from this case that the LOSC should be interpreted in the light of the contemporary legal meaning of the terms slavery and slave trade and not only in the light of the meaning when the LOSC was drafted. Therefore, the above remarks with regard to the subsequent developments in law and the current legal parameters of slavery and slave trade become germane to the interpretation of this provision. This is also in keeping with another principle of treaty interpretation, namely the principle of effectiveness (*'ut res magis valeat quam pereat'*).[87] This entails that the interpreter of any treaty provision, *in casu* of article 110 (1) (b), should aim at this interpretation, which would give full effect to the provision concerned, *ergo* at the interpretation that will most effectively suppress slave trade on the high seas.

Reportedly one such case was the *MV Etireno*, 'which in April 2001 sailed for several days near West African coasts with its mysteriously disappeared burden of more than two hundred slave children to be sold to cotton and cocoa plantations in countries such as Gabon and Ivory Coast'.[88] Although the Benin government called for international assistance in locating the

---

[84] Such cases are inter alia: (a) ITLOS: the *Mox Plant* case (*Ireland v United Kingdom*) – Request for Provisional Measures Order (3 Dec 2001); PCA: Dispute Concerning Access to Information under Article 9 of the OSPAR Convention Final Award (2 July 2003) 42 ILM 1118; (b) the WTO United States: Import Prohibition of certain Shrimp and Shrimp Products – Report of the Appellate Body (12 Oct 1998) WT/DS58/AB/R; (1999) 38 ILM 118; (c) the ECHR decisions on the relationship between the right of fair trial and state immunity in *Al-Adsani v UK* 123 (2001) 34, and in *Fogarty v UK* 123 ILR 54 (2001).

[85] This very critical issue is beyond the compass of the present paper; see however C McLachlan, 'The Principle of Systemic Integration and Article 31(3)(c) of the VCLT' 54 ICLQ (2005) 279.

[86] See *Oil Platforms* (*Islamic Republic of Iran v United States of America*), judgment, ICJ Reports (2003), para 79.

[87] Here the principle of effectiveness is more intertwined with *'la régle de l'efficacité'*, ie, the rule that the instrument as a whole, and each of its provisions, must be taken to have been intended to achieve some end and that an interpretation which would make the text ineffective to achieve the object in view is prima facie suspect. See H Thirlway, 'The Law and Procedure of ICJ, 1960-89, (Part Three)' 62 *BYIL* (1992) 43, 44.

[88] See 'Benin Seeks Help Over "Slave" Ship', BBC News, 16 April 2001; available at http://news.bbc.co.uk/hi/english/world/africa/newsid_1276000/1276620.stm; see also Lenzerini, above n 37, 179.

ship, it was not boarded at sea but was forced to return after being refused entry to ports in Gabon and Cameroon.[89]

In conclusion, the provision of article 110(1)(b) of LOSC may afford the requisite legal basis for the right to visit on the high seas vessels reasonably suspected of transporting slaves in the contemporary meaning of the term. Such persons may be victims of human trafficking, who may end up facing conditions of slavery, such as domestic servitude. This has been corroborated by a series of UN and CoE documents as well as judgments of regional human rights bodies.

However, it should be underlined that due to the lack of the ownership trait of traditional slavery in its contemporary forms, it might be difficult in reality to board the suspected vessels without solid information about the future of these persons in the destination country. It is in this regard that any boarding on this basis should be based on concrete intelligence, beyond the standard of mere suspicion, that the people on board will definitely be exploited as modern slaves.[90] This may happen, apart from the isolated cases of chattel slavery, when there is a corroborated pattern of sea borne transportation of people from one place to another to work under conditions of servitude and be exploited by criminal organisations, against which there are proofs that they profit from these heinous activities.

Finally, it should be stressed once again that states have to fulfil their obligations under human rights treaties concerning the prohibition of slavery and slave trade and that there is nothing in the LOSC to intrinsically prevent an evolutive interpretation of the notion of slavery. Slavery does exist in the twenty-first century, and it falls upon states to suppress the slave trade on the high seas by asserting the interdiction powers under article 110(1)(b) of LOSC.

ii. Other Multilateral Treaties: Smuggling Protocol (2000) and 2008 CARICOM Agreement

The sole multilateral treaty providing for the right to visit on the high seas for counter-migration purposes is the Smuggling Protocol. However, the first multilateral effort to regulate the issue at hand was the Interim Measures Circular of the IMO (1998). In more detail, it was in the late 1990s when Italy, in parallel with its own bilateral initiatives with Albania, appealed to the IMO for a multilateral legal instrument to be created to deal specifically with smuggling people at sea.[91] In response, the Assembly

---

[89] Guilfoyle, *Shipping Interdiction*, 77.

[90] Such information on human trafficking routes or patterns can be authoritatively derived from the UN Office on Drugs and Crimes; see UNODC, Toolkit to Combat Trafficking in Persons (UN, 2008); available at www.unodc.org/documents/human-trafficking/Toolkit-files/07-89375_Ebook[1].pdf.

[91] See Gallagher, above n 11, 483.

of the IMO adopted on 27 November 1997 Resolution A867(20) on 'Combating Unsafe Practices Associated with the Trafficking or Transport of Migrants by Sea'. This resolution was followed, in 1998 by a Circular of the Maritime Safety Committee on Interim Measures for Combating Unsafe Practices Associated with the Trafficking or Transport of Migrants by Sea.[92]

Although the measures adopted were of recommendatory nature and therefore non-binding upon the parties,[93] it served as the forerunner for the Smuggling Protocol adopted two years later. The latter protocol is extensively based on the IMO Circular, and it was the outcome of a process that started from 1994.[94] In general, the Smuggling Protocol is designed to fight cross-border crimes by obliging signatories to adopt national legislative measures, to open information channels and to promote cooperation in enforcement of international law.

As far as the boarding provision of the Smuggling Protocol is concerned, it should be noted at the outset, that it reproduces the provision in the IMO Circular (para 12), while it is modelled upon article 17 of the Vienna Convention. *In casu*, the relevant measures are to be enforced against a vessel suspected of being engaged in the smuggling of migrants and may include measures against masters or crews involved in the smuggling.[95] However, since measures are to be enforced against a vessel, measures under the Protocol may not be undertaken against stowaways, a situation in which the vessel as a unit is not engaged in the illicit activity.[96] The right to visit as such of a foreign-flagged vessel is stipulated in article 8(2) as follows:

> A State Party that has reasonable grounds to suspect that a vessel exercising freedom of navigation in accordance with international law and flying the flag or displaying the marks of registry of another State Party is engaged in the smuggling of migrants by sea may so notify the flag State, request confirmation of registry and, if confirmed, request authorisation from the flag State to take appropriate measures with regard to that vessel. The flag State may authorise the requesting State, *inter alia*: (a) To board the vessel; (b) To search the vessel; and (c) If evidence is found that the vessel is engaged in the smuggling of

---

[92] See IMO Maritime Safety Committee, Interim Measures for Combating Unsafe Practices Associated with the Trafficking or Transport of Migrants by Sea (adopted on 16 December 1998) (hereinafter: IMO, Interim Measures).

[93] For an overview and a drafting history of the relevant IMO Resolutions, see R Pedrozo, 'International Initiatives to Combat Trafficking of Migrants by Sea', in M Nordquist, J Moore (eds), *Oceans Policy: New Institutions, Challenges and Opportunities* (The Hague: Martinus Nijhoff, 1999) 53.

[94] See above Introduction (n 9).

[95] The *travaux préparatoires* of the Protocol indicate that the word 'engaged' in art 9 should be understood broadly as including vessels 'engaged' both directly and indirectly in the smuggling of migrants; see UN Ad Hoc Committee on the Elaboration of a Convention against Transnational Organized Crime Interpretative Notes, para 100.

[96] See Hinrichs, 428.

migrants by sea, to take appropriate measures with respect to the vessel and persons and cargo on board, as authorized by the flag State.

Obviously, under this provision, any action against a foreign vessel on the high seas must be based on the express flag state authorisation. Neither tacit consent, nor simply the consent of the master of the vessel, is sufficient to trigger article 8(2) of the Protocol. This must be read against the background of the previously analysed treaty regimes with regard to drug trafficking and proliferation of WMD, where there are bilateral and multilateral agreements, which provide for the tacit consent model. This kind of requirement *ratione temporis* is not found in article 8(2), even though there is an obligation incumbent upon the state parties to 'respond expeditiously to a request from another State Party' (para 4), as well as to 'designate an authority or, where necessary, authorities for this purpose (para 6).

Furthermore, the requesting State shall take no additional measures without the express authorisation of the flag State, except those necessary to relieve imminent danger to the lives of persons or those which derive from relevant bilateral or multilateral agreements' (para 5). This provision shall be read in conjunction with article 17 of the Protocol, which encourages the state parties to conclude bilateral or regional agreements to suppress smuggling of migrants.[97] To the knowledge of the author, no such agreement has so far been concluded.[98] As far as the *ratione loci* parameters of the right of visit enshrined in article 8(2) are concerned, they are identical to the Vienna Convention, ie the ship must be located beyond the outer limit of the territorial sea for an authorisation to be requested from the flag state to board the vessel.

Finally, reference should be made to another multilateral treaty that provides for interception of vessels carrying migrants or other human beings. This is the all-encompassing 2008 CARICOM Agreement, which includes within its *ratione materiae* scope, on the one hand 'illicit traffic in persons' in article I(2)(a) and on the other, 'illegal immigration' in article I(2)(e). It is assumed that the former pertains to the act of 'human trafficking' and the latter to the 'smuggling of migrants'. Again, no further definition is provided in the text, or the requirement for the adoption of relevant legislative measures. As regards the interception measures, they include operations on the high seas, operations in the waters of the coastal states and routine security patrols.[99]

---

[97] This provision is again modelled on art 17 of the Vienna Convention.

[98] It might be argued that the bilateral treaties of Spain with Senegal and Mauritania, which postdate the Smuggling Protocol, correspond to the agreements envisaged above. Nonetheless, apart from not referring at all to the latter Protocol, they do not exclusively deal with smuggling of migrants. See below.

[99] On the content of these provisions see the relevant discussion under Ch 5 and Ch 7.

iii. Bilateral Treaties

Following the legacy of the bilateral treaties signed by Great Britain and other states for the suppression of slave trade in the nineteenth century,[100] there has recently been a number of bilateral agreements concerning the suppression of illegal migration, which provide for, among others, the right to board vessels on the high seas. As was noted in Chapter 2, it seems that the latter agreements are the continuation of the slave-trade boarding agreements in the twenty-first century, since they share the same *ratio juris*: the enforcement of public policy in the form of 'international morals'. Nevertheless, they might have their historical roots in the slavery agreements, yet they resemble more the practice of bilateral counter-drug agreements. This holds true since both the counter-migration and counter-drugs agreements share parallel 'negative' purposes, ie they both aim at hindering the illicit flow of persons or narcotic drugs respectively as well as at maintaining the public order of international society. In addition, they both use more or less the same interception procedures and very often are concluded jointly.

a. The US Agreements

It is a truism that the majority of these agreements have been concluded by the US. What historically propelled the US action and led to the conclusion of the first agreement of this type was the Haitian exodus.[101] Following an Executive Order by President Reagan initiating the Haitian Migrant Interdiction Operation, the US concluded a bilateral agreement with Haiti on 23 September 1981, in the form of an Exchange of Letters relating to the Establishment of a Cooperative Program of Interdiction and Selective Return of Certain Haitian Migrants and Vessels.[102] The Agreement applied to private Haitian vessels on the high seas, and permitted the US authorities to exert the right of visit when there was reason to believe that such vessels were involved in the irregular carriage of passengers outbound from Haiti. The US had permission to board such vessels to determine their registry, condition and destination, as well as to determine the status of those on board. When the circumstances suggested that a violation of

---

[100] It is an interesting query to pose whether these treaties are still in force. The proper answer must be that they were limited *ratione temporis* and possibly *ratione materiae* and since the transatlantic slave trade ceased to exist, as we knew it, the treaties must have been equally extinct. This might be a case, in which the doctrine of obsolescence or desuetude does apply.

[101] From the abundant academic literature on the Haitian interception policy and its legal repercussions, see inter alia: B Frelick, 'Haitian Boat Interdiction and Return' 26 *Cornell Journal of International Law* (1993) 675; D Martin, 'Interdiction, Intervention and the New Frontiers of Refugee Law' 33 *Virginia Journal of International Law* (1993) 473.

[102] See 33 UST (1981) 3559.

US immigration laws had been or was being committed, the vessel and persons on board could be detained and returned to Haiti upon prior notification to the Haitian government. Therefore, not only the right to visit, but also further rights were accorded to the US authorities in the light of this agreement, such as the right fully to exercise its enforcement jurisdiction in this regard, ie arrest and detention on the high seas. This agreement afforded the legal basis for an extensive programme of interdictions effectuated concerning Haitians between 1981 and 1994.[103] However, upon his return to power in 1994, President Aristide terminated the Agreement according to its terms.[104] This certainly casts doubt on the legality of the latest Operation Able Sentry, starting in February 2004.[105] Absent an agreement to this effect, the interdiction operations, which took place on the high seas, off the coast of Haiti, seem to be on a tenuous legal ground.

This agreement is not the only which the US have concluded in the broader Caribbean area. After a certain period of extended interdiction operations on unstable legal ground,[106] they reached an agreement with Cuba, namely the US-Cuba Joint Communiqué on Migration (9 September 1994). It enunciated inter alia that 'The two governments will take effective measures in every way they possibly can to oppose and prevent the use of violence by any persons seeking to reach, or who arrive in, the US from Cuba by forcible diversions of aircraft and vessels'.[107] Besides Cuba, the US has similar agreements with the Dominican Republic (May 2003),[108] Bahamas (2004)[109] and Ecuador.[110] Also, very recently US extended their cooperation in this respect with Suriname, the Netherlands Antilles and Aruba (January 2006).[111]

---

[103] Approximately 25,000 Haitian migrants were interdicted in the period between 1981 and 1991. After Haitian President Aristide was overthrown in 1991, there was another series of interdictions by virtue of Executive Orders 12,587 (1992) and 12,807 (1992), presumably issued on the same legal basis, ie the 1981 Agreement. See GW Palmer, 'Guarding the Coast: Alien Migrant Interdiction Operations at Sea', in MN Schmitt (ed), *The Law of Military Operations* (Newport, RI: Naval War College Press, 1998) 165.

[104] See Palmer, ibid, 177 (fn 33).

[105] In this Operation, at least 905 Haitians were intercepted off Haiti and returned to Port-au-Prince. See in this respect Van Selm and Cooper, 76. The operation was in force at least until 2006; see S Legomsky, 'The USA and the Caribbean Interdiction Program' 18 *IJRL* (2006) 677, 682.

[106] See eg Operation Able Vigil discussed in Van Selm and Cooper, 79.

[107] See also the Cuba-US Joint Statement on the Normalization of Migration, Building on the Agreement of Sept. 9, 1994, May 2, 1995, 35 ILM (1995) 327. For further comments see Palmer, above, n 103.

[108] See US-Dominican Republic Agreement.

[109] See US-Bahamas Agreement.

[110] See US–Ecuador Agreement.

[111] In January 2006, Suriname, the Netherlands Antilles, and Aruba signed a Mutual Legal Assistance Agreement allowing for direct law enforcement and judicial cooperation between the countries; see www.state.gov/p/inl/rls/nrcrpt/2007/vol1/html/80857.htm.

b. European Agreements

1. The Italian Practice

However, such migration interdiction agreements are found also in the European milieu and more specifically in the Mediterranean Sea. Italy has been very active in seeking cooperation with other neighbouring countries in order to tackle illicit immigration.[112] First, in mid-1990s, when Italy was faced with a major influx of immigrants from Albania, it concluded an agreement with Albania with an Exchange of Notes of 25 March 1997 for the control and suppression of clandestine migration by sea.[113] It followed to a certain extent the US-Haiti Exchange of Letters and conferred the right upon the Italian Navy to stop Albanian vessels on the high seas and send them back to Albanian ports. The Italian Navy was also given the right to carry out its mission in Albanian territorial waters and to stop any private vessel, irrespective of its nationality. Thus, Albania effectively delegated to Italy its coastal State powers of preventing illicit migration. The Protocol of 2 April 1997 established the technical modalities applicable when the mission was carried out in Albania's territorial sea, which actually followed the pattern of shiprider agreements. The Italian Navy enjoyed the full scope of the right of visit as well as the jurisdiction to arrest and to divert.[114]

The most notable partnership of Italy in this regard, however, was with Libya. First, on 29 December 2007, Italy and Libya signed a bilateral cooperation agreement in Tripoli on the fight against clandestine immigration. On the same date the two countries signed an additional Protocol setting out the operational and technical arrangements for implementation of the said Agreement. Under Article 2 of the Agreement:

> Italy and the Great Socialist People's Libyan Arab Jamahiriya undertake to organise maritime patrols using six ships made available on a temporary basis by Italy . . . Surveillance, search and rescue operations shall be conducted in the departure and transit areas of vessels used to transport clandestine immigrants, both in Libyan territorial waters and in international waters, in compliance with the international conventions in force and in accordance with the operational arrangements to be decided by the two countries.

On 4 February 2009 Italy and Libya signed an Additional Protocol in Tripoli, intended to strengthen bilateral cooperation in the fight against clandestine immigration. That Protocol partially amended the agreement

---

[112] On the Italian practice vis-à-vis immigration in general see A Di Pascale, 'Migration Control at Sea: The Italian Case', in B Ryan and V Mitsilegas (eds), *Extraterritorial Immigration Control: Legal Challenges* (Leiden: Martinus Nijhoff, 2010) 281–310.

[113] For academic commentary see T Scovazzi, 'Le Norme di Diritto Internazionale sull'Immigrazione Illegale via Mare con Particolare Riferimento ai Rapporti tra Albania e Italia', in A de Guttry and F Pagani, *La Crisi Albanese del 1997* (Milano: Angeli, 1999) 239.

[114] See also Ronzitti, 1275.

of 29 December 2007, in particular through the inclusion of a new article, which stated:

> The two countries undertake to organise maritime patrols with joint crews, made up of equal numbers of Italian and Libyan personnel having equivalent experience and skills. The patrols shall be conducted in Libyan and international waters under the supervision of Libyan personnel and with participation by Italian crew members, and in Italian and international waters under the supervision of Italian personnel and with participation by the Libyan crew members.

On 30 August 2008 in Benghazi, Italy and Libya signed a Treaty on Friendship, Partnership and Cooperation, article 19 of which makes provision for efforts to prevent clandestine immigration in the countries of origin of migratory flows.[115]

This series of agreements served as the legal background for Italy's controversial 'push-back operations'. In nine push-back operations between 6 May and 6 November 2009, a total of 834 migrants intercepted in international waters were collectively and indiscriminately shipped to Libya by Italian border authorities, while 23 people were returned to Algeria.[116] Some of those people were the applicants in the *Hirsi* case before the ECtHR (2012).

With regard to the exact legal basis for these push-back operations, neither of these agreements expressly prescribed rules for the interception and deflection to Libya of seaborne migrants halted by Italian authorities on the high seas.[117] They referred only to the strengthening of their cooperation and to joint patrols, but there was no provision on interception by Italian warships on the high seas. However, in the 2009 push-backs, migrants were either shipped to Libya by Italian vessels, or transferred by Italian authorities onto Libyan vessels. On the other hand, the official position of the Italian government had consistently been that these interception operations on the high seas and the transfer of the people to Libya were conducted pursuant to the aforementioned agreements.[118]

---

[115] On these agreements see *Hirsi* case, paras 19–20.

[116] *Submission by the Office of the United Nations High Commissioner for Refugees in the Case of Hirsi and Others v Ital*, App no 27765/09 (ECtHR), 3. See also, CPT, Report to the Italian Government (2010).

[117] See inter alia A Terrasi, 'I Respingimenti in Mare di Migranti alla Luce della Convenzione Europea dei Diritti Umani' 3 *Diritti Umani e Diritto Internazionale* (2009) 591–607. See also, generally, S Trevisanut, 'Immigrazione Clandestina Via Mare e Cooperazione fra Italia e Libia dal Punto di Vista del Diritto del Mare' 3 *Diritti Umani e Diritto Internazionale* (2009) 609–20. The author is grateful to Ms Maria Giullia Giuffré for these articles and for information on the present topic.

[118] For instance, in a press conference on 7 May 2009, the Italian Minister of the Interior specifically posited that interception operations on the high seas and diversion of migrants to Libya followed the entry into force, on 4 February 2009, of the bilateral agreements with Libya. See A Kronos, *Immigrati, Maroni: 'L'accordo con la Libia funziona. Avanti con i respingimenti'* (Brussels: chiarimenti da Italia e Malta, 2009) www.adnkronos.com/IGN/News/Politica/?id=3.0.3718416369. See also *Hirsi* case, para 93.

It is the view of the present author that serious problems concerning the law of the sea could arise only in relation to vessels that were intercepted and were flying a third State's flag; for such vessels, there was no legal basis for interdiction. As far as the Libyan vessels were concerned, it could be argued that since Libya did not object to such interception, and to the contrary did accept the return of these people, any potential responsibility of Italy for acting beyond the bounds of these agreements was excused (article 47 ILC Articles). Finally, as regards stateless vessels, it is evident that the interception as such on the high seas was lawful, but it is questioned whether the return of these people pursuant to the 2008 Treaty included also people intercepted beyond the modalities of the said agreements. These remarks concerning the law of the sea dimension of the push-back operations are without prejudice to the concomitant responsibility of Italy under human rights law.[119]

Finally, pursuant to the agreement of technical and police cooperation concluded with Tunisia on 5 April 2011, Italy supplied its south Mediterranean partner with 12 new and refurbished patrol boats.[120] In turn, Tunisia committed itself to patrolling its coastal waters and accepting the repatriation of migrants who arrived in Italy after 6 April 2011 and removed from the country on the basis of accelerated identification procedures. On 21 August 2011, for example, 104 migrants were collectively returned to the ports of departure by means of the classified agreement between Italy and Tunisia.[121]

As to the interdiction procedure, it is reported that

> boats are usually sought by the Navy (*Marina Militare*), which informs the *Guardia di Finanza* (Tax and Customs Police) in charge of controlling irregular migration and defending national frontiers. These two bodies coordinate each other to watch over the crafts (called in military jargon 'targets'), check their route, their speed and their general conditions of navigation. Once a boat is supposed to be sailed away from Tunisia, it is reached by Navy or *Guardia di Finanza*'s vessels, which transfer migrants on Italian patrol boats and, then, on Tunisian guard ships.[122]

---

[119] Noteworthy is that the application of these agreements was suspended following the events in 2011; see *Hirsi* case, para 21. However, it is reported that on 15 December 2011, Italy and the new Benghazi-based Libyan National Transitional Council (NTC) reached an agreement on the reactivation of the Italy-Libya Friendship Treaty; see Italy-Libya: Reactivation of the Treaty of Friendship (15 Dec 2011) available at: www.esteri.it/MAE/EN/Sala_Stampa/ArchivioNotizie/Approfondimenti/2011/12/20111215_ItaliaLibiaTrattatoAmicizia.htm.

[120] See Italy-Tunisia Reach Migration Agreement: 6 Month Residency Permits for Tunisians Already in Italy; Accelerated Return Procedures for Newly Arriving Tunisians. *Migrants at Sea*, 6 April 2011.

[121] R Cosentino, 'Respingimenti in atto da mesi sulla rotta Tunisia-Lampedusa', 30 Aug 2011, *Terrelibere.org*, available at www.terrelibere.org/terrediconfine/respingimenti-in-atto-da-mesi-sulla-rotta-tunisia-lampedusa.

[122] ibid. The translation and the relevant information were kindly provided by Ms Giuffré, in a draft paper titled 'State Responsibility beyond Borders: What Legal Basis for Italy's Push-Backs to Libya?' 24 *IJRL* (2012) (forthcoming) (on file with the author).

2. The Spanish Practice and FRONTEX

There have been other relevant agreements in the European milieu, concluded by Spain, which are especially germane to interception operations coordinated by FRONTEX.[123] These agreements have furnished the principal legal basis for many FRONTEX Operations, such as HERA II, III and JO EPN HERA 2009 in the territorial waters of African states. The existence of such agreements is requisite for this kind of operations, since FRONTEX has not, as a matter of EU law, a mandate to operate beyond the external borders of the Union.[124] These operations take place in the territorial waters of third states; therefore, the consent of the coastal states is *sine qua non* for the entry and exercise of enforcement jurisdiction on the part of EU states.

In more detail, there have been two agreements between Spain and Mauritania and Spain and Senegal, both of which afforded the legal basis for Operation HERA II. In addition, according to a Memorandum of 19 October 2007 from the Spanish Embassy in London to the House of Lords, there is a third similar agreement in the form of a MoU between Spain and Cape Verde.[125] Nonetheless, it is regrettable that FRONTEX has not officially provided any further information about these agreements,[126] as well as that the Member States' agreements are often not publicly available. This actually undermines the legitimacy of these Operations and substantiates the argument for more transparency and public accountability of FRONTEX and its Operations.[127]

These agreements are, first, a recent MoU between Spain and Mauritania signed at Madrid on 16 October 2007, which provides for the active participation of Spanish authorities in the suppression of illicit migration from Mauritania, as well as in rescue-at-sea operations. Apart from technical assistance and coordination, Spain is also called to contribute with its officials or with its own vessels to the interdiction operations in Mauritania's internal and territorial waters.[128] It was preceded by an earlier agreement between the two states, which is, most probably, the bilateral agreement referred to by FRONTEX. Under that agreement, Spain

---

[123]   See above Introduction (n 60 and corresponding text).

[124]   art 1(4) of FRONTEX Regulation. See also Weinzierl and Lisson, 26.

[125]   The Memorandum states that 'Spain has signed MOUs with Senegal, Mauritania and Cape Verde so that they accept the deployment of Spanish or European forces on their territorial waters'; see HL Report, 243.

[126]   Both of these agreements have not been made publicly known by FRONTEX. In a communication with the author, FRONTEX has only stated that the pertinent Operations are based on existing bilateral agreements of Spain with Mauritania and Senegal, without giving any further information.

[127]   See European Council on Refugees and Exiles (ECRE) and British Refugee Council joint response to Select Committee on the European Union, Sub-Committee F (24 September 2007), at 12; available at www.ecre.org/resources/policy_papers/995 (hereinafter: ECRE/BRC Report).

[128]   See Spain-Mauritania MoU; Table of Cited Treaties.

and Mauritania had agreed to launch joint coastal patrols in order to avert the flow of thousands of immigrants to the Canary Islands, while Spain would give Mauritania four patrol vessels and would help train their crews.[129] In addition, there is the Agreement between Spain and Senegal signed in Dakar on 5 December 2006 'on co-operation in the field of the prevention of emigration by unaccompanied Senegalese minors, their protection and re-insertion'. The actions envisaged to fulfil the agreement's goals include, inter alia, controlling migrant smuggling rings.[130]

Assuming that the preceding agreements correspond to the bilateral treaties referred to by FRONTEX, it is still problematic that there are other states involved in these interdiction operations alongside Spain, which certainly raises questions with regard to the legal basis for their involvement. Even though FRONTEX and concomitantly EU Member States are entitled to provide assistance, for example, to Spain pursuant to article 8 of the FRONTEX Regulation, this does not alter the legal status of the agreements in question as bilateral and hence as *res inter alios acta* for the third states involved.[131] According to the relevant rules of international law, these agreements would have furnished the legal basis for the involvement of third states, had they provided for such a right to be exercised on the part of these states (article 36 of VCLT), in which case even tacit acquiescence on their behalf would suffice. Given that neither of these agreements, to the knowledge of the author, contains such provision, it could be alternatively and *ex hypothesis* maintained that either Senegal, Mauritania or Cape Verde have apparently consented on an ad hoc basis to this involvement of third states' vessels or, more controversially, that Spain has assigned part of its boarding powers to the latter states, without the consent of Senegal or Mauritania. However, the latter approach is not evidenced in state practice or in the academic doctrine and should, in principle, be rejected.[132]

It is rather the ad hoc agreements, either in written or oral form, between the North and West African states, mainly Senegal, and the other EU Member States, which grant the right to the latter states to intercept vessels

---

[129] See 17 *Resenha Migrações na Atualidade, No* 62 (Março 2006), 25 available at http://csem.org.br/pdfs/resenha62.pdf.

[130] See Spain-Senegal Agreement.

[131] See arts 34–38 of VCLT. The maxim *pacta tertiis nec nocent nec prosunt* expresses the fundamental principle that a treaty applies only between the parties to it. For academic literature see inter alia I Sinclair, *The Vienna Convention on the Law of Treaties*, 2nd edn (Manchester: Manchester University Press, 1984), 98.

[132] At the outset, it must be stressed that the Vienna Convention is silent on the assignment of treaty rights and also that assignment must be distinguished from *novation*, which denotes the substitution by a third state to a party's rights after an agreement between the initial parties to this effect; see McNair, above, 341. FA Mann concurs in his authoritative treatise of this matter that 'non-assignability is likely still to be the rule in international law and assignability the exception'; see 'The Assignability of Treaty Rights' in ibid, *Studies in International Law* (1973), 363.

in the formers' territorial waters.[133] These would often take the form of oral agreements between administrative agents of state parties, which, is has been consistently observed that even though they don't fall under the scope of VCLT, they are subject to the basic tenets of treaty law. It is important to stress here that the FRONTEX has the power under article 14(2) of FRONTEX Regulation to conclude 'working arrangements'. As was stated by the Executive Director of FRONTEX, General Laitinen, 'we do not establish a partnership with a country or a government but [between] the border control authority of that third country and Frontex'.[134] These 'partnerships' are, in principle, based on administrative or 'technical low-level agreements' between FRONTEX and a third non-Member State, which might take the form of Memoranda of Understanding or Technical Protocols. Provided that these Agreements are in written form and set forth international obligations incumbent upon the parties, they would fall under the scope of VCLT.[135] However, even though it seems that the contracting parties are virtually free as far as the adopted measures are concerned, it is according to *jus gentium* that all these agreements have to be construed restrictively and not open to broad and unfettered application.[136]

Conversely, the FRONTEX operations on the high seas are predominantly based on the search and rescue rules. Another tactic observed in this regard is that of diverting the vessel to the contiguous zone or territorial sea of an EU Member State, usually Spain, especially in the context of HERA II and III Operations, where enforcement jurisdiction can lawfully be exerted.[137] Nevertheless, this diversion of boats to a certain destination is indisputably a form of physical interference to the vessel; *ergo*, it must fulfil the conditions of the right to visit to be regarded lawful.

Rcently, the European Council issued Council Decision 2010/252/EU, supplementing the Schengen Borders Code as regards the surveillance of the maritime external borders in the context of the operational cooperation coordinated by Frontex.[138] According to its Preamble, the main objective of

---

[133] This is implied by the reference in the 2006 General Report of FRONTEX that 'informal contacts' have been established between the EU Member States and the African States; see Annual Report 2006, 13. It was also affirmed by FRONTEX officials in a conversation with the author under conditions of anonymity (30 January 2008).

[134] HL Report, at 46.

[135] See statement of Ms Coehlio (ECRE) in this respect in HL Report, 46.

[136] *cf* eg the *Wanderer* case.

[137] These remarks rely in one part on information provided by FRONTEX officials under conditions of anonymity (30 January 2008) and in other, on the Letter to the European Parliament by the Standing Committee of experts on international immigration, refugees and criminal law (the Meijers Committee); see HL Report, 235.

[138] Council Decision of 26 April 2010 supplementing the Shengen Borders Code as regards the surveillance of the sea external borders in the context of operational cooperation coordinated by the European Agency for the Management of Operational Cooperation at the External Borders of the Member States of the European Union (2010/252/EU) [2010] OJ L111/20, para 1.3, Part II, Annex, (hereinafter: 2010 Council Decision); see commentary by V Moreno Lax, 25 IJMCL (2010) 621. The Decision was very recently annulled by the

the Decision is to establish 'additional rules for the surveillance of the sea borders by border guards operating under the coordination of the [Frontex] Agency'. 'Henceforth, maritime surveillance operations conducted under the auspices of Frontex are to be governed by the binding rules contained in Part I of the Annex'.[139]

As far as operations on the high seas are concerned, by virtue of paragraph 2.5.2,

> where the vessel is encountered in the high seas beyond the contiguous zone, as a rule, the authorisation of the flag State to interdict the suspected ship is required. Pending the authorisation of the flag State, no other measures than those necessary to relieve imminent danger to the life of persons shall be taken.[140]

With regard to vessels with no nationality or assimilated to ships with no nationality,

> units participating in the joint patrol mission shall proceed to verify identity. If, after having checked the requisite documents, suspicion remains that the ship is in fact flagless, the participating unit concerned shall proceed to a full on-board examination. Where suspicion proves to be well founded and there are reasonable grounds to believe that the ship is involved in the smuggling of persons by sea, every participating unit must adopt suitable measures of interception.[141]

In general, these rules concerning maritime surveillance operations coordinated by FRONTEX are in line with international law of the sea.[142] Only the last point concerning stateless vessels is problematic, and more particularly the fact that it falls short of stipulating what kind of 'suitable measures of interception' Member States are called upon to adopt. To reiterate once again, it is the view of the present author that statelessness does not entail *ipso facto* the assertion of jurisdiction over persons on board. The Council Decision is not clear on what Member States are permitted to do, albeit it seems implying that also enforcement measures may be adopted. Although the European Court of Justice (ECJ) annulled Council Decision 2010/252, and thus also the guidelines therein, the ECJ decided that the effects of the Council Decision B have to be maintained until a new act can be adopted in accordance with ordinary legislative procedures.[143]

A different, yet very significant question in respect of the FRONTEX operations would be under whose jurisdiction these persons would fall,

---

Court of Justice of the EU; see ECJ, *European Parliament v Council of the European Union*, 5 September 2012, Case C-355/10 (2012).

[139] Moreno-Lax, ibid, 623.
[140] para 2.5.2.6, Part I, Annex, Supplementing Decision.
[141] para 2.5.2.5, ibid and V Moreno-Lax, above n 138, 624–25.
[142] On the surveillance operations of FRONTEX see J Coppens, 'Migrants in the Mediterranean: Do's and Don'ts in Maritime Interdiction' 43 *Ocean Development & International Law* (2012) 342, 356.
[143] See above n 139.

as well as whether the flag state or the coastal state would be responsible for any violation of international law.[144] The response to both questions would usually be given by the text of the relevant agreements, which would often set out the exclusive or concurrent jurisdictional powers and concomitantly responsibility of the flag or coastal state. Absent such treaty provision, it is submitted that, as far as the FRONTEX operations on the high seas are concerned, the default rule must be that they will be under the jurisdiction of the individual EU Member State, which proceeds to the interception in question. In the cases of joint patrols with the coastal state, the question of jurisdiction will be addressed on ad hoc basis and in accordance with the relevant rules on attribution of state conduct. Thus, the determinative factor would be whether the interception is carried out under the exclusive instructions of the coastal African state, which entails that the latter would be responsible under article 6 of the ILC Articles or the EU states' vessels retain their individual autonomy in this regard and incur their own responsibility.[145]

In the context of the RABIT operations, the principle is that the boarding party and its personnel will be subject to the national law and jurisdiction of the coastal or host state.[146] As far as the joint operations conducted under the 2011 FRONTEX Regulation, it is provided that such operations would be subject to an operational plan drawn by the Executive Director of FRONTEX and the host Member State, in consultation with the Member States participating in a joint operation,[147] while at the same time is set forth that

> The home Member State shall provide for appropriate disciplinary or other measures in accordance with its national law in case of violations of fundamental rights or international protection obligations in the course of a joint operation or pilot project.[148]

3. Concluding Thoughts

In conclusion, it is observed that these bilateral agreements and the Smuggling Protocol are markedly different in many respects. This is apparently the outcome of their different law-making procedure, ie the bilateral negotiations between a powerful state (eg the US) and weaker neighbouring countries for the former and the international setting of the IMO or of a multinational conference for the latter. Also, it is the result of their divergent objectives, namely, the ad hoc regulation of a massive flow of migrants (like a *traité-contrat*) in comparison with the imposition of

---

[144] See also relevant discussion in E Papastavridis, 'Fortress Europe and FRONTEX: Within or Without International Law?' 79 *Nordic JIL* (2010) 75, 91–92.
[145] See art 4 (de jure organs) of the ILC Articles.
[146] See arts 10 and 11 of the RABIT Regulation and also HL Report, 237.
[147] See art 3a para 1 of the 2011 FRONTEX Regulation.
[148] ibid, art 3 para 1a.

international criminal law obligations to states for the suppression of illicit exploitation of migration (like a *traité-loi*) respectively. Overall both these bilateral treaties and the Smuggling Protocol reflect the 'negative' aspect of interception since they focus predominantly on the suppression of the illicit migration. However, they consistently reflect the rationale behind their adoption as *mare clausum* exception to the *mare liberum*, namely the will of the states and a fortiori of the international community to regulate illicit immigration in the contemporary world politics.

B. Customary Law Bases for Interference

There was an extensive discussion above of the legal bases for the interception in question provided by the LOSC as well as by the relevant multilateral and bilateral treaties. Similar to the previous sections, it is questioned whether general international law can offer additional justifications for such operations. This enquiry is divided twofold: first, are there customary rules that permit such interception on the high seas, and second, have the relevant treaties crystallised a customary norm to this effect, which would endow third states with boarding powers?

To start with the latter query, it would be reasonable to hold that, apart from the relevant provision of the LOSC, all the other bilateral and multilateral treaties postulating the right to visit in this regard fall short of reflecting or crystallising norms of customary nature. First, it is obvious that the Smuggling Protocol or the other pertinent treaties were not codifying pre-existing custom, since the smuggling of migrants, which is the latter's raison d'être, was not formerly prohibited by international law. Secondly, they should not be considered as crystallising[149] or even generating[150] such norm for the following reasons: on the one hand, the bilateral treaties lack the requisite fundamental norm-creating character,[151] since they resemble more executive agreements (or *traités-contrats*) for the purpose of tackling certain ad hoc instances of illicit migration. On the other hand, the Smuggling Protocol, which might be considered as having a norm-creating character, has only recently entered into force and even if it has been broadly signed or ratified, it is unlikely that its provisions have engendered such a widespread practice and *opinio juris* necessary to create customary norms. In any event, even if the prohibition of the

---

[149] A crystallising effect is ascribed to treaties, which bring to maturity an emerging customary rule, that is a rule that was still in the formative stage; see Cassese, *International Law*, 2nd edn (Oxford: Oxford University Press, 2005) 168.

[150] See *North Sea* case, para 71.

[151] According to the court in the above-mentioned case, the treaty or 'provision concerned should, at all events potentially, be of a fundamentally norm-creating character such as could be regarded as forming the basis of a general rule of law'; see ibid, para 72.

smuggling of migrants attains such a customary law status, it will not *ipso facto* entail that also the relevant boarding provision will have a similar status.

Nevertheless, there are other customary rules that may provide the requisite justification for interception of human beings on the high seas. These rules could be the law of state responsibility and more specifically the circumstances precluding wrongfulness as well as the rules on rescue-at-sea, which, even though not qualifying as interception as such, are of extreme practical importance in the present context. As has been already noted in relation to FRONTEX, there has recently been an attempt to portray maritime interception as a humanitarian practice and thus to blur the lines between interception and rescue at sea.[152] However, this attempt to conflate migration control tactics with humanitarian rescue operations is not only dubious, but also legally unsound, since rescue-at-sea and interception fall under different rubrics according to international law: the former under article 98 of the 1982 Law of the Sea Convention and the relevant maritime conventions and the latter under article 110 of the 1982 Convention and other pertinent treaties.[153]

i. The Rules of State Responsibility

The first circumstance that a state may invoke in respect of interception of potential migrants or refugees on the high seas is consent:[154] a state may lawfully give its consent to the boarding of a vessel flying its flag on the high seas, ergo being under its exclusive jurisdiction (art 92 LOSC). As a result, the boarding state will be exculpated or excused for its wrongful act, ie the infringement of the freedom of navigation enjoyed by the foreign-flagged vessel, as long as the boarding remains within the bounds of the consent given. In addition, it may give its consent for the further exercise of enforcement jurisdiction by the boarding state, namely the seizure of the vessel or the arrest of the persons on board.[155]

---

[152] See eg B Miltner, 'Irregular Maritime Migration: Refugee Protection Issues in Rescue and Interception' 30 *Fordham ILJ* (2006–07) 75, 86 et seq.

[153] According to UNHCR, 'States should avoid the categorization of interception operations as search and rescue operations, because this can lead to confusion with respect to disembarkation Responsibilities'; see UNHCR, 'The Treatment of Persons Rescued at Sea: Conclusions and Recommendations from Recent Meetings and Expert Round Tables Convened by the Office of the United Nations High Commissioner for Refugees'; submitted in the Ninth Session of United Nations Open-ended Informal Consultative Process on Oceans and the Law of the Sea (23–27 June 2008) A/AC 259/17, para 20. See also Conclusion on Protection Safeguards in Interception Measures No 97 (LIV) adopted by the Executive Committee on International Protection; available at www.unhcr.org/excom/EXCOM/3f93b2894.html. In accord is also V Moreno-Lax, 'Seeking Asylum in the Mediterranean: Against a Fragmentary Reading of E.U. Member States' Obligations Accruing at Sea' 23 *IJRL* (2011) 174, 200.

[154] See ILC Articles, Commentary, 173.

[155] This can happen either *uno actu*, ie the consent of the flag state may include the right to visit and simultaneously the right to bring the vessel to the port of the boarding state and

Consent is the most plausible justification that might be used for inter-ference on the high seas in the present context. It is suggested, nonethe-less, that there should be regard also to the other applicable circumstances. First, self-defence should be disallowed as potential justification, since it is rather absurd that a vessel carrying illegal migrants or refugees could ever be considered as an imminent threat of an armed attack. Likewise, *force majeure*[156] and distress[157] should also be excluded in the present con-text. It may be fitting to note here that it is a totally different issue when a vessel is claiming distress, due to a human overload or the ill-health of the persons on board, in order to enter into the territorial waters or into the port of a coastal state;[158] or when a vessel is boarded on the high seas in a rescue-at-sea operation, since it is not the author of the wrongful act, ie the boarding party, but the other vessel that is actually in distress.

Contrary to the foregoing grounds, there might be room for the applica-tion of the state of necessity.[159] It is conceivable that all the conditions of the state of necessity could be satisfied in certain cases where a state takes enforcement action on the high seas against foreign merchant ships. In the context of our enquiry, it can be invoked only *in extremis,* ie in cases of a grave and imminent peril presented by the vessel and the persons on board; when, for example, the latter have been infected by a lethal virus or there are other grounds of public health necessitating that the vessel should be stopped on the high seas and precautionary measures taken. Needless to say, all the conditions of the provision of article 110 of LOSC and customary law concerning the right of visit should be scrupulously followed.

Lastly, reference should be made to the plea of countermeasures, ie the suspension of the performance of an international obligation by an injured state in order to induce a wrongdoing state to resume compliance with their legal obligations.[160] It is rather unlikely that this kind of argument could be upheld with regard to illegal migration by sea, since there is no primary rule which prohibits the transportation by sea of such persons. Nonetheless, it has been submitted that there is a duty incumbent upon states in international law not to create conditions in their own country calculated to cause an exodus of substantial numbers of its people, which resembles the principle of *sic utere tuo ut alienum non laedas,* applicable

---

prosecute any offences or it can be given in consecutive stages. See, for example, the case of the *F/V Jin Yinn,* which was boarded on the high seas by the US Coast Guard for smuggling aliens, pursuant to the consent given by the flag state, Taiwan, which, however, gave no further consent to the US to prosecute the smugglers; cited in R Canty, 'Limits of Coastal Guard Authority to Board Foreign Flag Vessels on the High Seas' 23 *TMLJ* (1998) 123, 134.

[156] ILC Articles Commentary, 183.
[157] ibid, 189.
[158] See eg the *Tampa* case.
[159] See art 25 of the ILC Articles.
[160] See art 49 of the ILC Articles.

when activities in one state cause environmental pollution in the territory of another state.[161] In response to the failure to abide by this obligation in the refugee context, the argument follows that 'the international community, acting individually or collectively, is entitled to undertake reprisals (or counter-measures)'.[162] This contention, however, is on the one hand, premised upon a far-fetched analogy with principles of environmental law, and on the other, it fails to take into account the provision of article 12(2) of the Universal Declaration of Human Rights that 'everyone shall be free to leave any country, including his own' and, ergo, it should, in principle, be refuted.

Moreover, the pertinent Smuggling Protocol has not yet attained the status of an international customary rule, which it would provide support to the plea of countermeasures in order to induce the wrong-doing state to resume its lawful, ie non-smuggling, behaviour.[163] Nevertheless, the same is not true for the case of slave trade or human trafficking leading to slavery, which constitutes indubitably rules of general international law. As a result, the countermeasures claim could persuasively provide a supplementary legal basis for the boarding of vessels on the high seas which are engaged in modern-day slave trade, whereas the principal legal basis for the latter would be supplied by the provision of article 110(1)(b) of LOSC and its corresponding customary rule.

ii. Rescue-at-Sea

a. The Regime under LOSC

The duty to assist persons in distress at sea is a long-established rule of customary international law. It extends to both other vessels and coastal states in the vicinity, and all persons, including irregular migrants, remain protected. Rescue obligations are sustained by purely humanitarian considerations.[164] It has been codified in LOSC, which prescribes relevant duties for both the flag and the coastal states. First, with regard to flag states, article 98(1) of LOSC provides that:

> Every State shall require the master of a ship flying its flag, in so far as he can do so without serious danger to the ship, the crew, or the passengers . . . to render

---

[161] See *Trial Smelter* case, 3 RIAA (1941) 1905.

[162] See Shearer, above n 7, 459.

[163] As far as the relationship between the treaty parties is concerned, the primary legal basis for the boarding would be provided by art 8 of the Protocol and not by the law of countermeasures, which can operate only as a secondary source in this regard.

[164] See eg UNHCR ExCom, 'Problems Related to the Rescue of Asylum-Seekers in Distress at Sea', Conclusion No 23 (XXXII) (1981), para 1; UNHCR ExCom, 'Report of the Working Group on Problems related to the Rescue of Asylum-Seekers in Distress at Sea', Conclusion No 26 (XXXIII) (1982); UNHCR ExCom, 'Rescue of Asylum-Seekers in Distress at Sea', Conclusion No 38 (XXXVI) (1985), para(a).

assistance to any person found at sea in danger of being lost . . . and to proceed to the rescue of persons in distress, if informed of their need for assistance, in so far as such action may be reasonably be expected of him.

Although the aforesaid provision is located in the Part of LOSC concerning the high seas, it is submitted that the duty in question applies in all maritime zones. A germane question would reasonably be what qualifies as 'distress'. At the outset, 'distress' is not defined by LOSC; yet it has been defined in the SAR Convention as 'a situation wherein there is a reasonable certainty that a person, a vessel or other craft is threatened by *grave and imminent danger* and requires immediate assistance'.[165] Further clarifications have been provided in relevant jurisprudence and authoritative commentaries. For example, in the case of *The Eleanor,* it was held that distress must entail urgency, but that 'there need not be immediate physical necessity'.[166] The International Law Commission has confirmed that a situation of distress 'may at most include a situation of serious danger, but not necessarily one that jeopardizes the very existence of the person concerned'.[167]

In light of the foregoing, there is certainly cogency in the argument that the overcrowded and unseaworthy vessels are de facto in distress and hence there is an obligation of assistance. This is consonant with the raison d'être of these operations, which is exclusively the protection of human beings. According to the European Commission, 80 per cent of the illegal traffic in the Mediterranean towards the EU is undertaken in small unseaworthy vessels, such as *cayucos* and *pateras*, which put the lives of its passengers 'objectively in danger'.[168] It may then be inferred that persons on board such crafts are *per definitionem* in distress and in need of assistance. Very recently, in the 2010 Council Decision, it was indicated that the existence of a situation of distress should not be determined exclusively on the basis of an actual request for assistance. A number of objective factors, such as the seaworthiness of the vessel, the number of passengers on board, the availability of supplies, the presence of qualified crew and navigation equipment, the prevailing weather and sea conditions, as well as the presence of particularly vulnerable, injured, or deceased persons, should be taken into account.[169]

On the face of article 98(1), the responsibility to rescue and provide assistance rests initially with the master of the ship that comes to rescue and entails the duty to deliver the people onboard to a place of safety. Every flag state must require the master of a ship flying its flag, both state

---

[165] See para 1.3.13, SAR Annex; below (emphasis added).
[166] See *The Eleanor* case (1809) Edw 135.
[167] See *Yearbook of the International Law Commission*, Vol II (1973) 134, para 4.
[168] See above n 17, 9 and 28.
[169] See 2010 Council Decision, para 1.3, Part II, Annex.

and private vessels, to proceed with all possible speed to the rescue of persons in distress when informed of their need of assistance. The obligation of the flag state is essentially an obligation of conduct, ie the flag state has to provide for the duty in question in its domestic legislation; article 98(1) is non-self-executing and requires implementing legislation to acquire the force of law.[170]

With regard to coastal states, article 98(2) of LOSC stipulates:

> Every coastal State shall promote the establishment, operation and maintenance of an adequate and effective search and rescue service regarding safety on and over the sea and, where circumstances so require, by way of mutual regional arrangements cooperate with neighbouring States for this purpose.

On the face of this provision, it is evident that LOSC sets out a general obligation of conduct on the part of coastal states to maintain search and rescue services as well as a general obligation of cooperation with other states to this end. Nevertheless, there is a conspicuous dearth in LOSC of specific rules of reference concerning the discharge of these obligations by the coastal states in the Convention. On the one hand, this is very typical of LOSC, as a framework convention; on the other, in contrast to matters such as shipping standards and environmental protection, there is no reference to rules established by the 'competent international organisation', ie the IMO.[171] In any event, the obligations under LOSC concerning rescue-at-sea are exhausted by these two paragraphs of article 98. Notwithstanding that these broad principles are fleshed out by more detailed agreements established under the auspices of IMO, state parties to LOSC are bound only by the said provisions. The relevant IMO conventions can only be used as an interpretive tool qua 'subsequent agreements', pursuant to article 31(3)(a) of VCLT,[172] albeit they would not entail the responsibility of LOSC parties for the breach of article 98.

---

[170] For example, Barnes reports that 'in the UK the master has a duty, upon receiving a distress signal, to proceed to their assistance, unless he is unable . . . Failure to do so is a criminal offence'; see ibid, 'Refugee Law at Sea' 53 *ICLQ* (2004) 47, 50 (fn 12). See also M Davies, 'Obligations and Implications for Ship Encountering Persons in Need of Assistance at Sea' 12 *Pacific Rim Law and Policy Journal* (2003) 109, 120.

[171] According to Barnes, 'This perhaps indicates that those negotiating the convention considered matters of search and rescue to be either adequately dealt with through the articulation of such general obligations, or that search and rescue was adequately dealt with in existing treaty rules and custom'; R Barnes, 'The International Law of the Sea and Migration Control', in V Mitsilegas and B Ryan (eds), *Extraterritorial Immigration Control* (The Hague: Brill, 2010) 103, 137.

[172] On art 31(3)(a) of VCLT see H Fox, 'Article 31(3)(A) and (B) of the Vienna Convention and the "Kasikili/Sedudu Island" case', in M Fitzmaurice et al (eds), *Treaty Interpretation and the Vienna Convention on the Law of Treaties: 30 Years on* (Leiden: Nijhoff, 2010) 59.

b. Other Applicable Treaties (SOLAS and SAR)

The relevant legal regime is supplemented by other treaty instruments, such as the 1974 Safety of Life at Sea Convention (SOLAS),[173] which covers a wide range of matters ranging from construction standards to operational rules to security measures. It also specifically deals with safety of navigation and rescue obligations. Chapter V, regulation 10(a) of SOLAS echoed article 98(1) of LOSC, with the additional requirement requiring the master to record any reason for failing to render assistance, which may provide a check on decision-making; regulation 15(a) dealt with coastal state obligations. The other relevant IMO Convention is the 1979 International Convention on Maritime Search and Rescue (SAR Convention).[174] The SAR Convention aims to create an international system for coordinating rescue operations and guaranteeing their efficiency and safety. Contracting states exercise SAR services in the area under their responsibility and are invited to conclude SAR agreements with neighbouring states to regulate and coordinate operations and rescue services in the maritime zone designated in the agreement.[175]

In May 2004, in the wake of the celebrated *Tampa* incident[176] and the initiatives that this led to,[177] the SAR and SOLAS Conventions were amended to impose for the first time an obligation on states to 'cooperate and coordinate' to ensure that ships' masters are allowed to disembark rescued persons to a place safety, irrespective of the nationality or status of those rescued, and with minimal disruption to the ship's planned

---

[173] See International Convention for the Safety of Life at Sea, adopted 1 November 1974, entered into force 25 May 1980 (1184 UNTS 278); as at 31 October 2012 SOLAS had 162 contracting states; see at www.imo.org/About/Conventions/StatusOfConventions/Pages/Default.aspx.

[174] See International Convention on Maritime Search and Rescue, adopted 27 April 1979, entered into force 22 June 1985 (1405 UNTS 23489); as at 31 October 2012 the SAR Convention had 103 contracting states; see at www.imo.org/About/Conventions/StatusOfConventions/Pages/Default.aspx (hereinafter: SAR Convention).

[175] See S Trevisanut, 'Search and Rescue Operations in the Mediterranean: Factor of Cooperation or Conflict?' 25 *IJMCL* (2010) 523, 524.

[176] In August 2001, in response to an Australian-coordinated search and rescue operation, the Norwegian *MV Tampa* rescued 433 asylum-seekers from a sinking Indonesian-flagged vessel 75 nautical miles off the Australian coast. When the *Tampa* began heading towards the Australian port of Christmas Island, the Australian authorities asked the captain to change course towards Indonesia and, eventually, intercepted the vessel before entering Australian waters. Australia defended its non-acceptance of 433 Afghan asylum-seekers and the boarding of *MV Tampa* on the basis of national sovereignty and security; see the relevant discussion in CM Bostock, 'The International Legal Obligation Owed to the Asylum-Seekers on the MV *Tampa*' 14 *IJRL* (2002) 279.

[177] See inter alia IMO Assembly Resolution on the Review of Safety Measures and Procedures for the Treatment of Persons Rescued at Sea, 22nd session, Agenda Item No 8, IMO Assembly Res A.920(22), November 2001 and UNHCR, 'Note on International Protection', 53rd session, UN doc A/AC 96/965 (11 Sept 2002).

itinerary.[178] As recognised by the IMO Maritime Safety Committee, the intent of the amendments is to ensure that a place of safety is provided within a reasonable time. The primary responsibility to provide a place of safety or to ensure that a place of safety is provided rests with the government responsible for the SAR region in which the survivors were recovered.[179] Moreover, according to the International Aeronautical and Maritime Search and Rescue Manual, the survivors 'must be delivered in a place of safety as quickly as possible'.[180]

Consequently, the most significant aspect of these amendments is the requirement for the states parties to promptly provide a place of safety to these people. Hence, from an obligation of cooperation and conduct, which the original treaty provisions set forth, the coastal state responsible for the SAR region is now faced with an obligation of result, ie to ensure that a 'place of safety' is furnished.[181]

The term 'place of safety' is defined neither by SOLAS nor by the SAR Convention, albeit by the 2004 IMO *Guidelines on the Treatment of Persons rescued at Sea*: a 'place of safety' means a 'place where the survivors' safety of life is no longer threatened and where their basic human needs (such as food, shelter and medical needs) can be met'.[182] Paragraph 6.13 continues to provide that 'An assisting ship should not be considered a place of safety based solely on the fact that the survivors are no longer in immediate danger once aboard the ship.'[183] Whilst these guidelines are not themselves constitutive of any binding obligations, they provide an important means for interpreting the obligations set forth in LOSC, SOLAS and the SAR Convention. 'It is arguable that they may contribute to the formation of new customary rules on the treatment of persons rescued at sea.'[184]

---

[178] See IMO, MSC Res 153 (78), MSC Doc 78/26 add 1, Annex 5 (20 May 2004) with regard to the amendments to SOLAS and IMO, MSC Res 155 (78) with regard to amendments to SAR Convention. Both amendments entered into force on 1 July 2006; see further information at www.imo.org/OurWork/Facilitation/IllegalMigrants/Pages/Default.aspx.

[179] Consequently, art 4.1-1 of SOLAS reads as follows: 'Contracting Governments shall co-ordinate and co-operate to ensure that masters of ships providing assistance by embarking persons in distress at sea are released from their obligations with minimum further deviation from the ship's intended voyage, provided that releasing the master of the ship from the obligations under the current regulation does not further endanger the safety of life at sea. The Contracting Government responsible for the search and rescue region in which such assistance is rendered shall exercise primary responsibility for ensuring such co-ordination and co-operation occurs, so that survivors assisted are disembarked from the assisting ship and delivered to a place of safety, taking into account the particular circumstances of the case and guidelines developed by the Organization. In these cases the relevant Contracting Governments shall arrange for such disembarkation to be effected as soon as reasonably practicable.' Similar provisions are included also in the SAR Convention in para 3.1.9.

[180] IMO, International Aeronautical and Maritime Search and Rescue Manual, Vol III, s 2.

[181] In accord is R Barnes, above n 169, 139.

[182] Resolution MSC 167(78), adopted 20 May 2004; available at http://docs.imo.org.

[183] ibid.

[184] Barnes, above n 169, 142.

c. The Problem of Disembarkation

This obligation of the state parties to SOLAS and the SAR Convention to provide 'a place of safety' as soon as reasonably practicable does not necessarily mean that the state responsible for the SAR region is obliged to disembark the survivors in its own area. In other words, on the face of the provisions in question, there is no residual obligation of the coastal state to allow disembarkation on its own territory when it has not been possible to do so anywhere else.[185] This has rightly been criticised as the most notable shortcoming of the relevant treaty regime, as it falls short of adequately addressing incidents, such as the *Pinar*[186] or the *Tampa*.[187]

To address this problem, there have recently been certain initiatives to enhance the relevant obligations of coastal states and read into them such a 'residual' obligation of disembarkation on their territory. In January 2009, the IMO Facilitation Committee (FAL) adopted certain 'Principles relating to administrative procedures for disembarking persons rescued at sea', which included the following principle: 'If disembarkation from the rescuing ship cannot be arranged swiftly elsewhere the, the Government responsible for the SAR area should accept the disembarkation of the persons rescued'.[188] They were, however, rejected in March 2010 at the 14th session of the Sub-Committee on Radio communications and Search and Rescue (COMSAR).[189]

In a similar vein, the 2010 Council Decision, which was recently annulled, proposed with respect to search and rescue in the context of FRONTEX operations that priority should be given to disembarkation in the third country from which the interdicted ship departed or through whose territorial waters or search and rescue region it transited. If that were not possible for any reason, it is suggested that priority be given to disembarkation in the Member State hosting the FRONTEX operation, unless a different course of action proves necessary to ensure the safety of

---

[185] For a contrary opinion see Trevisanut, above n 176, 530.

[186] In April 2009, the Turkish merchant vessel *Pinar* rescued 153 persons off the coast of the Italian island of Lampedusa in the Maltese Search and Rescue (SAR) zone. The *Pinar* had to take the rescued persons, who were irregular migrants, on board, and was then refused permission to enter Italian territorial waters. The Italian authorities justified their refusal by arguing that the responsibility for the reception of the rescued persons fell on Malta. On its side, Malta denied its responsibility and refused to give access to its ports; see 'Maroni Claims Malta Sent 40,000 Migrants to Italy,' *Times of Malta*, 21 April 2009.

[187] See relevant discussion in V Moreno-Lax, 'Seeking Asylum in the Mediterranean: Against a Fragmentary Reading of EU Member States' Obligations Accruing at Sea' 23 *International Journal of Refugee Law* (2011) 174, 195 et seq.

[188] IMO, FAL 3/Circ 194, 22 January 2009, Principle No 3; available at www5.imo.org/SharePoint/blastDataHelper.asp/data_id%3D24818/194.pdf.

[189] For a detailed discussion of these proposals see J Coppens and E Somers, 'Towards New Rules on Disembarkation of Persons Rescued at Sea?' 25 *IJMCL* (2010) 377, 388 et seq.

the persons involved.[190] This had elicited polemics by states that usually host FRONTEX operations, such as Malta.[191]

Finally, there is currently an ongoing discussion in the context of IMO, and more particularly in the COMSAR, with a view to adopting a regional Memorandum of Understanding concerning measures to protect the safety of persons rescued at sea.[192] The purpose of this draft MoU was, initially, the coordination of the search and rescue services as well as the delineation of the respective responsibilities solely of Spain, Italy and Malta, albeit there have been thoughts of including other Mediterranean states too. As far as the default obligation for disembarkation is concerned, the draft MoU is resoundingly silent.

iii. Concluding Remarks

What can be reasonably inferred from the foregoing is that states in general are not keen on accepting such a residual obligation for disembarkation, notwithstanding its obvious need. The denunciation of the amendment proposals, on the one hand, and protests at the EU non-binding Guidelines, on the other, as well as the dearth of any reference to such obligation in the draft Mediterranean MoU, warrant the assertion that, as the law stands, the obligation of ensuring a 'place of safety' for persons in distress does not include an ensuing obligation of disembarkation for coastal states. In addition, in view of the discord both in state practice and in the opinions of the states concerned, it is clear that no corresponding customary law has emerged, other than the well-established rules already enshrined in article 98 of LOSC.

With these remarks the discussion of the possible legal justifications for interference on the high seas in respect of human being was concluded. It was asserted, accordingly, that the international law furnishes various bases for states in order to tackle the contemporary scourges of human trafficking and smuggling of migrants. However, these claims serve two-fold purposes: on the one hand, negatively, to avert the flow of migrants to the developed world and thus maintain the public order of the respective states and on the other, positively, to save the lives of thousands of people in distress and under circumstances of severe exploitation and thus maintain the *ordre public* of international society as a whole. This entails that there are further legal justifications available to states concerned, such as the 'slave trade' and the rules on rescue-at-sea.

---

[190] para 2.1, Part II, Annex.
[191] See Moreno-Lax, Commentary, 627.
[192] See the discussion at the 15th session of COMSAR (7–11 March 2011) www.imo.org/mediacentre/meetingsummaries/comsar/pages/comsar-15th-session.aspx.

III. ADDITIONAL INTERNATIONAL LEGAL ISSUES IN THE COURSE OF INTERCEPTION OPERATIONS OF HUMAN BEINGS

Similar to the previous chapters, the present section will discuss some additional legal issues concerning the interception of human beings on the high seas. This is consistent with the basic tenet that the right of visit, whatever may its legal justification be, is subject to the legal order of the oceans, ie a network of international regulations, which aim to uphold the rule of law in the oceans. This legal order includes various rules of the law of the sea as well as of general international law. Such rules are the prohibition to use force and human rights law, which will be canvassed in the ensuing paragraphs. As in the drug trafficking context, more emphasis was placed upon the rules concerning jurisdiction, in the present context, more emphasis will be placed upon human rights and refugee law. However, it is not possible within the confines of the present thesis to address all the relevant legal issues. Thus, the focus will be centred on the principle of *non-refoulement*, which is of cardinal importance to thousands of people travelling the oceans of the world.

A. Use of Force and Interception of Human Beings

In the previous chapters, there has been considerable reference to the issue of the permissibility of the use of force in interception operations at sea. In the present context, there is room for a different assertion, namely that the use of force should be a priori prohibited and only in very exceptional circumstances allowed. In other words, the rebuttable presumption should shift from permitting the use of force in strictly controlled circumstances to being against it. This argument rests upon the consideration that the purpose of the enforcement operations and consequently the target of the use of force *in casu* are human beings, usually victims of trafficking or smuggling of migrants and not terrorists, drug smugglers or illegal anglers, as in other interdiction operations.[193] Elementary considerations of humanity, to which reference is made also by the *Saiga II* case,[194] as well as the proper application of the principles of necessity and proportionality buttress the thesis that the operations against the trafficking of human beings in all its forms should abstain from the use of force, save in self-defence cases, in contemplation of the human 'cargo' on board the intercepted vessels and the danger present for innocent persons being injured or even losing their life. Especially

---

[193] See eg the *Rigopoulos v Spain* case.
[194] See above Chapter 3 (n 152). See also the *Corfu Channel* case, 22.

the proportionality principle requires the enforcing state to weigh the gravity of the offence against the value of human life, which in all cases falls short of justifying the intentional sinking of vessels and the loss of human beings.[195] This was exemplified by the *Kates I Rades* case, where an Albanian vessel was sunk in the Adriatic Sea by an Italian warship in the course of a counter-smuggling operation, with the result that 58 persons drowned.[196]

B. The Principle of Non-Refoulement and Human Beings on the High Seas

One of the most controversial, yet extremely significant issues concerning the interception of human beings on the high seas is the question of non-refoulement, ie whether the boarding state has any obligation whatsoever not to reject or return (*'refouler'*) asylum-seekers intercepted on the high seas. The legal contours of the principle of non-refoulement in general have already been delineated in Chapter 3.

In the context of the present enquiry, a thorny question had been whether the principle in question applies extraterritorially, *in casu* on the high seas. According to one strand of legal doctrine, which is largely expressed by the decision of the US Supreme Court in the case of *Sale v Haitian Centers Council*, it falls short of applying on the high seas and it is inextricably linked with the territorial scope *ratione loci* of the Refugee Convention. In this case, the Supreme Court, by an 8-1 majority, construed both the Refugee Convention and the US implementing statute as inoperative on the high seas.[197] It held, therefore, that neither US domestic law nor US treaty obligations prohibited the Coast Guard from interdicting refugees on the high seas and *'refouling'* them to countries in which their 'life or freedom would be threatened' on any conventional grounds. Reliance was placed on the *travaux préparatoires* of the Refugee Convention, particularly assertions by the Swiss and Dutch delegates that the

---

[195] In accord seems to be Ivan Shearer, who claims that 'a deliberate sinking will in no circumstances be warranted if the offence involved is a customs (ie purely regulatory) offence . . . It is suggested that fisheries, revenue, immigration and other regulatory offences would fall into the same category'; see ibid, 'The Development of International Law and Respect to the Law Enforcement Role of Navies and Coast Guards in Peacetime', in MN Schmitt and LC Green (eds), *The Law of Armed Conflict: Into the Next Millennium* (Newport, RI: Naval War College, 1998), 441.

[196] See *Xhavara* case.

[197] See *Sale, Acting Commissioner, INS v Haitian Centers Council* 113 S Ct (1993) 2549 (hereinafter: *Sale* case). See an interesting account of the case in H Koh and M Wishnie, 'The Story of *Sale v. Haitian Centers* Council: Guantanamo and *Refoulement*', in D Hurwitz et al (eds), *Human Rights Advocacy Stories* (New York,: Thomson Reuters/Foundation Press 2009) 385.

Convention was only to apply to persons within state territory and that closure of borders was permissible.[198]

This decision, however, encountered piercing criticism not only from Justice Blackmun in his dissenting opinion[199] but also from the majority of the academic literature, which held the contrary and preponderant view that non-refoulement is prohibited wherever it takes place and not only within a state's borders.[200] Indeed, there are several reasons why, on the one hand, this decision and a fortiori its restricted or 'territorial' approach was at odds with international law and on the other, why the opposite view holds more legal merit.[201] First and foremost, it is argued that the 'territorial' approach, which this decision puts forward, deviates significantly from the hermeneutic paradigm of article 31 of VCLT. On a first account, it fails to place the appropriate emphasis upon the literal interpretation of the phrase 'return in any manner *whatsoever'*. The latter is the core element of the relevant prohibition of non-refoulement entailing that the relevant state action is prohibited *wherever* it takes place, whether internally, at the border, or through its agents outside territorial jurisdiction.[202]

On a second account, the ordinary meaning of the terms 'return' and '*refouler*' does not support an interpretation which would restrict its scope to conduct within the territory of the state concerned, nor is there any indication that these terms were understood by the drafters of the 1951 Convention to be limited in this way.[203] In addition, the decision fails to take into serious consideration the predominantly humanitarian object and purpose of the provision in question, which should be germane to the interpretation of humanitarian treaties.[204] Lastly, this reasoning runs counter to the obligation for a bona fides interpretation and application of the said provision set forth in articles 26 and 31(1) VCLT as well as to the principle of effectiveness which is intertwined with the interpretation of such treaty provisions.[205]

---

[198] See ibid, 2565–66. Nonetheless, the Swiss delegates spoke only about mass migrations, saying nothing about the non-applicability of art 33 outside that context; see P Weis, 'Legal Aspects of the Convention of 28 July 1951' 30 *BYIL* (1953) 478, 482.

[199] See Mr Justice Blackmun, Dissenting Opinion, reprinted in 6 *IJRL* (1994) 71.

[200] See inter alia: Goodwin-Gill's 'Comment' in 6 *IJRL* (1994) 102; LD Rosenberg, 'The Courts and Interception: The US' Interdiction Experience and its Impact on Refugees and Asylum Seekers' 17 *Georgetown Immigration LJ* (2002-3) 199.

[201] It is the author's choice to present this view in the form of counter-arguments to the *Sale* case, which, even if it is only a domestic court's decision, is treated as the *locus classicus* and main point of reference in this regard by the majority of the academic doctrine.

[202] Emphasis added. See Goodwin-Gill and McAdam, 248.

[203] See the recent UNHCR Advisory Opinion on the Extraterritorial Application of *Non-Refoulement Obligations* under the 1951 Refugee Convention and its 1967 Protocol, 26 January 2007, available at www.unhcr.org/refworld/pdfid/45f17a1a4.pdf (hereinafter: UNHCR, Advisory Opinion). See also Wooters, 50–51.

[204] See G Fitzmaurice, 'The Law and Procedure of the ICJ 1951-4' 33 *BYIL* (1957) 203, 207.

[205] This was one of the arguments put forward by the UNHCR in its *amicus curiae* brief in the *Haitian Refugee Center, Inc v Gracey*; see Motion for Leave to file Brief *Amicus Curiae* of UNHCR in Support of Haitian Refugee Center, Inc et al 8 July 1985, section II, 19-24.

Moreover, subsequent developments in the context of the Haitian interdiction programme as well as generally in the field of refugee and human
rights law rebut rather than reaffirm the *ratio decidendi* of the *Sale* case,
while lend credence to the contrary thesis expressed above. First, the
Supreme Court decision was not upheld by the Inter-American Commission
of Human Rights, which found the United States in breach of article 33(1)
of the Convention. Also, the Commission ruled that this practice breached
the asylum-seekers' right to life, liberty and security of their persons and
the right to asylum protected by article XXVII of the American Declaration
of the Rights and Duties of Man.[206] In addition, various declarations and
resolutions in different fora,[207] including UN bodies[208] or the UNHCR
EXCOM,[209] laws and practices of the states, and especially certain actions
by the US government[210] have adequately substantiated the thesis that non-
refoulement is prohibited wherever it takes place, and not only within a
state's borders. Most significant has been the consistent jurisprudence of
human right bodies, such as the Strasbourg Court, that human rights do
apply on the high seas.[211]

In UNHCR's view, 'the reasoning adopted by courts and human rights
treaty bodies in their authoritative interpretation of the relevant human
rights provisions is relevant also to the prohibition of refoulement under
international refugee law, given the similar nature of the obligations and
the object and purpose of the treaties which form their legal basis'. Thus,

> an interpretation which would restrict the scope of application of Article 33(1)
> of the Refugee Convention to conduct within the territory of a State party

---

[206] See *Haitian Center for Human Rights v United States*, Case 10.675, Report No 51/96, Inter-
American Commission of Human Rights Doc OEA/Ser L/V/II 95 Doc 7 rev (13 March
1997), paras 156–58.

[207] See eg the General Principles endorsed by the IMO Facilitation Committee, which
make specific reference to the 1951 Convention relating to the Status of Refugee, see 1965
Convention on Facilitation of International Maritime Traffic, as amended, 10 January 2002,
section 4.2.

[208] The Sub-Commission on the Promotion and Protection of Human Rights has observed,
for example, that the principle of non-refoulement not only applies without geographical
limitation, but also prohibits the indirect return of a refugee where he or she may be persecuted; see Sub-Commission on the Promotion and Protection of Human Res 2000/20, preamble para 11.

[209] See inter alia UNCHR EXCOM Conclusion No 6 (XXVIII), at para (c) and Conclusion
No 97 (2003). The latter contains eight guiding principles to ensure 'adequate treatment' of
intercepted persons, among which is, of course, the principle of non-refoulement, which
must be protected wherever the interception has taken place, ie even on the high seas. The
Conclusions adopted by the UNHCR EXCOM do not have the force of law, albeit they may
contribute to the formulation of *opinio juris*. See in this respect C Lewis, 'UNHCR's
Contribution to the Development of International Refugee Law' 17 *IJRL* (2005) 67.

[210] In the final years of the Clinton Administration, US delegates in UNHCR Executive
Committee quietly dropped their opposition to language in the latter's Conclusions affirm-
ing that the principle in question includes non-rejection at the frontiers; see B Frelick,
'"Abundantly Clear": *Refoulement*' 19 *Georgetown ILJ* (2005) 679.

[211] See the discussion in the relevant section of Ch 3.

would not only be contrary to the terms of the provision as well as the object and purpose of the treaty under interpretation, but it would also be inconsistent with relevant rules of international human rights law. It is UNHCR's position, therefore, that a State is bound by its obligation under Article 33(1) of the 1951 Convention not to return refugees to a risk of persecution wherever it exercises effective jurisdiction.[212]

It follows from the foregoing analysis that there is cogent support for the argument that the intercepting states bear responsibility for the treatment of the persons on board the intercepted vessels and a fortiori should respect and conform to the principle of non-refoulement.[213] This means that whenever these states stop and visit a vessel suspected of smuggling migrants or refugees or even engaged in human trafficking or modern slave-trade, they should always take into consideration their treaty as well the customary obligation of non-refoulement. Consequently they should, first, always provide for a refugee status determination process and secondly, abstain from returning persons determined to have a valid claim to places where they may face persecution or torture.[214] Even when actions are taken in line with international legal duties to establish search and rescue zones and to respond to distress calls by rescuing refugees at risk on the high seas, the responsibility for those rescued would devolve on that state particularly if the rescue occurs in the context of interception measures.

Also, the rescuing vessels would be bound by the obligation of the law of the sea to bring those shipwrecked to a place of safety. The bringing of those shipwrecked to a place of safety is an action that also must be measured against the prohibition of refoulement. This means that rescued persons, too, may not be brought to third countries without first having their applications for international protection examined in the rescuing state.[215] Noteworthy is in this regard that paragraph 1.2 of the 2010 Council Decision stipulates as a general principle that

> No person shall be disembarked in, or otherwise handed over to the authorities of, a country in contravention with the principle of *non-refoulement*, or from which there is a risk of expulsion or return to another country in contravention of that principle.

Moreover, having in mind that the obligation of non-refoulement is both an obligation of result and conduct and there is a break in the chain of causation when a state has failed to ensure that an asylum seeker

---

[212] UNHCR, Advisory Opinion, 17.
[213] On the question of attribution of human rights violations to States see H Dipla, *La responsabilité de l'Etat pour violation des droits de l'homme: problèmes d'imputation* (Paris: Pedone, 1994).
[214] See also a very interesting discussion of states' positive and negative obligations in Wooters, 313–46.
[215] See Weinzierl and Lisson, 16.

receives protection from refoulement elsewhere,[216] indirect or chain refoulement, namely causing a person to return to another place from which refoulement occurs subsequently, should be equally prohibited.[217]

The case of *Marine I* is telling:[218] the Committee against Torture considered that Spain maintained control over the persons on board the *Marine I* from the time the vessel was rescued and throughout the identification and repatriation process that took place at Nouadhibou and, by virtue of this control, that the alleged victims were 'subject to Spanish jurisdiction'.[219] The complaints in this case concerned, first, the conditions on board the vessel and in the abandoned fish processing plant, and secondly the possible exposure to torture and other cruel treatment of the migrants returning to India, in violation of the prohibition of refoulement laid down in article 3 CAT. The applicants invoked only the relevant provisions of CAT; nonetheless, it is hard to see why the latter complaints would not also trigger the application of the prohibition of non-refoulement, as enshrined in article 33 of the Refugee Convention, article 3 of ECHR and article 7 of ICCPR. In addition, it is not difficult to hold that the complaints concerning the reception and detention conditions in Mauritania, the lack of access to legal representation and the possibility of access to Mauritanian courts come under the scope of article 5 of ECHR and article 9 of ICCPR. In the present case, it was difficult to verify these allegations; let alone, that the Committee declared the application inadmissible.

The obligation to respect the principle of non-refoulement has been also recognised by the EU in respect of FRONTEX operations; suffice to refer to the 2011 FRONTEX Regulation, which recognises that

> The Agency shall fulfil its tasks in full compliance with the relevant Union law, including the Charter of Fundamental Rights of the European Union ('the Charter of Fundamental Rights'); the relevant international law, including the Convention Relating to the Status of Refugees done at Geneva on 28 July 1951 ('the Geneva Convention'); obligations related to access to international protection, in particular the principle of *non-refoulement*; and fundamental rights.[220]

---

[216] See P Mathew, 'Address: Legal Issues Concerning Interception' 17 *Georgetown ILJ* (2003) 230.

[217] See J Crawford and P Hyndman, 'Three Heresies in the Application of the Refugee Convention' 1 *IJRL* (1989) 155, 171. *Cf* also the *MSS v Belgium and Greece* case.

[218] The facts of the case are the following: On 30 January 2007, the Spanish Coast Guard received a distress call from a vessel named *Marine I*. It had developed engine problems and was drifting on the high seas off the coast of West Africa. The *Marine I* was within the Senegalese 'Search and Rescue' (SAR) area, but the Senegalese authorities requested Spain to proceed with the rescue operation, claiming not to have the means to assist. On 4 February, a Spanish maritime rescue tug reached the *Marine I* and provided immediate relief by handing out water and food supplies. On 12 February, after an agreement between Spain and Mauritania, the ship was towed to Nouahdibou, where the identification and repatriation procedure took place under the control of Spain; see K Wouters and M den Heijer, 'The *Marine I* Case: a Comment' 22 *IJRL* (2009) 1–19, 2.

[219] See Committee against Torture, *JHA v Spain*, no 323/2007, 21 November 2008, para 8.2.

[220] See art 1 para 1(2).

As far as the principle of non-refoulement in the human rights context as such, it attains even more significance in the context of the practice of the US and some European countries of intercepting vessels in the territorial waters of the state of departure.[221] The persons on board such vessels have not yet crossed an international border and hence they fall short of qualifying as refugees.[222] This was corroborated recently by the *Roma* case, in which even though the House of Lords accepted that the principle of non-refoulement forms part of customary law, the appellants could not take advantage of that norm because they had not yet left their country of origin and could not be said to be at the frontier of the UK.[223] In light of this decision, the intercepting states have not any obligation prima facie vis-à-vis the said persons stemming from the principle of non-refoulement according to the Refugee Convention. Nonetheless, the same is not the case with regard to the same principle in the human rights framework, which will indisputably compel these states to not return persons facing a risk of being subjected to torture and to analogous treatment. Otherwise, they will incur international responsibility for the violation, among others, of article 3 of the ECHR or article 7 of the ICCPR, since, in light of the case law discussed above, the intercepted persons will come under their jurisdiction.[224]

A linked question would be whether, for example, EU Member States conducting joint border and migration controls with third countries are exempted from responsibility for possible human rights violations, on the basis that they are under the authority of the coastal state. According the rules on state responsibility, the actions of one state's organs are only attributable to another state when these organs are made available to the second state in such a way that the other state exercises exclusive command and control, and when the actions of these state organs appear to be the sovereign actions of the second state.[225] However, as was persuasively maintained, 'for joint patrols with third countries in the territorial sea and contiguous zones of these third countries, such effective control by other States does not exist. For this, the contractual transfer of individual control rights to which only the coastal states are entitled is insufficient'.[226]

---

[221] See eg the practice of EU Member States in FRONTEX Operations, such as HERA II and III. See also in general A Fischer-Lescano, T Löhr and T Tohidipur, 'Border Control at Sea: Requirements under International Human Rights and Refugee Law' 21 *IJRL* (2009) 256 and M den Heijer, 'Europe beyond its Borders: Refugee and Human Rights Protection in Extraterritorial Immigration Control', in Ryan and Mitsilegas (eds), above n 169, 169.

[222] According to UNCHR Handbook, 'international protection cannot come into play as long as a person is within the territorial jurisdiction of his home country', at para 88; cited in Wooters, 49.

[223] See *Roma* case, para 16 (Lord Bingham).

[224] In accord seems to be also Wooters, 219.

[225] See art 6 of ILC Articles and Commentary, 221.

[226] Weinzierl and Lisson, 17.

Hence, EU Member States assume full responsibility concerning human rights violations in this regard.[227]

IV. CONCLUDING REMARKS

The present analysis demonstrated that the international society has accepted the arguments for *mare clausum* assertions of authority on the high seas in respect of the influx of illicit migrants. However, as regards the basic distinction that was made between 'negative' and 'positive' interceptions, it was readily apparent that the former has monopolised the relevant practice of the states concerned. This illustrates that the *ordre public* considerations of the participants in international policy-making with regard to the oceans are informed primarily by realistic political and societal demands rather than by humanitarian or moral appeals.

---

[227] *cf* the *Xhavara* case, in which, in agreement with older jurisprudence, the Court found that Albania was not responsible for migration control measures conducted by Italy on the basis of an agreement between Albania and Italy.

9

Conclusions

THE PRESENT BOOK has endeavoured to address certain international legal questions concerning interception on the high seas in the twenty-first century. Interception or the right of visit under LOSC is considered the most significant exception to the fundamental principle of the freedom of the high seas. This latter is conceptualised mainly as having a negative nature, namely 'the prohibition of interference in peacetime by ships flying one national flag with ships flying the flag of other nationalities'.[1] This prohibition and the concomitant principle of the flag state's exclusive jurisdiction on the high seas are arguably challenged by the recent extensive practice of interdiction of vessels on the high seas. Indeed, states have significantly engaged in such practice either in order to counter the threats of international terrorism and of WMD proliferation, or to suppress transnational organised crime at sea, such as illicit trafficking of narcotic drugs and smuggling of migrants, or even to suppress piracy and IUU fishing on the high seas.

Several partnerships in various forms have been established to this end between states, besides numerous agreements concerning the interdiction of suspect vessels in this regard. Interestingly, neither of the aforementioned activities was included in the provision of LOSC concerning the right of visit on the high seas (article 110). Therefore, it was questioned whether general international law can accommodate such claims for interference with foreign navigation on the high seas and provide the necessary legal justifications, and if so, whether the principle of non-interference has been curtailed and lost its relevance in the contemporary legal order of the oceans.

The central thesis was put forward in Chapter 2, which outlined the historic and contemporary role of the right of visit in the legal order of the oceans. The latter notion is central to the present enquiry, since it reflects the idea that the oceans are not *legibus solutus*, but they are subject to a certain regulatory and organisational scheme premised upon fundamental legal tenets, both of a negative and of a positive nature, such as the right of visit on the high seas. This legal order also imports the idea of *'la juridicité'* of the high seas: that the oceans are regulated not only by the *lex*

---

[1] *Memorandum*, 67.

specialis of the law of the sea, but also by general international law, where applicable. As history well attests, the role of the right of visit has been decisive for the legal edifice of the oceans; not only has it been a basic tenet of the relevant *jus gentium*, but more significantly it has been the principal vehicle with which the claims to further jurisdictional powers on the high seas have been conveyed. Accordingly, it was observed that the rationales behind the historical and contemporaneous claims to interfere with vessels on the high seas were identical with the classical *mare clausum* claims.

Drawing valuable insights from the celebrated doctrinal controversy between *mare liberum* and *mare clausum*, as well as from the relevant practice of the main naval powers, the following assertions were made: the freedom of the high seas was never an absolute principle but has always been qualified by '*mare clausum*' claims for jurisdiction and for police powers on the high seas. These claims have served certain firmly established and coherent purposes: first, the maintenance of international peace and security, which has been the *ratio juris* behind the acknowledgment of the belligerent right of visit and of the maritime interdiction operations established pursuant to the relevant Security Council Resolutions. Secondly, the protection of the *bon usage* of the high seas, which has been the objective of various treaties concerning IUU fishing as well as of the customary rules for the suppression of piracy *jure gentium*. Finally, the maintenance of the '*ordre public*' of states and of international society, which has been exemplified by the recognition of the right of visit in cases of illicit trade in alcohol and in narcotic drugs or of slave trade.

Contemporary interference on the high seas does not deviate from this scheme; on the contrary, the numerous boarding agreements and the corresponding interference practices in today's oceans share similar *rationes juris*. Thus, for example, the boarding agreements in the context of the PSI purport to maintain international peace and security by regulating the transfer of proscribed weapons, similar to the St Germain Convention in the early twentieth century, while the counter-migrant smuggling operations reflect legitimate *ordre public* concerns of states and of international society, similar to the nineteenth-century claims for the abolition of the transatlantic slave trade. A significant change that has been observed has been the gradual 'internationalisation' of the above claims, ie from purely individualistic claims of states, to collectively shared legitimate concerns of states and of the other participants in the law-making process of the order of the oceans.

In conclusion, the various cases of interferences on the high seas, both historical and contemporary, could be conceptualised and categorised as follows: at a first level, there are the cases of interference, which find their justification in the need to maintain the peace and security of states and of international society. Currently, these cases concern mainly the threats posed by international terrorism and by the proliferation of WMD. At a second level, there are the cases involving interference, which aim to maintain a *bon usage* or 'internal order' of the oceans, in the sense of a reasonable and non-abusive use of the freedoms of the seas without detriment to the 'usufruct' itself. Illegal fishing and piracy remain the principal threats to this internal order of the oceans; consequently, the exercise of the right of visit to address these threats looms large. The protection of submarine cables and potentially the protection of the marine environment complement the foregoing legitimate concerns regarding the 'usufruct' of the oceans. Lastly, at a third level stand the interferences that pertain to the general welfare and to the *ordre public* of states and of the international society, which aim thus to maintain the 'external order' of the oceans. Drug trafficking and the smuggling of migrants are the most important cases, in which the right of visit on the high seas is exercised for reasons of *ordre public*.

Nonetheless, it should be mentioned that these levels or categories are neither hermetically sealed nor isolated; on the contrary, there is patently a degree of permeation between these categories. Finally, it is submitted that the recent practice has not brought about substantial changes to the legal order of the oceans, in the sense of curtailing the fundamental tenet of the exclusivity of flag-state jurisdiction. It is also doubtful whether such change will occur in the near future, since these rationales are well embedded in the legal order of the oceans.

The foregoing analysis addressed the central question, ie how current interception operations can be conceptualised and theoretically justified under the legal order of the oceans. Another important question, however, had been whether there is a new law of interdiction. In more detail, it has been questioned whether technological developments in the field of maritime surveillance as well as the extensive practice of interdiction by states have modified the legal contours of the right of visit. It was submitted that the relevant legal framework has not been dramatically altered, besides the customary right of approach. This framework is complemented by various legal rules concerning law enforcement at sea, international human rights law and the assertion of jurisdiction over crimes at sea. These rules were thoroughly canvassed in Chapter 3.

The main part of the book has been devoted to the most significant issues that have given rise to substantial interception activities, ie the threats to international peace and security, posed mainly by international terrorism and WMD, piracy *jure gentium,* drug trafficking and finally illicit migration and human trafficking on the high seas, were in turn canvassed.

With respect to the question of interception in the context of international peace and security, the belligerent right of visit and search was considered, first in Chapter 4, with particular emphasis on its application in recent international and non-international armed conflicts. It was argued that there is certainly legal merit in the invocation of this right in contemporary conflicts at sea for reasons of legal certainty and of foreseeability. This was followed by an analysis of interference on the high seas for the purpose of enforcement of Security Council Resolutions. In this context, the question of implicit authorisation of interception measures was also addressed. This was, in principle, disallowed, since it runs counter to the normative framework of Security Council Resolutions and to the fundamental principle of non-interference on the high seas.

The crux of the matter, however, was how states have collectively or unilaterally responded to the interrelated problems of international terrorism and of WMD, and which bases international law affords for interdiction on the high seas in this regard. Accordingly, the legality of the relevant initiatives of both international organisations and states was considered in Chapter 5. Thus, treaties and operations, such as the 2005 SUA Protocol and NATO's Operation Active Endeavour, as well as initiatives, such as the PSI, were discussed. It was concluded that, besides the various relevant treaties, these initiatives as well as the relevant operations do not engender any new legal basis for interdiction of WMD and of terrorist vessels. This notwithstanding, states may unilaterally invoke certain justifications under general international law, such as self-defence, countermeasures and state of necessity, in strictly defined circumstances. Chapter 5 concluded with a brief reference to additional international legal matters, including the permissibility of the use of force and the assertion of enforcement jurisdiction over the relevant offences on the high seas. The latter question is of paramount importance, it being observed that there is a considerable deficit of national legislation in respect of WMD.

Chapter 6 was devoted mainly to the piracy *jure gentium* and the unprecedented scourge of piracy off some of the African coasts. Piracy has traditionally been deemed a threat to the fundamental freedom of navigation and commerce, and as such has come to the fore recently. States as well as the international community as a whole have adopted numerous measures, besides interception operations, which aim both at the suppression of piracy and armed robbery at sea and at the effective assertion of jurisdiction over suspect pirates. These measures were critically assessed in Chapter 6 against the background of LOSC and general international law. The chapter was concluded with a brief discussion of the problem of IUU fishing on the high seas and the respective inspection schemes that have been adopted both at a global level (Straddling Stocks Agreement) and at a regional level (RFMOs).

The issue of illicit drug trafficking at sea has raised considerable legal questions in recent decades and has given rise to various multilateral and bilateral boarding agreements, as well as to significant interdiction activities, especially in the Caribbean region. The legal analysis of this issue was premised upon the distinction between treaty law and customary law justifications for interference with drug smuggling vessels on the high seas. It is true that drug trafficking is the problem that has engendered the most bilateral and regional boarding agreements in this regard, as well as having raised various interesting questions pertaining to treaty law and to coastal and flag state jurisdiction over drug offences. All these matters were addressed in the context of the analysis of the relevant treaties.

Accordingly, on the one hand, Chapter 7 observed that states have been very flexible and 'progressive' concerning the legal content of the agreements under scrutiny: these agreements, based upon the consent of the states involved, are designed to surmount the legal obstacles that state sovereignty usually places to such operations and guarantee the maximum effectiveness in suppressing drug trafficking. Nonetheless, they are conspicuously unequal, in the sense that they are drawn with the purpose mainly of facilitating US counter-drug policy, and they may seem problematic in relation to the position of third states. In addition, possible customary law justifications, such as consent of the flag states and countermeasures were scrutinised. Finally, there was an extended discussion regarding the exercise of legislative and enforcement jurisdiction over drug trafficking offences on the basis of relevant US legislation and practice. As was concluded in the respective section, 'it is not the objective of suppressing drug trafficking, but it is the method of not respecting in some cases basic tenets of international law, such as the freedom of the high seas and the requirements of due process, legal certainty and foreseeability, which hardly merits general approbation'.

A similar structure was followed in Chapter 8 in assessing the interception activities on the high seas in relation to human beings. Accordingly, the treaty law justifications were addressed first, such as the LOSC, the Smuggling Protocol and the relevant bilateral treaties. In this context, of particular interest was the argument for the reinvigoration of the 'slave-trade' basis of interference under article 110(1)(b) of LOSC, as well as the analysis of the various bilateral accords and interception operations coordinated by FRONTEX in the Mediterranean Sea. In respect of the former, it was propounded that there is room for an evolutionary interpretative claim for reinvigoration of the 'slave trade' provision of LOSC, to include victims of human trafficking under certain narrowly defined conditions. While this claim does not purport to equate *de lege lata* 'human trafficking' to 'slavery', it is in line with the pragmatic needs of human beings who are under conditions akin to slavery, as well as being consistent with the contemporary legal order of the oceans. In addition, the customary rules of 'search and rescue' on the high seas, on which basis FRONTEX largely runs its operations on the high seas, and various secondary rules, such as consent, state of necessity and countermeasures, were scrutinised.

It was generally submitted that the contemporary practice of maritime interception of human beings has to serve a twofold purpose: on the one hand, it should aim at combating illicit migration by sea when it is linked with organised criminal activity, ie smuggling of migrants, while on the other it should equally help to suppress human trafficking and other contemporary forms of modern slavery, as well as rescuing human beings on board unseaworthy vessels. Both of these aspects of maritime interception, ie the 'negative' one of controlling illicit migration and the 'positive' one of saving lives in distress or persons from exploitation, should be able to coexist. More importantly, interception as a whole should be practised in a humanitarian fashion and the protection of human beings should be placed at the centre of interest of the states involved. This would be in harmony with the overarching purpose of maintaining a legal order of oceans premised, inter alia, upon elementary considerations of humanity. Accordingly, it was asserted that there is no room for the use of deadly force, save in self-defence, or various refoulement practices in the framework of interception of human beings.

In conclusion, the right of visit on the high seas has always been central to the construction and development of the legal order of the oceans. It seems that it has attained a greater prominence recently, but the truth is that it has always served as the point of reference for all claims to sovereignty and jurisdiction on the high seas as well as for the resolution of all ostensible conflicts between *mare clausum* and *mare liberum*. It is therefore rightly considered a fundamental underpinning of the *civitas maxima* of the oceans, which will continue to safeguard, but also qualify, the freedom of the high seas.

Bibliography

BOOKS

Allen C, *Maritime Counterproliferation Operations and the Rule of Law* (Westport, CT: Praeger Security International, 2007).

Anand R, *Origin and Development of the Law of the Sea: the History of International Law Revisited* (The Hague: Martinus Nijhoff Pub, 1983).

Anderson D, *Modern Law of the Sea, Selected Essays* (Leiden/Boston: Martinus Nijhoff, 2008).

Babacan A and Briskman L (eds), *Asylum Seekers: International Perspectives on Interdiction and Deterrence* (Newcastle: Cambridge Scholars, 2008).

Bales K, *Disposable People: New Slavery in the Global Economy* (Berkeley, CA: University of California Press, 2004).

Bannelier K et al (eds), *Le Droit International Face au Terrorisme* (Paris: Pedone, 2003).

Bantekas I, *International Criminal Law* (Oxford: Hart Publishing, 2010).

Barnes R, *Property Rights and Natural Resources* (Oxford: Hart Publishing, 2009).

Bertin-Mourot E, Lelier F, Terroir E, *Terrorisme et Piraterie* (Paris: L'Harmattan, 2005).

Bohn M, *The Achille Lauro Hijacking: Lessons in the Politics and Prejudice of Terrorism* (Washington DC: Brassey's, 2004).

Bosch O and Van Ham P (eds), *Global Non-Proliferation and Counter-Terrorism: The Impact of United Nations Security Council Resolution 1540* (The Hague: Clingendael Institution, 2007).

Brownlie I, *International Law and the Use of Force by States* (Oxford: Clarendon Press, 1963).

——, *Principles of Public International Law*, 7th edn (Oxford: Oxford University Press, 2008).

Busch N and Joyner D (eds), *Combating Weapons of Mass Destruction: the Future of International Non-Proliferation Policy* (Athens, GA: University of Georgia Press, 2009)

Capps P, Evans M and Konstantinidis S, *Asserting Jurisdiction: International and European Legal Perspectives* (Oxford: Hart Publishing, 2003).

Caron D and Scheiber HN (eds), *Bringing New Law to Ocean Waters* (Leiden: Martinus Nijhoff Publishers, 2004).

—— and —— (eds), *The Oceans in the Nuclear Age: Legacies and Risks* (Leiden: Martinus Nijhoff Pub, 2010).

Chalk P, *Low Intensity Conflict in Southeast Asia: Piracy, Drug Trafficking and Political Terrorism* (London: Research Institute for the Study of Conflict and Terrorism, 1998).

Churchill RR and Lowe AV, *The Law of the Sea*, 3rd edn (Manchester: Manchester University Press, 1999).

Clingan Th (ed), *The Law of the Sea: What Lies Ahead?* (Hawaii: Law of the Sea Institute, 1988).

—— (ed), *The Law of the Sea: Ocean Law and Policy* (San Francisco, CA: Austin and Winfield, 1993).

Colombos CJ, *International Law of the Sea*, 6th revd edn (London: Longmans, 1967).

Coomans F and Kamming MT (eds), *Extraterritorial Application of Human Rights' Treaties* (Antwerp: Intersentia, 2004).

Crawford J, Pellet A and Olleson S (eds), *The Law of International Responsibility* (Oxford: Oxford University Press, 2010).

De Guttry A and Ronzitti N (eds), *The Iran-Iraq War and the Law of Naval Warfare* (Cambridge: Grotius Publications, 1993).

Doswald-Beck L (ed), *San Remo Manual of International Law Applicable to Armed Conflicts at Sea* (Cambridge: Cambridge University Press, 1995).

Dubner BH, *The Law of International Sea Piracy,* 2nd edn (The Hague: Martinus Nijhoff Publishers, 1988).

Elferink O and Rothwell D (eds), *Oceans Management in the 21st Century: Institutional Frameworks and Responses* (Leiden: Martinus Nijhoff Pub, 2004).

Ferron de O, *Le Droit International de la Mer* (Paris: Librairie Minard, 1958).

Fielding LE, *Maritime Interception and United Nations Sanctions* (San Francisco, CA: Austin/Winfield Publishers, 1997).

Freestone D, Barnes R and Ong D (eds), *The Law of the Sea: Progress and Prospects* (Oxford, Oxford University Press, 2006).

Fulton TW, *The Sovereignty of the Sea* (London: W Blackwood, 1911).

Gavouneli M, *Functional Jurisdiction in the Law of the Sea* (Leiden, Boston: Martinus Nijhoff, 2007).

Gidel G, *Le Droit de la Mer,* Vol I (Paris: Etablissements Mellottee Chateauroux, 1932).

Gilmore W, *Combating International Drug Trafficking: The 1988 United Nations Convention Against Illicit Traffic in Narcotic Drugs and Psychotropic Substances* (London: Commonwealth Secretariat, 1991).

——, *Agreement Concerning Co-operation in Suppressing Illicit Maritime and Air Trafficking in Narcotic Drugs and Psychotropic Substances in the Caribbean Area,* Foreign and Commonwealth Office (London: The Stationery Office, 2005).

Goldstein L, *Preventive Attack and Weapons of Mass Destruction: A Comparative Historical Analysis* (Stanford: Stanford University Press, 2006).

Goodwin-Gill GS and McAdam J, *The Refugee in International Law,* 3rd edn (Oxford: Oxford University Press, 2007).

Gosse P, *The History of Piracy* (New York: Tudor, 1946).

Gray C, *International Law and the Use of Force,* 3rd revd edn (Cambridge: Cambridge University Press, 2008).

Grewe W, *The Epochs of International Law* (translated and revised by M Byers) (Berlin: De Gruyter, 2000).

Grotius H, *The Free Sea* (ed D Armitage) (Indianapolis, IN: Liberty Fund, 2004).

Guilfoyle D, *Shipping Interdiction and the Law of the Sea* (Cambridge: Cambridge University Press, 2009).

Hurwitz A, *The Collective Responsibility of States to Protect Refugees* (Oxford: Oxford University Press, 2009)

Jennings R and Watts A, *Oppenheim's International Law,* 9th edn (London: Longmans, 1992).

Jones S, *Maritime Security: A Practical Guide* (London: The Nautical Institute, 2006).

Joyner D, *International Law and the Proliferation of Weapons of Mass Destruction* (Oxford: Oxford University Press, 2009).

——, *Interpreting the Nuclear Non-Proliferation Treaty* (Oxford: Oxford University Press, 2011).

Klabbers J, *The Concept of Treaty in International* Law (The Hague: Kluwer Law International, 1996).

Klein N, *Maritime Security and the Law of the Sea* (Oxford: Oxford University Press, 2011).

——, Mossop and Rothwell D (eds), *Maritime Security: International Law and Policy Perspectives from Australia and New Zealand* (Abingdon: Routledge, 2010).

Larson DL, *Security Issues and the Law of the Sea* (Lanham: University Press of America, 1993).

Lehr P, *Violence at Sea: Piracy in the Age of Global Terrorism* (New York: Routledge, 2007).

Lowe AV, *International Law* (Oxford: Oxford University Press, 2007).

Lubell N, *Extraterritorial Use of Force against Non-State Actors* (Oxford: Oxford University Press, 2010).

Lucchini L and Vœckel M, *Droit de la Mer* (Paris: Pedone, 1990).

Mallia P, *Migrant Smuggling by Sea: Combating a Current Threat to Maritime Security through the Creation of a Cooperative Framework* (Leiden: Martinus Nijhoff Pub, 2010).

Mansell J, *Flag State Responsibility: Historical Development and Contemporary Issues* (Berlin: Springer, 2009).

McDougal MS and Burke WT, *The Public Order of the Oceans: A Contemporary International Law of the Sea* (New Haven, CT: Yale University Press, 1962).

McLaughlin R, *United Nations Naval Peace Operations in the Territorial Sea* (Leiden: Martinus Nijhoff, 2009).

Mensah TA (ed), *Ocean Governance: Strategies and Approaches for the 21st Century* (Hawaii, The Law of the Sea Institute, 1996).

Mueller GOW and Adler F, *Outlaws of the Ocean: The Complete Book of Contemporary Crime on the High Seas* (New York: Hearst Marine Books, 1985).

Murphy MN, *Small Boats, Weak States, Dirty Money Piracy and Maritime Terrorism in the Modern World* (London: Hurst and Co, 2010).

Nordquist MH (ed), *United Nations Convention on the Law of the Sea, A Commentary*, Vol III (Dordrecht: Martinus Nijhoff Pub, 1985).

—— and Moore JN (eds), *Security Flashpoints: Oil, Islands, Sea Access and Military Confrontation* (The Hague: Martinus Nijhoff Pub, 1998).

——, Koh TB and Moore N (eds), *Freedom of Seas, Passage Rights and the 1982 Law of the Sea Convention* (Leiden: Martinus Nijhoff Pub 2009).

—— et al (eds), *Legal Challenges in Maritime Security* (Leiden: Martinus Nijhoff Pub 2009).

O'Connell DP, *The International Law of the Sea*, Vol II (ed IA Shearer) (Oxford: Clarendon Press, 1984).

O'Day A, *Weapons of Mass Destruction and Terrorism* (London: Ashgate, 2004).

Ortolan T, *Règles Internationales et Diplomatie de la Mer*, Tome II (Paris, 1864).

Palma MA, Tsamenyi M, Edeson W, *Promoting Sustainable Fisheries: The International Legal and Policy Framework to Combat Illegal, Unreported and Unregulated Fishing* (Leiden: Martinus Nijhoff, 2010)

Parritt BAH (ed), *Violence at Sea: A Review of Terrorism, Acts of War and Piracy, and Countermeasures to Prevent Terrorism* (Paris: ICC Publishing, 1986).

Pazartzis Ph, *La répression pénale des crimes internationaux: justice pénale international* (Paris: Pedone, 2007).

Petrie D, *The Prize Game: Lawful Looting on the High Seas in the Days of Fighting Sail* (Annapolis, MD: Naval Institute Press, 1999).

Politakis GP, *Modern Aspects of the Laws of Naval Warfare and Maritime Neutrality* (London: Keagan Paul International), 1998.

Potter PB, *The Freedom of the Seas in History, Law and Politics* (London: Longmans, 1924).

Rayfuse R, *Non-Flag State Enforcement in High Seas Fisheries* (Leiden: Brill Academic Publishers, 2004).

Ronzitti N (ed), *Maritime Terrorism and International Law* (Dordrecht: Martinus Nijhoff), 1990.

Rothwell D and Bateman S (eds), *Navigational Rights and Freedoms and the New Law of the Sea* (The Hague: Martinus Nijhoff, 2000).

Rubin AP, *The Law of Piracy*, 2nd edn (New York: Transnational, 1998).

Ruyver De B et al (eds), *Multidisciplinary Drug Policies and the UN Drug Treaties* (Antwerp: Apeldoorn, 2002).

Sarooshi D *The United Nations and the Development of Collective Security* (Oxford: Oxford University Press, 1999).

Schaller C, *Die Unterbindung des Seetransports von Massenvernichtungswaffen* (Berlin: SWP, 2004).

Scheiber HN, *Law of the Sea: the Common Heritage and Emerging Challenges* (The Hague: Martinus Nijhoff, 2000).

Schloenhardt A, *Migrant Smuggling: Illegal Migration and Organized Crime in Australia and the Asia Pacific Region* (Leiden: Nijhoff, 2003).

Schneider B and Davis J (eds), *Avoiding the Abyss Progress, Shortfalls and the Way Ahead in Combating the WMD Threat* (London: Praeger Security International, 2006).

Simma B (ed), *The Charter of the United Nations A Commentary*, 2nd edn (Oxford: Oxford University Press, 2002).

Smith GP II, *Restricting the Concept of Free Seas: Modern Maritime Law Re-evaluated* (Huntington, NY: Krieger Pub, 1980).

Smith H, *The Law and Custom of the Sea* (London: Steven and Sons, 1959).

Sohn LB, *Cases and Materials on the Law of the Sea* (Ardsley, NY: Transnational, 2004).

—— and Gustafson K, *Law of the Sea in a Nutshell* (St Paul, MN: West Publishing Co, 1984).

Stark F, *The Abolition of Privateering and the Declaration of Paris* (New York: Columbia University, 1897).

Stokke OS (ed), *Governing High Seas Fisheries: The Interplay of Global and Regional Regimes* (Oxford: Oxford University Press, 2001).

Torr J, *Weapons of Mass Destruction: Opposing Viewpoints* (Farmington Hills, MI: Greenhaven Press, 2005).

Tuerk H, *Reflections on the Contemporary Law of the Sea* (Leiden: Martinus Nijhoff, 2012).

Van der Kruit PJJ, *Maritime Drug Interdiction in International Law* (Utrecht: Druk OBT/TDS, 2007).

Van Gingel B and Van der Putten F-P (eds), *The International Response to Somali Piracy: Challenges and Opportunities* (Leiden: Martinus Nijhoff, 2010).

Van Selm J and Cooper, B, *The New 'Boat People'. Ensuring Safely and Determining Status* (Washington DC: Migration Policy Institute, 2006)

Valencia M, *The Proliferation Security Initiative*, Adelphi Paper 376 (London: The International Institute for Strategic Studies, 2005).

Vidas D (ed), *Law, Technology and Science for Oceans in Globalisation: IUU Fishing, Oil Pollution, Bioprospecting, Outer Continental Shelf* (Leiden: Martinus Nijhoff, 2010).

—— and Østreng W (eds), *Order for the Oceans at the Turn of the Century* (The Hague: Kluwer Law International, 1999).

—— and Schei J (eds), *The World Ocean in Globalisation: Climate Change, Sustainable Fisheries, Biodiversity, Shipping, Regional Issues* (Leiden: Martinus Nijhoff, 2011).

Walter C et al (eds), *Terrorism as a Challenge for National and International Law: Security versus Liberty?* (Berlin: Springer 2004)

Wendel P, *State Responsibility for Interferences with the Freedom of Navigation in International Law* (Berlin: Springer, 2007).

Witt J-A, *Obligations and Control of Flag States: Developments and Perspectives in International Law and EU Law* (Berlin: Verlag, 2008).

Wooters CW, *International Legal Standards for the Protection from Reloulement* (Oxford: Hart Publishing, 2009).

ARTICLES AND ESSAYS

Abi-Saab G, 'The Security Council as Legislator and as Executive in its Fight against Terrorism and against Proliferation of Weapons of Mass Destruction: the Question of Legitimacy' in Wolfrum R and Röben V (eds), *Legitimacy in International Law* (Berlin: Springer, 2008) 109–30.

Ahlström C, 'The Proliferation Security Initiative: International Law Aspects of the Statement of Interdiction Principles', in *SIPRI Yearbook (2005): Armaments, Disarmament and International Security* (Oxford: Oxford University Press, 2006) 741–765.

Alexander CD, 'Maritime Terrorism and Legal Responses' 19 *Denver Journal of International Law and Policy* (1991) 529–67.

Alexandrowicz CH, 'Freitas versus Grotius' 35 *British Yearbook of International Law* (1959) 162–82.

Allain J, 'The *Jus Cogens* Nature of *Non–Refoulement*' 13 *International Journal of Refugee Law* (2001) 533–58.

——, 'Insisting on the *Jus Cogens* Nature of *Non–Refoulement*', in Van Selm J (ed), *The Refugee Convention at Fifty* (2003) 81–95.

——, 'The Nineteenth Century Law of the Sea and the British Abolition of the Slave Trade' 78 *British Yearbook of International Law* (2007) 343–88.

Allen C, 'Limits on the Use of Force in Maritime Operations in Support of Weapons of Mass Destruction Counter–Proliferation Initiatives' 35 *Israel Yearbook on Human Rights* (2005) 1115–80.

——, 'A Primer on the Non–Proliferation Regime for Maritime Security Operations Forces' 54 *Naval Law Review* (2007) 51–77.

Anand RP, 'Freedom of the Seas: Past, Present and Future', in R Gutiérrez Girardot et al (eds), *New Directions in International Law: Essays in Honour of Wolfgang Abendroth* (Frankfurt: Verlag, 1982) 215–33.

Anderson A, 'Jurisdiction over Stateless Vessels on the High Seas: an Appraisal under Domestic and International Law' 13 *Journal of Maritime Law and Commerce* (1982) 335.

Anderson EH, 'The Nationality of Ships and Flags of Convenience: Economics, Politics and Alternatives' 21 *Tulane Maritime Law Journal* (1996) 139–70.

Antonopoulos C, 'Force by Armed Groups as Armed Attack and the Broadening of Self–Defence' 55 *Netherlands International Law Review* (2008) 159–80.

——, '"The Legitimacy to Legitimise": The Security Action in Libya under Resolutuion 1973 (2011)' 14 *International Community Law Review* (2012) 359–79.

Bahar M, 'Attaining Optimal Deterrence at Sea: A Legal and Strategic Theory for Naval Anti-Piracy Operations' 40 *Vanderbilt Journal of Transnational Law* (2007) 1–86.

Balkin R, 'The International Maritime Organisation and Maritime Security' 30 *Tulane Maritime Law Journal* (2006)1–34.

Ballet F, 'Safety on the High Seas: Human Security as an Element of Ocean Governance' 18 *Ocean Yearbook* (2004) 543–57.

Bardin A 'Coastal State's Jurisdiction over Foreign Vessels' 14 *Pace International Law Review* (2002) 27–76.

Barnes R, 'Refugee Law at Sea' 53 *International and Comparative Law Quarterly* (2004) 47–77.

Barrios E, 'Casting a Wider Net: Addressing the Maritime Piracy Problem in Southeast Asia' 28 *Boston College International and Comparative Law Review* (2005) 149–63.

Barry IP, 'The Right of Visit, Search and Seizure of Foreign Flagged Vessels on the High Seas Pursuant to Customary International Law: a Defence of the Proliferation Security Initiative' 33 *Holfstra Law Review* (2004) 299–330.

Bassiouni C, 'Universal Jurisdiction for International Crimes: Historical Perspectives and Contemporary Practice' 42 *Virginia Journal of International Law* (2001) 81–162.

Bastid-Burdeau G, 'Migrations Clandestines et Droit de la Mer', in *La Mer et Son Droit, Mélanges Offerts à Laurent Lucchini et Jean–Pierre Quéneudec* (Paris: Pedone, 2003) 57–66.

Beasley JA, 'Grotius and the New Law of the Sea' 18 *Ocean Yearbook* (2004) 98–116.

Beck A, 'Vessels, Aircrafts and Persons Entitled to Protection during Armed Conflict at Sea' 65 *British Yearbook of International Law* (1994) 211–301.

Becker M, 'The Shifting Public Order of the Oceans: Freedom of Navigation and the Interdiction of Ships at Sea' 46 *Harvard International Law Journal* (2004) 131–230.

Beckman R and Davenport T, 'Maritime Terrorism and the Law of the Sea', in M Nordquist et al (eds), *The Law of the Sea Convention: US Accession and Globalization* (Leiden: Martinus Nijhoff, 2012) 229–57.

Bederman DJ, 'Counter Intuiting Countermeasures' 96 *American Journal of International Law* (2002) 817–31.

Bedjaoui M, 'Peuples en Mer: Une Ere Nouvelle de Colonisation des Espaces Maritimes', in *La Mer et Son Droit, Mélanges Offerts à Laurent Lucchini et Jean-Pierre Quéneudec* (Paris: Pedone, 2003) 67–77.

Bellayer-Roile A, 'La Lutte contre le Narcotrafic en Mer Caraïbe, une Coopération Internationale à Géométrie Variable' 111 *Revue Générale de Droit International Public* (2007) 355–86.

Bennett A, 'The Sinking Feeling: Stateless Ships, Universal Jurisdiction, and the Drug Trafficking Vessel interdiction Act' 37 *Yale Journal of International Law* (2012) 433–61.

Bergin A, 'The Proliferation Security Initiative: Implications for the Indian Ocean' 20 *International Journal of Marine and Coastal Law* (2005) 85–95.

Berman F, 'Preemption and Weapons of Mass Destruction' 9 *International Peacekeeping* (2005) 173–82.

Biad A, 'La Lutte contre le Trafic des Armes de Destruction Massive par Mer' 9 *Annuaire de Droit de la Mer* (2004) 197–210.

Birnie PW, 'Piracy Past, Present and Future' 11 *Marine Policy* (1987) 163–83.

Blakeslee FS, '*United States v Mynard* and Enforcement of United States Drug Trafficking Laws on the High Seas: How Far United States Jurisdiction Really Reach?' 2 *Pace Yearbook of International Law* (1990) 169–94.

Blanco-Bazán A, 'Suppressing Unlawful Acts: IMO Incursion in the Field of Criminal Law', in T Malick Ndiaye and R Wolfrum (eds), *Liber Amicorum Judge Thomas A Mensah* (Leiden: Nijhoff, 2007) 713–33.

Boczek BA, 'Peaceful Purposes Provisions of the United Nations Convention on the Law of the Sea' 20 *Ocean Development and International Law* (1989) 359–89.

Boisson P, 'La sûreté des navires et la prévention des actes de terrorisme dans le domaine maritime' 55 *Droit Maritime Français* (2003) 723–36.

Bostock CM, 'The International Legal Obligation Owed to the Asylum-Seekers on the M V *Tampa*' 14 *International Journal of Refugee Law* (2002) 279–301.

Bothe M, 'Terrorism and the Legality of Pre-emptive Force' 14 *European Journal of International Law* (2003) 227–40.

Bourgon S, 'The Impact of Terrorism on the Principle of "*Non-Refoulement*" of Refugees: the *Suresh Case* before the Supreme Court of Canada' 1 *Journal of International Criminal Justice* (2003) 169–85.

Brilmayer L, Klein N, 'Land and Sea: Two Sovereignty Regimes in Search of a Common Denominator' 33 *New York University Journal of International Law and Politics* (2001) 703–68.

Brolan C, 'An Analysis of the Human Smuggling Trade and the Protocol against the Smuggling of Migrants by Land, Air and Sea (2000) from a Refugee Protection Perspective' 14 *International Journal of Refugee Law* (2002) 561–96.

Brown Weiss E, 'Invoking State Responsibility in the Twenty-First Century' 96 *American Journal of International Law* (2002) 798–816.

Brunnée J and Toope SJ, 'The Use of Force: International Law after Iraq' 53 *International and Comparative Law Quarterly* (2004) 785–806.

Byers M, 'Policing the High Seas: The Proliferation Security Initiative' 98 *American Journal of International Law* (2004) 526–45.

Byers M, 'Gunboat Diplomacy: Policing the Seas and the Skies' 59 *The World Today* (2003) 14–15.

Cable J, 'Conflict at Sea' 9 *Marine Policy* (1985) 261–68.

Canty R, 'Limits of Coastal Guard Authority to Board Foreign Flag Vessels on the High Seas' 23 *Tulane Maritime Law Journal* (1998) 123–37.

——, 'The Law of Piracy: Is There Room for Terrorism?' in Fitzhugh TC (ed), *International Perspectives on Maritime Security: A Cooperative Effort of the Maritime Security Council, US Department of Transportation, United States Maritime Administration and the US Coast Guard* (Washington DC: US Department of Transportation, 1996) 211.

Chetail V, 'Le droit des réfugiés à l'épreuve des droits de l'homme: bilan de la jurisprudence de la Cour européenne des droits de l'homme sur l'interdiction du renvoi des étrangers menacés de torture et de traitements inhumains ou dégradants' 37 *Revue Belge de Droit International* (2004) 155–210.

Churchill R, 'The European Union and the Challenges for Marine Governance: from Sectoral Response to Integrated Policy?', in Vidas D, Schei P (eds), *The World Ocean in Globalisation: Climate Change, Sustainable Fisheries, Biodiversity, Shipping, Regional Issues* (Leiden: Martinus Nijhoff, 2011) 395–436.

——, 'Conflicts between UN Security Council Resolutions and the UN Convention on the Law of the Sea– and their Possible Resolution' 38 *Israel Yearbook on Human Rights* (2008) 185–93.

Clark H, 'Staying Afloat in International Law: The Proliferation Security Initiative's Implications for Freedom of Navigation' 21 *Ocean Yearbook* (2007) 441–74.

Condorelli L, 'The Imputability to States of Acts of International Terrorism' 19 *Israel Yearbook of Human Rights* (1989) 233–46.

Constantinople RG, 'Towards a New Definition of Piracy: The *Achille Lauro* Incident' 26 *Virginia Journal of International Law* (1986) 723–53.

Coppens J, 'Migrants in the Mediterranean: Do's and Don'ts in Maritime Interdiction' 43 *Ocean Development & international Law* (2012) 342–70.

Costa M, 'Extraterritorial Application of Maritime Drug Law Enforcement Act in the *United States v Suerte*' 18 *Temple International and Comparative Law Journal* (2004) 131–54.

Crépeau F, 'The Protocol against the Smuggling of Migrants: The Crowning of an Intense Cooperation on Migration Containment', in Canadian Council on International Law (ed), *Globalism: People, Profits and Progress* (2002) 125–33.

Curtis RC, 'The Outer Limits of Jurisdiction on the High Seas: *United States v Romero-Galue* and *United States v Alvarez-Mena*', 5 *Wisconsin International Law Journal* (1986) 222–40.

Dalton J, 'A Comparison between the San Remo Manual and the US Navy's Commander's Handbook' 36 *Israel Yearbook on Human Rights* (2006) 71–88.

Davide H, '*Hostes Humani Generis*: Piracy, Territory and the Concept of Universal Jurisdiction', R McDonald and D Johnston (eds), *Towards World Constitutionalism* (Leiden: Nijhoff, 2005) 715–36.

Davidson S, 'Dangerous Waters: Combating Maritime Piracy at Sea', 9 *Asian Yearbook of International Law* (2004) 3–29.

——, 'International Law and the Suppression of Maritime Violence', in Burchill R et al (eds), *International Conflict and Security Law Essays in Memory of H McCoubrey* (Cambridge: Cambridge University Press, 2005) 265–85.

Davis-Mattis L, 'International Drug Trafficking and the Law of the Sea: Outstanding Issues and Bilateral Responses with Emphasis on US-Caribbean Agreements' 14 *Ocean Yearbook* (2000) 360–85.

DeFrancia C, 'Enforcing the Nuclear Nonproliferation Regime: The Legality of Preventive Measures' 45 *Vanderbilt Journal of Transnational Law* (2012) 704–83.

de Wet E, 'The Legitimacy of United Nations Security Council Decisions in the Fight against Terrorism and the Proliferation of Weapons of Mass Destruction: Some Critical Remarks', in Wolfrum R and Röben V (eds), *Legitimacy in International Law* (Berlin: Springer, 2008) 131–54.

Diaz L and Dubner H, 'On the Problem of Utilizing Unilateral Action to Prevent Acts of Sea Piracy and Terrorism: A Proactive Approach to the Evolution of International Law' 32 *Syracuse Journal of International Law and Commerce* (2004) 1–50.

Dinstein Y, 'Piracy *Jure Gentium*', in H Hestermeyer et al (eds), *Coexistence, Cooperation and Solidarity: Liber Amicorum Rüdiger Wolfrum* (Leiden: Martinus Nijhofff, 2012), 1125–43.

Dipla H, *La responsabilité de l'Etat pour violation des droits de l'homme: problèmes d'imputation* (Paris: Pedone, 1994).

Discussions of Panel IV: 'Caribbean Drug Challenges' in Nordquist MH and Moore JN (eds), *Ocean Policy: New Institutions, Challenges and Opportunities* (1999) 173–239.

Doolin J, 'The Proliferation Security Initiative: Cornerstone of a New International Norm' 59 *Naval War College Review* (2006) 29–57.

Donnelly D, 'Foreign Affairs, Drug Interdiction and Immigration' 21 *Suffolk Transnational Law Review* (1998) 269–92.

Dragonette C, 'Maritime Terrorism: Underway as Before?', in Fitzhugh TC (ed), *International Perspectives on Maritime Security: A Cooperative Effort of the Maritime Security Council, US Department of Transportation, United States Maritime Administration and the US Coast Guard* (Washington DC: US Department of Transportation, 1996) 159.

Dubner H, 'Piracy in Contemporary National and International Law' 21 *California Western International Law Journal* (1990) 139–50.

Feinstein B, 'The Interception of Civilian Vessels at Sea in the Fight against Terrorism: Legal Aspects: An Israeli View' 2 *Finnish Yearbook of International Law* (1991) 197–267.

Fenrick W, 'The Exclusion Zone Device in the Law of Naval Warfare' 24 *Canadian Yearbook of International Law* (1986) 91–126.

Fidler O, 'International Law and Weapons of Mass Destruction: End of Arms Control Approach?' 14 *Duke Journal of Comparative and International Law* (2004) 39–88.

Fitzmaurice M, 'The Identification and Character of Treaties and Treaty Obligations between States in International Law' 73 *British Yearbook of International Law* (2002) 141–85.

Fleck D, 'Rules of Engagement for Maritime Forces and the Limitation of the Use of Force under the UN Charter' 31 *German Yearbook of International Law* (1988) 165–86.

Foster CE, 'The *Oil Platforms Case* and the Use of Force in International Law' 17 *Singapore Journal of International and Comparative Law* (2003) 579–88.

Francioni F, 'Peacetime Use of Force, Military Activities and the New Law of the Sea' 18 *Cornell International Law Journal* (1985) 203–26.

——, 'Use of Force, Military Activities, and the New Law of the Sea', in Cassese A (ed), *The Current Legal Regulation of the Use of Force* (Dordrecht: Martinus Nijhoff, 1986) 361–83.

Francioni F, 'Maritime Terrorism and International Law: The Rome Convention of 1988' 31 *German Yearbook of International Law* (1988) 263–88.

Franckx E and Van Assche C, 'Contemporary High Seas Fisheries Law' in Franckx E and Devine D (eds), *Contemporary Regulation of Marine Living Resources and Pollution* (Antwerp: Maklu, 2007) 29–70.

Freestone D, 'Problems of High Seas Governance', in Vidas D and Schei PJ (eds), *The World Ocean in Globalisation: Climate Change, Sustainable Fisheries, Biodiversity, Shipping, Regional Issues* (Leiden: Martinus Nijhoff, 2011) 99–130.

Frelick B, 'Haitian Boat Interdiction and Return: First Asylum and First Principles of Refugee Protection' 26 *Cornell Journal of International Law* (1993) 675–94.

——, '"Abundantly Clear": *Refoulement*' 19 *Georgetown Immigration Law Journal* (2005) 245.

Frowein J, 'The Security Council and the Security on the Seas', in Hestermeyer H et al (eds), *Law of the Sea in Dialogue* (Berlin: Springer, 2011) 179.

Fu K-C, 'Policing the Sea and the Proportionality Principle', in M Nordquist et al (eds), *The Law of the Sea Convention: US Accession and Globalization* (Leiden: Martinus Nijhoff, 2012) 371–81.

Garmon T, 'International Law of the Sea: Reconciling the Law of Piracy and Terrorism in the wake of September 11th' 27 *Tulane Maritime Law Journal* (2002) 257–72.

Garvey J, 'The International Institutional Imperative for Countering the Spread of Weapons of Mass Destruction: Assessing the Proliferation Security Initiative' 10 *Journal of Conflict and Security Law* (2005) 125–47.

Gauci G, 'Piracy – Legal and Theoretical Problems', in *Maritime Violence and Other Security Issues at Sea*, World Maritime University, University of Wales, Swansea – Proceedings of a Symposium, Malmö, 26–30 August, 2002, Sweden (Malmö: WMU, 2002) 39–53.

Gautier P, 'L'Etat du Pavillon et la Protection des Intérêts lies au Navire', in Kohen M (ed), *Promoting Justice, Human Rights and Conflict Resolution through International Law, Liber Amicorum Lucius Caflisch* (Leiden: Brill, 2007) 717–45.

——, 'From Piracy to Maritime Violence: The Quest for All–Encompassing Terminology' 2 *Journal of International Commercial Law* (2003) 177–94.

Gazzini T, 'The Rules on the Use of Force at the Beginning of the XXI Century' 11 *Journal of Conflict and Security Law* (2006) 319–42.

Geraghty AH, 'Universal Jurisdiction and Drug Trafficking: a Tool for Fighting One of the World's Most Pervasive Problems' 16 *Florida Journal of International Law* (2004) 371–403.

Gilmore WC, 'Narcotics Interdiction at Sea: UK–US Cooperation' 13 *Marine Policy* (1989) 218–230.

——, 'The 1988 United Nations Convention against Illicit Traffic in Narcotic Drugs and Psychotropic Substances' 15 *Marine Policy* (1991) 183–92.

——, 'Narcotics Interdiction at Sea: The 1995 Council of Europe Agreement' 20 *Marine Policy* (1996) 3–14.

——, 'Drug Trafficking at Sea: The Case of *R v Charrington and Others*' 49 *International and Comparative Law Quarterly* (2000) 477–89.

Giuffré M, 'Watered-down Rights on the High Seas: Hirsi Jamaa and Others v Italy' 61 *International and Comparative Law Quarterly* (2012) 728–50.

Gjerde K, 'High Seas Fisheries Governance: Prospects and Challenges in the 21st Century', in Vidas D and Schei J (eds), *The World Ocean in Globalisation: Climate Change, Sustainable Fisheries, Biodiversity, Shipping, Regional Issues* (Leiden: Martinus Nijhoff, 2011) 221–45.

Goldie LFE, 'Terrorism, Piracy and the Nyon Agreement', in Dinstein Y (ed), *International law at a time of perplexity: Essays in honour of Shabtai Rosenne* (Dordrecht: Martinus Nijhoff, 1989) 225–48.

——, 'Commentary to the Nyon Agreements', in N Ronzitti (ed), *The Law of Naval Warfare* (Dordrecht: Martinus Nijhoff, 1988) 489–502.

Golitsyn V, 'Maritime Security (Case of Piracy)', in H Hestermeyer et al (eds), *Coexistence, Cooperation and Solidarity: liber amicorum Rüdiger Wolfrum* (Leiden: Nijhoff, 2012) 1157–76.

Gonzalez-Pinto J, 'Interdiction of Narcotics in International Waters' 15 *University of Miami International and Comparative Law Review* (2008) 443

Gooding GV, 'Fighting Terrorism in the 1980's: The Interception of the *Achille Lauro* Hijackers' 12 *Yale Journal of International Law* (1987) 158–79.

Goodman TH, 'Leaving the Corsair's Name to Other Times': How to Enforce the Law of Sea Piracy in the 21st Century through Regional International Agreements' 31 *Case Western Reserve Journal of International Law* (1999) 139–68.

Gowlland-Debbas V, 'The Limits of Unilateral Enforcement of Community Objectives in the Framework of UN Peace Maintenance' 11 *European Journal of International Law* (2000) 361–83.

Goy R, 'Le Renforcement par l'Organisation Maritime Internationale de la Sécurité en Mer et au Port' 9 *Annuaire de Droit de la Mer* (2004) 157–95.

Graham T, 'National Self-Defence, International Law, and Weapons of Mass Destruction' 4 *Chicago Journal of International Law* (2003) 1–18.

Green LC, 'Terrorism and the Law of the Sea', in Dinstein Y (ed), *International law at a time of perplexity: essays in honour of Shabtai Rosenne* (Dordrecht: Martinus Nijhoff, 1989) 249–71.

Greenwood C, 'War, Terrorism, and International Law' 56 *Current Legal Problems* (2003) 505–30.

Gualde VG, 'Suppression of the Illicit Traffic in Narcotic Drugs and Psychotropic Substances on the High Seas: Spanish Case Law' 4 *Spanish Yearbook of International Law* (1996) 91–106.

Guesnier F, 'Acts of Terrorism as Crimes against Humanity under the Rome Statute', in Yee S (ed), *International Crime and Punishment*, Vol II (2004) 55–86.

Guilfoyle D, 'Interdicting Vessels to Enforce the Common Interest: Maritime Countermeasures and the Use of Force' 56 *International and Comparative Law Quarterly* (2007) 69–82.

——, 'Maritime Interdiction of Weapons of Mass Destruction' 12 *Journal of Conflict and Security Law* (2007) 1–35.

——, 'The Proliferation Security Initiative: Interdicting Vessels in the International Waters to Prevent the Spread of Weapons of Mass Destruction' 29 *Melbourne University Law Review* (2007) 733–64.

——, 'Piracy off Somalia: UN Security Council Resolution 1816 and IMO Regional Counter–Piracy Efforts' 57 *International and Comparative Law Quarterly* (2008) 690–99.

Guilfoyle D, 'Counter-Piracy, Law Enforcement and Human Rights' 59 *International and Comparative Law Quarterly* (2010) 141–69.

——, 'Legal Challenges in Fighting Piracy', in Van Gingel B and Van der Putten F-P (eds), *The International Response to Somali Piracy: Challenges and Opportunities* (Leiden: Martinus Nijhoff, 2010) 127–52.

——, 'Combating Piracy: Executive Measures on the High Seas' 53 *Japanese Yearbook of International Law* (2011) 149–77.

——, 'Human Rights Issues and Non-Flag State Boarding of Suspect Ships in the High Seas', in Symmons CR (ed), *Selected Contemporary Issues in the Law of the Sea* (Leiden: Martinus Nijhoff, 2011) 83–104.

——, 'The *Mavi Marmara* Incident and Blockade in Armed Conflict' 81 *British Yearbook of International Law* (2011) 171–223.

Haines S, 'The United Kingdom's Manual on International Law Applicable to Armed Conflicts at Sea' 36 *Israel Yearbook on Human Rights* (2006) 89–118.

Halberstam M, 'Terrorist Acts against and on Board Ships' 19 *Israel Yearbook of Human Rights* (1989)331–42.

——, 'Terrorism on the High Seas: The *Achille Lauro*, Piracy and the IMO Convention on Maritime Security' 82 *American Journal of International Law* (1988) 269–310.

Hall J, 'The Treatment of Asylum-Seekers and Migrants in the Context of the Global War on Terror' 98 *Proceedings of the American Society of International Law* (2004) 258–60.

Hannesson R, 'Rights Based Fishing on the High Seas: Is it Possible?' 35 *Marine Policy* (2011), 667–74.

Happold M, 'Security Council Resolution 1373 and the Constitution of the United States' 16 *Leiden Journal of International Law* (2003) 593–610.

Harrington C, 'Heightened Security: The Need to Incorporate Article 3 *bis*(1)(a) and 8*bis*(5)(e) of the 2005 Draft SUA Protocol into Part VII of the United National Convention on the Law of the Sea' 16 *Pacific Rim Law and Policy Journal* (2007) 107–36.

Hathaway J, 'Human Rights Quagmire of "Human Trafficking"' 49 *Virginia Journal of International Law* (2008) 1–59.

Häussler U, Crisis Response Operations in Maritime Environments', in Odello M and Piotrowicz (eds), *International Military Missions and International Law* (Leiden: Martinus Nijhoff, 2012), 161-210.

Hayashi M, 'The 1995 Agreement on the Conservation and Management of Straddling and Highly Migratory Fish Stocks: Significance for the Law of the Sea Convention' 29 *Ocean and Coastal Management* (1995) 51–69.

Hedigan J, 'The European Convention on Human Rights and Counter–Terrorism' 28 *Fordham International Law Journal* (2005) 392–431.

Hegelsom, G–J, 'Implementation of Caribbean Maritime Counter–Narcotics Cooperation Report', in Nordquist MH and Moore JN (eds), *Ocean Policy: New Institutions, Challenges and Opportunities* (1999) 295–303.

Heintschel von Heinegg W, 'Visit, Search, Diversion and Capture in Naval Warfare: Part II, Developments since 1945' 30 *Canadian Yearbook of International Law* (1993) 89–136.

——, 'The Legality of Maritime Interception Operations within the Framework of Operation Enduring Freedom', W Heere (ed) *Terrorism and the Military: International Legal Implications* (The Hague: Asser Press, 2003) 43–60.

——, 'Current Legal Issues in Maritime Operations: Maritime Interception Operations in the Global War on Terrorism, Exclusion Zones, Hospital Ships and Maritime Neutrality' 34 *Israel Yearbook on Human Rights* (2004) 151–78.

——, "Maritime Interception/Interdiction Operations within the Framework of Operation Enduring Freedom", in *Les Nouvelles Menaces contre la Paix et la Sécurité Internationales* (Paris: Pedone, 2004) 149–64.

——, 'The Proliferation Security Initiative: Security v Freedom of Navigation?' 35 *Israel Yearbook on Human Rights* (2005) 181–203.

——, 'How to Update the San Remo Manual on International Law Applicable to Armed Conflicts at Sea' 36 *Israel Yearbook on Human Rights* (2006) 119–47.

——, 'The United Nations Convention on the Law of the Sea and Maritime Security Operations' 48 *German Yearbook of International Law* (2006) 151–86.

——, 'Terrorism, NATO, Rules of Engagement' in D Karpen et al (ed), *Maritime Security – Current Problems in the Baltic Sea* (Berlin: Nomos, 2007) 103–120.

——, 'Manoeuvring in Rough Waters: The UK Manual of the Law of Armed Conflict and the Law of Naval Warfare', in Fischer-Lescano A et al (eds), *Frieden in Freiheit: Festschrift fur Michael Bothe zum 70 Geburtstag* (Baden-Baden: Nomos, 2008) 427–44.

——, 'Security at Sea: Legal Restrains or Lack of Political Will? Comments on the Keynote Address by Admiral Hogh', in M Nordquist et al (eds), *Legal Challenges in Maritime Security* (Leiden: Martinus Nijhoff Pub, 2008) 133–48.

——, 'The Law of Military Operations at Sea', in TD Gill and D Fleck (eds), *The Handbook of the International Law of Military Operations* (Oxford: Oxford University Press, 2010) 325–74.

Hesse GH, 'Maritime Security in a Multilateral Context: IMO Activities to Enhance Maritime Security' 18 *International Journal of Marine and Coastal Law* (2003) 327–62.

Hinrichs X, "Measures against Smuggling of Migrants at Sea: A Law of the Sea Related Perspective" 36 *Revue Belge de Droit International* (2003) 413–51.

Hodgkinson S et al, 'Challenges to Maritime Interception Operations in the War on Terror: Bridging the Gap' 22 *American University International Law Review* (2007) 583–671.

—— et al, 'International Law in Crisis: Seeking the Best Prosecution Model for Somali Pirates' 44 *Case Western Reserve Journal of International Law* (2011) 303–16.

Holmes JR and Winner A, 'The Proliferation Security Initiative', in N Busch and D Joyner (eds), *Combating Weapons of Mass Destruction: the Future of International Nonproliferation Policy* (Athens, GA: Georgia University Press, 2009) 139–55.

Jacobsson M, 'Terrorism at Sea', in *Maritime Violence and Other Security Issues at Sea*, World Maritime University, University of Wales, Swansea – Proceedings of a Symposium, Malmö, 26–30 August, 2002, Sweden (Malmö: WMU, 2002) 157–64.

——, 'Maritime Security: an Individual or Collective Responsibility?', in Petman J, Klabbers J (eds), *Nordic Cosmopolitanism Essays in International Law for Martti Koskenniemi* (Leiden: Martinus Nijhoff, 2003), 391–416.

Jesus JL, 'Protection of Foreign Ships against Piracy and Terrorism at Sea: Legal Aspects' 18 *International Journal of Marine and Coastal Law* (2003) 363–400.

Jimenez-Kwast P, 'Maritime Interdiction of Weapons of Mass Destruction in an International Legal Perspective' 38 *Netherlands Yearbook of International Law* (2007) 163–241.

Jimenez-Kwast P, 'Maritime Law Enforcement and the Use of Force: Reflections on the Categorization of Forcible Action at Sea in the Light of Guyana/Suriname Award' 13 *Journal of Security and Conflict Law* (2008) 49–91.

Joyner CC, 'The 1988 IMO Convention on the Safety of Maritime Navigation: Towards a Legal Remedy for Terrorism at Sea' 31 *German Yearbook of International Law* (1988) 230–62.

——, 'Suppression of Terrorism on the High Seas: The 1988 IMO Convention on the Safety of Maritime Navigation' 19 *Israel Yearbook of Human Rights* (1989) 343–69.

Joyner DH, 'Restructuring the Multilateral Export Control Regime System' 9 *Journal of Conflict and Security Law* (2004) 181–211.

——, 'The Enhanced Proliferation Control Initiative: National Security Necessity or Unconstitutionally Vague?' 32 *Georgia Journal of International and Comparative Law* (2004) 107–23.

——, 'The Proliferation Security Initiative: Non–proliferation, Counter proliferation, and International Law' 30 *Yale Journal of International Law* (2005) 507–48.

Kaye S, 'State Practice and Maritime Claims: Assessing the Normative Impact of the Law of the Sea Convention' in Chircop A, Johnston D (eds), *The Future of Ocean Regime-Building: Essays in Tribute to Douglas M Johnston* (Leiden: Martinus Nijhoff, 2009) 133–58.

——, 'The Proliferation Security Initiative in the Maritime Domain' 35 *Israel Yearbook on Human Rights* (2005) 205–29.

Kearley T, 'Raising the Caroline' 17 *Wisconsin International Law Journal* (1999) 325–46.

Kern HL, 'Strategies of Legal Change: Great Britain, International Law, and the Abolition of the Transatlantic Slave Trade' 6 *Journal of History of International Law* (2004) 233–58.

King G, 'The Security of Merchant Shipping' 29 *Marine Policy* (2005) 235–45.

Kinley G, 'The Law of Self-Defence, Contemporary Naval Operations and the UN Convention on the Law of the Sea', in ED Brown, R Churchill (eds), *The UN Convention on the Law of the Sea: Impact and Implementation* (Hawaii: The Law of the Sea Institute, 1987) 10–40.

Kirsch P, 'The 1988 ICAO and IMO Conferences: An International Consensus against Terrorism' 12 *The Dalhousie Law Journal* (1989) 5—33.

Kirtley W, '*Tampa* Incident: The Legality of *Ruddock v Vadarlis* under International Law and the Implications of Australia's New Asylum Policy' 41 *Columbia Journal of Transnational Law* (2002–2003) 251–300.

Kladi-Efstathopoulou M, 'Droit de Visite et Rescherche et Droit de Poursuitre en Haute Mer: Aproache Juridique Contemporaine' 57 *Revue Hellénique de Droit International* (2004) 261–73.

Klein N, 'Legal Implications of Australia's Maritime Identification System' 55 *International Comparative Law Quarterly* (2006) 337–68.

——, 'The Right of Visit and the 2005 Protocol on the Suppression of Unlawful Acts against the Safety of Maritime Navigation' 35 *Denver Journal of International Law and Policy* (2007) 287–332.

Knight WS, 'Seraphin de Freitas: Critic of *Mare Liberum*' 11 *Transactions of the Grotius Society* (1926) 1–11.

Koh HH, 'Reflections on *Refoulement* and *Haitian Centers Council*' 35 *Harvard International Law Journal* (1994) 1–20.

—— and Wishnie M, 'The Story of *Sale v Haitian Centers* Council: Guantanamo and *Refoulement*', in Hurwitz D et al (eds), *Human Rights Advocacy Stories* (Thomson: Foundation Press, 2009) 385–432.

Kolb R, 'Self–defence and Preventive War at the Beginning of the Millennium' 59 *Zeitschrift für Offentliches Recht* (2004) 111–34.

Kontorovich E, 'The Piracy Analogy: Modern Universal Jurisdiction's Hollow Foundation' 45 *Harvard International Law Journal* (2004) 183–237.

——, 'A Guantanamo on the Sea: The Difficulty of Prosecuting Pirates and Terrorists' 98 *California Law Review* (2010) 243–76.

——, 'Beyond the Article I Horizon: Congress's Enumerated Powers and Universal Jurisdiction over Drug Crimes' 93 *Minnesota Law Review* (2009) 1191.

—— and Art S, 'An Empirical Examination of Universal Jurisdiction over Piracy' 104 *American Journal of International Law* (2010) 436–53.

Krajewski J, 'Out of the Sight, Out of Mind? A Case for Long Range Identification and Tracking of Vessels on the High Seas' 56 *Naval Law Review* (2008) 219–50.

Kramek JE, 'Bilateral Maritime Counter–Drug and Immigrant Interdiction Agreements: Is this the World of the Future?' 31 *University of Miami Inter-American Law Review* (2000) 121–61.

Kraska J, 'Brandishing "Legal Tools" in the Fight against Maritime Piracy', in M Nordquist et al (eds), *The Law of the Sea Convention: US Accession and Globalization* (Leiden: Martinus Nijhoff, 2012), 258–90.

Kuruc M, 'Monitoring, Control and Surveillance Tools to Detect IUU Fishing and Related Activities', in Vidas D (ed), *Law, Technology and Science for Oceans in Globalisation: IUU Fishing, Oil Pollution, Bioprospecting, Outer Continental Shelf* (Leiden: Martinus Nijhoff Pub 2010) 101–8.

Kwiatkowska B, 'Creeping Jurisdiction beyond 200 miles in the Light of 1982 Law of the Sea Convention and State Practice' 22 *Ocean Development and International Law* (1991) 153–87.

Lamb S, 'Legal Limits to United Nations Security Council Powers', in Goodwin-Gill and Talmon (eds), *The Reality in International Law: Essays in Honour of Ian Brownlie* (Oxford: Clarendon, 1999) 361–88.

Landsidle J, 'Enhancing International Efforts to Prosecute Suspected Pirates' 44 *Case Western Reserve Journal of International Law* (2011), 317–23.

Larsaeus N, 'The Relationship Between Safeguarding Internal Security and Complying with International Obligations of Protection: The Unresolved Issue of Excluded Asylum Seekers' 73 *Nordic Journal of International Law* (2004) 69–97.

Larsen MD, 'The *Achille Lauro* Incident and the Permissible Use of Force' 9 *Loyola of Los Angeles International and Comparative Law Journal* (1987) 481–97.

Laursen A, 'The Use of Force and (the State of) Necessity' 37 *Vanderbilt Journal of Transnational Law* (2004) 485–526.

Lauterpacht E and Bethlehem D, 'The Scope and Content of the Principle of *Non–Refoulement*: Opinion', in Feller E, Türk V and Nicholson F (eds), *Refugee Protection in International Law* (Cambridge: Cambridge University Press) 87–177.

Lavalle R, 'The Law of the UN and the Use of Force under the Relevant Security Council Resolutions of 1990 and 1991 to Resolve the Persian Gulf Crisis' 23 *Netherlands Yearbook of International Law* (1992) 3–65.

Le Hardy de Beaulieu L, 'La Piraterie Maritime à l' Aube du XXIème Siecle' 115 *Revue Générale de Droit International Public* (2011), 653–74.

Lee R, 'Double Jeopardy on the High Seas: International Narcotics Traffickers Beware' 10 *Georgia Journal of International and Comparative Law* (1980) 647–71.

Leemans E and Rammelt T, 'Mare Liberum or Mare Restrictum? Challenges for the Maritime Industry', in Vidas D and Schei J (eds), *The World Ocean in Globalisation: Climate Change, Sustainable Fisheries, Biodiversity, Shipping, Regional Issues* (Leiden: Martinus Nijhoff, 2011) 265–92.

Lehrman Th, 'Enhancing the Proliferation Security Initiative: The Case for a Decentralised Non-proliferation Architecture' 45 *Virginia Journal of International Law* (2004) 223–76.

Lehto M, 'Terrorism in International Law – an Empty Box or Pandora's Box?', in J Petmann and J Klabbers (eds), *Nordic Cosmopolitanism: Essays in International Law for Martti Koskenniemi* (Leiden/Boston: Martinus Nijhoff, 2002) 291–313.

Lepage K, 'Terrorisme et Armes de Destruction Massive', in Doucet G (ed), *Terrorisme, Victimes et Responsabilité Pénale Internationale* (Paris : Pedone, 2003) 36–40.

Letalik N, 'Arrest of Vessels and the Law of the Sea', in Krueger RB and Riesenfeld SA (eds), *The Developing Order of the Oceans* (1985) 687–712.

Letts DJ, 'The Use of Force in Patrolling Australia's Fishing Zones' 24 *Marine Policy* (2000) 149–57.

Liakouras P, 'Intelligence Gathering on the High Seas', in Strati A, Gavouneli M, Skourtos N (eds), *Unresolved Issues and New Challenges to the Law of the Sea* (Leiden: Nijhoff, 2006) 123–48.

Liljedhal J, 'Transnational and International Crimes: Jurisdictional Issues', in *Maritime Violence and Other Security Issues at Sea*, World Maritime University, University of Wales, Swansea – Proceedings of a Symposium, Malmö, 26–30 August, 2002, Sweden (Malmö: WMU, 2002) 115–31.

Lobach T, 'Combating IUU Fishing: Interaction of Global and Regional Initiatives', in Vidas D (ed), *Law, Technology and Science for Oceans in Globalisation: IUU Fishing, Oil Pollution, Bioprospecting, Outer Continental Shelf* (Leiden: Martinus Nijhoff, 2010) 109–29.

Lodge M, 'Developing a Model for Improved Governance by Regional Fisheries Management Organizations', in Vidas D (ed), *Law, Technology and Science for Oceans in Globalisation: IUU Fishing, Oil Pollution, Bioprospecting, Outer Continental Shelf* (Leiden: Martinus Nijhoff, 2010) 157–74.

Logan SE, 'The Proliferation Security Initiative Navigating the Legal Challenges' 14 *Journal of Transnational Law and Policy* (2005) 253–74.

Lowe AV, 'Some Legal Problems Arising from the Use of the Seas for Military Purposes' 10 *Marine Policy* (1986) 171–84.

——, 'Self-Defence at Sea', in Butler WE (ed), *The Non-Use of Force in International Law* (Dordrecht: Kluwer Academic Publishers, 1989) 185–202.

——, 'National Security and the Law of the Sea', in XVII *Thesaurus Acroasium, The Law of the Sea with Emphasis on the Mediterranean Issues* (1991) 133–97.

——, 'The Commander's Handbook on the Law of Naval Operations and the Contemporary Law of the Sea', in H Robertson (ed), *The Law of Naval Operations* (Newport, MD: Naval War College, 1991) 109–47.

Malirsch M, Prill F, 'The Proliferation Security Initiative and the 2005 Protocol to the SUA Convention' 67 *Zeitschrift für ausländisches öffentliches Recht und Völkerrecht* (2007) 229–40.

Mallia P, 'The Fight against Piracy and Armed Robbery against Ships off the coast of Somalia', in Martínez Gutiérrez N (ed), *Serving the Rule of International Maritime Law: Essays in Honour of Professor David Joseph Attard* (London: Routledge, 2010) 216–32.

Marcopoulos A, 'Flags of Terror: An Argument for Rethinking Maritime Security Policy Regarding Flags of Convenience' 32 *Tulane Maritime Law Journal* (2007) 277–312.

Martin D, 'Interdiction, Intervention and the New Frontiers of Refugee Law' 33 *Virginia Journal of International Law* (1993) 473–81.

Mathew P, 'Australian Refugee Protection in the Wake of *Tampa*' 96 *American Journal of International Law* (2002) 661–76.

——, 'Address: Legal Issues Concerning Interception' 17 *Georgetown Immigration Law Journal* (2003) 221–49.

Matlin DF, 'Re-evaluating the Status of Flags of Convenience under International Law' 23 *Vanderbilt Journal of Transnational Law* (1991) 1017–55.

Mbiah K, 'The Revision of the Convention for the Suppression of Unlawful Acts Against the Safety of Maritime Navigation, 1988, and its Protocol of 1988 Relating to Fixed Platforms Located on the Continental Shelf', in *Maritime Violence and Other Security Issues at Sea*, World Maritime University, University of Wales, Swansea – Proceedings of a Symposium, Malmö, 26–30 August 2002, Sweden (Malmö: WMU, 2002) 193–219.

McCredie JA, 'Contemporary Uses of Force against Terrorism: The United States Response to *Achille Lauro*–Questions of Jurisdiction and its Exercise' 16 *Georgia Journal of Comparative and International Law* (1986) 435–67.

McDorman TL, 'Regional Port State Control Agreements: Some Issues of International Law', 5 *Ocean and Coastal Law Journal* (2000) 207–25.

——, 'Maritime Terrorism and the International Law of Boarding of Vessels at Sea: A Brief Assessment of the New Developments', in Caron D and Scheiber HN (eds), *The Oceans in the Nuclear Age: Legacies and Risks* (Leiden: Martinus Nijhoff, 2010) 239–64.

McGinley, 'The *Achille Lauro* Affair – Implications for International Law' 52 *Tennessee Law Review* (1985) 691–738.

McLaughlin R, 'United Nations Mandated Naval Interdiction Operations in the Territorial Sea?' 51 *International and Comparative Law Quarterly* (2002) 249–78.

McMillan S, 'Piracy: An Old Menace Re-emerges' 27 *New Zealand International Law Review* (2002) 23.

McNulty J, 'Blockade: Evolution and Expectation' 62 *International Law Studies* (Naval War College, 1980) 172–96.

Mejia M, Defining Maritime Violence and Maritime Security', in *Maritime Violence and Other Security Issues at Sea*, World Maritime University, University of Wales, Swansea– Proceedings of a Symposium, Malmö, 26–30 August, 2002, Sweden (Malmö: WMU, 2002) 27–38.

—— and Mukherjee P, 'The SUA Convention 2005: A Critical Evaluation of its Effectiveness in Suppressing Maritime Criminal Acts' 12 *Journal of International Maritime Law* (2006) 170–91.

Mellor JC, 'Missing the Boat: The Legal and Practical Problems of the Prevention of Maritime Terrorism' 18 *American University International Law Review* (2002) 341–97.

Menefee SP, 'Maritime Terror in Europe and the Mediterranean' 12 *Marine Policy* (1988) 143–59.

——, 'The New "Jamaica Discipline": Problems with Piracy, Maritime Terrorism and the 1982 Convention on the Law of the Sea' 6 *Connecticut Journal of International Law* (1991) 127–50.

——, 'The Case of the *Castle John*, or Green beard the Pirate?: Environmentalism, Piracy and the Development of International Law' 24 *California Western International Law Journal* (1994) 1–16.

——, 'Anti–Piracy Law in the Year of the Ocean: Problems and Opportunity' 5 *ILSA Journal of International and Comparative Law* (1999) 309–18.

——, 'Foreign Naval Intervention in Cases of Piracy: Problems and Strategies' 14 *International Journal of Marine and Coastal Law* (1999) 353–70.

——, 'The Maritime Slave Trade in 21st Century' 7 *ILSA Journal of International and Comparative Law* (2001) 495–509.

——, 'Punishing Acts of Piracy and Maritime Violence: A Model National Law of the Twenty First Century' 2 *Journal of International Commercial Law* (2003) 195–208.

——, 'The Smuggling of Refugees by Sea: a Modern Day Maritime Slave Trade' 2 *Regent Journal of International Law* (2003–4) 1–28.

Mensah TA, 'Suppression of Terrorism at Sea: Developments in the Wake of the Events of September 11th, 2001', in Frowein J et al (eds), *Verhandeln für den Frieden Liber Amicorum Tono Eitel* (Berlin: Springer, 2003) 627–47.

Michaelsen C, 'Maritime Exclusion Zones in Time of Armed Conflict at Sea: Legal Controversies Still Unresolved' 8 *Journal of Conflict and Security Law* (2003) 363–90.

Michel K, 'War, Piracy and Terror: The High Seas in the 21st Century' 12 *Journal of International Maritime Law* (2006) 313–24.

Momtaz D, 'The High Seas', in Dupuy R–J, Vignes D (eds), *A Handbook on the New Law of the Sea*, Vol II, Hague Academy of International Law (Dordrecht: Martinus Nijhof, 1991) 383–422.

——, 'La Lutte contre « l'Introduction Clandestine » de Migrants par Mer', 4 *Annuaire du Droit de la Mer* (1999) 49–57.

——, 'La Libre Navigation à l' Epreuve des Conflits Armés', in *La Mer et Son Droit, Mélanges Offerts à Laurent Lucchini et Jean-Pierre Quéneudec* (Paris: Pedone, 2003) 437–54.

Montero Llacer FJ, 'Open Registries: Past, Present and Future' 27 *Marine Policy* (2003) 513–23.

Moreno-Lax V, 'The EU Regime on Interdiction, Search and Rescue, and Disembarkation: The Frontex Guidelines for Intervention at Sea 25 *International Journal of Marine and Coastal Law* (2010) 621–35.

——, 'Seeking Asylum in the Mediterranean: against a Fragmentary Reading of EU Member States' Obligations Accruing at Sea' 23 *International Journal of Refugee Law* (2011) 1–47.

Morabito RE, 'Maritime Interdiction: Evolution of a Strategy' 22 *Ocean Development and International Law* (1991) 301–11.

Motomura H, 'Haitian Asylum Seekers: Interdiction and Immigrant Rights' 26 *Cornell Journal of International Law* (1993) 695–717.

Muhammad P, 'The Trans–Atlantic Slave Trade: Forgotten Crime against Humanity as Defined by International Law' 19 *American University International Law Review* (2004) 883–947.

Muntarbhorn V, 'Asylum-Seekers at Sea and Piracy in the Gulf of Thailand' 16 *Revue Belge de Droit International* (1981) 481–508.

Murphy JF, 'Defining International Terrorism: A Way Out of the Quagmire' 19 *Israel Yearbook of Human Rights* (1989) 13–37.

Murphy M, 'Piracy and United Nations Convention on the Law of the Sea: Does International Law Help Regional States to Combat Piracy?' in Lehr P (ed), *Violence at Sea: Piracy in the Age of Global Terrorism* (London: Routledge, 2007) 155–82.

Myjer E, 'The European Convention on Human Rights, The Fight against Terrorism and the Ticking Bomb Situation', in Kohen M (ed), *Promoting Justice, Human Rights and Conflict Resolution through International Law, Liber Amicorum Lucius Caflisch* (Leiden: Brill, 2007) 379–97.

Nascimento A, 'El control de buques méchantes en alta mar por parte de los effectivos de la armada española que participan en la operación Libertad duradera: el episodio del so sane' 55 *Revista Española de Derecho Internacional* (2002) 267–78.

Nelson D, 'The *Virginius* Revisited', in *Maritime Violence and Other Security Issues at Sea*, World Maritime University, University of Wales, Swansea – Proceedings of a Symposium, Malmö, Sweden, 26–30 August 2002 (Malmö: WMU, 2002) 1–8.

Nevans M, 'The Repatriation of the Haitian Boat People: its Legal Justification under the Interdiction Agreement between the United States and Haiti' 5 *Temple International and Comparative Law Journal* (1991) 273–301.

Obokata T, 'Trafficking of Human Beings as a Crime against Humanity: Some Implications for the International Legal System' 54 *International and Comparative Law Quarterly* (2005) 445.

O'Connell D, 'International Law and Contemporary Naval Operations' 44 *British Yearbook of International Law* (1970) 19–85.

Odier F, 'La Sûreté Maritime ou les Lacunes du Droit International', in *La Mer et Son Droit, Mélanges Offerts à Laurent Lucchini et Jean-Pierre Quéneudec* (Paris: Pedone, 2003) 455–68.

O'Keefe R, 'Universal Jurisdiction' 2 *Journal of International Criminal Justice* (2004) 735–60.

Oude E and Alex G 'The Genuine Link Concept: Time for a Post Mortem?', in Dekker IF and Post HGH (eds), *On the Foundations and Sources of International Law* (2003) 41–63.

Oxman BH, 'Human Rights and the United Nations Convention on the Law of the Sea' 36 *Columbia Journal of Transnational Law* (1998) 399–445.

—— and Coombs M, 'Jurisdiction – Constitutionality of the United States Jurisdiction over Criminal Acts Occurring on the High Seas' 95 *American Journal of International Law* (2001) 438.

Pallis M, 'Obligations of States towards Asylum Seekers at Sea: Interactions and Conflicts between Legal Regimes' 14 *International Journal of Refugee Law* (2002) 329–64.

Palmer GW, 'Guarding the Coast: Alien Migrant Interdiction Operations at Sea', in Schmitt MN (ed), The Law of Military Operations, *Liber Amicorum* Professor Grunawalt 72 *International Law Studies* (1998) 157–79.

Pancracio JP, 'L'Affaire de *l'Achille Lauro* at Le Droit International' 31 *Annuaire Français de Droit International* (1985) 221–236.

Papanicolopulu I, 'The Law of the Sea Convention: No place for Persons?' 27 *International Journal of Marine and Coastal Law* (2012) 867–74.

Papastavridis E, 'Interpretation of Security Council Resolutions under Chapter VII in the Aftermath of the Iraqi Crisis' 56 *International and Comparative Law Quarterly* (2007) 83–117.

——, 'Interception of Human Beings on the High Seas: A Contemporary Analysis under International Law' 36 *Syracuse Journal of International Law and Commerce* (2009) 145–228.

——, 'Case Comment: ECHR, *Medvedyev v France*' 59 *International and Comparative Law Quarterly* (2010) 867–82.

——, 'Enforcement Jurisdiction in the Mediterranean Sea: Illicit Activities and the Rule of Law on the High Seas' 25 *International Journal of Marine and Coastal Law* (2010) 569–99.

——, 'Fortress Europe and FRONTEX: Within or Without International Law?' 79 *Nordic Journal of International Law* (2010) 75–111.

——, 'Piracy off Somalia: The Emperors and the Thieves of the Oceans in the 21st Century', in A Abass (ed), *Protecting Human Security in Africa* (Oxford: Oxford University Press, 2010) 122–54.

——, 'The Right of Visit on the High Seas in a Theoretical Perspective: *Mare Liberum v Mare Clausum* Revisited' 24 *Leiden Journal of International Law* (2011) 45–69.

——, 'Extraterritorial Immigration Control: The Responsibility of States for Human Rights Violations' 6 *Annuaire International des droits de l'homme* (2012) (forthcoming).

Patel BN, 'Security Council Resolution 1540 and Non-Proliferation of Weapons of Mass Destruction' 11 *African Yearbook of International Law* (2003) 301–11.

Peppetti J, 'Building the Global Maritime Security Network: A Multinational Legal Structure to Combat Transnational Threats' 55 *Naval Law Review* (2008) 73–156.

Perez D, 'United States Haitian Interdiction Policy: *Sale v Haitian Centers Council, Inc*', 3 *Journal of Transnational Law and Policy* (1994) 247–63.

Perrakis S, 'Recent Tendencies in the Evolution of National Law and Practice in the Field of Asylum and Refugees', in Council of Europe, *The Law of Asylum and Refugees: Present Tendencies and Future Perspectives: Proceedings of the Sixteenth Colloquy on European Law* (1987) 59–64.

Perry T, 'Blurring the Ocean Zones: The Effect of the Proliferation Security Initiative on the Customary International Law of the Sea' 37 *Ocean Development and International Law* (2006) 33–53.

Piedimonte Bodini S, 'Fighting Maritime Piracy under the European Convention on Human Rights' 22 *European Journal of International Law* (2011) 829.

Pirtle C, 'Military Uses of Ocean Space and the Law of the Sea in the New Millennium' 31 *Ocean Development and International Law* (2000) 7–45.

Plant G, 'Legal Aspects of Terrorism at Sea', in Higgins R and Flory M (eds), *Terrorism and International Law* (New York: Routledge, 1997) 68–96.

——, 'The Convention for the Suppression of Unlawful Acts against the Safety of Maritime Navigation' 39 *International and Comparative Law Quarterly* (1990) 27–56.

Polere P, 'La Piraterie Maritime aujourd'hui' 57 *Le Droit Maritime Français* (2005) 387–404.

Politakis GP, 'From Action Stations to Action: US Naval Deployment, "Non-Belligerency", and "Defensive Reprisals" in the Final Year of the Iran-Iraq War' 25 *Ocean Development and International Law* (1994) 31–60.

Pugash JZ, 'The Dilemma of the Sea Refugee: Rescue without Refuge' 18 *Harvard International Law Journal* (1977) 577–604.

Raab D, 'Armed Attack after the *Oil Platforms* Case' 17 *Leiden Journal of International Law* (2004) 719–35.

Ralph D, 'Haitian Interdiction on the High Seas: the Continuing Saga of the Rights of Aliens outside United States Territory' 17 *Maryland Journal of International Law and Trade* (1993) 227–51.

Rassam Y, 'Contemporary Forms of Slavery and Evolution of the Prohibition of Slavery and the Slave-Trade under Customary International Law' 39 *Virginia Journal of International Law* (1999) 303.

Rayfuse R, 'Countermeasures and High Seas Fisheries Enforcement' 51 *Netherlands International Law Review* (2004) 41–76.

——, 'Regulation and Enforcement in the Law of the Sea: Emerging Assertion of a Right to Non-Flag State Enforcement in the High Seas' 24 *Australian Yearbook of International Law* (2005) 181–200.

——, Warner R, 'Securing a Sustainable Future for the Oceans beyond National Jurisdiction: The Legal Basis for an Integrated Cross-Sectoral Regime for High Seas Governance for the 21st Century' 23 *International Journal of Marine and Coastal Law* (2008) 399–421.

——, 'Moving Beyond the Tragedy of Global Commons: The Grotian Legacy and the Future of Sustainable Management of the Biodiversity of the High Seas', in Leary D and Pisupati B (eds), *The Future of International Environmental Law* (Tokyo: United Nations University Press, 2010) 201–24.

Reuland R, 'Interference with Non-National Ships on the High Seas: Peacetime Exceptions to the Exclusivity Rule of the Flag State Jurisdiction' 22 *Vanderbilt Journal of Transnational Law* (1989) 1161–1229.

Rigeaux F, 'La Compétence Extraterritoriale des Etats' 69 *Annuaire de l'Institut de Droit International* (2001) 13–94.

Roach JA, 'Initiatives to Enhance Maritime Security at Sea' 28 *Marine Policy* (2004) 41–66.

Roach JA, 'Proliferation Security Initiative (PSI): Countering Proliferation by Sea', in M Nordquist et al (eds), *Recent Developments in the Law of the Sea and China* (Leiden: Nijhoff, 2006) 351.

Robertson H, 'Interdiction of the Iraqi Maritime Commerce in the 1990-1 Persian Gulf Conflict' 22 *Ocean Development and International Law* (1991) 289–99.

Romero J, 'Prevention of Maritime Terrorism: the Container Security Initiative' 4 *Chicago Journal of International Law* (2003) 597.

Ronzitti N, 'The Right of Self-Defence at Sea and its Impact on the Law of Naval Warfare' XVII *Thesaurus Acroasium, The Law of the Sea with Emphasis on the Mediterranean Issues* (1991) 265–94.

——, 'Le Droit Humanitaire Applicable aux Conflits Armés en Mer' 242 *Recueil de Cours de l'Academie de Droit International* (1993-V) 9–196.

——, 'Coastal State Jurisdiction over Refugees and Migrants at Sea', in N Ando et al (eds), *Liber Amicorum Judge Shigeru Oda* (The Hague: Kluwer Law International, 2002) 1271–86.

Ronzitti N, 'The 2006 Conflict in Lebanon and International Law' 16 *Italian Yearbook of International Law* (2007) 3–19.

——, 'The Proliferation Security Initiative and International Law', in Fischer-Lescano A et al (eds), *Frieden in Freiheit: Festschrift fur Michael Bothe zum 70 Geburstag* (Baden-Baden: Nomos, 2008) 269–84.

Roos LL, 'Stateless Vessels and the High Seas Narcotics Trade: United States Courts Deviate from International Principles of Jurisdiction' 9 *The Maritime Lawyer* (1984) 273–95.

Rosand E, 'Security Council Resolution 1373, the Counter-Terrorism Committee, and the Fight against Terrorism' 97 *American Journal of International* (2003) 333–41.

——, 'The Security Council as Global Legislator: *Ultra Vires* or Ultra Innovative?' 28 *Fordham International Law Journal* (2005) 542–90.

Rosenberg LD, 'The Courts and Interception: the United States' Interdiction Experience and its Impact on Refugees and Asylum Seekers' 17 *Georgetown Immigration Law Journal* (2003) 199–219.

Rothwell DR, 'The Proliferation Security Initiative: Amending the Convention on the Law of the Sea by Stealth?', in Caron D and Scheiber HN (eds), *The Oceans in the Nuclear Age: Legacies and Risks* (Leiden: Martinus Nijhoff, 2010) 285–93.

—— and Klein N, 'Maritime Security and the Law of the Sea', in Klein N, Mossop and Rothwell D (eds), *Maritime Security: International Law and Policy Perspectives from Australia and New Zealand* (Abingdon: Routledge, 2010) 22–36.

—— and Stephens T, 'Illegal Southern Ocean Fishing and Prompt Release: Balancing Coastal and Flag State Rights and Interests' 53 *International and Comparative Law Quarterly* (2004) 171–87.

Roucounas E, 'Facteurs Privés et Droit International Public', 299 *Recueil des Cours de l'Académie de Droit International* (2002) 9–419.

Rubenstein P, 'State Responsibility for Failure to Control the Export of Weapons of Mass Destruction' 23 *California Western International Law Journal* (1992–3) 319–72.

Rubin AP, 'Evolution and Self-Defence at Sea' VII *Thesaurus Acroasium* (1977) 107–39.

——, 'Piracy', in Bernhardt R (ed), *Encyclopedia of Public International Law* (1989) 259–62.

Russ GR, Zeller D, 'From *Mare Liberum* to *Mare Reservarum*' 27 *Marine Policy* (2003) 75–78.

Sakhuja V, 'Terrorism at Sea: Then and Now', in The Indian Maritime Foundation, *Proceedings of the Seminar on 'Terrorism and Piracy at Sea'* (Pune, May 2002) 16–22.

Salamanca Aguado E, 'International Terrorism and Maritime Security: Multilateralism vs Unilateralism', in Rafaël Casado Raigón (ed), *L'Europe et la mer* (Busseles: Bruylant, 2005) 105–417.

Schachter O, 'The Lawful Use of Force by a State against Terrorists in another Country' 19 *Israel Yearbook of Human Rights* (1989) 209–31.

Schaffer RP, 'The Singular Plight of Sea-borne Refugees' 8 *Austrian Yearbook of International Law* (1983) 213.

Schaller C, 'Keeping Weapons of Mass Destruction from Terrorists – An International Law Perspective', in Giegerich T (ed), *A Wiser Century?: Judicial Dispute Settlement, Disarmament and the Laws of War 100 Years after the Second Hague Peace Conference* (Berlin: Duncker and Humblot, 2009) 121–42.

Schreiber M, 'Convention supplémentaire des Nations Unies relative á l'abolition de l'esclavage', *Annuaire Française de Droit International* (1956) 555.

Scovazzi T, 'The Evolution of International Law of the Sea: New Issues and New Challenges' 286 *Recueil des Cours de l'Academie de Droit International* (2000-I) 39–244.

Shah N, 'Self-Defence, Anticipatory Self-Defence and Pre-emption: International Law's Responses to Terrorism' 12 *Journal of Conflict and Security Law* (2007) 95–126.

Shearer IA, 'Problems of Jurisdiction and Law Enforcement against Delinquent Vessels' 35 *International and Comparative Law Quarterly* (1986) 320–43.

——, 'International Law and Refugees in South–East Asia' 13 *Thesaurus Acroasium* (1987) 429–68.

Spearin C, 'Private Military and Security Companies v International Naval Endeavours v Somali Pirates' 10 *Journal of International Criminal Justice* (2012) 823–37.

Shulman M, 'The Proliferation Security Initiative and the Evolution of the Law on the Use of Force' 28 *Houston Journal of International Law* (2006) 771–828.

Sicilianos A-L, 'L'Autorisation par le Conseil de Sécurité de recourir a la force: une tentative d'évaluation' 106 *Revue Générale de Droit International Public* (2002) 1–50.

——, 'The Classification of Obligations and the Multilateral Dimensions of the Relations of International Responsibility' 13 *European Journal of International Law* (2003) 1127–45.

——, 'Entre multilatéralisme et unilatéralisme: l'autorisation par le Conseil de sécurité de recourir à la force' 339 *Recueil des Cours* (2008) 9–436.

Siddle J, 'Anglo-American Cooperation in the Suppression of Drug Smuggling' 31 *International and Comparative Law Quarterly* (1982) 726–47.

Sohn LB, 'Interdiction of Vessels on the High Seas' 18 *International Lawyer* (1984) 411–19.

——, 'Peacetime Use of Force on the High Seas', in H Robertson (ed), *The Law of Naval Operations* (Newport, MD: Naval War College, 1991) 39–90.

Song Y–H, 'The US-Led Proliferation Security Initiative and UNCLOS: Legality, Implementation and an Assessment' 38 *Ocean Development and International Law* (2007) 101–45.

Soons AHA, 'Enforcing the Economic Embargo at Sea', in Gowlland-Debbas V (ed), *United Nations Sanctions and International Law* (The Hague: Kluwer Law International, 2001) 307–24.

——, 'A New Exception to the Freedom of the High Seas: The Authority of the United Nations Security Council', in Gill TD and Heere WP (eds), *Reflections on Principles and Practices of International Law* (The Hague: Martinus Nijhoff, 2000) 205–21.

Sorensen CE, 'Drug Trafficking on the High Seas: A Move towards Universal Jurisdiction under International Law' 4 *Emory International Law Review* (1990) 207–30.

Sossai M, 'EU Counter-Terrorism Action and Due Process Guarantees', in K Chainoglou et al (eds), *International Terrorism and Changes in International Law* (Navarra: Aranzadi, 2007) 227–92.

Spadi F, 'Bolstering the Proliferation Security Initiative: A Comparative Analysis of Ship-Boarding as a Bilateral and Multilateral Implementing Mechanism' 75 *Nordic Journal of International Law* (2006) 249–78.

Sproule D, St-Denis W, 'The UN Drug Trafficking Convention: An Ambitious Step' 27 *Canadian Yearbook of International Law* (1990) 263–93.

Starkle G, 'Les Epaves de Navires en Haute Mer et le Droit International Le Cas du 'Mont-Louis' 18 *Revue Belge de Droit International* (1984–5) 496–528.

Stein T, 'Pre-emption and Terrorism', 9 *International Peacekeeping* (2005) 155–71.

Stephens D, 'The Legal Efficacy of Freedom of Navigation Assertions' 34 *Israel Yearbook on Human Rights* (2004) 127–50.

Stieb JD, 'Survey of United States Jurisdiction over High Seas Narcotics Trafficking' 19 *Georgia Journal of International and Comparative Law* (1989) 119–47.

Strang KA, 'Foreign Search and Seizure: The Fourth Amendment at Large' 25 *San Diego Law Review* (1988) 609–30.

Stribis I, 'La Sécurité des Transports Maritimes face au Défi du Terrorisme: les Initiatives Interétatiques de prévention de prolifération des ADM', in Hague Academy of International Law (publ under the direction of Glenon M, Sur S), *Terrorism and International Law* (Leiden: Martinus Nijhoff) 585–654.

Suarez VS, 'Post September 11 Security Challenges to the Legal Regime of the Maritime Carriage of a Nuclear and Radioactive Materials' 18 *International Journal of Marine and Coastal Law* (2003) 423–43.

Sucharitkul S, 'Quelques Questions Juridiques à l'Egard des 'Boat People' en tant que Réfugiés Politiques' 35 *Annuaire Français de Droit International* (1989) 476–83.

Sur S, 'La Resolution 1540 du Conseil de Securite (28 Avril 2004): Entre la Prolifération des Armes de Destruction Massive, Le Terrorisme et les Acteurs non Etatiques' 108 *Revue Générale de Droit International Public* (2004) 855–82.

Syrigos A, 'Developments on the Interdiction of Vessels on the High Seas', in Strati A, Gavouneli M, Skourtos N (eds), *Unresolved Issues and New Challenges to the Law of the Sea* (Leiden: Martinus Nijhoff, 2006) 149–201.

Szurek S, 'La Lutte Internationale contre le Terrorisme sous l'Empire du Chapitre VII: Un Laboratoire Normatif' 109 *Revue Générale de Droit International Public* (2005) 5–49.

Taft WH IV, 'Self–defence and the *Oil Platforms* Decision' 29 *Yale Journal of International Law* (2004) 295–306.

Talmon S, 'The Security Council as World Legislature' 99 *American Journal of International Law* (2005) 175–93.

Tams C, 'The Use of Force against Terrorists' 20 *European Journal of International Law* (2009) 359–97.

Tancredi A, 'Di Pirati e Stati "falliti": il Consiglio di scurezza autorizza il ricorso alla forza nelle acque territoriali della Somalia' 91 *Rivista di Diritto Internazionale* (2008) 937–66.

Tannewald N, 'The United Nations and Debates over Weapons of Mass Destruction', in Price RM and Zacher MW (eds), *The United Nations and Global Security* (London, Palgrave Macmillan, 2004) 3–20.

Thomas I, 'L'affaire du « *Monica* »' 106 *Revue Générale de Droit International Public* (2002) 391.

Thomas T, 'The Proliferation Security Initiative: Towards Relegation of Navigational Freedoms in UNCLOS? An Indian Perspective' 8 *Chinese Journal of International Law* (2009) 657–80.

Tiribelli C, 'Time to Update the 1998 Rome Convention for the Suppression of Unlawful Acts against the Safety of Maritime Navigation' 18 *Sri Lanka Journal of International Law* (2006) 149–66.

Totten C and Bernal M, 'Somali Piracy: Jurisdictional Issues, Enforcement Problems and Potential Solutions' 41 *Georgetown Journal of International Law* (2010) 377–424.

Trapp K, 'Back to Basics: Necessity, Proportionality and the Right of Self-Defence against Non-State Actors' 56 *International and Comparative Law Quarterly* (2007) 141–56.

Travalio G and Altenburg J, 'Terrorism, State Responsibility and the Use of Military Force' 4 *Chicago Journal of International Law* (2003) 97–119.

Treves T, 'Intervention en Haute Mer et Navires Etrangers' 41 *Annuaire Français de Droit International* (1995) 651–75.

——, 'The Convention for the Suppression of Unlawful Acts against the Safety of Maritime Navigation' 2 *Singapore Journal of International and Comparative Law* (1998) 541–56.

——, 'Piracy, Law of the Sea, and Use of Force: Developments off the Coast of Somalia' 20 *European Journal of International Law* (2009) 399–414.

Trevisanut S, 'Droit de la Mer', in TTreves, PBertoli (eds), 'Chronique de jurisprudence italienne' 133 *Journal du droit international* (2006) 1035.

——, 'The Principle of *Non-Refoulement* at Sea and the Effectiveness of Asylum Protection' 12 *Max Planck Yearbook of United Nations Law* (2008) 205–46.

——, 'Search and Rescue Operations in the Mediterranean: Factor of Cooperation or Conflict?' 25 *International Journal of Marine and Coastal Law* (2010) 523–42.

Tsamenyi M et al, 'The European Council Regulation on Illegal, Unreported and Unregulated Fishing: An International Fisheries Law Perspective' 25 *International Journal of Marine and Coastal Law* (2010) 5–31.

Turner RF, 'State Responsibility and the War on Terror: The Legacy of Thomas Jefferson and the Barbary Pirates' 4 *Chicago Journal of International Law* (2003) 121–40.

Van der Mensbrugghe Y, 'Le Pouvoir de Police des Etats en Haute Mer' 11 *Revue Belge de Droit International* (1975) 56–102.

Van Dyke JM, 'Military Exclusion and Warning Zones on the High Seas' 15 *Marine Policy* (1991) 147–69.

Van Hooydonk E, 'Les Lieux de Refuge pour les Navires en Détresse' 56 *Le Droit Maritime Français* (2004) 808–15.

Van Zwanenberg A, 'Interference with Ships on the High Seas' 10 *International and Comparative Law Quarterly* (1961) 785–817.

Vidas D, 'Responsibility for the Seas', in Vidas D (ed), *Law, Technology and Science for Oceans in Globalisation: IUU Fishing, Oil Pollution, Bioprospecting, Outer Continental Shelf* (Leiden: Martinus Nijhoff, 2010) 3–40.

Vohrah LC, Askin KD, Mundis DA, 'Contemporary Law Regulating Armed Conflict at Sea', in Ando et al (eds), *Liber Amicorum Judge Shigeru Oda* (The Hague: Kluwer Law International, 2002) 1523–42.

Walker G, 'Application of the Law of Armed Conflict during Operation Allied Force: Maritime Interdiction and Prisoner of War Status', in Wall AE (ed), *Legal and Ethical Lessons of NATO's Kosovo Campaign* (Newport, RI: Naval War College, 2002) 85–105.

Warner R, 'Jurisdictional Issues for Navies Involved in Enforcing Multilateral Regimes beyond National Jurisdiction' 14 *International Journal of Marine and Coastal Law* (1999) 321–32.

Warner-Kramer D and Canty K, 'Stateless Fishing Vessels: The Current International Regime and a New Approach' 5 *Ocean and Coastal Law Journal* (2000) 227–43.

White M, '*Tampa* Incident: Shipping, International and Maritime Legal Issues' 78 *Australia Law Journal* (2004) 101–13.

Wilheim E, 'MV *Tampa*, the Australian Response' 15 *International Journal of Refugee Law* (2003) 159–91.

Williams MJ, 'Bilateral Maritime Agreements Enhancing International Cooperation in the Suppression of Illicit Maritime Narcotics Trafficking', in Nordquist MH and Moore JN (eds), *Ocean Policy: New Institutions, Challenges and Opportunities* (The Hague: Martinus Nijhoff, 1999) 179–200.

Wilson D, 'Interdiction on the High Seas: The Role and Authority of a Master in the Boarding and Searching of his Ships by Foreign Warships' 55 *Naval Law Review* (2008) 157–211.

Wolfrum R, 'Military Activities on the High Seas: What are the Imports of the United Nations Convention on the Law of the Sea?' in Schmitt MN and Green LC (eds), *The Law of Armed Conflict* 501–51.

——, 'Fighting Terrorism at Sea: Options and Limitations under International Law', in Frowein J et al (eds), *Verhandeln für den Frieden Liber Amicorum Tono Eitel* (Berlin: Springer, 2003) 649–68.

Wood MC, 'The Interpretation of Security Council Resolutions' 2 *Max Planck Yearbook of United Nations Law* (1998) 73–95.

Young C, 'Balancing Maritime Security and Freedom of Navigation on the High Seas: A Study of the Multilateral Negotiation Process in Action' 24 *University of Queensland Law Journal* (2005) 355–414.

Zemanek K, 'Was Hugo Grotius Really in Favour of the Freedom of the High Seas?' 1 *Journal of History of International Law* (1999) 48–60.

Zou K, 'Maritime Enforcement of United Nations Security Council Resolutions: Use of Force and Coercive Measures' 26 *International Journal of Marine and Coastal Law* (2011) 235–61.

OTHER SELECTED MATERIAL

Conclusion on Protection Safeguards in Interception Measures No 97 (LIV), adopted by the Executive Committee on International Protection of Refugees of the United Nations High Commissioner for Refugees, www.unhcrorg/excom/EXCOM/3f 93b2894html.

Council of Europe, Explanatory Report to the 1995 Council of Europe Agreement on Illicit Traffic by Sea, implementing article 17 of the UN Convention against Illicit Traffic in Narcotic Drugs and Psychotropic Substances, Document CDPC (94) 22, Addendum of 27 June 1994; http://conventionscoeint/Treaty/en/Reports/Html/156htm.

Council of the European Union, Council Conclusions on integration of maritime surveillance (Brussels 23 May 2011), www.consiliumeuropaeu/uedocs/cms_data/docs/pressdata/EN/genaff/122177pdf.

European Council on Refugees and Exiles (ECRE) and British Refugee Council joint response to Select Committee on the European Union, Sub–Committee F (24 September 2007), 12; www.ecre.org/resources/policy_papers/995.

FAO, International Plan of Action to Prevent, Deter and Eliminate Illegal, Unreported and Unregulated Fishing, adopted at the Twenty-fourth Session of CDOFI, Rome Italy (23 June 2001

FAO, Model Scheme on Port State Measures to Combat Illegal, Unreported and Unregulated Fishing (Rome: FAO, 2007).

2005 Rome Declaration on Illegal, Unreported and Unregulated Fishing adopted by the FAO Ministerial Meeting on Fisheries, Rome, 12 March 2005, available at ftp://ftp.fao.org/fi/document/ministerial/2005/iuu/declaration.pdf).

Council of the European Union, 'Council Conclusions on integration of maritime surveillance' (Brussels, 23 May 2011); available at www.consilium.europa.eu/uedocs/cms_data/docs/pressdata/EN/genaff/122177.pdf.

François, *Regime of the High Seas,* UN Doc ACNA/17, reprinted in *Yearbook of the International Law Commission* (1950-II), 36.

Guiding Principles applicable to unilateral declarations of states capable of creating legal obligations, with commentaries thereto (2006), http://untreaty.un.org/ilc/texts/instruments/english/commentaries/9_9_2006pdf.

Human Rights Committee, General Comment No 31 26 May 2004, CCPR/C/21/Rev1/Add13.

IMO Maritime Safety Committee, 'Interim Measures for Combating Unsafe Practices Associated with the Trafficking or Transport of Migrants by Sea' (adopted on 16 December 1998).

IMO, International Aeronautical and Maritime Search and Rescue Manual, Vol III

International Institute of International Humanitarian Law, San Remo Manual on International Law Applicable at Armed Conflicts at Sea (1994), reprinted in L Doswald-Beck (ed), *San Remo Manual on International Law Applicable at Armed Conflicts at Sea* Cambridge: CUP, 1995).

International Law Association, Helsinki Principles on the Law of Maritime Neutrality, Final Report of the Committee on Maritime Neutrality, Report of the 68th Conference, Taipei, 1998.

J Morrison and B Crosland, 'The Trafficking and Smuggling of Refugees', *New Issues in Refugee Research,* Working Paper No 39, 62; www.unhcr.org/research/RESEARCH/3af66c9b4pdf.

Meeting of State Representatives on Rescue at Sea and Maritime Interception in the Mediterranean (Madrid, 23–24 May 2006), www.unhcr.org/refworld/pdfid/45b8d8b44pdf.

Memorandum on the Regime of the High Seas, by the Secretariat (14 July 1950), UN Doc A/CN4/32, reprinted in *Yearbook of the International Law Commission* (1950-II), 67.

Practical Guide for Competent National Authorities under Article 17 of the UN Vienna Convention (UN Office for Drugs and Crime, 2003).

Regime of the High Seas, Draft Articles, A/CN4/79, section II, reprinted in *Yearbook of the International Law Commission* (1955-I), at 27.

Regulation V/19-1 of the SOLAS Convention, as amended by Resolution MSC 202(81) (adopted on 19 May, 2006), MSC 81/25/Add1, Annex 2.

Report by T Hammarberg, Commissioner for Human Rights of the Council of Europe (Strasbourg, 7 September 2011) – CommDH (2011), https://wcdcoeint/wcd/ViewDocjsp?id=1826921.

Report of the International Expert Group on Piracy off the Somali Coast commissioned by the Special Representative of the S–G of the UN to Somalia, 15, www.imcsnetorg/imcs/docs/somalia_piracy_intl_experts_report_consolidatedpdf.

Report of the International Law Commission covering the work of its 8th session (A/3159), reprinted in *Yearbook of the International Law Commission* (1956-II), 258

Report of the International Law Commission to the General Assembly 11 GAOR Supp (No 9) at 21, UN Doc A/3159 (1956), reprinted in *Yearbook of the International Law Commission* (1956-II), 29.

Report of the Secretary-General's Panel of Inquiry on 31 May 2010 (September 2011).

Report of the Secretary-General's Panel of Inquiry on the 31 May 2010 Flotilla Incident (September 2011), www.unorg/News/dh/infocus/middle_east/Gaza_Flotilla_Panel_Reportpdf.

Report of the Working Group on Contemporary Forms of Slavery 1996, UN ESCOR (48th Session).

Report on the Meeting of the Working Group of Government Representatives on the Question of the Rescue of Asylum-Seekers at Sea held in Geneva, 5–7 July 1982 (EC/CSP/21).

Report by T Hammarberg, Commissioner for Human Rights of the Council of Europe (Strasbourg, 7 September 2011) – CommDH (2011) 26, available at https://wcd.coe.int/wcd/ViewDoc.jsp?id=1826921.

Report with Evidence submitted to the House of Lords by the Sub Committee F (Home Affairs) of the European Union Committee; see House of Lords, European Union Committee, *FRONTEX: The EU External Borders Agency, Report with Evidence*, HL Paper 60 (5 March 2008), www.publicationsparliamentuk/pa/ld200708/ldselect/ldeucom/62/62pdf.

Revised Performance Standards and Functional Requirements for the Long-Range Identification and Tracking of Ships, Resolution of MSC263(84), adopted on 16 May 2008, MSC 84/24/Add2 Annex 9.

UN Basic Principles on the Use of Force and Firearms by Law Enforcement Officials; adopted by the 8th UN Congress on the Prevention of Crime and the Treatment of Officers adopted in Havana, Cuba (27 August–7 September 1990); available at www2.ohchr.org/english/law/firearms.htm.

UNHCR, Advisory Opinion on the Extraterritorial Application of *Non-Refoulement Obligations* under the 1951 Convention Relating to the Status of Refugees and its 1967 Protocol, 26012007, www.unhcrorg/refworld/pdfid/45f17a1a4pdf.

UNHCR, Selected Reference Materials, Rescue at Sea, Maritime Interception and Stowaways (November 2006), www.unhcrbg/other/law_of_the_seapdf.

United Nations Economic and Social Council, *Commentary on the United Nations Convention against Illicit Traffic in Narcotic Drugs and Psychotropic Substances 1988* (UN, 1998).

UNODC, *Transnational Organized Crime in the Fishing Industry. Focus on Trafficking in Persons, Smuggling of Migrants and Illicit Drugs Trafficking* (Vienna, 2011).

United States Coast Guard, *Guide to the Law of Boarding Operations* (June 2008) (on file with the author).

UNODC, Issue Paper, Smuggling of Migrants at Sea (Vienna, 2011).

United States *Commander's Handbook on the Law of Naval Operations*, NWP 1–14M (Edition July 2007).

UNHCR ExCom, 'Problems Related to the Rescue of Asylum-Seekers in Distress at Sea', Conclusion No 23 (XXXII) (1981).

UNHCR ExCom, 'Report of the Working Group on Problems related to the Rescue of Asylum-Seekers in Distress at Sea', Conclusion No 26 (XXXIII) (1982).

UNHCR ExCom, 'Rescue of Asylum-Seekers in Distress at Sea', Conclusion No 38 (XXXVI) (1985).

UNHCR, 'The Treatment of Persons Rescued at Sea: Conclusions and Recommendations from Recent Meetings and Expert Round Tables Convened by the Office of the United Nations High Commissioner for Refugees'; submitted in the Ninth Session of United Nations Open-ended Informal Consultative Process on Oceans and the Law of the Sea (23–27 June 2008) A/AC 259/17.

US National Plan to Achieve Maritime Domain Awareness for the National Strategy for Maritime Security (October 2005), ii, www.dhsgov/xlibrary/assets/HSPD_MDAPlanpdf.

US Navy, 'Navy Maritime Domain Awareness Concept' (May 2007), www.navy-mil/navydata/cno/Navy_Maritime_Domain_Awareness_Concept_FINAL_2007pdf.

World Drugs Report – Executive Summary (2007), issued by the UN Office on Drugs and Crime, www.unodcorg/pdf/research/wdr07/WDR_2007_executive_summarypdf.

Index